Terry Tales

Growing up in the fifties in Litchfield, Minnesota

with

The History of Downtown Litchfield: The First One Hundred Years

By Terry R. Shaw

TERANDLO PUBLISHING

Cover design by Terry R. Shaw

Published by
Terandlo Publishing
1601 15th Avenue Southwest
Willmar, Minnesota 56201

Printed in the United States of America
Library of Congress Control Number: 2003095563
International Standard Book Number 0-9744109-9-3

Table of Contents

Dedications

Oliver Wendell Holmes once said "The average person goes to his grave with his music still in him." As a musician, songwriter and performer, I think how sad that must be, and I pity that person. I think it's just as sad for a man to go to his grave with his stories still in him. One day I asked my daughter, Andrea, to tell me about her favorite childhood memories. At the top of her list were the camping trips we took as a family when she, her sister Christine, and her brother Adrian, were little. More specifically, she said she loved the campfire stories of my own childhood and hometown that I would tell as we sat toasting marshmallows. Andrea kept after me to write those stories down so they wouldn't be lost to my and my brothers' grandchildren. When she presented me with my first grandchild, Ethan Ryan Peterson, I decided the time had come. To Ethan and to all of the grandchildren of Dennis, Michael, Terrance and Patrick Shaw, this book is for you.

My grandson Ethan Ryan Peterson at 1 year old and my brother Pat Shaw at 56.

It dawned on me, as I wrote these stories, that I did everything and went everywhere with my youngest brother and best friend, Patrick Francis Shaw. Pat, I'm sorry for some of the things I did to you, you were not adopted as I told you, and this is for you too.

My wonderful wife Lois spent many evenings looking at my widening back and my balding head while I typed my daily research notes into my computer. Then she listened to me complain and cry as programs crashed, information was lost and much needed hair was pulled out. For putting up with me and telling me you still love me, you're included in my dedications.

My wife,
Lois Shaw

Finally, as I was writing these stories, I let a few people read them in advance, asking for suggestions and comments. The one common response I got was, "Your mother was sure a remarkable woman." Yes she was and, more than anyone else, this book is dedicated and a tribute to Helen Elizabeth Rheaume Shaw Young, born on September 19, 1918 and died on August 25, 1991. She was a wonderful, remarkable woman who, against all odds, persevered and triumphed in my hometown of Litchfield, Minnesota.

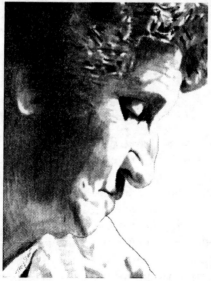

A drawing I made of Helen Shaw Young.

Forward

This book was the outgrowth of two true stories I wrote called *The Typewriter* and *Nickels*. I let my daughter Andrea, an English teacher, read them and she gave me some help fixing them up. She then asked me where some of the other childhood stories were that I had told her when she was little. Back to the drawing board I went and the additional stories grew into part of this book. Writing those stories, I wrote about places in Litchfield that were either background for or an important part of my stories. I decided that as long as I'm writing about Johnson's Drug Store, for example, why not tell a little of the history of the building?

The deeper I got into that research, the more discrepancies I found in the facts. I decided that someone should pull all the facts together and set the record straight, if that's possible. As Mom used to tell me, "If a job's worth doing, it's worth doing well." Before long, my stories got lost in the forest of facts about the buildings. I wanted the facts to stay in because I knew my book was turning into an important historical piece, but I didn't want them to overwhelm the stories. So I put the facts into an appendix and footnoted the stories to it. Now the book is at two levels, my tales and the historical stories and facts.

I decided I would take the reader on a walk around Litchfield in a particular year and let my stories unfold as they came up naturally. I picked the year of 1959. It was still in the innocent fifties and I was a not so innocent teenager, fourteen years old to be exact. I continued my research of the buildings up to the year of 1971. That covered Litchfield's first one hundred years and also coincided with the year that I left town and stopped calling Litchfield my home. I had trouble writing that last sentence because, really, I've never stopped calling Litchfield my home. I've just temporarily lived in other places, such as Glencoe for twenty-six years and now temporarily in Willmar.

To those friends and relatives whom I might have embarrassed by reporting their stories, I apologize, but I hope I got the facts right. To those history buffs who will read my appendix and say I've got some facts wrong about a certain store's location or history, all I can tell you is that I did my best and I welcome your input. There were some people, like Cairncross, Topping, Koerner and Chapman, who moved all over town, sometimes staying in one place for only a few months. They made my job very difficult. To those who say I have too much personal information in the book, well that's how it started and that's how it has to stay. To those who aren't familiar with Litchfield and say the book has too much history either of the town or of the stores, I simply have to tell you that you really should get to know this wonderful town.

"A hometown never truly becomes beautiful until you've left it once and then returned." I read that somewhere. But I can say that I've always loved my hometown of Litchfield, Minnesota, always thought it was beautiful, and my leaving and coming back to visit has only increased that love.

In addition to this book, I've written two other books, one about the Beatles and one about Buddy Holly, which I've given away free on the internet. Someone asked me why I was doing all this writing, without a monetary reward. In his song *Blue Moon Nights*, John Fogerty sings,
"Heaven only knows I don't wanna be...
just a fool...passin' through."
That's how I feel. Maybe, because of these writings, someone will know that I wasn't just "passin' through" on this road of life. I stopped along the way and I tried to make a contribution.

Terry R. Shaw

Terry Tales

Growing up in the fifties in Litchfield, Minnesota

By Terry R. Shaw

Chapter One
My World

My generation has been named the "Baby Boomers" generation because we were a part of the post-World War II crop of babies born from 1945 to 1964. I feel blessed to have grown up a Baby Boomer in the fifties in a small town in mid-America. The years of my childhood were fun, innocent and without fears. No fears, that is, except for the "Duck and Cover" drills in school, teaching me what to do if there were a nuclear attack from the Russians. I was to *duck* under my desk and *cover* my head. I presume I was to do this so that my charred lifeless body could be found under the desk instead of sitting in it. But movie monsters, snakes, spiders and the bogeyman were much more terrifying to me than the threat of the communists because my world didn't include Russia or Washington D. C., or any other place that I couldn't get to by walking or riding my bike.

My "Frankenstein" bike, thrown together from parts of other bicycles, was my most prized possession because it expanded my world. It had no fenders, no chain guard, no handlebar grips, and very little for a seat. If I rode through a mud puddle, I got sprayed with a streak of muddy water up my back. The local police department gave out safety reflectors to kids to put on their bike fenders. I had nowhere to put them.

But that bike was so important to me. I vividly remember meeting my mother at the corner of our block, as she was walking home from her job at the turkey plant to eat her noon lunch, and having her watch me peddle wobbly down the street in front of her for the first time. I didn't need anything else in my world. There was enough entertainment and adventure for me right in my own backyard and that bike had just made that backyard much bigger.

Terry
Shaw
with his
bike.

My parents were divorced, which was rare in the late forties and early fifties, and I started smoking in the seventh grade, which wasn't rare for us Boomers in those days. I respected my mom and my teachers.

1

I went to church every Sunday, I did my best in school and I dressed up for both. I didn't expect an allowance for doing chores around the house, two gifts at Christmas were enough to satisfy me, and a perfect day was one that included a 10¢ bottle of soda pop or one of those store bought chocolate-covered cookies with marshmallow inside that I only got at a relative's house. My heroes were movie stars, Davy Crockett, my teachers and my mother.

The fifties was an innocent time, but it was also an exciting time. I was there for the birth of so many wonderful things in the fifties. I was there for the birth of rock and roll, with the debuts of Elvis and the Beatles. I was there for the birth of the space program, with the launching of Sputnik, and, because of it, an increase in the Cold War. I was there for the birth of the peace movement and civil rights. I was there for the beginnings of drive-in movies, canned soft drinks, television, the Barbie doll, microwave ovens, satellites, stereo records, portable transistor radios, 3-D, K-Mart, Wal-Mart, Disneyland and McDonald's.

For a period of time, I was able to listen to one episode of *The Lone Ranger* on the radio with William Conrad starring as Matt Dillon and then see an entirely different episode on TV with fellow Minnesotan James Arness in the lead. We played marbles during recess at school and other games with unusual names such as *Red Rover, Red Rover* and *Captain (or Mother), May I*. At home we played *Cops and Robbers, Cowboys and Indians, War, Night Tag, Annie, Annie Over, Blind Man's Bluff* and *Hide 'n Seek*. If we couldn't find anybody in *Hide 'n Seek*, which we always liked to play in the dark, we'd return to the "home base", which was usually a tree, and yell, "Ally, ally oxen free!" What it really meant, we had no idea. But to us it meant, "I give up. Everyone can come in now." We Boomers started fads like Hula Hoops and Davy Crockett coonskin caps and dances like the *Twist*, the *Limbo*, and the *Stroll*, the real first line dance.

We stopped to pick up a penny on the ground, no matter what condition or what puddle it was in. Hours could be spent just lying in the grass with a friend, looking at the clouds and saying, "That one looks like…" Major decisions were made by saying "Eeny-meeny-miney-mo" along with "My mother told me to choose you." Mistakes were corrected by simply yelling, "Do over!" We would do anything stupid on a dare and if we backed down, we were forced to do it anyway by something called a "double-dog dare." I was a typical Baby Boomer kid growing up in the fifties and I never wanted to live anywhere else than in my little hometown of Litchfield, Minnesota.

We all have fond memories of our hometown. For most of my earliest years, my entire world consisted of my hometown. The children of today have a much larger world. Many go to Disney World for spring break, for example, and Washington, D.C. or the Grand Canyon for summer vacation. It was a very rare occurrence when I had an opportunity to leave Litchfield. When I did leave, it was for the weeklong stay my brother Pat and I had at Uncle Buck and Aunt Wilma Owens' farm in Osakis, Minnesota in the summer of 1955, or the few times I visited my cousin Tommy Wolf in Fairmont, Minnesota in the late fifties, or the occasional trip sixty-five miles east to Minneapolis and St. Paul or "the cities[1]", as we called them.

One of my first trips to the cities was on March 4, 1958 when the Nelsan-Horton American Legion and the Litchfield Shrine Club took my school patrol group to the Zurah Shrine Circus. Before that trip, and my few visits to relatives, Litchfield, Minnesota was my entire world.

Going to the Shrine Circus, I'm the third boy from the left.

---

[1] In the old town newspapers of the 1890s, the Twin Cities were often referred to as "Sodom and Gomorah". For example, the September 24, 1891 *Litchfield Ledger* stated "Postmaster Koerner was in Sodom and Gomorrah on business last Thursday and Friday."

3

My family moved to Litchfield from Mankato, Minnesota in September of 1946. My mother, Helen Elizabeth Rheaume Shaw, had three little toddlers under her wing, four-year old Dennis William, two and a half year old Michael Eugene, and myself at seventeen months. Mom was very pregnant with her fourth and final child, Patrick Francis, who was due to arrive in November. My dad, Florian Shaw, had bought the house we moved into from his aunt and uncle, Mildred "Millie" and Edward "Ed" Birkemeyer.

Dad did some "re-decorating" and moved his growing family into the house without Mom having ever seen it. She told me she walked into the kitchen that early fall day and saw that Dad had painted the walls a tractor orange and had slapped some ugly decals on the cupboards and the refrigerator. She sat down on the doorsteps and cried.

1947:
Terry,
Mick,
Pat and
Dennis
Shaw

Two and a half years later, after my father had left us and he and Mom had divorced three days before my birthday on April 20, 1949, Mom was on her own in this strange town, miles away from her parents and brothers and sisters, supporting four little boys totally on her own. Dad, who didn't pay Mom any child support, lived across town for a short time in a small cement block house at 715 South Street East. The house is still there, out by the Super Valu store. Then he and his new wife, Gertrude "Sunny" Papesch, moved to Eden Valley, Minnesota to run a short-lived produce and repair radios and TVs.

From that point on, I could count on my hands the number of times I saw my father until he had a massive stroke and died in 1961. At sixteen years old, I was ushered into his room at the University of Minnesota

4

hospital to say good-bye. He was in a coma so I never got to say it. I was actually relieved. I had been given instructions by Mom to talk him into seeing a priest before he died. I had no clue as to what to say to him, he being virtually a stranger to me. I just stood and looked at him lying in the bed with tubes in his mouth, nose and arms. I was emotionless and lost standing there at the foot of his bed.

Less than a week later, Mom got a phone call early on a Sunday morning. She put the phone down, walked to the kitchen table and sat down for a minute. Then she stood up and walked over to where I was sitting on the floor by the furnace grate in the living room reading the comic section of the Sunday newspaper.

"Your father just died," she said.

I looked up at her and muttered, "Oh." It had no more effect on me than if she had told me that a neighbor had died.

1963: Pat, Mick, Helen, Terry and Dennis Shaw.

Dennis, Terry, Mick and Pat Shaw in 2003.

Despite our family and financial situations, my early years growing up in Litchfield were wonderful and exciting. Mom and us four boys lived near the very center of the town. Our little bungalow house at 222 Swift Avenue North[2] was only three blocks from Sibley Avenue North, Litchfield's main street[3].

A painting I made of the house on Swift Avenue North. The addition from the right side window and on was added after 1961. To the left of the chimney had been the kitchen door with red steps down to the driveway and a shingled canopy over the door.

To a small group of friends, which included my youngest brother Pat and I, growing up in the center of Litchfield was almost like growing up in the center of an amusement park. Several large green parks, a huge public swimming beach, rows of stores with interesting alleys running behind them, and other structures in town offered us a myriad of possibilities for entertainment. Each store, each building, and each park in town brings back memories to me.

Using the layout[4] of 1959 Litchfield, I'll walk "uptown" from that house on Swift Avenue and tell an occasional story along the way. For the most part, what was known as "downtown Litchfield" consisted of a nine block rectangular area with Sibley Avenue North, running through the center. The downtown area was bordered by Marshall Avenue North on the east and Ramsey Avenue North on the west. Both streets paralleled Sibley. The north boundary was the courthouse and Central

---

[2] Originally, when the house was built in 1939, it was assigned the number 218, but it was switched to 222 in 1947.

[3] Sibley Avenue was first paved around 1918-1919.

[4] See the "MY WORLD – Litchfield 1959" map on page 364 of the History of Downtown Litchfield Appendix.

Park at Fourth Street and the south boundary was the railroad tracks next to Depot Street, which branched off to First Street.

To get uptown, I could go to the corner of Swift Avenue and Third Street, turn right and walk along the south side of the street, but I usually shortened the first block by cutting through Pat McCormick's[5] backyard. McCormick's house, yard and garage were directly behind our garage. I had to walk between his garage and a huge old gray barn that was directly behind our neighbor Alma Colmen's big garden south of our garage. The old gray barn wasn't a standard looking barn and there were lots of old block and tackle hanging from the rafters in it. We thought it was odd for such a huge barn to be in the city limits, but we never gave it any more thought.

In researching this book, I found an old plat book from 1897. In that book, certain landmarks such as hotels, livery stables and schools were noted on the city blocks. Icehouses were also indicated. There were two in Litchfield at that time. One was near the elevators south of the railroad tracks, close to where Litchfield Lumber is today. The other one was in the middle of the south side of Third Street between Swift and Miller Avenues. That would have been no more than twenty feet north of our garage. Was the old gray barn that icehouse[6], which had been moved fifty yards south to serve as someone's garage?

Aunt Doris Shaw Johnson in front of our garage and the "ice house".

Anyway, I would walk between the garages, past McCormick's house and arrive at the "old power plant", which was a block away from us on the corner of Miller Avenue and Third Street. The power plant

---

[5] Pat McCormick was Litchfield's assistant fire chief from 1960 to 1961 and fire chief from 1961 to 1964 and 1967 to 1972.

[6] I believe he owned the one here was owned by John Happ, as his woodshop was just east up Third Street and the Happ and Company store was a little further uptown near the corner of Sibley Avenue and Third Street. See page 374 of the "History of Downtown Litchfield Appendix."

was a large brown brick building with a tall water tower just east of it with "LITCHFIELD" painted on the cone topped cylindrical tank on the top. The site is now a vacant lot with a newer, different shaped water tower.

On the roof of the old power plant was the town whistle. It was technically a siren, but we called it "the whistle". Today you hear a siren only in an emergency or on the first Wednesday of every month for testing purposes. In Litchfield in the fifties, we heard an ear-piercing siren six times a day. On the west wall inside the power plant was a very accurate clock that George D. Tuttle would set and maintain. Right below the clock was the button for the whistle. Someone had to actually push that button and hold it for fifteen seconds six times a day at precisely the correct time. People set their watches by that whistle and they were very upset if it was off by a minute or two.

To the Shaw boys and anyone else who lived near the power plant, the siren was deafening. People claimed they could hear it miles out of town. It started low and slowly worked its way up to a high pitched and long held scream. Then it would take just as long to wind back down to a whisper and then blessed silence. I thought of the times the whistle went off in this way:

6am - "Get up!"

7am – "Go to work! ("School kids – get up!")

Noon - "Dinner time!"

1pm - "Go back to work!"

6pm - "Supper time!"

10pm - "You kids better get off the streets and get home to bed!"

The smokestack, the water tower, and the old power plant on which sat the whistle.

8

When there was a fire, the whistle would go up and down rapidly for minutes. Pat and I would hop on our bikes and pedal to the fire station, which was only a block and a half away at the corner of Ramsey Avenue and Third Street. If we were quick enough, which was rare, we'd get to see the fire engine, with men hanging on the sides, come screaming out the station door. The door was always left open and we'd run inside and read the small blackboard on the right wall beside the door. Scribbled on the blackboard would be the address of the fire. If it were in town, we'd hop back on our bikes and peddle there to watch the fire being put out. We saw a big fire in town only a couple of times, but it was thrilling chasing the truck, nevertheless.

Before the days of two-way radio, dispatchers and beepers, how did the firemen and policemen know where to go if the siren went off? The telephone operators at the telephone office told them. Strung between the Greep and Trueblood Department store and the hotel at the intersection of Highways 12 and 22, was a large red light. The fire station man on duty, usually caretaker Herman Krueger who had been fire chief, would get the initial call and he'd notify the siren operator and the telephone operators. The operators would turn on the red light. Firemen would hear the siren, see the red light and know they could call the operator to get the location of the fire rather than drive all the way to the fire station.

The "red light" is at center left.

The same was true for what we'd call a "911" call today. If someone called the operator in distress, she'd throw the red light switch on and the police would know to check in with her. Or if the Chief of Police needed to get hold of his on-duty patrolman, he'd call the operator and she'd throw the switch. It was a pretty good system. It worked and the telephone operators sure deserved a pat on the back. Litchfield's red light is on display in the Meeker County Historical Society building.

The hotel switchboard operator backed up the system. The hotel had a special phone on the top of the switchboard. The information would be called in when the siren went off or a message was left for the police. Old John Fisher, the late night clerk at the hotel, could never get the messages right and he caused quite a bit of excitement on different occasions. KLFD radio, which the town didn't get until the late fifties, would also broadcast the fire's location when it was on the air during the daytime.

East of the old power plant, on the corner of the same block, was a gravel lot where the new fire hall stands today. In the winter, the city street crew piled snow in that lot. We spent many hours playing *King of the Hill* on a mountain of snow there.

Speaking of winter, I must tell of a couple of crazy things we did as kids in the winters in Litchfield. One was "frozen water skiing" and the other was "hitching a ride". "Hitching a ride", sometimes called "street sliding", was simple enough. Roads weren't salted back then and they would be snow covered or just plain glare ice. On a not too busy side street, we'd stand on the side of the road until a slow moving old car came by. When it had just passed us, we'd run behind the car and grab the back bumper. Squatting down, we'd go for a ride, letting the car pull us down the street. Kids have been doing this for ages. In an 1882 *Litchfield Independent* newspaper, there was an article about the danger of youngsters grabbing the backs of passing horse-drawn sleds coming through town.

"Frozen water skiing" was a little more dangerous. We only did this when we were older and one of us had a car. We'd tie a long rope to the car's rear bumper and drive out on frozen Lake Ripley. We'd take turns being pulled behind the car on the ice. The danger was that the ice wasn't always smooth and you also might run into an abandoned fishing hole. A "safer" version had a saucer sled tied to the back of the car.

Another favorite thing to do on the ice with a car was "screwy Louies" or getting up speed on the ice and slamming on the brakes while whipping the steering wheel in one direction or the other.

I don't remember anyone getting hurt being pulled behind the cars or going into the freezing water for an unexpected dip. It was either dumb luck or we had some forgiving Guardian Angels watching over us, answering our mothers' prayers. As Archie Bunker once said on TV's *All In The Family*, "God watches over drunks and dingbats."

Besides the mountain of snow, the empty gravel corner lot by the old power plant had one very small building in the middle of it. Erected in 1951, the building was made of wood and was raised off the ground by cement blocks. We dubbed it the "paper shack". Those of us lucky enough to have paper routes went there every morning or afternoon to pick up our *Minneapolis Tribune* or *Minneapolis Star* newspapers to deliver to our customers. I had a paper route. It was relentless, daily hard work, especially on Sundays with the heavy newspapers, and anytime that the weather had turned bad. I never had a day off.

Mom always found time to help me deliver my Sunday papers when there was a snowstorm. We'd walk along the mile and a half long route in the snow pulling my heavy sled. We'd pull it up Fifth Street, which went up a hill west of town, and deliver a paper to the house on Arnold Kline's horse farm and then one to John Odenkamp's crop farm, further out of town. After the final Sunday paper had been delivered to the Martin Huiko house at the top of the Fourth Street hill, Mom would hop on the sled behind me and we'd slide down the hill. Yes, Litchfield was my world, but my mother, Helen Shaw, was the center of that world.

Aerial view of downtown Litchfield in the thirties. Our house would be built later in the upper left quarter of the picture, a block north of the smokestack.

Chapter Two
Turkeys and Mom-isms

Across Third Street, north of the paper shack, was a blacksmith's shop[7]. There was always a beehive of activity and lots of noise coming from the small building. Two or three grungy looking men with dirty faces and dressed in bib overalls were always pounding on or welding on some kind of metal structure. Pat and I would stop to watch the men weld, hoping we wouldn't go blind in the process. We had been told that to look at the light from a weld would cause you to go blind. Sometimes we'd see one of those guys do a quick spot weld without his black spaceman hat on and we'd wonder why he'd risk his eyesight for his job. I only knew one of the men, the owner Andy Anderson[8]. He lived two blocks from us at 301 Austin Avenue North with his wife, three daughters and four sons. One of his sons, Eugene, was called Skeeter. He was older than us but a friend and a character. There's a lot more about Skeeter in later chapters.

Turning south from the paper shack onto the west side of Ramsey Avenue brought me to the Litchfield Seed Company, an alley and then the small Black & White Inn café with an alley entrance. Pat Woods owned the cafe, later called the Hide-A-Way, which had originally been on Sibley Avenue across from Central Park where Janousek's café went. Pat Woods and his wife Borghild "Borgie" split. Pat left the business to Borgie in the divorce. Jim Gunter[9], who had worked for Pat, married Borgie, (wink, wink), and then ran the Black & White. Borgie's daughter, Anita Woods, was a waitress there. She dated Conrad "Connie" Olmstead, a guitar player in my brother Dennie's[10] rock band. Connie looked just like Buddy Holly, complete with the curly dark hair and black-rimmed glasses.

At the southwest corner of this block, at the intersection of Ramsey Avenue and Second Street, was a large white building housing the turkey processing plant's freezer lockers. The building was connected to the main processing plant, across the street to the south, by a large overhead tube that was used to transport frozen turkeys and chickens to the lockers. When the tube was being used, the roar from the rattle and

---

[7] 124 Third Street West. Today the drive-thru window for the Central National Bank is at this location. The bank's address is 301 Ramsey Avenue North.

[8] 114 Third Street West. See page 375 of the History of Downtown Litchfield Appendix.

[9] Jim Gunter lived at 514 Swift Avenue North across the street from my Grandpa Bill Shaw.

[10] Mom always wrote Dennis' name as "Dennie" instead of "Denny" and it stuck.

12

clatter of the frozen birds racing down the track of rollers inside the tube on their way to the other side of the street was so loud that it could be heard uptown and by us in our backyard two blocks away. The tube was gravity powered, the tracks inside slanting towards the locker building. There were times when there would be a "traffic jam" up there and some little worker, like Freddie Williams, whom you'll meet later, would have to climb through the tunnel to get the mess going again.

God knows how long some of those frozen turkeys hung around in freezers before they were eaten. When Dennie was in the Marines in the mid-sixties, he was on a ship heading back to the United States from Japan. He was given the job of exercising and working prisoners from the brig each day. One day he had to watch them unload a freezer in the hold of the ship so that the freezer could be disinfected and then reloaded. Dennie noticed some boxes that looked familiar. He walked up to them and saw that they held frozen ELPECO turkeys from Litchfield, Minnesota. The dates on the boxes were 1955 and 1956.

We called the turkey plant "the Produce" because the official name was the Litchfield Produce Company[11]. Earl B. Olson of Willmar, Minnesota finally owned it. In one of life's funny twists, Earl B. became my neighbor when I moved to Willmar when I was fifty years old. Earl B. is a nice old guy, but we sure hated his turkey plant. It stunk of wet turkey feathers, blood, turkey poop, ammonia and who knows what else.

Left: Frozen turkeys. Right: The Produce complex: At the bottom middle is the locker plant and the B&W Café. Above the locker plant, at the middle left, is the turkey plant, which is connected by the tube. Top right is Anderson Chemical.

---

[11] See page 448 of the History of Downtown Litchfield Appendix.

Several times each year a strong ammonia smell would drift into our backyard from a leak at the Produce. It would gag us and burn our eyes. I can still remember the smell today. It overcame two women working there when a pipe sprung a leak in August of 1952. The women were taken to the hospital. In October of 1956, a broken ammonia pipe caused an explosion at the Produce. Woman ran out of the building with their hair and clothes on fire. Fourteen were sent to the hospital.

Besides the ammonia smell, loose turkeys drifted into our backyard also. Pat and I would chase them into the garage, more afraid of the giant birds than they were of us. Mom had asked us to try to catch any that came into our yard. They were probably attracted to Mrs. Colmen's huge garden. We kept them in the garage until Grandpa Bill Shaw could come over to wring their necks or chop their heads off.

If he chopped their heads off, he did it over by the north side of the garage where our doghouse and a tree stump was. Grandpa would swing the turkey's head against the garage to stun it. Then he'd lay the bird's neck across the stump. Clunk...his ax would come down. Then he'd throw the body onto our lawn to bleed. The headless turkey always jumped up and ran around in circles. Pat would scream in fright and I would laugh at him and tease him. I was scared too, but it was funny and fascinating at the same time. I always wondered if a human being would do that. Sometimes Pat ran behind a tree and closed his eyes, but I stayed and watched and enjoyed the executions for the "fright show" that followed.

Grandpa
William
"Bill" Shaw
in our
backyard.

Grandpa did chickens for Mom too. The chickens usually had their necks wrung. Grandpa would grab the chicken's head and swing the body 'round and 'round until the neck snapped and the body flew off. Once a headless rooster actually got up off the lawn and seemed to chase

14

after Pat, splattering him with blood, before the ghoulish bird finally dropped over. Pat screamed and ran and screamed and ran.

After that episode, we could get Pat crying by just pushing a plain feather from any bird into his face. We all did it, but Mom caught Dennie doing it and she smacked him on the back of his legs with a long green fiberglass yardstick that she got free from Baril's paint store uptown. That yardstick and one of our leather belts were Mom's choice of weapons when we needed disciplining. And the backs of our thighs were her targets instead of our butts. Either she knew it stung more or her aim was terribly off. But she had to catch us first.

I would run upstairs and hide under the bed at the top of the stairs. It wasn't really a bedroom that Pat and I shared. It was the hallway leading to Dennie and Mick's room. Mom would go to one side of the bed, bend down and swipe at me with the belt. I'd scoot away. She'd get up and come to the other side of the bed and I'd scoot to the opposite side. Finally, she'd say, "Well, you have to come out to eat sometime. I'll get you then!" She'd turn and go downstairs.

I would lie under the bed with the rest of the dust bunnies that weren't already wiped up by my clothes. Ten or fifteen minutes later, I would quietly and sheepishly go back down the stairs where I'd find Mom standing in the kitchen by the stove or at the kitchen table doing her cooking. I'd walk up behind her and give her a hug around the waist saying, "I'm sorry Mom. I won't do it again." It always worked. Rule number one: Know your enemy's weaknesses.

Mom caught me smoking under the basement steps behind the coal auger, our favorite place to hide from her or each other. She smacked the backs of my legs with that green yardstick all the way up the stairs. When I got to the top, I turned around, looked her in the eye with my tears held back as best I could and said, "Ha! Didn't hurt!" Rule number two: Never let the enemy think that they got the best of you.

Remember that hated turkey plant? We hated that turkey plant because at some point in our young lives my brothers and I put in time there doing some hated job. Dennie shoveled shaved ice onto the birds in a cart after the turkeys had been cleaned and put into plastic bags. Then he pushed them into a freezer for a quick freeze. When the turkeys came out in an hour, frozen rock hard, some ladies weighed them and sealed them up into shipping boxes. That was one of the few clean jobs.

Mick and Pat worked in clean up. It was not a clean job, hosing down blood, guts, and crap, literally. I stacked those shipping boxes before they went into the locker freezers, but I soon finagled my way into just gluing the labels onto the boxes. I was in college at the time and I guess the foreman thought you needed a college education to label boxes. Well, you did have to be able to read and I can't swear that all of my co-workers could. At least not read English. I learned how to swear in Spanish that summer.

Because of our various jobs at the plant and all of the turkeys we chased into our garage and then ate at Sunday dinners, none of us four boys are too fond of turkey today. And, as I've written, we hated that turkey plant. Most of all, we hated it because we saw what it did to our mother. Mom started working at the plant in late 1952 to support us four boys by herself. I don't know what she did before that job, but I do know that she worked somewhere. She always refused aid from anyone except for health care from Aid to Dependent Children.

Mom graduated Salutatorian in her high school class and she should have gone on to college. Instead, she stood in an inch of water on the eviscerating line on the second floor of the turkey plant cutting the oil sacks off the asses of turkeys, which moved by her hanging from a conveyor line. I remember going up there to see Mom a couple of times. It was cold, wet, noisy and scary, with water on the floor and the stink of cold turkey flesh all around. I had asked Pat how to get up there. I knew he had gone up a couple of times too. I was scared walking by all the carnage going on, but I needed some money for something for school.

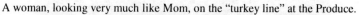

A woman, looking very much like Mom, on the "turkey line" at the Produce.

Somehow I picked my mother out of a row of women, all looking the same, dressed in white uniforms with their hair done up under nets. They were all talking loudly to be heard over the noise of the plant. It was cold up there, even though it was quite warm outside.

"Mom," I said, coming up behind her. "Mom!" I said louder. She turned and glanced at me but had to keep her eyes on the turkeys coming by and the sharp knife in her hand.

16

"Terry, I told you not to bother me when I'm working. Do you want me to get fired?"

"But Mom, I need a dollar for school and I forgot to..."

"What do you expect me to do now? I can't leave the line," she explained. "You'll just have to either wait outside for me to go on break in half an hour or wait 'til I get home."

"But, Mom..."

"Those are the choices, Terry. I don't have my purse here and I can't leave the line for any reason."

I turned and left, hating that turkey plant and the smells and the coldness of it all and mad at my mother for something that was beyond her control.

Mom always complained about her aching legs and feet. Her legs became covered with tiny blue spider veins and her feet swelled up so that her Sunday shoes didn't fit. I could see that she was in pain as we walked the five blocks to church every Sunday morning. Her hands were dry, cracked, cut and bleeding all of the time. They were never soft to the touch when she would take us by the hand and walk us to the front pew at church or caress our foreheads if we were sick in bed. Every night we'd sit in front of our little TV in the living room and Mom would go through her nightly ritual of greasy up her hands and legs, which she always had raised up on a footstool. I felt sorry for Mom. She was too proud to go on welfare so she worked at that turkey plant all week and on some Saturday mornings too.

Just when Mom had built up enough time at the Produce to earn a much needed and well-deserved paid vacation and raise, the plant went bankrupt in the early spring of 1957. The Produce shut down and Mom was devastated. She had lost the job she hated but needed and she was without an income. I don't remember her crying about it, just complaining. Mom had the attitude that I've inherited... "Que sera, sera" or "Whatever will be, will be". She just knew that she'd finally have to ask for help and it bothered her. She felt defeated. I remember her trying to get some other work and saying something about how she would be ahead staying home and drawing her unemployment and getting some help than working for lower pay somewhere else. She finally gave in and went on welfare after her unemployment had run out.

Not one to sit around, Mom decided she would refinish the living room floor. I can't remember what was on the floor before she went to work on it, but for some reason Mom thought she could rent a big sander, take off the old finish and inexpensively have a beautiful natural wood floor. She rented the sander but she couldn't figure out exactly how to run it. Uncle Alan came over and showed her and then left, not volunteering to help. Mom started sanding but she didn't move the electric monster fast enough and she gouged some little dips into the floor. Fifteen-year old Dennie puffed up his chest and said, "Let me do it. I can run it, Mom."

The sander was awkward and heavy and would take off on you. Dennie slammed it into the baseboard a few times before he got the hang of it. He cracked some of the trim and Mom was not happy about it. The sandpaper got gummed up quickly and often, so Pat and I took turns standing on the big green thing to give it weight and make it dig down better.

Fifteen-year old Dennis Shaw taking a test in high school.

Somehow the floor got sanded and sealed and then Mom was in her familiar position on her knees wiping in the floor wax. Then came the fun part of the whole project. The whole family, plus Mom's friend Kathryn Van Nurden, put burlap sacks on our feet and we skated around to work the wax finish into the floor. It took hours. After we buffed it with towels, it was like glass, dips, gouges and all.

Pat was the first one to forget about it and slam down to the floor, cracking his head, by running in the living room in his socks. Everyone was slipping all over the place, Mom included. You quickly learned to stay off the throw rugs and take off your socks. Bare foot was the way to go. For that reason, or because of the dips and gouges that stood out when the sun hit the floor, Mom eventually covered the floor with wall-to-wall carpeting when she married my stepfather Floyd Young. But she had shown us another side of her we didn't know existed. Mom wasn't afraid to try anything.

Earl B. Olson bought the turkey plant from the creditors and started it up again in September of 1957. Our proud mother went back to work at the job she despised, giving up the dreaded welfare and the stay at home do-it-yourself projects.

On Saturday afternoons, Mom cleaned Dr. Gregory Olson's house while Pat and I mowed his lawn or raked his leaves. When we'd get home, we'd help Mom clean the house and then she'd bake for us. There was always a sheet cake or cookies in our house. She used to make her own noodles and drape them over a chair by the furnace grate to rise. I couldn't figure out why she couldn't just buy the noodles. How much could they have cost? But, Mom loved to cook, even if she rarely had time to do much of it. After she married Floyd, she worked as a cook at the high school and then became head cook at the Ripley Elementary School. She was finally able to do something she enjoyed doing. But that came later.

Left: Helen Shaw Young cooking at home.   Right: High School cooks Helen Young, Rhoda Lundblad and Evelyn Wick.

Bedsides cleaning our house and baking for us, Mom also washed our clothes on Saturdays. When she did the laundry in the winter, she "freeze-dried" our jeans by throwing them over the wrought iron railing on our front steps. When they were frozen stiff, she'd bring them in and stand them up in the basement to thaw out. They looked as stiff as they were the day she bought them for us at the Greep-Trueblood Department Store.

We hated new blue jeans. They were always over starched and stiff as a board. I would take mine, soak it in water and then kick it around the block a few times to "break them in". I had seen Spin and Marty, two teenage characters on *The Mickey Mouse Club* show on TV, do it so

19

I knew it'd work. I'm sure that Mom loved washing those jeans before I had even worn them one time.

Blue jeans were the "uniform of the day" for us. Dress pants were for Sunday church only. We never wore shorts or "cut-offs" in the summer in the fifties. It was blue jeans year 'round. Because our bikes had no chain guards, I was forever catching my jeans in the chain. I would have to fall over to my right, and then stand and crouch to peddle the bike with my hand and walk my jeans out of the chain. There would be a black tattoo of the chain track on the bottom of my jean leg. Of course, if I had only rolled my pant leg up, it would never have happened. But I chose the possibility of catching the jeans in the chain rather than look like a "square", a "dork" or a "fairy", which were our terms for a nerd. "Fairy" had nothing to do with being gay in those days, by the way. If you wore glasses or got good grades in school or helped your mother with the housework, you were a fairy. I had all three strikes against me. "Terry the Fairy" was what they called me.

In our small town in the fifties, we never wore baseball caps either, except when actually playing baseball, for fear of being called a "square" or a "dork". I didn't even wear one then. We didn't want to look like a dork and we didn't want to mess our hair up. Cool hair was important in the fifties. I spent hours training my hair to go back on the sides with some sticky goo from a jar labeled *Butch Wax*. It was used for crew cuts and I bought it from the Roscoe the barber. My hair was going to go back on the sides, even if I had to glue it to my head.

I froze my ears many mornings walking the six blocks to the high school, many times with my head turned sideways so that the bitter Minnesota January wind wouldn't mess up my "do". I would arrive at the school door with frozen hair and red ears, but looking cool. I remember my ears burning during most of my first hour class as they and my hair slowly thawed out.

Being cool always went before safety and warmth. We never wore "rubbers", which is what we called boots or overshoes in the fifties, so we always had cold and wet feet and salt stained shoes. And we never wore gloves. If we saw someone with mittens on, we'd fall down laughing at them. We'd taunt the poor kid, "Did your mommy dress you today?" or "Are those pinned to your coat?" Some of the bullies would take a little kid, pull off one of his mittens real hard and he'd hit himself in the head with his other mitten-covered hand. The two mittens, of course, were tied together with a long string around the kid's neck inside his coat. I guess it was so he wouldn't lose them.

We never went barefoot in town either. My wife tells me that she used to love the feeling of stepping barefoot into a warm cow pie on the farm. No, thank you. In town, there was too much broken glass and nails around where we played. I don't think the city crew swept the streets much back then. But if there was a good rain, Swift Avenue North would always flood between Third and Fourth Streets and Pat and I would take off our shoes and socks, roll up our jeans and wade around in the water. Why we never stepped on the broken glass on the streets, I never knew. It never even entered our minds.

Mom, who was scared to death of lightning, would yell out the front door, "You kids are gonna get electrocuted!" Then she would grab her little bottle of Holy Water and run around the house sprinkling it. I guess she had reason to be afraid. Lightning struck our kitchen window once and Mary Jensen and Alma Colmen, our neighbors on either side of us, had lightning strikes.

The transformer on the pole behind Jensen's took a hit and Alma had a tree in her front yard get zapped. I was always reading about lightning strikes in the *Independent Review* newspaper. There'd be a picture of someone standing by a fried telephone or TV set or they'd be pointing at some black spot on the wall. You don't hear much about those kinds of lightning strikes anymore.

Sunday mornings we always went to church, but in the afternoon Mom cleaned Abe's Place pool hall[12], which was half a block from the turkey plant. My brothers and I helped Mom with that pool hall job, knowing that we could get in a free game of pool or get a pack of cigarettes, when Mom wasn't looking. When we'd walk into the pool hall, we'd be overwhelmed by the putrid, acrid smell of old smoke, spilled beer, and God knows what else.

Mom would get on her knees in front of the bar cleaning spit and tobacco off the floor and bar foot rail. She'd empty the spittoons into the toilets and soak them in a bucket that had bleach and water in it. Then she'd have to clean the smelly, filthy bathrooms. Mom protected her boys from that disgusting part of life and she never asked us to help with that job, just the barroom floor.

We'd sweep or dust and help scrub the floor with mops soaked in the bleach and water solution. Pretty soon the bleach smell would start to burn our throats and our eyes. Finally we'd get a giant squeegee and push the bleach water out the back door. Good riddance! Mom only did

---

[12] 26-28 Second Street West. See page 442 of the History of Downtown Litchfield Appendix.

that job for a couple of years. I think it was too much for her and we were getting harder to talk into helping her, as we grew older. It taught us a lesson about drinking and what it did to people, though. None of us have a drinking problem today, even though Mick and I spent a large portion of our lives playing music in bars.

There's a saying that "If Mom ain't happy, ain't nobody happy." That's pretty true I guess, but not in our case. If Mom would've burdened us with her problems and aches and pains, we wouldn't have survived as well as we did. She kept her problems to herself. We were only occasionally reminded of them when we'd see her tending to her swollen feet and cracked and bleeding hands or hear her crying alone in her bedroom. How Mom endured the troubles she had, while raising four pretty normal boys on her own, is a testament to her own upbringing and her faith in God, her religion. It was a religion that added to her miseries, I might add. Being a devout Catholic, Mom was forced to remain single and alone while my dad was still alive. She really believed that, in the Church's and God's eyes, she was still married to him. And, for some reason, she still loved him.

Mom was a normal mother; she just had extra problems heaped onto her normal mother problems. She dispensed the advice and the guilt trips onto us like every mother did. All mothers say the same things to their kids, I suppose. I call them "Mom-isms". Mom had one favorite saying. It was used only when she had reached her limit of our sass or our disobedience.
"I walked into the valley of death to give you life, and this is the thanks I get."
She would finalize things with "Because I said so, that's why, and I'm your mother," and the real last word was "That's the end of that!"
Other Mom-isms she used were:
"You are not going out of this house looking like that."
"I will not sit next to you in church unless you cut your hair."
"It's so loud in here, I can't hear myself think."
"I don't care what all your friends are doing. If all your friends jumped into the lake, would you jump too?"
"I hope you tell in Confession how you treat your mother."
"I don't know why I even bother to cook for you. I've slaved over a hot stove ever since I came home from work, and now you tell me you're not going to eat any supper?"

"Please clean your plate. I work hard to buy that food for you. I swear you kids are the reason I'm fat 'cause I have to eat all the food you leave on your plates. I can't throw it away."

"There's kids starving in China who would give anything for that piece of liver or those beets."

"This is the worst pigsty I've ever seen."

"This room is a disaster area."

"Did a tornado come through your room?"

"You boys are giving me all these gray hairs."

"If you keep making those faces (or crossing your eyes), it will stay like that."

"Stop pouting! If your lip hangs any lower, you'll trip on it."

"How many times do I have to tell you...don't throw things in the house."

"Close the door behind you. Were you born in a barn?"

"Okay, who's been using my good scissors? You did WHAT with them?"

"There's enough dirt in those ears to grow potatoes in."

"I hope you put clean underwear on, in case you're in an accident."

"Stop picking at that. It'll get infected and I'm not paying for a doctor visit."

"Someday you'll be sorry you picked on your little brother."

"What are you digging for back there? Gold?"

"I'm not just talking to hear my own voice, you know."

"No, I can't give you any money. Money doesn't grow on trees, you know."

"What do you think I'm made of? Money?"

"This hurts me more than it hurts you."

"What are you boys doing up there? Don't make me come up there. If I have to come up there, I'm bringing the belt with me."

"I walked two miles to school in the rain and the snow, so don't give me any more excuses."

"I was just worried sick, and you didn't even have the decency to call me and let me know where you were. You could've been laying dead in a ditch somewhere." (To which Dennie once replied, "Then how could I have called you?" That earned him an immediate icy glare and tear in the corner of her eye and a controlled raised hand, loaded with a never delivered slap to the face.)

Some of her Mom-isms were impossible for us to do or they were just downright confusing:

"Will you just look at the dirt on the back of your neck!"

"Shut your mouth and eat your food."

"If you fall down from there and break your legs, don't come running to me."

"Lock the doors when you get home. I don't want to wake up dead in the morning." The scary thing is that we knew what she meant.

And then there was the curse. I laughed about the curse back then but I think it actually worked on us. Well I know it worked on one of us for sure, but that brother will remain nameless. The curse...isn't it self-fulfilling for all of us? If we have children, don't we make sure that the curse comes true? Here's the curse: "I hope someday you have a son (a daughter...children) just like yourself." Maybe Grandma Rheaume "cursed" Mom when she was being bad when she was little?

Of course Mom never got to say the Mom-ism "Wait until your father gets home," to us. I always felt cheated when I would hear about "Dad-isms" like "Pull my finger..." or "I'll pull this car over and turn right around if you kids don't quiet down," or "I brought you into this world and I can take you out of this world." Of course, we just eliminated the middleman because we also never got to hear, "I don't know, go ask your mother." Other than the short time Grandpa Shaw lived with us, we never had a man in the house until Dennie turned to manhood and left for the Marines. I shouldn't say "never". I do have a couple of vague memories of Dad in the house. They must be my very first memories because he left when I was three. Anyway, I remember being spanked for something and then spanked again because I wouldn't stop crying from the first spanking. I don't remember if Dad said that famous Dad-ism to me or not, but he probably did. "If you don't stop crying, I'll give you something to cry about."

Our stepfather, Floyd Young, never said much to us as far as rules or Dad-isms. It was probably because he came into our lives when we were teenagers and he was walking into and through a minefield. But he did say something to me once that I've never forgotten. I've passed it on to my children and I know from first hand that it is true. Once when I was complaining about being asked to come in by midnight, Floyd advised me, "Nothing good ever happens after midnight, Terry." Another time when there was a discussion about some ill-conceived ideas or plans that were thought up over beers in a bar, Floyd said, "Like most things conceived in a bar, it probably should have been aborted."

I've told my children a couple of my own Dad-isms. At least I think I came up with them. One is "Whenever you have to chose between spending time with your family, especially a family reunion, or with your friends, pick your family." Simply stated, "Family always comes first." The other one came when my wife and I were walking out the door one day a couple of years ago.

"We're going out for dinner," I said to my stepson Peter. "Would you like to go along?"

"No, thanks," he replied.

"There's two things you should never turn down, Peter," I told him. "An opportunity to go to the bathroom and a free meal."

I'm sure every mother used the same system when it came to calling her children by name. "Terry..." meant everything was okay and I should respond. If my real first name was used however, "Terrance...", I should start to be concerned. I was doing something wrong. If my middle name was thrown in, "Terrance Raymond...", my level of concern should rise and, finally, if my whole name was used, "Terrance Raymond Shaw!", I should probably stop at church for Confession on my way out of town.

Chapter Three
Jobs

The Shaw boys were quite independent growing up. The circumstance of our one-parent family and our finances forced this upon us at an early age. Mom provided my three brothers and I with the necessities of life: a roof over our heads, food on the table, a couple of changes of clothes per year, necessary school supplies, and one, yes one, new toy each Christmas. That was it. Anything additional that we wanted, we paid for by ourselves. Because of this, we all had little jobs around Litchfield to earn spending money, such as the paper routes and the Produce work.

I suppose I could demonstrate Mom's finances by pointing out that we didn't get a phone until 1951. Mom couldn't afford one. When we did get one, my great-aunt and great-uncle, Millie[13] and Ed Birkemeyer, paid for it. They still ran their Birkemeyer Automatic Sales Company out of our garage until 1954. The business sold and repaired jukeboxes, pinball machines and slot machines. The pinballs were slowly being pushed out of bars and restaurants. The slot machines had already been outlawed, although several places disregarded the law and kept them.

One morning in May of 1941, three men walked into the Bye-Way, a bar north of town, after waitress Beatrice Sweeney had opened the doors. The men told Beatrice that they were from the sheriff's office and were there to confiscate the slots Alden Bye had in the place. They calmly picked them up, full of money, and carried them out to their truck, where two more men sat. Thinking it looked suspicious, Beatrice called Sheriff Art Krueger to confirm it, which he didn't. He tracked the five men down and arrested them in Willmar. Of course, Alden got fined anyway and lost his three slots.

In the forties, the Bye-Way was used as a Youth Center on Friday nights. Parents would drop their teenagers off there for a chaperoned night of dancing, food and games. Some teens thought it strange that Alden would give up a big money night just for them. I don't know if Alden was a concerned citizen or if he was doing "community service" for his "crimes". Maybe it was both.

---

[13] Mildred "Millie" was Grandpa Bill Shaw's sister. She and Leonard Michaud, one of her two former husbands, built our house in 1940. Leonard had an automatic sales business, i.e. jukeboxes, pinball machines and slots. After Leonard died in September of 1941, Millie married her third husband, Ed Birkemeyer, who took over the business. Ed had been married before also. Millie and Ed moved to 318 Armstrong Avenue South after selling their house to my parents.

The Feds thought the slots might be coming from Uncle Ed so they and Sheriff Krueger raided our garage in 1943 and took all the slots that were stored up in the attic. Then the government started in on the pinball machines. The problem with the pinball machines was that you got "prizes" for racking up points and therefore it was somehow construed as gambling. Our absent father used to give us those prizes for Christmas gifts. They were adult prizes, so as a little kid, I got some strange gifts from him, such as a cribbage board. I learned how to play the game though. I think the Birkemeyers saw the writing on the wall, because they sold the business to my dad, who was working for them. Mom always told me that Attorney General Miles Lord, who was behind the outlawing of the machines, put my father out of business and was one of the reasons that he didn't send her any money for our support.

Anyway, we boys did anything and everything we could around Litchfield to earn spending money. Dennie had a variety of jobs. He worked for Bob Sparboe taking little chicks out of the hatching incubators and putting them into boxes for the ladies to "sex", that is to determine the sex of the chick. Also, Dennie and his friend, Bob Schreifels, who was my friend Andy's oldest brother, reclaimed copper wire out of the old motors Bob's dad Leonard was rewinding for his business.[14] They sold the copper wire to Ollie Prieve for two cents a pound. Any old batteries around town that weren't tied down and some from the town dump were carted off to junkyards to sell for the lead.

Dennie also worked at Vern Worden's mink farm, which was where the newer addition to the golf course is today. Dennie and a boy named Billy Tomlinson fed the mink. Vern, who started the business in 1942, would buy old decrepit cows, kill them, and chop them into pieces. Dennie and Billy would put the cow pieces into a nasty old grinder. In about twenty minutes, the whole cow, and other assorted stuff, consisting of chicken heads and what not, would come out of the grinder as five-gallon pails of "hamburger mush". Once in a while an old horse was the meat of the day. Vern would pull the skin off the nag with his John

---

[14] The shop was at the corner of Armstrong Avenue and Ninth Street East, right next to the Schreifel's residence. Leonard Schreifels bought the building for his business from Robert Kaping in 1944. Bob Kaping had moved into the building in April of 1938 after Glader and West had moved out. After selling to Leonard, Bob moved downtown with his business.

Deere tractor. Vern got bit by one of those horses in '55 and it turned out the horse had rabies. So Vern had to go through the series of shots.

When the Dakotas and Montana became overrun with jackrabbits, Worden sent some men with a semi-truck out there and they proceeded to do a "round up". The men circled a farmer's field and beat the grass and, eventually, the jackrabbits with sticks. They brought back the semi full of fresh mink feed. Worden found mink feed everywhere. He had fifteen tons of frozen rough fish, which were seined out of Canadian lakes, trucked to his mink farm in February of 1958.

Dennie had a job for the Litchfield Ice Company at Litchfield's old icehouse[15]. Now why would Litchfield need an icehouse in the modern fifties? Surely everyone had a refrigerator by then? No, they didn't. Pat and I would stay at our aunt and uncle's farm by Osakis, Minnesota in the mid-fifties and they didn't have indoor plumbing. They didn't have electricity until 1949 and then a toaster shorted out one morning and burned their house down. They lived in their chicken coup for a year until their house was rebuilt. I stayed in it with them and their daughter Bev.

"Wash ice" was still being sold. People bought blocks of it to melt and use for washing clothes. It was soft water. I know that the milkman had ice in the back of his delivery truck. His name was Earling "Red" Stark or just "Starkey". He had the whole bit, a white uniform including a military-looking cap covering his red hair, and a little white milk truck with sliding doors for him to hop out of. On hot summer days, Pat and I would wait for Red to stop his "milk wagon" in front of our house to deliver glass bottles of milk that had a cardboard stopper on the top instead of a cap. Mom would leave her empties on the kitchen doorstep with some dollar bills and a slip of paper sticking out of the neck of one. On the paper she'd write something like "3 whole, 1 pt. cream".

"Can we have some ice, mister?" Pat and I would ask Red when he was done with his delivery. He'd reach into the back of the little truck and hand us a couple of fist-sized chunks, which we'd suck on. We had no idea that it probably came from Lake Ripley and we were sucking on some frozen pee that our friends and we had deposited in the lake ourselves in the previous summer at the swimming beach. Was this nature's ways of recycling?

---

[15] 200 Commercial Street East. See page 486 of the History of Downtown Litchfield Appendix.

The icehouse was near the corner of Commercial Street and Holcombe Avenue, where Litchfield Lumber is today. An earlier version of the lumberyard[16] was across Holcombe, almost from the beginnings of Litchfield. About three and a half stories high and capable of holding ten million pounds of ice, the icehouse was a big gray wooden barn-type building. There were no windows but lots of doors on the two long sides of the building and big long wooden ladders and chutes covered in tin inside. There were lots of big pulleys and ropes hanging inside from the rafters, which supported a steep black tar shingled roof that had big vents on the top. Lots of pigeons nested up there in those rafters. A big front door, facing north, was wide enough to drive a good-sized truck inside to unload ice.

There was a little office on the ground floor of the building to the west of the big door. The inside of the icehouse was very dark and smelled of wet sawdust. But the cool wet wood smell was pleasant. There were big stacks or tiers of large chunks of ice, which were about two and a half feet wide, one foot thick and three or four feet long. The building could handle forty tiers of ice, which were covered with canvas tarps and sawdust.

Tony DeMars, a friend of Dennie's, lived by the icehouse. He had a younger brother, Pat, who was a friend of my brother Pat. Tony, or his father Russ, had some connection with old man Henry Martens who ran the icehouse, because Tony and Dennie enjoyed a very cool and very short-lived summer job there moving sawdust around covering blocks of ice. They goofed off a lot and didn't do too much work. The owner caught them smoking inside one day, and with all that sawdust around, he fired them on the spot.

Then Dennie worked for Bernie and Shirley Sandberg. They ran Sandberg's Precision Tool on the eastern edge of town, making steel molds for rubber injection molding of all kinds, like the gasket that would go inside the back cover of a watch to make it water proof. Dennie's job was to clean up the shop. He finally graduated to running a drill press.

Dennie got interested in Morse code, because our Uncle William "Bud" Rheaume had done it during WWII. Dennie started hanging

---

[16] 100-124 Commercial Street East. See page 485 of the History of Downtown Litchfield Appendix.

around the depot bugging the Western Union telegraph[17] operator and depot agent, Paul S. Whitaker[18]. Whitaker asked Dennie if he wanted a job after school. The Shaw boys never turned down a job. Dennie started working at the depot loading and unloading freight.

Dennie put a telegraph set up into his bedroom and wired it to go out to the garage. He talked of stringing a wire all the way down the street and across the railroad tracks to Ludwig Andreen's house, but the plan never materialized. He got an "On The Air" sign somewhere and put it up outside his bedroom door. It lit up and was just meant to be a "Keep Out" sign because he never was "on the air". Anyway, he told Pat and I to "stay the hell out of his room". I made the mistake of going in there one time, ignoring the "On The Air" sign. He was playing darts. He told me to leave. I defiantly stayed and mistakenly walked right in front of him while he was throwing a dart. He stuck the dart right between my eyes. He caught hell from Mom for that one and put me further down on his list of people he liked.

One summer Dennie got a job through the Farm Bureau Office to work on a dairy farm. He went to live at an old farmer's house. The dairy farmer would bring Dennie in on Saturday evenings so Mom could wash his clothes. Dennie had to hitch a ride back on Monday mornings with Tom O'Keefe, the fuel oil deliveryman. He had to be there in time to hook up the one hundred and twenty Holsteins to the milking machines. At the end of the summer, Dennie was paid $300.00. Mom was very upset about this. She reported the man to the Farm Bureau and called to chew him out for taking advantage of Dennie.

Of course, during this time Dennie was playing some weekend dance jobs with his rock and roll band, renamed The Chancellors after starting out as The Rockets. As rock and roll was in its infancy, Dennie's dance jobs were few and far between. He wrote a song called *Dear Barbara* and Larry Graf from Hutchinson recorded the group doing it on an acetate record on his home record cutting machine. Dennie played it on Litchfield's KLFD radio station where he is working for free as a guest teenage disc jockey.

---

[17] Litchfield's first Western Union telegraph office was in the Robertson building at the northwest corner of Sibley Avenue and Third Street. At different times, it had been under the hotel, over the Meeker County Bank, and over the "old courthouse". It was moved to the train depot in June of 1902.

[18] Whitaker's father, Al J. Whitaker, had been the depot agent in Litchfield since 1898. Al worked for the railroad for fifty-four years, starting in 1883 in another town. His father, J. A., had also worked for the railroad.

Mick had started playing rock by this time too, trying different instruments before settling on the bass, jumping from band to band. All of these bands practiced in our garage or in our basement in the wintertime. I hung around them, sitting high up on the basement steps, watching the drummers' every move. For a long time, the drummer was always Jerry Wheeler, who didn't really like rock and roll but was a fantastic drummer.

The Defiants in 1964: Mike Shaw, Jerry Wheeler, Loren Walstad and Dick Newman.

I had fallen in love with the drums and I used to play along with records in my room on my makeshift drum set, which consisted of boxes. The round Quaker Oats boxes were great sounding, by the way, and my sticks were two butter knives. They had unbelievable bounce. When the bands would leave the basement to go uptown for coffee breaks, I would sneak downstairs and bang away on the real drums, teaching myself to play them the correct way. Mick came home unexpectedly once and caught me. He yelled at me, an argument ensued, and he hit me, but my drumming is what eventually brought us back together. Music also brought Dennie and I back together in later years as we started co-writing songs. Before that there was this natural division in the family where Mick and Dennie did things together and Pat and I did things together.

Sylvester "Spotty" Loehr had an A & W Drive-In[19] out on east Highway 12. He used to pipe Minneapolis radio station WDGY's music or records from an old nickel jukebox in the building onto his public address system to entertain his patrons. The music was constantly being interrupted by announcements like "Judy, pickup for station two. Station three would like more napkins."

---

[19] See page 499 of the History of Downtown Litchfield Appendix.

Starting on August 22, 1960, Spotty began running occasional Teen Hops on Friday nights to drum up business. He had the dances under the west canopy of his double-winged drive-in. The dances went over so well that Spotty hired Mick's band to play one Friday night. About half-way through the dance, Mick asked Alvie Watkins, Terry Kohlhoff and I to get up on the hay wagon with his band and sing background on a couple of songs. We did some "doo-wops" and even threw in some back and forth dance steps together that we had kidded around with to some records at Terry's house, just like we had seen the acts do on *American Bandstand* on TV. That's probably where Mick had seen us do it before. That was the first of thousands of times that Mick and I would be on a stage together doing rock and roll music.

Spotty's A & W without the side canopies or "wings".

I wrote a song about how music was a thread that ran through our family and kept us together. My song blends into other songs that are part of my memories. That first night on stage with Mick became a verse in the song and it goes into the first song I remember singing in duet with Mick when he took me on as his drummer in his band, The Defiants. I replaced Jerry Wheeler, my idol.

THE SONG GOES ON
Brother Mick took up the drums and joined the music race.
Then he tried the guitar, but he settled on the bass.
How many bands, I can't recall. I listened to them all.
But, I remember one night at a drive-in in the fall.
Mick let me get up on the stage and sing some background stuff.
The bands still practiced at our place; on Mom, it sure was rough.
I'd sneak downstairs when they were gone and beat the drums
"crash...bang!"
When Mick asked me to join his band, together we both sang...
[Go into *Rip It Up* by the Everly Brothers.]

Mick had a job for about a week at the gas station to the south of the Community Building. It was a strange looking wooden building. What was strange about the structure was that it was round, about the size of a Merry-Go-Round, so we called it the "Merry-Go-Round building". Little did we know that long ago, in the late 1800s and early 1900s, it actually housed a steam powered Merry-Go-Round[1] owned by the Olson brothers.

An aerial view of the Merry-Go-Round building in the thirties. To the right is the Community Building.

A son of one of the Olson brothers, named Martin, lived on the east side of town in a strange looking place at 627 South Street East. Martin collected odd machines and shiny things like the colorful glass globes that are popular in gardens today. Martin built a mosaic wall of colorful tiles around his house and yard. The wall had a large tiled archway for the sidewalk, which led up to his front door. His backyard was a wonderland of glass globes, statues, bright and shiny objects and a full size replica of the Liberty Bell held up by posts that matched Martin's mosaic wall.

All the way in the back of the yard was a shed where Martin kept his machines. Some played music, like an automated fiddle player and some just did odd things. I guess you could call the shed a gizmo museum. Martin let anyone come into his yard to look at and admire his collection. Pat and I went there several times and I brought my own kids back there in the seventies to see it. They loved it.

Martin was eccentric in another way too. He loved to watch country and western music shows on TV like KSTP-TV's *Barn Dance*, which was on Saturday nights. Martin would dress up in his own country and western outfit when he sat down to watch those shows. "Not only can I see them," he'd say, "but they can see me too." All that remains today is the wall and arch in the front yard and the Liberty Bell in the back.

Norb's Cut Rate Service, owned by Norbert Kohmetscher, was the gas station in that odd building where Mick worked. Norb's brother Paul

---

[1] See page 536 of the "Litchfield Downtown History Appendix."

married Eleanor Young, who was a sister to Floyd, our future stepfather. I'd see Floyd working there in the evenings, helping Norb out. Pat and I also knew Floyd from watching him do street repair work for the city maintenance crew around by our street. He always had a pipe sticking out of the corner his mouth while he worked.

The reason Mick didn't last long at the service station job, I was told, was that his service was slow and he had trouble finding some of the gas tank filler caps. This was in the days when an attendant filled your gas tank, checked your oil, water and tires' pressure and washed all of your windows. It was also in the days when car companies took delight in hiding the filler caps, such as behind your license plate.

Pat, Mick and Dennie also did corn detasseling, a job I wanted no part of when I would see them come home from work early in the evening all hot, sweaty, tired, filthy and bug bit. They would walk up and down acres and acres of corn in the hot summer sun pulling the tassel, or the male part, out of the top of the corn stalk so that another crew could come along and shake pollen onto the silk, the female part.

The fields were muddy and the workers would literally carry around about five pounds of mud on each foot after an hour or so of walking through the fields. After eight or ten hours in the field, they could hardly walk. Mosquitoes, flies and bugs of every description would fly up their noses and get into their ears. "No thank you," I told Mom when she suggested I do it too. I was just as poor as my brothers, but, hating bugs, I drew the line there.

Left: Detasseling. Right: Crew: 2nd from left is Dennis "Ole" Olson, 4th is Dennie Shaw, 6th is Paul "Chuck" Loch, 7th is Wayne Herman, a friend of mine, and his sister Donna.

Dennie also worked at the Litchfield Seed Store stacking bags of chicken feed, seed, and salt blocks in the warehouse. One summer he picked peas for the Cokato canning factory. I stayed with my cousin Tommy Wolf in Fairmont, Minnesota for two weeks one summer to work for Stokely-Van Camp doing the same thing. Tommy and I generally goofed off and ate the peas or threw them at each other while the migrant workers got farther and farther ahead of us down the rows of the field we were working in.

We were paid by the weight of the picked peas, which we put in a bushel basket that we carried down the rows, so Tommy and I would throw a few clumps of dirt in with the peas to give it more weight. We got paid less if it had rained the night before because of the added weight from the moisture on the peas, so we just evened things out, as it was a wet two weeks that summer.

Around noon, Tommy and I would usually tell the foreman that we didn't feel well and we'd catch a ride into town on a pea truck. In town, we'd head for Ward's Park and have a picnic with the lunch Tommy's mom, Aunt Marietta, had packed for us. Then we'd go exploring the Winnebago Indian caves around Sisseton Lake.

Late on the following Friday afternoon, Tommy and I reported to the main office for our pay. We stood in the long line with the migrant workers, shuffling forward. When the worker finally got up to the pay clerk, he'd identify himself, the clerk would repeat his name, announce his pay, and count it out in front of him from a small white envelope that had his name on it. This is what Tommy and I heard as we worked our way up the line: "Gomez...$62.47. Next. Garcia...$55.23. Next. Rodriquez...$69.14. Next. Wolf...$3.27. Next. Shaw...$5.17. Next."

Dennie, being the oldest, broke ground for us and many of his jobs were handed down to Pat and I. He was the first, for example, to mow our neighbors Alma Colmen and Kate Pierce's lawns. Pat and I would carefully divide their lawns into perfectly equal sections and take turns mowing. Most people didn't have power mowers in those days, so we would have to use their old dull-bladed push mowers. It wasn't an easy job for a little kid because the push handles were up near our heads. We really earned those quarters that we charged.

Someone told Pat and I about the money we could make by selling babbitt to the junkyard. That was all we needed to hear. We started prospecting babbitt. Babbitt was a tin or lead based alloy used by the railroad to line the bearings of the boxcar wheels. Because it had a low melting point, it would heat up inside the wheels and drop out onto the tracks. It looked like large, nickel-sized clumps of solder.

We each made ourselves a couple of peanut butter and jelly sandwiches, threw them into a paper bag, grabbed an empty coffee can and set out west on the railroad tracks towards Chicken Lake woods, which was about two and a half miles away. The woods were to the north of Chicken Lake, which got its name because the shape of it looked like a chicken.

A map shows the shape of Chicken Lake.

At first I was leery of this venture. I had never heard of babbitt and I didn't have a clue what it was supposed to look like. But, we had hardly gone a block from the crossing by our house when Pat stopped, leaned over and picked up a shiny little nugget of something. "I'll bet this is it," he said, dropping it into the empty can. We were on our way to riches. We walked all afternoon and nearly filled the coffee can. Along the way, we ate our sandwiches and threw rocks at blackbirds on the power lines or at the glass insulators on the tops of the poles.

We had been to Chicken Lake woods before on snake hunts. Dennie had told us where to find the snakes after he had brought a few home for pets. We caught hell from Mom for bringing a bag of them home. We were going to show them at our backyard carnival, another moneymaking venture we did several times, complete with penny games of chance, a variety show in a tent made from Mom's sheets strung over the clothes line, wagon rides, and animals to look at, (once we had a real live badger).

We'd organize a parade to entice neighborhood kids to come to our carnival. Those parades must have been a sight to see. We would dress up our dog Sparky and put him in the red wagon. Then we would put together some costumes for ourselves and decorate our bikes. Mickey would lead us down the street with his trumpet, which he played for a year or so in the lower grades of school. One of Marion Hatrick's daughters, who lived down the street from us, would twirl her baton, I'd beat on some homemade drum and Pat would carry a flag or a gun or a stick. We would march for blocks, all the way down to the "little store" by Lincoln Park, trying to drum up business.

When Pat and I returned home with our babbitt, we put the coffee can on the stove at the medium setting, as we had been instructed to do, and we waited for the clumps to melt down. They did melt, very quickly in fact, and we grabbed Mom's potholders and set the can in the kitchen sink, which we had half filled with cold water. Cooled down, the large shiny and heavy block of metal slid easily out of the blackened coffee can. We put our treasure into a paper bag and biked it out to the Meis Brothers' junkyard to sell. Mr. Meis weighed it and gave us fifty cents for it, a quarter each, which seemed a fair wage for a full day's work.

My dependable source of income, of course, was the paper route I had inherited from Dennie. Called a "paperboy", I delivered thirty evening papers and fifty Sunday papers, earning about $2.50 to $3.00 a week. I put fifty cents of that away in a "bond", which was a savings account the paper kept for us, and about $1.00 of it went into the "Bank of Mom" for safe keeping. The rest was my spending money.

The Elmer Dilley family's dog bit me on my very first day on the job, a cold winter day. Dennie used to throw rocks at that dog every day, but only in self-defense, he later told Mom. The growling dog saw my yellow *Minneapolis Star* bag hanging from my shoulder and he came running, clamping his teeth around my ankle. I finished the route that day limping, bleeding, and crying. By the time I had reached my last stop, the new Power Plant at the corner of Donnelly Avenue and Third Street, my eyes had frozen almost completely shut from the tears. I stood next to the giant turbine engines until they thawed out. Then I limped home to my frantic mother, who kept ranting about rabies and shots!

I was always bored to tears walking that paper route at about 4 o'clock every afternoon. I got to the point where I could walk my route in my sleep. During the school year, I started doing my homework reading assignments while walking the route. People must have thought I was a strange kid, walking up to their house with my nose in a book, reaching into my yellow shoulder bag, pulling out a paper and throwing it in between their doors, without ever lifting my eyes up from the book.

In the summer I would sing to myself, making up songs, fantasizing movie plots or TV shows, with myself as the star, or even draw pictures. Occasionally I would hear a sonic boom or a loud roar overhead and I'd look up to the skies to see a jet flying westward over Litchfield, seemingly so low that I could reach up and touch it. That was thrilling. In January of 1958, the Air Force announced in the local newspaper that they were going to start doing some low-level training flights over Litchfield with Boeing B-47 Stratojet bombers flying out of a base in Lincoln, Nebraska. There was also an Air Force base thirty miles away in Willmar, Minnesota, and their pilots would also practice their low-level flights over Litchfield with smaller jets. The base became Ridgewater College.

Pat had a paper route too. He inherited his from Mick and it was one of the best paper routes in town. Possibly Mick was given that great route because of his celebrity[21] status. The route included the stores uptown and some of the nicer homes on Sibley Avenue South. Storeowners and "well-to-do" people meant a gift bonanza for Pat at Christmas time. He really raked it in, as opposed to me.

My route was a mile and a half long and included the 300 to 500 numbered blocks of Swift, Austin and Donnelly Avenues, and went out of town on Fifth Street West to a couple of farms. It was the "poor side of town", complete with the tarpaper shack of the Carlson family, who never paid me, and the smelly houses of extremely old people, (there's a particular smell to old people's kitchens, believe me). I was lucky to get a couple of boxes of chocolate covered cherries at Christmas time. But I grew to love that candy. I carry on the tradition by giving my carriers a box at Christmas also. If they only knew I was carrying on a very old tradition, they wouldn't think me so cheap. Right?

There was one problem with Pat's paper route; it was a morning route. That meant getting up before school and walking around Litchfield in the dark. The uptown was well lit, but by the time Pat got further south on Sibley Avenue to the residential area, he was in darkness. The Johnson-Hagglund Funeral Home was on Sibley South and Pat had to deliver the paper there. He would run up the funeral home steps, throw the paper in between the doors and run back to the street as fast as he could before a dead person in the front room saw him and rose up out of his casket to chase him down the street, like Frankenstein's monster or the Mummy. I wonder who planted that idea in his head? Possibly some cruel older brothers? An enterprising prankster could really have had some fun with Pat. It's amazing that I never tried, but that would have involved getting up in the wee hours of the morning. I've never been a morning person. Not even for a joke at Pat's expense.

---

[21] More about that is in Chapter Five Heart Heroes.

There were other easier jokes to be pulled at Pat's expense. The morning route meant that Pat had to go to bed earlier than the rest of us. Off and on, I would wait a few minutes after he had gone to bed and then sneak up the stairs in the dark. Assuring myself that he had fallen asleep, I would turn on the lights and yell, "Pat! Get up! You overslept!"

"Whaaaaaa?" he would say, squinting at me through his half opened eyes that he was rubbing with his fists.

"You overslept, you idiot! You're late for delivering your papers!"

Then the fun would begin. He'd jump up out of bed, throw his clothes on and run down the stairs, with me smugly following behind him. As he was throwing his boots and parka on by the kitchen door, Mom would come out of her bedroom.

"What in the world is going on out here?" she would say. I'd shrug my shoulders, giving her my best innocent look.

"Pat! What are you doing up?" Mom would ask him. Pat would stare back at her like a zombie. My laughter would burst out and give me away.

"You oughtta be ashamed of yourself, picking on your little brother like that," Mom would scold me. "I don't know what I'm gonna do with you, Terry."

Pat would shuffle back upstairs, a victim of one of his three older brothers once again. Dennie, Mick and I tormented that poor boy so much that he developed a stutter and a face tic, which caused him to blink his eyes all the time. He's recovered well today and seems to be fairly normal, and downright forgiving. I watch my back around him, though.

Dean Schultz ran herd over the paperboys for twenty-nine and a half years. In August of 1946, Dean ran a taxi in town with a stand at the hotel. Then he was put in charge of his first four paperboys, working out of his 1931 Model A car in front of the hotel. He succeeded Dan Brown, who also had a restaurant in town. The papers came in on the bus. That evolved into Dean working from the first paper shack, which was on Depot Street near Marshall Avenue. Then it was moved to the vacant lot near our house.

Dean also worked at the Post Office. He was a substitute carrier for twelve years, then a full-time worker. He became the town's postmaster in September of 1961. Dean played tuba in the city band that performed in the park every Friday night in the summer. While Dean worked, either at the Post Office or at the paper shack, he constantly "burr-burr-burred" with his lips, playing an unknown song on an imaginary tuba.

Every Thursday evening was "meeting night" at the paper shack. We would pay our bill for the papers and then Dean would talk to us about missing deliveries, picking up our papers late and try to fire us up to go out looking for new subscriptions. "It's more money in your pocket," Dean would tell us.

Dean didn't motivate us to go out and sell subscriptions very well until the *Star-Tribune* started offering promotions to tempt the new subscribers and us. They got two weeks' delivery free and we got prizes. You could work for small prizes, like a transistor radio, or you could save up subscriptions for a larger prize, like a trip or a Schwinn bike. But the Schwinn was way out of our reach. My oldest step-brother-to-be, Val "Larry" Young, sold enough subscriptions to get a bike though and he had his picture in the *Independent Review* newspaper standing next to it.

A memorable prize was a water skiing trip, called the Ski-O-Rama. Pat and I canvassed Litchfield on our bicycles and we were able to earn that trip by each of us selling the required number of subscriptions. We were driven six miles south to Lake Minnebelle, where two boats gave each of the dozen or so of us paperboys three chances to get up out of the water. Pat and I failed all three times, drinking our share of the lake in the process. We were then given a freshly grilled hot dog, a bottle of Orange Kist Soda or Gold Medal grape pop from the Litchfield Bottling Works[22] and some potato chips before being driven back to the paper shack lot.

Another trip we worked hard to earn was quite a big deal. We were driven to Minneapolis where we stayed overnight at a real hotel for the first time in our young lives. It was the quite seedy Andrews Hotel on Hennepin Avenue and Fourth Street. Many of us were to return there in the late sixties the night before our pre-induction physicals, when we got drafted during the Vietnam War. Early the following morning, the paperboys were driven to the Minnesota State Fair grounds in St. Paul. We were given admission tickets, a couple of dollars to eat on and then turned loose, totally on our own, for the entire day. Pat and I spent most of the day getting freebies like yardsticks and pencils in the Commercial Building, walking up and down the carnival on the Midway or trying to make our limited spending money stretch in the Penny Arcade tent. Pat had one of his pennies flattened by a machine, which stamped some saying on it. It was his big souvenir of our big trip. Late that same night,

---

[22] 526 Ramsey Avenue North. See page 375 of the History of Downtown Litchfield Appendix.

we were driven back home to Litchfield. The car rolled back onto the gravel lot by the paper shack, where we were awakened to stumble home in a sleepy stupor.

The trip gave us the courage to do it again on our own the next few years. Somehow Pat and I, Andrew "Monk" Schreifels, Stan Lunderby and the Wimmer boys talked our mothers into letting us take the Greyhound bus to the cities, stay overnight at a hotel, make our way to the fairgrounds and get safely home again. We stayed at the much cheaper Kennesaw Hotel with all the winos and drunks. Why the clerk never questioned a group of kids renting a room for a night, I could never figure out. Money talks, I suppose. We never did anything wrong to the rooms and nothing ever happened to any of us there. We were living in a much different time. Nothing happened except for some very sore feet one time. We missed our bus that went back over the bridge to Minneapolis. Not knowing what else to do and not having any money for a cab, we walked all the way back to our hotel room to get our stuff before scrambling to the bus depot. It was about ten miles.

As we got into high school, we quit our paper routes. Pat and I passed ours on to some neighbor boys, Pat and Mike Hughes. I would imagine that all the paper routes in town could be traced back to those original three or four boys Dean started with; like the lineage of the Popes. Dean Schultz quit the paper business in late 1958 and Eldon C. Palm took it over. The paper shack was moved uptown to the alley behind Johnson's Drug. Floyd Young, our stepfather-to-be, worked part-time for Eldon, bundling up papers in the morning before he went off to work at his regular city maintenance job. On weekends, Floyd worked at the Produce in cleanup. Floyd was a man who wasn't afraid of work. Of course he was raising five children by himself, after the early death of his first wife, Lorraine.

Floyd's nephew Charlie Young also worked for Palm dropping off the paper bundles to the stores. He brought the papers to the hotel one early Sunday morning and was so sleepy and in such a hurry that he left his car in gear. The car proceeded south down Sibley Avenue in the direction of the railroad tracks. When Charlie returned, his car was closing in on the railroad crossing. He let out a cry and took off running. The night clerk, John Fisher, heard his scream, ran outside, and watched Charlie set a new world sprint record to catch up with his errant auto. He caught it just in time. John asked Charlie every Sunday after that if he had put his car into "park".

Chapter Four
More Jobs and Dingle and the American Dream

Sunday mornings were busy for me. I got up around 4:30am and pulled our old red wagon to the paper shack to load up the heavy Sunday Tribunes. I would finish delivering them just in time to return home and walk the five blocks to St. Phillip's Church with Mom for the six o'clock Mass. After Mass, I picked up my assigned stack of Sunday Visitor newspapers in the back of the church and ran down the steps to the sidewalk in front. I sold the papers for five cents and got to keep one penny for each one I sold. I did this before and after each of the three Sunday services, earning, at the most, $1.00 a Sunday.

St. Philip's Church.

There were two other religious papers being sold, one being the Catholic Register. Pat sold that one and Monk Schreifels sold the other one. Monk, short for "Monkey" I suppose, was really Andy, but a shaggy black mop of hair, that didn't hide two huge ears that stuck straight out, gave him the appearance of a chimp. He came from a family of sixteen kids. They ate in shifts. One of those kids had a tragic life.

I was playing with Monk in the basement of his house one day when we were both thirteen. All of a sudden, I heard some banging in another room.

"What's that noise?" I asked Monk.

"Oh, that's Mikey," he answered.

"Mikey?"

"Yeah, he's my little brother," Monk said, nonchalantly. He opened up the door and there, tethered to a bed, was an eight-year old boy who obviously was not right in the head. The room was pretty messy and smelled foul. I remember thinking, "This is not right."

Monk never told me the story about Mikey or why he was tethered to the bed and I never asked. I found out later on my own. Michael "Mikey" Schreifels was playing in the front yard one day when someone's car came speeding around the corner onto Holcombe Avenue. The car was pulling a trailer, which broke loose, swung onto the Schreifel's yard and slammed Mikey into a tree. He suffered brain damage. The family decided to keep Mikey at home and care for him themselves. Whether the decision was right or wrong, I don't know. I had to make the same decision ten years later when my Down syndrome daughter, Christine, was born.

It was an easy decision for me, but it had to be difficult for the Schreifels family. They had problems with Mikey. He was constantly wandering off. He made his way down to Jewett Creek[23] once and fell in, almost drowning. That was why he was tied to the bed, because no one but Monk and I were home at that time and Mrs. Schreifels, rightfully, couldn't trust Monk to keep an eye on Mikey. My heart still went out to the boy, although I was afraid of him. The family finally put Mikey into a facility in Cambridge, Minnesota, where he died at the age of sixteen in 1967.

Monk, the Wimmer boys and Pat and I did a lot of crazy things to amuse ourselves while we waited around outside of the church for Mass to get over. In a small town in the fifties, most people never locked their cars and a lot of them just left their keys in the ignition. So we'd pick out a car and take it for a ride around the block a few times. We got some good parallel parking practice in, returning the cars to their exact spot. I scored perfect on that part of my driver's license test.

After each paper selling, Monk, Pat and I would go next door, north of the church, to the priest's rectory to pay for the papers. Father Richard O'Connor, who had replaced the deceased Father Foley, set out three labeled cups on his kitchen table. We'd drop our coins into the cup with our paper's name on it.

Sometimes during the 8 o'clock Mass, when Father O'Connor's housemaid went to church, we'd sneak into Father's study and nose around. We found his box of Dutch Master cigars and helped ourselves to one or two for smoking later. We'd head south down the street to Highway 12 where Ole Larson's Travelers' Inn restaurant[24] was. In a

---

[23] The creek was named after T. Carlos Jewett, who came to Litchfield on June 20, 1856. At different times he was the Meeker County Sheriff, the registrar of deeds, a Justice of the Peace, and a United States Commissioner to Alaska.

[24] See page 498 of the History of Downtown Litchfield Appendix.

warm booth, we would treat ourselves to a Coke or a hot chocolate, making sure to get back to church just before Mass got over. Occasionally Pat and I would splurge and share a "Mud Ball", a big, rich, chocolaty, messy sundae, with marshmallow crème on the bottom. There went our morning's profits and our appetites for noon dinner at home.

Pat and I were lounging around in Father O'Connor's easy chairs in his study one Sunday morning while Monk snooped around in a bookcase.

"Hey what's this?" he said, holding up a canvas bag. Pat and I recognized it as a First State Bank moneybag, the same kind we had at home to put our paper route collection money in.

"It must be the church collection money from the first Mass," I said.

Monk pulled the drawstrings, opened the bag and peeked inside. He reached in, drew out some bills and envelopes and held them up for us to see, grinning from ear to ear.

"This won't be missed," he said, taking a few of the bills, stuffing them into his pocket and putting the envelopes back in the bag.

"Don't!" I said, jumping out of my easy chair. "Father's probably counted that!"

"No way!" Monk replied.

This sacrilegious theft went on every Sunday. Pat and I were sure that Monk was going to be struck by lightning and go straight to hell. About three Sundays later, we were sitting over hot chocolates at the Travelers' when Monk suddenly held up his hands for us to see.

"Hey! What the heck's on my hands?" he inquired to our puzzled faces. His hands had turned an inky black. He grabbed some napkins and started wiping them but the black didn't come off.

"What the hell?" he mumbled, standing up to wash them in the restroom. When he returned, we could see that the washing had not done any good either.

"We gotta get back to church," I said, looking up at the clock. "Take care of that later."

We sold our papers from the back of the church that Sunday because it was too cold to stand outside. Father O'Connor, still in his vestments, came into the vestibule after Mass, looked around, and walked over to Monk.

"I'd like to see you in the parish house, Andrew," he said, just above a whisper.

It turned out that Father O'Connor had indeed known how much money was in the canvas bag after each Mass. He had enlisted the aid of someone at the bank who had given him some powder to dust onto the money. It chemically reacted with the sweat on Monk's hands and turned them black. We all lost our jobs selling papers at the church. Monk had to pay the money back and I'm sure he caught royal hell from his dad, who had once studied for the priesthood. We were replaced with a coin box and the "honor system", with the papers stacked on a table in the vestibule of the church.

I supplanted my lost Sunday income by selling the Sunday Tribune in front of the Northwestern Bank. It was another job that Dennie had passed down to me, just in the nick of time. Dean Schultz would drop off a bundle of papers in the doorway of Ray Johnson's Drug Store. I'd pick them up and carry them down the street to the corner by the bank. There I stood all morning shivering in the cold selling Sunday papers to people driving by. It was cold and boring but I made more money than I ever did selling the Sunday Visitor at church. Any papers left would be dropped off back in the drug store doorway before noon. Ray would sell them in the store when he'd open up at noon for a couple of hours. After noon dinner, Pat and I would go to Abe's pool hall to help Mom clean. "No rest for the wicked" as they say.

In the summer, Pat and I would get up on the roof of our garage and reach over to the chokecherry tree that grew behind it, grabbing all we could to put into the pots held between our legs. We sold the chokecherries to our neighbors. We'd take whatever we could get for them, which was usually a promise of a jar or two of chokecherry jam from Mary Jensen or Alma Colmen.

Picking chokecherries wasn't the only thing we did up on the roof of the garage. One day we decided to parachute off, with the aid of Mom's umbrella. Once again our Guardian Angels were working overtime and nobody broke anything. Well, unless you count the umbrella, which turned inside out on the way down. After that unsuccessful try, we made little parachutes out of cloth and string and tied rocks to them. They floated down reasonably well, so we took them a step further and threw them off the water tower, once I had found out that I could climb to the top of it. More about that in a later chapter.

Probably the most unusual job Pat and I had was the selling of the "dog bone bags". We knew that on a certain day during the week, I think it was on Saturdays, the First District locker plant slaughtered pigs. The building was only a block away from our house, across the tracks to the south. We'd go behind the plant and dig through the garbage cans looking for the meaty bones nestled beside pigs' eyes, noses and other unidentifiable parts. We put the bones into paper bags brought from home. Then we went door to door selling them to people for their dogs. We asked for twenty-five cents a bag. It seems that everything we did was for a quarter, which the older people insisted on calling "two bits".

Pat and I would try any job offered in the backs of our comic books also. Both of us tried to sell subscriptions to a national newspaper called *Grit*. It was a forerunner of *USA Today*, I guess. It was hard to sell to people, though. They got the paper in the mail and news that's a couple of days' old wasn't appealing. Lured by an ad in some magazine, we sent for and sold punches on a punchboard card for a chance to win a stuffed animal. The board and the animal cost a certain amount and we kept whatever we sold the punches for. It was a great deal, but the punches were hard to sell. I don't think the people trusted us to be honest in the final drawing. But we were.

When county fair time rolled around, the carnival that was to come to town for it would let kids sell advance tickets to the rides. We'd pick up several sheets containing ten ride tickets at Johnson's Drug and go around town selling them for $1.00. Some rides cost two tickets, like the Tilt-A-Whirl. For every ten sheets we sold, we got a free sheet for ourselves. Pat and I really worked hard on selling those sheets. We each earned about ten sheets of ride tickets.

During fair week, we used up Pat's tickets, saving mine for Saturday, the last night of the fair, when we were going to go "hog wild". After supper on Saturday, I reached up on the top of the refrigerator where I had put them for safekeeping. They were gone! We started searching and yelling and running around accusing everybody and everybody's friends.

Mom said, "Don't worry, honey, they'll show up."

"But Mom," I yelled, "It's the last night of the fair!"

"Well, what do you want me to do about it?"

"I don't know," I said, wishing she had some extra money to give me for the rides that night. But I knew she didn't. Giving up the search after an hour, Pat and I got on our bikes and rode to the fair with our heads down, wondering what we'd do all night.

About ten that night, we heard our names being paged over the loud speaker, telling us to report to the fairground offices. There we were told to call home.

"I found your tickets," Mom told me. "Mickey's friend Larry was over and he said that he looked at them and put them into the cupboard above the frig by mistake." Doggone that Larry Andreen!

"The rides close at midnight," I told Pat. "Find Monk and Jerry and Dougy (Wimmer) and meet me at the Scrambler when I get back." I ran to my bike and peddled home as fast as I could. We lived over a mile away from the fairgrounds.

When I returned, Pat had all the guys waiting by the Scrambler. "Let's go!" I yelled, and we jumped on the ride. When the ride was over, I just handed the attendant more tickets and off we went again. When the ride ended again, we ran to the Tilt-A-Whirl. We rode that ride over and over and then ran to the Ferris Wheel and then the dreaded Bullet. We were exhausted and sick boys by midnight when the rides closed down, but I had managed to use every single ticket, not letting one go to waste. My friends saw a new generous side of me.

It seems that Pat and I did everything together, but occasionally he'd come up with some jobs on his own. He was quite industrious for a little brother. One of those jobs was putting flyers on cars for Lindquist Sheet Metal. Lindquist's was the Lennox furnace dealership and in an effort to increase business, Pat was asked to go around town on Friday nights, during the band concert, and put flyers on the windshields of cars. That was a way of advertising that has, thankfully, gone the way of cigarette ads. Everyone would come back to their cars, pull off the flyer, glance at it and throw it on the ground. There was always paper blowing around on the streets of downtown Litchfield.

Pat and I used to head uptown, as soon as we woke up, to walk the streets looking for money or Popsicle premium coupons on old wrappers. We'd save them up to send in for a cheap plastic wallet or some other prize. About once a week, we'd walk the alleys behind the stores, searching for discarded treasures in the piles of cardboard boxes, like old window displays or new but broken merchandise.

I found a couple of dollars once, which was a huge find and we found some actual plumed hats. Now they were cool. They were the kind you would see in *Mutiny On The Bounty*, worn by the British admiralty. We found them behind the Coast To Coast store. We could never figure out how they got there. It was a fantastic find. I now know where they came from. The Knights of Columbus used to have a meeting room above the store, where I eventually had an apartment. When the rooms were being converted into apartments, the hats were found and tossed into the garbage in the alley.

Stewart's Jewelry and the *Independent Review* were two places we could count on to find something of value. Stewart's threw away old window displays with tiny electric motors that moved a wire arm back and forth. We always had big plans for those motors, but they never developed. Stewart's also threw away beautiful velvet cloths that had decorated a jewelry display case. These were used to decorate our peach grate "dressers" in the clubhouse in our garage.

The *Independent Review* threw out pieces of paper, no doubt cut off larger reams of newsprint. They were great for notes, for drawing on, or for Mom's shopping lists. If the back door to the *Independent* were open, I'd often go inside to watch the huge press print the newspaper. The press seemed to take up the entire back room. It was so large and noisy that it was scary. A man with an inky denim apron on would just glance up at me and continue working, making sure the paper was fed into the press correctly.

It was during one of our "alley treasure hunts" that Pat and I happened upon Ed "Eeks" Nelson[25] in his sign painting shop, the Nelson Sign Company. I have no idea why he was called Eeks. He had several brothers, one of whom was called "Rats", another was "Babe" and yet another was called "Cooney". I delivered the paper to his home on Fifth Street where his gray-haired mother was always baking the best smelling bread in her kitchen. She'd invite me in on cold winter days to warm up and have a hot slice of fresh bread dripping with butter. It was heavenly.

Eeks' shop was in the alley west of Sibley Avenue, in a long building behind Fred Maass' new dentist office, which was on Second Street West. Nelson's sign painting shop was basically a two-story garage, with a basement and a room upstairs. The huge garage door facing north was always open. Walking down the alley, Pat and I saw Eeks inside his shop lettering a name on a side door of a truck. We went in to observe and struck up a conversation with him. Eeks always had a cigarette dangling out of the corner of his mouth and he smelled of alcohol. But he could sure paint those letters with a steady hand.

"How can you do that, mister?" I asked, marveling at his work.

---

[25] See Eeks' picture on page 280.

"Lots of practice son," Eeks replied, out of the corner of his mouth.

"Wow, you sure are good."

"Yea," Pat added.

"What you boys up to?" Eeks asked, loading up his brush with more red paint.

"Nothin'. Just lookin' 'round in the alley," I answered.

"Lookin' for work?" Eeks asked, stopping to flick a long ash off his cigarette and reload his brush again.

"We can't do that," I said, pointing to the half-finished door sign.

"No," Eeks laughed, "I'm lookin' for someone to sweep out my shop every afternoon. You think you two could do that?"

"Sure," we said in unison.

So Eeks hired us to come back to his shop late every afternoon and sweep the place out. The agreed upon salary was to be the usual "two bits" each.

Eeks was never doing any painting by the time we came in every day to sweep in the late afternoon. In fact, he was usually not in sight. He had instructed us that if he wasn't around, we could usually find him in the basement. Pat and I would find his two big brooms and sweep the floor of the shop, pushing the dirt out into the alley. It was an easy enough job only taking a couple of minutes. When we'd finish, we'd go to the rear of the shop and down the stairs to the basement. There we'd find a round green clothed table lit by a single bulb overhead in an otherwise pitch-dark room. The table was surrounded by a half dozen men all smoking and playing cards.

"Hey boys, ya done sweepin'?" Eeks would ask us. "OK, fellers," he'd say to the men, "ya gotta ante up for my boys here." All of the men would throw a dime or a nickel into a pile and Eeks would hand it over to us to split. We always got more than the quarter we were supposed to get. It was a great job and I hated to give it up. I was instructed by a priest to not return to the job.

Eeks had calendars hanging all over his shop. The calendars had large colored photographs of naked women on them. Every Saturday afternoon, I went to Confession at St. Philip's Church so that I could go to Communion with Mom on Sunday. At each Confession I'd tell the priest the same old thing.

"Bless me Father, for I have sinned. My last Confession was one week ago. I disobeyed my mother, I swore, I teased my little brother, I lied, and I...I had impure thoughts 'cause I looked at some impure pictures." I always saved the worst for last. Father Foley would instruct me to obey my mom, not take God's name in vain, be nice to my little brother, avoid the impure pictures and say ten Our Fathers and ten Hail Marys.

One Saturday, a different priest was in the confessional, helping out Father Foley. The new priest, the young Father Dufresne from Kingston, stunned me by asking me where I was seeing these impure pictures. Father Foley had never asked me that question. Shocked, I told him.

"Well, then you should never go back to that place," Father Dufresne said to me. "Do you understand me son?"

"Yes, Father."

"Promise me then. Promise me that you won't go back to that place where you see those pictures."

"Yes, Father. I promise." That was the kicker. A promise to a priest was different than a promise to anyone else in the world, even your mother. Pat kept working at Eek's shop. Apparently, he didn't see the pictures or didn't bother to tell about them in Confession.

Every year, as summer approaches, my thoughts go to Lake Ripley and the Memorial Park beach. What fun my friends and I had swimming there every day, playing in the park and buying a treat from old Evan "Dingle" Rangeloff, Sr. at the candy stand. Dingle took care of the park and ran the candy stand.

The old candy stand and the newer one today.

After Dingle retired, I took over the candy stand while I was still in high school. I gave the business up when I went off to college and Mom and Floyd took it over. A new concession stand and lifeguard building was built. Mom and Floyd ran the beach for over twenty years until the late 1980s. Mom was also the beach "matron", complete with a police badge. There's a plaque on the concession stand building commemorating Mom and Floyd's service to the park. It reads, "In Memory Helen Shaw Young & Floyd Young, Sr. For their years of service in Legion Memorial Park".

IN MEMORY
HELEN SHAW YOUNG
& FLOYD YOUNG, SR.
FOR THEIR YEARS OF SERVICE
IN LEGION MEMORIAL PARK

The Mayor of Litchfield dedicated it and my brothers and I and our stepbrothers paid for it from coins we found that Floyd had saved going through the change they took in everyday. Liberty dimes, Indian head nickels and wheat pennies. There should be another plaque somewhere out at that park dedicated to Dingle. Here's a story about Dingle and his American Dream.

Litchfield had a baseball team in the early fifties called the Optimists. Dick Siebert managed it[26]. The Optimists were the State Champs in 1951, but they folded in 1955. A regular town team, the Litchfield Athletics or the "A's", took over. They played a Sunday afternoon game and occasionally a Sunday night game at the local ballpark. They were quite good and huge crowds would attend the games. The Lake Ripley lifeguard, our "buddy" Gene McHugh, whose brother Jim had been a lifeguard too, was a star slugger.

Pat and I got jobs selling candy and pop in the stands at the games. Mom and her friend Kathryn Van Nurden had the job of running the concession stand, which was under the bleachers. I subbed for them a couple of times in the concession stand and when they couldn't continue with the job, it was given to me, even though I was only fifteen at the time. Because of that experience, I applied for and got the job of running the concession stand at the Lake Ripley Memorial Park when Dingle retired.

Mom had read about Dingle's retirement in the *Independent Review* and saw in a Help Wanted ad that the city was looking for someone to take over the candy stand at the beach.

"You should go up to the Community Building and apply for that job," she told me.

"You're crazy, Mom," I said. "Why would they give that job to me?" After all, I was only sixteen.

---

[26] Siebert was the coach of the Minnesota Gophers baseball team for thirty-one years with three national championship teams. He had played first base for a major league team, the Philadelphia Athletics, which became the Oakland Athletics.

51

"You tell them about your experience of running the concession stand at the ballpark. It doesn't hurt to try, Terry. All they can do is tell you 'No'. What have you got to lose?"

So I applied for the job. A week later I got a phone call and was told that the candy stand was mine. I couldn't believe it. I was sixteen and had my own business. I called it "Terry's Last Stand".

I had a couple of problems that I immediately needed to solve. My Uncle Allen "Johnny" Johnson, who was married to my dad's youngest sister Doris, worked for Henry's Candy Company, driving his orange truck around town and occasionally dropping off a bag of candy at our house for us Shaw boys. He would want my business, I was sure. But my stepfather Floyd had a good friend and fellow Knights of Columbus member, Dick Smith, who sold candy for Jude Candy, a rival business. Dick offered to sell to me for less than Johnny did. Money...profits! I was torn. I decided to buy from both of them, alternating weeks. Lucky for me, Uncle Johnny soon got out of the candy sales business and bought his own little store[27] in the mid-sixties.

My second problem was more difficult. How was I going to stop losing profits when kids would steal my pop bottles? I knew they would. When Dingle ran the stand, he would let Pat and I walk the park at 4:30pm every day picking up candy wrappers and empty pop bottles. For our pay, Dingle gave us each a bottle of pop. I would drink it as slowly as possible, savoring the wonderful flavor. It was so much better than Kool-Aid, which was all we ever got at home. Pat and I started throwing some of the empty bottles into the ditch by Highway 22 as we walked the park. Before we went home for supper, we'd go back to the ditch and wrap the bottles in our beach towels. Then we'd bike back to town and take the bottles to the Super Valu store for the three cents deposit[28] on each bottle.

Remembering this, I came up with a solution to my second problem, thanks to a suggestion from Floyd. I charged a five-cent deposit on the bottle when I sold the pop. I never lost any bottles and actually made more money as some adults just threw the bottles in the grass when they

---

[27] It was called Johnson's Northside Grocery and it was at 820 Sibley Avenue North. Uncle Johnny went out of business in July of 1967 and moved to San Diego. Arden Burleigh bought the building and moved his photography business into it.
[28] In the horse and buggy days, kids would go around town, especially to the livery stables, and pick up discarded whiskey bottles. They would take them to the saloons where they would get a penny for each. The saloons recycled them, refilling them from the large whiskey kegs in their cellars or back rooms.

52

finished. Floyd gave me another piece of advice. Dingle had only sold a couple of different candy bars, vanilla ice cream cones and two or three flavors of pop. Floyd told me to increase the selection.

"You'll sell twice as much if the kids can see more candy," he told me. He was right. I added a bunch of things that I knew little kids loved, such as candy necklaces and jawbreaker gumballs. I added things for adults too, like bags of chips, peanuts, and popcorn and kept a carton of Winston cigarettes hidden away for the occasional request for cigarettes. I had no license to sell them so I couldn't display them.

"Sorry, I don't sell cigarettes, but I can sell you a pack of my own, I suppose," I'd say, even though I smoked Kent.

Speaking of Dingle's selections, we loved to ask him what flavors of ice cream he had so we could hear his same old joke.

"Ice-a cream?" he'd ask in his broken English. "I gotta da three flavors today. I gotta da plain, da white and da vanilla. Which you want?"

How did Evan get the nickname "Dingle" or "Dingo", as some people called him? Like most nicknames in Litchfield, we never knew the origin. We just heard everyone call him that so we did too. I do know now and I can pass the story on to you. Dingle had a son, Evan Jr., who graduated in 1951 from LHS. In the eighth grade, a teacher asked the class what dog in Australia didn't bark. Evan, Jr., who was a little too talkative in class every day, raised his hand and answered "Dingo".

The teacher responded, "I wish you would be a dingo for just one day, Evan."

The name stuck and it also caught on with his dad, Evan Sr. Eventually it evolved into "Dingle". So they each had two nicknames and were called by both, although I only heard Evan, Sr. called the name.

Dingle had a hobby of collecting coins. His job at the candy stand was perfect as kids came to him daily with handfuls of change given to them by their parents. I didn't know about the hobby and I always thought Dingle was checking to see if the coins were real as he carefully looked at each one before tossing it into his change box. After I had the candy stand for a few weeks, Dingle came to me one afternoon. After some small talk, some compliments about what I had done with the place and some advice about running the stand, Dingle said, "When you getta da coins ready for da bank, you come to me instead at my house. I give-a you da dollar bills for them."

"Okay, Dingle," I said, as a light bulb went on inside my head. "Dingle wants to look through the coins for Liberty dimes, Indian head nickels and wheat pennies," I thought to myself. From that point on, I couldn't stop myself from looking at the coins a little closer myself as I took them in and counted them at the end of the day. I don't remember ever finding anything of value, and of course, Dingle must've been doubly frustrated. I remember the arrangement didn't last long.

We never quite pinpointed where Dingle's heavy accent came from. It was different from the Scandinavian accents we were used to hearing around Litchfield from the old Swedes and Norwegians. I wish now that I had asked Dingle about it and where he was from. Digging through old Litchfield newspapers, I found out that Dingle, or Evan Rangel Petchoff, had been born in Glovonasky, Bulgaria in 1898 to a large family of sheepherders. He had five brothers and sisters. They were quite poor and Dingle, being the youngest boy, felt even poorer because his mother made all their clothes and Dingle got the worn out hand-me-downs. He kept hearing about a place called America where the streets were paved with gold and every man lived like a king wearing a new suit every day.

Finally, at the age of fourteen, Dingle had had enough. He told his family, "I will go to this America and become rich and then I will make you all rich."

"Go tend your sheep," laughed his father, Rangel Petchoff. "It costs much money to go to America. You are just a child and you have none."

"How much money will it cost father?"

"I don't know. At least three thousand leva (over a thousand dollars today). You are crazy, boy. Go away."

Unbelievably, Dingle somehow talked a cousin into borrowing him some gold coins by telling him he would pay him back an extra thousand leva. Again, Dingle's father laughed at him but he finally said, "Well, you might as well try it," knowing that was the only way to get the crazy idea out of Dingle's head and shut him up. Dingle would surely be back in the morning.

Dingle had his mother, Kola, pack three days worth of meat and bread, and at 9pm on March 9, 1912, Evan Rangel Petchoff, Dingle, set out to walk to America. He had been told that America was west of Bulgaria. West of Bulgaria was the Rila Mountain, so Dingle naturally assumed that America was on the other side of the mountain. He walked all night and in the early morning, when he got over the mountain, he found himself at the hostile Serbian border. Bulgaria had just fought a long war with Serbia.

Some growling patrol dogs discovered Dingle as he tried to cross the border. He had a little meat left, so he gave it to the guard dogs to quiet them down before their masters, the border guards, could catch up to them. He made it across the border. He walked all that day and the following night and, in the light of the following morning, he realized that Serbia was exactly like the country he had just left. He had seen nothing but rolling hills and shepherds. No America. Bravely, he walked up to and talked to one of the shepherds, telling him of his plight.

"I'm looking for America. Where is it?" a frightened Dingle inquired.

The shepherd laughed at him and said, "America is much further away. You will need gold to go to America."

"But, I have gold," a naïve Dingle said, jingling the coins in his pocket.

"Wait until tonight," the shepherd said. "Tonight there is a man coming here who can take you to America."

That night Dingle met the man, who was huge and frightening. He asked Dingle if he had any money. Dingle showed him his gold coins.

"Give it all to me," the man said. "I will take you to America."

Dingle handed the coins over to the man and found himself on a train with him to Belgrade, Yugoslavia. Dingle had never seen a train before and it scared the hell out of him. In Belgrade, Dingle was turned over to another man who fed him and then locked him into a room with some other people for three days. He and the others were then locked into a boxcar going to Brussels. There they were put into a building for nine days and finally sent to Rotterdam with even more people.

All this time, Dingle had no one to talk to. Everyone spoke different languages. Dingle decided that he wanted to go back home, but now he had no more money and no way to do it. After eleven days in Rotterdam, he and the others were put on a ship bound for Canada. He had never been on the water before and he immediately got seasick. He worked for passage on the ship, not able to speak with anyone else and not knowing where he might end up. Dingle was seasick, terribly homesick and scared to death. A Greek sailor befriended him and showed him each day how much longer the trip would be by counting on his fingers.

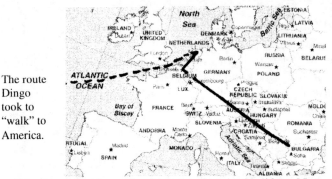

The route Dingo took to "walk" to America.

Dingle arrived not in America but in Halifax, Nova Scotia, with three pennies in his pocket. He later said, "I arrived in what I thought was America, a dirty kid with dirty clothes, no money, and a sausage and a loaf of bread under my arms." A few days later when his food was gone, Dingle went to a restaurant and asked to buy some bread and onions for his three pennies. The restaurant owner, who normally threw bums out into the street, laughed at Dingle but took pity on him. There was something about this dirty teenaged boy that he liked. He took Dingle's three pennies, threw each one into a corner of his restaurant and then gave him a room and food for a month until Dingle could get a job working on the railroad.

One day Dingle was sick and couldn't go to work with the railroad crew he was on. The crew was dynamiting a pass that day and there was an accident. The entire crew was killed. Dingle and some other workers decided to go to America, which they did. Dingle finally made it to America. He continued working for the railroad and mailed $40 back to the restaurant owner in Halifax.

Dingle left the railroad and ended up in Mahnomen, Minnesota, where he worked as a farm hand. He heard of the Balkan Wars going on back in Bulgaria and later found out that his entire family had been killed, except for a sister named Kava. Somehow Dingle and Kava made contact by mail and started writing to each other. The letters stopped when World War I broke out, so Dingle volunteered for the service. He thought he could go to Europe with the Army, get discharged there and then visit Bulgaria, where he would look for Kava or any other relative he could find before returning to the United States.

The eight-man unit he trained with was sent to Europe, but Dingle was kept stateside for a while. When his old unit landed in France, the entire unit was wiped out. Once again Dingle's life had been spared. It seemed that he was leading a charmed life. He was sent instead to Texas to guard the border to Mexico. There he was awarded a medal for capturing a spy who was trying to poison the water. Dingle snuck up behind the man in a culvert, put a bayonet to his back and brought him in.

During the war, a local woman, Mrs. Frank Lawrence, had written to servicemen who had no one to write to. Dingle had no one and now he did. He wrote back to Mrs. Lawrence and a friendship developed. During their correspondence, Mrs. Lawrence described our wonderful area of Minnesota. When the war ended, Dingle came to Meeker County. Mrs. Lawrence had her husband meet Dingle at the train depot in Minneapolis and offer him a job on their farm by Greenleaf. Dingle worked for them for a while but he soon quit farming and came to Litchfield to work for the park service.

The city had bought land by Lake Ripley for a Memorial Park[29] in January of 1922. That following summer, WPA workers built mounds in the park in the shapes of things like ships and hearts. People remember playing as kids on the "ship" mound at the north end of the park. They built concrete walkways and did landscaping. Dingle was put in charge of the park and he scoured the country for the hundreds of trees that are in the park and he and the WPA workers planted them, Dingle planting most of them by himself. He and the workers named every one of the trees for a veteran of World War I. They made a map[30] so that the personalized trees could be located. Families of deceased veterans would come to the park, Dingle would find their tree for them and they would picnic by it. Remember that the next time you go to the Legion Memorial Park.

About thirty feet south of the candy stand, in front of a tree near the sidewalk, used to be a heavy looking white block. It was a two and a half foot cube of concrete or limestone. Painted or scratched into the surface on the top was something like this: "Here lies Prohibition. 1933". We used to sit on it and sip our pop or talk to friends. What we never knew, and apparently very few people knew, was that this block was a time capsule made by Dingle, the WPA workers and the American Legion. What they put inside will never be known, as it suddenly disappeared around 1980 and has never been found or opened. Possibly the map of the trees was put in there. One of Dingle's sons, Virgil,

---

[29] Bengt Hanson had owned it before the turn of the century.

[30] One of Dingle's daughters got the map after he died. She put it away and it hasn't been rediscovered to this day.

investigated into the disappearance and found out that the Legion, not knowing that it was a time capsule, was doing some maintenance at the park and hauled it off to the dump.

Evan "Dingle" Rangeloff, Sr. mowing the Memorial Park. Notice the bathhouse behind him.

Dingle didn't quite walk to America, but he got here nevertheless. The streets weren't paved with gold, and Dingle didn't put on a new suit everyday. But when he and his wife Lillie and his kids lived on his own land on the north shore of beautiful Lake Ripley, I'll bet he thought he was living like a king. His son Evan Jr., the original Dingle, said that Bulgarian was never spoken in their home because his father was a citizen of the United States of America and proud of it.

Dingle went to work from that house on Lake Ripley everyday, maintaining the skating rink and warming house on Marshall Avenue South, mowing the huge Memorial Park grass, cleaning the bathrooms and the changing rooms at the beach and selling candy to kids who made fun of his accent and stole pop bottles from him, not knowing what he had been through. The American Dream? Dingle achieved and lived his American Dream in Litchfield, Minnesota. He died two weeks after his seventieth birthday in 1968.

Chapter Five
Heart Heroes

Mid-block between the turkey plant and the paper shack on Ramsey Avenue was the Litchfield Seed House[31], owned by Alden Martinson. I never had any reason to go in there except when my brother Mick, called Mickey at the time, won a dog there.

The "Purina Store", as we called it because of the large Purina sign and checkerboard painted boards on the building's front, was where the VFW now stands. The store was celebrating its 15th anniversary on March 12, 1955. They had an open house, complete with free eats and giveaways, including a drawing for some black lab puppies. All of the kids in town went in to sign up for the drawing and get the free food. If something were free in Litchfield, the Shaw boys and their friends would be there.

Store manager Jack Lawrence rigged the drawing by taping Mickey's entry inside the lid of the box. Much to Mom's objections, Mickey's name was the first one of the half dozen that were drawn out of the box. Jack, Dennie's Boy Scout troop leader, thought he was doing something nice for Mickey, the town celebrity. Mom didn't think so.

Mickey was a year older than I. We were both born in St. Joseph's Hospital in Mankato, Minnesota, he on February 16, 1944. In the forties, mothers stayed in the hospital for about ten days after a birth and they weren't allowed to dress their own babies for the trip home. Nurses came, took the baby and his clothes, went and bundled him up for the cold trip home and brought him back to the mother. There were lots of visitors and lots of commotion in Mom's hospital room on the day she was to go home with her newborn baby.

The nurse returned and handed Mickey to Mom, who was put into the customary wheelchair, and Dad wheeled her out to the car, followed by the room full of visitors. When they got home, Mom took Mickey into the bedroom to undress him. All of a sudden, Dad and all of the visitors, who had followed them to the house, heard Mom scream. Rushing into the bedroom, everyone saw the frantic mother standing next to the bed and the new baby. She yelled at them "This is not my baby!"

"How do you know that?" someone asked.

"Because I know my baby and this baby still has his umbilical cord and Mickey's has fallen off!"

---

[31] 221 Ramsey Avenue North. See page 377 of the "History of Downtown Litchfield" appendix.

Mom and the wrong "Mickey" were rushed back to the hospital, where they found another frantic mother and several red-faced nurses. Babies were traded, mothers were calmed down and everything was right with the world again, for the time being.

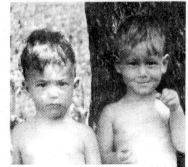

Terry and Mickey Shaw, the correct baby, just after the move to Litchfield.

Almost from the beginning back at home, Mom noticed there was something wrong with her new baby. Mickey was born a "blue baby". His lips and fingernails were a purplish blue color and he didn't have the stamina to do the things that other babies did. Mom noticed that when she fed him his bottle, Mickey often appeared to be out of breath, gasping for air. She took him to the doctor who told her that Mickey might have a heart condition, but he would probably outgrow it.

When I was born a year later and started growing, I began to surpass Mickey in size. When we were older, we'd go walking somewhere and he'd stop in the middle of the block and squat down, hugging his knees to his chest, trying to catch his breath. Motorists would stop to ask what was wrong and offer to give him a ride home. Mom asked me to pull Mickey in my wagon. When we got old enough for bikes, I had to "buck" him places, as he could not ride his own bike very far without getting exhausted. Mickey and I began resenting and disliking each other.

In 1950, Mickey had his preschool physical and the doctor told Mom something she already knew but dreaded to hear; Mickey had a bad heart condition. The doctor advised Mom to take Mickey to the University of Minnesota Heart Hospital in Minneapolis, Minnesota for a more detailed diagnosis.

There, after many tests, a University Hospital doctor sat down with Mom and told her that her son had "Tetrology of Fallot"; a hole between the two ventricles, the pumping chambers, of his heart. Not enough blood was getting sent out to the lungs to get oxygenated. Oxygen is what turns blood red and this was why Mickey was "blue" and pale looking. In addition, Mickey had a blocked artery from his heart to his lungs. If not corrected, the problem would only worsen and Mickey would certainly die before he reached the age of sixteen. Then the doctor dropped a bombshell on Mom telling her that there was no operation to correct the problem. Her son was going to die and there was nothing she or anybody else could do about it.

Mom was devastated, but she didn't give up. The next couple of years, she kept bringing Mickey back for monthly checkups hoping to hear some good news for a change. I don't know how Mom managed all these trips. By this time, she and my father were divorced and Mom didn't have a car or drive. Somehow she managed.

Mom read everything she could get her hands on about developments in surgeries and she kept searching. Then, in July of 1952, she was told that some doctors at the University of Minnesota were experimenting with heart defect repair operations. So Mom wrote a letter to the Director of the Pediatric Heart Clinic there, begging and hoping for help. In August, she received a very disappointing reply letter stating that she was misinformed and there was no such thing as a heart surgery to repair the defect. The letter went on explaining that some doctors at the hospital had been experimenting with it but they had not had any success. It seemed that Mom had finally "hit the wall."

For two years, Mom lived with the thought that she had done everything she could for Mickey and there was nothing left for her to do but pray for a miracle. In late March of 1954, a heart specialist named Doctor C. Walton Lillehei, later world-renowned as the "Father of Open-Heart Surgery", contacted Mom. He asked to see her and Mickey to see if he could possibly help. Mom, Mickey and our father went to the University of Minnesota Heart Hospital to meet this specialist who was holding out a ray of hope. Lillehei saw Mickey and did more tests and then sat down with my parents.

"Is there anything you can do?" my mother pleaded.

"Well, yes…maybe there is," Dr. Lillehei told her. A cold shiver shot through Mom's body in anticipation. Lillehei went on, "I've been doing some open-heart surgery for two years now[32], but we can't do that same type of operation on Michael."

---

[32] Dr. Lillehei and Dr. F. John Lewis performed the world's first successful open-heart surgery on September 2, 1952 at the University of Minnesota. Five-year old Jacquelin Johnson had her heart repaired in a five and one-half minute surgery using hypothermia.

Dr. Lillehei had been doing heart surgeries using hypothermia, which means bringing the patient down to near-death by cold so that the heart is barely moving. Lillehei had to get in and out in a matter of minutes or the patient would have brain damage. Hypothermia was not suited for birth defect repairs in the heart because of the length of the surgery, which was usually three hours or more. What was needed was a heart-lung machine, but it was a year away from being invented[33].

Doctor C. Walton Lillehei, the "Father of Open-Heart Surgery".

"I've had some success operating on dogs[34] and recently on two children with a new type of operation where we do something called 'controlled cross-circulation' using a donor," Dr. Lillehei continued. "That means having another person, or donor, surgically connected to the patient so that the donor's heart can pump blood to the patient, keeping him alive while the patient's heart is stopped for the surgery." Lillehei didn't add that this type of operation was extremely dangerous for the both the patient and the donor.

"As I've said," Lillehei went on, "I've had two successful operations using this technique, but I must warn you, there are no guarantees." The first operation had been earlier in March of that year. A baby boy's heart had been successfully repaired but he had died eleven days later from pneumonia. Since then, Dr. Lillehei had done the operation on a young girl, Pamela Schmidt[35] who was still surviving.

"I'd like to try this operation on Michael, but, again, I can't guarantee you anything."

---

[33] In 1955, Dr. Lillehei and Dr. Richard Varco, with help from Dr. Richard DeWall, invented the first practical heart-lung machine, called the bubble oxygenator. In 1958, Dr. Lillehei implanted the first artificial heart valve and also developed the first portable pacemaker with Medtronic founder Earl Bakker.

[34] Dr. W. G. Bigelow of Toronto, Canada had been successfully experimenting on dogs. Doctors Lillehei, Lewis and Taufic of the University of Minnesota started doing it also, with some success.

[35] She went on to marry and became Pam Stacherski.

My mother and father weighed their options and decided to let Dr. Lillehei try the operation. The University's Heart Fund would cover the costs, especially in that it was still an experimental learning operation. First, a donor would have to be found. In the previous two operations, it had been the child's father. A strong male was desired and one with an exact blood type match was mandatory.

"We have a problem here," Dr. Lillehei told my parents. "Michael's blood type is AB negative, which is a rare blood type. His father's blood doesn't match, nor does yours, Mrs. Shaw." What a roller coaster of emotions Mom must have been riding that day.

The search began for a donor. All of Mickey's adult male relatives were blood typed. No one matched. Litchfield's Knights of Columbus, American Legion Post, VFW, and local Red Cross combined under the leadership of Harold Duerr of Litchfield to conduct a statewide search. Unbelievably, in June, two brothers were found with the same rare blood type. To top it off, they were local citizens.

Amazingly, Vernon Holtz, one of the two brothers, lived about seven blocks from us. His brother, twenty-nine year old Howard, lived in Forest City, near Litchfield. They were approached and told of Mickey's dilemma and of the dangers of the operation. They could die. Without hesitation, they both volunteered.

Howard was picked to be the donor because he had the best match. Why does someone risk his or her life for a complete stranger? The Holtz brothers are both heroes and should have been given medals just like any other person who risks his life to save another. Dr. Lillehei later said that Howard Holtz' willingness to serve as the donor for my brother was "an unusual type of heroism".

Howard Holtz
and Mick after
the operation.

Mickey went into the Heart Hospital on Tuesday, August 24, 1954. One week later, on August 31, Howard was connected to my brother in the operating room for what turned out to be a five-hour ordeal. The operating team led by Dr. Lillehei, consisted of Doctors Richard Varco, Herbert E. Warden and Morley Cohen. During the operation, besides repairing the hole in Mickey's heart, they took an artery out of his left arm to replace the blocked one to his lungs. This was a forerunner of the by-pass operation that would save my life forty-six years later, while I was hooked up to a heart-lung machine similar to the one Dr. Lillehei would invent in 1955. Mick would have his own triple by-pass operation in 1996.

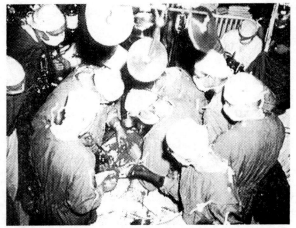

Doctors Lillehei, Richard Varco, Herbert E. Warden and
Morley Cohen operate on Mickey Shaw on August 31, 1954.

The operation was a success. News of the accomplishment was sent coast to coast and around the world. Mom started collecting newspaper clippings from all over. Two days later, Mickey was sitting up in bed and, the following day, my mother was pushing him down the hall in a wheelchair. Two more days and he was walking on his own. He came home on the following Tuesday, only two weeks after he had gone into the hospital. To us at home, it seemed like he had been gone for months. I remember a lot of different relatives and friends taking care of us at home. Mickey came home a celebrity with boxes and boxes of new comic books and toys that well-wishers had given him in the hospital.

Mickey hated shots and had screamed every time a nurse had come into his room with a needle. My parents had promised him a new bike if he didn't complain about all of the shots and medicines he had been given, so one day a shiny new bicycle was delivered to him at our home. A reporter from the *Minneapolis Star* newspaper was there to interview Mickey and take his picture getting onto his new bike.

64

The *Independent Review* ran a story about the operation on September 16, 1954. Mom also put a "Card of Thanks" from Mickey in that issue thanking Howard, the doctors, the Red Cross and all of the people who had sent cards and gifts. The *St. Paul Dispatch* came out also and ran a front-page article about Mickey in the October 27th newspaper along with a picture of Howard and Mickey. The *Independent Review* ran another article in the November 11, 1954 edition along with the *Dispatch's* picture. When the National Medical convention met in Atlantic City in late November, the story of the operation was told to all the people present. The *Associated Press* picked the story up and sent it by wire to all the newspapers in the country. Since Mickey's operation, it had been performed twenty more times, but his was the only case where the patient and donor were strangers and not relatives. Now Mickey was a national celebrity. I was jealous. Some people have all of the luck.

Mom started getting letters from concerned parents from all over the United States whose children had the same problem. They wanted reassurances that the operation they were contemplating would go all right. Mom sat down in our living room every night, tired after putting in a long day at the turkey plant, and wrote the parents all long reply letters with her cracked and bleeding hands. I know it had to have been very difficult for her, both physically and mentally, but she did it.

Six months later, Meeker County Heart Fund Co-chairmen, R. L. Hartwick and Doctor C. L. Johnson, asked my mother to go on a fund-raising tour of Minnesota. The statewide goal was $310,000. Mom, like most people, was deathly afraid of public speaking, but she agreed to do it. She wrote a long speech and practiced it in front of an audience of one…me.

Mom had another fear. She couldn't stand the sight of blood. It made her squeamish and feel faint. She used to gag as she fixed our skinned knees and cuts. She found out that she was going to be giving her speech in front of audiences with a color movie of Mickey's operation projected on a screen behind her…a giant color movie of her son's chest being carved open from armpit to armpit. But Mom was a real trooper and she did it. Attorney Leland Olson, who was an amateur radio operator friend of Dennie's, told him that Mom got a standing ovation at the fundraiser he attended. She had to make that speech many times.

The *Independent Review* ran a large article about kicking off the Heart Fund drive in the February 17, 1955 edition. The article was accompanied by a picture of Howard Holtz watching Mickey do something he had never been able to do before…shovel snow. Think of all the fun he had been missing! The fund-raising tour was very successful. There's a photograph somewhere of Mickey presenting an over-sized check for a million dollars to the president of the Heart Fund, far exceeding the state's goal.

Howard Holtz looks on as Mickey pretends to shovel for the camera.

The November 10, 1955 issue of the *Independent Review* had an article about Mickey being a guest at a Heart Association workshop at the University of Minnesota on November 5, 1955. No doubt Mom was there too. Mickey was there for surgeons and other doctors attending the workshop to see the results of the world famous groundbreaking operation. My brother was being used as a medical "show and tell" display.

On Tuesday, November 18, 1986, Mick, Dr. Lillehei, Howard Holtz and Mom were reunited in Litchfield for the filming of a BBC and Boston PBS documentary about the developments in surgery since the end of World War II. Mick and Dr. Lillehei were filmed walking through Central Park. Then the entire group was filmed sitting around Mom's kitchen table discussing the operation.

A book called "The King of Hearts" has been written about Dr. Lillehei. Through the years, he stayed in contact with my brother, calling him on the phone many times out of the blue. "How are you doing, Michael?" he would ask. He attended Mick's Twenty-fifth

Wedding Anniversary party in 1990. Mick called him to ask his advice before having his angiogram in 1996 and Dr. Lillehei consulted with Mick's surgeon before Mick had his triple-bypass.

 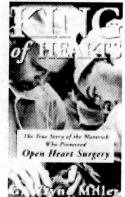

Howard Holtz, Mick and C. Walton Lillehei in 1986 and the book about Dr. Lillehei.

Dr. Lillehei died from pneumonia in 1999, just as that first baby boy had that Lillehei had operated on just before Mickey's surgery. Mick said of Dr. Lillehei at that time, "I loved him. He never forgot about me." Remembering what Dr. Lillehei had said about Howard Holtz' heroism, I'd say that Dr. Lillehei, in his search for ways to help people with heart problems all over the world for generations to come, showed another type of heroism. He saved my brother's life and indirectly he saved mine.

"He's your responsibility," Mom told Mickey, after he had won that black puppy at the Litchfield Seed House in the rigged drawing. "I don't have time to take care of any dog!"

Mickey named the dog Prince. Prince was the first of our three family dogs that Mom didn't have time to take care of for us, but did anyway. Prince got distemper and one Sunday morning, while Mom marched us four unaware boys the five blocks to church, a veterinarian came to our garage, where Mom had put Prince, and he put the dog to sleep.

Prince was followed by a white dog named Tuffy. I don't remember what happened to him. The last dog we had was named Sparky and he was a very intelligent water spaniel mixture. He used to tug on Mom's dress when he had to go outside. He was a member of the family and he slept between Pat and I. Mom would give him a "You're not supposed to be on that couch," look and Sparky would sheepishly get down without a word being said.

Terry Shaw and Sparky.

Someone poisoned Sparky on our front lawn one very cold and sad December night. Mom called me at the library.

"You'd better come home. There's something wrong with Sparky," she told me. "He's lying outside in front of the house."

I ran home and looked at Sparky lying there motionless, except for a light breeze moving his fur. That image froze in my mind and would come back to haunt me one day. We argued about what to do with Sparky. How could we bury him in the dead of the winter? Finally, Mick called his friend Larry Andreen, who had a car, and we took Sparky out to the town dump. We didn't know what else to do with him. We wrapped Sparky in an old blanket. Pat, with tears streaming down his face, lifted him out of the trunk and carried him to his final resting place. He deserved so much better. We felt terrible. Sparky was our last pet.

Chapter Six
Neighborhood and Family Characters

I suppose each town boasts of the odd characters who walk its streets. Over the years I've talked with many people about the characters I knew in Litchfield. The general consensus seemed to be that Litchfield certainly had more than its share of odd balls. Maybe it was something in our water. Some of the characters were my childhood friends, some were my teachers, some were neighbors, others were bums I knew and people we thought were crazy or "loony", and still others I only heard stories about. Unfortunately, if you had a physical or mental handicap, you were likely to be called a character, although those weren't the sole requirements. You generally had to do something odd along with your appearance.

Some of the characters like Benno McCarney or Len "Buck Buck" Inselman lived across town or on the edge of town, but it seemed that a lot of the characters lived in the northwest corner of Litchfield, where the Shaws lived. I suppose some people thought of the Shaws as characters too. I imagine some of the characters we'd see walking around that part of town were bums riding the rails.

The railroad tracks and a couple of "Hobo Woods" or "Hobo Jungles" were near us. One of them was across the tracks from us, next to the Swift Avenue crossing by the Andreen's house. There was a tree house built in a large oak tree towards the center of that small half an acre vacant lot. We'd see evidence of bums staying there. There would be dead cooking fires and empty tin cans strewn about. We used to play *War* in that woods, building forts out of plywood taken out of the railroad cars parked along the Land O' Lakes side track.

The other "Hobo Woods" was west of town, north of the railroad tracks across from Fortun's farm place. Jewett Creek flooded there almost every spring. Every so often there'd be a story in the paper about a dead "transient" found along the tracks between Litchfield and the cities, or a story about a "mysterious man" around town looking in people's houses or following young girls.

Eugene "Skeeter" Anderson, who I mentioned earlier, was five years older than I. He lived one block from us and sometimes he hung around with my brother Dennie, getting into trouble with him. The June 6, 1957 *Independent Review* newspaper had an article in it about a reward being offered "for information leading to the arrest of the parties who partly dismantled and threw bricks around from the backyard fireplace of Pete Lindberg". I hereby apply for that reward. It was Skeeter and Dennie. After forty-six years, they both finally 'fessed up to the deed. Dennie says he learned to smoke and tell dirty jokes and tall tales from Skeeter, besides get into trouble with him.

Skeeter would stop by our front yard to tease Pat and I. He'd be walking by, see us playing in the dirt between our yard and the street, walk over and say to us, "I'll bet you a nickel that you two Shaw boys can't get me down and pin me." We'd jump up and attack him. If we did get him down (and we usually did), he'd get up and run away laughing. "Suckers!" he'd say. We fell for it many times, but it was fun anyway and Skeeter was a likeable guy. It was a valuable commodity having an older friend. He liked us and he'd defend us from bullies and buy us cigarettes. I visited Skeeter at his house one day and he let me read the racy parts in his paperback copies of *Peyton Place* and *Lady Chatterley's Lover*. Skeeter was a valuable friend for a young teenage boy to have.

Eugene "Skeeter" Anderson today, a postal worker in Utah.

Skeeter was with a group of us younger boys at a park one day in the summer. I had never been in a fight before, but a boy named Bobby Welsand pushed me to my limit that day. Bobby and I started wrestling and I was able to get him down and sit on his chest. The other boys crowded around us, yelling at us both.

"Say uncle! Say uncle!" I screamed at Bobby.

He shook his head from side to side, "No!"

"Hit him! Hit him! Let him have it!" Skeeter yelled at me.

"Yeah, hit him," the others joined in.

"No!" I yelled back.

"Hit him, hit him!" Skeeter kept yelling.

Driven by the chanting, I raised my right fist and hit Bobby once, then twice in the face, more to shut Skeeter and the rest of the kids up than anything else. Bobby started crying. Suddenly, I realized what I

70

was doing. I felt so bad about hitting someone that I stood up, turned away and walked home. I didn't want the rest of the kids to see that I had started to cry too because of what I had done. I told my mother about it. It was kind of like going to Confession. That was the last time I ever hit anybody.

A lot of the characters in town lived near Skeeter. Across the street to his south was an old Dane, Pedar J. "Pete" Marstad, whom we called "Pete Mustard". In his seventies at that time, Pete was a retired local cop and he played the guitar. Pete had a heavy Danish accent and was extremely hard to understand. All the more strange that he was a policeman.

The story was told that Pete pulled over a car, which had a burned out tail light, as it passed through town. He tried to tell the driver why he had stopped him, but the guy had no idea what Pete was trying to say because of his heavy accent. The guy just kept shaking his head that he didn't understand. Pete finally had to pull the man out of his car, walk him to the back of his car and point at the taillight.

Across Austin Avenue to the east of Skeeter was another old Swede, Peter A. "Pete" Lindberg, the victim of Skeeter and Dennie's prank with the fireplace bricks. Pete played the fiddle and his wife Ellen used to cut Pat's and my hair in her kitchen for Mom. Pete had some kids, Lemoine, who was called "Pete" also, David, and Gwen. Lemoine was a character of the highest degree and there's more about him in a later chapter. When Gwen was three, she was playing in the basement with David, who was chopping at some wood with a small axe they had found. Gwen was holding the wood for David and he took off the tips of two of her fingers.

In May of 1943, Pete, who had a well drilling business in the forties and fifties, was working on a well pit for the Produce. There was an accident and Pete lost most of his thumb. Two of his other fingers were crushed. Despite this handicap, Pete could still play his fiddle, and play it quite well.

Pete would gather all his musician friends into his screened porch facing Third Street and they'd play their fiddles. One of the musicians was Pete's neighbor, Axel Roman, who played the piano. Axel, coincidentally, had a finger cut off by a fan in the Curtis Restaurant in July of 1921. So, at least two of the group were missing digits. Sometimes there were six or seven of them in that porch and it was almost like a band concert. They used to get quite a crowd of onlookers.

I suppose it was good, but to us preteens in the early days of rock and roll, we thought it was just funny and old-fashioned.

Pete and his friends formed a group called The Old-Time Fiddlers[36] and they played some dances. People entertained their neighbors like that in the fifties. Old man Eldor Ericson, across the street from us, played a concertina and a violin. His two daughters, one was Elaine, played in a band in the thirties. The rest of the band consisted of the Draxton family and it was called The Draxton Dance Orioles. Because they had no amplification in those days, Elaine sang through a megaphone.

In the twenties and thirties, Elmer S. and Rudolph Noreen had a band in town. They would play at house parties and at their Noreen's Pavilion[37] near downtown. It was located where the Produce plant went on the south side of Second Street. The Wheeler family had an orchestra too. Our dad played accordion, bass, guitar and piano. He played the guitar in a band out of Eden Valley called The Valley Ramblers. It's no wonder that the Shaw boys grew up to become musicians, both professionally and part-time. There was music all around us.

Dad playing guitar in the Valley Ramblers.

One of the few good memories I have of my father, before he left us, is of him playing guitar in the living room and my mother singing along to *You Are My Sunshine*. He was a self-taught musician and one of those people who could pick up any instrument and play it. He played the accordion and piano also and he had a big old white metal stand-up bass, but his first love was the guitar.

---

[36] The Old-Time Fiddlers group consisted of Pete Lindberg, Gottfred Carlson, Emanuel Jensen, Charles Lindstrom, Morris Mortenson, Joe Belmares, Axel Roman, Rudy Rydholm, and Carl Helland. Myrtle Lindstrom joined in on the piano.

[37] 123 Second Street West. See page 446 of the History of Downtown Litchfield Appendix.

I remember him setting his guitar amp out on the front steps and playing in the evenings. Neighbors would gather around outside of our house to listen to his impromptu concerts. My song about music in the family actually starts with this memory.

THE SONG GOES ON

The first thing I remember was my daddy's old guitar,
plugged into an old amp that he used when playin' bars.
He'd set the amp out on the steps so everyone could hear.
The neighbors would soon gather 'round and sit and share a beer.
He played accordion and bass and tried piano too.
In my small eyes there wasn't anything he couldn't do.
He and Mom would sing duets, that's something that I miss.
Mom would harmonize my dad and it would sound like this...
[Go into *You Are My Sunshine* in harmony.]

A very young Florian Shaw playing his accordion and guitar.

Another memory I have of Dad is of him walking around the living room in a leg cast using two chairs to support himself. I was four and a half years old. While driving alone back to Litchfield on west Highway 12 on January 28, 1950, a dark, early Saturday morning, Dad hit eighteen-year-old Gene Staunton's car head on. The roads had been icy. Gene, who eventually would run Northside Standard in town, ended up in a coma with some brain damage. Dad had a cut head and a broken leg. Both of them lay out in the cold night for several hours before someone came along and found them.

Florian
Shaw's car.

Dad didn't have a place to stay when he got out of the hospital and was recuperating. He had money problems because of the accident and the divorce from Mom, so my mother took him and his new wife in. Yes, even though Dad had divorced and left Mom and us four boys in the previous year, she took him in. Charity does indeed begin at home. I wasn't sure if this childhood memory was correct, so one day before my mother died, I brought it up to her.

"Mom," I said, "I have a strange memory from when I was a little kid." I told her what the memory was. "Is this correct?" I asked. "Am I remembering this right?"

"Yes," she said, as if I had asked her if I was remembering correctly that Grandpa Bill had lived with us for a while.

"What?" I gasped. "How could you do that, Mom?"

"What was I supposed to do? He was your father. He had no money and no place to go. His leg was broken, he had no insurance and he couldn't work and…"

"But Mom…" I continued in disbelief, "His second wife too?"

No, Mom wasn't crazy or stupid. She was a Christian and she felt it was the right thing to do. Mom never seemed to begrudge or bad mouth Gertrude "Sunny" Papesch Shaw, the lady who broke up our home. At least she didn't badmouth her to us. She knew that Sunny took care of us and was kind to us when we went to visit our father in Eden Valley. We rarely saw him. He was always too busy for us, so we spent more time with Sunny. Mom invited Sunny to my graduation party.

On Thursday, September 7th of that same year, Dad was recovered, out of our house and back working for Uncle Ed Birkemeyer's Automatic Sales Company. They were coming home from the Twin Cities at 5:30 in the afternoon and a truck pulled out in front of them, just outside of Delano, Minnesota. Ed was driving and he went for the ditch instead of hitting the truck. His car sheared off a utility pole and rolled over several times.

Luckily, Ed came out of the accident with just some scratches. Dad broke that same leg again, along with three ribs. The leg healed stiff. The rest of the few times I ever saw him, he walked around stiff-legged like Chester on TV's *Gunsmoke* and Arthur Godfrey, who Dad looked like anyway. A clot from the leg broke lose and caused the massive stroke that killed Dad in 1961.

Often the neighbors would congregate on the street to listen to the music coming from the porches and front steps of houses, share a beer and talk, especially during the days when we burned leaf piles on the street. That's a smell you never forget. Everyone would rake their leaves off their lawns onto the street and then two or three neighbors would make a huge pile and do a "controlled burn" that evening. Each year the city pleaded in the newspaper with the people not to do it as it weakened the tar, but they continued to do it until the practice was finally outlawed.

Although some of our neighbors didn't really qualify as characters, they were interesting, nevertheless. Next door on the corner north of us was Mary Jensen, a cook at the Wagner School. She liked to make jams and jellies, so Pat and I sold the chokecherries we picked from our tree to her. She lived with her brother Carl who dated Skeeter's Aunt Vera. Vera lived a block away from us across from the old power plant. Skeeter and Dennie had some parties at her house when she was gone.

Floyd E. "Curly" Housman, a widower, lived upstairs over Mary Jensen. Curly was completely bald. We always wondered where some of those nicknames came from. Curly of the Three Stooges was bald too. Our Curly was a foreman at the Produce and therefore one of Mom's bosses. He was a nice man. On hot summer nights, he'd come to his open window and see Pat and I playing on the front lawn or in the street and he'd talk to us and sometimes throw a coin or two down to us. He always appreciated Mom's hard work. Except for the times she ran Mickey to the Heart Hospital, she never missed a day of work at the Produce.

Curly's brother, John, was the custodian at St. Philip's School and also for the church. John was a big man and, on Litchfield's "Crazy Days" in the summer, he would always win the "Pancake Eating Contest". He retired "Undefeated Champion" when the town turned it into a "Pie Eating Contest" for kids. His secret was that he didn't use syrup and drank water to get the pancakes down.

Every year in July, the Litchfield stores had a sale day called "Crazy Days". The merchants would dress up in "crazy" costumes and bring their wares out to the streets to sell for "crazy" prices. Everyone knew they were just cleaning out their inventory of hard-to-sell items, but occasionally there were some real bargains. If you could use that wrongly mixed gallon of paint, that carpet piece or that string of Christmas lights, you could get them for under the store's cost.

One time the Northwestern Bank sold silver dollars for fifty cents…for an hour, when the bank opened its doors in the morning. You can bet Pat and I were there in front of the bank standing in line that morning. "One to a customer, please," we were told. Pat and I would scour the town for deals on Crazy Days to spend our hard-earned cash on. We bought our own TV set for our garage clubhouse on Crazy Days.

Mom would buy Christmas gifts of clothes for us on Crazy Days. She continued to do that later in her life for her grandchildren. We'd be amazed that she would be able to predict every kid's clothing size for December in the middle of July.

Crazy Days in July 1959. Left to right: Pat Shaw, an unknown lady and Lucille Wheeler at the Gambles store.

Alma Colmen, who lived next door south of us, was a widow who had a teenage daughter named Mary Gale. Mary Gale babysat Pat and I a few times. Mom paid her to give Dennie a couple of piano lessons on the big old upright piano that we had in the living room also. Dennie wasn't interested so that was dropped. The piano went out in the garage and Mom eventually sold it. The only person who had ever played that piano was our dad and then Grandpa Bill when he lived with us for a short time.

Even though my mother and father were divorced, Mom kept in contact with Dad's side of the family, I suppose for our benefit. She could have separated us from that side, but she didn't. I saw my paternal aunts and uncles as much as I saw my maternal ones. When Grandpa Bill, my father's father, needed a place to live, an arrangement was worked out where he lived with us and cared for us while Mom went to work at the Produce.

Mary Gale had a crush on our uncle Dean Shaw, my absent father's brother. When Dean came back from Korea, he stayed with us for a couple of weeks before he decided to move to Missouri to work at the Fisher Body plant. Mom was again opening up her house to more of her ex-husband's family. Dean looked like Clark Gable without Gable's protruding ears. Mary Gale made quite a pest of herself, hanging around our house while Dean was around, trying to get his attention. She had pigtails and glasses and, at that point, was a clumsy teenage girl.

One day Mary Gale was taunting Dean for "primping" his hair before our bathroom mirror. Dean got upset with her and he punched a hole the size of his fist through the plasterboard wall. Mary Gale[38] left crying. Dean patched the hole, but you could always see a fist-sized bulge on the wall to the right of the mirror where he had performed his macho demonstration. It's probably still there. Dean, who got the Purple Heart in the Korean War, died on New Year's Eve of 1991, a year after surviving his third by-pass surgery.

Aunt Mary Alice and Uncle Dean.

Dean on his homemade Cushman scooter.

Alma Colmen didn't like us Shaw boys too well when we were young. She had a big garden right next to our garage, so we were always chasing after one kind of ball or another into it, stepping all over her

---

[38] Mary Gale eventually married Kenny Angier who was the Assistant Manager at the J.C. Penney Store. They moved to North Dakota when Kenny was promoted and transferred to another store in the fall of 1960.

plants. Along side our driveway was her flower garden. At least she tried to have a flower garden.

Alma had an old longhaired dog she called Puppy. Puppy didn't like kids and he barked all of the time, straining at his leash in our direction. Alan Shaw, my absent father's baby brother, lived in our garage for a short time before going into the service. He took our BB gun once and shot at Puppy to shut him up. It didn't work. Alma came running out of her house and had a few choice words for Alan, but he had some better ones for her. I thought Alan was cool. He used to dress in the fashion of guys we'd call "Hoods". White t-shirt with a pack of cigarettes rolled into one of the short sleeves, super tight blue jeans and black Engineer boots. I used to imitate his swearing to impress my friends. "F**kin'-ay…I'm goin' up-f**kin'-town."

Our driveway ran very close to Alma's house. In fact, her bedroom window was right next to our driveway…one foot away. Alan would deliberately park right outside her window at night and play his car radio very loudly or rev his engine to aggravate her as much as possible. The feud continued to escalate until Mom, the peacemaker, stepped in. Alma was really a saint, and in her final years she was quite a good friend to the family keeping watch on things whenever Mom and Floyd were away visiting relatives.

Uncle Alan was around our house a lot, working on his car or visiting his dad, Grandpa Bill, after he had moved out of our garage. He let me "help" him fix his car. I handed him the tools while he lay on his back under the car. Alan had unique solutions to some of our problems. Pat, who liked to put things into his mouth, had some coins and marbles in there one time and he swallowed everything and started choking. Uncle Alan just picked him up by the heels and shook him until the stuff dropped out.

Alan Shaw in 1952 and 1956.

Alan was on the wild side, and never thought much about safety, even if one of us Shaw boys were with him.

"I need a haircut," he said to me. "Wanna go for a ride to Eden Valley?" Apparently Alan didn't trust the Litchfield barbers with his hair.

"Sure!" I said. I jumped at any opportunity to go for a car ride, and I thought I might get a glimpse of my absent father, who lived in Eden Valley. We drove there about ninety miles an hour, Alan got his haircut while I read comic books, we both got a piece of gum, and we turned right around and drove back to Litchfield at ninety miles an hour again. No visiting Dad.

On the way, Alan rolled his window down and said, "Grab the wheel." Stunned, I reached over and grabbed the steering wheel. I was scared to death. I had never driven a car before. Alan stuck his head out his window into the roaring wind and rubbed it with both hands to get the little loose hairs out. When he finished, he took the wheel from my shaking hand, mumbled "Thanks", rolled the window back up and lit up a cigarette. He probably offered me one too.

Alan had a cruel sense of humor, not only shooting at Alma's dog but also wiring up a cat's dish to give it a shock when it came to drink. He hated cats and tried to run over them with his car when he saw one walking across a street. He fed Dennie axle grease one time telling him it was licorice. But he was "cool" and we looked up to him, for some reason.

Alan also stayed with Uncle Buck and Aunt Wilma Owens on their farm at Osakis. I remember going there a couple of times and even staying with them for a week. Alan had a '49 Crosley[39] station wagon. A Crosley was a short-lived tiny compact car about thirty years ahead of its time. The little two-seater, which looked more like a kiddie car, was made from 1949 to around 1952. It sold for $350 and got over fifty miles per gallon. Alan put the tail gate down and Pat and I sat on it and hung on for dear life while Alan drove Uncle Buck down some gravel road as fast as he could get the little car going. Alan died in 1972 when a motorist pulled out in front of his semi-truck.

---

[39] Crosley entered the auto business with a plant in Cincinnati that produced the tiny car that was sold alongside Crosley radios in appliance stores, of all places. Crosley built the Voice of America radio station to counter Nazi propaganda and was so successful Hitler called the station "the Cincinnati Liars". After the war, Crosley produced sedans, wagons and the "Hot Shot" two-seater. He changed his company's name from the Crosley Radio Corp. to Crosley Motors Inc., but Crosley auto production ended in 1952.

1949 Crosley

Now that I think of it, our little section of Litchfield was full of Scandinavians. The southwestern part of town, around Donnelly and Austin Avenues South, was called "Swede Hollow" though. It was also called "Shanty Town" for a while. On the corner across the street from our house were Signy L. Ericson and her old Norwegian husband Eldor. Eldor Gerhardt Ericson sharpened lawn mower blades in a shop in his garage, where he had repaired cars as a business.

The Ericsons had a son named Rollin, who became a guard at the Stillwater Prison. Rollin had a "wild" reputation, was friends with Uncle Alan, of course, and, like Alan, did spur of the moment crazy things, like walking barefoot through the burning leaves in our fall street bonfires. More than one Sunday morning his car would be left on the Ericson lawn with the front end nosed into the bushes in front of the front porch step and skid marks in the sod leading up to it. Eldor would yell, "Who the hell parked this machine on my lawn?" knowing full well that it was Rollin's car, parked there after a night of drinking with his buddies.

Skeeter was in Eldor's shop one day fooling around with Rollin at the workbench. Rollin picked up a big old magnet that was on the bench and told Skeeter to "Watch this!" He threw the magnet at Eldor's leg. It stuck! Eldor had polio as a kid and one of his legs was withered and shorter than the other, so all his life he wore a metal brace on it.

Eldor's health was failing and one day Pat and I heard a terrific bang outside of our living room. We ran out the front door and saw half of Eldor's car sticking out of Mary Jensen's living room. That was cool. Eldor had backed out of his driveway a little too fast and missed the brake, probably because of that leg brace. Maybe it had locked up on him. Eldor died in January of 1957.

We called his wife Signy "Grandma Ericson" because the nice gray-haired lady in an ever-present apron was always giving us one of her great chocolate chip cookies with a glass of lemonade. She loved kids. Her own grandkids caused her some tears though, I'm afraid. She had a blond granddaughter who lived across town and the pretty little girl

80

would often come by to visit. Her name was Sheila but everyone called her "Dodo".

Sheila "Dodo" Lindell with her dog "Tiny" in 1956.

Dodo was the daughter of Bob and Elaine Lindell, and both Dennie and Mick had a crush on her. A week older than Pat, Sheila would die in 1968 at the young age of twenty-two from an aneurysm.

Sheila's dad was uptown one Monday evening in February of 1950, and he had a little too much too drink. He noticed that the unoccupied and brand new Pontiac police cruiser had the keys left in the ignition. Obviously the patrolman was doing his lock checks of the stores down the street. Bob took the car for a little joy ride home. The car was eventually found at his house at 318 Litchfield Avenue and Bob was taken to the jail to sit, sober up and ponder about what he just done. He got off with a $50 fine.

One of Sheila's cousins, David was a friend of Mick. David was riding his motorcycle out by Lake Ripley in October of 1960. Behind him on the back of the cycle, was Brendan "Jopey" Wimmer, a brother of my friends, Jerry and Dougy. David and Jopey hit some loose tar and oil on the road where men had been working that day. The men had left a warning light but it either wasn't turned on or it was broken. Jopey had some cuts and bruises but David messed his leg up pretty badly. He sued the county and won the case. He was going to be getting a nice sum of money when he reached twenty-one. Unfortunately, he met a tragic end in a car accident in 1962 at the age of eighteen. You'll read more about that in another chapter.

Jopey had poor judgment in picking friends to ride with. A year later, in November of 1961, he was riding in a '55 Chevy driven by Vernon Shoutz on Highway 12. Somehow Vernon rolled the car. It was a total wreck. Neither boy got hurt. Jopey led a charmed life.

Chapter Seven
More Neighborhood Characters

Harold "Smokey" Schmidt and his family moved into the house kitty-corner[40] from Skeeter at 325 Third Street in late 1955. Smokey was a garbage collector and the town's dogcatcher. Mom had Smokey as her chief suspect in the future poisoning of our dog, Sparky. Anyway, Dennie occasionally did things with Smokey's son Harland and Pat and I played with his younger son, Henry or "Hank".

Before the Schmidts moved in, two old bachelor brothers, Clarence and Ervin Ellis, lived there. In the early fifties, they still had an outhouse in backyard, which the city asked them to remove. On July 20, 1955 at 6:30am, sixty-two year old Clarence, who was depressed over his failing health, sat at his kitchen table and put a shotgun under his chin. The following blast not only took most of his face off, but it went through the ceiling wounding Ervin, who was upstairs in the bedroom. We mistakenly heard that Ervin was downstairs cleaning his shotgun and he had accidentally killed Clarence upstairs. You know how people get their stories mixed up.

The first thing I remember doing, when Hank asked Pat and I over to play after they had moved in, was ask him to show us the bedroom upstairs where the guy had been killed. Hank had heard the story wrong also and he happily took us up there to impress us. It was a dark unlit room at the top of the stairs that Hank had to walk through to get to his bedroom every night. Even though it was daylight, it was still quite dark up there. But, there was enough light so that we could see that the floor had been repaired so we had no reason to question the facts of the story.

"How can you sleep up here?" I whispered to Hank, not wanting to wake up the ghost of old Clarence.

He shrugged his shoulders. "Where am I s'posed to sleep?" he whispered back.

I had no answer for him except "Let's get outta here."

The Schmidts had a big garden right behind Grandma Ericson's place with lots of ground cherries in it, which we liked to eat. They also had a menagerie of animals that they raised. Bunnies, ducks and chickens. "Ma" Clara Schmidt, whose hair, which hung down the sides

---

[40] I've had arguments with people over this hyphenated word, meaning "diagonally across". Some say kiddy-corner, some say caddy-corner and still others say catty-corner. They are closer to being correct. It is supposed to be cater-cornered from the French word quatre for "four", which got Anglicized to "cater" as in "catawampus", or out of joint.

of her head, was the blackest, straightest hair I've ever seen, would kill the rabbits to eat, which shocked us when we heard about it. Bunny rabbits...to eat? Clara would also clean anybody's ducks and geese after a hunt, if the hunter didn't want to do it or know how. She charged for the service, of course. Sparky followed us over to the Schmidt's yard one day and raised such a racket barking at those shivering rabbits that Clara called Mom up and raised holy hell with her. Mom got quite upset about the whole thing and told Clara that she shouldn't have a barnyard full of animals in town anyway.

Skeeter's folks went on vacation one summer for about two weeks. What they were thinking, leaving teenager Skeets home alone in that house is a good question. Maybe they just had to get away from him for a while to recharge their batteries. Anyway, Skeets had the parties. He had a great big one on a hot summer night with lots of beer drinking and girls. Everyone parked his or her car all over the Anderson's lawn. It looked like an used car lot. The next day Skeets was walking uptown past Pete Lindberg's house and Clara was in her backyard with all her animals. She hollered over, with the wink of her eye, "Skeeter! When the cat's away, the mice have a good time playing!" But she never told his parents about the parties.

Clara's husband Smokey would go into Janousek's for a burger and, when he was finished eating, he'd stand up and reach into the pocket of his bib overalls, pull out a handful of pennies, nickels and dimes and lay them all on the counter. Huge Helen Anderson, cook and waitress, would count out what Smokey owed and push the rest back to him. Smokey had never gone to school and had never learned to count money, nor read and write.

Smokey took the law into his own hands where stray dogs were concerned. He didn't mess around. Sometimes he didn't quite think his actions out either. He was called one night about a stray just a few blocks from our house. When he tried to pick the mangy dog up, it growled and snapped at him, trying to bite him. So Smokey calmly went back to his car, opened the trunk, took out his shotgun and blew the stray to doggy heaven, right in the middle of a residential area of town. Some of the pellets ripped through the screen and two outer windows of Mrs. Delores Nagel's apartment at 720 Miller Avenue North, three hundred feet away from Smokey. The pellets continued on into her apartment and shattered a large mirror on a wall in her living room.

Police Chief George A. Fenner was called about someone shooting in town and then he got a call about vandalism at the Nagel place. He had called Smokey earlier that evening about a complaint about a dog and George put two and two together. Searching through the pile of broken glass, Fenner found the stray shotgun pellets. He commented that maybe Smokey was using too powerful of a shell. Apparently he didn't mind that Smokey was blasting away in town. It wasn't the first time.

Garbage collector and dogcatcher, Harold "Smokey" Schmidt.

Smokey would get called not only for stray dogs but also for other critters that were disturbing the peace or the garbage. One summer evening in about 1964, he took his trusty shotgun and blew away three raccoons rummaging through the garbage cans in the back of the hotel. He shot six times. The people downtown must have thought World War III was starting. Smokey completely ruined the garbage cans he was trying to protect. There was garbage, raccoon carcasses and blood all over the alley. Hotel manager, Vic Forte, thought two shells would have been sufficient but Smokey probably shot the other four just to be sure. Remember, he couldn't count. He removed the dead bodies but left the rest of the mess for someone else to clean up. Vic called him to shoot an occasional muskrat that got into the basement of the hotel too. Down there, Smokey used a quieter and safer .22 pistol. I wonder if Smokey took any of his kills home for Clara to clean for supper?

The Carlson boys lived by the new Municipal Power Plant on Donnelly Avenue, a block away from Skeeter. There are power transformers on that lot today. A large poor family, the Carlsons lived in a tiny wood and tarpapered dirt-floored shack that was surrounded by a fence to keep their animal collection in the yard. I delivered the afternoon paper there. I would have to carefully lift the rope "lock" on the fence gate and make my way inside, careful to not let any chickens out, and walk past a goat or two while a bunch of hound dogs bellowed, jumped, and slobbered on me. It was like a scene out of an old Ma and Pa Kettle movie or a "You just might be a redneck if..." joke from Jeff Foxworthy.

"Ma" Henrietta and "Pa" Louie Carlson would be sitting in big wooden chairs in front of the shack, while a couple of their older boys worked on cars in the backyard. The Carlson boys were Dicky, Wayne, Dale, Jim, Marlin, whom we called "Bud", and Ralph.

Dicky looked like a dark haired James Dean and he wore a black leather jacket, black "engineer" boots, skintight blue jeans with three inch cuffs, and a white t-shirt with a pack of Luckies rolled up in one sleeve, when the jacket wasn't on, just like my Uncle Alan. Dicky looked cool but, true to his juvenile delinquent persona, he got himself into constant trouble. In June of 1962, Dicky and his friends Dennis Nygaard, goofy looking Martin McCarney, and Arnold Haugen were arrested for breaking into the Hack Brown's Riverside Inn in Manannah, Minnesota. They pleaded guilty but Arnold got off for lack of evidence.

In March of 1948, there was a string of break-ins in town, mostly on our end of Litchfield. Beckstrand's Standard service station, the Seed House, the Produce warehouse and the paper shack were all hit. Four teenagers were picked up and they all confessed. The oldest of the gang was Marlin Carlson. The others were Orville Plowman, Gerald Koerner and Carlson neighbor George Vanderpas. They were sentenced to go to the Red Wing boys' detention facility until they reached the age of twenty-five.

Ralph Carlson got in trouble in January of 1949 when he assaulted bank teller Clarice Ditlerson on her way home from work and made off with her purse. He was caught the next day and confessed. He was sent to prison for about five years, of which he only served a couple. Ralph and his brother Dale had a big old green Hudson Hornet car. On Saturday, July 16, 1955 at 1:30am, when Dale was nineteen and Ralph was twenty-three, they were coming back from Coney Island[41], a bar ten miles south of downtown Litchfield on Highway 22. About a half a mile north of the Lake Minnebelle turn off, they hit another car head on. It had three members of the Lindner family in it. The Carlson boys were driving without their headlights on. The Lindners luckily came out of the accident with only bumps and bruises. The Carlson boys weren't so

---

[41] Coney Island became the Roadside Inn and is now the Highway 22 Inn.

lucky. Each lost a single eye in the accident, both the left eye. Dale was in the hospital for about a week while they tried to save his eye, but finally Henrietta had to sign a paper saying they could remove it. It was so odd to see both of those guys walking uptown on Third Street with their black patches over their eyes. Dale kept his for quite a while before he finally got a glass eye.

In the fall of the same year, Dale smashed his '48 Nash at 10:15pm in almost the identical spot. He and three other teenage passengers were following Tom Gandrud's car too close. When Dale whipped out to pass, he caught Gandrud's left rear bumper with the front of his car. Gandrud's car flipped over several times. Gandrud's female passenger was thrown from the car. Unbelievably, no one was seriously hurt.

Thirteen-year-old Hank Schmidt got up one Saturday morning in November of 1959 to make deliveries for his paper route. At 6am, he was walking by our corner of Swift Avenue and Third Street on his way to the paper shack, when a speeding car ran him down. The car never stopped. Cut on his arm, Hank got up from the pavement and ran home to his mother Clara, who called the police. Hank told the police that the car was a Ford and something sharp on the bumper had torn his coat and cut his arm. He was taken to the doctor for stitches and the police drove around the neighborhood looking for a Ford with something wrong with the bumper.

Amazingly they found one parked a block away from the Schmidt's house. The Ford with a broken and jagged headlight chrome cover was parked in front of the Carlson "ranch". Yes, Dale Carlson had struck again. This time, at twenty-three, he was fined $100 and had his license taken away. Dale moved to Glencoe in the seventies where I taught his daughter Patty in school. She babysat for my children a couple of times and I had occasion to talk to Dale. But I never mentioned his past.

There were two traffic problems the citizens of Litchfield seems to always be concerned with, if you can gauge it by the number of editorials and letters published in the local newspaper. One was double-parking[42]. The other was speeding in town. Even in 1906, the following editorial was in the paper for the citizens to read: "There is a general complaint that auto drivers hit up too fast a clip on our streets. We believe eight miles an hour is the speed limit for horse propelled vehicles, and the same rate (should be used) for those using Rockefeller's power fluid." (Gasoline)

---

[42] The city added parking meters in October of 1947 to eliminate the parking problem.

Louis Carlson never seemed to have any money when I would come collecting for the paper. "Ain't got it this week," he'd lie to me. "You catch me next week. I'll pay ya then." I kept pleading with Dean Schultz to let me cancel the Carlson's paper because it was eating away at my weekly earnings. Dean wouldn't let me do it. One day in 1957, I saw Wayne standing in the yard. He was back home after having spent two years in the Army. I told Wayne that his dad owed me many weeks back pay for the paper. He paid me everything they owed. I couldn't believe it. I suddenly had a lot of extra money.

Another family lived between the Carlson's place and the new power plant. They were the Tony Vanderpas family. Kids called them the "Vanderpants" family. Nine kids, Maxine, Jean, George, Raymond, Ruben, John, Tommie, and Dwayne and Dwight, twins the same age as Pat, were crammed into their shack. They were all tall "towheads", so blonde that they looked like they had white hair, and the older ones were already six feet tall. They moved to Torrance, California in the early fifties. They weren't necessarily "characters", just the size of the family and their financial situation made them stand out. There were a lot of poor people in Litchfield, it seemed, and many of them, like the Vanderpas family, made the Shaw boys forget that we were poor. We always had the necessities of life and didn't have a dirt floor in our house. Mom did a good job of providing.

Mrs. Vanderpas' sister's boy David, whom we called "Goose" because of his unusual walk, was "slow" and rode his bike around town. David was a big, clumsy kind of guy, sort of like a blond Jethro on *The Beverly Hillbillies*. He was very soft spoken and a nice kid. Just the sort that other kids picked on. Some kids would tease him about his bike and try to throw things through the spokes. David made you feel a little uneasy when you talked to him because he would just stare at you with a "deer in the headlights" kind of stare that made you wonder if anyone was inside there. Then he would finally blink and you'd know he was at least alive.

David really concentrated on riding his bike. We would wave at him and smile but it was rare to get a response. He stared down at his front tire making sure he was riding correctly. People would say "Hello David" and he would answer, "Hel.....looooo..." in a very slow and deliberate way. When it rained, he would put on a yellow slicker outfit that made him look like the Gorton fisherman. David became a custodian at a nursing home in Litchfield.

Directly across the street from us, in a tiny house with a fence around a small yard and garden and a rain barrel by his front door, was a kind old German widower named John Scheiwe, pronounced "Shayvee". John mowed the city parks on a giant riding lawn mower and worked with Dingle Rangeloff getting the beach ready for us swimmers. Skeeter's first job was helping John mow. John would be in his garden, hear the noon whistle blow, pull out his pocket watch from his bib overalls, shake his head and then complain that the "Danged thing is late again!" It bothered him if the whistle wasn't on time.

Grandpa Bill was a friend of John's. They had in common the fact that they had both lost their wives and were alone in this world. They would play cards at John's house and watch TV together at our house. John didn't have a television or a phone. Two kinds of TV shows would get them terribly upset. One was Friday night wrestling with Minneapolis wrestlers Butch Levy, Hard Boiled Haggerty and Haystack Calhoun. John and Grandpa believed that wrestling was real and they would get so upset with "those blind referees!" The other show that got them riled up was any western that would have horses fall down (with trip wires) when the riders, usually Indians, got shot.

"How can they treat those animals that way?" they would yell at the small television screen. I loved going over to John's little house when Grandpa was there. John always found me a piece of candy or a cookie. He got ill, moved to a nursing home in Paynesville in 1956, and died two years later.

Down the street north from us in the next block of Swift Avenue lived the Oster family. There was Lee, who was my age, a younger sister and their parents. Jon Oster, the father, was a bridge builder and was gone for weeks at a time. Somehow we had found out that his beautiful wife liked to sunbath in her backyard in the nude. She'd string blankets between trees and her clothesline and lay out there. That was all we needed to hear. We'd climb up on our neighbor Rose Hughes' garage, which was one house away from Oster's backyard, and we became young "peeping Toms". More fodder for the confessional.

We would see many of the neighborhood characters walking uptown on west Third Street. Most days we'd see "Billy the Badger", the Carlson boys, or Roy Peipus walking east on Third.

William "Billy the Badger" Nelson lived by Skeeter also and had one blue eye and one brown eye. He was a ditch digger and a gravedigger by trade, which was reason enough for us kids to fear him and leave him alone, besides his odd looking eyes. He dug the graves at the Lake Ripley Cemetery. I always wondered how he got out there because I only saw him walking all the time.

Billy, another old Scandinavian, looked like an overgrown Yul Brenner in bib overalls. He always wore a dark blue cap, the kind of cap that Elmer Fudd wore in the cartoons that had the sides that could be pulled down to make earmuffs. He talked with a heavy accent and chewed and spat tobacco. We learned that "Goddag" meant "Good day" so we'd yell that to him, keeping our distance. Billy would yell back "God dag a dag" or something. I think it meant "Good day to you too!" We just knew that it sounded funny, and we'd laugh.

Billy told people that he had dug most of the sewer system in Litchfield by hand and when Minnegasco came to town, he dug most of their trenches. I don't know why but Billy moved out of his house in 1967 and lived at the Litchfield Hotel for a couple of years. He kept two or three shovels in his room at the hotel, along with a large dirt "pick". A pick had a sharp point on one end and flat spade on other end. Old John Fischer, the hotel night clerk, teased kids working at the hotel that Billy the Badger would come after them with the pick if they didn't treat him nice. Billy was "sweet" on Florence Rethlake, a maid at the hotel.

There were a couple of other gravediggers around town. You would think we had a lot of deaths in Litchfield with all the gravediggers around, but many of them worked before the days of the machine diggers. Wilton "Tiny" Fredrickson was one, although he was the night cop at one time also, and George "Bing" Schultz was the other.

Again with the nicknames in Litchfield. I have a theory on the nicknames. I think it was a carryover from the pioneer days. So many of the people in Litchfield were of Scandinavian descent and had the same last name like Johnson, Nelson, Olson and Peterson, that, from the early days on, people were given nicknames, usually showing their profession or their appearance, just so people could tell them apart. So we had "Music Ole" Ole A. Olson, "Feed Ole" Olaf M. Olson, "Pool Room Ole" Ole B. Olson, "Merry-Go-Round" Ole Olson, "Milk" Nels Olson, "Plaster" Nelson, "Paint" Jenson and "Blacksmith" Anderson. Some nicknames were Swedish words, such as "Svart Nels", who was Nels Nelson. He had a big black beard and svart meant black in Swedish. Then there was "Slaktare" Peterson, who was a butcher and that's what slaktare meant.   Billy the Badger was a digger like a badger.   Years later, when a machine did the grave digging, it too was dubbed a "badger".

Like our neighbor Curly Housman, who had the wrong nickname being that he was bald, Tiny Fredrickson was a huge man at six foot two inches and way over three hundred pounds.   He was a caretaker and gravedigger at the cemetery.   It was said that Tiny's brother, "Gangster" Fredrickson, had been an actual gangster at one time.   I don't know if that's true or not.   He lived out of town by Star Lake and carried a sawed off shotgun, which impressed people.   Tiny played a big part in keeping Litchfield's famous Christmas decorations tradition alive.   More about that in a later chapter[43].

Bing Schultz was also called "Ding" by some people and that name fit him better as a "ding dong" was what we called crazy or stupid people.   Bing rode down Swift Avenue on his fancy Schwinn bicycle. Besides digging graves, Bing had been a ditch digger and he had been a very good one.   People marveled at his perfect ditches with perfectly slanted sides, I was told.   He had black saddlebags on the back of his bike and they were always full of something.   His bicycle had that metal cover between the two support bars and it had fenders with reflectors on them, unlike our bikes.   Talking to himself all the time, Bing rode his bike all around town with one pant leg rolled up.

He hung around Bull Johnson's pool hall a lot.   He was a great pool player so guys would treat him to a game and a beer, just to try to beat him.   Bull would give him a beer if he would swat flies around the bar. Occasionally Bing would stand outside the pool hall and swat flies on the south wall in the summer.   Thousands and thousands of flies congregated there probably attracted by the beer smell or urine stains.   Bing never did get them all but he gave it a good try.   He probably picked up some of the dead flies for food for his pet.   Bing had a pet toad named Johnny that he claimed "understands me when I talks to him."   He told Jim Sullivan about the pet toad in the Horseshoe Café one day and Jim told him he was nuts.   Bing went berserk and had to be asked to leave.

Bing got confused a lot and he would often end up in people's homes instead of where he currently lived with his old spinster aunts, Frieda and Pauline, at 324 Fifth Street East.   After they died, Bing got even more confused.   Photographer Arden Burleigh heard a noise in his

---

[43] See Chapter Thirteen The Bandstand.

basement one morning and went down to investigate. There stood Bing, obviously rising from his sleep. A lady in town went up to bed one evening and found Bing curled up in her bed. She never did figure out how he got into the house without her noticing.

One cold March day in 1969, Bing told some people that he was going to go hunting wolves and he took off on foot. He never returned and the police were notified. A search party of fifty people, including the local snowmobile club, started looking for Bing. A day later, the sheriff and his deputy found a dead and frozen Bing curled up in an old abandoned house four and a half miles east of Litchfield. Bing had died of exposure in the house where he had grown up. Bing had gone home.

We envied that bike of Bing's, with the saddlebags, fenders, handlebar grips, shiny reflectors and cushioned seat. Pat had a friend who had a bike like Bing, minus the saddlebags. His name was Jim Bares, pronounced "bare-ess", and he originally lived only a block away from us. I would always say to him, "Hey, Jim Bares, don't 'jimbaress' me!" I was always turning people's names around into what I thought were funny sayings. Popelka became "Poppycock", Justin Caine became "just in case" and anyone named Ben became Ben Dover. I thought it was clever, but, when I was teaching, some of my students thought I was making fun of their names and I had to quit doing it.

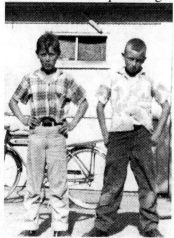

Jim Bares and Pat Shaw with Jim's bike in front of our garage clubhouse.

Another daily bike rider we'd see in Litchfield was Camellia Carlson, who was sort of a "bag lady". She wore old discarded clothes but she insisted they be bright and colorful. Bright reds and oranges, shocking pinks, yellows and lime greens. She looked like Carol

91

Burnett's clown cleaning lady on her TV show riding down the street with her flesh-colored stockings rolled down by her ankles. Camellia was no relation to the Carlson family by the way.

A few blocks from our house was the Litchfield Bottling Works where they bottled off brands like Orange Kist. We called it the pop factory and we could buy pop for half price in the front part, although I didn't do it very often. I hoarded my money. An old blind guy named Oscar Anderson, who owned the factory, sat in there taking our nickels after we helped ourselves to a bottle from the cooler. He went blind in 1950, but continued to run the factory alone until he sold it in 1967. He was able to do it because he trusted people, was kind to everyone and was great to his help.

Oscar and a bottling plant ad from 1948.

A man came in one day to buy a case of pop and handed Oscar a five-dollar bill.

"What ya givin' me there?" Oscar asked.

"A five," said the man, who obviously was just discovering that Oscar was blind. Oscar gave the man back his change.

"How do you know I didn't give you a dollar and say it was a five?" the man asked.

"I can feel the whiskers on old Abe's face," said Oscar. "No, I trust people, that's all." But Oscar learned to question the kids that came in. They weren't always so trustworthy. Oscar seemed to have a sixth sense concerning the kids and the pop. If you took two bottles and gave him one nickel, he'd know somehow.

"You haven't got two bottles there, do you son?" he'd say. But if you bought several bottles and handed him two quarters, for example, Oscar would make the correct change. He knew the size and feel of every coin.

We were a little bit afraid of anyone who was blind. I don't know why that is, but little kids are. You fear anything that's different from the norm. So we always stayed away from Oscar and stretched our arms to the limit to hand him the nickel. And we yelled at him, because he was blind, you see. People always do that.

"I'm blind," he'd say, "not deaf!" Oscar died in 1970.

When I did break down and treat myself to a bottle of pop, I drank it as slowly as humanly possible. It was the most wonderful taste I'd ever experienced, so I let it pour into my mouth and then slowly run back into the bottle. Over and again I did this, just getting the smallest essence of the flavor on my tongue. Finally when the pop had lost all of it's fizz and was warm, I drank it down slowly, re-enjoying the sweetness.

Roy Peipus would come limping down the two blocks on Austin Avenue to Skeeter's house and then turn onto Third Street, heading uptown. He limped but he walked very fast. Roy was something else. I thought he was old, but he was only six years older than I was. He contracted polio when he was a baby and was paralyzed for a while. His left foot was turned in on a shorter leg so that when he walked he stepped only on the toes of his left foot. He carried his left arm at his side with his hand sort of pointing forward. The hand wasn't good for much. His speech was slurred and spittle flew out of his mouth when he talked.

Max Peipus, Roy's deceased father, had been a street cleaner in the old days when there were still horses mingled with the cars on the streets. Max walked the streets pushing a big barrel on a cart, carrying a huge broom over his shoulder. Roy's brother Delos worked as a typesetter for the *Independent Review* newspaper.

Roy was our friend because he would buy us anything we wanted, like cigarettes or booze, if we gave him the money. He had some pet white rats that he kept in his garage. Once, when they had babies, Roy gave Mick, Pat and I each a little white rat. Mom went berserk when we brought them into the house in a cardboard box. She was one of those people who would jump on chairs when they see a mouse or a spider. We had already named the rats. It was 1957 and the song *Tammy* was popular, so that's what I named mine. Anyway Mom screamed, "Get those things right out of my house this instant!"

We took the rats out to the garage and found an old birdcage somewhere to keep them in. They grew rapidly and one day Mom found out that we still had them. She said, "That's the end of that," a favorite saying of hers. We were given orders to get rid of them in any way or means possible. We nailed some old boards together that we had found in the garage attic and made a little makeshift raft. We took the raft and the rats in their birdcage down to Jewett Creek. Gently we took our pets out of the birdcage, put them on the raft and set them adrift, knowing they would find a better world in Chicken Lake woods or wherever Jewett Creek flowed to.

We were always dragging animals home for pets. There were Prince, Tuffy and Sparky, the dogs, Tiger the cat, Tammy and her brothers and sisters and her mice and hamster cousins, the snakes, my five dollar badger I owned for a week, goldfish and Dennie's parakeet Bimbo. Dennie had a long-playing record he bought with the parakeet to teach it to talk. The idea was to put the bird near the record player, put the record on and leave the room. Leaving the room was hard for me to do when Dennie was borrowing my record player in my room. So I listened to "Canaries are cute, but they CAN'T talk... Canaries are cute, but they CAN'T talk... Canaries are cute, but they CAN'T talk..." on one side of the record and "It's absolutely preposterous...It's absolutely preposterous..." on the flip side for hours. Bimbo never did learn to say a darn thing before he got out of his cage and died or flew away. But I have never forgotten that canaries are cute, but they CAN'T talk, which is absolutely preposterous.

Roy Peipus lived with his mother Katy on Austin Avenue North close to Fifth Street West, repairing lawn mowers in his garage. He had a huge collection of girlie magazines in that garage. He'd let us look through the magazines and he'd tell us tales of his "conquests" of women. He carried a "rubber", or condom, in his wallet, so we knew that he knew what he was talking about. But, if you ever saw Roy you'd wonder about the stories he told us of his sexual conquests.

We always greeted Roy with, "Hey Roy, how's it goin'?" to which he would always reply, "She gotta go." We'd ask him to go to the Red Owl store and buy us some cigarettes. He'd pull a small notebook out of his breast pocket and write down our list. I still see him walking down Sibley Avenue almost every time I go through Litchfield now.

I met up with him in early June of 2002. Although the limp was less pronounced and he had a black wool hat pulled down on his head in the middle of the summer and a gray beard, I knew it was Roy. I stopped to talk to him and asked if I could take his picture, but he declined. His memory of buying us cigarettes when we were kids had faded away also.

"I don't tink I did dat," he said. "Must've been when I was a kid."

Chapter Eight
Friends Who Were Characters

In the fifties, girlie magazines were hard to come by. The only places I knew where you could buy *Playboy*, *Adam*, *Stag* or *Galaxy* magazines in Litchfield were Boyd Pankake's little neighborhood store and the hotel. Roy Peipus would've bought them for us, but at a dollar a copy, they were just too expensive for me. I usually waited for one of my richer friends to give me his magazines when he had to get them out of his house before his mother found them. I had no place to keep them either so I just passed them along. Today's *Victoria's Secret* catalogs put some of those girlie magazines to shame. We certainly had to use our imaginations more in the fifties.

I found Dennie's stash in his closet once and Mom caught me looking at them. She went ballistic and immediately took them out to the big empty oil drum in our backyard where she burned our trash. She burned them all. Dennie was upset with me again.

Reverend Ross, a minister from one of the smaller churches in town, tried to get a protest together against the hotel for selling them but the *Independent Review* wouldn't cover the story. He had to be forcibly removed from the hotel lobby once for trying to preach to people about the magazines. He even went so far as to buy the entire inventory but the hotel easily replenished it. A lady in town walked back and forth outside the hotel one day with a sign protesting the magazines but she also gave it up. They couldn't fight it.

Another supplier of contraband in town besides Roy was Floyd Strom. He was a hired farmhand for somebody. He came to town every Saturday morning and stayed at the hotel until Sunday night. He was a simple, friendly man, but he was lonely and wanted to be everyone's friend. So he bought kids girlie magazines, cigarettes and booze if they would give him an extra dollar. He wasn't worried about going to jail or prison because, as he used to say, "I've spent time in both places and I wouldn't mind going again."

One of my friends who always seem to have plenty of girlie magazines to share with us was Alvin Cecil "Alvie" Watkins. He had a lot of older brothers and no mom at home, so he had a constant supply of hand-me-down magazines that could be kept in his house. Alvie was a character. Short, but a gifted athlete, he never went out for sports in high school. We couldn't figure him out. He was as good or better than any of our school's stars. Maybe it had something to do with his grades. The school newspaper said of Alvie in their "Senior Predictions": "Al Watkins grabs his diploma and runs!"

Alvie
Watkins
today.

He was the "baby" in a family of eight kids. His dad, Emery, and two of his brothers worked at Fenton's Chevrolet. His mom lived in Hutchinson and was a waitress. I don't know when they divorced. Emery can be seen in a close-up in the 1953 film made about Litchfield. They all lived in a tiny two-bedroom house at 828 Holcombe Avenue North, right on the corner. They had moved here from Forest City, Minnesota. Alvie's brother Maynard told me, "I don't think we all lived in that little house at the same time, but there were three to a bed sometimes." Maynard ran on the track team. I never saw Maynard walking. He ran everywhere. We thought he was nuts. But he followed sports like a man possessed. Still living in Litchfield, today Maynard's an expert on Litchfield sports over the years.

Two of the eight children, Donald and Dorothy, were twins. They were born in different towns on different days of different months! Donald was born at home in Forest City on November 30th just before midnight. After complications, Alvie's mother was rushed to the hospital in Litchfield where, on December 1st of the next day, and obviously the next month, Dorothy was born.

Alvie had other talents besides his athletic prowess. We were all sure he would grow up to be a comedian. He kept us in stitches all of the time. Talking non-stop while he chalked up his cue stick, walking quickly around the pool table dropping ball after ball, beating the crap out of us, Alvie told joke after joke after joke. He later played on a Willmar pool team that went to the finals in an international pool tournament.

Besides talking non-stop, Alvie was always singing. His favorite performer was Jerry Lee Lewis and he combed his pile of blonde hair high up on his head, just like Jerry Lee. We'd be downtown at the bandstand or out at the Lake Ripley beach and Alvie would jump up on a bench or picnic table and entertain us by telling us jokes and singing the latest hits.

"Tell your mama, tell your pa, I'm gonna send you back to Arkansas," he'd sing. He loved to be "on stage" and his "act" was complete with dance moves. Alvie was as good a dancer as he was a joke teller. Mick had Alvie get up and sing a couple of songs with his current band, The Embers. Alvie sang and did *The Twist* and then he did some Jerry Lee Lewis songs. The audience loved him. Soon the band's posters were advertising the group as The Embers featuring Little Al Vee and then as Little Al Vee and The Embers.

▼▼▼▼▼▼▼▼▼▼

PLAYLAND
BALLROOM
KIMBALL, MINN.

Put Joy in Your Life
—Go Dancing!

—

FRIDAY, JULY 13
Carnival Days
THE AMBERS
Featuring Little Al Vee
Rock 'n Roll
Ultra Modern

Left: Poster with "Embers" misspelled. Right: The Embers. I painted the drumhead.

Alvie's whole family was athletic. In 1957, the Presbyterian championship softball team consisted of Alvie's brothers Maynard, Harold, Arnold "Ray", Marvin (whom we called "Muck") and a couple of actual churchgoers. I'll bet fourteen-year old Alvie hung around the games, wishing he could get in to play also. In the early sixties, Alvie, Maynard, Donald, Ray and Muck had a very good bowling team competing in the local league for Becker Shoe Service. Their substitute bowlers were, of course, their brother Harold and their dad, Emery. Then in March of 1967, the Miller Motors bowling team consisted of Emery and the six Watkins boys. They scored the second highest single game total in twenty-five years. Sadly, Marvin took his own life in July of 1989 and Donald, who lived in Hutchinson, followed the same way during the Halloween blizzard in October of 1991.

One block south of us lived the Andreen brothers, Ludwig and Larry. Ludwig Andreen was Dennie's age and they did some of Dennie's wild electronic things together. They also almost blew themselves to kingdom come one day in our garage when they cooked up an amateur nitroglycerin mix. Mick became friends with Larry. Larry was a wild kid, a loose cannon. The first time I met him, he totally grossed me out.

Pat and I had been to Chicken Lake woods snake hunting and we had a bag of garter snakes. We were over in Hank Schmidt's backyard showing them off. Larry was there, tagging along after Mick. Everyone, including myself, was afraid to touch the snakes, except for Larry. He just reached into the bag, grabbed one, and held it up in front of our stunned and awed faces.

"What's the big deal?" Larry said to us. "They don't bite. I bite!" Larry took the snake, put the head of it into his mouth and chomped down, biting the head completely off. He spit it out at my feet. I remember thinking, "This guy is strange, really strange!"

Mick became really close to Larry and so he was over at our house a lot, living only a block away and not getting along too well with his parents. One night Larry asked me if I wanted to go for a ride in his car. Having nothing else to do, I said "Sure," and off we went. Right away I knew that I had made a mistake. Larry took off north down our street squealing his tires, laying rubber. We turned left on Fifth Street and went out to the paved road west of town, County Road 11, where Larry floored the gas pedal of his car. 50, 60, 70, 80, 90 miles per hour.

All of a sudden Larry started weaving in and out of the broken centerlines, laughing. He scared the hell out of me and I asked him to stop it. I thought we were going to flip over. Larry just kept laughing and kept it up until he ran out of road. I was never so happy to get back home again as I was that night. From that day on, I turned down every offer for a ride from Larry. That decision turned out to be a possible lifesaver for me, as you will see later.

Terry Kohlhoff was a bit of a wild kid too. He was two years younger than me, but he acted much older and so he was invited into the clique. He seemed to have access to anything we wanted, like beer or cigarettes. The cigarettes probably came from his dad and grandpa's Super Valu store. And there was many a time that he told me about secret keg parties and their locations. He always seemed to be "in the know". His driving was suspect too. We'd be driving down the highway, he driving, me riding shotgun. He'd say, "Grab the wheel!" and, stunned, I would, steering with my left hand while he stuck half his body out his window, waving to the shocked oncoming traffic.

I was parked on a gravel road one night with a young lady in my stepfather Floyd's silver-gray and huge finned 1958 Buick. Suddenly the car started moving on its own down the road towards the ditch. Had I left the car in neutral somehow? I sat up and slammed the breaks on. Suddenly lights came on behind me. I turned around and saw Terry Kohlhoff sitting in his car, grinning from ear to ear.

One Saturday afternoon, Terry pulled into our driveway on a motorcycle.

"Hop on. I'll take you for a little ride," he said.

I did, and off we went, with me on the back hanging onto his waist for dear life. No helmets and no brains. We headed out of town on Highway 22 towards Hutchinson. When we had driven ten miles to Coney Island, Terry pulled onto their gravel parking lot and stopped.

"Time for a beer," he said. Now, Terry Kohlhoff was sixteen and I was eighteen, but we walked into the place and climbed up on two stools at the long but empty bar. Apparently Terry knew the bartender, because he looked his way and said "Two taps," holding up two fingers. The beers appeared in front of us on coasters, with foam oozing down the sides of the glasses. Terry threw a fifty-cent piece onto the bar, saying, "Keep the change."

We sipped the beers while Terry talked to the bartender about fishing and what not. As we were finishing, Terry said to the bartender, "Well, gotta get going. Any chance of me getting a case to go?"

"What kind?" the man said, as if Terry had asked him for a candy bar.

"Hamm's, Grain Belt, whatever ya got."

"Okay," the man said, turning to go into a back room. He came back holding a cold case of Grain Belt and Terry gave him the money.

Outside in the parking lot, I looked at Terry and said, "Okay. Now just how the hell are we gonna get this home?"

"You're gonna hold it," he said, nonchalantly. It started to dawn on me that this ride had been planned.

So there we were, two teenagers riding down the highway at breakneck speed on a motorcycle with a frightened idiot on the back holding a case of beer. I had no way of holding onto Terry this time. I squeezed my legs together onto his thighs, hoping I wouldn't burn them on the tailpipe and all of the time thinking to himself, "I'm gonna either die or end up in jail." The Gods of the Idiots were with us that day because we made it to Terry's house on the east side of Litchfield safely. He transferred the beer into his car trunk and gave me, the foolish fool, a ride back home.

It seems that Mick and Dennie's friends were always involved in accidents or mishaps. I mention their friends several other times in this book and talk about the mishaps. Dennie had a friend named Dennis "Ole" Olson, from another Swedish family that lived in our neighborhood. He went boating on June 2, 1960 with Dick Nygaard and James Vernon. Dick was looking for a boat motor for some type of boat race he was going to enter. He wanted to try out this very old, large, high torque boat motor and asked the others to go along. Dick put the boat into too sharp of a turn. When he over corrected, he lost control and the boat flipped over, landing upside down. Neither Dick nor Dennis had life jackets on or were swimmers.

"I remember being under water and thought to get my shoes off," Dennis told me. "We all got back to the overturned boat but the overturned hull was unstable and difficult to hang onto. Dick became separated from the boat and went under." Lennart Holen, who owned the Sinclair gas station by the high school and was on Lake Ripley fishing, got to them with his boat. But by then, Dick had drowned.

Left to right: Ray Salmela, Dennis "Ole" Olson, and brother Dennie. Notice the rolled up blue jeans.

Ole and my brother Dennie were fishing at Ripley on another day. They had no boat and they were just fishing from shore over by the boat landing by the golf course. They saw an incredibly large northern floating belly up off shore. It was barely alive, occasionally flapping its
100

tail fin, and they thought it was just dying of old age. The fish looked to be a monster, about thirty pounds. They saw another fisherman, Bob (last name withheld), who was loading his boat onto his trailer. Excited, they told him about it. The next thing they knew, he took the boat back out and netted the monster, which he took to town to have Stan Roeser take a picture of for the paper. The readers saw a picture of Bob holding up the huge fish he had caught on Lake Ripley. Moral: Don't believe everything you read in the papers.

Lake Ripley has a reputation of being a decent fishing lake. Nothing spectacle, but you can generally get some good sunnies, bass or walleyes. Once, in the thirties, it had gotten overrun with bullheads and carp. A tragedy turned into a blessing for both the lake and the town.

Minnesota had a number of drought years back then and in 1936 it had gotten so bad that you could drive through weeds and sweet clover half way across the lake from the north shore, where the golf course is today. Some older residents remember seeing haystacks where the middle of the lake is. The lake had pretty much dried up and the deepest point of what was left was only six to eight feet deep. In the winter of '36, there was a hard freeze and the lake "froze out". In April of the following spring, the dead fish washed up on the shores. Hugo Esbjornsson got a loader and scooped up forty tons of the fish. About twenty truckloads were taken to the Cleveland family farm to use for fertilizer. Mayor Leo Baumgartner contacted other towns that were seining out their shrunken and now overstocked lakes and Ripley was restocked with only good fish.

One Monday morning in 1964, I was riding back to the cities from Litchfield with my college roommate, Dick Blonigan. Dick grew up in Litchfield about four blocks from our house and his mother worked at the Produce next to Mom. Dick wasn't going to college. He worked in Minneapolis selling televisions and antenna systems. We had both found that we were in need of someone to share rent with, so we hooked up. Whenever Dick sold an antenna, he'd tell the customer that for an additional $20, he'd install it. He'd get me to crawl up on the roofs of the Minneapolis houses and put the antenna up while he did the hookup inside the house. He paid me $10.

Dick was two years older than my brother Dennie, but they had become friends when Dick played trombone for a short time in Dennie's band. Dick also did the bookings. The trombone was Dick's first love and the cause of some of his problems. Dick did band promoting on the side and this morning, as we rode together, he asked me to open up his glove compartment. Dollar bills spilled out onto my lap and the car's floor. Dick had put on a dance on the previous Saturday night in St. Cloud with The Trashmen. They were a Minneapolis band with a national hit called *Surfin' Bird*.

"Put those in stacks of a hundred for me," Dick said. I counted out the money and every so often, Dick would pull over in a town at a bank and run inside to exchange the stacks for hundred dollar bills.

Dick Blonigan today in San Jose, California.

Dick always had a weight problem and, for some reason, he dropped out of high school to join the Marine Corps. Washing out because of his weight after five months of service, Dick went back to and finished high school. Then his weight ballooned. I would guess he was close to three hundred pounds. We made quite the pair walking down Hennepin Avenue in the cities, he being so big and me as skinny as a rail. It was sort of a Laurel and Hardy look, I imagine. To top it off, I was in my Beatles phase and sported near shoulder length hair.

We'd stand at a downtown street corner amid a crowd waiting for a light change and, to fool around and embarrass Dick, I'd grab his hand and put my low-haired head lovingly on his shoulder. He would go nuts. Dick loved blues music and he would drag me down to Mattie's Bar at Nicollet Avenue and Lake Street to listen to Mojo Buford and his Chi Four perform. They were an all-black band and Mattie's was an all-black nightclub. Dick and I would be the only white people in the entire bar. I was nervous, but Dick didn't seem to care.

I knew that Dick had been in trouble with the law, just out of high school. In fact, he had "done time", as they say. One night I talked him into sharing his life of crime with me. As I said, Dick's first love was his

102

trombone. Today, living in San Jose, California, he plays in a symphonic brass orchestra that travels the world and has performed for President Clinton at the White House and the Pope at the Vatican.

When Dick was nineteen, he had gotten into a money bind and, as hard as it was, he had pawned his beloved trombone in a Minneapolis pawnshop. Things hadn't worked out and on a Saturday night, knowing that on Monday morning the pawnshop was going to sell his trombone to get their money, Dick snapped.

He drove his red and white '55 Oldsmobile out of Litchfield west to Cedar Mills, where he parked right in front of the liquor store. Dick put a small white handkerchief over his large face and, at 7:15pm, with only a pocketknife in his left hand, he walked into the liquor store. Sixty-nine year old William Schulz was sitting behind the counter. Thinking someone was pulling a practical joke on him, William looked up at the comically looking huge teenager with the tiny handkerchief over his broad oval face, holding a little jackknife out in front of him.

William laughed and said, "What the hell do you want?"

"I want the money in that drawer," the nervous desperado replied, stabbing the air with his knife. Realizing the teenager must be serious and might be crazy enough to use the little knife, Schulz thought he'd better do what he was told. Better to play along and be safe, even if it might be a practical joke. Nervously, he took the money out of the drawer and starting counting it out on the counter in piles, as if he were making change.

"One, two, three…"

"Never mind counting it," a frantic Dick said. "Just hurry up and hand it over."

Dick scooped the money up, all $75 of it, (the newspaper reported $123), and he turned and ran out the door to his car. Schulz followed him to the door and wrote down the license plate number of the red and white car pulling away in the direction of Litchfield. He called Sheriff Eldon Hardy. Meeker County and Kandiyohi County sheriffs' deputies converged on Litchfield.

Meanwhile, Dick was having trouble with his car. The lights kept dimming on him. Thinking his battery was dying, he got back to Litchfield and pulled into Beckman's Standard Service on Sibley Avenue North to have it looked at. Of course the deputies spotted the red and white car immediately and they surrounded Dick with their revolvers drawn. Dick denied any knowledge of the robbery until the cops said,

103

"Okay Dick, we can clear this up. Let's take a ride to Cedar Mills and see if the store clerk can identify you."

"You might as well save your gas for that trip," Dick said, not wanting to burden the officers. "I'm your man." Dick lucked out and only got probation. He broke probation though, and that's when he did some time.

As long as I've known Dick, he's been the perfect gentleman and an honest and true friend. When times got rough for me for money in college, Dick offered to pay three-fourths of the rent so that we could continue to be roommates until I graduated from college. That night he hosted and paid for a graduation party for me. His heart is as big as his body, but Dick was, and still is, quite a character.

Chapter Nine
Teachers Who Were Characters

Some of the town's characters were our teachers. There was the ancient spinster 9th grade Science teacher Ruthie Burns, with her odd wink while she stuck her tongue out of the corner of her mouth, the sleeping Vocations instructor Kermit Johnson, who we'd awake by "accidentally" dropping a book off our desk, and the Trig and Geometry teaching Rolly Scharmer, who threw erasers at sleepers in his class. The two of them should have gotten together. Rolly used to get so excited in class, running back and forth writing next to his blackboard, explaining theorems and solving problems. His excitement was infectious, at least for me. I tried to capture it and pass it on when I taught years later.

Then there was the *Esquire* magazine reading Phy Ed teacher Howard "Howie" Felt, who had a wooden paddle he smacked our behinds with while we bent over and grabbed our ankles after some indiscretion in class. The loud crack would echo in the big cold gym, which doubled as the stage for the auditorium.

Howie Felt was also the football coach and he was known for his inspirational speeches at pep fests or in the locker room. The Wimmer boys told me that the team would gather in the equipment shed by the football field at half time and listen to Howie's tirades. Sometimes tears would flow from his eyes. He would get the entire team so fired up that they busted the door down several times while running out of the building, screaming at the tops of their lungs.

Howard "Howie" Felt in 1955 and 1959.

At a pep fest in school one fall afternoon, Howie was standing next to English teacher Wally Stubeda in the back of the auditorium, waiting for his cue to go up on the stage and address the school.

"Wanna see me go up there and cry?" he said, leaning over to Wally. Then he winked. Wally looked at Howie, not knowing what to say. Howie, who then heard his introduction, ran down the side aisle, took two stairs at a time and grabbed the microphone on the stage. He started giving a speech about beating our rivals, the Willmar Cardinals, and about loyalty and tradition and before long his voice started cracking, reaching a crescendo, and suddenly he was in tears, unable to finish. He left the stage a broken man and he gave Wally another wink as he left the auditorium that afternoon. (The Cardinals stoned our bus and burned our "Go Dragons" sign when we beat them once in the district tournament. But I married two former "Cardinal" students.)

I had Howie for Phy Ed and Health classes in high school. All we ever did in Health, which was co-ed, was make posters against smoking or drinking, so I got an "A". Sex education was "self-taught" except for one time when the boys only were escorted into the upstairs projection room to see an ancient U.S. Government issued film on VD. In Phy Ed, Howie would have the current sport's starters pick teams to play touch football or basketball and then have the rest of the "unpicked" students, I was one, play some games on the sides of the gym or field. No matter what we did in class or how hard we tried, if we weren't out for a sport, we got a "C" in Phy Ed from Howie. After teams were picked, Howie would sit down in a chair and read the paper or his *Esquire* magazine. In those days, that was like someone reading a *Playboy* magazine in public.

At the end of Phy Ed class, we would run downstairs to shower. On the floor in the locker room was a two-foot square box half filled with talcum powder. You were supposed to put your feet in it after drying off after your shower, to keep your feet dry and prevent athlete's foot. I never saw anyone do it. Then we were to run back upstairs to the gym to line up at attention. Howie wouldn't let us leave the gym to go to our next class unless we all stood at attention and shut up. One day, after he had finally released us, I was walking down the hall along side of Howie. He looked at me and said, "How's it goin' there ole Shaw, Shaw, Shaw, Shaw, Shaw?" Before I could answer, his left leg swung up behind me like a whip and caught me in the hind end, propelling me down the hall in front of him.

"Sorry there, ole Shaw, Shaw," Howie yelled down the hall to me. "That ole leg of mine is acting up again."

One day in the fall during Health class, Howie marched us out to a small woods a few blocks from the school on the south side of town. He carried a shotgun with him over his shoulder. He was going to teach us about gun safety. When we got to the woods, we saw that Howie had made a circle of logs around an unlit campfire.

"Sit down, boys and girls," Howie told us. We complied and Howie started walking around the circle behind us talking and pointed the gun towards the ground. Of course, a bunch of us were screwing around, as usual, elbowing ribs and making faces to the students across from us.

"Now someday, boys and girls," Howie lectured, "you're gonna be out hunting with your buddy and settling down to camp and suddenly…" **BOOM!** The shotgun Howie was carrying went off behind a small kid with glasses, who jumped up about two feet in the air off his log. "…your huntin' buddy is gonna forget to put the safety on his gun," Howie continued, as if nothing had happened, "and it's gonna go off, just like that." Howie had our full attention for the rest of his lecture. I can only hope that Howie had a blank shell in that shotgun and I'll bet that kid hoped he had an extra pair of underwear in his locker back at school.

Apparently Howie could get by with very little sleep. An old relative of a friend was in the hospital and he didn't want to be there. He would try to leave whenever he got a chance. He needed to be watched. Someone at the hospital told the family that Howie Felt was available for such duty. So he was hired and he sat in the room and read through much of the night. If the man got up and started moving for the door, Howie stopped him. He did this on consecutive nights and could still teach his classes.

During the summer, Howie did a lot of umpiring. He was a colorful character doing that too, very vocal and demonstrative in his signals. He was umpiring a Legion game against Benson and was catching a lot of flak from a Benson fan named Gallagher. The guy was relentless and used some language Howie didn't like. All of a sudden, Howie stood up from his crouch behind the catcher and yelled "Time!" He pushed the batter and catcher aside, stepped on home plate and turned to face the stands. He pointed to Gallagher, then pointed to the parking lot and yelled "You…outta here!" He folded his arms across his chest and stood there motionless, like a cigar store Indian. Minutes and minutes passed and nobody moved a muscle except for Gallagher's lips, which he kept flapping, now protesting Howie's stoppage of the game.

"You got no rights over fans. We can disagree with your calls…" Gallagher went on and on.

Howie wouldn't give in and restart the game. Now it had been about ten minutes and obviously Gallagher wasn't going to leave. Finally, Howie walked over to the Litchfield dugout and informed the coach, "This game will not continue until that man is removed. I want you to call the police." Nobody went against Howie Felt. The coach left, the police were called, Gallagher was removed, and the game continued…a half an hour later.

The children would be lead in singing Christmas carols by Howie at the annual Jaycee sponsored Santa Claus Day program at the high school auditorium every year. The last day of classes before Christmas vacation in 1958, there was a Christmas program for the school kids in the auditorium during the final class period. The program consisted of traditional pieces played by the high school orchestra, songs sung by the Glee Club, a piano solo by someone, and so forth; the usual stuff. The students were anxious for English teacher Floyd Warta to make his appearance as Santa, as he usually did, so that the program would get over and they could get their free bag of candy and nuts donated by the Chamber of Commerce and get started on their vacation.

The lights were suddenly dimmed and Howie Felt walked out of the wings to center stage. The students expected him to make some kind of a speech, introducing Santa or just tell them which class could exit the auditorium first after the program. Instead, the stunned students heard this big, loud and gruff man sing *O Holy Night* in a Capella. He had a beautiful voice and hit the high note at the end of the song without a hitch. The assembly was incredibly silent except for Howie's voice. Once again Howie had tears in his eyes on that stage, but this time he was joined by a lot of students.

Howie had no time for overweight students or athletes who wouldn't play hurt. He got both in a kid named Steve P. in 1961. Steve got hurt in a football game and refused to go back in. Howie yelled and yelled and rode him so bad that the Steve broke down in front of the squad, which only made things worse. Steve told his parents, who went directly to the school board. The board had dealt with Howie before with several other complaints and Howie had been warned. This was the final straw. He was asked to come before the board where he was sharply reprimanded. Howie argued and a verbal fight ensued. Suddenly Howie said, "If you don't like the way I coach and run things, then to hell with you. I resign." Assistant coach John Klug finished out the season and Howie took a leave of absence from teaching, but he never came back.

The oddest teacher was Floyd Warta, a very talented but eccentric man in his fifties. He came to Litchfield in 1937 and taught English and Speech at the high school, but most importantly for me, he directed the school plays. He was a large, balding, roly-poly, happy-go-lucky kind of a guy and was the only teacher I can remember being called by his first name by his students. He was always laughing when he talked, kind of a giggle at the end of each sentence, and spittle would fly out of his mouth along with the words. He would either lean way forward on a podium or way back in his chair with one arm behind his head scratching the opposite ear while he lectured to his classes.

Floyd was a sloppy dresser. He was wearing large colorful ties with plaid or multi-colored shirts long before it became the fashion. Often his shirt, stained with his previous meal, would get unbuttoned at the bottom of his large stomach. Once a student went up to him and politely pointed out that Floyd's shirt was open down by his trousers. "Oh, hee hee," said Floyd, "I belong to the Belly Club and that's my button. Hee hee hee." Dr. Karl Danielson gave Floyd his old raccoon coat to use for a costume in a play. Floyd chose to wear it himself and it became his trademark.

Floyd
Warta
dressed up
in 1967.

You could pretty much do anything you wanted to in Floyd's class, as long as you got your work done. If you paid attention and tried, he was an excellent teacher. If you didn't, then you didn't exist in his class and Floyd ignored you completely. One day, to prove the point, John Hawkinson got up in the middle of one of Floyd's podium lectures and strolled across the room to the window, walking right in front of Floyd. John calmly leaned on the windowsill, resting his chin in his hand, and gazed out the window. Floyd didn't blink. He just kept lecturing. John stood at the window for a few minutes and then returned to his seat. Floyd didn't say a word to him. You see John didn't care about Floyd's class, so he didn't exist.

On a cold November afternoon, Floyd was lecturing to his class about poetry. With the winter sun beating through the window and the school's steam radiators working overtime, it was very warm in the room. Students began to drift off, helped by Floyd's long recitation about a boring subject. Still talking, Floyd slowly stood up from his chair and ambled over to a humongous dictionary that was on a stand in the corner of his room. He picked up the heavy book, held it up to the front of his face and let it drop to the floor. It sounded like a cannon went off in the room. Everyone woke up with a start and sat up straight in their chairs. The door opened up and Assistant Principal Harry Lindbloom and Vocation teacher Kermit Johnson stuck their heads into the room.

"Anything wrong, Floyd?" Lindbloom inquired, looking around.

"Not a thing, not a thing," Floyd said, "Just making a point to my class, hee hee." The men stared at Warta, then looked at the students and then back to Floyd, who waved them off with a "Goodbye" flick of his chubby little hand. They closed the door. Floyd walked over to the window, flung it open, shook his fist out the window angrily at the sky and started reciting a poem.

"Winter is a rushing in. Loudly sing, goddamn." I don't know if he made it up on the spot or if someone had written it, but as he continued reciting this odd poem full of curses, with his fist still raised out the open window, it started to gently snow. Perfect dramatics.

Floyd built beautiful sets for his plays and put on fantastic productions. After a co-lead in my first play in the ninth grade, a one-act Christmas play called *Why The Bells Chimed*, then bigger roles in *The Miracle Worker* and *The Vagabond*, Floyd gave me the lead in my senior year play, *Fair Exchange*. In the play I was a juvenile delinquent, brandishing a gun and talking tough. I was supposed to slap the character played by my perennial classmate Cathy Osdoba. Floyd demanded realism. During rehearsal one evening, we finally arrived to the slap scene. I gave Cathy a love tap and continued my lines.

"Stop!" Floyd screamed from his front row auditorium seat. "What the hell was that?"

I mumbled something and Floyd got up out of his seat, did his slow penguin-like walk to the side steps of the stage, which he climbed with some effort. He sauntered over to Cathy and I, deep breaths hissing through his clenched teeth.

"Slap her like you're supposed to!" he hissed at me.

I gave Cathy a firmer love tap.

"No, no, no!", Floyd yelled at me. "Like this." He cupped his hand and hit the fatty part of Cathy's cheek, making a loud "pop" sound. "See how I did that? Didja hear it? Did that hurt?" he asked, turning back to Cathy.

"No," she said. Did I see a tear forming in the corner of her eye?

I had to stand there and practice my slap on Cathy over and over as her cheek turned redder and redder. During the performance, I got into my character and really gave her a good whack, forgetting to cup my hand. Funny, but she remains a friend to this day.

Terry Shaw threatens Cathy Osdoba
with a gun in "Fair Exchange".

Floyd had two hobbies. He went, by himself, to every single movie that came to town and he built model ships. One night, a bunch of us were playing pool in Bull Johnson's pool hall. We were shocked to see Floyd come walking in, dressed in his large raccoon coat with a black fedora tilted to one side of his head. He had just been to the movie at the Unique Theater. He went up to the bar, ordered a dime glass of beer, shot it down in one big gulp, turned and walked out. We were stunned. In those days, we thought teachers had something in their contracts about drinking because they were never, ever seen in bars. At least in the towns they taught in. Floyd walked to the beat of a differe⸝ ⸝⸝mmer. Arden Burleigh photographed Floyd at work on a mode⸍ study. Arden had an eye for interesting characters ar⸍ certainly an interesting character.

In 1969, Floyd grew a long white beard for Litchfield's centennial and he never shaved it off the rest of his life. It matched his thinning white hair and huge stomach so well that he started playing Santa Claus in national television commercials and magazine ads for Artic Cat, Dunkin' Donuts and others. Floyd had finally reached his dream of being a professional actor.

Floyd making model ships in 1967 and as Santa Claus for Dunkin' Donuts.

Alice Volkenant taught German, which I never took, but I heard a lot of stories about her nevertheless. She taught at Litchfield for a very long time and the longer you teach somewhere, the more stories there are about you. Alice dedicated her entire life to being a teacher. That is all she ever did, all she had in her life and all she ever wanted to do with her life. She was a spinster and never married, living upstairs over a large brick house next door to the Red Castle building. She had about four thousand books, all neatly arranged in her living room like a library. She was always impeccably dressed and well-groomed, but quite high-strung and nervous all the time. Alice looked the part of the dignified lady, always having the mandatory handkerchief tucked in the sleeve of her dress.

Alice had an ongoing feud with Floyd Warta over a play and I believe they didn't talk directly to each other for over twenty years, even though they both were in the English Department. She, Ruthie Burns, and Bernice "Ski Jumps" Slinden, other spinster teachers, were the best of friends and, because neither Alice nor Ruthie drove, they depended on Bernice to get them around. After church, Alice and Ruthie often walked to the Colonial Café for their Sunday dinner, which Alice liked to order in German if a certain waitress was working. Alice was already old when we were in high school, at least by our standards, and old women teachers were considered harmless and fair game for pranks.

Alice
Volkenant
in 1966.

Alice was a clock-watcher, habitually glancing at the clock on the wall in her classroom, to the point of it being a distraction. During evening play practice week, my classmates Eric Olson and Dean Wilson snuck into Alice's room and "jocked" her clock, which meant they found an old smelly jock strap in the locker room and draped it over the clock on her wall. They both had Alice for first hour German class the next morning and could hardly contain themselves when she strolled into the full classroom of snickering students the next morning. When Alice looked up to the clock for the first time that morning and saw that jock strap, she just didn't know what to do. She decided the best thing to do was to ignore it and pretend it wasn't there, so that's what she did. She never acknowledged the jock's presence the entire period, but couldn't stop herself from continuing her habit of glancing at the clock and the jock about every thirty seconds.

Every afternoon Alice would draw the shades in her room because the afternoon sun beating through the west windows would get intense. Eric and Dean went into her room again another night of practice week and tied the window shade strings of her three west windows to the stalks of Alice's three potted red geranium plants sitting on each windowsill. Every morning when Alice came into her room, the first thing she would do was go the windows and tug on the shade strings, quickly in succession, one…two…three…letting the shades fly back up When she did it the following morning, her three geraniums were pul'   ⁀ out of their pots. They hung in the air like bad men lynched   movie. Alice was fit to be tied.

Alice also taught one class of Latin. She discouraged Catholics from taking the class, however, because she thought they had an unfair advantage over the other students because they "spoke it in church". What she didn't realize is that, for the most part, we didn't have a clue what we were saying, which is why the church went away from it.

One Monday morning, Alice's entire first hour class took their desks, which faced the north blackboard, and turned them to face the south. When Alice came into the room and saw her desk in the normal place but all of her students facing the rear of the classroom, she simply grabbed her notes, walked to the front of the class and carried on like nothing was wrong. When the second hour class came in, she had the students turn their desks around to face the right way, telling them, "The custodians must have turned them the wrong way after they cleaned over the weekend." Alice wasn't really a character, I guess. She just had funny things happen to her, which she took in stride, endearing her to her students.

Another favorite teacher, who wasn't really a character but interesting nevertheless, was Phyllis McCoy Koenig, who taught an unbelievable fifty-three years, twice my teaching career. She easily bested Hazle Walters (forty-six years) and Esther Settergren (forty-two years). Grandfathers would be stunned when their grandchildren would say their teacher was Mrs. Settergren.

"Really?" they'd ask. "I had her too!"

Phyllis Koenig in 1963.

Phyllis was from Mankato, Minnesota, as my family was before our father moved us to Litchfield. Exactly a year later, in September of 1947, Phyllis came to start her teaching career. She married Bob Koenig, who worked at the Post Office. Bob died suddenly in July of

1967 leaving Phyllis to raise her little children by herself. She reminded me of my mother, because of her family situation and her toughness.

Phyllis supplemented her salary for teaching English at the high school by conducting the Modern Woodmen Insurance club meetings. Mom bought $1000 insurance policies for each of her boys from some man who went to our church. Along with the insurance policy came a membership in the Modern Woodmen children's club. Once a month, during the school year, we would meet at the Community Building basement or in Phyllis' kitchen to play games, make crafts and have a treat. Brother Pat and I went religiously. It was free!

When I was in high school, I would go over to Phyllis' house at night along with Marty Foss, Wayne Herman, Billy Maass and Jeannie McCarney. We'd just sit and talk to her. Phyllis wasn't the "enemy" as many of the other teachers seemed to be. She seemed to understand teenagers and really care about us. She made it fun to learn about Shakespeare and vocabulary and nouns and verbs. She didn't care if we lit up a cigarette in her presence out of school either, so we'd often do that while we sat around talking to her at her house. She'd light up with us.

Some of the teachers were paid to do a school survey for the district in October of 1958. They had to call people on the phone and get details about how many children they had in the district, what schools they were attending, their names, ages, and so forth. Not everyone had phones, so occasionally the teachers would have to drive to the homes and sit down with the people and do the survey. Phyllis had to call on a phone-less family, who will remain nameless. They lived by the Wimmers' house. Pat and I saw the family a lot because we were always over at the Wimmers' picking up Jerry and Dougy to go somewhere. All of the members of this particular family were characters. The two kids were "slow" and in Special Ed when they were in school. We didn't tease them but we laughed about the family behind their backs because the mother and the dad, Earl, were completely bonkers. They were dirt poor, as close as you could get to the people in the movie *Deliverance* in Litchfield, I suppose.

They lived in a Quonset hut house. I could never figure out how they got separate rooms in that rounded tin shed. Later, I found out that they didn't. Their former paperboy told me that when he walked into the "house" to collect, he was immediately in the living room. In the ce of that living room was a toilet. No walls, no curtains, no privacy. Just a plain white stool. Earl had been told that he couldn't have an outhouse in the city limits anymore and, because of the Quonset's plumbing situation, the middle of his living room was the cheapest place he could find to put the toilet.

We'd ride by the hut on our bikes and say something to Earl and he'd come running after us with a rake, yelling and swearing. Anything would set him off. We were afraid of Earl but we always knew that we could outrun him on our bikes. The mother took after a friend of the paperboy once and chased him down the street with a butcher knife.

Phyllis had three such calls to make one evening and she told her husband Bob that she'd be home in time to make supper for him and the kids. She went to the mentioned family's Quonset hut and tried to stay outside because of the odors coming through the screen door. But she was invited in and reluctantly she entered, holding her breath for as long as she could. She started to ask her questions.

All of a sudden Earl jumped up and started ranting with one of his tirades. For some reason he thought Phyllis was prying into their family situation and that she was from St. Phillip's School, where his kids had been refused admission. The reason was the parochial school didn't have a program to handle such kids, but Earl didn't understand that. Anyway, he grabbed his gun and threatened Phyllis. She got up to leave. Earl told her to sit back down. He wasn't going to let her leave. Nothing Phyllis could say would calm Earl down or change his mind. She didn't know what he had in mind for her or how serious he was about the gun.

Meanwhile, Bob Koenig began to wonder what had happened to Phyllis, so he set out in his car looking for her. Knowing the houses she was to call on, Bob drove around in that neighborhood and saw Phyllis' car parked in front of Earl's hut. Bob figured out what was going on and knew enough about Earl to realize he couldn't handle the situation by himself and that he might actually make matters worse. So he went downtown and got Chief of Police George Fenner,[44] who obviously had dealt with the family and Earl many times before. George was able to defuse the situation and a relieved Phyllis got to go home to teach many, many, many more days. About a hundred thousand more days.

---

[44] George Fenner came to Litchfield in 1949 and started a furniture business with a man called C. I. Eddy on Depot Street near Greep's on Depot Street. He joined the police department on April 1, 1951 and became the Chief of Police on January 15, 1953. George died at the age of sixty-nine.

116

Chapter Ten
Some of the Town Characters

A lot of the guys we thought were characters in town were handy men types just doing little jobs around town to get by. August W. "Auggie" Lindegren was one of those guys. The fact that he always wanted to be paid in cash and didn't trust banks, fueled the legend that he had a lot of money stuffed away somewhere. I remember reading in the paper about an old bachelor farmer being found dead in his house with a bullet hole in his head and no weapon found. That fall when neighbors emptied his grain bin, a large bundle wrapped in newspaper fell out. It contained over $7000 in small bills. Apparently he wouldn't tell his attacker where his stash was.

Anyway, Auggie would do odd jobs for anybody in town for cash, and he gave you a slip telling you each charge and fee, like 50¢ for this and 25¢ for that. Auggie never did anything for free. He usually worked for housewives whose husbands couldn't or wouldn't fix a leak or a squeaky door. What made Auggie a character was the trust the women put in him. He would get from them and dispense to them juicy gossip as he made his way from housewife to housewife. He "understood" women and their ailments, they told him, and he would dispense advice and folklore remedies for their cures. The ladies loved Auggie.

Pat and I would be sitting in our living room, watching television, when we'd hear a jingling sound and the clippety-clop of horse's hooves on the street. We'd run outside to see Axel Bjur, who worked for Hugo Esbjornsson, bringing Hugo's team of Clydesdales down Swift Avenue. The horses were huge with gigantic hairy hooves. Hugo sent Axel around tilling people's gardens with his team. It was so much fun watching him work those huge horses around Alma Colmen's garden every spring. When Hugo ran his lumberyard, he delivered the lumber with a team of horses and a wagon. It wasn't until his son John took over that a delivery truck was bought.

Another man who had horses was Clarence "Breezy" Simmons. His weren't the huge type, just regular workhorses. He also kept them in town behind his house on Armstrong Avenue and Third Street, down by Alvie's house. Mom used him once for our tiny garden and he would regularly do Skeeter's dad's garden. Breezy's son Dick was voted Skeeter's class President in 1958. Dick and Skeeter used to have parties at Skeeter's aunt's house when she was gone for the weekend. The house was near our house and Mick and Dennie would go over there and join in on the fun.

Breezy was also an insurance agent. Skeeter had a '49 Ford and he kept getting stopped by John Rogers and ticketed for open bottle and speeding. He lost his license once and was supposed to get dropped from his insurance. Breezy made excuses to the company and put it off long enough for Skeeter to enlist in the Air Force. He did Skeets a huge favor. Breezy's wife made wallets and belts out of leather, complete with the customer's name stamped on the outside. Mr. Simmons would display them at the Red's pool hall in the glass case by the door and take orders on them.

Speaking of things coming down the street, one night in the summer of 1957, Pat and I heard the roar of a large engine combined with a whooshing sound. We ran to the screened window of the front door and saw a truck coming down Swift Avenue with a man sitting up on the back. With a steering wheel, he was aiming, and moving back and forth, a giant bent rectangular tube that looked like a cannon. He was shooting a fog all over Mrs. Colmen's yard. When the truck was in front of our house, the man "shot" us. We quickly closed the door until he passed, but all of the windows in the living room were wide open. The man was spraying for mosquitoes. A sweet smell permeated our living room.

Spraying for mosquitoes in '57.

Some people would be out in their gardens or on their porches when the spray truck came by. The sprayers didn't care. They went right down the street spraying away. No warnings, nothing. I went back and checked the newspaper. Nope. No warnings that the truck would be coming down your street on a certain day at a certain time. Sometimes a group of us would be playing ball in the yard or in a park, and the truck would come by and just spray us. It burned your eyes and smelled sweet. By the way, neither the guy driving nor the guy spraying wore any kind
118

of protection like a facemask. Sometimes there'd be a cigarette dangling from their mouths. Litchfield bought its own spray truck the following year and Ernie Radunz, who lived down the street from us, ran the sprayer. Sometimes an army of kids would follow the truck down the street oblivious to the dangers of the fog they were walking in. I was reminded of the spray trucks a couple of years ago when New York environmentalists got up in arms over the spraying in their city for the West Nile virus. They were worried about what it would do to their pets and the homeless. We lived in a different time in the fifties.

From our park bench, we would see seventy-five-year-old Leonard T. "Len" "Buck Buck" Inselman pull into town and park by the *Independent Review* office to sell his melons out of his car trunk. Len lived at the very western edge of town on a large lot at 609 Fifth Street West, just up the hill from the Carlson "ranch". Born in 1884, Len had been a plumber in the earliest days of Litchfield. In fact he had helped dig and lay in the original downtown sewer system. Len had in his possession something of great value and importance...the layout of the city's water and sewer system. A fired city employee had angrily destroyed the originals, the only other copies, I was told. Anytime the city wanted to dig, Len would have to be called in to supervise. He charged them for his services, of course.

Len would stand by the rear of his car and yell, "Melons, fresh melons, f**k, f**k..." Then he'd let fly with a bunch more expletives usually dominated by that "f-word", along with some facial and neck tics or twitches, before yelling "Melons..." again. That why we kids started calling him "Buck Buck", because that's how it sounded. He'd say something normal again and then let fly with more expletives and facial tics. We had heard that Len's father had caught him saying the "f-word" once and had beaten him so severely that the word stuck permanently into his daily vocabulary. That was just one of the several rumored reasons for his behavior. Another was that he had fallen while painting the water tower and banged his head. Years later, while watching a television show, I learned of something called Tourette syndrome that caused the same behavior. No doubt, that's what poor old Len had.

Len grew really great watermelons called New Hampshire Midgets and some muskmelon. The muskmelons, although small, were really juicy and sweet. But those watermelons were truly outstanding. Kids were always trying to raid Len's melon patch at night or in the wee hours of the morning. During the late summer, it was almost a nightly occurrence and a rite of growing up. It was a silly thing to do because if the kids had asked Len for a melon, he would have given it to you. But he didn't like anyone taking them from him without his permission. So I suppose the kids did it for the "bootleg power"...that is, the melons tasted twice as sweet if they weren't supposed to have them.

As far back as in the early thirties, kids were raiding Len's patches. Way back in August of 1931, there was an article in the newspaper about Len catching six youngsters raiding his melons. We thought it was something the kids had thought up to do in the fifties, but there was an article in the *Litchfield News-Ledger* in September of 1880 about kids raiding Dan Pineo's patch for his melons. Dan let the paper know that he had a shotgun and wouldn't be afraid to use it. Word going around was that Len had a shotgun too, loaded with rock salt, and he wasn't afraid to use his either. Dickey Carlson, Roy Peipus and my brother Dennie were shot at once. Dennie told me that Dickey was the only one who felt the sting of the rock salt.

Len caught one group of younger boys with armloads of his melons once and he made them eat every single one before letting them go. They got very sick. Another time Len was chasing some boys through his neighbor's backyard. Poor old Len got clotheslined...literally. He ran right into the clothesline and ended up on his back. Somehow one of the boys was caught anyway and the police hauled him off to jail to scare him and to call his parents. The boy's dad told the police, "Keep him there overnight. Maybe he'll learn something."

Len carried a paper in his billfold from his doctor explaining his malady in case he would have to deal with strangers. He also carried an extra handkerchief. If he was doing a job and there was a lady present, he would pull out the extra handkerchief and stuff it into his mouth so that he wouldn't offend her. He was a kindly old man, but he never went to church nor mingled with the public, except to sell his melons, fish in the fishing tournaments or box.

In the late twenties, Len was quite the boxer. Nobody ever thought to tease him about his "tic" to his face because of his boxing skills. In fact, it was said that only one man could beat him. That man was barber George Earley, who held matches in his basement barbershop under whatever drug store was currently at the northeast corner of Sibley Avenue and Second Street. Local merchants would go down there to bet on the matches.

There was another room connected to the barbershop that had showers in it. Patrons used to go there and pay to take a shower. Many of the barbershops in the old days had baths and later showers for their customers.   The room had a mini-gym or a workout room with a punching bag hanging from the ceiling. Occasionally a couple of the guys would get it in their heads to have a real live boxing match. Old timers said Len didn't have his "tic" until he started boxing. Maybe something was jarred loose?

Len was known to be a great fisherman. In fact he was a consistent winner in the Sportsman's Club's annual fishing contest and his ability to catch oversize walleyes was almost legend.   People were always pestering Len on the street while he sold his melons, or on the lake while he was fishing, to tell them where he was catching the fish or what he was using.   He always refused to tell, although he couldn't always control his mouth. County Attorney Leland Olson saw Len on the lake with a full stringer of fish. Lee came along side Len's boat.

"Say, Len," Olson said, "That's quite a catch you got. What are you using today?"

"Can't tell ya, f**k, f**k, jitterbug...can't tell ya, f**k, f**k, jitterbug. That's a secret."

Jarvis Brown pestered Len so much that Len came up to him one day and handed him a small nickel spiral notebook with *What I Know About Fishing – by Len Inselman* printed on the cover. Jarvis thanked him and hurried home to read it. When he opened it up to read the fishing secrets, he found nothing but blank pages.

Len T. "Buck Buck" Inselman with his catches.

Len finally married in his later years, but his years of being a bachelor had made him into a great cook. He made especially good donuts and bread. He developed some friendships too in his later years and would be invited on fishing trips, probably more for his fishing expertise and his cooking skills than for his conversational skills.

One day Eeks Nelson was standing in the doorway of his sign painting shop in the alley behind the Northwestern Bank sunning himself and having a cigarette. Down the alley came Len going through one of his "tic" episodes. He passed Eeks and continued on meeting a woman carrying a full shopping bag coming towards him from the other direction. She stopped in her tracks in horror at the words coming out of Len's mouth. After watching Len amble past her on his way, the woman shook her head, turned and continued walking towards Eeks.

"My goodness," she said to Eeks, "what's wrong with that man?"

"He voted for Hoover and he's been that way ever since," Eeks replied with a straight face, taking a long drag off his cigarette.

Len tried to stay healthy and fit his entire life. In August of 1964, he bought something he hadn't had for years but thought would help him exercise. He bought a brand new bike. On his maiden trip, he fell and broke his hip. So much for that. Six years later, in December of 1970, Len "Buck Buck" Inselman died.

Some of the town characters would sit on the benches in Central Park facing Sibley Avenue, just like us kids. That activity has gone on since the beginnings of the park, and surely goes on today. Old Col. T. Carlos Jewett, the Indian fighter and Commissioner of the Alaskan territory who had lived next to the Forest City Stockade during the Sioux Uprising and whom our favorite creek was named after, spent his retirement sitting in the park everyday handing out advice and philosophies. In late 1890, the *Ledger* newspaper quipped, "Col. Jewett's 'office' is once more lighted by electricity, the bandstand lamp having been put in running order." But usually the sitters were just bums or kids with nothing else to do, like us. We would talk to the sitters or tease them and run away. Roy Peipus sat on a bench everyday and "The Man About Town – Mr. Charles Brown" was usually there in the evenings. Everyone called Charles Brown that title. One day we walked by Burleigh's Studio, next door to the Unique Theater, and there in the window was a giant photograph of Charles Brown with that same saying underneath the portrait.

Charles Brown was a distinguished looking gentleman in his late eighties with a wide brimmed Derby hat, a velvet-collared coat and a cane. He seemed to know something about everything and everyone and he didn't mind telling people his philosophies and opinions. We could never get him to talk about his past though. All we knew about him was that he had repaired household appliances at one time, going door to door. What we didn't know was that he had been in Stillwater prison for a few years for "carnal knowledge" with a thirteen-year-old girl in town in the summer of '46, when he was seventy-five.

We spent a lot of time talking to Charles as he sat on a park bench, leaning on his cane. One of us would invariably say something that angered him though and he'd lash out at us with the cane. We learned to keep a cane's length away from The Man About Town, Mr. Charles Brown.

I've written about nicknames in town. There was one character named Benno (pronounced "Bean-o") McCarney. I always thought that was his nickname until recently when I discovered it was his middle name. James Benno McCarney, with a head full of wavy black hair, was a "happy go lucky" sort of a guy, although later in life, just before he died in a nursing home, he turned mean and messy. According to a lady who worked there, if Benno wasn't got to in time in the morning, he was likely to "shoot" a surprise all over the attendant and the bed. But, when he was younger, he never seemed to have a care in the world or a penny in his pocket. He just smiled all the time and laughed at everything. His favorite saying was "by Judas Priest!" That was his form of profanity.

Benno
McCarney
in a rare
suit in
1959.

Benno chewed tobacco and everyone said he must have been a levelheaded guy because the juice always ran out of both corners of his mouth instead of just one. He was also called "Litchfield's worst driver". Benno's car always had four different colored fenders. He was constantly having "fender benders". Benno would just go to the junkyard and get another fender and replace the one he'd dented. He didn't bother to paint the replacement to match his car. Why bother? He might have to replace it in a month or so. He just put it on. The doors were often different colors too. So, Benno drove a multi-colored mid-fifty's Chevy that had been blue once upon a time.

Benno was driving out to Manannah one Sunday to see Hack Brown. He hadn't pushed the hood of his car down to lock it securely after checking the oil. When he picked up some speed, the air got under the hood and lifted it up and over the windshield and roof. Benno tried to straighten the bent hood, but he couldn't get it quite right, so he tied it down with some rope. He showed up at a family get-together a week later with a replacement hood sticking out his trunk. Naturally it was the wrong color.

"Just give me a little hand for a few minutes fellas, by Judas Priest," he instructed the men, who were all standing around. The men, all dressed up in their Sunday best, complied and helped Benno remove the old hood and put on the new one. It took most of the afternoon and the women were upset with the men, who were upset with Benno, who just drove off into the sunset in his patchwork quilt car.

Benno was married and his wife sat in the back seat when they went anywhere. Either she didn't want to be seen with him or it was for her own safety because of all of Benno's accidents. She had to be a saint to put up with him. She hired herself out to do housework for people. The mother of a large family that lived on a farm got hurt and Benno's wife was hired to stay on the farm and do the housework and cook for the family. During her stay there, Benno just happened to show up every night uninvited to eat supper with the family. "By Judas Priest, it looks like you're about to eat," he'd say. "If you don't mind, I'll join you." Benno would attend every funeral in town, just to get the free meal in the church basement afterwards.

Benno wore other people's worn out old clothes and nothing matched, just like his car. He didn't care. He just wore whatever people gave him. Someone gave him a pair of black high top Keds sneakers and he wore them with his dress clothes, which consisted of a black suit jacket and brown shiny pants.

"When Emmett Kelly dies, Benno," Ed Carroll, another fall down-drunken Irishman told him, "you are going to come into a lot of clothes." Emmet Kelly was the famous "sad faced" clown, "Weary Willie", who dressed in a ragged bowler hat, ragged tuxedo tails and Keds sneakers.

Benno belonged to Litchfield's Council of the Knights of Columbus for many years. In October of 1959, three charter members were picked to meet Bishop Alphonse Schadweiler at a banquet. Benno was picked, I don't know why. He showed up with a suit coat on but, again, his pants didn't match his coat, his tie was a disaster, with spots of chewing tobacco and traces of several meals on it, his socks were two different colors, and his zipper was half way down, showing off part of his boxer shorts. But Benno was the one of the group who got his picture in the newspaper shaking the bishop's hand.

Some people called Benno "Cookie". He would be working with some guys doing odd jobs for the city and they would take an afternoon coffee break in Fransein's Café. Everyone would order a cup of coffee and a slice of pie or a donut except for Benno, who either didn't have the money or was too tight to spend it. He would order a glass of water and one cookie. Now cookies sold two for a nickel back then so usually Fransein would just give it to Benno instead of messing with the pennies. I never said that Benno was stupid.

Once at a funeral, Benno was determined to lead the rosary for his friend, the departed. He knelt by the casket but he couldn't remember how to start the rosary. He became so distraught that the only thing that came out of his mouth was "By Judas Priest, I can't even remember how to say the rosary!" Ed Carroll, sitting in the crowd and not paying attention, yelled out "Amen!" when he heard the word "rosary" and got up and left.

Kate Hughes, who chewed tobacco and lived by the Wimmers, made different brews in her basement. She could make moonshine out of anything that, as she said, "had ever been connected to a root". She made the brews for medicinal purposes only, of course. Her potions were good for colds, flu, and aches and pains. Her specialty was a potato brew that was as clear as water, but extremely potent. She had learned this in Ireland, where she had grown up. Benno was a frequent visitor of Kate's for tea. Kate didn't drive so Benno would give her rides around town to the store, wakes, funerals, and Mass in the winter.

Benno got a terrible cold, which might have been pneumonia. He was very sick but refused to go to the doctor. Dr. Danielson finally came to Benno's house at the request of Benno's wife. Danielson gave Benno a shot of something, a prescription to fill, and told Benno that if he didn't get better fast he would have to go to the hospital. Not wanting to go to the hospital, Benno called on Kate for some of her medicine. Kate "medicated" Benno back to health in a matter of two or three days by "chasing those demon germs" out of his body with hot tea, her potato brew, sweat and a lot of sleep. Dr. Danielson stopped by the house to see if Benno was improving and was astonished to see him sitting up at the kitchen table looking like new.

"That shot and prescription I gave you must've worked, Benno," Dr. Danielson said.

"Never filled it, by Judas Priest," Benno said. "The shots cured me." Dr. Danielson probably left wondering about the plural word "shots" Benno had used.

For some reason, Benno drank his coffee and tea out of the saucer rather than the cup. He slurped it so loud that it annoyed most people, except for Kate. Father Foley wouldn't sit at the same table with him. Benno had a major gastro intestinal problem later in his life. He passed gas all the time and didn't seem to care about it or had no control over it. It was horrible. His clothes and body started to reek. While serving as a pallbearer at a funeral in Manannah, Benno let go with a long loud "breaking the wind" incident during a solemn moment close to the end of service. It echoed throughout the small church. The smell was horrible, but no one dared move, as service was still going on. Kids were quietly snickering, men were smirking, women were holding their noses, offended and disgusted, and everyone gagged. Father Dufresne heard it at the altar, but did not dare acknowledge it either. The only one in the church who didn't seem to notice or cringe his face up was the deceased in the casket and, because the lid was closed, no one was sure about him. After the service, Toby Foley asked Benno what had happened.

"I just couldn't hold it any longer, by Judas Priest," Benno explained. "I had to let it go." The Wimmer boys, who were there also, heard Benno's excuse and it became their catch phrase for a long time. They'd let one rip and say, "I just couldn't hold it any longer, by Judas Priest."

Benno ended up in the nursing home and then at the Meeker County Hospital. All of his smelly clothes were thrown away at the hospital. Florence Hughes went to his house, got some of his other clothes and washed them. By this time his wife had just given up and quit washing his things. A grateful Benno said, "Thanks, Florence. I shouldn't have to wash clothes ever again before I am sent to heaven, by Judas Priest." True to his word, those same clothes were all that people saw Benno wear until he died about a month later.

Some of the town characters were "bums", as Mom would call them. Bums in the sense that they didn't do much to get by. Not all of the bums in town lived in the woods. Some lived around town and were called bums because they never seemed to do a thing to support themselves, and they drank a lot and didn't seem to care about their appearance. One such bum was old Henry "Hank" Campbell, who had once been a farmer. People said his name in one word...Hankamel. Hank looked like Jimmy Durante, with his huge nose and fedora hat, or straw hat in the summer, tipped to the side on his head. He always wore an old Army overcoat. On top of his appearance, Hank spoke funny because he had no teeth. He continually chewed and spat tobacco juice. He was one of the perennial park bench sitters that we had learned to keep a good "spitting distance" away from.

Hank used to walk around town with his hands clasped behind his back dispensing information to people. He actually shuffled around instead of walking normally. He always seemed to have his left foot forward as he walked. Hank considered himself a "self-appointed constable" and he would watch out for people's stores and cars, telling strangers to do this or do that. Hank never spit on the sidewalk. He always walked over to the curb to spit in the gutter. He would also stop suddenly and pick up cigarette butts on the ground and put them in his pocket. He was either keeping his town clean or accumulating tobacco for a smoke later.

A likeable old guy, Hank had friends in town who helped him out. Frank Fransein was one. Hank would come into Fransein's restaurant every morning and Frank would give him a free day old sweet roll. One day Hank said to Frank, "No, I don't want that one. I want that one over there," pointing to a fresher roll in the glass showcase.

"You'll take the one I give ya," Frank said.

"I'll take my business elsewhere then!" Hank spat back, leaving.

One place he took his "business" to was Dan's Café, which was down towards the park on the east side of Sibley Avenue. Hank would walk into Dan's and go into the bathroom where he proceeded to wash his socks out in the sink. Then he would drape them over the radiator to dry, leave the café and come back later to retrieve them. Other places Hank did his laundry were in the bathroom in the basement of St. Philip's Church and in the fountain in the park. The church was never locked in the early days and Hank would often find refuge down in that basement from the cold or stormy weather. He would generally sleep elscwhere though.

Hank lived in some different people's garages in the summer in exchange for doing odd jobs. He lived in Elsie Phelps garage a lot. But in the winter when it was too cold in the garages, he would just disappear at night. No one knew where he slept, but it wasn't the church basement.

For a long time, the small entrance room of the courthouse was never locked. Just the main building was. Late one night, Judge Reuben Erickson had to go to the courthouse to get some paperwork to commit someone. When he entered through the outside door, he tripped over a body. It was Hank, curled up on the floor. The mystery of where Hank lived in the winter was solved. Where he went after they started locking the entrance doors though, no one knew, although he had stayed in the back of the fire hall at times. There was a room back there with a couple of cots. The police, whose office was on the second floor, would let drunken men sober up back there instead of taking them to the jail. The drunken women were taken to the hotel.

Sometimes Hank would sit in a booth in Dan's or Fransein's and have a cup of coffee. In those days the mustard in the booth was in a small fat jar with a wooden spoon in it to apply it to your food. One of the waitresses in Fransein's noticed Hank licking the spoon one day. From that point on, the mustard had to be kept behind the counter.

Sitting in a local tavern, Hank leaned over to the man sitting next to his stool. Holding out his brown beer bottle, Hank said, "Look in there."

"What for?" the man asked.

"Look in there."

"What am I s'posed to see?"

"Well, a hundred and sixty acre farm went down there," Hank replied, "ya oughtta see somethin'!" Hank had owned a three hundred and twenty acre farm with his brother, Tom, and lost his half. Hank knew that he had drunk away his fortune. He liked his little joke on himself so much that he told it over and over. Once, while in Dr. Danielson's office for a county paid check-up, Hank was told by Karl to say "Ahh...", as the doctor probed his wide-open mouth with a tongue depressor.

"Don't see anything down there, Hank."

"Really? Ya shudda," Hank said.

"Why's that, Hank?"

"Well, a hundred and sixty acre farm ..."

Hank loved to travel and he didn't let the fact that he didn't drive hold him back. He hitchhiked or bummed rides. A driver would pick him up and say, "Where ya headed, Hank?"

"Where you goin'?" Hank would always answer.

"Well, I'm headin' for Howard Lake (or wherever)."

"Well," Hank would say, "that's where I'm goin' too."

If the driver returned later in the day, he would invariably see Hank standing along side the road with his thumb out.

Roy Ekbom was traveling to a local farm auction with his father one weekend. They spotted Hank shuffling along the gravel road.

"I s'pose we should offer Hank a ride," Roy's father said. "Say, Hank," he called out his window as he stopped the car beside him. "If you're goin' to the auction, I can give you a lift."

"Sure thing, Mr. Ekbom," Hank said, as he crawled onto the back seat and rolled down the window to spit a brown liquid outside. When they got to the auction, Roy noticed that the rear fender was covered in tobacco juice. Later in the afternoon, as the auction was winding up, Roy was told to go find Hank and offer him a ride home. He was nowhere to be found, so the Ekboms headed for their car, which was parked off in a pasture. There they saw Hank patiently sitting in the back seat, waiting for his ride home, spitting out the window.

Andy Quinn, whose son "Acey" was in my high school class, had to go to the cities and then to western Minnesota with his truck one day on business for his farm operation. As he was passing through Wayzata at six in the morning with his load, whom should he see along the roadside, but good old Hank. After Andy dropped off the load in Minneapolis, he headed for Appleton to get a load of oats. You guessed it. Like a scary episode on TV's *Twilight Zone*, there stood Hank on the shoulder of the highway just outside of town.

One day a local priest picked Hank up. As they were driving along, the priest started in on Hank for not doing anything with his life and just being a bum.

"Say Father," Hank said. "Do you like bein' what you are...doin' what you do?"

"Well, sure I do Hank."

"Well, so do I," Hank spat back.

Virgil "Peg" or "Peg Leg" Mortenson wasn't a bum, but he was a character. He had a wooden leg and one eye, which alone qualified him as a character, if not a pirate. A darkened lens on his glasses concealed his missing eye. I don't know when or how he acquired the wooden leg, but I heard it was a railroad accident. The leg eventually wore down so much from walking on it that Mortenson couldn't move normally with it anymore. He sort of swung it ahead or kicked the leg forward in order to walk. He had an old truck, which he drove through the alleys of town, picking up cardboard boxes. He flattened them, baled them up and sold them.

Another citizen with a wooden leg was Curly O'Connor. Curly was way before my time, but I heard about him from old P. J. Casey, the lawyer. Curly carved his wooden leg himself and he liked to tip a few with the boys at the local watering hole. When he would get good and drunk, he had trouble working the wooden leg. So the police would cart Curly to the cooler in a wheelbarrow.

Jeannie Peterson, whose father Harold A. Peterson was a dentist in town for many years, had something about her appearance that qualified her as a character. She looked normal except for her two arms, which were covered from wrist to shoulder with watches. She had a thing for watches and apparently no one could turn her down when she said she needed a new one. She did some babysitting and earned some of her own money, but I'm sure her dad paid for most of the watches.

Kids are scared of and fascinated with death. We found a dead cat once and poked at it with a stick for the longest time. I wondered if humans went through the same process that I was witnessing. The stiffness, the maggots, the stink. There was an eighty-seven-year-old hermit bachelor that lived in a small worthless shack down by Jewett Creek at the north edge of town. His name was John Paulson and, in April of 1957, he was burning some brush and garbage behind his shack. The fire got away from him and he ran into his shack for some water, ran out to the fire with a bucket full, and collapsed into the fire from a heart attack.

A few days after his charred body was taken away, I think it was Pat who came up with the idea of going to his place to "check it out." Anyhow, Pat and I and some other brave friends ended up in his backyard. There's strength in numbers, you know. At first we explored the shack, which was left open but had nothing of value inside, and then we picked around the rather large burn spot in the yard. I remember thinking to myself, "Just a couple of days ago, a human being died on this exact spot where I'm standing." It gave me the shivers.

To the edge of the large burned area was a big log with a large round burned spot in the middle next to a smaller one beside it. An idea leapt into my head. What if...?

"Hey guys," I said. "I'll bet this is exactly where the old guy's body burned. Right here. See?" I pointed to the burned spots on the log.

"What'd ya mean?" someone said.

"Well, look," I went on. "He fell into the fire and burned right? What if he fell onto this log? Like this..." Then I laid down with my head in the large burned spot on the log and my hand on the smaller one. I don't know what had possessed me to do that. If one of them had done it, I would've gotten the willies. But it seemed logical and I felt like a detective.

"Wow!" someone said. "That's creepy. Get up outta there and let's go." We left, our exploring done and my detective work complete. I wonder if I was right?

Some of the town's best-known and wildest characters haven't even been mentioned yet. They'll crop up in later chapters. For example, there was Robert Hilner "Bugs" Bokander, speaking of old guys and death. Bugs gave Litchfield's teenagers an unintentional thrill one Halloween night in 1958 while we attended a record hop[45] in the rear of the Western Cafe.

---

[45] In the old newspapers of the early 1870s, dances were often referred to as "hops", as in "There is to be a social *hop* at the Town Hall this evening," in an 1881 *Litchfield News-Ledger*. I always thought it was a fifties' term.

Chapter Eleven
The Crossings and the Big Accident

The Great Northern train tracks run right through Litchfield, splitting the town exactly in half. The railroad was the reason for Litchfield's existence, but it caused many problems. A lot of trains didn't stop and just roared through Litchfield. A turn of the century local newspaper writer wrote, "Eight passenger trains per day on this line now, while freights are thicker than leaves in Vallambrosa[46]." In the forties, an average of thirty-five trains came through town every day.

There were four crossings[47] in Litchfield connecting the north and south sides of town. There was the Davis Avenue crossing way out on the east side of town, the Holcombe Avenue one that got the southside kids to the high school, the main Sibley Avenue crossing uptown by the depot, and the crossing a block from our house on Swift Avenue that had been closed but reopened in late 1958.

There were many accidents and deaths recorded at these crossings over the years. Two passenger trains, the Great Northern Western Star and the Great Northern Flyer, came through town at speeds of up to eighty miles an hour, if they didn't have a Litchfield stop scheduled. There were also the freight trains that came through town at a good clip or were always stopping and blocking one or more of the crossings.

Ads for the Western Star and the Flyer.

"Pacific Fast Mail"

WESTERN STAR
STOPS DAILY IN GLACIER PARK, JUNE 15 THROUGH SEPTEMBER 15

"The Great Northern Flyer"
EVERY DAY

Only morning train to Montana and the Pacific Coast from St. Paul and Minneapolis

There was a Quonset hut at the Swift Avenue crossing, where the Produce used to stack empty wooden turkey crates. Pat and I used to lie in the summer morning sun on a wooden loading platform there, watching the railroad men switch train cars. Trains have always fascinated kids. My first train ride was on a fall Saturday morning when

---

[46] A tree covered mountain area in Italy.

[47] There were five railroad crossings at one time. There was also a crossing at Miller Avenue until it was closed.

I was in college in Minneapolis. I usually came home on Friday afternoon, hitching a ride or taking the bus. But this weekend I stayed for a party, and so I took the Saturday morning train home. I remember it cost $2.10 and I enjoyed every second of it. It was so comfortable and smooth riding.

Trains fascinated dentist Harold A. Peterson too. He had always wanted to be an engineer, not a dentist. Whenever he could, he would stand on the depot platform and watch the freights come through. Somehow he got to be friends with a couple of the engineers and when they'd see him standing there, they would sometimes slow down and let him hop on for a ride. They showed him how to run the engine and he'd take over and sometimes end up in the Twin Cities. Then his wife would have to drive down there to retrieve him.

But the freight train traffic in town and the switching of cars to sidetracks meant frequent blocked crossings. It was frustrating and it always seemed to happen when Pat and I were in a hurry to get home or go to the lake for a swim in the summer. There were many times we took our lives in our own hands and scrambled under the railroad cars to get to the other side. It was either that or wait fifteen minutes for the train to move or walk a couple of blocks to the next crossing, hoping that it also wouldn't be blocked. To a little kid, fifteen minutes is an eternity.

Pat and I would crouch down and scoot like crabs under the boxcars. We even dragged our bicycles under the cars. Only once do I remember the train starting to move while we were under it. Trains start with a sudden jerk, a backward movement, and then a slow crawl forward, so we always made it across safely. We knew to always crawl under the center of the car, never by the big shiny wheels. We never told Mom about our daring crossings, because every so often we'd read in the *Independent Review* about some car, truck or person getting hit either in town or, more often, out at one of the country road crossings. Many times the mangled body of a bum would be found along side of the tracks. The coroner never knew if the bums fell off or were pushed off the train. Of course, there were suicides too. I read in the local newspaper about one man who laid his neck across the track just as the train was closing in on him. There was a determined man.

Mid-block on Depot Street East, around the corner from Greep's, was the Western Café. They held dances for teenagers in the back of the Western where the old bowling alley had been when the building had been the Bowling Cafe. A man named Don Bruns[48] ran the café in the front of the long narrow building. I don't know if it was Don's idea to have dances for teenagers in the back or not, but we did have dances there for a while.

Once in a while a band performed back there. Mick's band was one, and at the time Jerry Wheeler, my drumming idol, was playing for him. Jerry was the grandson of Litchfield pioneer barber Ray Wheeler, who played the drums also in the Wheeler Orchestra with Jerry's mom and dad. Everyone always wanted to hear Jerry do a drum solo. We would stand in front of the band and chant "Drum solo...drum solo..." They usually only had record hops in back of the Western, however. Someone would play records through a makeshift sound system and we'd dance. I think the dances were free or for a quarter admission, intended to keep the delinquents off the street and sell food in the front café, I suppose.

I attended all of the dances because I had discovered that I had a talent for dancing. I was one of a handful of boys who could actually do all of the different dances, the Twist, the Stroll, the Calypso, the Bunny Hop, and, my favorite, the Lindy. My talent made me extremely popular with the girls...at the dances. While the rest of the guys stood against one wall, (we always separated into two gender lines), and talked about cars, sports, and the girls across the floor from them, I was out on that floor "cutting a rug" with the most beautiful girls in town. I was the only guy who could actually keep up with La Vonne Merdice "Mert" Fortun, a gorgeous blond with really fast feet. The girls usually asked ME to dance, not the other way around. For an hour or so each week at the hops, I was in my glory and in heaven.

Of course, once the dance was over, I'd walk home alone, satisfied with my hour or so of glory, while the girls went off with the "jocks" or the older guys who had cars. Merdice never had a problem getting a ride home. My friend Billy Maass was always "sniffing" around Merdice.

Merdice and her family used to live near us in Evergreen Park, just south across the tracks. Later her family moved out by Worden's mink farm. Merdice had a younger sister named Annette. They were a year apart. They found their dad's .22 revolver and started playing with it one morning in April of 1949. The gun went off and the bullet traveled through four-year old Annette's chest and into her brain, killing her

---

[48] Don had also managed the Milk Bar downtown. He eventually ended up being a policeman in Glencoe, where I taught school for twenty-five years.

instantly. Merdice never talked about it. In fact, I didn't even know about it until I was researching this book. There is nothing sadder than the death of a little child.

There was a Halloween dance at the Western Café on October 30, 1959. I was fourteen and dancing with Merdice when someone ran in at about 10:45pm and announced, "Hey everybody! Bugs Bokander just got splattered against the depot!"

Bugs was Robert Hilner Bokander. I don't know why he was called "Bugs" but it might have had something to do with his appearance. Bugs had thumb-sized boils all over his body. The visible ones were on his neck, face and the back of his head. Ray Nelson, the barber, used to cringe when Bugs would come into his shop for a haircut. It was difficult to cut around the bumps.

Bugs had been a ditch digger by trade and had been arrested in 1931 for following women and girls in town and window peeking. Now, in Litchfield in 1959, he was a sixty-three year old bum and wino. He hung around the pool halls and cleaned the tables off at closing time for a beer. Dirty and unshaven Bugs was buddies with another character named Martin McCarney.

Martin walked hunched over and a little stiff legged, with his arms hanging down like a bad impression of an ape. He spoke funny. For example, he would say to the telephone operator, "Why helloooooo operatee. How are you this fine evening?" Martin drank a lot and a car hit him one evening after he had stumbled out of Abe's pool hall. He had sustained some brain damage from that accident along with back injuries. He aggravated his injuries many times by falling down the flight of stairs from his room at the Lien Apartments and Rooms, the old Litchfield House by the library, where Bugs also lived. I guess you could truly call Martin a "fall down drunken Irishman".

Bugs and Martin went to a Saturday night dance at the Hilltop bar in Manannah one cold winter night. I don't know how they got there because neither man drove. Anyway, Ray O'Keefe, Martin's cousin from Forest City, gave Bugs and Martin a ride back to Litchfield. Befuddled by the booze and thinking it was later in the morning, Martin said he had to go to church and asked to be dropped off at St. Philip's.

Rather than argue with Martin, Ray, knowing it was only about 1:30 in the morning, dropped them both off in front of the church as a joke.

The church doors were never locked back then so Martin and Bugs, who wasn't Catholic, went inside. Finally realizing they were "early" for Mass, they went downstairs to the church lunchroom and lay out on the tables where the custodian John Housman found them sleeping in the morning.

Aroused and hung over, Martin and Bugs meandered upstairs to the six o'clock Mass. That day a kneeling Bugs Bokander took Holy Communion from Father Foley right next to Martin at the communion rail. After church, Housman and his wife offered Martin and Bugs a ride to the Lien Apartments because it was so cold. Mrs. Housman turned in the car and said, "Mr. Bokander, I didn't know that you were Catholic."

"I am today, Mrs. Housman," Bugs responded. "I am today."

With the announcement at the dance that "Bugs Bokander just got splattered against the depot!", we all stopped dancing and ran the half a block west to the Litchfield railroad depot[49]. The Great Northern depot was a large sandstone block building to the south of the tracks. The blocks were light in color and very porous.

Arden Burleigh's painting of the depot. ©1989

A witness to the accident, my classmate James McLane[50], told the police that Bugs had tried to beat the train across the tracks and failed. Bugs was heading home to the Lien Apartments. Westbound No. 31, the Western Star, hit him at seventy-eight miles an hour, officials later determined. James heard a noise that sounded like the cracking of a whip. When we arrived, men from the volunteer fire department were hosing his blood and body parts off the east side of the depot before the blood could soak in and permanently stain the building.

Dennie was working as a "Teenage Guest Disk Jockey" at KLFD, our local radio station. James Murray "Jimbo" Harrison was the regular

---

[49] See page 481 of the History of Downtown Litchfield Appendix.

[50] Three years later, James was in the back of a pickup with our classmate Lennie Hawkinson when Lennie fell out. He hit his head on the pavement and died instantly. They were picking up wood for our homecoming bonfire.

136

announcer working with him. The station, which kept moving around town, was above Reed's Printing at that time. Dennie and Jim had shut down the station at sundown, as the station's 500-watt power dropped at that time, but they had stayed in the building working late on some projects.

Jim's father, a medical doctor from Worthington, Minnesota, was in Litchfield visiting Jim. Dennie and Jim were on their way to meet Jim's father at the Black Cat Café for a cup of coffee late in the evening when they heard the news about Bugs. They rushed down to the depot to observe the accident. When they saw what the commotion was about, Jim walked up to Chief Of Police George Fenner. Wanting to volunteer his father's services, Harrison said, "George, do you need a doctor?"

"Hell, no," George replied. "I need a shovel!"

Parts of Bugs Bokander were all along the loading dock and also on the track for at least a hundred yards. We were kept back so we never got to see anything up close, but it sure made for a memorable Halloween night.

In the newspaper issue following Bugs death, the *Independent Review* published a long list of Litchfield's crossing fatalities. Before Bug's demise, the crossings had claimed six lives in town and seven out of town. Carl Wickstrom and his thirteen year old daughter, Lilah Mae, left church early on the south side of town because they had to get to the drugstore to pick up a prescription before the store closed at noon. The church service had run long this cold January morning in 1946.

As fate would have it, when they got to the Miller Avenue crossing, a westbound mail train was coming. Carl gunned his '38 Chevy, trying to beat the train and still make it to the drugstore in time. Maybe there was ice on the approach, because he didn't move as fast as he anticipated and both he and his daughter were killed instantly.

Two women, Hilda Linden and Lillian Harder, also died at that same Miller crossing after having been hit by a freight train in March of 1951. They were leaving work at the First District plant and tried to beat the train at the crossing. The Miller crossing was closed shortly after this accident.

Two of the six fatal town accidents had happened at the same Sibley Avenue crossing where Bugs was killed. One was four years before Bug's accident and the other was a year, almost to the day, before.

On September 16, 1955, at 4:30pm, a seventy-eight year old Swede named Ole Nelson was walking south across the tracks towards his home. He was carrying a bag of groceries he had just purchased at the

Fairway Market. Maybe he was carrying the bag up by his head or shifting it noisily in his hands because he didn't see or hear the oncoming freight train. It hit him so hard that he stuck to the engine and his lifeless body was carried for a half a block down the tracks.

Eighteen-year-old Jim Bachman, home on leave from the Army in late October of 1958, tried to beat the train with his beautiful fender skirted '49 Chevy at 4:35pm one day. Fifteen-year-old Lyle Rosenow, another friend of Dennie's, witnessed the accident and told the police that Bachman took off south from the traffic light by the hotel and never slowed down for the tracks, even though the signal lights were flashing. Bachman had just dropped thirteen-year-old David Lindell off at his home at 4:30pm. Ironically, David, a friend of my brother Mick, would be killed in a traffic accident five years later.

Jim Bachman's mother was just leaving Dr. Vold's optometry shop by the alley in the Greep's' block, only a block away. Wondering what had happened, she walked up to the crowd of gawkers at the Sibley Avenue crossing and saw her son's demolished car. The gawkers, who now included Lyle, Dennie and Dennie's friend Connie Olmstead, waited around to see the mangled bloody car being towed on a flatbed truck to Minar Motor, just a block away west of the hotel.

Mick Weber, a classmate of brother Pat, had his dad Clarence Weber's 1960 Plymouth Valiant at school on Friday, November 3, 1961. Clarence Weber, whose daughter Judy would marry my stepbrother Val "Larry" Young, didn't have good luck with his kids and cars.

On August 25, 1959, Clarence's eleven-year old son Teddy[51] took the family car for a joyride from their house two blocks from us at 411 Swift Avenue North. Driving out on Fifth Street West towards Arnold Kline's horse farm, Teddy put the car into the ditch.

Anyway, Mick Weber had promised to give football teammates Ralph Koelln and Kenny Fenner, Police Chief Fenner's son, a ride home after school at three o'clock. Ralph and Kenny went to the school parking lot and found Clarence's car and got in, waiting for Mick, who had given them the car keys. Mick never showed up. For some reason, he had forgotten about the arrangement and had walked uptown.

Along came my friend, Jerry Wimmer. "What's up guys?", Jerry asked. They told him and the three of them concocted a scheme where

---

[51] Teddy Weber developed polio at the age of four in 1952. There was an outbreak of polio in Meeker County at that time.

Ralph would drive Kenny home, drive himself home from Kenny's and then turn the car over to Jerry and have him return it to the parking lot and explain it all to Mick, who would have realized his mistake by then and gone back to school. Jerry was an amazing athlete, but a terrible driver. We already had one bad experience involving Jerry's driving.

The Wimmer boys' mother, Margaret, was a cousin to our neighbor, Rose Hughes. Mrs. Wimmer would often drive across town to visit Rose. Jerry and Dougy would come along, pay their respects, grab some cookies and then run over to our house to play basketball or have a smoke in the garage.

One night Jerry said, "Let's take Mom's car for a spin." None of us had driver's licenses but we went around the block a few times in the old thirty-something Chevy. We got away with it, and so on subsequent visits we ventured farther and farther out around Litchfield.

On a fall Sunday afternoon, Jerry and Dougy showed up in our driveway with the car.

"Mom's gone and she left the keys in the car. Let's go for a ride!" Jerry said.

Pat and I hopped into the back seat and we took off to pick up Monk Schreifels. He jumped into the front next to Dougy to "ride shotgun". Jerry drove out east of town on the county road that goes past the fair grounds and the Meis Brothers' junkyard. Taking a corner too fast, Jerry lost control of the car and we headed for the ditch. We all screamed and the next thing I knew we were dangling on the side of the ditch at a dangerous angle but right side up.

"Everybody out before we tip over!" Jerry yelled. We scrambled up the seats and out the left side of the car.

"I can't get out!" we heard Monk yell. We looked back and, despite the danger of the situation and the trouble we were obviously in, we all burst out laughing. We couldn't stop laughing. Through our tears, we could see that Monk's head had gone through the passenger side window, making a neat hole just the size of his head in the safety glass. Unhurt, but dazed and scared, he couldn't pull his head back into the car to get out.

Somehow we managed to push his head back through the window without cutting his face. We were able to talk a farmer into pulling the car out of the ditch also. The car was undamaged except for the broken window and the clumps of grass and dirt stuck to the bottom. How Jerry explained the window to his mother, I never found out. I imagine he said he was playing ball in the backyard and had accidentally batted a ball through the window. I'll bet that happened all of the time at the Wimmer's house anyway.

The story of our joy ride was no secret to our friends, so it was all the more amazing that Ralph and Kenny thought to ask Jerry to return the Weber's Valiant to the school. Everything went well dropping off Ralph and Kenny, but as Jerry's luck would have it, driving back to the school alone, he managed to stall the car right in the middle of the Holcombe Avenue railroad crossing.

Hearing an oncoming freight train, Jerry panicked and jumped out of the car. He tried to push the car off the tracks, first from the front and then from the rear. Unfortunately, he had left the car in gear and it wouldn't budge. Jerry was very excitable. I can just imagine what he went through, struggling to push the car, his face turning redder than his bright red-orange hair. He must have finally realized that there was nothing he could do because he wisely turned and ran, just as the horn blasting and speeding Great Northern freight train plowed into the "borrowed" car.

The train slammed the Valiant into the automatic crossing signal lights, shearing them off their standard. The car sailed another fifty yards before it came to a rest beside the tracks and the rest of the train that had finally come to a halt. Jerry just stood there, paralyzed, staring at the car. He must have been thinking, "My life is over. I'm dead. They will put me in jail." Before long people ran up, asking Jerry if he was okay. He just stood there, staring at the car and crying. After he had completely broke down, he was taken to the doctor, who sedated him. Jerry was never the same after that and all of us, to this day, are a little more cautious when we drive across a railroad track crossing.

Jerry Wimmer at 13 and what was left of the Valiant.

I wish I could have told Jerry what I know now about that same crossing. In September of 1950, eighty-two year old City Assessor and former banker Peter Rodange didn't see or hear the oncoming speeding troop train and he drove his old Nash across the tracks in front of it. Peter almost beat the train. It caught his car's rear end, demolishing the old car and throwing Peter out. He came away with a broken nose and some broken ribs and seemed to be recovering in the hospital, but he died one week later.

One year later on December 4, 1951, almost exactly ten years earlier than Jerry's accident, a learned man, Judge Herman M. Hershey, who had owned a music store in town, had the same thing happen to his '39 Ford that had happened to Jerry's car. It stalled on the tracks, the judge couldn't move the car, and he turned and ran and watched a freight train demolish his car.

Back in 1929, Nancy Angell, the wife of Litchfield's pioneer photographer, Clark Angell, Sr., tried to beat a freight train on foot at this crossing. She lost the race and got a ride on the engine for a long ways before her crushed body dropped off onto the railroad tracks. Her daughter was Litchfield's librarian, Alice Lamb. These stories might have comforted Jerry a little. Just a little.

About this time, Mick and I were driving to ballrooms all over central and southern Minnesota to see rock stars, such as the Ventures, the Everly Brothers, Jimmy Gilmer and the Fireballs, Roy Orbison, Conway Twitty, the Beach Boys and Jerry Lee Lewis. For some reason, Pat didn't share our passion for music and rarely came along. This is when I started becoming friends with Mick. Mick usually drove his '48 Merc and generally the group going to the dances consisted of he and I, Terry Kohlhoff and Alvie Watkins.

The White Cardigan boys: Terry and Mick Shaw, Terry Kohlhoff and Alvie Watkins.

141

We found out that Conway Twitty was going to be at the Lakeside Ballroom in Glenwood, Minnesota on Friday, August 31, 1962. Conway wasn't doing country yet and he sang like Elvis with his current hits of *It's Only Make Believe, Lonely Blue Boy,* and *Mona Lisa.* Mick had other plans for that night so Terry Kohlhoff said that he'd get his dad's car and drive. Alvie didn't have a car and he hadn't driven much since he was fifteen and had borrowed his brother Harold's '49 Chevy on June 1, 1959. Alvie rolled the car on northeast Highway 24. He and passenger Allan Snow survived with just scratches.

Terry and Alvie picked me up at my house and we headed uptown to leave on Highway 12 west. When we got to Central Park, we saw Larry Andreen sitting on the hood of his parked '53 Olds, smoking a cigarette. He waved at us to pull over. We did and jumped out of Terry's car to talk to him. Larry asked us what we were doing and we told him.

"Are you sure you don't want to party with me tonight?" Larry said, sliding down off the hood of his car. "Check this out," he continued, walking to the rear of his car and opening the truck. Inside were three cases of beer.

"No thanks," we said. "We gotta get goin'."

I remembered Larry's insane driving and still wanted no part of it. As we took off for Glenwood, I related my story to Al and Terry about Larry scaring the hell out of me with his driving.

"Yeah, he's a loose cannon," they said. "He's an accident looking for a place to happen."

The show and dance were great. After Conway's second show we decided to leave the dance early and head home. It was about midnight and we were hungry, so we talked of stopping at the Diamond Café truck stop just east of Grove City. We got there about 1:30am and it was closed so we just kept heading towards Litchfield. Passing the junction of Highways 12 and 22, by Eleanor Revering's "El's Corner" bar[52] which we still called "the Bye-Way" by the way, we headed up and around the final right bend to home.

---

[52] In August of 1937, Dan Brown started a bar there calling it the Harvey Tavern or the By-Way because of the two highways that met here in Harvey Township. Alden R. Bye bought it in July of 1938 and changed it to the Bye-Way Inn. The Bye's daughter Bev was in my class at high school. Al and Eleanor Revering bought the bar in June of 1948, first calling it Al's Drive Inn, then El's Corner in 1953, El's Drive-in '56 and then the Sky Line Club in April of 1956. Al, who had owned a garage and blacksmith shop in Grove City, Minnesota, was terminally ill, so he bought it so that Eleanor would have a steady income after he died.

Just north of Nystrom's truck stop on west Highway 12, now the Maverick Bar and Grill, we saw lights and a couple of cars pulled over on the shoulder at the top of the hill. Just ahead of them were two more cars, right in the middle of the road. There obviously had been an accident. Terry pulled his car over to the shoulder. A man was running towards us, so we rolled down our windows.

"Do you have any blankets?" he yelled at us. We said we didn't and he continued running down the road. I looked back in the direction of town and thought I recognized one of the two cars in the middle of the road.

"Say, isn't that Larry's car?" I asked.

We jumped out of the car and ran up to the accident. What we saw will stay in my mind forever. One of the cars had six people in it. Some of the six were lying still, but two women, the driver, eighteen-year-old Betty Lohse, and the front right passenger, were sitting up and screaming with blood running down their faces. I remember Betty's entire face was red, covered with blood. She was screaming, "Please help me. God, somebody please help me." Two men were tugging on her door. The middle person in the back seat was alive also. So oddly, starting at the driver's seat, every other person in the car survived. Mrs. Austin Casey, Edward Lohse and John Damsgaard were the three dead in this car.

Larry's car was diagonal across the road facing the east ditch. The doors were open and there were three bodies lying on the pavement. A boy I didn't know, nineteen-year-old Robert "Bobby" Clayton, was lying on his back on the road by the right rear tire. He was perfectly still. Eighteen-year-old David Lindell, Mick's friend and a grandson of our neighbor "Grandma" Ericson, was also lying on his back on the road by the open passenger door. His eyes were closed, but he was moaning "Oh...oh...oh...oh..." rhythmically over and over and over.

There were men on one side of him trying to lift him onto a stretcher. When they lifted him up, he suddenly stopped moaning. The official announcement was that he had died on the way to the hospital, but I felt in my heart that I had just witnessed my very first death.

I walked around the car and saw our friend, seventeen-year-old Larry Andreen, lying motionless face down in a pool of oil on the road. The light summer night breeze was gently blowing the hair on his head. I stared at the moving hair wondering where I had seen that before? Then it hit me. When our dog Sparky had been poisoned and lay dead on our front lawn, he had looked the same way, with his fur moving gently in the night breeze. Larry had let us put Sparky in his trunk that night to take him to the dump.

I remember thinking something very odd at that moment staring at Larry's lifeless body. "How are they going to clean all of that oil off of his face when they put him in the casket?" When I saw him lying in the casket two days later, that odd question came back to me and I looked very close at Larry's face. Somehow, they had, of course. In moments of stress, your mind thinks of the oddest things.

Larry's '53 Olds. His body was on the road by the missing side door.

The people in the other car had all been at the Bye-Way earlier that evening. Obviously drinking was involved on both sides, but witnesses said that Larry's car had swerved out of control hitting both shoulders before turning to get hit broadside by Lohse's car on Larry's side of his car.

Earlier that night, around midnight, a classmate and former girlfriend of mine, Cheryl Furman, was coming back to Litchfield on south Highway 22 with her future husband, Bob Olson. As they passed the boat landing by Lake Ripley, Bob said, "There's Larry Andreen." He and Dave and Bobby were outside of Larry's parked car, acting drunk. Cheryl and Bob continued on into town when suddenly Larry's car sped pass them at a pretty fast clip on the residential street. They might have been the last people to see Larry and the others alive.

We were finally told to get out of the way of the ambulances and fire trucks, so we worked our way around the scene and drove home slowly and quietly, nobody saying a word except for our good-byes as Terry dropped us off. I told Alvie and Terry, "I'll wake up Mick and tell him about Larry."

144

I went into Mick's bedroom and gently shook him awake. He looked up at me and I said, "There's been an accident. Larry and Dave are dead."

"Yeah, I know," Mick said, but he obviously wasn't fully awake and didn't understand me, because the next morning when he came downstairs, I mentioned it again and shocked him. He stood there stunned in the kitchen, looking at me while I went over the whole grisly scene. He broke down and began to cry, so he quickly went outside so I couldn't see him. I didn't follow him. I didn't know what to do. I could see him in the window, walking around and around the outside of the house.

The phone rang and it was Terry Kohlhoff. He told me where Larry's car had been taken. I went outside to find Mick and told him.

"Would you like to go and look at Larry's car?" I asked.

"Yeah," he said, turning away and looking down at the ground so I couldn't see his red eyes.

We drove to the gas station on Sibley Avenue where Larry's car had been taken. There was a crowd of people gathered around the car. Mick stood and stared at it. I stayed close by him and didn't talk. I still didn't know what to say to him. Somebody in the crowd said, "Yeah, those damned teenagers and their drinking." Mick started crying again. I put my arm around him, turned him away and got him out of there.

Mick, Alvie and his brother Maynard, Terry Kohlhoff, Billy Maass and I were the pallbearers. It was my first time for that also. It seemed that the happy carefree days of growing up in Litchfield were put on hold for me the night of that accident. We had all suddenly grown up.

Chapter Twelve
Dealerships, the Bakery, and Janousek's

Back on Ramsey Avenue, at its intersection with Second Street, there were two interesting places at the opposite corners across from the turkey plant. The north corner had Litchfield's old red brick fire hall and the south corner[53] had the Litchfield Produce Company, a part of the Produce where Mom worked. Besides preparing eggs for shipment, the Litchfield Produce made ice cream and Popsicles. What an odd combination.

In the summer, Pat and I would hang around the open doors and ask for a free sample. Sometimes we'd get an unfrozen Dixie Cup. It'd be mushy and usually strawberry-flavored, which I hated, but it was free. We did the same thing over at the Land O' Lakes plant, where they also made ice cream.

The Litchfield Produce building eventually became the Lund-Hydeen Pontiac dealership[54]. The car dealership also had a Skelly gas station in the front, which accounts for the diagonal driveway still there across the corner. Many times car dealerships also sold gasoline. How convenient. In 1959, Litchfield had an unbelievable seventeen gas stations.

Sometimes Pat and I would go to the gas station there and buy a gallon of gas for a quarter to burn in inventive ways. We started by just pouring a puddle on the driveway with a trail of gas leading up to it. We'd light it and watch the flames race to the puddle. Wow! Then we put an old cup full of gas on the driveway with a trail up to it. That was better. Then we got the idea of making a bomb by filling a pop bottle with gas, putting a rag fuse in it and pouring a trail on the driveway up to it. Boom! There was glass everywhere. We had made a Molotov cocktail and didn't know it. We were smart enough to realize that the bomb wasn't a good idea and we didn't make another one.

I was by myself one late morning in the backyard playing with my gas when I ignited and started the doghouse next to the garage on fire. Grandpa Bill Shaw, who was staying with us at the time, came running out of the house with some rugs and beat the flames out. He saved the garage and whipped my hind end all of the way into the house, where I was instructed to sit on the couch all day until Mom came home from

---

[53] In the early 1900s, a blacksmith shop had been there in an old wooden building.

[54] 37 Second Street West/130 Ramsey Avenue North. See page 450 of the History of Downtown Litchfield Appendix.

work at five o'clock to inflict her punishment on me with the green yardstick or the belt. That was a long day of just sitting. We didn't have a television then. I had to just sit and watch Grandpa iron clothes, spit tobacco juice into a can, and listen to the soap opera *Ma Perkins* on the radio.

The old fire hall[55], across the street from Lund's, had a huge upstairs. Fire Chief Herman Krueger[56] had an office up there and originally Chief George Fenner, elected in 1953, and his "I don't like kids" deputy John Rogers had their headquarters up there too until 1963. Pat and I were hauled up there once for shooting our BB guns in town, although it was over by the new power plant at the edge of town. My first and only arrest. They took the BB gun away and I never got it back. The Police Department was moved to the City Hall, or Community Building as we called it, in April of 1963. That's where the office of Mayor Fred Richter was. I don't know what became of the offices over the fire hall but the rest of the upstairs was a huge empty hall, used for meetings.

In the late forties, the upstairs had been a Youth Center Club Room. The forties' teenagers called it "the Teen Center". They had ping-pong tables, board games, and a jukebox up there. Parents took turns chaperoning it, which is what killed it, of course. Dennie and Mick used to get permission for their bands to practice up there on Sunday afternoons, when they decided to give Mom's ears a rest.

The old
fire hall
in 1889.

---

[55] Before the fire hall was built in 1886, Litchfield just had a Babcock Fire Extinguisher pump, which it bought in 1876. It was parked on Second Street near the southeast corner of the block. Then, in 1883, a Cataract Hand Engine and one thousand feet of hose were added. The first fire chief was Per Ekstrom. See page 443 of the History of Downtown Litchfield Appendix.
[56] He was fire chief from 1947 to 1955.

Back across the street, west from the hall at the corner of Second Street and Ramsey Avenue, was the frozen turkey part of the Produce[57], where I worked as a college student labeling and stacking boxes of frozen turkeys.

Still heading west on Second Street was Laura's Lunch Time Inn, which sold 3.2 beer along with lunches. Laura was the daughter of Kate Pierce of Kate's Café uptown and the mother of Bobby and Bonnie Welsand. Bonnie was yet another classmate of mine. Kate had owned this café and sold it to Laura and her husband Kenny, who died. Laura then married one of the Carlson boys, Marlin, whom we called Bud.

Pat played with Bobby sometimes and would meet him at the café. He walked into Laura's one morning to discover our father doing his route for the jukebox and pinball business he had taken over from the Birkemeyers. Busy counting change from the machines, he hardly acknowledged Pat and barely spoke to him.

Mom would go to Laura's on Friday evenings with her friend Kathryn Van Nurden. That's where Mom met my stepfather, Floyd Young, one of the best things that ever happened to her. He came over to their booth and asked if he could sit down. Mom, who was sitting on the outside of her bench and had her feet up on Kathryn's bench, dropped her feet and said, "Sure," but she didn't slide over, so Floyd had to sit by Kathryn. But that was the start of the romance.

Mom came into the bathroom one night, where I was standing in front of the mirror combing my hair. What else would a teenage boy in the early sixties be doing?

"Terry," she said, "Floyd Young has asked me out for dinner some night. Do you think I should go?" The reason she asked was because my father was still living and Mom, the devout Catholic, believed that she was stilled married to him. She wanted somebody's okay to go out.

I misunderstood and looked at her stunned, saying, "Are you nuts! He's the same age as Dennie!" I thought she was talking about Floyd Young, Jr., or Snooky, as we called him. After Mom set me straight, I gave her my permission with a shrug of my shoulders and a mumbled "I don't care."

West of the café was an alley and then what used to be Roy Swanson's auto repair shop. Roy moved there in February of 1932. He

---

[57] Various businesses had been at this corner before the produce, most notably some car dealerships.

had a Hudson car dealership there starting in November of 1950 and had been in the Kopplin building south of the depot.

At the corner of Second Street and Miller Avenue was the Litchfield Machine Shop, which became the Lindquist Sheet Metal shop, which was a Lennox furnace dealership. During the late fifties and sixties, it was Chet's Machine Shop. Across Second Street was the Anderson Chemical Company plant and the turkey processing plant.

Back on Third Street, east of the paper shack heading back uptown across Ramsey Avenue, was the huge red brick Dahl's Goodyear Tire Store[58]. Occasionally we would ask the men inside the tire shop to fix a bicycle tire for us, but they were generally too busy for bike tires for kids. We'd wind up at Beckman's Standard Service gas station[59] where the attendant would fit us in between checking oil and water levels, checking tire inflation and washing all of his customer's car windows for a couple of dollars worth of gas. The customer probably got a free glass too or some Gold Bond stamps.

We had a phenomenon back then called "Gas Wars". All of a sudden the gas stations would go to "war" and try to drive each other out of business by lowering their prices. With seventeen gas stations in town, it happened a lot. For the longest time, gas was less than thirty cents a gallon, but a war would break out and the fun would begin. I remember a Grove City station dropping to ten cents a gallon one week in the late fifties. When Super America opened up in Litchfield in March of 1963, a war started up and some stations in town sold gas at five gallons for a dollar.

We bugged and bugged the guys at Dahl's to give us a tractor inner tube to take out to the Lake Ripley beach. We finally got one, got it patched and inflated and triumphantly and very difficultly biked it out to Lake Ripley beach. Imagine a young kid trying to hold a huge tractor inner tube on a bicycle while peddling and avoiding cars for the mile ride from our house.

"What do you guys think you're gonna do with that thing?" the lifeguard asked us, when we came rolling the tube down to the beach.

"Gonna play on it in the water," I responded.

"No, you're not," he said. "Not on my beach."

---

[58] 224 Ramsey Avenue North/35 Third Street West. See page 379 of the History of Downtown Litchfield Appendix.

[59] Today it's the HandiStop Service Station. See page 385 of the History of Downtown Litchfield Appendix for a list of the 1959 gas stations.

"But…"

"No buts. I ain't gonna chase after you after you float out in the middle of the lake. Get it out of here." We took the huge tube over by the boat landing away from the public beach where there were the yucky weeds. It wasn't the same and we gave up on it.

The Goodyear tire store had a huge lot to the south of the building where they piled old tires, especially those big monster tractor tires. We would climb on them and try to roll them into "forts" on Sunday afternoons when no one was around to chase us away.

South of Dahl's on Ramsey Avenue was the Nelson Implement Company[60]. It was a family affair run by Sigfrid W. Nelson, his son Lloyd and grandsons Dick and Stan. It had originally been just west of the hotel on Depot Street and moved here during the early 1920s. They had a feed grinder in the back to grind up grain for the farmers. Now this location is a parking lot.

North of the tire store, across Third Street, was Nelson's Buick car dealership[61]. Jim and L. Miles Nelson's dealership was a small operation and didn't get much of our attention except for a couple of things. In September of every year, the new cars would be unveiled, literally, in the various dealership showrooms.

For a week or so prior to the unveiling, we'd peek in the showroom windows and see the new models covered up with a large cloth. On the "unveiling" days at each dealership, (they were all on different days), the huge cloths would come off. We would go around to all of the dealerships to "ooh" and "ah" at the new designs with the tail fins getting bigger and bigger and then smaller and smaller each year. We went there to get a free doughnut or two also, of course.

There were eight car dealerships[62] in Litchfield at that time. My friends and I went around town visiting them all on each "unveiling" day to get the "freebies". There was Nelson's Buick, Fenton Chevrolet-Cadillac[63], Lund-Hydeen Pontiac, Quinn Motors Dodge-Plymouth, Stock

---

[60] Ferdinand H. "Frank" Brecht bought the Overland car and Republic truck business part of Nelson's Implement in March of 1910. He sold from the same building Nelson did.

[61] 24-28 Third Street West. See page 380 of the History of Downtown Litchfield Appendix.

[62] See page 381 of the History of Downtown Litchfield Appendix.

[63] Starting in the late 1930s, it had been Carpenter Chevrolet. Ben H. Carpenter sold it to Hugh D. Fenton in February of 1939. Al Fenton took over the business in 1950.

150

Motors Chrysler-Plymouth, Kvam's Oldsmobile-Packard-Studebaker and Oliver tractors[64], O. R. Schwartzwald's Motors, which sold Nash, and finally Horace J. Minar Motor Ford[65]. Minar Motor took up half the block[66] around the corner west of the hotel.

Most of the dealerships sold other things besides cars. For example, Schwartzwald's, which began in February of 1947 out on East Highway 12, sold International Harvester tractors in addition to Kelvinator refrigerators and ovens and Whirlpool laundry equipment. Most of the early car dealerships were actually farm implement businesses. In later years when cars and implements were sold separately, the farm implement businesses were also diversified. Ed Hamm's Implement business, for example, sold sewing machines and RCA televisions and radios.

To the west of Nelson's was a vacant lot[67] full of the used or "dead" cars. We would sit in the cars on Sunday afternoons, pretending to shift and drive them. The cars were never locked. It was a reflection on the times. Dennie slept overnight in one of those cars when he was angry with Mom over something. He was trying to prove a point. He also used to make out with some girl late at night in one of the cars with the radio playing. You could turn the radio on in some of the older cars without the key being in the ignition. Dennie got caught. One of the Nelsons couldn't figure out why the batteries were getting run down in the cars so he did a "stake out" one night and caught Dennie. Nothing came of it, except more yelling between Dennie and Mom.

Being the first of the Shaw boys to become a teenager during the rebellious fifties, Dennie had to constantly break new ground and pave the way for our freedoms to come. If Mom told Dennie to be in the house at ten, he'd come in at eleven. So it became eleven for us too. Because Mom had a tough time taming us on her own, while working at the Produce all day, we did have a lot more freedom than our friends did. Because of those experiences, all my children had earlier curfews.

Staying on the north side of Third Street, heading east again, there was an alley right after Nelson's Buick. The alley only went half way

---

[64] Where Culligan is today.

[65] See page 383 of the History of Downtown Litchfield Appendix.

[66] 22-28 Depot Street West. See page 477 of the History of Downtown Litchfield Appendix.

[67] See page 380 of the History of Downtown Litchfield Appendix.

through and behind the 300 block of Sibley Avenue. It met with and formed a "T" with the east-west alley, which ran through the same city block. The Meeker County jail was at the junction of the two alleys.

Still heading east, I reached the intersection at Sibley Avenue. Litchfield's first traffic signal light was installed at this intersection in the late forties. It worked great except for one problem. Someone lost the key that had to be used to turn the lights to the "middle of the night" mode. In that mode, Highway 12 drivers were supposed to get a flashing yellow light and Third Street drivers, a flashing red light. So for several years, angry drivers had to sit in their cars for no reason in the middle of the night and wait for the light to change at this deserted intersection. In November of 1953, the key was found and an article was put in the *Independent Review* to inform the relieved citizens.

By the way, two of the downtown intersections in Litchfield used to have a ten-foot tall pole right in the center. They were put there in 1914 and were called "turnarounds" or "center posts". They were there to slow down the traffic through town. The State Highway Department made the city remove them in August of 1924. This was before my time, but as late as the forties.

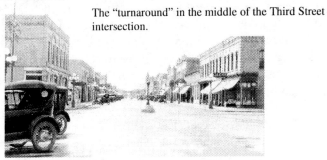

The "turnaround" in the middle of the Third Street intersection.

The first building across from Central Park at this intersection was called "the Robertson block" because Dr. James Wright Robertson built the large brick building at the corner in 1906. One of the first stores at this corner was Emil C. Gross' jewelry store. He had a clock on a pole on the sidewalk out front. I remember Olson Realty or the Ed Olson Agency sharing this corner building[68] with the Sparboe Chick Company. Around the corner in the rear was Taylor C. Waldron's law office. My classmate, Mike Miller, lived with his mom above the store, where the Robertson Hospital had been. The privately owned hospital, which

---

[68] 301 Sibley Avenue North. See page 386 of the History of Downtown Litchfield Appendix.

opened in December of 1908 and closed in February of 1915, was Litchfield's first hospital. Also there was an outlet store for the Litchfield Woolen Mills[69] run by Boyd Anderson in half of the main floor after it moved up from the basement. Sometime in the early fifties, the clock and the pole it stood on were removed.

Gross Jewelry Store in the Robertson Hospital building at Third and Sibley.

The store building to the right of the Ed Olson Agency stood vacant in 1959 and I don't remember much about it[70]. In 1909 it was Happ and Company, a grocery and dry goods store owned by Joe A. Happ. This store was the first in Litchfield to have an electric sign out front. Mr. Happ made it himself.

Hamilton A. Johnson's Furniture Store was in the next building[71]. I remember my step-grandpa, Charles Young, working in there. They did some furniture repair and restoration there and Grandpa Charlie was good at working with wood. But stronger in my memory was Wayne Rayppy's New Bakery in this location. Rayppy's New Bakery started in the corner building at Sibley Avenue and Second Street where Sandgren's Shoe Store went. Wayne moved across the street to the building south of the First State Bank. When the bakery across from the park was for sale, Wayne bought and ran it briefly in 1950. And so, for a while, he owned two bakeries at one time in town. One day a woman, not knowing this, came into the bakery across from the park and was giving Wayne a hard time about his price for a loaf of bread.

---

[69] Started in 1885 by Henry Klauser and Waterman, the Woolen Mills was located on the northeast edge of town by Jewett Creek. It looked ancient in the fifties and it's still going.
[70] 305 Sibley Avenue North. See page 392 of the History of Downtown Litchfield Appendix.
[71] 307-309 Sibley Avenue North. See page 395 of the History of Downtown Litchfield Appendix.

153

"Lady, if you don't like the prices here," Wayne said to her, "why don't you go down the street to the other bakery and get your bread."

"I will!" she replied. She turned and left the store in a huff.

Wayne went out the back door and ran down the alley to his other bakery. When the lady came walking in, Wayne was standing behind the counter. She looked at him with her mouth hanging open. Wayne looked her in the eye and said, "Prices are the same here lady."

Wayne had a fire at the bakery next to the bank. He had already had one fire there on April 12, 1954. The first fire had only shut him down for about ten days. This time on December 30, 1961, Wayne and his helpers were installing a new oven in the bakery. Sparks from welding ignited insulation in the walls and the place went up so fast that people in the offices above them didn't have time to grab their coats as they left. Keller's Barber Shop below the bakery was flooded with the firemen's water. The fire sent the bakery back to the vacant building where Wayne had owned the other bakery and where Johnson's Furniture had been.

On the left, Rayppy's New Bakery. On the right, Janousek's.

Rayppy's son Gary, who went to New York to do Shakespeare on Broadway and now works at the Brave New Workshop and Guthrie Theater in Minneapolis, had a reel-to-reel tape recorder, which was a rare luxury in those days. Dennie used to borrow it to record his band or himself doing some of his early compositions, such as a song he wrote called *Dear Barbara*.

What great smells came out of Rayppy's bakery! There is no better smell in the world than freshly baked bread. Pat and I didn't go in there for bread, however. We would go into the bakery to buy cheap day-old Bismarks or a bag of broken cookies for a dime. If they were sugar cookies, we'd take them home, put the pieces in a bowl and pour milk over it. The resulting mush was wonderful. I still take graham crackers and do that to them.   Another reason to go into the bakery was for something to eat during our noon lunch break from high school.

Our high school was only four blocks away and we had an open forty-five minute lunch period. It had been an hour long until the spring of 1958. You could eat at school or anywhere else you wanted to as long as you made it back to school in time for your next class. Many town kids went home but we didn't. We would sprint to the bakery and buy a bag of day-old sweet rolls or Bismarks for a quarter. I think we got about six in the bag. We'd take the bag across the street to eat the rolls in the bandstand at the park, so we could have a smoke afterwards.

Hot lunch was twenty-five cents a day, so Mom would give us each $1.25 on Monday mornings for the upcoming week. If we wanted to, we could buy a week's worth of the green plastic hexagonal lunch tokens for $1.00 or a single token for a quarter in the entrance hall at school each morning. If we bought the week's worth, we'd have a quarter left over to buy a pack of cigarettes. But the thoughts of the lunchroom food and more raisin and carrot salads, (who ever came up with that recipe?), usually drove us to other options.

Here's a typical hot lunch menu for a week in the fifties: Monday - BBQs, scalloped corn, cheese slices and pears. Tuesday – Beans, sandwiches, and cabbage and apple salad. Wednesday – Chicken rice soup, cheese sandwiches, fruit salad and a cupcake. Thursday – Hamburger gravy on mashed potatoes, green peas and a bran muffin. Friday – Vegetable plate, bread, butter, honey and cheese slices. Now it doesn't sound so bad.

If we didn't buy sweet rolls at the bakery, we'd go to Janousek's Cafe, or Kate's Café, or "have a beer". Someone found out that Lennart Holen's Sinclair Oil gas station a couple of blocks south of the high school had "near beer" in its dime pop cooler, so we made the trek over there a few times to have a beer. "Near beer" was a non-alcoholic beer, which was legal for us to buy. To tell the truth, I think we stopped doing that because, at the time, we thought beer tasted like crap. We had better things to do with our money, like buying cigarettes.

North of the bakery or Johnson's Furniture was one of our favorite places in Litchfield, Janousek's Cafe[72]. It shared a small building with Arthur Hyneman's Insurance office. The real name of the hamburger

---

[72] 311-311½ Sibley Avenue North. See page 397 of the History of Downtown Litchfield Appendix.

stand was Janousek Brothers' Café but the only identification outside was a large neon sign hanging above the door, which said "EAT 10¢ HAMBURGERS". One brother, Paul, had this cafe and the other brother, Henry or "Heinie", had an almost identical cafe in Hutchinson, Minnesota.

Johnson's and Janousek's.

Janousek's was only wide enough to accommodate a large long grill up by the front window, a long counter with red stools and a wall with coat hooks. On that wall was a painting of Paul in a fishing boat. The other brother painted it and he was very talented. In the rear of the café were a refrigerator and two freezers, one for the beef and one for the ice cream. The small greasy dime hamburger was wonderful. I've yet to have one better. For a quarter more, we could add a Coke and some fries. A 35¢ meal. Most people upsized it to two burgers, however and paid an extra dime. Or for a quarter, we could buy a huge thick chocolate malted or just an entire double order plate of homemade French fries.

Often for our school lunch break, Pat and I would opt for the mountain of fries at Janousek's. We would share the steaming pile, which always too hot to eat quickly. We'd be blowing on them and dousing them in a sea of ketchup, knowing our time was limited. We always had trouble finishing the plate before we'd have to sprint back to school, especially if we wanted to allow ourselves five minutes for a quick cigarette in the park.

The Janousek brothers owned a farm where they raised their own beef cattle and grew onions, potatoes and cucumbers for making pickles. This was the reason they could sell burgers for only a dime. The pickles were brewed in the basement of the restaurant. One day Paul went down there to get some more pickles and never came back upstairs. Finally one of the waitresses went down to check on him. He had passed out on the floor from the fumes. He spent quite a while in the hospital recovering.

156

Helen Anderson and Rita Dougherty were the day waitresses and Laura Young, a sister-in-law to my future stepfather, and Eva Sutter did the evenings. Helen and Rita were very big women. The restaurant was so small and Helen and Rita were so large that when they both worked, they had to stay in their own areas. They couldn't pass each other behind the counter.

Rita usually stayed up front doing the hamburger frying on the large grill by the front window and Helen stayed towards the back, doing the deep-frying and making malts. Rita wouldn't sell hamburgers to the Catholic kids on Fridays[73]. She knew us all from attending St. Philips herself and she absolutely refused to sell us meat on Fridays. Many times in the summer, we simply lost track of what day it was. But after being reminded by Rita, we weren't about to be condemned to hell for an eternity for a dime hamburger. Rita also wouldn't fry potatoes after about 11am.

"You boys have some fries," she'd tell us. "I'm not making any more hash browns now." I don't know what her reasoning was, but it was Rita's way or the highway.

Helen Anderson and her husband Bill married late in life because Bill was a non-Catholic and had been married and divorced. His first wife finally died, so Father Foley married them. My mother could relate to their dilemma. Bill and Helen lived in a small brick house about a block from us, right next to the railroad tracks. I thought it was bad enough living a block from the tracks with all the noise of boxcars switching and diesel engine horn blasts, but their house couldn't have been more than ten feet away from the tracks. They must have had a lot of bums bothering them for handouts. Why would anyone want to live there?

Obviously, Bill got a deal on the place. He bought the house for something like $100 from the county, who owned it. Why so cheap, besides the location next to the tracks? The little brick house had been a "pest house" or "contagious house" used by the county hospital to put up quarantine patients who had TB, diphtheria or some other contagious

---

[73] For centuries Catholics abstained from eating meat on Fridays. It was Church law and a sign of penance. Pope Nicholas I (858-867) was the pope who put it into effect. Early in 1966, Pope Paul VI authorized local Church officials to modify this abstinence requirement in their countries as they saw fit. The Pope was acting in line with recommendations made at the recently completed Second Vatican Council. Thus, in one country after another, meatless Fridays were virtually abolished. Catholics may perform an act of penance of their choosing.

disease. Before the turn of the century, another such house had been out by Lake Ripley, where the golf course is today.

Auctioneer Chet Berg gave Bill five gallons of white paint and five gallons of yellow paint that he had leftover from an auction he ran. So Bill mixed them in equal amounts and painted the whole inside a light yellow color after it had been sanitized from top to bottom with Clorox bleach.

On a hot summer night, Pat and I would run into the Janousek's via the back screen door and order a "malt", which is what we called a malted milk. The waitress would pour the malt into a large heavy "malt glass" and set the metal mixing container down next to it on the counter in front of the customer. You could count on having another half of a glass of "malt" in the container, so Pat and I would share the malt. Eventually the diner changed its name to "EAT 15¢". Even with the inflation, it was still a bargain and the best hamburger in the world.

Litchfield's Janousek's had been the original site of Pat Woods' Black & White Inn, which was moved to Ramsey Avenue between the Seed Store and the turkey plant. When it was Woods' in the early forties, I was told that it was one of only two places in town where you could buy a condom. The other place was the hotel. The pharmacies didn't stock them. The Black & White had just six stools at a counter and one booth. Don Larson, future owner of the Viren-Johnson Clothing Store worked there in the late thirties, while in high school. He said the recipe for their hamburgers was five pounds of hamburger mixed with three pounds of crackers or breadcrumbs. I heard once that White Castle had a similar recipe.

I remember the next building[74] down from Janousek's on Sibley Avenue as the Skelgas Sales and Service store and the Farm Bureau. Skelgas sold bottled gas and Norge appliances and did electrical contracting. At one time Harry Radunz had a tire repair shop and junk business there, most of it in the alley.

Harry was a practical joker with a smart answer for everything. If you asked him how tall he was, he'd say, "Five feet, seventeen and a half inches." Harry stood tall and wide at six foot and five and a half inches and about three hundred pounds. One day he soldered a dime to a wire and then took the contraption out to the sidewalk in front of the shop. He

---

[74] 313 Sibley Avenue North. See page 399 of the History of Downtown Litchfield Appendix.

wedged the wire into a crack and was able to turn it just enough so that it couldn't be pulled out. Then he sat back and watched as victim after victim strolled by, stopped and tried to pick up the dime.

Harry
Radunz
in 1946.

In Chicago on a business trip in February of 1930, Harry went to a movie one night. After the movie, he was strolling down a street by a motorcycle shop when he saw two men ahead of him enter the building. He stopped to look in the window at the cycles. Inside the shop, he saw one of the two men pull a gun on the man behind the counter and yell, "Stick 'em up." Before Harry or the bandits could do anything, the man behind the counter pulled a gun out of his pocket and fired at the men, killing one and wounding the other. Harry came home to Litchfield, having had enough of Chicago.

Elmer "Cooch" Curtis, who worked for Harry, rescued some wild geese from a frozen pond after the Armistice Day blizzard. The freezing drizzle and snow came up so fast that chickens, hiding by trees, were frozen right to the bark and many duck and geese were frozen into the water. Cooch brought a rescued goose into Harry's shop to show it off. Harry tied a string around one leg, took the goose outside and started to walk it up and down Sibley Avenue, just to see people's reactions. He went up and down the west side of Sibley with that goose all afternoon.

Harry was notorious for his drinking. Cooch once said, "Harry drank more in one day than I did in a month." In April of 1933, when prohibition ended, Harry supposedly walked into the Black Cat Cafe, sat down and drank nineteen bottles of beer. When the Black Cat closed down for the evening, Harry wandered over to the hotel and sat up all night in the dining room. The dining room also sold beer. Ironically a Minnesotan had spearheaded the passage of his bill called the (Representative Andrew J.) Volstead Act of 1919 or the National

159

Prohibition Act. Volstead, from Granite Falls, Minnesota, was called the "Father of Prohibition."

An interesting sideline to the prohibition is a story about the Garfield school. The Garfield school, a four-classroom brick structure built in 1886, was at the corner of Marshall Avenue and Pacific Street. It was shut down when the Longfellow school was built in 1909. When Litchfield imposed their own prohibition, voting to go dry in April of 1914, all of the saloons in town were closed down. Three saloon owners got together and leased the old school to store their bars and bar fixtures in. One night in 1915, the old school mysteriously burned down. The local temperance group was thought to be behind it, but nothing could be proven.

Harry was tight but his wife Helen was tighter. Helen had been married before and her ex was serving time for forgery. She wanted to know where every penny went. Harry, no doubt needing extra money for his drinking, wouldn't take all of the money home from the tire shop. He would hide some in various places such as inside an inner tube box. Employees, like Ollie Prieve, were put on notice to never throw away any boxes in the shop without first checking them out.

Harry loved to go hunting and fishing with his buddies, but he'd have to sneak money out of the house for his trips. One Saturday morning he wrote Helen a note that he was going to Mike Radtke's barbershop to get a haircut and from there he was going fishing with his friends. He was sitting in the chair at Mike's when Helen burst into the barbershop.

"Okay Harry," she said, "give me your wallet." Harry reached around his backside, pulled out a wallet and handed it over.

After Helen left, Mike asked, "Thought you said you were goin' fishin' from here. How you gonna buy bait and drinks afterwards?"

"Gave her the little one," Harry said, holding up a fat wallet from his other back pocket.

Even though he watched his money, Harry drove a big white Cadillac. When he'd be somewhere where people didn't know him and he was asked what he did for a living, Harry always replied, "I'm in the junk business." He didn't care what people thought, but Helen did and she would get terribly upset.

"Don't tell them that," she'd say, "Tell them you're in the tire business. What's wrong with you?"

Deb Thomas, who owned a trucking business, told his wife to send a bill to Harry for some hauling work he had done for him. She didn't know Harry's last name or address, so she put "Harry by the junk yard" on the envelope and mailed it. Surprisingly, Harry got it. To save the cost of the postage stamp, Harry turned around, put a check in the envelope, "sealed" it with a paper clip and wrote on the front "Return to sender for a better address." Deb got the check.

Harry couldn't read and, for a long time while he had his shop on Sibley Avenue across from the park, he had his sister-in-law, Mrs. Koktavy, come in everyday from the bakery, which she and her husband owned down the street, and give him instructions. Driving home to Litchfield one night in April of 1954, Harry fell asleep in his big Cadillac. He ran off the road, broke some ribs and other bones, but was pinned in the car and died before help found him.

There was an alley[75] after Skelgas. In the alley, behind all of this, was the small brick Meeker County jail, built in August of 1912. We would stand in the alley and talk to the prisoners through their barred windows. They'd ask us for a cigarette or to run to Janousek's to get a hamburger for them. I'm sure the smells from Janousek's drifted across the alley to the jailhouse and just drove them crazy.

The Meeker County jail.

Our friends, the Dollerschell boys and their parents, lived in the front of the jail. Robert, the older of the four or so boys, took Dennie in the jail for a tour. He pointed out one cell where someone had hung himself. The boys' dad, Russ, was the jailer and their mom cooked for the prisoners. She was also the day dispatcher when the police got receivers in the patrol cars. I heard she was a great cook, so the Meeker County prisoners didn't suffer any. But they just had to have a Janousek's burger after smelling them. Didn't we all?

---

[75]   315 Sibley Avenue North.   See page 401 of the Litchfield Downtown History Appendix.

In the mid-forties, there was a spot in the alley in front of the jail and behind Janousek's that kept sinking, causing a dip in the road. The city crew kept filling it in with more dirt, making the alley very uneven. Finally in May of 1949, they decided to have a road grader level the uneven alley off. When the grader got to the place where the ground kept sinking, it uncovered a grave marker or headstone. On it was simply the name "Nisse" and the dates "1825 – 1889". Was this the only one? Had there been a graveyard at this location at one time? The city crew never bothered to find out, leaving well enough alone. It was probably a discarded marker from the marble works that William Grono owned in the area in the late 1800s.

The Uptown Skelly Service station[76] followed the alley. It was finally torn down in the late-fifties. Nothing replaced it, just more lawn for the Meeker County Court House, which finished the block.

A Burleigh painting of the Court House, which was torn down in 1975. © 1980

Forest City was originally the Meeker County seat because it had a river for shipping goods. But the addition of the railroad through Litchfield changed the population makeup of the county. A referendum was held and the difference of only eighty-nine votes changed the county seat to Litchfield. So, we had the courthouse[77]. The big brick courthouse across from the park was torn down in 1975 to make room for a larger new one. Directly across Sibley Avenue from all of these stores was Central Park.

---

[76] 317 Sibley Avenue North. See page 401 of the History of Downtown Litchfield Appendix.
[77] See page 403 of the History of Downtown Litchfield Appendix.

Chapter Thirteen
Christmas Decorations, the Bandstand, and the GAR Hall

I suppose if my wife drove herself and me to Minneapolis from Willmar on a cold December day and I fell asleep in the car and woke up entering a town, I'd know immediately if I was in Litchfield for two reasons. The main reason would be the distinctive Christmas decorations. For as long as I can remember, Litchfield has had the same unique Christmas decorations.

In the early 1910s, a big municipal Christmas tree was put up in the middle of the "railroad park" at the southeast corner of Depot Street and Sibley Avenue. It was only lit for two hours each night. A couple of years later, it was put in the intersection at Sibley Avenue and Depot Street. Obviously, when the number of cars in town increased, that tradition had to be stopped.

Christmas decorations in 1914.

Vic Sederstrom, who had a realty and insurance business in town, started putting the famous hanging decorations up around 1935. He and his wife were driving out to California for Christmas in 1934 and they passed through Fremont, Nebraska. Fremont had decorated their little town so beautifully that Vic was extremely impressed. He said to his wife, "Litchfield should do that too." His son Loren said that was all he talked about the rest of the way out to California and on the drive back home.

Vic got funding from the Commercial Club, similar to the Chamber of Commerce today, and started the tradition. For years he had to do most of the work himself. He would work on the garland strings in the alley behind his realty business. At first he got help putting up decorations by going to the pool hall nearby and asking for help. He "paid" his helpers with a drink and a bag of the Christmas candy that he also bagged up for the annual children's Christmas program he had organized. It's no wonder that people started calling Vic "Mr.

Christmas". Eventually Vic, his son Loren, his brother Vern, and Chet Berg were the usual workers and then the city street department took over the job.

There's about twenty-seven of those garland strings around town, each with seventy-two bulbs. Laid out, they are almost three-fourths of a mile long. My wife calls them "The Sunglasses" and some people have said they look like an upside down strapless bra, but most people think they just look like a pair of regular glasses. "Litchfield's Spectacles" are what some out of towners have enviously called them.

There's something interesting about the lights they used for the "glasses". At one time, either the majority was yellow or they all were yellow. They quit using yellow bulbs for a long time because some ladies' club objected, saying they looked like "bug lights". So every other color was used. Now they use yellow again.

I was always proud of those "glasses" that my stepfather Floyd Young helped put up every year when he worked for the city street department. He also decorated the water tower. When Floyd worked for the city, it took at least a week and a lot more manpower to put the decorations up. They didn't have all the boom trucks and equipment that they use today. Currently, it takes two days to put them up and one day to take them down, weather permitting.

To appreciate the decorations, you really have to see them at night. It has always put most of the other towns' decorations that I've seen to shame. Some are downright ugly, cheap looking and sparse. Because of our decorations, Litchfield was given the unofficial title of the "Prettiest Decorated Town West of Minneapolis". There's something to be said for the tradition Litchfield has established and kept going. But they almost lost it.

The decorations basically unchanged for about seventy years.

Although the Chamber of Commerce paid for the decorations, the city street maintenance department was asked to maintain them and put them up. This took time, equipment and money. For over thirty years, from the sixties and on, Larry Dahl took each of the five thousand or so twenty-five-watt bulbs out and cleaned and tested them about a month before they went up. You see, with all the truck traffic through Litchfield, the bulbs would get covered in diesel soot.

In October of 1959, under a budget crunch and an auditor's scrutiny, the city public examiner said, "No, we can't afford to do it anymore. Besides, it's illegal." Well, the Chamber members and many local citizens were outraged and they took up collections to save the tradition. Kids literally emptied their piggy banks. The first week, over $700 was collected by the "Dollars for Decorations" campaign.

Walter Wogenson, who ran the seed house, and night policeman Wilton "Tiny" Fredrickson put the decorations together and up, stringing the bulbs into the garland and hanging them. They built a two-wheeled cart and clamped two big ladders onto it. They dubbed it "Charlie Pollequin's ladder." I don't know what that meant. Tiny pulled it down the street behind his 1937 Allis Chalmers tractor and they clambered up to attach the "glasses" to the light poles. Tiny was six foot two inches and way over three hundred pounds, so it was quite a site for people to see this immense man high up on a ladder hanging Christmas decorations.

Mae Fransein, of Fransein's Café, and Julia Larson, of the hotel's Colonial Café, told the men that they could eat free in their restaurants for as long as it took to get the job done. The next year it was put on the local ballot to appropriate tax dollars for the job. It won overwhelmingly and the City of Litchfield and Public Utilities currently own, operate and pay all costs related to the decorations. Today, nine men work for three days using three city utility trucks to put up both the garlands and the park decorations.

Larry Dahl said that when the decorations come down each year, the citizens go into a two or three day depression. Year after year, the depression appears without exception. There may be magic in those lights after all. Imagine the depression the whole town went into in 1942 when the government asked them to not put up the lights at all to conserve energy during the war.

The other "landmark" that would tell me I was "home" was decorated every Christmas too. It was the bandstand in Central Park. It was built in 1913. For a while, it was converted into "Santa's house", until a portable permanent one was built and put at the park's entrance. The sidewalks leading up to the bandstand were decorated with candy cane lights, earning the name "Candy Cane Lane".

Every time I drive through Litchfield, I glance over at the park and take a loving and nostalgic look at that bandstand. It's the only thing that never seemed to change in my hometown. I had spent hours in and around it growing up. You can imagine my surprise and horror in the late summer of 2001 when, driving through town, I glanced over and saw that it had been torn down!

My mind was put to ease when my Litchfield friend Dick Holtz told me, "It's okay. They're gonna build it up again, just like it was." The new one, almost identical at a cost of over $100,000, was dedicated on June 3, 2002. I can tell you every little thing that's different about today's bandstand from the one I played in. The shingles are supposed to be the same ones, but the top rail of the "fence" that goes around the sides isn't painted green, nor is the floor. There was a large green "box" with a top lid to the left of the south steps where the band's chairs were stored also.

The bandstand in 1952 and the new bandstand, minus the green rails I remember.

Litchfield's second bandstand, built around 1910. The first one had no roof.

The bandstand sits almost in the center of the park. It was actually Litchfield's third bandstand. The first was basically just a platform. Village Council President Jesse V. Branham, Jr. was instrumental in getting that first bandstand built. He drew up the plans for Central Park and was Litchfield's first "mayor" although that term wasn't used in

Litchfield until 1887. His father, Jesse, Sr. who came to the area in 1857, was one of the pioneer residents of the county. When the Sioux attacked in 1862, Jesse, Sr., at the age of fifty-nine, was the only person of the six hundred assembled in Forest City to volunteer to ride a horse to St. Paul to get help. That's about a hundred miles or more on horseback. Jesse, Jr. was a scout with Captain Strout and it was Jr.'s idea to build the stockade at Forest City. While his father rode to St. Paul, Jesse, Jr. rode around the county like Paul Revere alerting settlers that the Indians were attacking.

I'm going to interrupt my story to tell of a phenomenon that occurs on a hill not far from that stockade, just north of Forest City. The hill has acquired the name of "Indian Ghost Hill". The phenomenon defies gravity, or appears to. I've visited the hill several times and the only explanation I can come up with is that it's an optical illusion. Some people suggest there is a gravity anomaly or a magnetic vortex there. When you drive to the site and reach the top of the hill[78], turn your car around so that you're facing north and observe that it's downhill in front of you and behind you towards the curve in the road. Then drive back down the hill. Put your car in neutral, turn your engine off (or not) and release your brake. As crazy as it sounds, your car will be "pulled" backwards, back up the hill. The folklore that is told is that ghosts of the Indian children killed there push your car back up the hill as a warning to not think about building a home on that land, which was thought to be sacred by the Indians.

The last time I visited the site, I did two "experiments". I brought along a carpenter's level. When I was at what I thought was the top of the hill, I kept checking the ground with my level until I found a perfectly level spot. I scratched a line in the gravel with my heel and drove down the hill, thinking when I was pulled back, my car should stop or really slow down at or near my line. Nope. I rolled right past it, quite far past it. Then I drove down the hill and turned my car to face the hill or south and put the car in neutral, thinking I should be pulled up the hill just as before. Nope. I rolled away from the hill. I turned my car around again to face north, and, sure enough, I was pulled up the hill again.

---

[78] Take County Road 2 north out of Forest City, going over a bridge. Go 1.5 miles from bridge to 330th Street, turn right and go .5 mile to 660th Street, turn right again and drive up the small hill. The hill is just before the curve to the left. Turn around to face north and observe that it's downhill behind you and in front of you. Drive about half way down the hill and stop. Put your car in neutral and take your foot off the brake. The farther you go down the hill the faster you will be pulled back up the hill.

On August 17, 1862, while fighting Indians, Jesse, Jr. stopped to reload his rifle and was shot in the chest. The bullet passed through his lungs, and came out his back. He never fell, but was able to walk instead to his team of horses and go for help. A doctor was summoned after Jesse collapsed at a house.

"I can do nothing for this man," the doctor said, after taking one look at Jesse. "Make him as comfortable as you can. He'll be dead in three hours."

Obviously, he was wrong. Jesse, Jr. lived long enough to see his son, Hiram S. Branham, become the mayor in 1889, although I only found that fact in one source, the newspapers. The history booklets about Litchfield made for centennials and other celebrations make no mention of that fact. The years Hiram served are skipped over. Possibly he was erased from the books because he embarrassed the city. You see, Hiram was co-owner of the Stevens and Company Bank, which failed due to some shady dealings. One night in December of 1890, while his brother D. E. or "Abe" was visiting him, Hiram went into his bedroom and put a bullet in his chest just below his heart with a .32 revolver. The next morning, he died at the age of thirty-four. One of the officers of the bank was arrested for embezzlement and many people lost their money.

Jesse V. Branham, Sr. and Jesse V. Branham, Jr.

The second bandstand in Central Park was octagonal in shape and it had a roof. The bandstand I knew, the third one, which was built in 1913, was constructed of wood and concrete with four columns supporting the roof on each side. It was painted white with a green roof and a white wooden "fence" between the columns, the top and bottom rails of the fence being green. All of it sat high up on a concrete base and floor.

I suppose Central Park was in the actual center of the early town of Litchfield, but the majority of the stores have always been to the south of it. What a great park it was and is. The St. Paul, Pacific and Manitoba Railroad gave the land to the city in 1870. It was and is an entire city block filled with tall, shade trees. In 1876, it was plowed up in preparation for the planting of those trees. A crop of potatoes was also put in.

An 1874 lithograph of
Central Park, facing east.

A wooden fence surrounded the park in June of 1883. The fence got so plastered with bills and posters that it was torn down in June of 1885. The fountain was added in May of 1894. A various times, things for children popped up in the park, such as a toboggan slide in the early 1900s, although the adults tended to hog it with a Toboggan Club. The park was used as a grazing pasture for the town folk's milk cows that were kept in sheds in people's backyards. It got so bad that an ordinance was passed in the spring of 1910 prohibiting the "staking and pasturing of cows in parks and streets in town." In the fifties, you'd have to look hard to find a place in the park that wasn't shaded by all of the trees. There were large and extremely heavy wooden green picnic tables and green wooden benches strewn throughout the park. Of course, most of the benches were pulled and carried up close to the bandstand on concert nights.

Every Wednesday night in the summer, Litchfield hosted a band concert in the bandstand. It was changed to Saturdays to coincide with the night the stores stayed open and changed again to Fridays in March of 1953, for the same reason. M. B. Larson, the high school band instructor, conducted the band, which started playing at 8:30pm. For years, each concert began with *America* and ended with *The Star Spangled Banner*, a sure way to get a standing ovation, I suppose, although half of the audience stayed in their cars parked around the park square. When the band finished their piece, you'd hear the combination of applause and horns honking.

We always attended the band concerts, not so much to listen to the band but to meet our friends and run around. I would stand up on the outside of the bandstand, clinging to the green rail, and watch my drumming idol Jerry Wheeler play his snare drum, our neighbor Bob Lindell play his trumpet or my paper route supervisor Dean Schultz blow his tuba. There were always bugs and mosquitoes buzzing around the musicians and I marveled that they could play anything at all. I'm sure they swallowed many of those bugs during the concerts.

You could buy a bag of popcorn for a nickel from the popcorn stand wagon at the southwest corner of the park. Merlin Johnson and his wife owned it and they later sold it to Carl Gustafson. Sometimes we'd try to smuggle a bag of their popcorn into the movie theater where they charged a dime. When I first started going to movies, you weren't allowed to have food in the theater at all. Then we'd have to load our pockets up with penny candy from Axel Johnson's little store down by the Unique Theater across from the hotel.

During the day, we would sit on a bench facing Sibley Avenue and watch all of the cars going by. Sibley Avenue was also Highway 12 so every vehicle heading east towards the Twin Cities had to come through downtown Litchfield. We could name the make and year of every car and often made a game of it. The cars didn't all look the same, as they do now. We'd jerk our arms up and down when a truck came rumbling through, trying to get the driver to give us a blast on his air horn. We had a lot of time on our hands back in the fifties and the park, with its wonderful bandstand, offered many diversions and time killers for us.

The bandstand was our hangout. Everyone met there to decide where to go and what to do. We played and smoked up there, convinced that no one could see us. We didn't really care, though. We would have mad bicycle races around the outside of the bandstand. I say "mad" because it was quite dangerous with half a dozen bicycles speeding around on the dirt, trying to edge each other out. We wore the grass completely away around the bandstand. There were always crashes. I wasn't very good at bicycle racing, and I was scared of the crashes, so I volunteered to be the race starter and finish judge.

On a sunny summer Saturday morning, when I was thirteen, I walked uptown to the bandstand to meet up with my buddies and have a smoke. When I arrived, I found none of my buddies there. There were just three older boys, Brendan "Jopey" Wimmer who was Jerry and

170

Dougy's older brother, Don "Pokey" Schreifels who was Monk's older brother and Billy Johanneck, a neighbor of the Wimmers, who had one eye looking in the wrong direction.

I should have left, but I hung around, probably thinking I was going to impress them with my smoking. They warned me a couple of times to "Beat it, Shaw!" but I stood my ground replying, "You don't own the bandstand!" I decided to go to the bathroom. We often peed behind the bandstand, but down in the dirt. That day, for some unknown reason, I decided to pee right up there on the concrete floor. I went to the southeast corner and did my thing. Mistake.

"Hey, Shaw!" Jopey yelled at me. "What the hell do you think you're doing? Clean that up!" I replied the wrong answer because all of a sudden two of them were on me like hungry dogs on a meaty bone. They pushed me down, grabbed me by my feet and picked me straight up off the floor. I was suspended upside down looking down at my yellow puddle on the floor.

"If you won't clean it up, we'll have to!" Billy said.

They proceeded to mop the floor with my dark hair, their laughs covering up my screams. Finally setting me down, quite gently actually, they left me alone to pick myself up crying and sputtering something about telling on them. This was met with more laughs and a few threats. I ran down the steps to walk home with pee dripping down my head. The hot summer sun cooked it into my scalp as I slowly walked the three blocks home. Thank God my mother was there to console me and give me a shampoo in the kitchen sink.

"Well, I hope you learned your lesson," she said for the thousandth time to me. This time, I had. I can honestly say that I have never peed in that bandstand again and I never will.

The park had a set of swings set back about thirty feet from the sidewalk on the Third Street side. We would get swinging as fast and as high as we could and then "bail out" or jump from the swing trying to "fly" to the sidewalk. No one ever made it to the concrete sidewalk, thank God. I don't remember anyone ever breaking a leg either. The strange things that kids will do. Some older boys would stand up on the wooden swings, holding tight to the two chains, and get swinging to tremendous heights, trying to go all of the way around. I saw Tom Sederstrom do it. When he reached the top of his circular route, gravity took over and he and the swing came down with a slam that threw him off the swing towards the sidewalk. He didn't break anything either, and he didn't make it all the way to the sidewalk, but he convinced the rest of us to never try that stunt. In April of 1968, Tom got into a fight with Joe Hamm at the new VFW club and lost an eye.

Next to the swings was the "Vomit Comet"; a small round orange metal merry-go-round that would spin so fast you'd be thrown off by centrifugal force. It couldn't have been three feet in diameter. If you could hold on for dear life and not fall off, you would usually get sick and lose your lunch onto the green grass, hence the name. I didn't like it and kept to the swings.

Across the park to the north on the corner of Fourth Street and Sibley Avenue was, and still is, the beautiful Trinity Episcopal Church, which was built in 1871. It was Litchfield's very first school[79], although parochial. I always wanted to see the inside of that church, thinking that it must look like the quaint old churches I saw in the movies.

Next to the church, at 25 East Fourth Street, after an alley, was the home of one of my favorite teachers and a town character, Floyd Warta. His little house with the white fence was "charming", if I can use that word. I was invited in one time for a cast party after the last night of one of the plays. Usually the cast parties were at a senior performer's house.

On the eastern corner of Floyd's block was the Litchfield Clinic[80]. Opened by Dr. Harold Wilmot in March of 1950, it was a feared place in town for kids. We knew if our mother was taking us there, a shot was going to be involved. In the fifties, they were always coming up with some new inoculation for some old dreaded disease that we have since eradicated, so we were always getting shots. Once we got to go to the high school auditorium where we were handed a pink sugar cube that had an oral vaccine for polio in it. That was better.

Four doctors were at that clinic to inflict pain upon us, Dr. Harold and his brother Dr. Cecil A. Wilmot, Dr. Donald Dille, whose son Steve

---

[79] Another source states that the first school was established in March of 1870. The first teacher, from 1872 to 1873, was Flora Mitchel. In an interview in the *Independent Review*, an old pioneer remembered the first teacher as being Mrs. Ben Amber whose husband was a blacksmith in town. Still another source claims that the first teacher was John Blackwell. The December 29, 1889 issue of the *Litchfield Saturday Review* states that it was Flora. A January of 1872 issue of the *Litchfield Republican* states that Mary Berquist taught primary school, Miss A. F. Simons taught intermediate school and Mr. Bailey taught grammar school at that time.

[80] 35 Fourth Street East. Built in the summer of 1949, it's the Sparboe Company offices today.

172

was in my class, and Dr. Frederick Schnell. Harold was a brilliant doctor but was known to take a drink or two. But it was said around town that people would rather have a drunken Dr. Harold operate on them than any other sober doctor. Generally some old lady in a white uniform, who told us to drop our pants and bend over the doctor's examining table, administered the shots. I learned to ask her to give my butt a good pinch before she stuck the needle in. Try it next time. It works.

I woke up one summer morning, when I was twelve, and discovered that I couldn't bend my left arm. There was a hard lump of something inside on my elbow bone. Mom took me to the clinic and one of the doctors there decided he had to cut my arm open and pull out the hard puss-like growth. He did it rather painlessly, and I was quite pleased with myself for my bravery. I have a tiny half-inch scar there. When I was in the ninth grade, I woke up to discover that the lump was back. This time, however, it was on my left knee. I panicked because I didn't want to miss school. I had a perfect record of never missing a day of school. I thought I could just do what the doctor had done. I got a scissors, a tweezers, a bottle of peroxide, some mecurachrome, a couple of Band-Aids and I operated on myself.

My knee was already numb, so I poked at the lump with the scissors until I had opened the skin. I took the tweezers and pulled out the offending lump, doused the wound with peroxide, swabbed on some mecurachrome, (Ouch! The first time that my self-operation had hurt!), bandaged the whole mess up and limped off to school. It never came back nor got infected, but I still have a dime-size circular scar today from that operation.

There was a national treasure right under my nose as I grew up in Litchfield, and I had no idea what it was. East of Central Park was, and still is, the Frank Daggett Post #35 of the GAR at 308 Marshall Avenue North. As a young boy, I'd see it almost daily as I played in the bandstand or on the park swings and I never knew what the heck it was. It looked like a small brick fort and it had a pair of real cannons on its small front lawn. My friends and I would occasionally sit on the cannons or pretend to fire them. Only later in my adult years did I learn that the GAR Hall was originally a meeting hall for Civil War veterans and that the cannons actually came from the Civil War, my favorite period in history. I was teaching art in Glencoe, Minnesota and another teacher had asked me where I had grown up.

"Litchfield," I answered.

"Oh," he said, "that's where that Civil War building and museum is."

"What?" I felt embarrassed that I didn't know about it. I wondered why in the world my history teachers had never mentioned the building or taken us there on a field trip while we were studying the Civil War. After all, it was only two blocks from the high school I attended in the early sixties. Perhaps my teachers also didn't know what was right under their noses?

Why do I call it a national treasure? Litchfield's Hall is one of only two original and authentic GAR Halls remaining in the United States and it's the only one in Minnesota. The building is on the National Register of Historical Places. The Meeker County Historical Society Museum building was added to the rear of it in 1960, but the Hall was left exactly as it was when the "Boys of '61", as they called themselves, met there well over one hundred years ago in 1885. Whether you're a Civil War buff or not, if you don't spend a few minutes in the GAR Hall, you are really missing something special.

The GAR Hall, yesterday and today.

After the Civil War, twenty-seven veterans from Meeker County founded a chapter of the Grand Army of the Republic, a service organization much like the American Legion or VFW clubs of today. Dr. B. F. Stephenson started the GAR in Illinois in 1866. The membership was limited to honorably discharged veterans of the Union Army, Navy, Marine Corps and the Revenue Cutter Service who had served between April 12, 1861 and April 9, 1865. With a motto of "Fraternity, Charity and Loyalty", the organization's purpose was to maintain fellowship for the men who fought to preserve the Union and to help handicapped veterans and the widows and orphans of dead veterans.

174

Meeker County's original organization was called the Edward Branham Post #39 and had fourteen members, most of them business owners. A new Post, named after Lt. Frank E. Daggett, the Post's commander and ranking member and later a Grand Commander of the Minnesota GAR, was started in July of 1883. He had been actively associated with abolitionist John Brown and the commander of two all-black heavy artillery regiments during the Civil War. Daggett, who was only five feet six inches in height and weighed nearly two hundred and fifty pounds, came to Meeker County in 1872 and was the editor of the *Litchfield Ledger*, one of the earliest newspapers in the county. He died in 1876 at the young age of thirty-nine.

The Post met in the old county courthouse, which was next to the grand Howard House hotel on Sibley Avenue. A meeting hall was needed to accommodate the local membership, which had grown to one hundred and forty veterans. A suitable lot by Central Park at 308 Marshall Avenue North was bought from Reuben S. Hershey. Henry Ames, a Post member and owner of a brickyard northeast of Litchfield, donated the bricks to build the Hall. Construction began in early 1885. The total cost was $5000. The Hall was finished in the fall and was dedicated on November 14, 1885. One week after the dedication, on November 21, 1885, the members deeded the Memorial Hall, as they called it, to the Village of Litchfield with the stipulation that it be kept as it was "in memory of the 300,000 soldiers who fell in defense of the Union" and be opened to the public for reading. So, the Hall naturally became the first public library in Meeker County.

The city has tried to keep the meeting room as it was at the last meeting. In that meeting room, which had been repainted in the color scheme it was, you'll see huge portraits on the north wall of most of the original members and the same chairs that were used by them in 1885. At their first meeting, the members were instructed to bring their own chairs from their homes to the Hall. So all the chairs, now painted gray, are different from each other, but generally they are just ordinary kitchen table chairs. The original organ is also there along with some other original furniture. A large chandelier, first lit by kerosene, hangs over the center of the room. It was brought to Litchfield from Boston in 1885, although some romantic historians believe that it came through Boston from a New Orleans bordello. More romantics want to believe it was a spoil of war brought here after the Civil War. I really doubt it but it sounds good.

In 1889, the Post was given an oak log from the actual Acton cabin where five members of the Jones family became the first settlers who were killed in the Dakota Indian War of 1862, commonly called the Sioux Uprising. The log was taken to a sawmill in Forest City and made into lumber from which an altar or podium, in the center of the room, and a gavel, which were both used during meetings, were made. The altar is thirty-two and a half inches square and thirty-six inches high. It has a cushioned top covered with heavy leather. In the northwest corner of the meeting room is a miniature model of the Jones' cabin and it was also made from wood from that log.

The Civil War cannons I used to see on the front lawn have been brought inside the Hall and have been replaced outside by replicas. The original ones are the first things you'll see in the entrance room, called the Ante Room and Library, which has a guest book for you to sign. The entrance room is a Civil War museum in its own right with tall glass showcases displaying rifles, uniforms, flags and other Civil War artifacts, such as munitions, medals and ribbons. The Hall actually had many more artifacts but it was broken into in the late forties and many of the Civil War rifles were taken.

The GAR Hall's entrance and meeting rooms today.

Litchfield's Hall serves as the entrance to the Meeker County Historical Society Museum. The museum is behind the Hall where a wooden twenty by forty-five foot kitchen had originally been added. The museum is another treasure of Litchfield's where I've spent many wonderful afternoons discovering even more treasures or just pouring through old issues of Litchfield's newspapers, which date all the way back to the beginning of the city. Many visitors come to do genealogical research in the museum. It has county plat books, records of obituaries and lists of cemetery markers.

There are many artifacts from the pioneer days of the county, including an actual 1868 log cabin you can walk into and explore. John Blomberg built the cabin in Acton Township and sold it to O. G. Samstad, who raised eleven children in it. His descendants donated it to the museum. When they took it apart to transport it to the museum, they found a huge honeybee's nest in the ceiling and over six hundred pounds of honey in the walls. A man named Shorty Wolters was called to come and deal with the bees before there could be any more dismantling. Upstairs in the museum is a replica of pioneer O. A. Jacobson's Crow River Store.

The United States' GAR members started the celebration of Memorial Day in 1868. W. A. Olmstead, who died in 1933, was the last Civil War veteran and GAR member to live in Litchfield, and Albert H. "Al" DeLong, who died in 1936, was the last Meeker County veteran. Al was an Indian scout. He and Vincent Coombs went to Acton after the Jones family was massacred to bury the bodies and pursue the Indians into Kandiyohi Woods. The last GAR member and Civil War veteran in the United States was Albert Woolson, who was from Duluth, Minnesota. He died in 1956 at the age of 109.

One member of Litchfield's GAR was unusual, at least for our very Scandinavian town. He was black and his name was Allison or Albert Van Spence, known only as Van. Van was born to African slaves in Alabama on January 16, 1837. He was sold away from his parents at the age of seven. By the time he was nineteen, he had been sold two more times. Drafted into the Confederate Army when the Civil War broke out, Van deserted and "escaped" to the north where he enlisted in the Union Army. It was at this time that he met Lt. Daggett, who was as short and wide as Van was. They became friends. Van became the personal servant of Major General George Thomas until the war ended. He ended up in Wisconsin where he met and married another freed slave named Missouri Jay Blair. Because of Van's friendship with Daggett, he and his wife came to Litchfield in 1880.

Van became an officer in the GAR, a custodian at the county courthouse and the town's lamplighter. The city paid him 50¢ a night for his lamp lighting. As the courthouse custodian, he cut wood for its rooms' fireplaces and the heaters in the basement. Van proudly marched in every annual Memorial Day parade out to the cemetery. He entertained the veterans at the Hall with his great singing voice, singing such songs as *Old Black Joe, Roving Little Darkey, I'se Gwine Back To Dixie*, and *That Feller What Looked Like Me* while his daughter Ada accompanied him on the organ, which is still on the small stage in the Hall. Van even dressed up as Santa Claus for the Hall's Christmas celebrations. He roasted ox for the GAR encampments and several times he sent off to places like West Virginia to have opossum sent to him. He must have had it as a child and missed it. Van was known by the kids in town to always have a bag of candy on him, so he was very popular with them.

Van Spence roasting an ox and in his uniform.

Van and Missouri had a house at 401 Marshall Avenue South and their children attended Litchfield schools. Their son, Van Artis, called "Tonk" or "Art", wasn't allowed to participate in sports, but he was the mascot for the Class of 1900's State championship football team. That team, which included A. W. Robertson whom went on to star for the Gophers, outscored their opponents that season 361 to 6. I will get some arguments about Art participating in Litchfield High sports, but a picture I found of the championship team clearly shows him sitting on the floor in a different outfit from the team's striped uniform and the rest of the team is either standing or sitting on chairs.

The 1900 team with "Tonk" Van Spence.

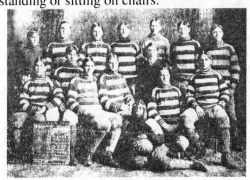

178

Van must have had family in Savannah, Georgia because in November of 1883, twenty-seven years after he had left the south, he took his family there for a visit. When the old lamplighter "retired" in 1904, he moved to Minneapolis where he shined shoes in a barbershop until he died. His body was brought back to Litchfield and, for some reason, was buried in an unmarked grave in a Ripley Cemetery plot that he had bought for his wife, daughters Ory May, Eva Van, Zula Viola, and son Frank Daggett Henry Spence. "Doc" J. H. Bacon, a fellow GAR member who had been wounded at the Battle of Bull Run, wrote a poem, which he read at the graveside. It contained a very politically incorrect verse: "'Tho born a slave and black his skin, he was always welcome, for he was white within." In the winter of 1968, a group in town petitioned the Army and finally, in April of 1969, Van got a proper marker for his grave.

Surely, Van Spence was treated well by the people of Litchfield. After all, he stay here most of his life. All accounts of him in the newspapers are of a positive nature. Maybe the fact that he had fought in the war for the north had something to do with it. But, there was another black in town besides Van, his wife and his kids. She was known as "Black Jenny" or "Aunt Jenny" and she was treated with less respect.

Black Jenny was Jenny Gardner and she was originally a housemaid for the Harmon Pennoyer family in Greenleaf. They had vacationed in the south in October of 1886 and convinced Jenny to come back up north to work for them. Farm kids around the area had never seen a black woman, and Jenny was very black, so they would go out of their way to go by the Pennoyer place and peek in on her working in the house. She'd see them and say, "Run along, you chiluns."

When Black Jenny moved to Litchfield, she lived over the laundry in the Snell building on Second Street East, where she worked. Kids in town used to taunt her and call her names, especially the ruffians who hung around the livery stable across the street from the laundry. When they came around, she'd shush them away with "You git!" and swipe at them with her broom or laundry stick. Jenny body is buried in Van Spence's plot at the cemetery, although they were not related.

Several times over the years, stories popped up in the local newspapers about cross burnings in Litchfield. I don't know whom they were burning crosses against, although the Germans and the Catholics have been mentioned. I believe that some of the times it was just a juvenile prank. In December of 1923, however, a five-foot high cross was burned at the eastern corner of the "railroad park", which would put the location across from where Burger King is today. The purpose of the burning was to celebrate the induction of the one-hundredth member into Litchfield's chapter of the KKK.

In November of 1925, a cross was burned on the lawn between Reverend M. O. Silseth's and lawyer Nelson D. March's houses on Sibley Avenue South, only a block and a half from the railroad tracks. One August evening in 1926, six white robed and hooded men entered the Church of Christ during the service and marched down the aisle to Reverend J. W. Umphres, who was a visiting revival evangelist. They handed him what looked to be a purse, then turned and left. Then in 1927, a burning cross appeared on the lawn by the Catholic Church. During the town's controversy over the sight of the new high school, W. W. Shelp's house was singled out for a burning cross on December 6, 1929. During the Christmas holidays in 1937, a flag with a swastika appeared on the flagpole at the new high school and, in April of 1940, one showed up out by the Bye-Way café and bar.

As late as in 1964, the Lenhardt Hotel was given orders by the government to remove some signs on the doors of the restrooms in the basement. The signs are now in the Meeker County Historical Society Museum. One states "COLORED WOMEN" and the other states "WHITE WOMEN". A woman, who was a waitress at the hotel in 1962, said that the White Women sign was not usually visible to a person going down the stairs to the ladies' room because the door was usually left open after the room had been used. So travelers stopping at the hotel to use the restroom would sometimes only see the Colored Women sign. The help at the hotel generally used the Colored restroom because they knew it would be cleaner. It got less use, you see.

The actual signs from the hotel basement restrooms.

Similar signs were displayed in the train depot. The telegraph operator there told my brother Dennie that there was a big "to do" one time when a black porter got off the train and used the wrong restroom.

He had "forgotten" that he wasn't supposed to use it. He was told not to use it the next time he was in Litchfield.

A reliable source, who worked at the hotel, told me that blacks, Indians and Mexicans who came in on the bus were asked to sit at the counter and not go into the main dining room. There usually weren't any rooms found for black people at the hotel either, but if one was, you could be sure that it was up in the hot top level. There were no elevators at the hotel nor was there air-conditioning except in the dining room and lobby. My mother told me about a black veterinarian, who had reddish hair and freckles by the way, who worked with her briefly at the Produce. He was a Federal Meat Inspector. Turkeys were prone to have a disease called Coccidiosis and he was there to guard against it. He told Mom that he was turned down at both the hotel and the motel in town and he had to find a place to live out of town. When I mentioned that fact in Willard Erickson's history class in high school, when we were studying racial prejudice, both Mr. Erickson and the class laughed at me. Mr. Erickson told me that I was making the story up and I slithered down in my seat, wishing I had kept my mouth shut. As you can see, my hometown wasn't perfect.

Chapter Fourteen
Our Garage and Rock and Roll

Back on Sibley Avenue, the first store at the southwest corner of the intersection was Jacks' Ben Franklin[81], which was owned by James Carlton "J. C." Jacks. Litchfield's location was the second Ben Franklin store franchised in the United States. J. C. died and his son Paul took over. After Paul died, his wife Gladys ran the store. She was there when I was a kid and is still living. I never went in the store very much. Eventually Gladys fixed up a large place above the store for herself over the addition she had added on to the back of the store.

Looking south down Sibley Avenue in the mid-fifties. On the left is Penny's and, on the right, Johnson's Drug Store follows Jacks' Ben Franklin.

Next door south of Jack's was Johnson's Drug Store[82]. It was one of my favorite places in Litchfield to kill time. Entering Johnson's Drug, I saw the normal things you'd see in a drug store to the left of the store. But to the right, by the front window, were the magazine racks. I could hide over there with my friends and read the latest *Superman*, *Batman* or *Mad Magazine* comic books. Sometimes one of us would bravely pick up a *Popular Photography* magazine and quickly riffle through it, hoping to find the standard black and white picture of a nude female. We'd hold the picture up for the others to see and we'd all snicker. It seemed that each issue had one such "artistic photograph".

Invariably store clerk Margie Olson would come over and kick us out saying, "This isn't a library, you know!" We'd leave for a few minutes and then be right back in the store at it again. To the right rear of the store was the pharmacy where Ray Johnson dispensed his medicines and to the left rear was the soda fountain.

---

[81] 239-241 Sibley Avenue North. See page 403 of the History of Downtown Litchfield Appendix.

[82] 237 Sibley Avenue North. See page 406 of the History of Downtown Litchfield Appendix.

The soda fountain was a long red linoleum topped counter with about six red covered padded metal stools in a row to the north of it. The "soda jerk" or waitress[83] could make you sundaes, malted milks, ice cream cones and phosphates. A phosphate was a soda. You'd order a Coke, for example, and she'd put a paper cone cup into a metal holder, go to a row of metal pumps, and pump two squirts of Coke syrup into the cup. Then she'd go to a carbonated water or phosphate dispenser and finish the drink. It cost a nickel and you could order any combination of drink you wanted, cherry Coke, root beer Coke, a cherry root beer, an orange root beer or whatever you could think up and care to try.

My favorite phosphate was a "Suicide". I liked the Suicide because I got more syrup for my nickel. For a Suicide, the waitress went down the line and put one squirt of each of the dozen or so flavors into the cup and then added the phosphate. The result was a heavier, syrupy, sweet concoction that was similar to a Dr. Pepper. I was told that drinking the syrup without the phosphate made a great diarrhea elixir. I never had to find out if that was true. The soda counter was a meeting place for teens after school for many years until Ray removed it in 1960.

Inside Johnson's Drug. On the left is the soda fountain counter.

I was standing in the drug store one summer day reading comic books when a bunch of my friends came running in. I looked up to see what the commotion was all about. The resulting story necessitates telling you about our garage.

My three brothers and I were the envy of every kid in town. We were poor by most standards, but every kid in town envied us our garage. The thirty-two foot long garage was a two-car affair, which was very rare

[83] The waitresses were Cheryl Caswell or Elaine Housman in the early fifties and Margie Olson, Larraine Peterson, Roseanne McLaughton and still Elaine Housman in the mid-fifties.

for 1940, when it was built. Each eight-foot wide car section was a separate room with a wall between. There was a small plain wooden door between the two car sections. A large wooden door that pulled up was in the front of each section. Rectangular metal boxes full of sand in the rear of each section were the weights on a pulley that swung each door up.

The garage had an additional feature. It had a sixteen-foot wide section attached to the left of the car sections. It was built to be an office. The office had two windows, a front door and a plain wooden door in the wall between it and the middle car section. All three sections had a concrete floor. The office was nice enough that my Uncle Alan Shaw lived in it for a few months before he went into the Army in 1956. The Birkemeyers, who owned the house and garage before us, had operated their Birkemeyer Automatic Sales and Service out of the office.

The garage, as it looks today. It's the same except the wooden wall between the two car sections has been removed.

After my father left us, Mom got the house and garage in the divorce settlement, although very little had been paid on them. My mother didn't have a car or even drive so the garage sat idle. Uncle Alan stored his beat up car in there for a time. He was always fixing the thing and I remember "helping" him by handing him tools as he lay underneath it.   After Alan left, Dennie, being the oldest, took claim to the office section. It was his private place, "Den's Den". He had our old sofa in there, a fuzzy brown thing with big arms on the sides. Pat and I used to sit on the arms and pretend they were our horses when we played Cowboys and Indians in the house. Dennie had some other furniture too, Dad's piano taken out of our house because no one could play it, lots of electronic parts for God knows what and an actual old pinball machine with the tilt ball removed so that you could rack up unbelievable scores.

184

Dennie was always building radios, amps or something else with those electronic things.

Dennie in front of the door to his part of the garage.

He nailed the inside wooden door shut so that we couldn't gain access to his section from the middle section. You had to come in through the front door and it locked with a real key. We weren't allowed in there. Dennie strung wires from the house to the garage. I think originally the wires were for a telegraph system, but later it was for a "private" phone. The phone was an old style wall one with the hand crank and the mouthpiece on the front and it worked. The phone company found out it was on the line because it took more ringing current than one phone was supposed to take. They called Mom and told her to disconnect it or pay for an extension. She and Dennie had a very short conversation about it and Dennie promised to disconnect it.

Before he could, Chief of Police George Fenner showed up at our house to retrieve the phone. Someone on the corn detasseling crew Dennie was working on had ratted on him and told a deputy that Dennie had found the phone in an old house on a farm where they had been detasseling. Ludvig Andreen and Dennie had seen the phone one day while eating their lunch on the porch of the old abandoned house. Even though the windows of the house were busted and there were holes in the walls, the owner noticed the phone missing and reported it. Mom was at work, but neighbor Alma Colmen told her that the police had been here talking to Dennie. Then it hit the fan.

Dennie started playing the guitar in his early teens. When he graduated from his acoustic guitar to an electric one, a blonde semi-hollow Kay K-161 ThinTwin ordered from the Spiegel catalog in February of 1958, he formed a band with Connie Olmstead called The Rockets, with the slogan "Rock with The Rockets." I don't know if you could call what they played "rock and roll", but it sure wasn't "old-time" like our Uncle Robert Rheaume played with Whoopee John.

Back row: Terry and Pat
Front row: Mick, Helen and Dennie, smokin' with his Kay guitar.

The members of Dennie's band were always changing and sometimes the band included some very odd instruments for rock and roll, such as Dick Blonigan's trombone. I remember Sherman Robb's drums. The bass drum was so big it almost hid him. There were no toms and his cymbal was no bigger than a dinner plate. Sometimes Dave Thompson played sax and Bob Peifer, Jr., whose dad was an assistant manager at the Produce and who married Darlene Oliver, sister to my first love, plunked away on the piano, when one was available. I don't remember them having a bass player.

Sherm Robb, Dick Blonigan, Dave Thompson and Dennie at the Community Building.

For the band's first "booking", they performed two songs at a March of Dimes Benefit Dance and Talent Show held at the Litchfield Armory in September of 1958. Later they changed the name to The Chancellors and Dennie painted "The Chancellors" on the door of his section of the garage. It stayed there long after he went into the Marine Corps in June of 1960.

"Dennie" didn't seem like the proper name for the leader of a band, so the Wimmer boys, who were always at our place, started calling him "Des". I don't know where they came up with the nickname, but Pat and I picked up on it and started calling him that too. I think Dennie kind of liked it, although he didn't admit it. Anyway, he never hit us when we called him that. When he did an early enlistment into the Marines, while still in high school, the Wimmers and Pat and I started calling him "Desico Marino".

It took a long time for rock and roll to get to Litchfield. Once it did, the Shaw boys grabbed hold of it and never let it go. We started seeing movies with rock and roll in them as early as late 1956, yet the half-dozen dance halls around us never had a rock dance for teens. Finally in September of 1957, the Silver Horseshoe[84] ballroom in Darwin, Minnesota ran a newspaper ad for a "Teen-agers Only" dance featuring Jerry Wheeler and His All Modern Band. This wasn't rock and roll, believe me, but it wasn't "oom pa pa" old-time either and the tidal wave was finally on the way. Jerry, of course, was the drummer I eventually replaced in my brother Mick's band.

On Tuesday, May 13, 1958 most of the youth in Litchfield were conned into thinking that a national touring band from Texas was real rock and roll. A dance, at the four-year-old Armory Building, sponsored by the Chamber of Commerce and WDGY radio, was attended by about four hundred of the town's young people, including the Shaw boys. We heard WDGY's "Brother" Bill Bennet introduce The Big Beats, who did instrumental renditions of *In The Mood*, *Sentimental Journey* and *Raunchy*. It was close enough to rock and roll for us, but still light years away from the Jerry Lee Lewis and Chuck Berry songs we were listening to on the radio.

---

[84] The Silver Horseshoe went the way of most ballrooms when times got hard. It burned down one night in November of 1960.

At the Big Beats' dance at the armory. Back row: With half a face is Sheldon Berquist, then Dick Osdoba, smiling at the camera is Dennis Shaw, with the glasses is Connie Olmstead, at his left front is Anita Woods. In the center rear is Jerry Wheeler.

The turnout was so great, that the band was brought back on June 12, 1958 along with The Crescendos. The big turnout also inspired someone to bring in a real rocker. On Saturday, July 19, 1958, one of the fathers of "bop", Gene Vincent and his Blue Caps, came to Litchfield. Gene Vincent was most noted for his songs *Be-Bop-A-Lula* and *Lotta Lovin'*. He performed with and was idolized by the Beatles in Liverpool. Now we were getting somewhere.

The Big Beats: Don McCord-guitar, C.W. Kendall-piano, Jerry Zapata-drums, Earl Slocumb-bass and Larry Pigg-sax.

The Big Beats returned to the area several times. They were at the Armory again on Saturday, August 23, 1958. The newspaper ad, giving the admission price as 90¢, stated "No Slacks, Blue Jeans, or Leather Jackets. Dress Right, Feel Right, Act Right." Ah, the old dress code. It carried well into the sixties. The Big Beats were in Willmar with Sonny James of *Young Love* fame on August 30, 1958. Over a thousand teenagers showed up at the National Guard Armory for the artists, who also signed autographs earlier that day at Margie's Record Shop in downtown Willmar. Five hundred people showed up there and Willmar Chief of Police R. H. McLane had to come to control the crowd. The area teens were starved for rock and roll.

The Litchfield Armory dances inspired Dennie and his partner, Connie Olmstead, to put on their own dance at the armory. A local DJ was hired to emcee and it went over well enough that they started to get a few jobs in some local ballrooms in the winter of 1958 and summer of 1959.

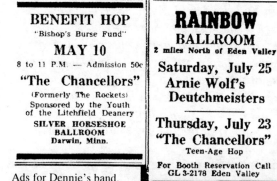

Ads for Dennie's band.

This is what the earliest days of rock and roll were like. The ballroom owners just didn't get it. They didn't understand the power the teens had to generate big money for them. They just kept having old time dances. So anyone who wanted to bring in "rock" groups, promoted the dances themselves in armories and town halls. The first time I saw a local ballroom bring in a legitimate rock performer was in October of 1958. The Playland Ballroom in Kimball brought in Dale Hawkins who had a hit called *Suzy Q*, which is now a rock standard. But those dances were few and far between. The next legitimate rock star that came around was Buddy Knox (*Party Doll*) in May of 1959 in Glencoe and Eddie Cochran (*Summertime Blues*) in Kimball in September of 1959. Small time "garage bands" like Mick's and my band, The Defiants, played most of their dance jobs in self-promoted venues. I think we played in every armory in southern Minnesota. And there is no place less suited for music than an armory that echoes so bad you can't understand what song is being played.

The Chancellors practiced in Dennie's section of the garage. Many times, when neighbors called to complain, Mom went out to the garage to plead with Dennie to "Please turn it down. I can't hear myself think!" After much yelling, Dennie would break into a Sonny James' song called *You're The Reason (I'm In Love)*. It seemed to magically shut Mom up and sometimes bring a tear to her eye, as did another song; *I Can't Help It (If I'm Still In Love With You)*. She would turn on her heels and head back to the house, beaten again. I told about those episodes in my song.

THE SONG GOES ON
The next thing I remember was my brother Dennie's band.
They practiced in the old shed and I was their biggest fan.
His guitar was from a catalog, and it was called a Kay.
He'd come right home from school and go up to his room to play.
He wrote some songs, we were impressed because they sounded fine.
The band just had a few jobs, but they practiced all the time.
Mom would yell, "Please turn it down. I can't hear myself think!"
Dennie would start singing this and Mom's heart just would sink...
[Go into *You're The Reason (I'm In Love)* by Marty Robbins.]

Mom seemed to lose control over us when we grew to her height. Dennie had long ago surpassed her in that area. His greasy pompadour hair-do, which was piled high on his head, culminating into a "duck-tail" both on the top of his head and in the back, added a few more inches to his six foot one inch height. Mick began to nose into Dennie's musical sessions. Mick didn't get shooed away as Pat and I did. We were content to play in the actual car sections or in the dirt behind the house with our toy cars and trucks.

There was an attic to the garage. On a hot summer day, Pat and I ventured to climb the wooden ladder, which was nailed to the side of one wall, and carefully step through the piles of old jukebox, pinball and slot machine parts. It was stifling hot up there and dark, so we didn't stay long. Each time we went up there, however, we found something new to play with or to intrigue us. I thought of it as a treasure hunt but we never found anything of real value. Dennie had long ago taken any of the remaining treasures out. He had found an actual working slot machine up in the attic. It suddenly disappeared when he unwisely told the Birkemeyer's son, Dick, about it.

Dick was a bit on the wild side. When he was nineteen, he shot himself in the right leg while trying a quick draw of his revolver out of his holster. He was hunting pheasants and rabbits with some friends.

Dennie also found a bag of slugs or tokens that were used in some machines in lieu of money. The slugs began popping up all over town and there was an editorial written by John Harmon in the *Independent Review* about the "low-lifes" who were ripping off town merchants using slugs. Lennart Holen, who ran the Sinclair Gas Station on Depot Street East, caught Dennie and his friends using them in the pop machine and they had to make restitution.

When Dennie left for the Marines, Mick took over the "good part" of the garage. Now his bands practiced out there and Mom had to tell him to quiet down. He didn't know the magic song to sing to her, so there was just a lot of yelling going on. But Mom still lost. Pat and I laid claim to the middle section of the garage and we went to work turning it into our clubhouse. I don't remember where we got things, but we had two beds, several chairs, a table, a radio, lamps and an old sofa. We even had an old television set, bought on Crazy Days for $2. But without a real antenna on the roof, we were lucky to get one snowy channel, Channel 7 from Alexandria. We found some old purple and green flowered wallpaper behind Baril's Paint Store uptown and we nailed and stapled it to the bare wooden walls. The large front garage door, which we nailed shut also, had one small rectangular window. The window opened in and could be propped up with a stick. Mom gave us an old curtain to put on the window. It was very "homey". It was our clubhouse and every kid in town wanted to join the "club".

Pat and I were allowed to sleep out in the garage one night. That one night turned into two and soon we were spending our entire summer nights out there. Before long we had a friend or two sleep over. It was the perfect setup. The friend would tell his parents that he was sleeping over at the Shaw's and that our mother would be home. The only thing they didn't tell was that we'd be in the garage and Mom would be in the house. We would sit and smoke and tell jokes until all hours of the night out in that garage clubhouse. Occasionally we did some juvenile things such as lighting farts or lighting each other. Someone had found out that you could squirt lighter fluid on your clothes or even on your bare arms, light it and not get burned, provided you patted the flames out in time. Dickey Whalen, one of our gang, would dare us to do some of those things for money. Ever since his mother remarried to businessman Harlan Quinn, Dickey always had money.

Another favorite "game" was to make our selves pass out by hyperventilating. We would bend over, grab our knees and take ten quick deep breaths. Then we stood up, closed our eyes and blew as hard as we could into our thumb, as if it were a whistle. The next thing we'd know, we'd be waking up on the ground or on the bed with everyone standing around us laughing.

"Gee! How long was I out?" we'd inquire. The answer of "Only a few seconds," was disappointing. It seemed much longer. You'd see the "white light" that people claim they see when they come back from a near-death experiences. You always had to do it with a partner. His job was to catch you as you passed out. A terrific bang on the head and the subsequent headache taught me that lesson when I woke up in somebody's flower garden one time.

As soon as it was dark and Mom was asleep, we would go on garden raids around town, looking for something to eat. Garden vegetables or apples from backyard trees were the usual menu items, but occasionally we found ground cherries or watermelons. Rarely did we do anything really "delinquent" or destructive. One Friday night in May of 1961, however, things got out of hand.

I can't remember who was involved that night but there were five of us and Pat wasn't along for some reason. It wasn't the usual crowd that stayed over in the garage. Anyway, we were walking the streets very late that night. We ended up by the vacant lot by the highway south of the high school. There was a single light on a wooden pole that illuminated the entire lot. The pole leaned toward the south at about a thirty-degree angle. Someone got the idea to "help" the pole go the additional one hundred and fifty degrees or in other words bring it down. We started pushing on the pole and swaying it back and forth when suddenly its wires touched some other wires on another pole, sparks flew and the lights for a few blocks all went out. We took off running across the highway to the railroad track, laughing that nervous "I'm afraid" laugh all the way.

Trudging east along the tracks, we kicked rocks and talked. Then we started picking up the rocks and throwing them at some of the old buildings along the tracks. When we got behind Schwartzwald Motors, one of the guys tossed a railroad rock at one of the old cars behind the building. Crash! He had broken a window. There was some laughter

192

and everyone grabbed rocks and started throwing...except for me. I wasn't a "goody two shoes" but I wasn't stupid. I knew this was not going to be good. Crash! Crash! I stepped in front of the gang and said, "Listen you guys. I'm going back to the garage. You're all gonna get in trouble for this."

"What's the matter, you big baby," someone said.

"Okay, whatever, but I'm leaving, and remember this...when you get caught, I wasn't with you tonight. Okay?"

"Okay, scaredy cat."

"Nice friends," I thought to myself as I left and walked home. Sure enough, they got caught and had to go to court. But the "honor among thieves" thing must be true. They never ratted on me. They, or their parents, had to come up with the money for the windows of three cars and one truck.

Most of the time, we just did innocent pranks. Four of us, this time Pat was included, went to Sid's Mobil gas station, now the Lehr Agency, on the corner of Fifth Street and Sibley Avenue one evening and, one by one, we went inside and asked to use the bathroom. In the small narrow bathroom, we closed the door and went to the water cup dispenser over the sink. The cups were small white paper cones. We grabbed as many cups as we could and stuffed them into our shirts and left. Meeting down the street, we headed for a quiet side street, such as Fifth or Sixth Street between Marshall and Holcombe Avenues. The street couldn't have too much traffic because we needed some time to set up our prank.

Scrambling out into the street, we made a perfect line from curb to curb with the cones turned upside-down. With the cup's points sticking straight up under the dim streetlights, it looked very odd and I'm sure dangerous to any car that came around the corner. We headed for cover in the bushes or behind trees and waited. Before long a car would come along and screech to a halt in front of our "barrier". Nobody ever got out of his or her car to check it out. They would just make a U-turn and head in a different direction. It was hard to muffle our laughter.

When a car full of teenage boys screeched to a stop in front of the barrier, some of us just lost it, snickering out loud. We were sure we had been heard, but the car also turned around and headed away. We quieted down our giggles and waited in the dark for our next victim. Suddenly I heard the thump, thump, thumping sound of feet running on the concrete sidewalk. I turned to see several large boys descending upon us. Pat and I took off running towards a house, while the other two boys scrambled in different directions. One got caught and I could hear his cries of pain as he was being pummeled. Pat and I never turned around to look. We scrambled up to the closest house's steps and began pounding on the door.

"Mom!" I yelled, improvising, "Mom…let us in!" Our pursuers stopped in their tracks, turned and left. When someone came to the door, we apologized and said that some big guys were chasing us. We were invited in but declined, knowing that the teenagers had left in their car. We weaved our way home that night from tree to tree and dark street to dark street. We usually stayed off the business streets of town anyway. Litchfield had a ten o'clock curfew, which was announced to all by a loud shrill whistle from the power plant a block from our house, and enforced by John Rogers driving around in the "prowl car".

Another prank was to defecate into a paper bag, put it on the steps of a house, light it on fire and ring the doorbell. We'd run and hide behind trees to watch our victim come out of the house, see the burning bag and stomp the fire out. Of course the feces in the bag splattered all over our victim's shoes.

In the fall, we'd pick out houses of very old people and go "Trick or Treating". The only problem was that it wasn't Halloween and we didn't have any costumes on. The old ladies would look surprised, say "Oh, okay. Just a minute then," and go find us a cookie or a piece of candy. The prank backfired one night when an old gentleman, Luther Nelson, at 423 Miller Avenue, asked us in while he looked for some candy for us. Then he calmly locked the door behind us. He started lecturing us and said, "I'm going to call my friend Chief Fenner on the phone." One of our gang took off running through his kitchen and out his back door, but after seeing that, the old man grabbed his cane and blocked our way out. We started crying and swearing we'd never do it again. He let us go after finishing his lecture. It turned out that he had been the Chief of Police[85], prior to George Fenner's predecessor, Fred Ross.

We stopped doing that prank and went on to safer ones, such as crank phone calls.

"Do you have Prince Albert in the can?" we'd ask a clerk at one of the drug stores. "You do? Then you'd better let him out."

"Is your refrigerator running, ma'am? It is? You'd better go catch it then."

---

[85] Luther Nelson had also been assistant fire chief from 1934 to 1937 and fire chief from 1937 to 1939.

"Good evening. This is the phone company and we're checking the phone lines in your area. Would you whistle into your phone for us?"

My favorite prank was to call a bar and ask for a fictitious Joe Smith. After a pause, we'd be told, "Nope, I checked. There's no one here by that name." After a minute or so, we'd call back and ask for Joe again. "Nope, he's not here," would be our answer. We'd wait a few minutes and a different kid would call and ask for Joe Smith. We did this over and over until we decided it was time for the kill. One of us would call the bar and say, "Hello. This is Joe Smith. Have there been any calls for me?" We would cry from laughing. Well, you had to be there. Phone pranks are a thing of the past. You can't do crank calls anymore because of caller ID.

You're probably wondering why I interrupted my story about Johnson's Drug Store to write about our garage. One of our overnight guests in our garage was a boy named Jeffrey B. I'm holding back his last name, as I don't know what happened to him and I'm covering my tracks. You'll meet Jeffrey in the next chapter.

Chapter Fifteen
The Fugitive and Smoking

We lived in a small world in Litchfield, Minnesota in the fifties, but it was a very different world from the one our parents lived in at the same time. As much as parents think they know their kids and what they're up to, they usually don't have a clue. Oh, they know the basics. They can sense a lie, they know if their kid is basically good, but if the kid really wants to hide something from them, they can. Mom was a good parent. She cared. She made sure we made it to church every Sunday. She tried to punish us for transgressions and teach us right from wrong, but she sometimes didn't know what was going on right under her nose. I'll elaborate by telling you about the garage gang.

Monk Schreifels, Dougy and Jerry Wimmer, and Dickey Whalen were the friends of ours who came over to our garage the most frequently. When I look back on it now, it was logical that they would be the ones to stay over. Monk came from a family of sixteen kids and he needed breathing room, our garage was better than Dougy and Jerry's bedroom, with four athletes crammed into that one room, and Dickey didn't get along with his new stepfather.

Dougy and Jerry were brothers from a family even poorer than ours. They lived in a very old house on the east side of Litchfield. Their father, Joseph A. "Joe" Wimmer, spent most of his time in the State Hospital in Willmar, coming home only occasionally for visits. He was a paranoid schizophrenic, prone to sudden attacks on his wife. He had another brother Louie, who lived in town and yet another brother named Leo, who had blown his wife away with a shotgun on the steps of a church in Minneapolis as she came out of Mass.

Jerry told us that his dad had been an auctioneer and it was probably true. We'd be over at their house when Joe was home and Jerry would say to him, "Hey, Joe. Auction off this rake for us." Joe would do it. He taught us tongue twisters and crazy rhymes that he used to exercise his auctioneering tongue. "Once a fella found a fella in a bag of beans. Said a fella, to a fella, 'Can a fella tell a fella what a fella means?' " and "Are you the guy that told the guy, that I'm the guy that sold the guy the bag of rotten peanuts?" I taught them to my children and to my students and who knows how far they'll keep going.

Jerry was a tremendous athlete and he would get a full athletic scholarship to Moorhead State College. He dropped out in his first year. Dougy had the thickest glasses I'd ever seen. He had an unusual talent.

He could throw up at will. We used to treat him to the cheap hamburgers at Janousek's and then have him throw up on the police car parked on Sibley Avenue or Third Street. Where did we get the money for the burgers? Dickey Whalen, of course.

Dougy Wimmer, Jim Bares and Andy "Monk" Schreifels.

Dickey was a short munchkin kind of kid with tiny little ears. He had physical problems. He never talked about them, so we didn't ask. It obviously had something to do with his joints because his fingers and legs seemed stiff all of the time. He walked stiff legged, he had trouble picking up things and his growth was stunted.

Dickey's divorced mother had recently married Harlan Quinn, a rich businessman in town. From that point on, Dickey had money, which he lavished on his friends. He told us that he raided his new stepfather's wallet nightly for twenty-dollar bills. Dickey would change the bills into coins so he could throw them into snow banks or down the street to watch us scramble for them. He treated us to meals at Fransein's Restaurant or at Janousek's. Eating out was a real treat for Pat and I. We had never eaten in a restaurant before Dickey Whalen came along.

We decided to go camping one day so we got another friend, Charlie Koelln, to drive us to the Army Surplus store in neighboring Hutchinson. Charlie graduated with me but he was older and had his license and a car. Dickey bought us camping supplies there. Mess kits, pup tents, sleeping bags, and machetes, you name it, and we bought it.

We trekked the six miles out to Lake Minnebelle[86], set up our tents and built a fire. Before we had a chance to cook ourselves our first meal,

---

[86] Legend has it that the lake was named after two young girls, Minnie and Belle, who fell through the ice and drowned in it. Over the years, the lake has been know by four different names: Minniebelle, Minnie Belle, Minne Belle and Minnebelle. Road signs, maps and history books have used all the different ways.

Dickey's mom showed up. She said she was worried about us staying outdoors overnight by ourselves.

"Wouldn't you rather stay at our lake cabin on Lake Manuela?" she asked. "I'd feel a lot better about you boys if you were there." That was like asking us if we wanted to stay at their expensive home by ourselves. The cabin was really a house, stocked with liquor and food. We jumped at the opportunity. I don't remember ever being asked back there again, though.

One day in the late seventies, I turned on my television in Glencoe, Minnesota and there was Dickey Whalen doing a commercial for Grain Belt beer. In the commercial, bartender Dick Whalen said, "When I left home for a while and then came back, the first thing I did after I got off the plane, was go get myself a nice cold Grain Belt." Sure, you did Dickey.

We had another friend named Jeffrey B. who had gone through St. Philip's School with us. Jeffrey was crazy. I mean really crazy. He had something wrong with his brain. In school, he was constantly in trouble. Outside of school he was always shoplifting things like candy bars or comic books. Jeffery would walk out of the Sward-Kemp drugstore with his yellow paper route bag stuffed with stolen candy. He took huge chances, so when we saw him in a store, we wouldn't stand by him. He'd just grab things, stuff them into our pockets and walk away from us laughing. We quickly learned to start avoiding Jeffrey.

June of 1958. First boy on the left: Dickey Whalen. In the center leaning over: Jeffrey B. Behind him is a Dollerschell boy and to the right of him is James Ouast. Pat's friend.

At St. Philip's School, we were expected to attend morning Mass before school every day. It wasn't required, but you knew you were expected to be there. Of course, it had the opposite effect on some of us than it was supposed to have. Church lost some of its mystique. You got bored easily.

198

Just like at the dances, boys sat in the pews on the right side of the church and girls on the left side. So on the right side of the church there was always more talking, fidgeting and giggling over passed notes, whispered jokes and elbow nudges. Because of this behavior, the school's principal, Sister Margaret Claire, started sitting in the first pew on the right side near the middle aisle. We started drifting slowly back to the second or third pew, but quieted down, nevertheless.

I was sitting in the pew one school morning, relieved to finally be off my knees, trying to stay focused on the Mass. I was in the second pew on the aisle, right behind Sister Margaret Claire. I heard some snickering behind me, but paid it no mind, as it had become as common as mosquitoes in Minnesota in the summer. Out of the corner of my eye, I saw a movement coming down the pew towards me, like falling dominoes. Finally I felt an elbow nudge me in my side. I turned to the boy sitting next to me and he jerked his smirking head over his left shoulder, meaning, "Look back to the third pew."

I looked over my right shoulder towards the middle of the pew and I couldn't believe what I saw. Jeffrey was jacking off! He had his thing out in church, right in front of the boys on either side of him, right in front of God! If ever there was going to be a bolt of lightning crashing through the ceiling, it was going to be now. We all would get fried right along with Jeffrey. The hair stood up on the back of my neck. Jeffrey suddenly stopped and put his "toy" back into his pants. I turned around to see that Father Foley was heading for the pulpit. Saved by the sermon. Thank you God.

I left you in Johnson's Drug Store several pages back. I was standing by the magazine rack there reading comic books when I heard a racket as a group of boys came running in, laughing and talking. I looked up to see the Wimmers, Pat, Monk and Jeffrey. Jeffrey was on a mission to steal some M & M candies. He quickly accomplished his task and the group left, giggling. I followed them outside and around the corner by Jacks' Store where we always parked our bikes. Jeffrey took out an old empty prescription bottle from his pocket and poured some of the candies into it. With a shout of "Okay! Let's go!", Jeffrey led us back on Sibley Avenue to McGowans' Millinery[87]. I had no idea what was going on.

---

[87] McGowan was always spelled "McGowin" in the newspaper ads and articles until Mary McGowin died in May of 1920. Then Mary's sisters, Sadie and Lizzie, took over

The Millinery was south of Johnson's Drug, after the Red Owl store. Mary McGowin came to Litchfield from Ireland and started her own dressmaking store with a Miss Kennedy in 1885. Kennedy left shortly and Mary brought in her two sisters, Lizzie and Sadie, starting the McGowin Millinery. When Mary died in 1920, the sisters took over. Elizabeth or "Lizzie" had been a teacher for fifteen years and the Meeker County Superintendent of Schools and Sadie had taught in Salt Lake City, Utah. Lizzie was born in 1870 so when we were around in 1958, she was already eighty-eight years old. Both of them were spinsters and ancient, as far as we were concerned.

Left to right: Sadie McGowan, a customer, and Lizzie McGowan in the thirties.

Their store had women's clothing and tons of hats, but everything looked like it was from the twenties. The ladies were known to wear the goods to church and then put them back on the shelves for sale. We rarely saw a customer in there. We should have stuck out like sore thumbs because the millinery, by definition, was a women's clothing store, specifically hats. But we went in occasionally to talk to the old ladies and just look around at the odd looking goods.

The old spinsters lived in the back of the store through a curtained doorway. They had given up their house on Third Street across from the park swings. People would see them walking down Sibley Avenue early in the morning with coats on over their nightgowns, which hung out from under the coats, and the store's hats, with the price tag still on them, on their heads. They would go to Janousek's Café to buy some fresh milk for cooking. When we'd pop into the store in the afternoon, we could smell what they were cooking for supper. If it was something pungent, like sauerkraut, the entire store reeked of it and I'm sure the clothing in there took on the smell.

---

the business and started using "McGowan" in their store ads. See page 411 of the History of Downtown Litchfield Appendix.

Girls used to go into McGowans' during their lunch break from school and try on hats. Sadie and Lizzie would get excited, thinking they had a sale and then the girls would say, "You know, we'd better think about it. We'll be back tomorrow." Then they would leave to giggle down the street while the old ladies put the hats back on the wood head forms.

We walked into the store and, standing by the counter, I said "Hi," to Sadie who was on the other side. Lizzie was "helping" her customers, my pals. Lizzie couldn't see much anymore. Jeffrey left the group and walked over by Sadie and me.

"Excuse me, lady," he said, "Can you tell me what time it is?"

"Yes," she said looking at her tiny pocket watch. "It's a quarter past four."

"Okay...oh, no!" Jeffrey said, pretending he had just remembered something while he pulled the prescription bottle out of his pocket. "I have to take my medicine! Can I have a glass of water please?"

"All right. Just a minute." Sadie shuffled off to the store's back living quarters for a glass of water.

Lizzie was still occupied with the guys who were asking her all kinds of dumb questions about a hat. Jeffrey quickly and calmly stepped behind the counter and opened a drawer that he apparently knew contained the store's cash. Flipping open a King Edward cigar box, he stuffed some coins and several bills into his pocket. He scrambled back around the counter to stand next to a stunned open-mouthed me.

"You're nuts!" I whispered. "I'm leaving."

I left the store, not wanting to be involved. How was I going to tell this in Confession next Saturday? A few minutes later, all of the boys came out of the store and headed quickly for the bandstand in Central Park. I ran to catch up with them. The money was split up, but I didn't take any. I found out that Jeffrey had pulled this stunt at least once before. Why the McGowans had never caught on, I don't know.

One unusually hot day, in May of 1960, we were over at Jeffrey's house on Marshall Avenue North. We were outside on the lawn, fooling around with the garden hose, spraying each other and running around laughing. Monk took hold of the hose and started spraying Jeffrey. Jeffrey could dish it out, but he couldn't take it. Swearing at Monk, he ran into the house. Suddenly, he appeared at the open window of his living room and started taunting Monk. Monk casually turned and sprayed at Jeffrey, getting water inside the house.

Jeffrey ran away from the window but Monk just kept spraying. We were really laughing now. Jeffrey returned to the window with a pistol. A real gun! Our jaws must have dropped all at the same time in unison with Monk's water hose. We all froze in place staring at the gun. It got very quiet. Jeffrey calmly raised his arm, aimed the pistol in Monk's direction and fired a bullet over his head.

Monk turned and ran. We looked in shock at Jeffrey as he left the window. We thought he was going to come out after the rest of us. Somebody yelled, "I'm outta here!" and we scrambled. We knew Jeffrey was crazy but this took things to a whole new level. We ran down the middle of the street as fast as we could, not daring to turn around and look to see if we were being pursued or not.

Not much more came of the incident. We didn't talk about it nor did we pal around with Jeffrey anymore. He kept getting into trouble in school and it only seemed to get worse. Then one day we noticed his absence from school and word spread that his parents were moving him to Minneapolis. They were going to put him into a special school. We thought that was the end of Jeffrey.

A group of us were in the garage smoking and telling jokes one summer vacation evening. A couple of the guys were sleeping over as usual. There was a knock on the door. I stood up and asked, "Who's there?"

"Me," came back the answer.

"Me who?" I said, as I unlatched the door and swung it open. There stood Jeffrey. "Jeffrey! What the hell are you doing here? Did you move back to Litchfield?" we all asked at once.

"I ran away," Jeffrey said, nonchalantly, shrugging his shoulders as he entered our clubhouse. He sat on the corner of a bed and told us about the special school or "prison" that he was forced to attend.

"Did you really run away?" I asked. "How'd you get here?"

"I hitchhiked. Listen you guys. Can I stay here for a while?"

"Are you crazy? What about your parents?"

"Just let me stay here for a while, okay? They'll never find me here."

I don't know why, but we relented. Thus began our strange summer of hiding out a fugitive. Mom never questioned Jeffrey's being there. There were always kids hanging around the garage. We slept out in the garage every night anyway, so that was no problem. If Mom checked up on us, which she did every night at about nine o'clock, we just hid Jeffrey under a bed. As far as food goes, we sneaked peanut butter and jelly sandwiches to him out of the house. Dickey provided money for store bought treats. I don't remember how long we hid Jeffrey, but it seemed like weeks.

One night we were sitting around in the garage, listening to KDWB ("Channel 63, that's easy to remember.") on the radio, smoking and joking around. About midnight, Jeffrey said, "I'm hungry. Is there anything to eat?"

"No, and we're not going into the house, 'cause we'll wake up Mom." I said.

"Well, I'm hungry. I'm gonna go get a hamburger," Jeffrey said, as he rose up from his seat.

"Where the hell you gonna get a hamburger now?" someone asked.

"At the Shell Café on Highway 12."

"And how are you gonna get way out there?" I pointed out, because it was a good mile away.

"Gonna walk. Anybody goin' with?"

"You're nuts, Jeffrey," Pat said for the rest of us. "No way."

"Well, I'm goin'." Jeffrey left disappearing into the dark night. We lay on the beds talking in the dark garage until we all finally fell asleep.

When we woke up in the morning, Jeffrey still hadn't returned. That was the last we ever saw of him. He never returned the next day either. Days went by and then weeks. We could only speculate that the police had picked him up as he walked along Highway 12 towards Bill Johnson's Shell truck stop. There was that ten o'clock curfew, you know. Whatever happened to him, he must not have told on us for hiding him out. Nobody ever asked us a thing about him. I've often wondered if he's sitting in prison somewhere today or if he turned his life around and is a successful businessman and father.

Dennie and Mick were already smoking by the time I reached the age of twelve. I decided that I should try it too. It looked cool and grown-up and everyone I looked up to, adults in my world and stars in the movies and on TV, was doing it. It wasn't long before my friends and I were all hooked. Cigarettes weren't hard to come by in the fifties. If you had the money, you could always find somebody to buy them for you. A lot of the store clerks didn't care about your age either.

"I'm supposed to buy a package of Kent cigarettes for my mother, sir," I'd lie. Or I'd write a note for Pat that said, "Please give my son a package of Pall Malls. Thank you, Mrs. Shaw."

Pat and I seldom had the money to buy cigarettes though. We came up with a clever idea. Pooling our money, we purchased a cigarette-rolling machine for a dollar from Abe's pool hall, which was a few blocks from our house. Then we bought a package of cigarette papers for a nickel and a small blue tin of Bugler tobacco for twenty cents. We were in business. We began rolling our own cigarettes. It worked but the cigarettes always came out in different sizes and were unfiltered. I had ultra thin cigarettes long before Virginia Slims was even thought of. Plain tobacco cost money too so I made as many cigarettes as I could from the small slim tin.

The Bugler cigarette rolling machine and cigarette case.

When we didn't have the money to purchase even a tin of tobacco, we took to picking up discarded butts on the ground or in ashtrays. We had tried leaves from the yard but the smoke was hot and choked us. You could find the longest cigarette butts sticking out of the white sand filled ashtrays in the air-conditioned entrance lobby of the Hollywood Theater. We would tear off the paper and recycle the remaining tobacco. I tried rolling my own filter cigarettes using filters off discarded butts. By the time I was done smoking my "new" cigarette, the yellowish filter I had found would be an ugly brown.   Soon we were able to impress each other by blowing smoke rings or "French inhaling". We were cool and just like the adults.

Smokin' at 13 in Central Park.

204

With the acquisition of paper routes, we soon had the money to purchase "store-bought" cigarettes or "tailor-mades". Everyone had his own special brand. At first my brand was Wings, because they cost the least, seventeen cents a pack, but I settled on Kent and Pat smoked Pall Malls. They cost a quarter a pack. When our older brothers weren't around to buy cigarettes for us or told us to "Get lost, creep!", we found Skeeter Anderson or Roy Peipus to buy them for us.

We all had hiding places to keep the cigarettes in school. During the winter you could leave them in the pocket of your parka, but during the warmer days, when we had no jackets along, some of us would keep them inside the ankle of our sock. I kept mine in the front of my underwear. It served the dual purpose of also insuring that no one bummed a cigarette from me.

There was the usual collection of bicycles on our driveway in front of our garage late one summer afternoon. Inside the clubhouse were several of our friends and Roy Peipus, who had just returned from uptown with our cigarettes. There must have been six of us in there puffing away and we forgot about the time. Mom came home from work and saw smoke billowing out of the small garage door window. Suddenly there was knocking on the locked side door.

"What's going on in there? Why is this door locked?" she asked loudly.

"Nothing Mom. I'll open up," I said, as everyone, except Roy, scrambled to douse his cigarette.

"Who's smoking in there?" she yelled, as I did a final glance around the room and reached to undo the hook on the door.

"Just Roy, Mom," I lied, as I opened the door. She walked in waving her hands in the bluish gray air in front of her face.

"I think you should leave," she said to Roy. "You're much too old to be hanging around my kids. And the rest of you," she added, as she turned to face the crowd, "should go home to your parents. I should call up each and every one of them and tell them what you're doing over here."

As everyone got up to leave, Mom noticed Gary Young. Gary was a couple of years younger than the rest of us but he looked only about eight. He was very little for his age.

"And who do you belong to?" Mom asked Gary as she reached out her hand to grab his shoulder, stopping him from leaving.

"Floyd Young," the small boy replied.

"Well, you'd better get home to Mr. Floyd Young right this minute."

Pat and I ran around with Floyd's son Gary sometimes, Mick was a friend of Gary's brother Duane and Dennie hunted and fished with "Snooky" or Floyd Young, Jr., another of Gary's brothers. To top it all off, Mom would meet their dad, Floyd Young, Sr., in a couple more years and eventually marry him in 1961. It's a small world when you live in a small town.

Floyd and Helen Young.

When Gary became my stepbrother, he filled the musical void left by Dennie's departure. Gary played guitar also and it wasn't long before he got involved in a band and they started practicing in the garage too. Mom must've wondered when it would all end. In August of 1964, Mick and I promoted a "battle of the bands" at the armory with our band The Defiants playing along with Gary's band The LeSabres, who had Marv Stewart on the drums.

As we grew older, our interest in the garage clubhouse diminished. The rock and roll bands still practiced in the office part. Mom married Floyd and he needed the two car sections for his car and a boat. But, for a time in the mid-to-late fifties, every boy in town envied the Shaw boys because of our garage.

Chapter Sixteen
Groceries, TV, Longfellow, and Barbers

South of Johnson's Drug Store was the Thomas Furniture Mart, once called the Litchfield Furniture Mart.[88] For most of the early fifties, I remember this building having the Red Owl store. It was one of Mom's favorite places to shop, probably because it was the closest to our house.

There were several grocery stores in town. Some were the larger ones like the Super Valu, the Red Owl, Nordlie's IGA, Bernie's Fairway, Cox's Market, or the Red & White store out of town on east Highway 12. But many were small neighborhood stores in the front part of people's homes. They were sprinkled throughout the residential areas of town like Jackman's Grocery at 204 West Fifth Street, Wallace and Blanche Damhof's Park Grocery[89] at 431 East Fifth Street, Pankake's[90] at 502 South Litchfield Avenue, Schager's at 607 and 609 East South Street at different times, Don Jacobsen's Don' Northside Grocery[91], and Batterberry's across from the library.

I was told that the reason we had so many small groceries in town was because of the Seventh Day Adventists, whose church was a block and a half from our house on Miller Avenue. The church had stood where Washington High School went. The high school became the junior high. The church was moved to its present location when the school bought the lot. When we were little kids, we'd hear the Seventh Day Adventists praying on Saturday afternoons in the small church and we thought they were strange like "Holy Rollers" or something. We didn't know. Because they worshiped on Saturday, Sunday was a regular workday for them. However, no grocery stores were open on Sundays for them to shop at, so a family started up one in the front of their house. It was so successful that many others started up.

In an emergency, Mom would ask one of us to bike down to Jackman's Grocery over by Lincoln Park, which was three blocks from us. Lincoln Park was basically a big empty city block lot where the

---

[88] 231 Sibley Avenue North. See page 409 of the History of Downtown Litchfield Appendix.

[89] George Ley moved to this address in August of 1946 and sold the business to Wallace and Blanche Damhof in September of 1951. In July of 1962, the Damhofs sold to Mrs. Helen Wigen, who became Helen Mattson and sold the store to John Carlson in April of 1969.

[90] It became Jeppesen's Grocery in March of 56 when L. P. Jeppesen bought it.

[91] It became Tom Breen's Grocery. In the forties Milton K. Langren had a store in his house on West Weisel Street and R. C. Thurber had one at 818 Marshall Avenue North.

Lincoln School [92]had been. Today Lincoln Apartments are there at 122 Fourth Street West. We called Jackman's "the little store". Ellen Jackman and her sister, both retired schoolteachers, owned it.

The old Lincoln School.

On Fridays, shopping night, Mom frequented all of the uptown grocery stores, going wherever the specials were. She would clip and save coupons all week. I was usually asked to go shopping with her. I'd get the red wagon and off we'd go walking uptown. Because we didn't have a car and Mom didn't drive anyway, we'd pull that wagon all over town, with Mom's shopping list in hand, just to save a penny or two on each item. Unfortunately, we had just missed the era of the home delivery. Silverberg's Fairway, Sam's Meat Market and Cox's Market had done home delivery at no extra charge. What a help that would've been for Mom. Cox's had very unique collapsible wooden boxes that they delivered their goods in.

Mom bought the most either at the Red Owl or the Fairway store until the Kohlhoffs built their new modern Super Valu[93] store over by Becker Shoes on Marshall Avenue North. The new Super Valu, which opened in December of 1954, had Litchfield's first automatic doors and it took some doing for some of the older people to get used to them. More than one old person went flying out into the parking lot when they went to push the door open and it swung away from their outstretched arms. I think the Kohlhoffs had to do something to slow the door's swing down.

---

[92] Lincoln school was built in 1890 and was used until the 1930s. It sat vacant for a while and then, in the 1930s and '40s, it was used as offices for several federal agencies, such as a recruiting office, the Farm Home Administration, a relief agency and the rationing headquarters. It was torn down in November of 1953 through March of 1954. Kitty-corner from Lincoln, in the house where ex-chief of police Luther Nelson lived, had been a boarding house in the twenties run by the Edblom family.

[93] 216 Marshall Avenue. See page 539 of the History of Downtown Litchfield Appendix.

The checkout ladies at the Red Owl would let Mom use coupons even though she didn't buy the items. One of the first stops in the Red Owl was to the right rear of the small store where the butcher counter was. I'd smell the meat in the display case and the sawdust on the floor behind the counter as we approached it. Mom would buy a ring of bologna and several pounds of hamburger from Butch Swenson. He'd wrap the meat in white paper right on the scale. Then Mom would ask Butch to "Give my boy a treat, won't you?" He'd reach into the glassed display case, grab a raw wiener and hand it to me. We kids used to go there also to get butcher paper to do murals on for school projects. They never charged us. Butch later went into partnership in the Nordlie market.

One checkout lady at the Red Owl had a son in my kindergarten class at the castle-like nunnery across the street from St. Philip's Church. He and I were picked to sing a duet of *O Little Town of Bethlehem* at the kindergarten Christmas concert. We rehearsed and rehearsed and on a bright December Sunday afternoon, on a platform in the church basement, I made my stage debut. The class finished singing *Joy To The World* and my partner and I stepped off the rear risers to the front of the stage. Some lady started our song on the piano and, with sweaty palms and shaking knees, we began to sing. The other kid started singing *Hark, the Herald Angels Sing!* Stunned, I stopped singing *O Little Town*, the correct song, and looked at him with my mouth hanging open. He didn't stop singing his song. I didn't know what to do. Frantically, I searched the audience with my eyes for our teacher. I found her sitting in the front row of chairs.

"Sister, he's singing the wrong song!" I yelled to her after I had found her. The audience roared in laughter and the idiot just kept singing "Glory to the newborn king..." even though the accompanist had stopped playing *O Little Town*. I turned red and stepped back into my place on the risers with the class, wanting to crawl under the stage instead. My partner just shrugged his shoulders and stepped back to his place, oblivious to the fact that he had just screwed up my stage debut! I never spoke to him again and I have obliterated his name from my memory banks.

After grocery shopping, Mom and I would pull the wagon back home. While she put away the groceries, my job was to squeeze the oleo. The dairy lobby in Minnesota had the politicians pass a law that outlawed oleo in the state if it looked like butter. So we bought Blue Bonnet margarine. It came in a yellow rectangular box that had cutouts of Howdy Doody characters on the back. Inside the box was a two-pound plastic "yellow quick bag" of off-white oleo. In the center of one side of the bag was a red-orange dye capsule. I squeezed the capsule until it popped inside the bag and kneaded the oleo until all of it was yellow. Mom would cut off a corner of the bag and squeeze every drop of that oleo out into an old Cool Whip container.

An ad for Blue Bonnet margarine.

Before we'd sit down to watch television, Mom would pull out the old black skillet and make some popcorn. She'd stand at the stove shaking that old skillet back and forth until every kernel had popped. She was an artist at it. There was never a burnt kernel and very few "old maids". Mom loved popcorn and it was our treat every Friday and Saturday night while we watched *Lawrence Welk*, *Perry Como* and *Gunsmoke,* in exactly that order on Saturday nights, on our small-screen black and white Emerson television set. After the Dave Moore, Bud Kraehling and Hal Scott's news, *Sea Hunt* would come on.

Television was still in its infancy and a novelty more than the norm, although in June of 1935, there was a service shop in town called Glader-Wilson Radio and **TV**. I can't imagine that they repaired any televisions, as there weren't any in town. In August of 1948, there was an article in the newspaper telling the public that Berquist Electric had a new Motorola television in its store. The article said that the television "projects a clear image of the radio program" and predicted that someday it would be as common as radios in everybody's homes. Then in September of 1949, John Colberg of Bell-Colberg Home Supplies had a press release in the paper telling the public that he had a new TV in his home and people were invited, by appointment, to come and view "this new entertainment".

We got our first television in 1953, when I was in the third grade at Longfellow School. Before that, I would listen to *Arthur Godfrey, Gang*

Busters, and *The Lone Ranger* on the radio during the week and a kid's radio show called *The Teddy Bears' Picnic* on Saturday mornings. Mom told us about the new TV the night before we got it and I couldn't wait to get home from school the next day. I told all my friends, "We're getting a TV at our house!" I hardly impressed them though, as almost all of them already had televisions at home for a couple of years. But it was a big deal for me.

I got off the bus, ran into the house, and saw the television standing along the north wall of our living room. It felt like Christmas morning. The TV had a deep reddish brown mahogany cabinet about a yard high and eighteen inches wide with two brass lions' heads holding rings in their mouths on fake doors in the bottom half. The entire bottom half served absolutely no purpose, as the tiny speaker was right on the top of the cabinet. The top half of the cabinet contained a small twelve-inch black and white screen, with gold letters spelling EMERSON on a pull down door that concealed controls right under the screen.

Our Emerson TV with Sparky, Terry, Dennis (in the rear) and Pat Shaw.

Mom had bought the television for about $150 from her friend Ernie Aveldson, who sold Emersons out of his house at 426 Holcombe Avenue North. Ernie was an electrician in town. He took Dennie pheasant hunting a couple of times and was a nice man. He died suddenly at the age of forty-six in July of 1957.

On top of the television was a note, which read, "Don't touch until I'm home. Mom" Rats! She didn't get home until 5pm! When she finally got home, Pat and I started pestering her to turn it on.

"We're not turning that TV on until we've eaten supper and all of the dishes are washed and put away," Mom said. When Mick and Dennie ambled in, just in time to sit down to the table, they started in on her too. It did no good. We rushed through the meal and we were extra

211

helpful that night clearing the kitchen table and washing the dishes. Mom had also started insisting that we pray the Rosary every night while we did dishes. Our minds already wandered while repeating the *Hail, Marys* over and over, but this night the prayers didn't do us a bit of good as we mumbled our responses to Mom's lead as fast as we could.

Finally, a little before 7pm, we all gathered in the living room, jockeying for the best place on the sofa, which Mom had pulled to the center of the room facing the TV. The single easy chair off to the side had been declared hers. She turned off all of the lights, except for a special "TV lamp" sitting on top of the television. The 40W light bulb was in a red upside-down cone, which was perched on the middle of a little red settee, on which sat two miniature plaster Chinese people, a boy and a girl, dressed in red with gold trim. Mom had been told to have a TV lamp so that her children's eyes wouldn't get ruined watching television.

The big moment had arrived. Mom reached down and turned the volume knob to the right with a click. The small screen started to flicker. A small white dot in the center of the screen slowly grew as the picture tube warmed up. This was taking an eternity. Suddenly the dot jumped to fill the screen. We had a full screen of…nothing. Nothing but snow, accompanied by a roaring hiss from the tiny speaker. Mom turned the volume down and then, clunk, clunk, clunk, clunk…she turned the channel tuner dial, which had numbers from one to twelve on it, until she came to a stop at a channel that wasn't all snow. Somewhere on the snowy screen was the faint image of…*The Goodyear TV Playhouse*. An hour-long drama without any cowboys or police shooting at bad guys. We had waited for this?

"Mom, isn't there anything else on?" I pleaded. I had heard about the cowboy shows like *Gunsmoke*, the police dramas like *Dragnet*, the comedy shows like *I Love Lucy* and *The Jack Benny Show*. Clunk, clunk, clunk, clunk…she turned the dial.

"I'm sorry, boys. That's all I can find. Just this one channel comes in."

"Why didn't you buy a better TV?" Pat cried.

"It's not the TV, dope," Dennie said. He knew about these things. "It's the antenna. Mom, we need a better antenna."

"Well, we'll just have to do with this for now," she said. We sat through the drama, bored to tears.

Over the next few days we did everything we could to improve the reception, including moving the TV set closer to the window, but all we could get was a snowy WCCO channel 4, a clearer KSTP channel 5, a snowy KMSP channel 9, and a very snowy WTCN channel 11.

Mom called Ernie and he came over and went up on the roof. He yelled down, "Is it clearer yet?" over and over until Mom finally told him to hold it and said to us, "Well, that's the best we're gonna get it, I suppose." It didn't get much better until a few years later when the stations started building bigger transmitters. Litchfield was just too far away from the transmitting towers in the cities.

Television shows didn't come on until 6am. Before that, all you got was a test pattern. I never knew what in the world you were supposed to do with that test pattern. I suppose use it to adjust your contrast, brightness and vertical and horizontal hold knobs. Those were the four controls you had, besides the volume/on and off knob. We'd be watching a TV show and suddenly the picture would start twisting sideways. One of us would have to jump up, run to the set and delicately turn the appropriate knob until the picture straightened out.

"There...there...there...that's it...no, back the other way, you dummy...no...here let me do it."

"Now the picture's rolling...put it back the way it was."

Then, at midnight, everything went off after the National Anthem was played with a movie of jets flying superimposed over the front of the American flag.

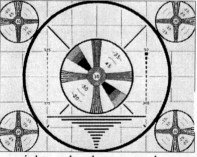

A typical test pattern.

I sat on the floor right up by the screen, because I couldn't see the television very well. I wouldn't be getting my glasses for two more years. Mom kept telling me to back up from the screen because I was going to ruin my eyes, but I would just inch forward back to where I had been. So I became the official knob turner. I became quite good at keeping a nice straight picture for my family. Plus I got to "surf" the channels after shows ended.

"There...leave that on."

"No, we ain't watchin' that junk."

"Mom…make him put it back to where it was."

There was a clever television show on Saturday mornings from 1953 until 1957. It was called *Winky Dink and You* and Jack Barry hosted it. There were lots of cartoon TV shows on the air in the fifties and they all had the same format. A host wore a costume, such as a cowboy suit, a spaceman suit, or railroad engineer outfit, like local celebrity Casey Jones, and the guy would perform skits and introduce cartoons. What was different about the Winky Dink show, which featured the adventures of Winky Dink, a star-headed cartoon boy, and his dog Woofer, was that Jack Barry wore a plain suit, and the show was interactive. For 50¢, I was able to send away for a light green plastic Winky Dink screen and "magic" black crayon. When I put the Winky Dink screen on our TV screen and wiped it with a cloth, it "magically" stuck.

Jack Barry, Winky Dink, and kids drawing on their Winky Dink screen on the TV.

Winky Dink would get himself into jams in the cartoons and end up being chased by some villain. Suddenly he would find himself at the edge of a cliff in front of a canyon. The cartoon would freeze and Jack Barry's voice would give us instructions. "Quick kids, connect the dots and draw a bridge for Winky Dink."

I'd grab my magic crayon, draw the bridge, Winky Dink would run across it, I'd erase the bridge, as instructed by Barry, and the villain would be foiled again. I saved Winky Dink's life many times. At the end of each segment, we were instructed to trace parts of letters at the bottom of the screen so that we could eventually complete and read a secret message at the end of the show. Dennie, whom Mom had entrusted to watch us while she worked at the Produce, would yell at me to give Pat a turn, but I had bought the screen with my own hard-earned money and I wasn't sharing. I guess *Winky Dink and You* was the world's first interactive video game.

Later Mom bought a similar screen somewhere after she believed an ad that it would magically turn our black and white TV into a color TV. Mom's screen had three colors that blended slowly into each other. The top third was blue, like the sky, and the bottom third was green, like grass. The middle third was red. It was perfect for watching programs that had scenes of sunburned people standing on someone's lawn on a sunny day.

I mentioned that I was going to school at Longfellow when we got our first television set. Longfellow, built in 1909, was in the center of the block between Weisel and St. Paul Streets on Sibley Avenue South. Most Litchfield students will remember Miss Hazle (that's how she spelled it) Walters as the principal and first grade teacher and Mrs. Esther Settergren as the second grade teacher. These two ladies were in the school system for a very long time. Mrs. Walters, a little old lady with white hair, who was in education for forty-six years, reminded me of Mrs. Rayburn, the principal on the old TV show *Leave It To Beaver*.

Longfellow School.

I went to Longfellow from second through fourth grades and so I only had Mrs. Settergren as a teacher. She taught for an amazing forty-two years. Dennie remembers her having a strong dislike for nail biters and a step-by-step method for curing them of the nasty habit.

Step One: Public humiliation. It was a warning loud enough for the entire floor of the school to hear. "Dennis! Stop biting your nails."

Step Two: Public humiliation and extra work. "Dennis, if you don't stop biting your nails, you will be staying after school tonight and you will write a report for me entitled, *Why I Should Not Bite My Nails*."

Step Three: Public humiliation and parental involvement. "Dennis, stop biting your nails and take this note home to your mother. Ask her to contact me about your problem."

Step Four: The Clincher. "Dennis, come up to the front of the classroom. Now, put your hands on my desk, palms up." Mrs.

Settergren would then take down a wooden pointer, which hung on the wall next to the world map, and she'd whack his palm with it. Then she removed a bottle of denatured alcohol from her desk and placed a sponge in a glass bowl. She would fill this with the alcohol and place a couple drops of red India ink in it.

"Dennis, stick your right hand in the bowl and squeeze the sponge. Now your other hand." Dennie said it burned like hell and the ink stained his nails.

"Hold your hands out in front of you, face the class and repeat ten times, 'I will not bite my nails, ever again'." Apparently, it worked because Dennie doesn't bite his nails anymore.

I remember absolutely nothing about my classes at Longfellow except for two things; the "art project" I did in one of the classes and the free vitamins. The project was a plaster of Paris impression of my hand, which I painted and Mom wondered what to do with. It looked like an ashtray, but Mom didn't smoke.

We went through a period where the teachers at Longfellow handed out awful tasting vitamin pills to us every afternoon when we came back from lunch. The pills were shaped like little brown footballs and I think they were mostly cod liver oil. Some kids had trouble swallowing them and would hide them in their pencil boxes or pockets. One little girl dropped her pencil box one day and a couple dozen little brown footballs rolled all over the floor. She had to pick each and every one up and then her mother was called in and she had to stand in Mrs. Walters' office and take them all. I'll bet she had to run to the bathroom several times that night.

One interesting thing about Longfellow school was the fire escape. It was a slide, which was inside a tube on the outside of the building. It was only used by the fourth, fifth and sixth grade students, who were upstairs, so only Dennie got to go down it on fire drills a couple of times. It was a traumatic experience for some of the younger kids. Dennie remembers a little girl named Holly Baker who was afraid to go down it. She peed all the way down and it made for a nasty, sticky slide for the kids that followed her.

During fire drills, two sixth grade boys were assigned to help their fellow students enter the chute. They stood on each side of the door to the slide. Occasionally, they had to give one of the students a little shove. Teachers were responsible for keeping order. In the fall, when it was still quite warm and humid, the janitors would sprinkle some kind of powder at the top so the kids would slide easier and girls' bare legs wouldn't stick to the metal slide.

Some kids found out how to go up the tube at night and get into the school. Dennie and a couple of his buddies tried to crawl up it, but they could never quite make it all the way up. It was pretty steep and slippery and you made a lot of noise as you were trying. Somebody told Mrs. Walters and she had Mr. Rude, the janitor, put a lock on the bottom door. All hell broke lose when the State Fire Marshal inspected the school and saw that the tube was locked. If a fire had broken out, the tube would've turned into a kid cooker. The tube was removed when the school was added on to.

In the background is the famous tube slide fire escape.

I do remember Longfellow's playground. There were all the usual things like the teeter-totter, monkey bars, swings, merry-go-round and uneven bars. But there was another piece of equipment that many people remember calling "The Giant". I called it the "May Pole" because of its appearance. A metal pole in cement held up a large circular metal "umbrella" from which hung chains with a large metal ring at the end of each. The whole thing went around so that you could grab a ring, run around in a circle as fast as you could and then lift your legs so that you swung out and around clipping any bystanders who weren't watching. And also, unfortunately, any unoccupied rings became lethal weapons both to the swingers and the watchers. Many a student ran into the building crying with a lump on his head.

The short period I went to Longfellow was the only time I rode the school bus. Catholics who went to St. Philip's weren't allowed to ride the school bus. I didn't think anything of it at the time but it bothers me now. Anyway, we didn't miss much. Bus riding wasn't, and probably still isn't, always a pleasant experience. There were the bullies and the teasing and the forgotten books and lunch bags. One day on the way to school, I was teasing some little girl with long pigtails. I thought she was cute and that's what you did with the girls you liked when you were little, you teased them. I did something, she did something back, and finally I did something she didn't like, like pulling her pigtails. She huffed and turned around. I laughed as loud as I could, with my head back and my eyes closed. She turned around and spit in to my mouth! I never closed my eyes in front of a girl I was teasing again. And I no longer thought she was very cute and desirable.

Under the Thomas Furniture Mart or the Red Owl was Mac E. Steen's Barbershop[94]. We never went there. Grandpa Bill Shaw cut our hair with a hand clipper, because Mom couldn't afford a regular barber haircut for us. Grandpa's clipper looked like the electric version except he squeezed the handles together like pruning shears. Apparently it needed sharpening because it always pulled our hair and we hated it.

When Grandpa stopped doing the haircuts, or we refused any more torture, we went to a house on Austin Avenue, across the street from Skeeter Anderson's house. The old overweight lady there, Ellen Lindberg, would cut our hair in her kitchen with a scissors and an old electric trimmer. Pat and I didn't mind, but by that time Dennie and Mick started to balk.

"I ain't lettin' some ole lady touch my hair!" Mick said. After all, a cool haircut in the fifties was a must. You either had a "heinie" or crew cut, as Pat and I did, or you had a pile of long greasy hair on top of your head, which you combed into a "duck tail" or "duck's ass" in the back and/or on the top of your head, as Dennie and Mick did. They paid for their own haircuts at a barbershop. Mom refused to pay for the little trim they got around their ears. Mick preferred Roscoe G. Keller, whose son David was in his class in school.

Dennie preferred "Mike the Barber" Radtke, the barber under the hotel, because he had *National Geographic* magazines to read with pictures of bare breasted native women. Mom was always after Dennie to "Please cut your hair. It's so long you look like a bum!" She had no idea what she was in store for when I discovered the Beatles in 1964.

---

[94] 233 Sibley Avenue North. See page 409 of the History of Downtown Litchfield Appendix.

Then she said to me, "I'm not going to sit by you in church if you don't cut your hair."

"Okay," I said, "then I won't go to church."

In the pool hall they started calling me "Miss" and I had to quit going into truck stops after midnight. That's when the drunks would stop in for a sobering cup of coffee and a sandwich. One look at me and they would start in. "Hey, who's the girl?"

Pat and I soon graduated to "real" haircuts too. Mom broke down and gave us each a dollar and off we'd go to get our "ears lowered". There were five barbers to choose from in Litchfield and they all had shops in the basements of stores. There was Steen's under the Red Owl, Ray Nelson under Sward-Kemp Drug, "Mike the Barber" under the hotel, Hubert's Barber Shop under Tostenrud's Jewelry with an alley entrance, and Roscoe G. Keller, whose shop was under the New Bakery next to the First State Bank.

We generally went to Roscoe because he was one of the nicest guys in town. He was like a much hipper "Floyd the Barber" on the *Andy Griffith Show*. He was funny, kind and best of all he let us come into the shop anytime and trade comic books with him. He had quite a pile of comics, so, for us, it was like hitting the jackpot. I knew I had passed some kind of "rite of manhood" when Roscoe finished my haircut one day, undid the cloth around my neck and then reached out to my shoulder to stop me from getting up out of the chair. He proceeded to lather up my neck with warm foam and then shave the back of my neck with his straight razor, which he ran up and down a leather strap connected to the chair. After the neck shave, Roscoe slapped on some great adult-smelling aftershave. I still got the usual stick of spearmint gum from him too. I walked out of Roscoe's a little taller that afternoon.

Roscoe moved "above ground" in the sixties and built a shop by the Unique Theater. He fell off the roof of his house later in his life and never recovered from the injuries. His son, David, took over the business. In the back of Keller's was Cynthia's Beauty Shop. When I moved back to Litchfield after my stint in the Army, my wife worked there as a beautician. When I remarried and moved to Willmar, David did the same thing, remarrying and moving to Willmar. I mention his great dad to him every time I see him.

Chapter Seventeen
The Watch, Christmas, and Parking

One door south of the Thomas Furniture Mart was the famous McGowans' Millinery[95]. After McGowans' store was Setterberg's Jewelry with Whitney Optometry sharing the building[96] with its giant clock on a pole outside on the sidewalk. I heard an interesting story about that pole.

In the 1910s, future bowling alley owner Art Krout worked after school and on weekends at Emil C. Gross' jewelry store, which was at this location then. Dogs used to come down the street, see the clock pole, sniff it, and then lift their leg and mark it. During the winter a large deposit of yellow ice started growing at the base of the pole. It drove Gross nuts. His watchmaker, Art Ganner, came up with an idea. He went into the basement and wired the pole with electricity. When a dog came along and urinated, his stream completed the electrical circuit and he got a jolt in a very sensitive spot. After the dogs went whimpering down the street enough times, the problem ceased.

In the spring, things started melting and there was a large puddle on the street in front of the pole. Along came a farmer with his team of horses, which he parked in front of Gross jewelry. Somehow the horses standing in the puddle made a connection with the pole and, of course, they got the resulting jolt. Rearing up, they started going crazy in front of the store. Luckily Art saw what was happening and he was able to disconnect the electricity before the horses could come through the store window.

In the early sixties, Setterberg's became Stewart's Jewelry, where I made my very first jewelry purchase. You learn "life's little lessons" as you grow up. Nobody can teach you them. You just have to learn them on your own. One of those lessons is about trust. There's an awful lot of trust floating around in a small town. We didn't lock things up in Litchfield in the fifties. We'd leave the house for hours and never think to lock a door. We never locked a car door when we parked on the street downtown. You trusted the town people and, most of all, you trusted your friends.

---

[95] 229 Sibley Avenue North. See page 411 of the History of Downtown Litchfield Appendix.

[96] 227 Sibley Avenue North. See page 413 of the History of Downtown Litchfield Appendix.

220

After I had my paper route for a few months, I decided that I was earning enough money to buy myself a luxury item, a watch. I've always been obsessed with time, the correct time. I wear an "old-fashioned" digital watch today. Isn't that strange to say that? Trusting Mom's judgment, I asked her to go shopping with me for my big purchase. We ended up at Stewart's Jewelry. I made my selection and the watch I picked cost about $9. I asked if I could buy it "on time".

"Sure," jeweler Marvin "Bill" Stewart said. "You just give me a dollar today and then come in every week and pay me another dollar." He slid the watch in its plastic case across the counter towards me.

"No, I don't want it until it's paid for," I said. "You keep it until then." It was a lesson I had learned from Mom.

"Never buy anything unless you have the money to pay for it," she had told us.

Only once or twice in my life have I ever bought anything again "on time". There are a lot of reasons for my mother's generation being called "The Greatest Generation" by authors and politicians. The lessons they learned in their teens in the Depression and in their early twenties during WWII were passed on to my generation, their children, the Baby Boomers. Mom always said she got fat because her kids didn't clean their plates and she couldn't throw the food away that she had worked so hard to buy. I say the same thing about free meals anywhere. I can't push myself away from that potluck buffet. Mom's generation saw what "buying on time" did to their parents and they refused to get over extended or live beyond their means. A good philosophy.

For two months I waltzed into Stewart's Jewelry every Saturday morning and paid my dollar. Finally the day came when the watch was paid for. I strapped it to my wrist and showed it off to all of my friends. We decided to go out to Lake Ripley for a swim. At the Lake Ripley Memorial Park beach there's a large cement block building called the bathhouse. It was built in June of 1950 by the P.T.A. and you can change your clothes, go to the bathroom, and shower the lake water off in there. A bare shower, three long wooden benches against three of the four walls and a wall of lockers to put your clothes in were inside the men's changing room.

We went to the beach so many times each summer that Pat and I put our own combination locks on two of the lockers. I changed into my cold and moldy swimsuit, which I kept wet in the locker, locked up my clothes and my new watch and went swimming with the guys. When I returned to get dressed later that afternoon, I had quite a shock. Someone had broken my padlock and taken my brand new watch, which I had owned for about six hours. I never did find out what happened to it. Who knew what was in my locker but my "friends"? I learned to be careful of which friends I trusted and I learned to never trust a cheap padlock again. Important life lessons.

The jewelry storeowner's son, Marv Jr., played drums with my stepbrother Gary in a band called The LeSabres. He also sat in with an early band Mick had before I joined up with Mick. Mick and I had seen Jerry Lee Lewis perform at the Lakeside Ballroom in Glenwood in the early-sixties. Jerry Lee, who I saw three times and never once saw sober, had two drummers playing for him. It made an impression on Mick. He suggested that we try it in our band, The Defiants. Mick ran the band, so I went along with the suggestion, although I didn't like it. I was nervous about it because Marv had taken drumming lessons and played in the high school band and I was self-taught and hadn't started playing until I was out of high school.

We played in the old armory in Olivia, Minnesota on a Saturday night. As usual, we had put on the dance ourselves. We got "the door", or the admission money, after paying the expenses of $15 rent and $5 for a policeman. We'd usually get a hundred or a hundred and fifty kids paying $1 each to get in at our dances. A friend or a girlfriend of one of us would take the money at the door for us. We thought it was great if we made $20 apiece.

The Defiants at the Willmar Armory. Terry Shaw, Loren "Wally" Walstad, John Collins and Mike Shaw.

222

Marv and I set up our drums on opposite ends of the stage. The stage was made up of large gray eight-inch high four by eight foot platform sections that were pushed together. We piled up extra sections on the stage's corners so that Marv and I were up higher than the band so that we could see each other. We had to be able to see each other. You couldn't depend on what you heard in an armory. It was like playing inside of an echo chamber or farm silo, which was used as the first echo chamber in recordings, by the way.

I don't think the experiment went that well because we never tried it again. Maybe the guys didn't like dividing up the money five ways instead of four. *Wipe Out* is the only song I remember doing that night. It was like a "battle of the drummers" between Marv and I on that song, especially with all of the echo in that armory. I finished the song after Marv so I'll have to say that he won the battle.

The building south of Stewart's Jewelry stood vacant in 1959 but soon it was the Montgomery Ward store[97]. The most interesting prior resident of the building was the famous Litchfield Milk Bar. James "Jim" Otto owned it but Don Bruns ran it or bought it from him, because he was the man in there. It was a teen hangout. The strongest drink you could get there, besides coffee, was a butterscotch malted milk, hence the name, "Milk Bar". They had booths, a counter with stools, pinball machines and a jukebox. It seemed ideal for teens, but it didn't last very long. I don't know why.

Coast To Coast[98] was the next store in the block. There were apartments over the store. When I got out of the Army and came home from Germany with my wife and baby daughter Christine, I rented an apartment[99] above the Coast To Coast. Our apartment had tremendously high ceilings and the walls were painted a dark brown and green. It was depressing. I asked Mrs. Ray McGraw, the owner and landlady, if she would mind if I painted the place.

"Oh, no," she said. "In fact, I'll pay for the paint if you'll do that." I enlisted the aid of my wife's parents and her aunt and uncle. We painted the entire apartment white in a few hours on a fall Saturday.

---

[97] 225 Sibley Avenue North. See page 415 of the History of Downtown Litchfield Appendix.
[98] 223 Sibley Avenue North. See page 416 of the History of Downtown Litchfield Appendix.
[99] My address was 221 Sibley Avenue North. The upstairs used to be called "Watson Hall".

After the painters left, I went to work with my artistic talents. In each of the three long and narrow rooms, I drew and then painted vertical stripes on one wall of each room. The stripes started about two inches wide in the center and increased in size as they went to each corner of the wall. The effect was amazing and made the room look much bigger. The living room had black stripes, the bedroom had green and the kitchen had yellow. My wife made matching curtains for each room out of colored burlap. We bought some cheap furniture and rugs to match the curtains. It was an ultra modern apartment out of a women's magazine. I can only imagine what the landlady and new tenants thought after we moved out.

At one time there was an alley next to the Coast To Coast building, where the Chamber of Commerce is located today, but Ray McGraw erected a one-story building[100] there in 1946. In May of 1956, Tobkin's Jewelry moved into that building. Litchfield sure had a lot of jewelry stores. What I remember about that building was that we used to go up on its roof from the back alley to watch parades and "shoot" our peashooters at cars passing by. We also dropped water balloons on people on the sidewalk below. We tried to aim for kids we knew, but occasionally an adult would get wet. Then we'd have to run and scatter and stay off the roof for a week or so. Throwing objects off buildings has always fascinated kids. I remember a carton or two of eggs being thrown at passing cars around Halloween too.

Little did I know that in about ten more years I'd be sitting up on that same roof with a wife and a little one-year-old daughter. My wife and I could crawl out onto the roof from a hall window by our apartment, so we used the roof as our patio to lounge around in the summer sun. Better than that, we had a bird's eye view of Sibley Avenue and Litchfield's wonderful Watercade and Memorial Day parades.

Occasionally, when I was a kid, a circus came to town, as they did on August 2, 1952. The circus would parade the elephants, giraffes and hippos down Sibley Avenue to drum up business. I think those days are gone forever. Mom took us to that circus, buying me my first candied apple for a dime. The general admission price for the circus was 45¢. The best show was the free one you could get before the big top went up. We would ride our bikes out to the site of the circus and watch the elephants being put to work pulling the ropes that brought the huge tent up.

---

[100] 219-219 ½ Sibley Avenue North. See page 419 of the History of Downtown Litchfield Appendix.

Following the one story building was, and still is, the *Independent Review* newspaper's building[101]. I loved going into the *Independent Review* office. There was something about the smell of newspaper and fresh ink that was appealing to me. I'd see reporter/photographer Stan Roeser walking the streets, his head held up higher than normal, as if he were sniffing out the local news. I think it had something to do with his eyesight. The *Independent Review* was actually a combination of two of newspapers, the *Litchfield Independent* and the *Litchfield Saturday Review.*

The *Litchfield Independent* began publication in May of 1876, during the famous Grasshopper Plague of 1873 to 1877, which Laura Ingalls Wilder wrote about in her *Little House on the Prairie* books. On June 12th, 1873, a swarm of Rocky Mountain Locust, not grasshoppers as often mistakenly reported, invaded the central and southwestern parts of Minnesota. They came in swarms so huge that they blocked out the sun, sounding like a rainstorm. The "grasshoppers" became so thick on the railroad tracks that it took three hours to go just five miles. Workers had to scrape them off the tracks and then pour sand on them. Farmers raked the critters into piles like leaves and set them on fire. They ate everything in sight, including the wool and cotton blankets the frantic farmers used to cover their crops. They even ate the wool off the backs of live sheep. Tree bark and even wooden tool handles were eaten.

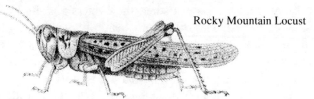

Rocky Mountain Locust

Many impoverished farmers and town people were forced to abandon their holdings and leave Meeker County. Governor Pillsbury declared April 26, 1877 a statewide day of fasting and prayer. Apparently it worked, because by the middle of August the "grasshoppers" were gone and the following year the farmers had their biggest crop of wheat ever. Was it the power of prayer or just the locusts moving on to find more food?

---

[101] 217 Sibley Avenue North. See page 420 of the History of Downtown Litchfield Appendix.

South of the *Independent Review* building was the Litchfield IGA Market[1], also called Nordlie's IGA. Next door[2] to it was what I knew as Sederstrom Realty. It had been a restaurant and ice cream factory. In March of 1952, the Northwestern Bank moved into that building for five months, while their building at the corner was being remodeled. They took out an ad assuring their customers that they had taken out extra insurance and their patrons money would be safe in the "Ice Cream Company building".

In the twenties, the Silver Grill was in the basement under the next building, which became part of Whalberg's store. The Silver Grill was quite an establishment, both in its décor and in its proprietors. What I heard was that Fred Kopplin[3] financed it, but he probably just spent a lot of money and time there. Other things I've heard about the Silver Grill make me think that it might have been a "speakeasy", although I have no proof of that. Customers came in from an ally entrance and walked down a stair, through a door and then through beaded curtains. There were beads everywhere, especially around the proprietors' necks.

Originally Emma Swanson had started the cafe upstairs with much fanfare. She served Pink Tea and had orchestras playing up there at times, but she wasn't one to be messed with. In the summer of 1919, a couple of men tried to break in and were met by Emma holding a revolver. She got off a couple of rounds, but the burglars luckily escaped with their lives.

Emma and her sister Esther, the owners and cooks in the basement version of the Silver Grill, were beautiful women with jet-black hair piled high on their heads. They always wore puffy sleeved long dresses. The restaurant, dimly lit with Japanese lanterns, had high booths that had lattice dividers that could be pulled across in front, insuring privacy in the booth. There was a nickelodeon down there and some customers would get up and dance to the music.

Karna Johnson Agren, candy man Axel Johnson's daughter and "Music Ole's" granddaughter, grew up on main street and she would go down to the Silver Grill in the daytime to see the ladies. One day she walked in unannounced and, to her horror, she saw that both women

---

[1] 215-215 ½ Sibley Avenue North. See page 424 of the History of Downtown Litchfield Appendix.
[2] 213 Sibley Avenue North. See page 426 of the History of Downtown Litchfield Appendix.
[3] Fred's father came to Litchfield in 1898. He bought a lumberyard from Charley Gourley. It was west of the Ideal office building, which he built.

226

were completely bald. Emma and Esther swore Karna to secrecy. Karna immediately went home and told her mother, who told Karna that the women had lost their hair to some disease and that she should never tell anyone. But word did get out because I've heard the story from several sources. One more thing that I've heard from different sources is that food and drink weren't the only thing you could get down in the Silver Grill. The Swanson sisters were very friendly ladies.

The upstairs of the building[105] was bought by Art Tostenrud in April of 1945, but stood empty for a while until Whalberg's, next door, bought it and expanded their operation. The old wooden building was torn down in March of 1954. So, where Dueber's is today was Warren Whalberg's "V" Store[106] in my day. Pat bought Mom a red ruby looking necklace and earrings for Christmas one year there. In his mind, he remembers buying them in a jewelry store. That was also the store where Pat bought me some tacks for a Christmas gift.

Whalberg's
V Store

Christmas was a special time for my mother and she had rules concerning the holiday. My brothers and I would each get one toy gift. The other gifts "from Santa" had to be clothes. The tree wouldn't go up until one week before Christmas and it wouldn't go up at all if her four boys didn't pitch in picking it out, carrying it home and decorating it. My favorite decorations were our bubble lights and we always topped the tree off with a lot of tinsel and Angel Hair. Only Mom could put the Angel Hair on the tree because it was made from spun glass and too dangerous for us to handle, she told us. A plastic Santa in his sleigh pulled by eight reindeer on top of a sheet of sparkling cotton usually went on top of the TV, with the manger scene on one of the lamp tables beside the sofa. Sometimes Mom would switch them around.

---

[105] 209 Sibley Avenue North. See page 428 of the History of Downtown Litchfield Appendix.
[106] 207 Sibley Avenue North. See pages 428 and 430 of the History of Downtown Litchfield Appendix.

We would open gifts on the twenty-third of December because of another rule. We had to be in Le Sueur, Minnesota for Christmas Eve Midnight Mass with Mom's parents, Grandpa and Grandma Rheaume, every year. Getting to Le Sueur without a car was quite a task for Mom, but somehow she did it. I remember taking the bus a couple of times, where we had to go to Minneapolis and then to Le Sueur from there. Grandpa or Uncle Bud drove up to Litchfield to get us a couple of times. Most often there was a family of three, Clinton Rohrbeck, and his wife Caroline and son Guy, who had relatives also in Le Sueur and they would give us a ride with them. The back seat of their old sedan would be crammed with Guy and us noisy kids, having to go to the bathroom, fighting amongst ourselves and yelling everything we said. God bless the Rohrbecks. We never missed a Christmas Eve in Le Sueur.

The Christmases there were always the same, which was comforting. We'd arrive on Christmas Eve afternoon, always the first of Mom's brothers' and sisters' families to arrive. The others would come on Christmas morning. Grandma would let us each have one of her homemade gingerbread men hanging on her Christmas tree. We'd go to Midnight Mass that night and then the next day the house would fill with hugging and kissing adults and running and yelling kids. We'd have a huge Christmas dinner and then anxiously wait for two things to happen later in the day.

Mom's family would sing Christmas carols, not just sitting around but lining up like a choir in the living room with Uncle Ray or "Babe" directing. They had an excellent choir. They all sang in their respective home church choirs and Ray was the choir director in Albert Lea, Minnesota. The Shaw boys knew that we had grown up when we were invited to join the choir and sing along in our late teens.

The other event we anxiously waited for was the arrival of Santa Claus. He'd have bags of candy and small gifts for all of us kids. I believed it really was Santa, of course, but found out later that it was always one of my uncles. They took turns. One year Pat and I had red pajamas and late one Christmas afternoon, Mom came to us and asked where they were.

"Why?" I asked.

"I'm gonna do a load of wash before we go home," she lied, "and I want to wash them."

"On Christmas day?" I thought to myself.

Santa arrived and he "ho ho hoed" around the living room, handing out the gifts and accepting the traditional glass of brandy offered to him from Grandpa. Santa would usually comment on how cold it was coming down from the North Pole in his sleigh and how the drink would warm him up. I stared at Santa in awe that Christmas and then slowly my gaze went down his tall plump body to his long legs. There wrapped around his ankles were our red pajamas. Extremely tall Uncle Ray had taken his turn as Santa and had found that the family owned Santa costume didn't quite fit.

There was one more Christmas rule of Mom's. My brothers and I had to buy gifts for each other with our own money. Mom wouldn't finance it for us. The gift had to cost at least a quarter. We could spend more if we wanted to, but nobody ever did. Dennie and Mick were easy to buy for. I bought them each a pack of cigarettes. Pat was harder to buy for. I would try to buy some cheap toy or some candy for him.

I eagerly opened my gift from Pat one Christmas, expecting a cheap toy or some candy back from him. When I had torn off the wrapping paper, I saw in my hands a piece of four inch by two inch cardboard with about two-dozen multi-colored pushpins sticking out of it.

"What the heck is this?" I asked him.

"It's a game."

"The heck it is. This is just some darned tacks!" I made sure Mom heard the anguish in my voice, trying not to say hell and damn.

"I thought it was a game," Pat said, looking to Mom for support.

"That's OK, honey," she said. "I'll take them back and get the money and you can buy Terry something else. Thank Pat for the gift, Terry."

"The heck I will. Darned tacks!"

"I thought it was a game!"

"Tacks?"

"I thought it was a game."

I comforted myself with some of my chocolate covered cherries I had received as Christmas gifts on my paper route.

Following the "V" store was the Litchfield Hardware Company, also known as Our Own Hardware[107]. The building, which had "A. Tharalson" high up on the facing above the upstairs windows, originally was in a backwards and upside down "L" shape, wrapping itself around

---

[107] 205 Sibley Avenue North. See page 432 of the History of Downtown Litchfield Appendix.

the bank next door. William "Bill" Harder[108] had a plumbing shop in the rear, which had its entrance behind the bank on Second Street. Above it was Evelyn's Beauty Salon, owned by Evelyn Pearson.

Finishing the block was the Northwestern National Bank[109]. During my younger days, Patrick "P. J." Casey's law office, Dr. Silverthorne's dentist office and Hanson's Studio, a photography studio, was above the bank. P. J. Casey, who opened his law office here in February of 1933, was assigned as my lawyer in 1967 when I got drafted into the Army. My college deferment had run out and I got "the letter" in the mail. I was given an automatic appeal with the services of a lawyer. It didn't do any good, however. Uncle Sam wanted me.

From the left: Meeker County Bank, Litchfield Hardware, Krueger Brothers' dry goods, and Peterson Brothers' tobacco and candy Shop.

Around the corner and downstairs under the bank had been Ray Wheeler's barbershop[110] in the old days and, as I said, the back entrance to the hardware and plumbing store. Heading west down Second Street, was Dr. Fred Maass' dentist office[111], which was the first building right after the alley. Although Fred Maass' son Bill, whom we called Billy, was a good friend of mine, we didn't go to Fred for our dentistry. I don't know why.

---

[108] Originally Bill Harder was in partnership with Pat J. Campbell. Harder bought Campbell out in March of 1949. Bill's son Jim was a star athlete for Litchfield High School in Dennie's class.

[109] 201 Sibley Avenue North. See page 435 of the History of Downtown Litchfield Appendix.

[110] M. E. Steen followed Ray here until July of 1946, when he moved under the Red Owl store.

[111] 24 Second Street West. See page 439 of the History of Downtown Litchfield Appendix.

I was over at Billy's house one evening when Fred and I began talking about art. He said that he had done some drawing in his day and he offered to show some of his sketches to me. They were fantastic. He was quite an artist. Billy would borrow Fred's big Chrysler Imperial and pick me up to "cruise" Sibley Avenue and drive around the lake listening to the radio. Some cars had great sounding dashboards and the Imperial was one. I'd play drums with my hands on the dash along with the radio and the Imperial had a nice rattle on the metal part, like a snare drum, and the padded part of the dashboard had a good bass drum sound. I suppose I was the only person who thought of these things.

Billy had a crush on Merdice Fortun. For some reason, Billy thought he needed to be with someone when he pursued girls. I don't know why. He wasn't as shy as I was. He came to pick me up one night and he had Merdice in the front seat and Gerry Kragenbring in the backseat.

"Let's go to Glencoe to the Pla-Mor for the dance," Billy said.

"Okay," I answered, totally surprised. I jumped into the back seat of the car next to Gerry. We were friends but there were no sparks flying between us. We went to the Pla-Mor Ballroom for the dance and came home early. Billy wasn't a dancer like I was. I was busy dancing with both girls. Billy had other things on his mind. He drove us around Lake Ripley and then we pulled onto the road that runs between the Ripley Lanes bowling alley and the cemetery across from Memorial Park. Down the gravel road, he turned left into a grove of trees. I had heard about this place but I had never been to it. It was known as the "Beehive" and was a parking place for teenagers. We had the only car in there that night.

Every town had a favorite parking place for lovers. A couple of towns I've been in, like Olivia, had a "gravel pit". Litchfield actually had two places. The Beehive was one and the other place was one of the parking lots at Lake Ripley beach.

Billy put his arm around Merdice and they hunched down in the front seat. I started to feel self-conscious with Gerry. What was I supposed to do? We weren't dating. Finally I decided that maybe I was expected by Gerry to do something. I didn't want her to feel funny, like I didn't like her or something, so I thought "When in Rome..." I leaned over and kissed her. We talked quietly and kissed a few more times. That was it. A half an hour later Merdice said she had to get home. Billy started up the car and we pulled out of the Beehive and took the girls home. It was such an odd experience for me. I chided Billy about it as he drove me home.

"Don't ever do that to me again," I said. "Let me pick who I go parking with, OK?" Gerry and I remained friends and we laughed about the incident but never dated. Billy never ended up with Merdice either.

Now that I knew where the Beehive was, my friends and I started "bushwhacking" it. That simply meant pulling in with your car's lights off, finding a car somewhere in there, pointing your car at it and then hitting it with the high beams until two heads came popping up over the dashboard. One night some students caught the Spanish student teacher there with another student teacher. That was the cause of some interesting classroom whispering the rest of the week.

Late one night in 1961, Val "Larry" Young, my step-brother-to-be, took his date and future bride, Judy Weber, out for a drive around the lake. Larry turned off his lights as he pulled into the Memorial Park parking lot facing the lake next to another car, whose occupants were obviously enjoying the view also. Larry shut off the engine and put his arm around Judy. Glancing past her face to the people in the next car, Larry thought he recognized the driver. He reached over and rolled down Judy's window.

"Dad!" he said. "What are you doing here?"

"What are you doing here?" the surprised Floyd Young said back. Floyd's date? My mother, who had finally found the man who would bring some happiness to her life. Larry, Floyd and their dates had a good laugh over the incident.

Next to Fred's dentist office was the Anderson Chemical Company office, which had been the Anderson Creamery. Finishing off the block was the old fire hall, which I've visited earlier in this book. Directly across the street was an Auto Parts store[112]. To the east of the Auto Parts were two businesses. The Paradise Café[113] was the first one and the next store was Wilfred F. Baril's Paint and Wallpaper Store[114], which began business in January of 1952. That's where Mom got the free yardstick she used to paddle our behinds.

---

[112] 37 Second Street West See page 449 of the History of Downtown Litchfield Appendix.
[113] 27-29 Second Street West. See page 450 of the History of Downtown Litchfield Appendix.
[114] 23-25 Second Street West. See page 451 of the History of Downtown Litchfield Appendix.

Chapter Eighteen
Nearness to Greatness

David Letterman used to have a segment on his late night TV show where audience members would talk about their "nearness to greatness". They would tell Dave a story about how they had bumped into a star at the airport, spilling his luggage, for example. If I were ever asked about my "nearness to greatness", I would tell about the time I stood at a urinal in Chicago's Second City Theater in 1972 peeing next to movie star Bill Murray.

"Hey! Great show, man," I complimented Bill, who had been in the Second City Improv show.

"Thanks, " he said back to me. This was before his breakthrough on *Saturday Night Live* and in the movies. My first "nearness to greatness", however, was in Litchfield, Minnesota when I was seven years old.

I was in the first grade at Washington High School and for some reason I was uptown around 2:30 in the afternoon on Thursday, October 23, 1952. I saw a huge crowd down by the train depot. "Maybe," I said to myself, "they're giving something away free." I ran down the street and mingled in with the crowd of 2,500 people standing on the tracks. A man was speaking from the platform of the last car of a small passenger train. I stood in the crowd, jumping up and down, trying to see over the adults' shoulders and hear what the dark haired man was saying.

"Who's this guy?" someone asked a neighbor.

"Richard Nixon," the other man answered. "He's running for vice-president with Ike Eisenhower."

Left to right: Pat Nixon, Minnesota Governor C. Elmer Anderson and Richard M. Nixon on his "Whistle Stop" campaign train.

I still had no clue who the man on the train was or what he was talking about, nor did I care. It didn't look like they were going to be giving anything away free so I turned and went home. The thirteen-car train was the "Dick Nixon Special" and it was the first time a presidential or vice-presidential candidate had been in Litchfield since October of 1896 when William Jennings Bryan came and campaigned from a platform erected at the depot. Unless, of course, you want to count the time Teddy Roosevelt's train stopped shortly after midnight for nine minutes in April of 1903. No doubt, Teddy was fast asleep. Or the time that Franklin D. Roosevelt's ten-car train roared through town at 8:30pm on October 4, 1937. A crowd of fifty on-lookers waved from the platform to the curtained windows of the train. Harry S. Truman, also asleep, sped through town at two in the morning on his way to Minneapolis on May 14, 1950.

There was an interesting sideline to William Jennings Bryan's visit in 1896. After the train left Litchfield it headed for Minneapolis. Picking up speed, it roared through Dassel, Minnesota where it struck and killed a man at the crossing. Because there were no warning signals, the man's wife sued the railroad for $5000 and won. I don't think she voted for Bryan either.

I wasn't impressed with Nixon and, because he didn't give anything away, I didn't like him. Besides, Mom always voted Democratic. The next time a presidential candidate was in town was on Saturday, March 3, 1956, when Democratic candidate Adlai Stevenson spoke at the Armory Building in his campaign against Nixon and Eisenhower. I wasn't there that day. They must not have given anything away free.

WCCO-TV had a wonderful children's show on everyday in the afternoon right after *Pinky Lee* and *Howdy Doody* and right before WTCN TV's *The Mickey Mouse Club*. It was called *Axel and His Dog* starring Clelland Card as Axel. Axel had a Hitler-like mustache on his face, a railroad engineer's cap on his head, and he talked with a heavy Swedish accent. He looked and sounded like half the old guys I knew in Litchfield. He would talk to Towser and Tallulah, his hand puppet pet dog and cat, which were manipulated by Don Stokes, and then he'd look through his cardboard spyglass down to the forest where he and his audience would see an episode of *The Little Rascals*.

The star of the little rascals was Alfalfa Schwitzer. With his slicked down black hair parted in the middle with a "rooster's tail" sticking up in the back, freckle-faced Alfalfa was the foil of everyone's jokes. Everything he did went wrong. Skeeter's older sister kept calling me Alfalfa, because apparently I looked like him, not having my glasses yet.

This was before we got a television, so I didn't know whom he was. I went home crying to Mom.

"That's OK, honey," she said, "You should be proud. Alfalfa is a movie star!"

"Oh, that's different," I thought, proudly marching away. Then we got the television in 1953 and I saw Alfalfa for the first time on Axel's show. Movie star, indeed.

Terry Shaw and his look-alike, Alfalfa, from the Little Rascals

Axel came to Litchfield three times. The first time was on Saturday, December 15, 1956 for Litchfield's "Santa Claus Day". I was eleven and Pat was ten. We walked up to the high school after lunch to see our idol in the school auditorium. He showed up at 2:30pm and did about half an hour joking around with Santa in front of the packed house. Then some men gave each of the three thousand kids in attendance a small bag full of candy and nuts. Vic Sederstrom and some other men in the Chamber of Commerce put in a lot of hours for us kids, filling those bags. One time the Girl Scouts volunteered to do it for them but the men turned them down. Filling Christmas candy bags was their job and they enjoyed doing it.

The other two times Axel came to town were both at Sandgren's Shoe Store, once at 10:30am on May 23, 1959 and the last time at 10am on Saturday, May 28, 1960. I was there both of those times to see the real live television star up close also. Each time at Sandgren's, Axel said "Hey dere kiddies, how are ya doin' in this fine town of Litchfield, Minnie Soda?" Then he talked to us, telling us stories and reciting a couple of "Birdies". Finally he sat on a stool and handed out pictures of himself. No autographs. The pictures were pre-printed with his name on them.

Clelland Card as Axel on WCCO-TV and in Litchfield in 1956.

Axel always ended his television show with a Birdie. There was a play that was performed recently about Axel. I saw it at the Science Museum Theater in St. Paul. The director came out before the show and asked if anyone could do a Birdie. I was the only one in the audience who raised a hand. I stood up and said, trying to duplicate Axel's accent, "Birdie wit da yella bill, hopped upon my vindow sill. Cocked his shinin' eye and says, 'Didja ever see a horse.... fly?' Peepoo! See ya tomorrow kiddies!"

The director said, "Maybe we've got the wrong guy playin' Axel!" Here are a few more of Axel's Birdies:

"What are you going to do with that turkey...neck?"

"What's keeping you in jail, Goldie...locks?"

"How do you like your bathwater, Luke...warm?"

"What did you do with the light...socket?"

"What did you get for your birthday, Bobby...socks?"

"What did you do after you ate the banana...split?"

"What would you do if your wife drank...liquor?" (Some of the Birdies were for Mom and Dad and the show's crew. Once in a while Axel got in trouble over them.)

Another WCCO-TV personality was actually raised in Litchfield and graduated from LHS, although he was born in Benson, Minnesota. He was Don Dahl, who was a sportscaster, Sunday *Business and Finance* show host, and the Sports Director for the TV station in the early sixties. He joined the station in 1958, and was best known for being the host of WCCO TV's *Bowlerama* show, the nation's first live televised bowling show. I never met Don or knew him.

Litchfield's Chamber of Commerce came up with a short-lived idea in 1957 to promote business downtown. They called it "Sellebrity Sales Days". Lasting three days, the idea was to have downtown merchants give out "Sellebrity Bucks" for every dollar you spent in their stores. At the end of the week on Saturday, they would have two auctions where you could bid your Sellebrity Bucks on donated items. Before the auctions, a real live celebrity would entertain you. They set up a hay wagon on Second Street, between the two banks but closer to the First State Bank facing north, and had a show and an auction at 10:30am and 2pm for the people. The celebrity on August 10, 1957 was Smiley Burnette.

 Gene Autry and Smiley "Frog" Burnette.

Smiley Burnette[115] was cowboy star Gene Autry's plump sidekick, Frog Milhouse, in the movies. In those movies, Smiley always wore the same outfit, so on Saturday, Litchfield held a "Look Like Smiley" contest for kids under twelve years old. Being exactly twelve, I didn't qualify.

That Saturday afternoon, G. A. Hollaar introduced Mayor Lund, who introduced Smiley. Smiley got up on the hay wagon and played the accordion and sang some songs that he had written for his movies. I never forgot that amazing moment when I looked up at that hay wagon and saw someone in the flesh that I had only seen before on the silver screen. I was near a real live movie star!

But all didn't go well for the auction. It turned out that some merchants had "favored" their friends with extra bucks, and in some cases many extra bucks. The town's people didn't like what they saw going on during the auctions. Eugene Tobkin, President of the Chamber of Commerce, wrote a front-page article for the *Independent Review* newspaper apologizing, "In the future, we will attempt to eliminate the

---

[115] Gene and Smiley both made their film debuts in the movie *In Old Santa Fe* and they went on to work together in more than eighty westerns. Smiley also provided the comic relief for other cowboy stars, such as Sunset Carson and Charles "Durango Kid" Starrett, and he appeared as railroad engineer Charlie Pratt on *Petticoat Junction* on television.

'chiselers' and 'cheaters'." But there were no future Sellebrity Sales Days. The chiselers and the cheaters had killed it. They never did it again.

A previous promotion, before my time, might have been tainted also and it was done for Christmas of 1913. The city bought a pony complete with a little buggy and harness and kids could earn "votes" to win the pony by having their parents buys at certain stores in town which gave away the votes at a rate of one vote for each penny spent. John M. Learn's son Leon won the contest and the pony with 2,648,710 votes. John Learn was the manager of the Lenhardt hotel and influential with all the businessmen in town.

Two houses north of Skeeter was an old house that I was told a witch lived in. When we were little kids, any old lady who kept to herself and didn't seem to like kids was dubbed a witch. I never saw her and even though the house was in my paper route territory, I never tried to sell her a subscription. But apparently somebody did, because one day Dean Schultz instructed me to start delivery there.

The first two free weeks, I threw the paper inside her front screen door and ran. But finally the day came when I had to collect from her. Tentatively, I tapped on her screen door. No answer. "Good," I thought, "she's not here. I'll tell Dean she's never home and he'll have to collect from her." Suddenly, as if by magic, she materialized behind the screen door. I felt the hairs stand up on the back of my neck as a shiver shot through my body despite the summer day's heat. She was an old lady in a long dark dress with her gray hair pulled back and up into a bun. She looked like the mother in the movie *Psycho*.

"Ah...I...I...I'm here to collect for the paper, ma'am," I said, hoping she didn't notice the tremor in my voice and my shaking hands.

"Oh...all right, son," she said. "Come on in."

I looked down at my feet and thought to myself, "Why? Why can't she just get the money and come back to the door?" I looked up to say I'd stay outside but she had disappeared. I slowly opened the screen door and walked into the house.

I found myself inside a small dark living room that had the unmistakable odor of an old person. The lady was slowly walking down a hall in front of me. To my left I saw an old piano with lots of pictures resting on a lacy cloth spread on its top. To my right were an old heavy wooden rocking chair and a dark green couch covered with lacy doilies. The right wall above the couch was covered with large black and white photographs in ornate wooden frames. I stepped over and peeked at them. The photographs, obviously very old, were of the same young beautiful woman in various poses and wearing huge hats. In some of the pictures, she was with other people.

"That's me," I heard the old lady say behind me. Frightened, I swung my body around and saw her walking towards me with a couple of dollar bills in her skeleton-like hand. "I used to be an actress," she added. "That was a long, long time ago."

"Really?" I didn't know what else to say. I wasn't scared anymore, but I couldn't talk, except to mutter "Thank you," as I took her money and gave her some change and her receipt slip. I thanked her, turned towards the door and left, feeling a warm relief wash over my body, like I did when I stepped out of the confessional at St. Philip's. As I walked home, I started kicking myself for not asking her for more details. Her name was Mrs. Ida Louise Ford. I don't know what her stage name was or even what her deceased husband's first name was. It was an eerie experience for me. She cancelled the paper after a couple of weeks or died because Dean told me to stop delivery there. I never saw her again.

When our band, Shaw, Allen & Shaw, started taking off, we were playing in a lot of small clubs in the area. Whenever we played in Litchfield, especially at the golf club, a gifted surgeon named Dr. William A. "Bill" Nolen was in the audience. He took a real interest in our band and invited us over for many late night snacks after gigs. I often wondered if his wife Joan shared his enthusiasm for our group when she had to feed us at 2:30 in the morning. Bill loved the old big band songs and kept after us to re-do some of them on an album, offering to finance it. We never took him up on the offer but we stayed friends with him over the years.

One day he excitedly told us that an article of his was being published in *Esquire* magazine. Shortly after that, a book of his, *The Making of a Surgeon,* was published and, as it climbed up the bestseller list, Bill started doing the talk show circuit. What a thrill it was to see a friend of mine on NBC's *Today* show, Mike Douglas' afternoon show, Merv Griffin's late night TV talk show, David Frost's show on January 25, 1971 and Johnny Carson's *Tonight Show* on January 21, 1971 and in December of 1972. He was so impressive on the TV shows, looking so relaxed and commanding attention away from the other stars on the panel. He handled himself like a pro and made Litchfield proud.

Bill was from Massachusetts and came to Litchfield in 1960. He was certainly the most intelligent person I've ever met, but he never wore it like a suit. He was down to earth and everyone liked him. He stood out in any room that he was in. His other books included *A Surgeon's World, Surgeon Under the Knife, Baby in the Bottle, Diary of a Publicity Trip*, and *A Doctor In Search of a Miracle*. He published dozens of articles in national magazines, sometimes baring his soul in them, because Bill was an alcoholic. Bill died suddenly and too soon in December of 1986.

There are some great people from town that either weren't from my fifties era or that I didn't meet. Some deserve a mention anyway. There was a stage actress from Litchfield named Mary Janet Angell Lamb Tacot, stage name Mary Angell. Born in 1902, she acted on Broadway and traveled across the country with a theatre company in 1924. Her grandfather was Clark L Angell, Sr., Litchfield's first professional photographer. After her mother died, her Aunt Alice Lamb, who was the librarian in town and lame from having TB as a child, raised her. Mary assumed Alice's last name and married a French soldier named G. A. Tacot. When they would come to Litchfield to visit Mrs. Lamb, Mary would walk down the street arm in arm with G. A., he in his uniform and she in a black dress and hat, high heels and stockings, loaded with jewelry, looking very New York and high class. They had a son named Charles and then they divorced.

Alice Lamb outlived all her relatives and had become an invalid. Mary had promised her that if and when Alice needed someone to take care of her, she would return and do it. She kept her promise. Charles didn't return with her. Mary spent the rest of her life caring for Alice. She became friends with Harriet Wagner. Harriet was the daughter of Charles W. "Hans" Wagner; the newspaper publisher that Wagner School was named after. Harriet lived in Puerto Rico, and when her parents got too old to care for themselves, Harriet asked Mary to do it, which she did. She met and was to marry Dr. Harold Wilmot, I was told, but she had a stroke around 1975, which rendered her without a voice. The marriage never happened. Everything Mary had was sold at a public auction so that she could qualify for admittance to a nursing home. One of her stage trunks is in the Meeker County Historical Society Museum. Mary died alone in the nursing home in 1990.

Mary's son, Charles, who lived in Los Angeles, married before Mary died and he had a daughter named Nicole. Nicole was in a girl backup singing group. The group was working at the Beatles' Apple Recording Studio in England in 1973 recording some songs, which were being produced by ex-Beatle George Harrison, when Nicole got reacquainted with Steve Winwood. They had met before in 1968. Winwood was a famous rock musician from England. He recorded the hits *Gimme Some Lovin'* and *I'm A Man* with his group called the Spencer Davis Group. Then he was with Traffic and Blind Faith. Nicole achieved her own "nearness to greatness" when she married Winwood in 1977. Mary was very proud of her granddaughter and showed clippings about her and Winwood to everyone at the nursing home. Unfortunately Nicole and Steve divorced in December of 1986.

In high school, our acting club was called the Gale Sondergaard Thespian Club. Gale Sondergaard was born in Litchfield in 1899 as Edith Holm Sondergaard. Her father, Hans Tjellesen Schmidt Sondergaard, was a well-known and prizewinning butter maker at the Litchfield Creamery. The house both she and Bernie Bierman lived in at different times is still in town on the southwest side at 326 Donnelly Avenue South.

Gale was a movie star and Broadway stage actress. She starred in many thirties and forties movies[116]. One was called *Anthony Adverse,* for which Gale won the Academy Award for Best Supporting Actress in 1936. She got caught up in the House on Un-American Activities Committee's witch-hunt of the late forties. She and her husband were blacklisted. It pretty much ended Gale's film career for the time being.

She was performing at the Guthrie Theater in 1967 and she made a trip out to Litchfield one day in November of that year. She visited friends, stood in the bandstand for a while, and then she spoke for about an hour to the high school Thespian Club, which had been named after her. She did a few more movies in the seventies before her death in 1985.

Bernie Bierman was the son of Litchfield clothing merchant William F. Bierman, whose store preceded Viren-Johnson's. Bernie was the captain of Litchfield's high school football team and a 1913 graduate. He coached at Tulane University and took that team to the Rose Bowl in 1932. Returning to Minnesota to coach the Gophers, Bernie brought on what has since been called the "Golden Era" of Minnesota football and the reason the team is now called the Golden Gophers. On the return train trip from a victorious Rose Bowl and National Championship in 1948, Bernie had the train stop in Litchfield. He then had his players

---

[116] *Maid of Salem, The Letter, The Cat and The Canary,* and *Anna and The King of Siam.*

greet the town folk. Future Vikings' coach and Hall of Fame legend Bud Grant was one of them.

Silent movie star Richard Arlen drove his white convertible into town in 1935. Julie Webster Hill, LHS Class of '23 graduate, was nursemaid to Arlen's son and he had driven Julie here for a visit. He had been in Minneapolis visiting his parents. P. J. Casey's wife Flo remembered seeing him here and she swooned all the way home.

Right: Richard Arlen

Left: Gale Sondergaard.
Center: Coaching legend Bernie Bierman

Maria Von Trapp and her family of singers, whom the Broadway musical and movie *Sound of Music* were written about, sang in a concert at the high school on March 11, 1950. Everyone remembers her as the large Austrian lady she really was, instead of the small pretty and dainty Mary Martin or Julie Andrews who portrayed her.

Of course, I didn't meet these last five people, so I wasn't "near their greatness". They deserved a mention anyway. I didn't repeat Floyd Warta who was "Santa Claus" in so many TV commercials and magazine ads. I should mention Bernie Acker, who worked with his velvet voice at KLFD. Bernie, who died in late 2002, did some films and was very involved in setting up Litchfield's community theater. Mick Shaw, my world famous brother, got his own chapter, Chapter Five, of course.

There's been other fame brought to Litchfield because of products starting here or being made here. I never knew about one of the most famous ones while I was living in town. It was Mrs. Stewart's Bluing. Mom used it and I did too as part of a recipe for something my students made when I was teaching Art in Glencoe, Minnesota. I always wondered about the old-fashioned small blue bottle with the picture of the old lady on it.

There's a house still standing and being lived in at 523 Holcombe Avenue South. In the late 1870s, Albert Emerson Stewart, a traveling salesman for a Chicago grocery wholesaler, and his wife Nancy Eleanor Taylor Stewart lived in that house and they concocted the mixture for the bluing in their basement. They decided to call it Mrs. Stewart's Bluing after Nancy. Not wanting to put Nancy's young face on the bottle, thinking an older face would instill more confidence in their product, Albert grabbed a picture of a Mrs. Taylor, Nancy's mother, from their mantel and gave it to the printer instead. A January 3, 1895 ad for the bluing didn't tell the housewives what it would do for their laundry, instead it stated, "Ladies...Buy Mrs. Stewart's Bluing and you will get the best. It is never put up in second-hand beer bottles." The Stewarts sold the rights to manufacture their product to Luther Ford of Minneapolis.

 Mrs. Stewart's Bluing and Mrs. Taylor who is "Mrs. Stewart".

Being there for the birth of rock and roll, I was able to see and sometimes talk to some of rock's innovators and legends. Again, it was such a different time. The rock stars played dances, not concerts, and they were totally accessible. When I saw the Everly Brothers or the Beach Boys in Mankato, Minnesota in the late fifties and early sixties, for example, only about thirty or so of us fans stood by the stage watching as they performed. The rest of the two thousand teenagers danced. Not me. I stood so close I was looking up their noses as they sang and saw that Don Everly had a tiny scar on the left side of his nose.

I stayed close to my brother Mick because he was so brave when it came to rock stars. He'd just walk right up to them and start talking. He was knowledgeable about their instruments or knew the ballroom owners personally so the stars usually listened to and talked to Mick. So I was right at his heels when he barged up to the Everly Brothers when they walked into the Kato Ballroom carrying their guitar cases and garment

243

bags. They stopped and talked to us. They were my idols with their beautiful harmonies and great melodic and tasteful songs. I was in heaven. One day as a member of Shaw, Allen & Shaw, we broke the attendance record set by the Everlys that night.

A drawing I made of the Everly Brothers for their fan club website.

I was with Mick when we saw Roy Orbison sing *Oh, Pretty Woman* at the Showboat Ballroom in Laverne, Minnesota during a snowstorm. There were only about two dozen of us die-hard fans there, but Roy did his show anyway. He stayed on stage afterwards and talked to us telling us he had just returned from England where he had headlined a show with a group called the Beatles. He was impressed with them and said we would be hearing more about them. "Not with a silly name like that," we thought.

We saw the Ventures and the Fireballs at Cold Spring, Minnesota and talked to them also. And we saw a drunken Jerry Lee Lewis there. He refused to play the ballroom's out of tune piano. So he played guitar all night. We saw Jerry Lee again in Glenwood, Minnesota where he was a little more sober. The grand piano, which was in tune there, was brought down to the front of the stage. I worked my way up to it and leaned on it as Jerry Lee played. He was singing one of his rockers called *Breathless* and some girls behind me were jumping up and down. When Jerry Lee got to the break where he sang, "You leave me…ahhhhhh…breathless-ah!", he leaned towards the girls, looked at them and hissed the word "breathless-ah". One of them fainted on my back.

"The Killer",
Jerry Lee Lewis.

Being prejudiced, I always felt, and am supported by the memories coming back to me as I write this book, that the greatest person I was ever near was my mother, Helen. Growing up and learning about saints in religion class, I always felt that I was living with a saint. If she were alive today, she'd be the first person to disagree and argue me that point. Nevertheless, I felt that she was the most "saintly" person I ever knew and I thank God for the forty-six years I got to be with her.

When I was really little, I would snuggle up close to Mom in church after she came back from Communion. The nuns had told me in Kindergarten class that it was Jesus' body in those flat wafer hosts and I wanted to get as close to God as I could. So I snuggled up tight to Mom 'cause He was in her body somewhere. Now that I think about it, I was close to Him everyday that Mom was alive when I hugged her and told her how much I loved her.

Terry and Helen
Shaw on First
Communion day,
1954.

Chapter Nineteen
The Hotel Block

Each city block in Litchfield developed a name. We called the blocks by the names of the prominent stores in them. The Johnson Drug Store Block and the Greep's Block were probably known only to my generation. But for all generations, the block on the west side of Sibley Avenue between Second and First Streets was always called the Hotel Block.

The first building on that block, starting at Second Street, was the First State Bank[117]. An old photograph shows that a basement window at the bank had the sign "Baths" in it. You could get "cleaned" upstairs and downstairs, I suppose. Well, the barbershops in the basements under stores in those days originally offered baths too and later added showers. The bank building and the building next door to its south were torn down and a new bank was built in the same place in early 1963. In the fifties there was a doorway between the original bank and the next building. In that doorway and up the stairs were a bunch of offices[118]. Below the bank was Roscoe G. Keller's Barber Shop[119].

West, behind the bank, where I remember a parking lot only, had been another early version of Litchfield's Post Office, which came to this location in 1892 and remained here until the bank expanded and took over that part of the building in June of 1931. Victor A. "Vic" Sederstrom's realty business was back there too. Later Marvel's Beauty Shop was back there somewhere in the early fifties. The bank building used to extend all the way west to the alley. At sometime before my time, the back half of the building was torn down to make the parking lot.

All of the businesses above and below the bank suffered damage when the New Bakery, next door to the south, had a big fire in 1961. Since December of 1941, Wayne Rayppy had been making his fresh bread there daily. The bakery moved down the street across from the

---

[117] 135 Sibley Avenue North. See page 453 of the History of Downtown Litchfield Appendix.
[118] 133 Sibley Avenue North. See page 456 of the History of Downtown Litchfield Appendix.
[119] 137 Sibley Avenue North. See page 452 of the History of Downtown Litchfield Appendix.

246

park where Johnson's Furniture was and the building[120] was torn down to make room for the bank's expansion.

South of the New Bakery was the Hagglund Furniture Store[121]. Reuben B. Hagglund had his undertaking business there also until the late thirties. E. Lee Buckley worked for him as an assistant undertaker. Lee would frequent Ray McGraw's Horseshoe Café on Second Street East.

Undertakers Reuben B. Hagglund and Lee Buckley.

Ray McGraw waited on customers with a white apron around his waist and a cigar sticking out of the corner of his mouth. He and Lee were friends and they loved to argue with each other and kid around. They'd argue over anything, just to argue. Most times it was good-natured banter over the food in Ray's restaurant or Lee's umpiring for the softball league. Ray used to say, "Buckley, one of these days I'm gonna shoot you!" One morning Lee popped into the restaurant and, sure enough, an argument started.

"This coffee is awful. Don't you know how to make a decent cup of coffee?" Lee asked.

"It's the same damned coffee everyone else is drinking," Ray spat back, "and no one else is complaining. Hell, you're a damned poor judge of anything anyway," he added, "the way you called balls and strikes at the game last night."

The argument shifted to a call Buckley had made umping a softball game. The other customers were used to this bantering and they ignored it until Ray started to really get heated up and loud. Obviously something was bothering him this morning because he started to go berserk.

---

[120] 131 Sibley Avenue North. See page 458 of the History of Downtown Litchfield Appendix.
[121] 129 Sibley Avenue North. See page 460 of the History of Downtown Litchfield Appendix.

"Damn you Buckley," he finally said. "I've had just about enough of you. You ain't ever gonna make a bad call like that again!" With that said, Ray reached under the counter, pulled out a gun, pointed it at Lee's chest and fired. Surprised and stunned, Lee fell back off his stool. He lay on the floor. The other customers then saw Ray reach over the counter and fire two more times into Lee.

Old man Kingsryder stood up from his booth, dropped the cane he hobbled around town with and actually ran out the door. Ray fired at him too. Kingsryder ran down the street towards Dr. Danielson's office yelling, "McGraw shot Buckley. McGraw shot Buckley. McGraw shot Buckley." Meanwhile, Lee, realizing he was still very much alive, heard Ray laughing over him. Ray had been firing blanks at Lee in a cruel joke. The arguments ended. I don't know if the friendship did.

Don Brock bought the furniture business from Hagglund in August of 1959 and started his Brock's Furniture in the building. It became Brock's Home Furnishings. Brock eventually moved to the building which Fenton's Motors had occupied at 627 Sibley Avenue North, when Fenton's moved way north out by the Dairy Queen.

Butterwick's Rexall Drug Store[122] was the last store before the alley on this block. I never went into Butterwick's. They must not have sold comic books or allowed any loitering by kids, plus it was a whole extra block away from our house. I know they didn't have a soda fountain there, although they did in the earlier days when the store was called Lofstrom's. Foster Butterwick owned it and his son, Forrest Butterwick, was a classmate of mine from first grade through high school. In high school, I teased him about his name, calling him "Trees Oleostring". Think about it. He was a real nice soft-spoken guy and extremely intelligent. Forrest was so skinny that when he stood still in the locker room shower, you could see his heart beating in his chest. Being tall, he played basketball for the Litchfield Dragons and I think he became a doctor. We always got along. What stands out most in my mind about Forrest was the day we met in first grade at Washington High School[123].

---

[122] 127 Sibley Avenue North. See page 462 of the History of Downtown Litchfield Appendix.
[123] The original high school building burned down in March of 1929. It was on the lot east of the Super America at the southeast corner of First Street and Holcombe Avenue.

The 1963 National Honor Society. Some students of note: Row 4 from the left: The 1st student is Richard Peipenburg who died in training for the Army, then James McLane who witnessed the two accidental deaths, 4th is Forrest Butterwick, 5th is Senator Steve Dille. Row 3: 4th student is Terry Shaw, 6th is Cathy Osdoba. Row 1: 5th student is Patty Peifer, whose dad managed the Produce.

Litchfield High School was once called Washington High and they not only had high school and junior high school in the building, but they managed to squeeze in some lower grades too. Mom began her school cook career there before going on the be the head cook at the new Ripley Elementary School. She was still at Washington in 1970 when I came back and student taught an Art class in the junior high for two weeks. Pat's class of 1964 was the last high school class to graduate from Washington High before it became just the junior high. I went to first grade there in a large room on the first floor by the south windows.

Washington High School where I attended first grade and graduated in 1963.

The very first day of school, our teacher introduced herself and then gave us each a sheet of paper. She asked us to draw and color something about ourselves on it. I eagerly started drawing my bicycle and our dog Sparky. Then I started coloring my drawing with my brand new eight-color box of Crayons. I can still remember the smell of the new Crayons today. As I was coloring away with my tongue sticking out of one corner of my mouth, I heard the unmistakable sound of someone crying

249

behind me. I turned in my seat and there sat Forrest, his head down on the desktop. He was sobbing.

"What's the matter?" I asked.

"I forgot my Crayons at home!" he answered through his sniffles.

"Oh...that's all right. You can use mine," I said, suddenly feeling compassionate.

"Oh...okay. Thanks."

That was our introduction. It's funny how the little problems of life are such big problems when you yourself are little. Another classmate I met that day was Stevie Dille, dressed in his cowboy outfit. He later became a teenage champion rodeo rider and he grew up to be State Senator Steve Dille.

Immediately following the alley after Butterwick's was Tostenrud's Jewelry[124]. It was memorable to me only because of another giant clock on a pole on the sidewalk. Gust Chellin, a mechanic and garage man, had a jewelry store there in 1909. He bought the huge street clock that was in front of Jacob's Jewelry store on Nicollet Avenue in Minneapolis and moved it out here. It was built in the 1870s. The clock blew down in 1929, but it was fixed. Eventually, in March of 1959, it was taken down and sold to someone in South Dakota. A replica of it is in front of Litchfield's new library on Marshall Avenue North.

The original Bernie's Fairway store[125] was the next store in this block. Bernie eventually moved around the corner when he remodeled part of the old Minar Ford building. For many years the two biggest groceries in town were Bernie's Fairway and Kohlhoff's Super Valu. Mom and I used to be able to walk and pull our wagon right down the west side of Sibley Avenue and hit the four groceries she shopped at, from Red Owl to IGA to Super Valu to Bernie's.

The next building was built in 1882. It had the Meeker County courthouse upstairs until 1890 when a new one was constructed across from Central Park. Not the one that's there now, though. Coincidently, on the 4th of July in 1890, Litchfield citizens switched on electric lights for the first time in an "Illumination Ceremony". This large building was changed to accommodate two businesses. I remember the two stores as

---

[124] 119 Sibley Avenue North. See page 465 of the History of Downtown Litchfield Appendix.

[125] 115 Sibley Avenue North. See page 467 of the History of Downtown Litchfield Appendix.

the Northland Tot Shop[126]and, next door to it, Viren-Johnson's Clothing store.

Northland Tot Shop was a children's clothing store, so of course, I never had any reason to go in there. Viren-Johnson's Clothing[127] was a men's clothing store, owned in the fifties by Art Tostenrud. I also never went in there because of what I considered high prices. Of course they had quality, but what does a poor teenager care about quality? I've been told that Art, although a very nice fellow, liked to tip the bottle while at work. Several times, when customers pulled a pair of slacks out of a stack, a thin bottle came crashing to the floor, exposing one of Art's hiding places. The other hiding place was inside the toilet water tank in the store's bathroom.

Above Viren-Johnson's and Boyd's was the office of Dr. Gregory Olson, our family doctor, who partnered with Dr. David Allison in 1954. Greg reminded me of JFK. Mom used to clean his house on Saturdays and Pat and I would do his yard work. Upstairs also was the office of Dr. Frederick C. Brown, our family dentist.

The word "dentist" struck fear into the hearts of any child of the fifties or before. I remember fluoride just being introduced in 1956. A new toothpaste called Crest came out with a slogan of "Look Mom...no cavities!" Every kid got a free tube of Crest in school. Again, it was a different era and schools allowed people to walk into classrooms and give out things, even the Gideon bible.

We all had cavities in those days. It was almost expected. Everyone's grandma and grandpa had just a few yellow teeth or false teeth and a lot of old guys like house mover E. M. Eastman walked around town with no teeth at all. The dentists went in to drill out our teeth at the drop of a hat and they really drilled them. If you had a cavity, the dentist took out the entire inside of your tooth. Maybe it was an "as long as I'm in there..." kind of policy. But all of us Baby Boomers are walking around today with a mouth full of caps, crowns and false teeth because over the years the over-drilled and over-filled teeth have weakened and broke. There was nothing inside our teeth but gray disintegrating fillings to hold them together. We all hated and feared the

---

[126] 113 Sibley Avenue North. See page 470 of the History of Downtown Litchfield Appendix.
[127] 109 Sibley Avenue North. See page 471 of the History of Downtown Litchfield Appendix.

dentist, no matter how nice he was. Dr. Brown was a very nice man, but we feared him nevertheless.

Mom would march all four of us Shaw boys uptown to the dentist on the same day. We'd climb the long and wide wooden staircase between Viren-Johnson and Northland Tot Shop to the second floor of the building where an array of offices was. Dr. Brown's office was to the right at the top of the stairs. We'd march in and line up on one of those shiny metal-tube legged green plastic covered sofas, all of us shivering with fear.

Dr. Brown would come out of his torture chamber, look down at the four frightened Shaw boys, clasp his hands together and say with a grin, "Okay boys! Who's gonna be first?" Nobody would look at Dr. Brown or say a thing. Mom would say something but, again, nobody would move. Finally, I'd volunteer, not because I was the bravest, but because I had finally figured out something. I had figured out that if I went in first and got it over with, the long wait afterwards, while my brothers were in there being tortured, would be a whole lot more comfortable. It worked!

I was in and out quickly and then I sat as comfortably as I could on the hard sofa and read comic books while my brothers sat shaking in fear of what lay in store for them. Pat always went in last, so he'd be sitting with me on the sofa the longest. I may have teased Pat a little about the long needle he was going to get, or the long dull drill bit Dr. Brown was going to use on him so that by the time he was called in, he was a sobbing, nervous wreck. I may have done that. I can't remember for sure. Pat may remember if I did.

Dr. Brown didn't seem to have the Novocain needle bit down. At least it didn't seem so for us boys. That needle was much more frightening than the drill. I suppose the needles were bigger back then, because it was agony getting that shot. We'd always be spitting a lot of blood into that little porcelain spit bowl. Pat got so freaked out by those shots that he refuses Novocain to this day. He goes without.

I never forgot that valuable lesson I learned of being first. It came in very handy the rest of my school career. I always volunteered to read my report first or get up and give my speech first in every class. The teachers looked at me in a more favorable light for making their job easier, and, because they had no one else to compare my work with, it meant a better grade for me. Most importantly, I could sit back, relax, and enjoy the rest of the kids making fools out of themselves, mumbling and ah-ing and fidgeting when their turns came. Ah, a little wisdom is a wonderful thing. Oh, the one place it didn't work, by the way, was in basic training in the Army. There you didn't want to volunteer to be first in anything. Just before I went in, two uncles told me to "Never volunteer for anything."

"Can anyone here drive a truck?" the sergeant would ask our squad. Two or three dummies would raise their hands and they'd be pushing a moving cart or "truck" loaded with heavy boxes around the rest of the day. At night I would crawl into the empty space created in a corner where two rows of lockers met, then pull the lockers back together and sit and write letters to Mom or my fiancée. The idiots lying around on their bunks always got "volunteered" to go clean the Day Room or the officer's offices.

Dr. Brown, who died from kidney problems, had a couple of sons, Fritz and Ed. They were younger than I but Fritz had some similarities with me. Both of us sold papers outside of the church and uptown on Sunday mornings and both of us had a daughter with Down syndrome. Fritz, who's an attorney in Edina today, married Judy Berquist. His brother Ed worked for Don Larson at Viren-Johnson and is Professor of Microbiology and Marine Biology at the University of Northern Iowa. He spent twenty years in Alaska as a Marine Biologist and Professor at the University of Alaska.

At the corner of Sibley Avenue and First Street was the grand Lenhardt or Litchfield Hotel[128]. It was a very impressive looking building and every postcard or picture of Litchfield's downtown always included it. That corner is still called "the hotel corner" by the locals even though nothing is there. Arden Burleigh made a wonderful painting of the hotel, of which I have a treasured print, given to me by brother Mick.

"Mike the Barber" Radtke had his barbershop in the basement of the hotel. The hotel had a coffee shop in the front right section called the Colonial Room or the Colonial Coffee Shop. It was out of my league until my mother remarried when I was sixteen. Then my stepfather Floyd occasionally treated me to a breakfast there after Sunday Mass. Mom and Floyd had their wedding reception dinner there too. For many years, Katie Turck was the cook there. Minnie Beckstrand was the pastry chef. Other chefs were Ralph Reed, Ole Larson, Jerry O'Keefe

---

[128] 103 Sibley Avenue North. See page 473 of the History of Downtown Litchfield Appendix.

and Stan Nelson, who was also a winter relief chef and did the banquet catering.

The painting of the hotel by Arden Burleigh. ©1980

There was a waitress at the hotel named Laurie Kempka. She was from Germany, spoke with a heavy accent and only had a work permit to stay here. She did not want to return to Germany under any circumstances. The word was she was looking for a husband so she could stay. Alice Volkenant, the high school German teacher, used to go to the hotel café to order her meal in German from Laurie. Laurie had a famous relative, but when she was asked about him she would clam up. She didn't want to talk about her Uncle Erich Kempka, Hitler's chauffeur, who testified in the war crime trials in Nuremberg about the fate of Martin Bormann.

On the flip side of that coin, the Produce would occasionally permit some special workers to come in for a few months every year and they would stay at the hotel. They were Jewish rabbis working for the Zion Meat Company located in the Bronx in New York. They would come to Litchfield to do the kosher killing of the turkeys with a special knife called a "shohet", which looked like an old-fashioned straight edge razor. In July of 1968, there were four of them at the hotel. They only ate kosher foods, so they couldn't eat in the hotel cafe. They had their food sent to Litchfield on the bus two or three times a week. They used dry ice to keep the lamb, veal, poultry, eggs and butter cold. The veggies and other groceries were in a separate box. Two of the men were always at the bus stop to pick up their freight. The rabbis only drank unpasteurized cow and goat milk. It seemed like a contradiction with all the trouble they went through to get the rest of their food. Pete Hughes' stepbrother supplied them with both types of milk when they wanted it.

254

Maybe they sterilized and separated the cream after they bought it? They dressed in black suits with a white shirt and a fedora hat, but only one of them had the long beard and hair you'd think you'd see.

For many years, another German, Edmundt "Ed" Lenhardt, owned the hotel. He dropped the "t" and became Edmund. Ed was the son of Erhardt M. Lenhardt, who bought the hotel in 1901. Ed and his family lived at the hotel for many years. There was a small apartment in the rear, which had one large room where Ed's wife and kids lived and a very small room where Ed lived. Ed added a deck to the rear of the hotel by the apartments in the early thirties so his kids had a better place to play than in the alley. Ed was known to have money in every pocket on his body and he carried a huge bulging wallet. He would cash checks for people who didn't make it to the bank on time. Ed's nephew Don Palmquist said he thought Ed cashed more checks in town than the banks did. Ed had long ago lost his reddish hair, so he went out and bought himself a red toupee. As he got older and his hair turned gray, he didn't change the toupee, which he often put on backwards, so it looked like he had a red beret on his head. But people seldom saw his toupee because Ed had a bowler hat on most of the time.

Ed's dad, Erhardt, had been Meeker County's first brewer. Erhardt, his wife Charlotta and their four-year-old daughter Fredriche came to the United States from Hildburghausen, Thuringen, Germany on July 4th in 1872. He and Joseph Roetzer started a brewery here in 1873 and a three years later Erhardt had it alone. It was quite the complex that Erhardt owned on the northwest shore of Lake Ripley. He had a residential house, a house for his up to eight hired men, a malt house, a bottling house with walls two feet thick, a cooper's shop to make barrels, an ice house, a stable and swine sheds and chicken coops. Then there were the brick lined caves to store the brew in.

Esther Williams, not the movie star, bought the site in 1936 and in the spring of 1970 she almost fell through her garden. She had John Rogers come out to investigate. Using his earth moving equipment, he uncovered two huge underground caverns or cellars. Both were brick lined with a ceiling fourteen to sixteen feet high. The cellars were twelve feet wide and about fifty feet long. They had little tracks and carts that the kegs were moved in and out with. Originally there had been five cellars.

Erhardt retired in 1910 and sold the business to his son Edmund and son-in-law William Shoultz. William bought out Edmund in 1911 and in

1914 the county went dry. Of course the brewery mysteriously burned down then in 1915. One building, the bottling house, was left standing and it remained on the site until it was torn down in the thirties.

Erhardt had thought ahead and stored cases and cases of his brew in his basement. Edmund also had some of his dad's original brew stored in his basement. Friends, who were over for a drink, were sometimes stunned at the bottles the brew was in, however. Some of it was in square green bottles with ceramic and wire stoppers on the top, perfect for storing beer, except for the two words embossed in the glass…"Embalming Fluid". Erhardt had been a very frugal man and he loved his brewery. He was always looking for bottles for his beer and he was known to go to the funeral homes to get the old embalming fluid bottles. On real hot summer days, the town people could hear him coming across the railroad tracks with his beer cart full of clanking bottles and the corks letting go as the beer inside foamed up. The embalming bottles didn't have that problem.

Erhardt got into a little trouble during WWI for raising money for the Germans. It was for the "starving German children", but not everyone understood or believed him, although he continued on with the cause after the war into the 1920s. Everyone was paranoid during that war about German heritage or anything German. The Heinz Company even sold sauerkraut with a label calling it "Liberty Cabbage".

Erhardt was a man of means and few people knew how charitable he was. During the depression, he kept bag lunches in the cooler at the hotel. No one was ever denied a meal when they came begging after jumping off a boxcar when the train had stopped by the depot. It was a tradition that his daughter-in-law kept going also.

A lot of Litchfield's "characters" lived at either the Litchfield Hotel or the Litchfield House. One character that not only lived at the hotel but worked there was Fred Roy Archer, known as little "Fritzie". Fritzie was before my time, but I heard a lot about him. He weighed ninety pounds, at the most. He was from England and had been a jockey there. The story told was that he had been deported because of a betting scandal. I don't know if that was true or not.

After coming to America, Fritzie had joined the Barnum and Bailey Circus and then the Ringling Brothers Circus, which came to Litchfield in August of 1885. The circus pulled out and left Fritzie here. He didn't have enough money to follow or find them, so he decided to stay. He got a job working for the Meisenbergs at the Ripley House hotel, where he had been staying. From there he went on to the Lenhardt Hotel where he became the "porter" for the hotel. He met all the trains with a two-wheeled cart and brought the luggage back to the hotel for the guests. Fritzie also did odd jobs, kept the furnace going and shined shoes from a stand out front. He had put the stand together from an antique wooden chair he had been given. He painted the chair a brilliant blue.

Fritzie loved modern inventions and he bought himself a Victrola phonograph and a radio. Some people think it was one of the first radios in Litchfield. He ran an extension cord down to his stand on the street from his third floor room at the hotel. He had painted that room a bright pink, by the way. He painted the radio the same brilliant blue he had painted his chair. When something important was broadcast on the radio, such as a prizefight, a crowd would gather on the street around Fritzie's shoeshine stand.

Fritzie had a cat named Topsy and he loved stray dogs. He always had a bunch of them hanging around him in front of the hotel because he fed them with the hotel café's scraps. His most unusual pet was a little bear, which he took for walks on a leash in the park. As the bear got older and bigger, Fritzie had to get rid of it. Fritzie loved children and he became a friend to the kids of hotel employees. Charlotte Hall Painter, whose mother was a chambermaid at the hotel, remembers Fritzie tying a rope between some trees in Central Park and teaching her how to tightrope walk and do some other circus tricks. He liked to dab in photography and had a dark room in the old "sample room" in the hotel basement where he took some kids and taught them how to develop pictures.

Fritzie had a talent for playing drums. He shared his talent with the entire town. Sometimes he'd just set up a snare drum, but most often he'd set up an entire "trap set" of drums on the sidewalk facing Depot Street. On some evenings or Sunday mornings, he'd go to the small park to the south of the hotel, where Burger King is today. He'd bring down his Victrola from his room and play along with the Sousa marches from his record collection. He'd play his drum both for himself and for the small crowds that would gather around him. Some people remember him playing the ukulele along with the drums.

Frank Viren helped Fritzie go home to England to visit his parents in May of 1908. Everyone thought they had seen the last of little Fritzie, but he returned a year and a half later, got his job back at the Lenhardt and lived out the rest of his life in town. Later, when he was no longer associated with the hotel, he moved his shoeshine stand to Second Street West across from the fire hall. Fritzie died in November of 1948 and is buried in the Lake Ripley cemetery.

Fred Roy "Fritzie" Archer with his shoeshine chair and his drums.

There were town drunks and bums, whom we'd tease and then run away from. Each one had a nickname and a rumored interesting life story that we never had the courage to inquire about. One of them, who lived at the hotel, was Frederick O. "Freddie" Williams, a short four-foot something little old dwarf of a man in his sixties with a head too big for his tiny body and an actual wooden foot. He was my classmate Mae Williams' uncle, I just found out.

Freddie had a speech impediment. "Id Tamby tymb," he'd say, reaching into his breast pocket for his pack of unfiltered Camels. He meant, "It's Camel time," or time for a smoke. Freddie chain-smoked and chewed snuff at the same time. He must have been on a constant nicotine high. He lived on the fourth floor of the hotel, in the poorer attic rooms where most of the help lived. In the old days, it was politically incorrectly called "nigger heaven". Why, I don't know, as the hotel never allowed blacks, Indians, or Mexicans to stay there or eat in the

258

dining room proper that I'm aware of. Freddie's wooden foot would occasionally catch on the steps as he went up the two flights of stairs to his room at the hotel. The foot would come tumbling down the stairs. Freddie would just sit on the next step until whomever was working the desk retrieved it for him so he could continue his trip up to his room.

Freddie hung around the pool hall, sitting high up on one of the tall chairs by the pool tables, so we saw him every day. He had an understanding with the bartender that any beer left in glasses or bottles would be poured into a glass that he'd retrieve once it was full. The bar regulars must have known about the arrangement because many would leave a little in their glass every time. We'd walk over to Freddie, waiting our turn to shoot, and ask him to repeat his story to us about the time that he took a girl for a boat ride out on Lake Ripley.
"I ted to her...you tum a trough or I pull da tork!" ("I said to her...you come across or I'll pull the cork!") We'd laugh every time he'd tell us that story. Born in 1894, Freddie died in July of 1970.

When we were in high school, "Tamby Time" was our code name for a nicotine fit. I'd lean over to Marty Foss' desk in study hall and, imitating Freddie, whisper, "Id Tamby tymb!" Marty would understand that I needed a cigarette, or at least I wanted him to think so. Strangely, we were proud of our cigarette addiction in the fifties.
Marty would invite me over to his house in the evenings to play pool in his basement on a table that his dad had taken in on trade for a used car. Marty's dad, Pete Foss, managed Minar Motors Ford. In the early days, especially during the depression, farmers wanting new vehicles couldn't always afford the down payment. Often they offered something in trade. At one time Minar Motor had in its possession fifty horses, one hundred and ninety head of cattle, various used farm equipment, seed corn, potatoes and lots of chickens. Apparently they wanted to move cars for old Henry Ford. Kopplin Oil Company took in produce also for the fuel oil they delivered to the farms.

A couple of different sources told me something interesting about our grand hotel. It was the town's unofficial stopover for "ladies of the evening". For several years, women came to town on the train and rented rooms at the hotel on weekends. They usually rented the better rooms on the first floor, one up from the street level. There were three rooms on that floor with full bathrooms and three with just a stool and a sink that were their favorites.

There were ways to get into the hotel other than by the front door. There was a side door and a back door. The back door, in the alley behind Viren-Johnson's, was the most popular means of entry if someone did not want to be seen. Otherwise, most of the gentlemen just came through the lobby and asked for the ladies by name and/or room number. The night clerk was told not to ask any questions, mind his own business and never tell anyone what happened there. Obviously, one of them spoke to me about it. A certain well-known doctor in town was a frequent weekend visitor and had a bottle of vodka kept for him under the front desk counter.

Two or three ladies came at a time on the train on Friday afternoons and left on Sunday mornings. They never caused any trouble and they had their meals sent to their rooms. They paid in cash and bought a lot of cigarettes from the night clerk. Most of the ladies were in their twenties or early thirties and not particularly good looking. The downtown stores were open on Friday nights because it was payday. Sometimes, as in December of 1958, the bank cashed the Produce checks with $2 bills. Some of the ladies changed stacks of $2 bills into larger bills at the front desk before leaving on Sunday morning. The "business" was still going into the sixties.

In the days of Dillinger and Capone, St. Paul, Minnesota was known to be a safe haven for mobsters around the country. When the mobsters needed to hide out or "take it on the lam", they would head for Minnesota. I heard stories that in later years, when even St. Paul wasn't safe, they started to trickle out to the smaller towns.

One hot summer day in the early sixties, a cab from Minneapolis deposited an impeccably dressed gentleman in front of the hotel. Vic Forte, hotel manager at that time, was waiting for him and put him in a room with a full bath, registering him as Pete Swanson. Pete wanted an air-conditioned room but there were none at the Litchfield Hotel. Only the lobby had air, so the desk clerk gave Pete two fans. The next day, two large expensive steamer trunks arrived on the train for Pete. He then rented the adjoining room to his, which had a door connecting them. Pete rented these rooms for the better part of two years.

Pete Swanson kept very much to himself and he was always talking to Vic privately. Pete didn't talk to people he didn't know. If someone would try to start up a conversation of small talk with him, about the weather or whatever, Pete just ignored them. When he finally opened up to some of the hotel employees, he told them he was originally from

Hancock, Michigan and he had ended up in Detroit doing "security work" for a wealthy family. He was "hurt on the job" and was sent to Hurley, Wisconsin to recover. Hurley was a known gangster resort haven for mobsters. Pete said he had to leave Hurley in a hurry over a woman and that Vic's brother had referred him to Litchfield. The Forte family was also from Detroit.

Every week Pete received a letter at the hotel postmarked from Detroit. Shortly after receiving it, he would come down to the front desk and ask to break a few $100 bills. He went downstairs to Mike Radtke's barbershop for a trim two times a week and gave Mike a big tip. He liked to walk out to Lake Ripley early in the morning and enjoyed sitting by the lake. He never went to a pool hall, club or movie and, when he first came to town, he had most of his meals sent to his room. Later, he started coming down to the Colonial Café at the hotel. Kathy McCann, a former waitress there, remembers Pete as the best tipper that lived in the hotel, or in Litchfield, for that matter. He always left a dollar tip, which was enormous in those days when most people left only a couple of dimes or a quarter, if they left anything. Kathy said that Pete always ate alone and sat in the same booth back by the kitchen, so he could always see the door to the dining room. If that booth were not available, Pete would just leave and come back later. He never complained about it and usually he ate a roast beef sandwich with a large glass of milk. For supper, around eight, he always ordered a top line meal, usually a steak.

Pete bought some exercise equipment and had it put in his other room. He lifted weights and he was in terrific shape. He told one employee that he did over a thousand pushups and sit-ups everyday. About twice a month, a taxi from Minneapolis would bring a "lady friend" to the hotel on a Saturday morning. Most of the time it was the same lady and she was a beautiful woman. Pete and the lady stayed in the room most of the time. On Monday morning, a taxi would return to pick her up.

Pete always used the pay phones in the lobby to make calls late at night when the lobby was empty. The hotel staff told him many times that he could use the phones in rooms 105 or 106, if they weren't occupied, but Pete always refused. One day he confided in an employee that his real name was Pete Santori and he showed off two revolvers that he traveled with. Then, just when he was starting to open up to people, he left town. He came down to the lobby one night with his suitcase in his hand and talked to Vic for a while. Then he sat in the lobby dressed in his new wool dress coat and fedora hat. Shortly, a car pulled up in front of the hotel and a man came into the lobby and talked quietly to Pete. They left together in the man's car. Pete's loaded steamer trunks and all his extra clothes remained in his rooms for another six months, as he had the rooms paid up. After that, the belongings were put in storage. I don't know what happened to them. After Pete's departure, Vic confided in an employee that Pete had been "hiding out" at the hotel, but he wouldn't elaborate.

Every Saturday morning there was a big poker game for a select group of card players in a room at the hotel. They played for cash only. No checks were allowed. Some of the big players were business owners in town. Vic Forte cashed and held checks for members of the card group quite frequently. Some, obviously, didn't want their wives to know about the game or to leave a paper trail, so they made their checks out for cash, usually in $100 increments. Most often they bought them back before the hotel had a chance to cash them.

One Saturday, two of the players came to the desk and asked to have checks for $1000 cashed during the middle of a game. It seems they both thought they had winning hands and the rules called for cash only. So the other players allowed them a "timeout" to go get more cash. Vic didn't have enough on hand to cover the checks but he was able to scrounge up about $700 for each of them, mostly in those $2 bills that were still circulating throughout town. The results of the big game are not known, but whoever won had a lot of $2 bills to hold on to until the banks opened up on Monday morning.

The fire department volunteers always hoped there would never be a major fire at the hotel. They knew that they didn't have the equipment, such as a "hook and ladder", to do anything for the top floors. That was one of the reasons it was eventually torn down. On Christmas Eve of 1966, the firemen had a scare though. A fire broke out in the kitchen and broke through the floors and walls on the second floor. Minnie Beckstrand and Lorraine Birkholz had come to work around 5am and lit a stove and then gone to another work area. When they came back five minutes later, they saw a roaring fire. Minnie called the fire department and night clerk John Fisher got the guests out of their rooms, down the halls and out the doors. Somehow the Colonial Café opened up later for Christmas dinners. The guests were lucky they didn't have to use the fire escapes. The "fire escapes" for the top third floor rooms was a long rope tied to the radiator in each room. The second floor was more elite. The rope was in a nice cloth bag.

John Fisher and Vic Forte inspect the fire damage at the hotel.

The only contact I had with the hotel, other than the Sunday morning breakfasts, was that it also served as the Northland Greyhound Bus Company depot. Every day, twelve buses came through Litchfield. Six were heading east and six were heading west. Litchfield was a rest stop for the bus line, so each bus stopped and stayed for about fifteen minutes. If you look at Arden's painting of the hotel, you will see a Greyhound bus parked on the Depot Street side of the hotel.

I used to take that bus to and from Minneapolis the first couple of years I went to college. I didn't have my first car until I was twenty-one. Mom and Floyd would give me two bottles of milk, two pounds of hamburger, a few potatoes and two cans of corn every Sunday night. I would pack them in my suitcase and live on that food for the next week at school. That was their contribution to my educational fund and it was very much appreciated. Once I got to the big Greyhound depot in Minneapolis, I had to lug that heavy suitcase eighteen blocks to my apartment. I couldn't afford a cab.

Chapter Twenty
Greep's and the Unique

If I went south from the hotel, I'd have to cross over the tracks by the depot and go by the Ideal Lumber Company[129]. The lumberyard would occasionally have some free giveaways. I'm sure that's the only reason the Shaw boys ever went there. Customer Appreciation Days, Grand Openings, store anniversaries, new car model unveilings, REA days, Crazy Days, anything the stores would celebrate or promote, would draw us in like flies on sh...ah, molasses.

On Sundays, we would sometimes play in the small buildings the lumberyard had made to sell, which were lined up near the railroad tracks. Again, no locks. Weyerhauser Lumber had a yard across the street from Ideal in the mid-sixties. I had a free buffalo barbeque in a bun there during their grand opening.

Across the street south of Ideal was Batterberry's. It was another one of those small "Ma and Pa" grocery stores. Hugh I. Batterberry owned it at one time, but it was Nelson's Grocery[130] by the time we went there for penny candy or a Popsicle on our way to the lake for a swim. We still called it Batterberry's though. The Nelsons sold Skelly gas out front also.

Batterberry's, which became Nelson's.

Our friend Skeeter Anderson worked at Batterberry's one summer in the mid-fifties. He took out the trash and stocked shelves. He said that taking out the trash was how he got his smokes. The trash basket was right under the counter where the cigarettes were kept so Skeeter would let a pack of Pall Malls accidentally fall into the basket when no one was looking. He'd take the basket out to empty behind the store.

---

[129] 126 Sibley Avenue South/25 Commercial Street West. See page 481 of the History of Downtown Litchfield Appendix.
[130] 200-202 Sibley Avenue South. See page 483 of the History of Downtown Litchfield Appendix.

There he would retrieve the cigarettes and hide them until he was finished working. Sometimes a candy bar would accidentally fall into the basket also.

Batterberry's was the unofficial hitchhiking pick-up spot in Litchfield for all of the boys heading out to the swimming beach. Pat and I went out to the beach almost daily in the summer. If we were too lazy to ride our bikes the mile trip out there, we would leave them behind Batterberry's and hitchhike. We always got a ride immediately and nothing ever happened to any of us. The bikes were still there when we'd return also. Again, we were living in a different time. But, of course, who would want to steal our "Frankenstein" bicycles, made from several different bikes?

Directly across Sibley Avenue from Batterberry's was Litchfield's library, the Carnegie Library. A grand block building, it fascinated me. I just loved it. It had a dome on it, but they kept having water leaks from it so it was removed. The librarian I knew was Gertrude Johnson[131] and she was very nice, even though she had to constantly scold my friends and I for talking. Her son, Jim, was a guitarist friend of Mick's. He's now an undertaker in Redwood Falls, Minnesota. Mrs. Johnson was known for entering and winning contests all of the time. She won cars, refrigerators, trips to Hawaii, freezers; just about anything anybody was giving away. I suppose it was something she did during the quiet days when no one was in the library, although she said she spent hours on it at home. Her ability to get something for nothing made her one of my heroes. Later in life, I too entered and won many contests.

Litchfield's Carnegie Library.

I spent many hours in the library reading magazines, looking for science fiction or detective novels or researching papers for school. I even went there a lot in the summer, just to entertain myself. I felt at home in there amongst all that knowledge. When the library was moved

---

[131] Gertrude Johnson resigned in June of 1972.

downtown into the First State Bank building, Bill and Laura Harper put the Library Square Restaurant, originally called Library Restaurare, in the building in June of 1983. Mom used to love to go there. It was rather ironic that a restaurant was in the library as the library had a rule against eating in the building. The restaurant failed, another one was tried and now I believe there are just offices in the building.

East of the library was the huge wooden Litchfield House[132]. It was officially called the Lien Apartments and Rooms in the fifties, but we still called it the Litchfield House. In the very early days of the railroad, it was "the" hotel in town. After the grand Howard House was built, it quickly went into decline. People would live there for longer periods of time. I suppose you'd call it a boarding house. A half a block long and two stories plus high, it was an imposing building.

The Litchfield House – Lien Apartments.

Back uptown, north across the track and across Sibley Avenue from the Litchfield Hotel was the Greep-Trueblood Department Store[133]. What a name and what a store. I have so many memories about that store that we called Greep's. Greep's was a huge brick building and it showed up in all the pictures and postcards of Litchfield, just like the hotel.

In the early days of Litchfield, there had been a duck pond at the corner where Greep's was and Sibley Antiques is today. After the duck pond was drained and land filled, Frank Belfoy's livery and another small building were on the lot. The small building was used as county offices. Richard Welch bought the lot from Belfoy's widow and built a big red brick building on it in 1892. It actually took in the lot next door to the north also. When the hole for the foundation was dug, the workers

---

[132] See page 485 of the History of Downtown Litchfield Appendix.

[133] 100 Sibley Avenue North. See page 488 of the History of Downtown Litchfield Appendix.

thought they had uncovered an ancient burial ground. A closer look showed that it was indeed a burial ground, but not for people. Late in 1876, during the Grasshopper Plague, county auditor Hamlet Stevens had dug a huge pit there behind his office. In the pit, he deposited the tons of locust that the city had paid a bounty of $5.00 a bushel on. In July of 1877, G. W. Harding and Frank Rawley filled seventy-nine bushels with the pests. The locusts were dumped into the pit for over a year.

Greep's had an antiquated but unique system of money transfer called a "receipt trolley". Above the wooden floors and counters was a cable system strung below the ceiling. You would bring your purchase to the counter, the clerk would write up the sale slip, reach up and unscrew a metal and wooden can off the cable, insert the slip and your money, screw the can back on the cable and pull on a cord. Zing! It magically went up the cable to Grace Lupfer or Gen Osdoba sitting upstairs. They would check the total of the sale and then put your change in the can with your paid slip. Zing! Down it came to the clerk. It was a great double-check system, virtually guaranteeing there would be no mistakes in the transaction. Penney's, when it was at the opposite end of town by Central Park, had the same system, but people seem to only remember Greep's.

The trolley system still on the ceiling at Sibley Antiques.

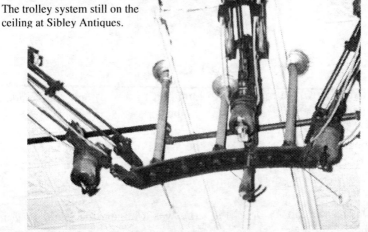

Pete Hughes worked at Greep's in the sixties and one summer he and the store's manager went to downtown Minneapolis to the old J. C. Penney store and picked up about a third of their "trolley" system, which Penney's had removed from their store. They brought it back to Litchfield and replaced the worn out ones in Greep's. In order to work properly, the wires had to be very tight. A special wench, borrowed from the city street department, was used.

My classmate Cathy Osdoba's two aunts, Gen and Peg, were clerks on the women's side of the store for many years. They actually owned the store after Pete Osdoba, their brother, had died. Gen's husband Phil Schelde managed the store and Peg's husband Don Palmquist sold shoes. The Osdoba family ran Greep's for forty-eight years.

The shoe department was in the back of Greep-Trueblood. We always got three new clothing items at the start of each new school year: a pair of stiff blue jeans, a long-sleeved plaid flannel shirt and a pair of Buster Brown shoes, which were sold exclusively at Greep-Trueblood. The neat thing about Buster Brown shoes, besides the fact that they were advertised on Andy Devine's Saturday morning television show which I watched religiously, was the fact that you got a free Buster Brown comic book and a Buster Brown toy just for buying the shoes. I still remember the commercial tag line: "Hi! I'm Buster Brown, and I live in a shoe. That's my dog, Tige, and he lives there, too!"

Buster Brown

Buster Brown (a midget with long hair or a wig) and Tige made an appearance on a little stage out on the sidewalk in front of Greep's predecessor, the Wells Brothers Company Department Store, on September 17, 1909. By the way, the Wells' house, which had been the Greenleaf mansion, was the sole house in the entire block on the site where the Meeker County Hospital was constructed in 1950.

On the woman's side of the store was a huge wide staircase going up to the second level. During Christmas season, the first landing of that staircase became "Santa's Place". Mom took us there and we stood in line waiting for our turn to walk up and sit on Santa's lap. Of course he always gave us some candy and a small gift. That was the only time I ever remember sitting on Santa's lap anywhere. Years later, Litchfield built a little house for Santa in Central Park where kids could come and see him. One year they had Santa's house in the bandstand.

268

On a summer morning during Crazy Days in the early sixties, I walked by Greep-Trueblood, looking at the men's clothing hanging from racks on the sidewalk. A red-haired guy was sitting on a stool in the doorway playing his guitar through a small amp and singing into a microphone. I stopped to watch him. He was a good-looking guy and a great singer, but he was just singing folk songs, which, at the time, I hated. If it wasn't rock and roll, I wanted nothing to do with it. His name was Jim Allen and he was dating my perennial classmate Cathy Osdoba.

Jim is immortalized in Arden Burleigh's painting of the hotel. In the painting, Jim is walking away from the bus, carrying a guitar case. No doubt, the girl walking next to him is Cathy. Arden probably put them in the painting because Cathy worked in his photography store at the time. The way that life takes funny turns brought Jim and I together a few years later.

When I returned home from my Army service in mid-October of 1969, I went walking the streets of Litchfield once again on a Monday afternoon, soaking in the warmth of my hometown. Jim came running out of his CJ Music Store, by Janousek's at that time, and he grabbed me.

"Hey, Terry!" Jim started. "Welcome home! Hey, how're ya doin'?" Meanwhile, I'm trying to remember who the heck this redheaded guy is and where I had seen him before.

"Say," Jim went on, "we're starting a band and you're gonna play drums for us."

"Who's 'we' and who's gonna be in this band?" I cautiously asked, thinking that this guy's got a lot of nerve telling me I'm playing drums in his band.

"Well, your brother Mick and I. Didn't he talk to you? No?…Well, we're gonna rehearse on Thursday at Mick's house 'cause we play on Friday here at the Legion Club."

"I haven't heard a thing about it…but if Mick's gonna be in it, I guess it's ok with me."

"Great. See ya Thursday night then." Off he went and I went home to call Mick.

As much as Mick and I didn't get along early in life, music had made us closer and I respected his taste, judgment and business sense in the music business. In the winter of 2000, the Minnesota Music Hall of Fame showed that they respected him too by electing him into the Hall. The following year, the annual "Rock and Roll Reunion", held in St. Joseph, Minnesota, presented Mick with a Lifetime Achievement Award.

Mick, Jim, and I played that first job at the Legion club without a band name, so the newspaper ad stated that the music would be by "Jim Allen & his band." That was the start of a seven-year non-stop run with the band that we started calling Shaw, Allen & Shaw. We played every single night for those seven years while I started my teaching career in Glencoe, Minnesota. I remember one December having Christmas Eve and one other day off. That was it. It ran me ragged, burning the candle at both ends, but being a teacher, I had my summers off. I devoted them entirely to my children with our camping trips, which included telling my kids these stories of my childhood while we sat around the campfire.

★★★★★★★★
FREE
MEMBERSHIP
Dance

American Legion
Clubrooms
Litchfield

SATURDAY NIGHT
Saturday, Oct. 25th

Music by
Jim Allen and his Band
(3 piece)
★★★★★★★★

Left: The first ad. Right: Jim Allen, Mick and Terry Shaw

The band became quite famous, recording two albums, appearing on television, receiving a national award from the Entertainment Operators of America (ballroom owners) convention held in Kansas and setting and breaking ballroom attendance records all over southern Minnesota.

Shaw, Allen & Shaw albums released in 11/71 and 12/72.

When Mick and I were teens, we used to hitchhike down to the Kato Ballroom in Mankato, Minnesota to see the biggest recording stars. You name the group, The Beach Boys, Jerry Lee Lewis, Roy Orbison; they all

270

played there, even Buddy Holly on his fateful last tour. Mick and I were there in the summer of 1962, when our idols, the Everly Brothers, just out of the Marines, set a Kato Ballroom attendance record. From that day on, my dream was to play the Kato. In 1975, Shaw, Allen & Shaw played the Kato for the first time. We broke the attendance record and our record stands today.

On our second album, Jim and I wrote all the songs except for two. Our recently hired keyboardist, Dewey Larson, wrote one and Dennie wrote the other, a song called *Love Is Gone*. The Shaw-Allen-Shaw band provided another verse for my song, which goes into the song that Dennie wrote for that album.

THE SONG GOES ON
Brother Pat, he never sang nor played in any band.
But he was always at the shows; he was our biggest fan.
Brother Dennie went out state to be a businessman,
while Mick played on and I "G.I.ed" across in German land.
I came home and Mick said, "Hey...we've got another band,"
and we took off on a never-ending string of one-night stands.
We made some records and it seemed that we could do no wrong,
and on one album we recorded one of Dennie's songs...
[Go into *Love Is Gone* by Shaw-Allen-Shaw.)

Around the corner from Greep's, heading east on Depot Street, was the original Northwestern Bell Telephone office[134], until the late fifties when they built their new office building on Ramsey Avenue North. Cheryl Caswell Almgren was one of the operators there.

"A-num-ber pa-leeze..."

"204-W please." (The Shaws' number. A "W" or a "J" indicated that you were on a party line.)

"Just a moment...I'll connect you." In the mid-fifties, Litchfield got dial phones with an Oxford exchange prefix and Cheryl had to find work elsewhere. Our number became Oxford 3-8278. The dial phones also meant that the operators couldn't listen in anymore to the juicy conversations between extra-marital lovers, such as a certain married Meeker County law enforcement officer, or one of our eye doctors and their female friends.

---

[134] See page 490 of the History of Downtown Litchfield Appendix.

Next to the telephone office was the VFW clubroom.[135] The next two buildings[136] heading east had an implement dealer and a vacant building, which had housed different restaurants in the thirties and forties, as did the next building. It was the Western Café, where I went to dances and had my first pizzeria pizza. It had been a bowling alley, first called the Litchfield Bowling Lanes and then the Bowling Café[137].

In May of 1939, a man named Frank Trappani bought a restaurant there from Walter McHugh. Right away he started getting into trouble with the law, selling to minors and allowing gambling to go on in the back. One day in late July, Mayor Leo Baumgartner, under pressure from people in town, had finally had enough. He walked in and took Trappani's beer license right off the wall saying, "I'm shutting you down Frank." Then Trappani did a really dumb thing. He sued the city.

In preparation for the trial, the city attorney uncovered some interesting things. An FBI agent told him that they were very interested in Mr. Trappani concerning a murder investigation in Chicago and a counterfeiting ring in Minnesota. A Secret Service agent confirmed the counterfeiting story. Trappani got wind of all this and he had one of those sudden mysterious fires in his restaurant in late August. Then someone "broke in" the café and removed all his goods. Trappani quickly sold the building to the Askeroth brothers in October and left town.   A couple of years later, in April of 1941, Frank, his brother Jasper, and two others were found guilty of counterfeiting $10 bills. June Brown, his former Litchfield waitress, was the prosecutions chief witness against Trappani.

On the corner of Depot and Marshall Avenue was Litchfield Implement[138].   Later, however, my classmate John "Fergie" Ferguson had his first car lot there.

The Greep's block must have been Litchfield's "Sin City" in the late 1800s. An 1875 photograph shows the Independent Printing Office before the alley and then there was Solomon's Saloon, the seedy Litchfield Exchange Hotel, and then Uncle Tom's Cabin Saloon. Add to the two saloons, the emergence of the filmed decadence of Hollywood in

---

[135] 21-23 Depot Street East. See page 491 of the History of Downtown Litchfield Appendix.

[136] 25 Depot Street East. See page 492 of the History of Downtown Litchfield Appendix.

[137] 27 Depot Street East. See page 494 of the History of Downtown Litchfield Appendix.

[138] 33 Depot Street East. See page 496 of the History of Downtown Litchfield Appendix.

a silent movie theater just before the alley, and you had the fuel for many of the sermons that were preached in Litchfield's dozen or so churches.

In 1889 and 1890, they were eight saloons[139] in Litchfield. Most of the saloons were on the east side of Sibley Avenue. In those days, the drug stores could also sell liquor, if they had a license, which they all did. An account in an 1892 copy of the *Litchfield Independent* newspaper tells of a fight involving a man named John Herman. It started in Nels Fredrickson's saloon, spilled out into the street and worked its way down to Swan August Scarp's saloon, where it escalated. After much damage, Herman and two others, Pat Hopkins was one, were thrown out. The next morning Herman's body was found on a road east of town with a bullet hole in the chest.

1875: Uncle Tom's Cabin saloon, Exchange Hotel, Solomon Saloon, the alley and the Independent Printing Office.

When the sight of drunks lying in the street, people flying out of doors and the fighting down Sibley Avenue and even the murders got out of hand, a religious group got up in arms and forced the city into a prohibition, which began on April 22, 1893. It didn't last long. It was over in a year in May of 1894. One man who came to town in the early 1910s, recalled how the first thing he saw, while walking down Sibley Avenue, was a man flying through the window of the saloon that was behind the site of Nicola's today. The city again voted to go dry in April of 1914.

Drinking does seem to go hand in hand with the "dark side", but church groups sometimes get funny ideas as to what is sinful. Some old

---

[139] They were Nels Fredrickson's, S. A. Scarp's, Nels Clements's, Albert Vitzthum Von Eckstaedt's, Ditlof Peterson's, Charles Forester's, John Konsbrick's and Rawson and Larson's saloons.

timers remember not being allowed to play baseball at all in Litchfield around 1919. All the games had to be played "on the road". It went back further than that. An April of 1889 town newspaper reported that at the council meeting, the town Marshall was instructed to prevent ball playing within the city limits on Sundays.

The Unique Theater[140] was next door to Greep's, heading back north on Sibley Avenue. Because the lot originally had a different building that was part of the Greep's building to the south, the Unique shared a foundation with Greep's. There was a door in the basement by the Unique's restroom leading to a storage room and from there into Greep's basement. The door was locked but left unblocked for the city steam system workers.

There was a hanging suicide in the basement of the Unique in the fifties. We never knew about it or we would have never gone to another scary movie there or at least to the bathroom in the basement. A man named Jim M. went to the theatre to ask Lloyd Schnee for some drinking money. After being refused, he went down to use the restroom and hung himself in that adjoining storage room using a drapery cord that he found. The next morning, a Greep's employee found him hanging there. When the Catholic Church burned down in 1920, Mass was held in the Unique for a year until the new church was built. The Unique wasn't allowed to show movies on Sundays anyway until April 14, 1929.

We kids thought of the Unique Theater as "our" theater. We called it the "Uni-Q". The Unique showed our kind of movies, that is movies starring the Bowery Boys, the Three Stooges, and Ma and Pa Kettle. Then there were the Roy Rogers and Gene Autry westerns and, finally, the science fiction and monster movies we both loved and feared. We

---

[140] 104-106 Sibley Avenue North. See page 500 of the History of Downtown Litchfield Appendix.

went to every single monster movie but some of us didn't watch the screen when the monsters appeared. Pat would dive under his seat when *The Creature From The Black Lagoon* or some other monster would show up on the screen, imploring me to "Tell me when it's gone! Tell me when it's over. Is it gone yet?" Invariably, I would lie and have him come up while the monster was still on the screen. Little brothers are put on this earth for older brothers to tease and torment.

The movie cost twenty cents, if you sat in the first seven rows, except on Saturday matinees, when all of the seats were twenty cents. Saturday afternoon matinees had a cowboy serial installment before the main feature starring Johnny Mack Brown, Rex Allen, Gene Autry with his sidekick Smiley Burnette or Roy Rogers with Trigger and Dale Evans. In the thirties and forties, you could take your matinee ticket stub over to the Land O'Lakes creamery after the movie and get a free ice cream treat with it.

Mom would give us a quarter on Friday nights for doing our weekly chores. Pat and I always went to the movies. I'd "buck" him there on my bike. Once, while I was teasing him by pretending to peddle into a parked car, he swallowed his quarter. He had put it in his mouth for safekeeping, because his elastic-waist trousers had no pockets. We didn't know what to do. We explained the problem to Mrs. John L. Reeves, who was sitting in the ticket booth at the theater. She, being a mother, understood and let Pat in with a promise that he'd pay double the following week.

With the five cents I had left from my quarter after buying my ticket, I'd buy a package of Stark Wafers. Stark Wafers was a roll of round quarter-sized candy wafers wrapped in almost clear cellophane. Another similar brand was Necco, which bought out Stark. Some of the candies tasted like soap, we thought, but if you sucked slowly on the discs and didn't chew them, they lasted for most of the movie. And yes, I did know what soap tasted like...thank you, Mom.

The Schnees just started selling candy and popcorn in their theaters when I was quite young. Before that we had to buy it at Axel's candy store down the street and sneak it in. The Schnees didn't want to put up with the noise and mess from it. But, they must have decided, "If you can't beat 'em, join 'em," because they soon installed a nice candy counter and popcorn machine in both of their theaters.

I had my very first date at the Unique Theater. In the seventh grade at St. Philip's Catholic School, I had fallen in love with Jeanette "Jan" Oliver, a beautiful sixth grade girl with short curly blonde hair, a winning smile and the most beautiful lips. Her dad, Vern[141], worked for the city street department with my future stepfather Floyd Young and the Olivers lived at 122 Fuller Avenue South. We had a seventh and sixth grades' club in our combined classroom at St. Philip's. I was elected the president and Jeanette was elected secretary. How nice! Instead of "Jeanette Oliver", she was "Jeanette Ah – love – her" to me.

Left: Jeanette Oliver, five years after our first date.
Right: The first date movie ad.

Somehow, at twelve and a half years old, I convinced Jeanette's mother that she could trust me to take Jeanette to a movie unchaperoned on Friday, December 20, 1957. With my limited resources, I chose the 7:30pm show at the Unique Theater, which was showing *Beginning Of The End*, a monster movie, of course. It starred Minnesota born Peter Graves and it was about giant grasshoppers. It was ironic that the Unique was next door to a former giant grasshopper gravesite. I paid the ticket lady forty cents and Jeanette and I sat in the first seven rows. To be specific, we sat in the two aisle seats in the second row on the left side. Luckily, for me, Jeanette turned down my invitation to buy her some popcorn. I didn't buy any Stark Wafers that night either, for the first time.

---

[141] Vern was never around much while I was "dating" Jeanette. Then, he suddenly disappeared from town. I found out in researching this book that he was caught and convicted of burglary of the Strout store in June of 1959. Maybe he got "sent up"?

Sometime after the cartoon, which was called *Woodman Spare That Tree*, the previews of the coming attractions, the newsreel and the comedy short called *Let's Talk Turkey*, I worked up the courage to ask Jeanette if I could hold her hand. I was so nervous that my hand was sweating like crazy. Regardless of the sweaty palm, once I got hold of her beautiful tiny hand, I wasn't letting go. I was in heaven. I would've tried to put my arm around her shoulder too, but I was deathly afraid of being seen by the other kids in the theater and then teased about it in school after Christmas vacation was over. Sitting by a girl was a daring thing to do and, for now, the touch of her hand was quite enough for my young and fast beating heart to stand.

Halfway through the movie, Jeanette excused herself to go to the bathroom. When she came back, I was too scared to ask for her hand again. I cursed the bathroom break and my shyness. It was a dumb movie too, with just real grasshoppers enlarged and superimposed on the screen.

I walked Jeanette home after the movie and we went to her basement family room where Paul "Chucky or Chuck" Loch, Jr. was sitting with Jeanette's eighth grade sister, Darlene. Chuck was a friend of my brother Mick and he was dating Darlene. He started grilling me right in front of everyone. (His picture is on page 34.)

"Didja kiss her? Huh? Didja?" Chuck asked. When I didn't answer him, he just kept on and on. Finally he asked, "Didja at least hold her hand?" I admitted that I had. That was a mistake. Darlene started to laugh at Jeanette and tease her. Jeanette got upset, started crying, and she ran upstairs. That was the end of my first date. Jeanette didn't talk to me for a week. The relationship went downhill from that point. Another one of life's lessons; don't "kiss and tell".

The Unique is gone today, but the memories aren't. The building was torn down in May of 1996 and it's just a vacant lot, but I'm sure dozens, maybe hundreds, of Litchfield teens and pre-teens had their first dates and maybe their first make-out sessions there.

Chapter Twenty-One
Art, Penny Candy, Glasses, and Nuns

When Pat and I would go to the movies at the Unique, I would lean my bike against the window of Burleigh's Studio[142] next door to the north. Our bikes were always there when we came out after the movie was over at 9:00 pm. "Small town trust." The building Arden Burleigh owned was an old wooden one. Arden was a photographer and he was also a very good artist. He painted beautiful realistic portraits and realistic paintings of landmarks around town, such as the hotel.

In 1961, high school principal Curtis McCamy called Arden and asked him to start an Art Department for the school. Arden had taught in Hutchinson for two years before becoming a full-time photographer. In 1962, the high school finally started offering Art classes for the very first time. I don't think Arden really wanted to teach the classes but he had pestered the school so much about its absence that he felt compelled to do it part time for a year.

It was quite an undertaking for Arden, considering he had three morning classes of thirty students each. He ran his photography studio in the afternoons, painted portraits in the evenings and did weddings on the weekends. But, Arden's hard work turned out to be quite a blessing for me. I learned more in my first year with Arden than I did in all my Minneapolis College of Art and Design classes combined. I do not exaggerate. Arden Burleigh was an inspiration to me.

Arden Burleigh with his daughter Bonnie.

I became an Art teacher, teaching for twenty-five years in Glencoe, Minnesota. I used many of Arden's lessons and techniques to teach my classes throughout my career. One that comes to mind was his "Contour

---

[142] 110 Sibley Avenue North. See page 503 of the History of Downtown Litchfield Appendix.

Drawing" course. In a couple of weeks, using Arden's techniques, I was able to turn my students' comical "monkey paw" drawings of their hands into beautiful accurate renditions. I never had one single student whose artwork didn't improve using Arden's methods.

I always told my students about Mr. Burleigh when I introduced my drawing class. I told them what Arden did the very first day of my very first Art class, which resulted in that wonderful drawing lesson. He came running into class late, huffing and puffing because he was a smoker, and he told us that he had been in the office checking on our supplies, which he had ordered for us. They still hadn't come.

"No problem," Mr. Burleigh went on, "because the basis of all art is drawing and for drawing all you need is a piece of paper and a pencil, and we've got that." Then he added, "But learning to draw is learning to see. What I'm going to do is not teach you how to draw better, but teach you how to see better." The resulting lessons he taught were what I based my drawing classes on for twenty-five years. I always credited Arden with the techniques I was passing on to those students. I made a point of writing a letter both to him and to the *Independent Review* newspaper when he retired. He was an excellent artist and an excellent teacher.

Auctioneer Col. Chester "Chet" Berg had his electric sales business in the building before Arden from 1939 to 1948. Chet lived two blocks north of us on Swift Avenue North. He had an artificial arm and a mean scar on his neck. It was the result of a work accident. Chet was doing work for the Municipal Power Plant after a big storm on August 4, 1941. Chet, Perry Riebe and Conrad Aveldson were sent out north of Darwin to repair some downed lines.

Back row: A young Chet Berg and Perry Riebe.
Front row: J. C. Bang, Ed "Eeks" Nelson and Claude Hamilton.

Chet went up the pole the downed line came from and Perry and Conrad went to the base of the pole the line was supposed to be connected to. Perry had the dead line in his hands and called to Chet for more slack. Trying to comply, Chet bumped the live wire and a charge of very high voltage went through his body, knocking him out and badly burning his arm, neck and the fingers of one hand. His cap had a burn hole right through the top. His unconscious body hung from his safety strap. The charge continued down the previously dead wire to Perry Riebe who was killed instantly. Aveldson, who was standing near by, was knocked to the ground but unharmed.

It took hours to get the unconscious Chet down from the pole. His burned arm had to be amputated and it took several months for Chet to recover. The story going around was that after he recovered, he had a nervous tic that caused him to jitter when he talked or get excited and one of his doctors told him to use it to his benefit and so he went to school to become an auctioneer. But most people will say that the story isn't true.

Chet's disability of having only one arm didn't hold him down, however. Before the accident, he had been a Golden Gloves boxer and an avid outdoorsman. Now he figured out ways where he could still fish and hunt. He became an award winning trap shooter. Once in July of 1959, after not participating for three years, Chet went down to the Twin Cities' Hopkins Gun Club and shot 188 clay pigeons out of 200 bringing home the championship.

Chet in 1958 and 1959.

Chet had an odd thing happen to him in the fall of 1946. At an afternoon farm auction south of Litchfield, Chet auctioned off a horse to Nick Arens. That evening, driving on Highway 22 near the Crow River

Bridge, Chet went out into the left lane to pass a car and ran right into the horse he had just auctioned off. One of the horse's legs was severed. It came through the windshield and ended up on the seat next to Chet. Nick had been trying to coax the horse across the road to his farm and the horse wasn't cooperating. They were standing on the opposite side of the road. Nick was able to jump out of the way, but it was a fatal decision on the horse's part not to be stubborn and not move.

The next store after Burleigh's in 1959 was Vold's Optometry. Before it was Vold's, it was Axel's Candy and Tobacco store[143], the small twelve-foot wide store that I knew most of my childhood. Axel Johnson and his wife Esther, who was Ole A. "Music Ole" Olson's daughter, ran the tiny store. They had a daughter named Karna, who married Kenny Agren and their son Gary ran around with my brother Mick. Axel had started out working for his father-in-law, "Music Ole". Then he worked at Tom Wandok's Litchfield Cigar Factory in early 1907, and finally he ventured out on his own buying the small confectionery from the Nelson sisters.

Axel also served as the town's fire chief from 1918 to 1922 and assistant fire chief from 1937 to 1938. People up town would hear the fire whistle blow and see old Axel sprint out of his store, run across Sibley Avenue avoiding the cars, and run down the alley by Butterwick's drug on his way to the fire hall. They were sure the thin, gray-haired old man was going to have a heart attack. Axel never took the time to lock up his store. He'd leave customers in there wondering what to do because Axel would yell to them, "Watch the place for me." He would make oyster stew to feed to the firemen at their meetings.

Axel had a gold mine with his location because of the Unique Theater being just a couple of doors away. For a long time the Unique was the only movie theater in town and, unbelievably in those days, the movie theaters didn't sell popcorn or candy. So Axel got all of that trade. For us kids, the biggest thing about Axel's store was that we could buy penny candy there.

There's no way to describe penny candy. It, obviously, cost a penny, but sometimes you'd get two for a penny. They were hard candies, suckers, bubble gum, miniature wax Coke-shaped bottles with

---

[143] 112 Sibley Avenue North. See page 504 of the History of Downtown Litchfield Appendix.

colored sugar water inside, Candy Buttons, which were strips of waxed paper with small colored candy "dots" on them, flavored wax lips and mustaches, yard long strings of red licorice, candy cigarettes with packages that looked like the real thing, candy necklaces, and long waxed paper tubes with flavored sugar inside. A nickel or a dime went a long way in Axel's store.

Penny candy and candy cigarettes.

In the window of the store was a big popcorn machine. As you went in, there'd be a long glassed counter to the left, almost the length of the store. The first section of the counter had the penny candy. Axel, standing behind the counter, had the patience of Job. A little boy would stand in front of the counter and stare at the candy for minutes trying to make his decision for his big purchase. Axel quietly stood on the other side of the counter smiling and looking down at the boy. Finally the customer's little mouth would open.

"I'll have two of those," the boy would say, pointing with a little finger.

"These?" Axel would ask, bending over and reaching his hand into the counter.

"No, the ones next to it," the boy would answer. "Yeah, those. Okay, I want two of those and then…how much are those there, Mister?"

"Which ones?"

"Those there, with the red things on them."

"These?"

"Yeah."

"They're two for a penny."

"Okay, I'll have…no, wait. I don't want those. How much are those yellow sticks next to it?"

"They're two for a penny also."

"Okay, I'll have one of those, and…"

"They're two for a penny, son, I can't sell you one…"

"Oh...okay. Then I'll have...how much did you say those red ones were?"

After the penny candy section, there was the candy bar section and finally the tobacco section. In the back was the "bar" where you could get cookies and doughnuts, coffee and cold tap beer. I wonder if Axel would pour himself a cold one after spending fifteen minutes with a kid to make a nickel sale.

Left: Axel Johnson Right: Axel and his wife Esther, in 1956 when he retired.

Axel and his wife retired in August of 1956 when Axel discovered that he couldn't make change anymore. He sold the building to Newell J. Vold. Of course, Newell had a son Lyle who was in my high school class, just like everyone else in town it seemed. Newel remodeled the building and it became Vold's Optometry where I got my first pair of glasses in the fifth grade. How I survived until then, getting good grades in school, I have no idea. My vision was 20/400, we found out at Vold's. 20/200 is legally blind, if uncorrected.

I remember walking out of the store with my mother on a Friday night with the new black "Buddy Holly" type glasses on my face. The stores stayed open in Litchfield on Friday nights, so all of the neon signs and streetlights in town were turned on. Looking around, I thought someone had shined the town up just for me. I was in awe, everything looked so clear, shiny and clean. I looked at my mother and I saw every wrinkle on her face. I thought she had aged twenty years on the spot. I told her too, not realizing what I was doing.

I hated those glasses. I was always breaking them and I knew Mom couldn't afford to buy me new ones. Kids started calling me "four eyes" and Grandpa Louis Rheaume called me "the Professor". One Sunday morning I was home alone watching television while my brothers and

Mom were off to church. I had gone to the six o'clock Mass earlier after delivering my Sunday papers.

Once again, the reception on our television was terrible. I sat in front of the television on the floor turning the channel tuner, looking for something to watch. I found a Mass service, a news program, and Oral Roberts giving a sermon. Those were what I had to choose from. I settled on Oral Roberts. He had just finished his sermon and people were lining up in the aisles to come forward to have Oral pray over and heal them. He'd touch their foreheads yelling, "Heal, in the name of Jee...zus, heal!" The "believer" would fall over and then get up and throw away his crutches or dance around saying he was healed. I was taken in by the moment. I was convinced it was real. Oral said, "Now I want to pray for those of you at home. If you have an ailment, if you have an affliction, come to your TV set and touch the screen and the part of your body where your ailment is. I'll pray for you and Jee...zus will heal you."

Oral Roberts healing a believer.

What ailment did I have? "My eyes!" I said to myself. "Yes! I'll get rid of these thick glasses!" I reached over and touched the screen and touched my closed eyes. Oral pleaded with Jesus to heal me. He begged for Him to have mercy on me and correct my problem. Oral was praying so hard for me, I was certain it would work. "God answers all of your prayers," the nuns had told me in my religion classes. Then they added, "Sometimes, though, you have to wait for the answer because God answers the prayers in his own time, not when you want him to." I opened my eyes. Oral's prayers hadn't worked. I couldn't see any better and I was upset. Oral Roberts was a fake!

In the year 2000, I opted for the new Lasik corrective surgery and shelled out almost $5000 for it. I came out of the operation with 20/15 eyesight. It was a miracle. The nuns had been right. God does answer all of your prayers...in his own time.

Speaking of nuns, I want to put in a good word for them. Over the years I've continually heard the horrors stories, usually told by comedians, of kids going to parochial schools with the sadistic nuns rapping their knuckles with rulers or pulling them out of their desks by their ears. I went to St. Philip's Conservatory[144], we called it "the nun's castle", at 307 Holcombe Avenue North for kindergarten and then to St. Philip's School from the fifth grade to the eighth grade and I never once saw any of the nuns in the school or the conservatory lay a hand on a student. The fifties were the days when teachers could spank you, pull your ear, pinch your arm, cuff the back of your head, and do other things to punish you and get your parents' backing and blessing. You'd probably get a couple of smacks from your parents thrown in for good measure.

The conservatory or Otho H. Campbell's residence.

Being poor, my mother couldn't afford to buy me a new winter coat when I had grown out of my old one in kindergarten. So she and her friend Kathryn Van Nurden made me a coat from one of my father's old green wool Army jackets that he had left at our house. I can vividly remember standing in the living room while they put it on me and tugged here and there and stuck pins in the jacket. Then they took it off and I was allowed to go play for a while until they called me into the living room again for another fitting. This went on for a couple of days.

Finally, when they finished, I looked at the coat and still saw an old green Army jacket. I was ashamed of that coat and I told Mom with tears in my eyes that I wasn't going to wear it to my afternoon kindergarten class. But, as moms will do, she somehow talked me into wearing it. Wiping away my tears, I refused her offer to walk me to the

---

[144] The Conservatory was originally Otho H. Campbell's residence, built in 1889. St. Phillips Church bought it in July of 1936 to used as three classrooms on the main floor and a residence for the nuns on the second floor.

285

nun's conservatory. A block away from our house, I started crying again and I cried all the way to the conservatory. I just knew that everyone there was going to make fun of me with my homemade coat.

When I arrived, the nun, who was my teacher, met me at the door.

"Why Terry Shaw," she said, with a huge grin. "You've got a brand new coat! Isn't it the prettiest coat I've ever seen?" Putting her arm around me, she gently led me into the classroom.

"Look class. Isn't Terry's new coat nice?" she said to the students as she walked me to my little chair. I don't know if my mom had anything to do with this, but I never forgot the wonderful thing that nun did for me that day.

At St. Philip's school, I had two outstanding teachers, Sister Margaret Claire and Sister Viola Irene. Both of those nuns nurtured my artistic talents asking me to draw things for their bulletin board displays. I never minded staying in during recess to help them with a project. They lavished me with praise. They encouraged me to help others with their homework when I was finished with mine. It planted the seed for my own teaching career and kept me from getting bored in school.

Sister Viola Irene had us put our books away every day during the last half hour of classes. She let us put our heads down on our desks, close our eyes if we wanted and then she read a few chapters from a book to us. I remember books about the Bobsey Twins. That nun had such a way with her readings that she made me love the printed word and a great story.

St. Philip's sent my eighth grade class of twenty-two students over to the ninth grade at the high school and sixteen of us made the honor roll the first quarter of the school year. Many of us sat in the front row at our graduation ceremony with a gold braid around our necks, indicating that we were Honor Students in the top ten percent of the class.

St. Philip's School

Now, Father Clarence R. Foley, the first priest I can remember at St. Philip's Church, was a different story. He had a temper and was old-fashioned and strict. He was hard of hearing, so he would yell his sermons, which weren't always about the Sunday Gospel or the theme of the day. Sometimes he'd go into a tirade about the need for money for repairs or about the filthy "condemned" movies they were showing at the Hollywood Theater. He could spend fifteen minutes chiding the women for not picking up their pots and pans that lingered in the basement for weeks after a potluck feed.

Even though Father Foley was hard of hearing, he could hear a crying baby and he would stop his sermon and demand the mother take her screaming kid out of the church. (I silently applauded him, by the way.) He would stop Mass and turn around to face us all and yell at someone leaving the service early to "Sit back down! This Mass is not over yet!" Once he caught my Aunt Doris on her way out with her little daughter Marilyn. Doris yelled back, "I've got a sick kid here, Father, and I am leaving!" She left and Father Foley, stunned no doubt that someone would talk back to him, especially in church, turned around and continued the Mass.

I felt self-conscious going to Confession because Father Foley talked so loud that I could hear him talking to the person in the confessional across from me. I didn't always want people to hear what he had to say to me or vice versa. I had heard that Jackie Vossen had told Father Foley something in Confession once when he was little which caused Father to come out of his middle partition, pull Jackie out of his curtained section and paddle his behind. I'm betting Jackie talked back to Father Foley, or, worse yet, swore in church. Swearing was the one thing that was sure to get Father's goat.

Father
Clarence
R. Foley

A woman from out of town went to the police one Saturday afternoon and told them that she had just gone to Confession at St. Philip's Church and the priest there was drunk. An officer was sent to investigate. He found Father Foley, a diabetic, in insulin shock in the confessional. The symptoms, slurring language for example, were very similar to drunkenness.

Some of our classes were doubled up at St. Philip's. The seventh grade class was so big that it was split with the eighth grade and the sixth grade. Father Foley came into my classroom at St. Philips School once a week to teach a half hour religion class. There was an extremely poor family in town called the Rogers family. They had a dirt floor in their house, that's how poor they were. Two of the kids, Lloyd and Clemet were in my classroom. Lloyd was in my class and Clemet was in Mick's eighth grade class. An older brother of theirs was in Dennie's class. I saw Father Foley throw Clemet Rogers against the blackboard one day during that religion class. Clemet deserved it.

Clemet had been a thorn in the nun's side all morning, making rude comments off to the side. He started in again during Father Foley's short lecture when he arrived later in the morning and the priest stopped talking and reprimanded Clemet sternly. With a smug smile on his face, I suppose to tell the rest of us to "Watch this...", Clemet said to Father, "I don't give a shit. Go to hell." We gasped when we heard the words come out of his mouth. Father Foley's face turned red and he was standing over Clemet in a flash.

"What did you say to me?" he asked the smirking boy. Before he could finish repeating it, Clemet found himself flying against the blackboard, spanked in front of the class and then marched out of the classroom. I don't remember him ever coming back.

There was a nun named Sister Lenore who came into our classroom a couple of times a week to teach us music. At least they called it music class, but all we really ever seemed to do was rehearse in Latin for singing Requiem Masses or other church ceremonies. "Requiem aeternam dona eis Domine..." we would sing, not understanding what we were singing. Lloyd refused to sing, either in school during music class or on Saturday mornings at the funerals. I always hated those Masses and I understood why Lloyd was doing what he was doing. But again, he, just like Clemet, first knocked heads with the nun and then with Father Foley. I'm sure Father Foley won again in round two vs. the Rogers boys.

Monk Schreifels, Clemet Rogers, Don Larson and Lloyd Rogers in 1956

Growing up in Minneapolis, Father Foley came to Litchfield in 1946. He was a force in getting the parochial school built[1] and was extremely proud of it. One day in April of 1960, he called up his old friend P. J. Casey, the lawyer, and asked him to come over. They walked around the school, talking about it and what it meant to finally get it built. A few days later, Father Foley died.

As I stated, the Rogers family lived in a shack with a dirt floor. The Good Cheer Club got together and had a free concrete floor poured into their house. The Good Cheer Club consisted of people from every church in town. It was organized by Mrs. Nelson D. March in December of 1922 in the days before there was a welfare program. The first members were Mrs. March, Axel E. Johnson's wife Esther, who was in it for all of its thirty-six years, Mr. and Mrs. Ole A. "Music Ole" Olson, C. H. Maxson, Marie Peterson and Mrs. James Campbell. Kitty Holm soon became a member and the club worked closely with the Red Cross headed up by Reuben B. Hagglund. If they found somebody in town in need, they saw to it that something was done to help them. They made up food baskets in the room over the old fire hall and stored donated mattresses and furniture, which was stored at Olson's music store. As the members aged or died, the club, which hadn't recruited new members, folded in 1958.

---

[1] The school was built in the summer of 1953 on a lot where pioneer Judge of Probate Francesco V. DeCoster had his home. DeCoster, who spoke Sioux, was a Civil War veteran and owned several different businesses in town after he came in 1871.

North of Vold's was another tiny restaurant called Kate's Café, once called Kate's Lunchroom[146]. Kate Pierce and her husband Melvin, neighbors of ours living across the street, bought the site, tore down the small wooden building that was there and put up a new brick one. Kate's Café was small like Janousek's, but Kate didn't specialize in hamburgers. She made regular home-cooked meals and therefore, to a teenager like myself, it was not near as good a place to go. Pat went in there with his buddies during their school lunch break, if he and I didn't have our lunch breaks at the same time. He'd order a plate of mashed potatoes and gravy for twenty cents.

Kate had a mouth like a truck driver and she had a unique menu. She cooked one or two things for noon dinner and if you didn't want one of those "blue plate specials", you didn't eat in Kate's. The "special" was always some kind of meat like roast pork along with mashed potatoes and gravy and a vegetable, usually succotash or corn.

Kate originally had a small restaurant and 3.2 bar on Second Street West in the mid-forties, which she called the Lunch Time Inn. It was right between the turkey plant and an automotive repair shop. What a spot for fine dining. She sold it to her daughter, the widow Laura Welsand, who was Bobby Welsand's mother. Bobby was the boy Skeeter Anderson had talked me into hitting.

An interesting sideline to Kate's Café on Sibley Avenue was that during prohibition it was called the Taxi Inn and you could get more than food and a taxi there. If you need some bootleg whiskey, for example, you'd call for a taxi and when it showed up at your door, you'd tell the driver what you needed. He'd take you somewhere where he had his stash and sell you what you wanted.

---

[146] 114 Sibley Avenue North. See page 506 of the History of Downtown Litchfield Appendix.

Chapter Twenty-Two
Pool, Sandgren's, and the Community Building

North of Kate's Café was the usual mid-block alley. After the alley was Putzier and Johnson's Recreation Hall[147]. It became just Johnson's Rec and then Dale's Rec in 1966. We simply called it "the pool hall". As Johnson's Rec, it was a bar and pool hall owned and run by Melvin "Bull" Johnson[148]. Old man Dewey Vick worked behind the bar.

Damaged photo of Dale's Rec from 1969.

Bull allowed teenagers to come into the back of his establishment to play pool. Initially we had to stay in the back and away from the front where the bar was. But slowly we worked our way up to the front booths where we played cribbage, until we got kicked out to the back again. We always came in through the south side door from the alley, but if we came in through the front we'd see a long high bar on our right and wooden booths on our left. It was a typical wooden bar about four feet high with metal-legged stools all along it and a brass foot rail on the bottom. There were still spittoons on the floor near it, so some of the customers obviously still chewed, and a long mirror opposite the bar.

Small square tables were spread around the front half of the pool hall, between the bar and the booths, where groups of old guys sat playing Whist, Euchre or Sheepshead, which the old Germans called Schafkopf. We stayed in the back where there were six regular pool tables and one billiard or snooker table. It cost ten cents for a game of pool. We racked up your own balls and paid on the honor system, which, unbelievably, we honored. Getting kicked out would have been a fate worse than death because the other pool halls in town wouldn't let us come in.

---

[147] 116 Sibley Avenue North. See page 507 of the History of Downtown Litchfield Appendix.
[148] Melvin "Bull" Johnson was assistant fire chief from 1962 to 1964.

Along the walls by the pool tables were heavy wooden chairs, which looked like adult "high chairs". The same old guys would be sitting in them everyday, watching the pool games and nursing 10¢ glasses of beer. Old Freddie Williams was one. Almost everyday after school, I ran down to Johnson's to play a game of Missouri Eight Ball with my buddies. We spent some evenings and most Saturday afternoons there too, especially when it rained. I got to be a pretty good pool player, but I always had trouble beating Alvie Watkins, who kept us entertained while we played. I used to call myself "Dr. Jekyll and Mr. Hyde" because I was a straight "A" student in the Honor Society in school, but outside of school I hung around the pool hall and smoked.

I spent a couple of study hall periods in school one week drawing a five-dollar bill, carefully copying one that I had. I had a talent for realistic drawing and when I finished, it looked astonishingly real. I showed it to my friends and they dared me to try to pass it. I took it the pool hall that afternoon after school and handed it to old Dewey Vick to pay for my games. After he had accepted it and started to give me change, I told him about it. He laughed and showed it to Bull, who was so impressed that he offered to buy it from me. I sold it to him for a dollar and he taped it up on the mirror behind the bar. My first Art Show. I met someone recently who told he that he had acquired it and kept it for years before finally throwing it away. I should have signed it.

The double lot next to the pool hall, where Penney's built a new store in 1958, originally had two store buildings on it. Don's TV service[149], run by Don Test, was in one of them, and north of it was a vacant building[150]. The vacant building had been the original Sandgren's Shoe Repair Shop[151]. Andrew W. Sandgren's shoe repair moved into the location in the late twenties. One morning in August of 1933, Andrew Sandgren didn't open up. When he wasn't found at home, the police were notified and asked to open up the shop. Inside they discovered Sandgren's body hanging in the back room. He had committed suicide. Andrew's son George came home and took over the business at this location before moving it to the corner north of here.

---

[149] In 1961, Don moved to the Ramsey Avenue side of the Dahl Tire Company building.
[150] 118 Sibley Avenue North. See page 510 of the History of Downtown Litchfield Appendix.
[151] 120-124 Sibley Avenue North. See page 512 of the History of Downtown Litchfield Appendix.

I frequented Penney's because they carried the latest styles of clothing and they were cheap. The sixties and the Beatles had brought about a clothing revolution for men. Being a late teen and a college student by then, I made every effort I could to keep up with the styles with my limited financial resources. My classmate John "Fergie" Ferguson worked as a clerk in Penney's and he guided me to the best buys. He went on to own Ferguson's Motors, a car dealership, out on east Highway 12.

Heading north from the Penney's site was the Black Cat Café[152]. In the forties and early fifties, the Black Cat had been a teen hangout. I don't know why my buddies and I didn't carry on that tradition in the mid and late fifties, but we didn't. I don't think I ever even sat in there for a Coke. It was probably because they didn't like kids in there after dark because they sold beer.

The Black Cat was a very nice café, however, and it was famous for its pies. The local citizens didn't know that you could get the same pies at almost every restaurant in Litchfield. Mrs. Edward Scarp, who had owned Scarp's Café at this location with her husband, who went blind, had a business out of her home[153] making and selling pies and pastries. Starting in 1930, she baked the treats out of her wood-burning stove in her home kitchen for nine different restaurants in Litchfield. She eventually moved up to a gas oven, but still used only one. She initially charged the restaurants 50¢ a pie. Her daughter, Iva Scarp Pearson, who was taken into the family during the twenties but never adopted, delivered the pies around town for Mrs. Scarp during her hour-long school lunch break.

Sam's Grocery and Meat Locker, which we called Sam's Butcher Shop[154], followed the Black Cat Café. Occasionally Mom would go into Sam's, but not very often. Next door to Sam's was Plate's Toggery[155]. Plate's was another men's clothing store, another one that I never went into.

---

[152] 126 Sibley Avenue North. See page 513 of the History of Downtown Litchfield Appendix.
[153] 121 Holcombe Avenue North.
[154] 130 Sibley Avenue North. See page 515 of the History of Downtown Litchfield Appendix.
[155] 132 Sibley Avenue North. See page 516 of the History of Downtown Litchfield Appendix.

At the southeast corner of Sibley Avenue and Second Street was Sandgren's Shoes[156]. Sandgren's was a favorite place for Mom to shop for us, after we had outgrown the Buster Brown shoes at Greep's. In July of 1947, Sandgren advertised that you could buy comfortable shoes at his store because he had "X-Ray Fitting". The fascinating machine he had for a time was a foot X-ray machine called a fluoroscope. An X-ray machine with absolutely no safeguards or lead aprons around the kids? It's unbelievable that it even got on the market. It was removed in the late fifties. Greep's had a fluoroscope once also. The customer would put on a new pair of shoes and stand up on the machine, inserting his feet into a slot. The clerk would then turn the machine on. Looking through a viewer on the top, you could tell how the shoes fit. There were two extra viewers for the customer's mom or wife and the salesman. Kids and husbands were never allowed to make such a big decision as to what they should put on their own feet.

Sandgren's sign and the fluoroscope machine.

In December of 1957, Paul "Chuck" Loch and I were still going with the Oliver sisters and the couples had exchanged gifts for Christmas.

"We should take the presents to Sandgren's," I said to Chuck, "and then we could look through the X-ray machine and see what's in them." We decided not to do it but Chuck told Jeanette that I had done it anyway. I was in the doghouse again, for two weeks that time.

One night Chuck Loch, Mick and Pat decided to raid Harlan Quinn's outdoor Christmas decorations. I don't know what they were thinking or why they singled his house out, but they took a lot of Christmas bulbs off of the trees outside of his house. The next day we were sitting in school at St. Philip's Parochial and Chief of Police George Fenner paid our classroom a visit. He spoke to Sister Viola Irene for a while and then Pat and I were called out into the hallway. Chief

---

[156] 134 Sibley Avenue North. See page 517 of the History of Downtown Litchfield Appendix.

Fenner started grilling us about the missing lights. At the time, I honestly didn't know what he was talking about but Pat started fidgeting and squirming. I was sent back into the room and Pat came walking in later. He looked like he had been crying.

Chief Fenner came back into the room and Sister told us that he wanted to talk to our class. George sat down on the corner of Sister's desk and gave us a speech about how Christmas decorations were the candles on Jesus' birthday cake.

"Some naughty boys have stolen the candles off of Jesus' birthday cake," George said. Everyone in class turned around and looked at me. I hunched my shoulders up and shook my head, silently miming "It wasn't me!"

Pat must've ratted on Mick and Chuck because all three of them were nailed and put on probation. They had a curfew of six o'clock every night for several months. This was going to put a damper on Chuck's pursuit of Darlene Oliver. Chuck started sneaking out nights. He'd make his way down the four blocks to our house where I'd join him outside. We'd sneak down to the Olivers', hoping not to get caught. All that trouble and neither Chuck nor I ended up with either of the sisters.

Pat and I and our combined seventh and eighth grade classes had our picture in the December 25th *Independent Review* newspaper that year, presenting a new television to the nuns for their residence. Our classes had collected the money to buy it for them. Pat and I did do some good things too.

The arrow points to Terry Shaw, the author. Left of me is Dougy Wimmer and right of me is Marty Foss. In front of me is Jeffrey B. To the left of him is Dickey Whalen and to the right are Pat Shaw and Jerry Wimmer.
At the extreme left is Andy "Monk" Schreifels. The first nun on the left is Sister Margaret Claire. The tall boy in the back on the right is James McLane; under him is Dee Dee Cox. Kathy Berle has her arm in a sling.

In May of 1966, twenty-one year old Chuck Loch was home on leave from the Navy. He and a girlfriend were out riding on his Honda motorcycle three miles east of Litchfield on Highway 12. Nineteen-year old Dickey Whalen was home on leave too, from the Air Force. He was driving his mother's '65 Chrysler around and had picked up four young girls to go riding with him. Coincidentally two of them were my cousins, seventeen-year old Marilyn and fourteen-year old Vivian Johnson. They lived by Dickey's mother and were the daughters of my dad's youngest sister Doris.

Dickey approached Highway 12 from the south on a gravel road. He stopped, looked quickly to one side, and gunned his car to cross over the highway. Chuck's motorcycle slammed right into the Chrysler's right passenger door. Chuck hit the windshield, shattering it and his body, and he continued across the car, landing on the pavement. His girlfriend flew all the way to the ditch across the road. No one in Dickey's car was seriously injured, nor was Chuck's girlfriend, miraculously. But Chuck sustained head injuries, multiple fractures of his left arm, and both of his legs were broken. He ended up losing the arm. Dickey was ticketed. Once again the threads of my life were intertwining.

If I turned the corner at Sandgren's and walked east on Second Street, I went by the side entrance to the rear of Sandgren's where Louie Vossen had a shoe repair service until February of 1958. Louie, who lived a block and a half from us, was bald and the rumor was that he had been bit by a monkey in the South Pacific during the war and lost all his hair. I never had the nerve to ask him if it was true. Louie's son Jack ended up playing guitar in bands too and was Cathy Osdoba's second husband.

Following the shoe repair shop was the Askeroth Paint and Wallpaper store.[157] I found out something interesting about Clarence "Skip" Askeroth, the owner of that business. In 1917, as a bugler in the Navy, Skip played in the Great Lakes Band. For a period of time, including the time Skip was in the service, that band was conducted and led by none other than the famous "March King" John Philip Sousa.

---

[157] 18-24 Second Street East. See page 520 of the History of Downtown Litchfield Appendix.

East of Askeroth's was an alley and following it was George Bauer's Horseshoe Cafe[158]. I can't remember going into the Horseshoe. It just wasn't a place kids hung out in. I think it was one of those restaurants where old guys sat around and talked all morning over a never empty cup of coffee. The name "Horseshoe" came from the shape of the lunch counter, with the open part of the "shoe" in the back by the kitchen.

I don't remember what was in the next couple of buildings in 1959[159]. It's hard to believe that I didn't venture down this street enough to remember the stores, but I didn't. Arriving at the corner of Second Street and Marshall Avenue, I came to Harlan Quinn's Dodge/Chrysler car dealership[160]. Harlan was a widower and was the gentleman that had married Dickey Whalen's mother. He unknowingly paid for many a meal at Fransein's for Dickey and his friends.

Pat and I were invited for a meal at the Quinn's house one night and we were quite impressed with how fancy everything was. After the meal, Harlan pushed back his chair and said, "Well, gentlemen, should we retire to the TV room for coffee and dessert?" We had never been treated like an adult guest before and we didn't know how to act. I think we giggled. I know we belly-laughed about it later. "Retire to the TV room..." It was like a foreign language to us "gentlemen", which nobody had ever called us before either.

Across the street, east of Quinn's, was the City Hall or the Community Building, which had originally been the Litchfield Opera House. Built in 1900, the building[161] was used for many things. In the front were offices, but the back had a large gymnasium with a stage. Because the sidewalks in town were so bad, we'd go to the Community Building for free roller-skating. You had to provide your own skates. Our skates were those terrible ones we called "clamp-ons" and the stores called "Adjust to fit". They clipped onto your shoes and you tightened them up with a "key". You could buy a pair at the Coast To Coast store for about $2.50. You'd hit a crack in the sidewalk, the skate would pull

---

[158] 26-30 Second Street East. See page 522 of the History of Downtown Litchfield Appendix.
[159] 32-34 Second Street East. See page 526 of the History of Downtown Litchfield Appendix.
[160] 40 Second Street East. See page 527 of the History of Downtown Litchfield Appendix.
[161] 126 Marshall Avenue North. See page 537 of the History of Downtown Litchfield Appendix.

off and you'd half-skate and stumble down the block trying to stay on your feet and not lose half your leg's or your hand's skin in the inevitable fall to the concrete sidewalk. Sometimes you'd pull off half of the sole of your shoe. Louis Vossen must have loved the business he got in his shoe repair shop from the kids' use of those skates.

We also went to the Community Building for gun training, club meetings or for a free lunch during REA Days. REA Day was a customer appreciation day for the Meeker County Rural Electric Association customers. Being "town people", we weren't customers but we went anyway. The "Day" was held on a Saturday in the spring, usually in late February or early March. All we kids knew was that we could get a free meal of a sandwich, potato salad, potato chips, a carton of Land O'Lakes milk and a Dixie Cup of the locally made ice cream. We could sign up for free giveaways also and pick up a free pencil or ruler. I usually signed up for everything even though I was only in my early teens.

The Community Building, City Hall, or the Opera House.

On Saturday, February 7, 1959, I was home in the late afternoon, after having eaten my free meal at the Community Building, when there was a knock on the door. It was Skeeter. He said that he had heard my name being drawn as a winner of something at the Community Building. Excited, I ran to Mom to tell her and ask how I could get my prize.

"Take your bike and ride out to the REA Building (out on east Highway 12) and ask them," she said. I ran out of the house, got my bike out of the garage, and peddled as fast as I could out there. Luckily there was very little snow on the ground. All the way, I had visions of some huge prize like a hundred dollars or a brand new TV. I ran into the building, puffing.

"Hi! I'm Terry Shaw. Somebody told me that I won something today."

298

"Let's see," the lady behind the counter said, shuffling through some envelopes. "Oh yes, here it is. You've won a $10 gift certificate to the Larson and Peterson Grocery store in Cosmos." She handed me the envelope.

"Oh...ah...thanks," I said turning for the door. "Cosmos?" I thought to myself. "How am I going to get to Cosmos?"

Disappointed, I went home and told Mom, saying something about it being worthless because we didn't have a car.

"Well, I can ask Kathryn Van Nurden if she'll drive us there, "Mom told me. "Will that be okay?"

"Sure!" I said, with visions of mountains of store-bought cookies, candy bars and pop dancing in my head.

"You'll need to offer her something for her gas, though," Mom added. "Maybe some of the groceries?"

"Oh, okay," I said dejectedly. There always seemed to be a catch whenever I got good news.

"And you should give something to Skeeter for telling you that you won too," she went on. "After all you wouldn't have anything if it wasn't for his and Kathryn's help."

In the blink of an eye, I had lost half my fortune. But Mom was right, as usual, and that's how it went.

"Oh," she added. "I'll expect you to share with your brothers too." Sure, why not...the family tax. That's life. The "haves" soon become the "have-nots".

Dances were held at the Community Building too. In the fall of 1960, the city started having weekly teen hops there and they held a contest to come up with a name. I submitted the winning entry, "Hop Stop". I was embarrassed about my entry for some reason so I put Jerry Wimmer's name on it. Jerry won ten free passes to the "Hop Stop". Jerry didn't dance, so he gave the passes back to me. The hops didn't go over very well and they were discontinued after about five dances. Too many kids were non-dancers like Jerry and there were too many parents there as chaperons. You felt like you were under a microscope. Somewhere there's a silent home movie of Dennie or Mick's band playing for a teen dance at the Community Building. I've seen it once.

In the fall of 1962, the back third of the Community Building was converted into an additional classroom for the crowded high school. I had my senior year Art class there at the Community Building. Jerry Trushenski had taken over the teaching duties from Arden Burleigh. I sat next to my seventh grade girlfriend, Jeanette Oliver, everyday, still secretly in love with her, wishing for the "good old days" when she felt the same towards me. But it wasn't to be.

This wasn't the first time that high school classes were held in other buildings in Litchfield. The original high school, built in 1880 or 1881, burned down on March 14, 1929. It was situated on the lot on Armstrong Avenue next to First Street. The school was made of brick and the gymnasium attached to it was made of wood. Just the brick school burned down. Go figure. The Board of Education had to scramble and use temporary classrooms all over town until the new high school was built in and dedicated in December of 1930.

The old high school before it burned down in March of 1929.

Shop and Music classes were in the town hall. Home Economics was in the Robertson building basement at the northwest corner of Sibley Avenue and Third Street, English class was over the bank at the southwest corner of Sibley and Second Street, French, Latin, Algebra, the sciences, and study and assembly halls were upstairs over Viren-Johnson's where the old court house rooms were, there were American History and Plane Geometry classes in Watson Hall over the Coast To Coast store, one class was in the Masonic Hall at the southeast corner of Sibley and Third, there were typing classes under the bakery next to the bank at the southwest corner of Sibley and Second Street, classes were held in the display room of the Motor Supply Company and under Jacks' Ben Franklin, and there were classes in the basements of churches. Basketball was played in the old dance Pavilion where the turkey processing plant went. The Pavilion only had twelve-foot high ceilings so you couldn't put any arch on your shots. Litchfield defeated Willmar 19 to 6 and Grove City 7 to 2 there. Can you imagine kids running all over town to get to their classes?

N. Thomas Woodward, a lawyer, taught the Typing class. He would come in and give the day's assignment to the students and then leave. So a lot of students, like Elaine Ericson Lindell, would run upstairs to grab a doughnut in the bakery or get one at the end of class on

300

the way to study hall. In the spring, the senior class had their picture taken on the steps at St. Philip's Church and they graduated from either the courthouse or the Opera House. Different students told of different locations.

At the corner of Marshall Avenue and Second Street, across the street diagonally northeast of Quinn's, was Erickson's Funeral Home[162]. It was one of those funeral homes that was actually a home and looked like one. I saw my first dead body there when Mom took me along to a visitation on a cold wintry Saturday afternoon. I don't remember who the deceased was, but I remember being scared to death at the sight. I shuddered when I saw someone reach out and touch the hand of the dead person. I stared at the body in the casket and wondered how in the world anyone could live in that same house.

Mr. Erickson had a son named Frederick who was a year older than my brother Dennie. Freddy was a brilliant student and a very talented cello player who went on to teach at Harvard University. But he was a bit odd in that he was missing an ear and he had something wrong with his mouth. It must have been a cleft palette or something. It made him talk funny. Freddy wore glasses and had some kind of contraption on his head to hold them up, because of his missing ear.

Of course kids can be cruel, sometimes unintentionally. A group of kids kept bothering Freddy about his missing ear.

"Hey, what happened to your ear?" someone started.

"Yeah, how come you ain't got no ear?" someone else added.

To shut them up, Freddy told them, "My dad forgot to tie a corpse down to his work table and it got up and came after me and cut my ear off with a scalpel."

The frightened boys never bothered Freddy again and they always ran to the other side of the street when they saw him walking towards them after that. To Freddy's credit, he never let his "disabilities" hold him down. He went out for Speech and was in the class plays. But I looked at him, being "different" and all, and thought to myself, "This guys sleeps in a house with dead bodies." It unnerved me. No amount of education or life experiences has changed my feelings about corpses.

Most undertakers I've encountered in my life were kindly older men, always elegantly dressed, with every hair on their head in place,

---

[162] 202 Marshall Avenue North. See page 538 of the History of Downtown Litchfield Appendix.

like Reuben B. Hagglund. It's a good thing I never met John O. Larson, from what I've heard. He had an undertaking business a few blocks to the east of Erickson's in the basement of his house at 329 East Second Street. He started the business in October of 1926 and called the house the Litchfield Funeral Home after he had set up the main floor as a showing room in August of 1927.

In those days, there weren't a lot of funeral homes where the body was shown. Bodies were usually prepared in the basements and backrooms of furniture stores or the undertaker's home and then brought to the house of the departed for the showing and the wake. John wasn't impeccably dressed, his hair wasn't perfectly combed and he chewed and spat tobacco. A couple of stories I've heard illustrate everything about him.

John was called to go to a farmhouse to pick up a body of someone who had died in his sleep. He asked someone from town, who later related this story, to go along with him. The weather turned bad and by the time they had arrived at the farm, they were in the middle of a Minnesota blizzard. Shown into the bedroom of the deceased by the family, the talk turned to the weather. The family bemoaned the fact that they didn't think John and his companion should venture out into the storm with their dearly departed. They were afraid, however, that they had no extra bedrooms to put the gentlemen up for the night. John lay down on the bed next to the deceased and said, "Oh, I can sleep here tonight. This will be fine."

John was told to meet a train in the dark of the early morning hours one time to accept the body of a deceased. He met the train at the depot, got the body bag and then threw it into his wheelbarrow and proceeded to cart it down dark Sibley Avenue towards his residence. On the way, he met up with a young morning paperboy named Don Larson, who was no relation to him.

"Whatcha got in the bag, mister?" Don, who would later own Viren-Johnson's, asked John.

"Oh, it's a dead one," John replied, matter of factly to the stunned lad. Don hurried on his way and John continued on to his home, where he slid the body down his coal chute to his workroom.

Don Larson had already met up with the strange mortician once before at a funeral. The little boy, standing with his brother and parents at the graveside, watched the undertaker chewing his cud as he was holding a container of dirt for the family to sprinkle over the casket after the minister had finished his prayers. Suddenly, John spit a brown liquid down near the edge of the grave. A stunned Don said out loud to his brother, "Did you see that? He spit on the grave!" Don's embarrassed mother quickly hushed him up.

John O. Larson had a son named Warren, who was a friend of John Esbjornsson II. Esbjornsson was a real character that you'll read about in a later chapter. His fellow Army Air Corps pilot friend Warren Larson went by the nickname of "Killer". I think it had something to do with his hunting skills. Twenty-seven year old Killer Larson went out to the airport one day in March of 1947 and rented a plane from Carl Ulrich at about four in the afternoon. He immediately flew out to Lake Ripley and was flying low over the water heading east when he suddenly banked right to buzz the golf course clubhouse. Unfortunately his right wing struck a cottonwood tree on shore and his plane was swung into more trees while flipping upside down. It crashed to the ground.

D. W. Albright was driving by and he stopped his car and ran up to the plane where he saw a badly injured Killer Larson inside. As he started to pull him out of the wreckage, the plane exploded and burst into flames. Albright was forced back to watch Killer be consumed by the flames. Dingle Rangeloff's place was close by and his wife called the alarm in to the fire department, but they couldn't do anything to save Killer or the plane. John Esbjornsson was a pallbearer but the experience didn't change him from continuing on with his wild ways.

What was left of Killer's plane.

Chapter Twenty-Three
Gunmen and the Beach

Directly across the street, north from Quinn's, was the Post Office.[1] It was where Dean Schultz and, eventually in the seventies, my pal Skeeter Anderson worked. In the late sixties, I played briefly in a Litchfield based country band named The Country Ramblers. The leader of the band, Keith Miller, was also a mailman at the Post Office.

Litchfield actually had nine different locations for its Post Office. In the early days of the town, the Post Office simply followed the postmaster around town, so the first one was in John A. C. Waller's or George B. Waller's home in 1869, depending on the source of the information. From 1870 to 1874, it was at the northwest corner of Sibley Avenue and Second Street where Litchfield's first official postmaster Horace B. Johnson had his clothing store. The Pizza Ranch is there today. Then the Post Office followed Postmaster Frank Daggett to the present location of the Main Street Café from 1874 to 1879. It went across the street to the north half of Dueber's from 1879 to 1891 and then, from 1891 to 1892, it was in the building just after the alley on Second Street East where the Second Street Business Center is. When a large new bank building was erected at the southwest corner of Sibley Avenue and Second Street, where Sparboe Farms is today, the Post Office moved into the rear of that building from 1892 until 1931 except for a few months in 1908, when it was moved to the present location of Dee's Family Hair Style while an addition was added to the rear of the bank building. Then it was moved to the present location of the Legion Club from 1931 to 1936, while the present Post Office building was erected. It has remained at its present location since 1936.

Sando's and the Post Office.

---

[1] 35 Second Street East. See page 541 of the History of Downtown Litchfield Appendix.

Heading back towards Sibley Avenue from the Post Office, I passed Sando's[164]. Leonard "Len" Sando sold TVs and Baldwin and Thomas organs in his small store and was an auctioneer also. I don't remember much about Sando's but I do remember the small white wooden building to the west of it, just after the alley.

That little white building[165] was a radio and television repair shop owned by Dick Baldwin. Dennie liked to hang around Dick and learn how to hook up speakers and other things electric. Dennie was walking by Baldwin's one day and he saw two guitars hanging up on the inside wall of that little building. Dennie bought the cheaper of the two, a Hohner, and he started turning blisters into calluses. Our absent father came by once on one of his extremely rare visits and showed Dennie some chords, but most of what Dennie learned was on his own with the help of a Mel Bay instruction book. Dad did show Dennie how to tune the guitar and, being a wiz with electronics, he built Dennie an electric pickup and helped him install it into the sound hole of the old Hohner. I don't remember Dad spending that much time around us, so Dennie must have been in heaven. Then Dad showed Dennie how to hook the guitar up to his old Ward's Airline Radio for amplification. Dennie immediately turned our big console in the living room into an amp, much to Mom's objections. Dennie was on his way to rock and roll, which had been given birth about the same time as Dennie's guitar playing.

Dick Baldwin also sold some guns, did gun repairs and was quite a hunter, which also got Dennie's interest. Dick didn't advertise that aspect of his business. He kept the guns in a very small room in the back. He sold a sawed off 12 gauge pump shotgun to Dennie's friend, Connie. It had been a riot gun at the St. Cloud prison. Maybe Dick got it from our neighbor Rollin Ericson, who had been a guard there. "Not much good for ducks," Connie told me, "but it was hell on pheasants,"

One day Roy Lindeen walked over to Baldwin's from Sandgren's Shoes across the street where he worked.

"Hey Dick," Roy said. "Come outside here." Dick came out of his shop and looked up to where Roy was pointing his hand. "See that

---

[164] 27-29 Second Street East. See page 542 of the History of Downtown Litchfield Appendix.
[165] 23 Second Street East. See page 543 of the History of Downtown Litchfield Appendix.

rooster up on the roof of Sward-Kemp's?" Roy asked. Sure enough, a real live rooster stood on the ledge of the side of the roof.

"How in the hell did he get up there?" Dick asked.

"Don't know," answered Roy. "Just noticed him and came over here to tell you."

"Want him?" Dick asked.

"Sure."

Dick went back into his little shop, came out with a .22 rifle, aimed and shot. The bird tumbled off the roof to the sidewalk by Nelson's Barber Shop stairs.

"There's your rooster," Dick calmly said, as he turned and walked back into his shop.

Dick Baldwin.

Someone found an old radio in the city dump. Knowing that Dick claimed he could fix anything, the person brought the radio into the shop and set it on the counter as a joke.

"My radio quit on me, Dick," he said. "Can you fix it?"

"Sure," said Dick, reaching under the counter and bringing up a ball peen hammer. Raising it over his head, he brought it down hard on the radio. "There, it's fixed. Now take the damned thing back out to the dump where you found it." Dick had recognized it as one that he had deposited in the dump just that morning.

Dick had a quirk in which he didn't want to be told a job needed to be done quickly. That would just get you a long wait. Dick also didn't want to be told what was wrong and what he should do to fix it. If you talked too much, he would likely say to you, "If you know what's wrong with it, why don't you fix it yourself?" Then he would hand it back to you, unfixed.

"I've got Dick Baldwin coming out here to fix the TV," a farmer told his wife. "When he gets here, just show him where it is and leave

306

the room. Don't say anything else." Unfortunately, the wife didn't listen, she talked too much, Dick turned and left, and the TV didn't get fixed.

Don Larson was in the shop visiting Dick when a woman drove up in a car, came in and asked for help carrying her broken TV into the shop. Don said he'd help and went out and lifted the TV out of the woman's trunk and carried it into the shop. The woman then made the mistake of telling Dick what she thought was wrong with the TV and Dick finally shut her up by telling Don, "Would you carry this back out for the lady. Apparently she knows what's wrong and how to fix it herself." Don complied and the stunned woman had to leave.

An old picture of Litchfield shows that Baldwin's shop location had a harness shop on it among other enterprises. The entire street in front of the shop became a "wood market" on some winter days during the years between 1870 and 1890. People would sell cords of wood to the townspeople. The wood was brought to town on horse drawn sleds. Stores also took cords of wood in on trade for just about anything.

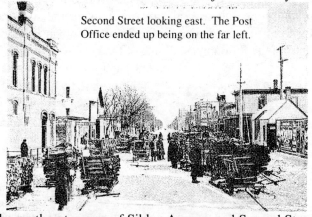

Second Street looking east. The Post Office ended up being on the far left.

At the northeast corner of Sibley Avenue and Second Street was the Sward-Kemp Drug Store[166]. We went into Sward-Kemp's occasionally to read comic books but they didn't have a soda fountain, so we preferred Johnson's Drug. In October of 1956, the downtown stores let school kids paint their store windows with Halloween scenes and decorations. St. Philip's Parochial School's sixth and seventh grade classes were represented by the artistry of Patty Peifer, Cathy Osdoba and myself. Our assigned store was Sward-Kemp Drug. Each afternoon, for an hour

---

[166] 202 Sibley Avenue North. See page 544 of the History of Downtown Litchfield Appendix.

after school, we stood out on the sidewalk and painted a scene we had designed on the store window with tempera paints. Our window design had something to do with the religious side of the "hallowed eve of All Saints Day" at the encouragement of the nuns. No ghosts or goblins or anything to do with the devil or witches could be found in our design.

On Friday of that week, a man came by and handed us "I Like Ike" campaign buttons. Dwight David "Ike" Eisenhower was running for re-election with Dick Nixon running as his vice-president.

"Here," he said, "Take these buttons home to your moms and dads." I didn't do it. Mom was a Democrat and I was reminded of that fall day when I saw Nixon at the train depot. I still didn't like Nixon.

On the Second Street side of Sward-Kemp were stairs leading down under the drugstore to Ray Nelson's Barber Shop[167]. Ray sold out to Jim Murphy in July of 1955 to move up north and run a resort, but he had come back. He had a gun and ammo collection hanging on the wall across from his mirror and counter in his barbershop. Ray had about thirty rifles of different types, a couple of hand grenades, a Japanese helmet, a canteen and a bayonet and other assorted nasty things, such as a German land mine and several knives. A lot of the stuff came from Romeo Rangeloff, a son of Dingle Rangeloff. Romeo had brought the stuff home from the Philippines. Some of the guns were quite rare, like a flintlock pistol. Ray let his customers handle them, though. Being a practical joker, he couldn't resist taking his collection a step further.

Ray
Nelson
with some
of his gun
collection.

The VFW used to store their guns and the blank ammunition in a back room in the shop. The veterans used them for funerals and parades. Ray took one of the 30-06 carbines, loaded it with a blank and bolted it onto the wall around the corner from his barber counter. Then he tied a string to the trigger and worked the string over by the chair where he

---

[167] 200 Sibley Avenue North. See page 544 of the History of Downtown Litchfield Appendix.

worked. Ray was a practical joker and he had thought up a real good one. One of the first victims of Ray's joke was Reuben B. Hagglund, the undertaker, who happened to be a good friend of Ray's. When Reuben came in for his bi-monthly haircut, Ray made small talk about the flintlock on his wall. Reuben walked over and picked it up. He took it over to the window to get a better look, raised it and looked down the barrel.

"Be careful with that one," Ray said. "It's so old that the trigger is very sensitive."

"Oh, I will," said Reuben. Just then Ray pulled his string and the resulting explosion surprised Reuben so much that he stumbled backwards, hit the other barber chair, spun around and ended up on the sofa by the opposite wall.

"Where'd the bullet go?" a worried Reuben asked, jumping up.

"There were no bullets, Reuben."

"The hell there weren't. I saw blue flames come out of the barrel!"

After Ray explained his joke, good natured Reuben had a good laugh and then came back many times to sit and wait for another victim. One day he brought in his associate E. Lee Buckley and set him up.

"Lee, you've got to take a look at Ray's old pistol there," Reuben said. "It's really something." Lee walked over and looked at the gun.

"You can hold it. It's okay with Ray," Reuben added, motioning to the nodding Ray Nelson. Lee picked the gun up and the joke was pulled.

"That's the second damned time I've thought I'd been shot!" an exasperated Lee said to his laughing audience. He was referring to a previous joke pulled on him.[168]

A variation to the joke was for Ray to say to his customer in the chair, "Did you hear a noise in my back room? Just a minute while I check it out." He would leave the customer and go behind the wall where the 30.06 was mounted on the wall. The "mark" in the chair would then hear an out of sight Ray loudly say, "What are you doing back here? What is that...a gun? Hold it! No...no...don't shoot!" Then there would be the gun blast.

Ray pulled his gun jokes many times for about twenty years. "It got rid of a lot of salesmen," he said in an interview. He also said that he probably lost a few customers over it but he was sure he gained many more. "Ollie Prieve came in the shop often, hoping to see a performance," Ray said. But," he added, "I didn't do it to a woman, 'cause women can't take a joke." Apparently he had had a bad

---

[168] See page 248.

experience with a woman. Generally the customer sitting in Ray's chair would get just as much a scare as the victim holding the gun.

Ray's sister, Mildred or Millie, took over the shop while Ray went in the Navy during WW II. During the war, he got stationed on Manus Island in the Admiralty Islands. He had some dental work that needed to be done and so he went to the base dentist. He was shocked to see Lt. Robert M. "Bob" Farrish. What was shocking was that Bob was the dentist Ray went to back in Litchfield, Minnesota. They had been assigned to the same base. Bob could only do some temporary work for Ray, so in '46 when Ray got home, he went back to Bob, who had also just come home, and Ray had the permanent work done.

Even though Ray was back home, Millie stayed on for a while working the second chair. She was in on Ray's joke and knew what to do. A customer was in one afternoon looking at the pistol and carelessly pointed it in Ray's direction.

"Be careful there, that trigger is sensitive," Ray warned. Knowing her cue, Millie pulled the string, the carbine exploded and Ray grabbed his chest and fell to the floor. The customer fainted and Ray and Millie had to revive him.

Mildred and Ray Nelson in front of Ray's barber shop.

Ray also kept a package of special cigarettes in his home. He had replaced several of the cigarettes in the pack with "loaded" ones that would explode in his victim's face. Ray must have missed the loud noises he had heard in WW II. He also played the violin and he and a brother, who played accordion, used to play for some dances around town. One place they played was the old Watson Hall, above the old Coast To Coast.

310

Ray and telephone office manager Bill Paddock got caught out duck hunting in the famous Armistice Day blizzard. They crawled for miles in the storm to a farmhouse and were saved.

Directly above the stairs leading down to Ray's barbershop, on the second floor of Sward-Kemp, were the windows of some doctors' offices. Doctors Harold and Cecil Wilmot's offices, before they built their clinic, and Doctors Karl and Lennox Danielson's offices[169] were up there. You went up through a doorway on Sibley Avenue and it was quite a climb up the white marble stairs to the doctors' offices. Dr. Lennox used to say, "If you can make the stairs, we have a chance to cure you." One of my childhood friends, a Wimmer boy, had to go up to Dr. Lennox's office for his high school sports physical. He was weighed, his height was noted, his blood pressure was taken and then, before being shown to the doctor, who was going to ask the young athlete to turn his head and cough, he was escorted into a small storeroom to pee into a cup. The bathroom was currently occupied, so the nurse was improvising.

The room was basically a small closet with an open window looking out onto Second Street. Wimmer did his duty and filled the cup, but he found that he had more "duty" to do and nowhere to do it. Desperately looking for a solution to his problem, he improvised. He did his duty out the open second story window. Nobody must have been walking by on Second Street because nothing came of the episode. But how did he miss the stairs going down to the barbershop? Can you imagine coming up the stairs with your fresh haircut from Ray, some Bay Rum on your neck and a new stick of Spearmint gum in your mouth only to suddenly have a "golden shower" rain down on your head? But this was Litchfield, Minnesota, my hometown, and anything could and did happen here.

Dr. Karl E. "Henry" Cassel[170] had his office up there also when Dr. Karl Danielson first came to town. They both spoke Swedish, so many of their patients were Swedes. Dr. Cassel weighed well over three hundred pounds and people would see him walk to work down Sibley Avenue from his home. He would go about half a block and then stop and rest. When he arrived to his office over the drug store, he would first go into the back of the store and have John Anderson, the owner at that

---

[169] 204-206 Sibley Avenue North. See page 546 of the Litchfield Downtown History Appendix.

[170] Dr. Cassel came to town in April of 1899.

311

time, pour him a couple of shots of medicinal brandy so he would be fortified for the steep climb up the stairs.

Henry and Karl ran over to Swede Grove often on the train to see some of their Swedish patients. They would get off the train in Grove City. The first time Henry was called to Swede Grove to see a patient, he stepped off the train, climbed into the awaiting horse drawn buggy and broke it. In later years, when he purchased an automobile, he found that he couldn't get behind the steering wheel, so he sat in the middle of the car and drove.

Karl and Henry were asked to go to the Swedish Hospital in Minneapolis several times to see non-English speaking patients. They went out to eat in a hotel restaurant after seeing patients on their first trip. Karl was astounded to see Henry put away two porterhouse steak dinners and one duck dinner before asking to see the desert menu. When Henry died in 1911, the undertakers were unable to get his casket through the doors of his house. So Henry went in and out through his living room window.

Dr. Karl Danielson swam in Lake Ripley every day of his life, including the frozen winters. He lived to be a shivering ninety years old. Ironically, Lake Ripley was named after Dr. Frederick Noah Ripley who froze to death in March of 1856 where Memorial Park is located. He lost his way in a blizzard. It was the first recorded death in the township of Litchfield.

After we had learned how to swim, Pat and I set a personal record one summer by going out to Lake Ripley every single day to swim, regardless of the weather. Upon hearing me say this once, my wife asked, "How does anybody besides you and Pat know you did that?" I told her that anyone could ask the lifeguard, Jim McHugh, because he'd be sitting in his chair under the tree to the left of the bathing house with his coat on and his legs wrapped in towels and he'd say, "You Shaw boys are nuts to go swimming on a cold day like this." Maybe we were, but the record was important to us. We didn't know that Dr. Danielson was besting us by going in the winter too.

Prior to that record setting summer, Mom had insisted that Pat and I take Red Cross swimming lessons. She signed us up for them against our protests. Even though it was in July of 1956, it was chilly in the mornings and we were frustrated because we were cold and the lessons were going so slowly. For one whole morning, all we did was hold our noses and dip our heads into the water. We quit the class, went over to another part of the beach and taught ourselves how to swim by copying the arm strokes of swimmers we had seen. It worked and we both can swim very well today. What Mom didn't know didn't hurt her either.

Back Row: 3rd from the left is Terry Shaw, 4th from the left is Pat Shaw during their record setting summer. Front Left: Bobby Hughes, neighbor boy.

I've always thought that Litchfield's swimming beach was one of the best around. It was huge and there were lots of things out there to keep us occupied. The park itself was immense, at least two city blocks long, with lots of places to throw a ball or chase each other around, snapping towels at each other. There were horseshoe pits, a merry-go-round, a teeter-totter, and a tall metal-chained swing set. Some idiot had the idea of paving underneath the swing set. Many a time little kids scraped the skin off their feet on those swings and would go running all bloodied and screaming to Dingle, or to me in my teens or to my Mom in later years.

In the water was the water wheel, two large rafts, which we always tried to sink by overloading with kids, and a tall platform structure with a diving board, way out in what seemed like the middle of the lake. The first time Pat and I got the nerve to swim out to it was quite a big deal. We had to go from the closer raft to the middle raft and then to the platform. It was too far out to just swim to from shore. We had to be careful of what bigger kids were out there because we were pretty much out of the lifeguard's vision and we could get dunked and held under the water quite easily. So we didn't "wise off" much out there.

The water wheel was just that, a huge wheel in the water. It stood up vertically, supported by a laddered platform. When your turn came, you stepped onto the wheel and let it take you into the water. Of course trying to run on the wheel, like a giant hamster, was a better trick to do, but invariably you'd end up slipping or falling and getting hurt. Knowing how slippery painted wood gets in the water, you had to wonder what kind of sadist thought this was a good thing to have for little kids to play on.

The
water
wheel.

The rafts were about ten foot square and there was about eight inches of space under them, if no one was on the raft. Someone told us about the space and we ventured to dive underneath one of the rafts and take the chance of breathing under it. When we found out we could do it, we used it for a hiding place. If the lifeguard yelled, "Closing time!" at 8pm and we wanted to swim some more, we'd just go under the raft for a while. After the guard had left, we would continue to swim until pitch dark. It was a great place to hide in later years too when we'd go skinny dipping, so we could avoid the cop's floodlight.

Skeeter and a friend had to "wait out" night policeman John Rogers one night for a couple of hours because Rogers had seen them taking off their clothes. He finally bagged the clothes, then sat in his prowler and waited for Skeets and his friend to come out when they got cold.

All these "toys" were painted with shiny white enamel and they would get pretty slippery, so the lifeguard was always yelling, "No running out there on the raft!" There were almost daily accidents on them, so I couldn't imagine what calamities the big slide caused in the earlier days.

Back in the late twenties and early thirties, there was a monstrous slide on the north side of the bathing house. It was a permanent structure, about two stories high. It looked like a section from a wooden roller coaster. Kids rented a "cart" from the candy stand for a nickel an hour. The cart looked like one of those "creepers" that mechanics use to scoot around under cars. It had little wheels that went into a track that kept you going straight down the slide. Kids walked up steep steps from the water end, just like they do today in modern water slides at amusement parks. Only one person was allowed on a cart or on the track at one time. The carts went down and shot out over the water at a terrific speed. God help any bathers who had wandered over in front of it when the slide was busy. Sliders' carts must have become lethal weapons.

When the lake started drying up in the mid-thirties, the slide became useless and maybe people had started getting more safety minded. It must have been a lot of work keeping the slide in good repair also. For whatever reasons, it disappeared. During that low water period, the swimming beach was moved to the south of the present beach in front of today's trailer park, where there are a number of drop offs. It was moved back to the present location in the summer of 1944. Of course, we didn't know about the slide back in the fifties, which is just as well 'cause we would've really been bummed out. I can't imagine the damage we would've done to ourselves and to each other on that thing.

The big water slide in the thirties. Already the lake is drying up and the water is receding from the slide.

Next door to Sward-Kemp heading north again, was Fransein's Café[171]. We went into Fransein's many afternoons after school to sit in the dark brown wooden high backed booths, drink a Coke, and have a smoke. We called the sessions "Tamby Time" in honor of old Freddie Williams. Several mornings in the summer, Dickey Whalen treated Pat and I to breakfast at Fransein's from money he had "received" from Harlan Quinn. I started feeling guilty about the money because I had a good idea how Dickey was "receiving" it. So I started selling Dickey

---

[171] 208 Sibley Avenue North. See page 547 of the History of Downtown Litchfield Appendix.

watercolor paintings of ducks I had made. It eased my conscience a little and turned me into a professional artist, I suppose.

Frank Fransein began Fransein's Café at this location in 1935. Frank had been a policeman in Willmar. One day he was standing on a downtown Willmar street corner when a friend of his walked up to him and said, "Frank, any damned fool can be a cop." Frank said that he choked on that statement all day and by evening he realized that his "friend" had been right. He quit the job the next day and started a restaurant in Willmar called the Magnet Inn. After a while, working as both cook and waiter, Frank decided it was easier being a cop, so he went back on the force. He thought it wasn't too bad a job getting paid to stand on a street corner.

Frank's wife died and he married his second wife, Mae. Something about the restaurant business kept pulling at Frank. He and Mae moved to Litchfield to manage Scarp's café. After the LaLondes bought it, they were out of work. Mae didn't like Scarp's anyway as it was overrun with cockroaches. Frank heard that the Schnees were going to build a new theater in the next block and there was a vacant building by that location. Frank wisely bought the building and started Fransein's, which initially was open from six in the morning until midnight, seven days a week.

Frank Fransein had a "nearness to greatness", if I can call it that, which he probably could've done without. When he was still living in Willmar, he was in the Bank of Willmar one hot summer morning in July of 1930 when three members of a gang of five, called the "Sammy Stein Gang", walked in dressed in suits and Panama and straw hats. Outside another gang member stood guard at the door with a machine gun, while yet another bandit sat in the getaway car on Fifth Street. In Paul Maccabe's well-researched book, *John Dillinger Slept Here: A Crook's Tour of Crime and Corruption in St. Paul 1920-1936*, Maccabe claims that the man outside the door was non other than George R. "Machine Gun" Kelly and it was Kelly's first bank robbery after leaving Leavenworth. I don't know if that was true or not. I do know that Kelly was in Minneapolis at that time. In fact, he later married Kathryn Thorne there in September of 1930.

Anyway that hot summer morning Sammy Stein walked up to the first teller cage where cashier Norman H. Tallakson stood.

"Lie down," Stein said to the cashier.

Thinking he was being made the butt of a joke, Norman said, "My, that's a nice gun."

"Get down, quick!" Stein yelled at him. "This is a holdup!" Everyone was told to get down. At first they too thought it was a joke. A bank holdup in Willmar, Minnesota? Ernest Person sat down on a sofa.

"Lie down there on the floor and keep quiet," Stein continued. "No fooling. We mean business." A swift kick to the stomach and a rap on the head of one of the customers got everyone's attention. This was no joke. Frank Fransein, the sitting Ernest Person and the other six customers dropped to the floor.

Ernest looked up and asked, "Should I keep my face down too?"

"Damn you, yes!" Stein yelled. "Or I'll fill you with lead!" He must have thought, "What's with these hicks?" On his way down, teller "Obbie" Nordstrom tripped the alarm. The bandits were annoyed but didn't panic. They calmly emptied the two teller's cages and then started on the vault, loading a sack. They got over $75,000 in currency and negotiable bonds and then grabbed customer Marie Wacker and employee George Robbins, who they thought had tripped the alarm, for shields and started to leave.

As they emerged outside, a shot was fired at them. Marie fainted. Jeweler Rudy Paffrath, who had a store down the street, had grabbed a .22 revolver he kept in his store when he heard the alarm, hid behind a car across the street and fired. The man with the machine gun sprayed the street, just missing several people and mostly hitting just the pavement. But a ricocheting bullet ended up in Mrs. Donna Gildea's leg and another went through her mother's chest. As Donna was dragging her mother, Mrs. Emil Johnson, to safety, another bullet struck Donna in the hip. They both later recovered.

Meanwhile, construction worker Sam Evans had run into a hardware store and borrowed a rifle and shells. He fired at the getaway driver and got him with one shot. The driver grabbed his neck and slumped over in his seat. The other bandits shoved him aside and drove down Litchfield Avenue East firing at anybody they saw moving. They just missed a service station attendant whose uniform they had mistaken for a policeman's. The bullet went through the "O" in the Pennzoil sign. The bandits escaped to Kandiyohi where another gang member had a different car waiting for them.

A couple of weeks later, three of them, including leader Stein, were found executed gangland style near White Bear Lake. Another, probably the driver because of a wound in his neck, was found in a shallow grave near Owatonna. The other two and the money were never found although one was said to have died in prison. How anyone knew that, I don't know. Frank Fransein soon moved to the quieter streets of Litchfield, where all of our banks put announcements in the newspapers that they had beefed up their security systems.

Frank's son Wally was quite a bowler and he had an incredibly awesome delivery. He was tall with long arms that he would use to whip the ball down the alley. He had a five-step delivery and he would loft the ball for the first ten feet or so. It would drop with a slam and come screaming down the alley. One winter league evening at the old bowling alley on Depot Street, Wally missed the pocket and left a 5-7 split. He let his next ball rip and it was a screamer. It was loud enough that everyone on his team and most of the other people in the place just stopped and watched. The ball smacked the first pin and slammed it to the right, smacking the other pin, which ricocheted off the side of the pit, bounced up and stuck into the acoustic paneled ceiling. There it hung and there it stayed for a couple of weeks.

Chapter Twenty-Four
The Esbies, the Hollywood, and KLFD

Fransein's Café was the second home of many of Litchfield's characters. Arnie Lunderby and his wife Anna, whose son Stan was in my class, would come in from working at the Produce for their noon dinner. Arnie had a hair lip and bulldog faced Anna was known to wear shorts and sandals almost year 'round, but not when she worked. They both would have their bloody aprons and turkey manure covered black rubber boots on. Finally Mae Fransein asked them to please clean up before they came in because it bothered the rest of her other customers. Several other Produce workers did the same and Mae had to talk to them too.

The Lunderbys were asked to not come back to the hotel's Colonial Café. They could have sat in a bath for a week and Julie Larson, the manager, would not have let them back in. They emptied the sugar jars, ate the preserves straight out of the jars with a spoon without ordering toast, took all of the paper napkins home and drank many "bottomless" cups of coffee. Then they complained that the prices were too high.

Anna had another "quirk". She was known to dance to her radio around the house in the nude without pulling the shades. This disturbed some people, but didn't affect Arnie who had a strange relationship with his wife. They lived separately in the small house. When they would push their shopping cart up to the check-out counter in a grocery store, they would have the items neatly arranged into "his" and "hers" piles. They paid for them separately, each cashing their Produce checks.

Hugo Esbjornsson would walk into Fransein's with King, his expertly trained and beautiful Dalmatian dog. In fact, Hugo wouldn't go anywhere without that dog. He would plop down on a stool by the lunch counter and the dog would jump up and sit on the stool next to him. No one dared to say a word about it to Hugo. The Esbjornssons were one of the pioneer families of Litchfield, they owned one of the lumberyards and they were one of the town's elite. They were known for their great dinner parties and eccentric men. Anyway, the dog never messed with anyone's food. It just sat there at attention while Hugo finished his coffee and sweet roll.

Hugo and King were sitting in Fransein's one day and Hugo was swearing up a blue streak. Behind him, sitting in a booth, happened to be a minister, who got up and walked over to Hugo.

"Excuse me, sir, but I'm a minister of God and I don't appreciate you taking the Lord's name in vain like that," he said to Hugo's back.

Hugo didn't turn around. Instead he looked down at King and said, "Tell that preacher to go to hell, King." King started barking at the stunned minister, who turned and left.

Hugo would go into a liquor store out of town with King and then he'd touch a bottle on a display, making sure the clerk didn't see him. When the clerk would ask Hugo if he could help him, Hugo would say, "Oh well, I think I'll have a bottle of brandy." Turning to King, he'd continue, "Get me a bottle of brandy, King." The dog would rush over to the bottle Hugo had touched, grab it with his mouth and bring it back to him. Hugo would deposit it on the counter in front of the stunned clerk. Sometimes he'd make a bet with the clerk and get the bottle for free.

Hugo was a tall handsome man, personable, always a gentleman with the ladies and a generous man, but he did things one way and one way only, Hugo's way. Whenever someone had the traditional barn dance after the raising of the barn built with lumber from Hugo's lumberyard, he would bring out a keg of beer, telling the people, "You let me know if that one runs out, and I'll bring ya another one."

Hugo loved to hunt but not follow the rules so he was always being picked up for and paying fines for hunting out of season or having too many of something. Once when he was coming back from out west with a trunk full of too many of one thing and a trailer full of too many of something else, a roadblock was set up to stop him. Apparently a game warden had found out about Hugo's cargo and called ahead to someone. Hugo busted right through the roadblock. A game warden jumped up on Hugo's running board and Hugo just brushed him right off. Either this time or another time he was finally caught and arrested along with one of the Robertson doctors. They spent a period of time in jail.

Hugo liked to have lots of the things he liked. He liked horses and women. He had a dozen or more horses and he had one too many wives. Well, he wasn't married to "the blonde", as town people called her, but he did keep another woman and even sire some children with her. Some say she was from St. Cloud and others say she was from Kingston. Hugo didn't try to hide her. She'd be seen with him on the streets of town and he took her to horse shows with him.

Irene Lindberg Esbjornsson, Hugo's real wife, loved to entertain with big dinner parties, complete with live music. The Esbjornssons were members of Litchfield's exclusive "400 Club". I don't know what that meant but there was a small circle of well to do people in town that belonged to it and entertained each other. One such party night, Hugo wasn't around to greet the guests, so Irene showed them into the dining room by herself. Suddenly the door burst open and Hugo rode his prized stallion into the house and into the dining room. Pictures were snapped, the gloved hands of the elegant ladies petted the horse and then Hugo rode him up and down the stairs and back out of the house again.

Hugo's "father", John[172] Esbjornsson I, who started the first lumberyard in Litchfield in 1869, planted the seed for his descendants' wildness and love of the ladies. Before he settled down, he was considered quite the ladies' man. In late July of 1877, he was involved in an incident, which caused the local newspaper to write a column about "a needless disgrace heaped upon the moral reputation of our, heretofore far and wide reputed, quiet, orderly and law abiding village."

John
Esbjornsson I

John was "keeping company" with Annie Hollingsworth, whose father owned a local saloon among other things. John and Annie had a rendezvous in Milwaukee, each leaving Litchfield by train on different days, for propriety's sake. They spent a couple of weeks there. Annie returned to Litchfield, expecting John to follow shortly. He didn't. Annie got concerned. Maybe she was aware of John's tendencies. She went back to Milwaukee on the next train to find him. Meanwhile, like a script from a comedy, John was already on his way back to Litchfield. On Saturday, a couple of days later, Annie returned again to Litchfield

---

[172] Pronounced "Yo-han".

distressed because she couldn't find John. She went to her parents' house on Sibley Avenue South to lament.

That evening, around 8pm, "Mr. E." as the newspaper described him, came walking down Sibley Avenue past the Hollingsworth residence. Annie, followed by Mrs. Samuel Hollingsworth and Annie's sister Mrs. Herrick, came out of the house and followed John down the street until they were all by the railroad track crossing. John was accosted and, as the newspaper described the scene, "a general angry conversation was indulged in." All of a sudden, two shots rang out in our quiet village and "Mr. E. was wounded just above the knee on the left leg and another shot passed in close proximity to his head."

The women all screamed and ran in different directions, with John in hot pursuit of Annie. He wanted to get the revolver she still carried in her hand. He caught her and was wrestling with her for the weapon when up ran Mr. Samuel Hollingsworth, who smacked John in the eye. Marshall Gordon, the city constable, ran up to the fracas and separated the combatants. The Hollingsworths were arrested and hauled off to jail, where they spent the weekend, because no bail bondsman could be found on a Saturday night. The only outcome that was reported in the newspaper was that "Mr. E.'s wound happily proved of no serious nature as it penetrated only the fleshy portion of the leg and struck no bones. Dr. Bissell extracted the bullet and he (John) is now able to be out upon the street."

Two years later, John married a fine lady from out east and from a well to do family. Her name was Eureca or Ericka A. Rosenquist. The Esbjornssons went back out east to visit her family and John went fox hunting with them. When he came home to Litchfield, he brought back the full foxhunting outfit including the small red hat. When he went riding around town in the outfit, he must not have heard the snickering behind his back. But, John lived by his own set of rules and he wouldn't have cared anyway. A few years later, John and Ericka went back to Sweden to visit John's sister, Mrs. Swanson. Being childless, they offered to take one of the sister's boys back to the States and raise him. They were given Hugo Swanson as a foster child. They never adopted him, but Hugo took their last name and eventually took over the lumberyard.

The way that John and his son Hugo lived, it was no surprise then that Hugo's son, John Esbjornsson II, turned out the way he did. He was considered "wild" in school, doing anything on a dare. When WWII broke out, he enlisted in the Army Air Corps and became a pilot. He flew over eighty missions over the infamous "Hump" from Burma to China after the Japanese had closed the Burma Road. It was extremely dangerous flying the Curtis C-46 Commando over the mountains on runs, transporting war materials, while trying to make it back to ill-equipped and poorly lit airfields. When John came home to Litchfield with an Air Medal with Oak Leaf Cluster, a Bronze Star, and a Distinguished Flying Cross with Oak Leaf Cluster, he became even wilder.

John bought a plane in '46, a surplus WWII single prop fighter trainer called a Vultee. It had a glass canopy on top, and John took his friends for scary rides, dive-bombing sites in town. He took his buddy Lemoine "Pete" Lindberg up so that Pete could jump out and parachute back down. I remember John dropping "Flying Disks" or heavy paper plates that had prizes or $1 off promotion coupons for businesses printed on them for Crazy Days or for the County Fair. In June of 1948, in the middle of a drought, the two of them took the Vultee up to drop ice in the clouds to make rain. They got the Chamber of Commerce to pay for their gas, but it didn't accomplish anything except for chunks of dry ice dropping onto the roofs of farm buildings. John and Pete would take off for weeks up to the boundary waters or northern Wisconsin to "test" a new water floatplane they owned together. They flew and flew one time until they ran out of gas and were stuck in the wilderness in the middle of a lake. You never knew what John was going to do next.

John Esbjornsson II and Pete Lindberg in John's Vultee.

Lemoine "Pete" Lindberg had flown in the war also and he ran the Litchfield airport beginning in November of 1947. Pete did crop dusting in South America, Canada and Texas, flew helicopters for a petroleum company and had been a pilot for a Nicaraguan airline for a while. In the early fifties, flying to Canada from a dusting job in Idaho, he decided to

323

stop off in Litchfield to see his parents, who were our neighbors. Pete shocked onlookers by flying low over downtown Sibley Avenue, (some say just off the ground), dive-bombing Central Park, veering northwest and getting a little too close to mail carrier Ralph Hawkinson's house at 412 Marshall Avenue North. John Esbjornsson must've loved that stunt, but Ralph didn't. Ralph drove out to the airport, gave Pete a piece of his mind and then reported him to the FAA. By the time the authorities caught up with Pete, he was in Canada.

On New Year's Eve in 1953, John and Pete brought a monkey to a cocktail party. The monkey got out and crawled up a tree. The two caused such a ruckus trying to get the monkey down that the police were called. Now they had to explain to the not amused cop, in their inebriated state, that they were making all of the noise because their monkey had escaped. Pete brought the monkey, named Dennis, home from Managua, Nicaragua just before Christmas in 1953. It was a Spider monkey he had brought with him to Texas in his plane and then driven from there to Litchfield.

Dennis the monkey and Pete Lindberg.

"A trip is never uneventful when a monkey is along," Pete said. "I put Dennis in the empty hopper of the plane used for dusting powder and gave him a dozen bananas to eat on the way. When I opened the hopper, he had taken the bananas, unpeeled them, and chinked up all the air holes in the hoppers." The monkey had been cold. In the car he ate Pete's insurance policy and half a carton of cigarettes. Dennis turned Pete's parent's home upside down, so Pete finally gave him away to someone in

324

the cities, hoping he would end up at the Como Park Zoo. Pete Lindberg died from cancer in 1979.

Not content to just duplicate one of Hugo's horse stunts, John II did "one better" than his father by riding his horse into public places. He rode the horse into the golf course clubhouse one night. Finding the patrons were apparently amused, John then rode the horse down the ramp and into the Legion club on Stag Night when the Legion was in the basement of the Kopplin building south of the Depot. He got away with it at the Legion so he did it again and again until he was asked not to do it. Another place he rode into was Benson's pool hall on Second Street.

John caught and killed a large snapping turtle. He brought it to the lumberyard where he chopped off the head and long neck. He was fooling around with it with some of the workers when he received a phone call from one of his customers, Jack Harris, the manager of the Super America station. John's lumberyard had installed some windows in Jack's home and one of them wasn't working properly. "I'll be right over and check it out," John said stuffing the turtle's head and neck into his pocket. At the Harris' house, while talking to Jack and his wife about the window, John suddenly pulled the long necked head out of his pocket and held it in front of his pant zipper. It was obvious what his crude joke was meant to be and Jack got upset and kicked him out of the house.

John married a brilliant and beautiful woman named Kay Payne, who must have been in fear for her life. John was reckless with his guns and fired his revolver through the kitchen floor of his house at 809 Marshall Avenue South several times. One story told is that, while Kay was sitting at the kitchen table, John shot up through the kitchen floor from the basement and the bullet almost passed between Kay's legs. One night the police were called because of all the shooting in his basement. He explained to them that his foundation had gotten weak because of outside pressure and he was putting holes in the walls to relieve the pressure.

John came home one night after having a little too much to drink and found Kay watching TV. Some words were said and then Kay decided to give John the cold shoulder and not talk to him any more. She just sat there and watched the TV. John left the room, came back with his shotgun and blasted the television into video heaven. One night at Chet Berg's cabin on Lake Washington, John pulled out his revolver, took five of the six bullets out of the chamber, spun it, and started playing Russian roulette with the gun. Or at least that's what he wanted Chet to believe. He had palmed the final bullet. At least he told Chet that he had palmed it after he had quieted Chet down.

One day John landed a large military plane at the airport in Litchfield. Word was that John, still a pilot in the reserves, took the plane without permission from Wold-Chamberlain Airfield in St. Paul. It was one of the older multi-engine planes like a C119 or C47 that were in abundance at the National Guard's airfield. The plane was a predecessor to the current huge C130 Hercules that you can drive vehicles into. Landing in Litchfield was no problem but the runway was too short to take off again. The Army Air Corps had to come to Litchfield to remove the wings and transport it by truck back to St. Paul. I don't know if John was charged or fined for this latest stunt or not.

John and Kay had two girls, Kristin and Jo, and a boy named John III. Unfortunately Kay developed a brain tumor and died. John thought it best that the kids live with their grandparents because he wasn't domestic and he didn't know how to take care of children. Kay's parents, the Paynes, kept the girls but they didn't feel they could handle young John III. Hugo Esbjornsson took him in under "court supervision". The judge had social services monitor the kids for about a year and then stopped when it was determined that the kids were being well taken care of. By voluntarily seeing that the kids went to the grandparents, John was able to visit the kids at any time. His visits were very sporadic and unpredictable, however, until the Paynes finally insisted he set up a time to see the girls.

One day in December of 1965, John was out on Hugo's farm cutting wood. He had rigged a circular saw on a tractor and was trying to adjust the guard when his hand slipped. His middle three fingers of his right hand suddenly disappeared. They weren't reattaching fingers in those days. When John's mother Irene passed away, John, Kay, Hugo and others went to Hagglund's funeral home to pick out a casket. They were talking in the selection room when suddenly John disappeared. He was found lying in a casket. "Trying it out," he told them. After all, he told the group, he wanted to be sure his mother would be comfortable in her eternal rest.

John III started getting his name in the papers too in the early sixties. For three years in a row, starting in 1961, he won the pie-eating contest on Crazy Days. He ended up teaching Biology in Alexandria. His dad, John II, took over the reins of the lumberyard from Hugo and it went belly up, as John was too busy with his other pursuits to be bothered with it. Of course Hugo had already started its downward spiral, not spending very much time at the yard himself. He was too busy fishing and hunting, or breeding horses and women.

After John I died, Hugo moved into his grand house at 703 Sibley Avenue South, which had been built in 1880. In 1954, he sold it to the First Evangelical Lutheran Church. They wanted it for a building site for their present church. Hugo had a certain period of time to get the house off the property. As the deadline approached and Hugo hadn't done anything, he was given some warnings. Suddenly, in the wee morning hours of May 27, 1955, the house caught on fire. Claude Mattison, a passing motorist, saw policeman John Rogers parked by the hotel and told him about the fire. Rogers got the fire department out. The fire department apparently came much quicker than Hugo thought they would and they outdid themselves because, much to Hugo's dismay, the house was saved. Fire chief Glenn Smith noticed Leland Olson, the county attorney, standing in the crowd of onlookers.

"Say, Lee," he said, "I think we've got a problem here. We've found 'sets' on all the floors." "Sets" were piles or cans of oily rags and lumber, and their presence and their placement in the house, coupled with the suddenly increased insurance, just didn't smell right. Hugo was indicted and brought to court for arson by his neighbor and friend, Leland Olson, who was also the father of yet another one of my classmates named Eric.

Hugo would see Leland walking to the courthouse for the trial in the cold November mornings and stop to offer him a ride. Leland would turn him down. The case was thrown out for lack of evidence but Hugo couldn't collect on the insurance. His wife sued the insurance company and the case bounced around in the courts until October of 1958, when a jury ruled in favor of the insurance company. Hugo had lost it all.

The Hollywood Theater[173] was north of Fransein's. This was a grand theater. We thought it was quite plush and a whole world away from "our" Unique Theater. It was air-conditioned, which must have been a wonderment in the mid-thirties, when it opened its doors. The air-conditioning was a huge plus in the fifties when all you could do at home was put a bowl of ice cubes in front of a table fan and pray for

---

[173] 210 Sibley Avenue North. See page 549 of the History of Downtown Litchfield Appendix.

some relief. There was a big lobby with a huge popcorn, pop and candy counter. Downstairs was a lounge with sofas, ashtrays and bathrooms.

Most of the movies were in Technicolor and Cinemascope or wide screen. If a movie had just been released, it would soon be at the Hollywood. The shows were changed every Sunday, Wednesday and Friday. The Hollywood had all of the latest things such as headphones for the hard of hearing, a "cry room", (we'd sneak in there for a smoke during the late show), and Cinemascope, which was introduced to us on December 25, 1954. They even had ushers. The ushers wore green uniforms with pillbox hats in the thirties and forties. They would come down the aisles guiding people to seats with a flashlight and telling us kids to take our feet off the seats in front of us. Those seats at both the Hollywood and the Unique originally were 10¢, if you sat in the first seven rows. The "regular" seats at the Hollywood were 35¢. The price only doubled twenty years later, when I was a kid.

When C. F. Schnee got too old to run the theaters, his sons, Fred and Lloyd, took them over. Fred ran the Hollywood and Lloyd, who had owned a theater in Paynesville, had the second-class Unique where Jerry Wheeler's dad, Donnie, was the projectionist. Jerry's mother, Lucille, was the ticket lady at the Hollywood. Five foot two inches Donnie Wheeler had a "nearness to greatness" of his own in 1945, when he was stationed at Ft. Knox, Kentucky. By the luck of the draw, Donnie was picked to dance with movie star Carmen Miranda, the dancer known for her towering hats made of fruits. She must have towered over short little Pvt. Wheeler.

The Hollywood Theater had a fire on May 23, 1956 in the ticket office area. It had started during the night due to a short in some wires. The ticket booth and the front lobby had damage and the rest of the theater had a lot of smoke damage. The Hollywood Shop Shoes store next door suffered enough damage that the owner, H. K. McIver, simply gave up and retired. For most of the summer, while the Schnees and their employees cleaned up and remodeled, the Unique showed all of the "A" movies. Luckily the Starlite drive-in was up and going in June, so Fred and Lloyd had a place to show all of the monster, cowboy and Bowery Boys movies.

The Schnee brothers opened Litchfield's first drive-in movie theater on June 28, 1956 with a movie called *Cockleshell Heroes* starring Jose Ferrer and Trevor Howard. A movie theater without walls or doors? The fun began. We had already been sneaking into the regular theater by opening the exit door to the alley and letting a few friends in. This was even easier. I was too claustrophobic to do the cramming in the trunk bit, but I heard of it happening a lot. We used to walk or ride our bikes all the way out there, a good mile or more, sneak in through a farmer's field and then sit on some chairs in front of the concession stand watching the movie. Or a friend would drop us off in a farmer's field, then drive in and pay for himself. After we sneaked in, we'd all jump into his car. One night we noticed that one of the farm fences near by was electrified. So we made a chain of about six of us holding hands and the first one in line touched the fence. Only the last guy in the line (who usually wasn't in on the joke) would get the shock. If the person after you broke the chain, you also got the shock.

Kids were always stealing speakers or driving off without taking them out of the car, which would result in a busted side window. The stolen speakers were usually thrown away. They were not standard eight-ohm speakers. They were some off the wall impedance and did not work very well when hooked up to other "applications". Dennie tried hooking them up to the radio in his friend's car for early versions of back seat speakers. They sounded like crap.

In the Hollywood Theater, a giant velvet-like red curtain would open and close at the start and end of each of the segments comprising the night's show. Unfortunately, most of the movies offered there didn't interest us kids. We wanted funny, we wanted cowboys and Indians and we wanted monsters. We didn't want Gene Kelly or Fred Astaire dancing or Rock Hudson and Doris Day falling in love. Still, I remember sitting at the Hollywood with my friends in the comfortable seats, laughing, until tears flowed, at Jerry Lewis movies or sitting in awe at the first Elvis movies.

I also remember a man sitting down next to me one night when I was at the movies by myself. He started putting his hand on my leg, and then slowly worked his way up towards my crotch. I moved my leg. He continued. I got very nervous. I didn't have a clue what he was trying to do. I got up and moved. I was scared to death that he would follow me. I didn't know what else to do and I didn't want to leave the show. It never occurred to me to tell an usher. Luckily he didn't follow me and I never looked back to see his face. In some respects, Litchfield lost some of its glitter for me that night.

Next to the theater, with the same façade, was Irene's Fashions and Bridal Shop[174], which moved in after the shoe business left. Again, it was a store with absolutely no interest to my friends or I. Howard's Dry Cleaners[175] was in the building north of Irene's. No interest.

The next two stores were the James J. Reed Printing shop[176] and George Farnquist's Marshall-Wells Store[177] sharing one large building. Rick's Plumbing and Heating[178] was in the back. Above Marshall-Wells was the Legion Club and KLFD, Litchfield's radio station, was above Reed's Printing. KLFD kept moving around town and this was their second location. The station started in the Nelson D. March house, recently occupied by the Nordlies, down by the library at 218 South Sibley Avenue. Later, it was in a street level store on the west side of Sibley Avenue and today it is finally on the east side of Sibley.

Frank Endersbee and Lee Favreau owned KLFD and Frank went on the air in January of 1959. KLFD was a small 500-watt daytime only AM radio station at that time. The joke was that the call letters meant "Keep Litchfield From Dying". Frank used to air organ music at the end of the broadcast day. Announcer Jim Harrison referred to that show to his friends as "Music For People Who Died Today".

Dennie did announcing there as an unpaid guest teenage disk jockey. The station would occasionally bring in high school kids to try to get more teens to listen. Dennie always claimed that Mom, his brothers and Aunt Doris Johnson were his only listeners. Dennie's job only lasted about two months. He used to sweep up, vacuum the studio and tear newssheets off the UPI Teletype machine in the back room. He got paid in 45rpm demo records that came to Endersbee unsolicited in the mail. Frank hated rock and roll and was glad to get rid of them. So we had a lot of 45s around our house with white labels that stated "Promotional Copy - Not For Sale" on them.

---

[174] 212-212½ Sibley Avenue North. See page 551 of the History of Downtown Litchfield Appendix.
[175] 214 Sibley Avenue North. See page 553 of the History of Downtown Litchfield Appendix.
[176] 218 Sibley Avenue North. See page 556 of the History of Downtown Litchfield Appendix.
[177] 220-222 Sibley Avenue North. See page 558 of the History of Downtown Litchfield Appendix.
[178] Before Rick's, John O'Neil had a plumbing business there and Jerry Nelson came after Rick moved out.

In the early sixties, KLFD starting having a Saturday afternoon one-hour teen show called the *Pepsi Platter Parade*. The deejays finally played some rock and roll music, although it was very "white". I picked up a copy of Billboard magazine in the radio station's lobby once and saw that *Mickey's Monkey* by Smokey Robinson and the Miracles, a black R & B group, was the number one record in the U.S. I had never heard of it, not even on the Minneapolis stations. Jon Kent, the *Platter Parade's* deejay, gave away gift certificates for six packs of Pepsi during the Saturday show. I would call in every time and win a six-pack. I knew a lot of rock and roll trivia.

In my junior year in high school, the station asked the school to send over three teens to do the Saturday show with the deejay. Marty Foss, Jeanette Oliver and I volunteered. We were put into a small windowed room next to Jon Kent's larger studio. We sat at a table introducing records by reading from a yellow script while we looked at Jon through the window for signals. When the song was over, Jon would ask us to adlib our thoughts about the record. It was kind of a Rate-A-Record, ripped off from TV's *American Bandstand*.

"It's got a good beat and it'd be easy to dance to," Jeanette or Marty would say, and then snicker when their mikes were turned off.

I told the truth though. "I didn't like it too much." I'd say. "It sounds like somebody trying to imitate Elvis and the lyrics are stupid."

Off the air, Jon asked us for trivia questions for the Pepsi giveaways. I was the only one who could ever come up with them, so it became my job. Marty and Jeanette got bored with the whole deal and quit coming, so pretty soon it was just Jon Kent and I every week. The following year, we continued with that format, just the two of us. Just like Dennie, I got a lot of free demo records, but mine were always obscure groups doing terrible rock songs that never made it. Somebody at the station was finally taking the good records.

Bill Diehl of WDGY radio used to come out to the armory and put on record hops. He would give away those same dumb demo records as prizes. Songs like *Go Man Go* by the Rockateens or something. You'd never, ever, get an Elvis or Everly Brothers' record.

Reed's Printing was on the street level underneath the radio station. It sold office supplies and did printing jobs and it had something to do with the course the rest of my life took.

Chapter Twenty-Five
The Typewriter

I was substitute teaching in a science class in Willmar, Minnesota when a student asked me the age-old question, "Why do I have to learn this junk? I ain't never gonna use it."

"Yeah, why?" a bunch of other students chimed in.

"How do you know you'll never use this? I asked them back.

"'Cause I ain't gonna be no chemist," came back the reply.

I told the students that you just never know if what you learn when you're younger will someday benefit you down the road. I told them about choices and decisions in life. Life is full of choices and decisions. Some of them are simple and easy and are made without much thought. Others are more difficult, but each one, in some way, affects the rest of our lives, our future. At the time we may not think that some simple choice or some school subject is important in the grand scheme of things, but you just never know. I then told the students my typewriter story.

On Crazy Days, July 23, 1959, Pat and I were walking the streets looking for bargains to spend our hard-earned cash on. We didn't find much, but as we walked past Reed's Printing, an office supply store, something caught my eye. A small black portable typewriter with its own case was propped up in the window with a "crazy" price tag of $4 on it. Why it intrigued me, I do not know. When I was ten, I had bought a small tin toy typewriter. It had a wheel with letters on it, which you dialed to the letter you wanted, and then pressed down to transfer the letter to the paper. It was slow, tedious and sloppy in the printing. I remember spending over an hour slowly typing out the entire lyrics to *The Ballad of Davy Crockett,* my favorite song at that time. I knew the lyrics by heart.

I had always been fascinated with the power of the typewritten page. I knew that it magically increased a school report's grade by at least a half a grade. I had spent hours clicking away on a typewriter at my father's house, whenever I had spent a rare summer week visiting him and "Sunny", his second wife, in nearby Eden Valley. Dad had a jukebox business and I was allowed to type up the little paper tabs that went into the song title slots in the jukebox.

I turned to Pat and said, "Let's buy it!" I always tried to get Pat to share in the cost when buying games or toys. I knew that I would end up using it with him anyway. Why not co-own it? I had even concocted a scheme where we had pooled our earned money at the end of each week and then divided it. It worked great for both of us, for a while, until he started out earning me. That little runt was a hard worker. Then he wanted out of our verbal contract. We had to go to arbitration (Mom) to resolve that conflict. She ruled in my favor.

"A promise is a promise," she told Pat. But, I relented and let him out of the arrangement. I did have a conscience and I valued his friendship.

"Come on, let's buy it!" I repeated to my brother's quizzical stare, again pointing to the typewriter in the window.

"What for?" he sneered.

Quickly I thought up and spewed out a list of reasons: homework assignments, a weekly neighborhood newspaper to sell, and letters to relatives.

"No way," Pat said, his favorite expression. For one thing, he wasn't into grades as much as I was.

Now I had to make one of those decisions you're confronted with in your life. $4 was a lot of money for me. I delivered thirty daily *Minneapolis Star* newspapers, fifty Sunday ones and then spent a Thursday evening collecting from my customers to earn just $3.00. And I put half of that away in savings. Would I really use the typewriter that much? Does it even work? What else could I do with that $4? What should I do?

"Come on, let's buy it," I again pleaded with my brother. "We'll have a lot of fun with it," I added, knowing that $2 would hurt me a lot less.

"Oh, all right," he sighed, following me into the store. "But remember, it's both of ours and I get to use it too." He knew deep down that I would hog it.

"Look what we bought, Mom," I said as we entered our house that noon. I got to carry the typewriter home. Pat didn't object to that.

"What is it?" she asked, staring at the small black suitcase in my hand.

"A typewriter!"

"What are you going to do with a typewriter?" she asked.

"Homework assignments!" I said, knowing that that would get her approval of our purchase.

Pat and I sat down on the floor in the living room in front of the coffee table on which I had set down our shopping bargain. I opened up the case and slid the cover off the base. The small black typewriter had the gold letters "Remington" printed in the center of the front. I took out some old notebook paper and wound it into the carriage. Pushing the carriage to the far right, I sighed and thought. "What am I going to write? Ah, my name. Of course!" Click...click...click...click...click.

"Terry" There it was. My name in print. "Now what?" I thought. "My last name." Click...click...click...click. "Shaw" Okay, now what?

"It's my turn!" Pat said.

"Hold your horses," I shot back, as I typed our address.

"Now, it's my turn."

"Just a minute," I said as I typed Mom's name. And so it went.

After a while I gave in and gave Pat his turn, knowing that he would soon tire of our new toy. And he did. Now it was mine. Before long, the "hunt and peck" method of typing began to wear me down. At this rate, I'd never get anything typed. Not a newspaper or a report for any class, that was for sure.

"Mom...," I yelled to the other room. "Do you know how to type?"

"No I don't," came the answer from the kitchen. "Your Aunt Millie does. Why don't you ask her to show you how to do it?"

Aunt Millie was actually my great-aunt. She was a younger sister to Grandpa Bill Shaw. She and the second of her three husbands had built our house. After he had died, she and her third husband, Uncle Ed, had operated a small business from our garage before retiring. Millie often stopped by to see us boys and talk to Mom, usually crying on Mom's shoulder after a fight with Ed. She'd come in the house like a ball of fire, loud and sure of herself, always chewing gum and clicking it in her mouth. She'd tear a stick in half and hand it to me. She seemed to genuinely care for me, calling me "Butchy" and taking me along on short business trips in her great big car.

The next time I saw Millie at our house, I enthusiastically showed her the typewriter and asked her to show me how to type.

"That's not something I can just show you, Butchy," she said. "But, I've got a book at home that you could learn from."

"Can I use it?" I begged.

"Sure, honey. I'll tell you what...you can keep it." True to her word, Millie was back the following day with a book titled *Touch Typing Made Easy*. "Easy". That was just what I wanted.

To the right: Back Row: Grandpa Bill Shaw, Aunt Millie, and Louise Connor, a second cousin. Front Row: Dennis, Terry and Michael Shaw.

Below: The Remington portable.

What possesses a 14-year-old boy to read a typing instruction manual and diligently do the exercises on his own in the summer? I don't remember what drove me but I did it. I practiced every day. First learning the home base letters and then slowly moving my fingers up and down the letter keys, I spent days and days doing the exercises. Slowly my skill and speed picked up. I mastered it and actually got pretty proficient at it. I timed myself. 40...50...60 words a minute!

I was confident enough to hire myself out to other students the following fall to type their Science, English and Social Studies' reports. Sometimes they expected me to not only type the report but also write it for them. I knew that certain teachers never actually read the reports, so I made sure the first and last pages were good and then, in the middle, I had my fun. I remember typing in a report for one of the Wimmer boys for Ruthie Burn's ninth grade Science class that "Donald Duck is a very good duck. He lives with Mickey Mouse." Nobody ever discovered what I was doing, not the teachers and, for sure, not my friends who paid for the report.

Nine years later in 1968, I was in my fifth year of college and my Selective Service deferment ran out. I got the dreaded letter from Uncle Sam. "Greetings, You are hereby ordered to report for induction..." My mother, who had remarried seven years earlier, was beside herself. The

Vietnam War was going on. She stood outside the bathroom as I stood in front of the mirror combing my hair.

"Can't you go to Canada or something?" she implored. At the time Mom had had two of her sons and a two stepsons who had been in the service and had just got out and she had one stepson who was still in the Army. Her brothers had fought in World War II and Korea. Uncle Bud had been torpedoed on a ship in the South Pacific. He had spent days clinging to the side of a raft, while his buddies drifted off into the ocean or were attacked by sharks. Uncle Sonny had his heel shot off, also in the Pacific. Bud and Sonny coincidentally ended up in the same hospital in Australia at the same time. Uncle Dean had a bullet pass through his hand. He had a scar on his belly in the shape of a half circle where they took skin to do a graph on his hand. His forefinger didn't close into his fist like his other fingers. No one had been killed yet, but Mom thought her luck was going to run out.

"I afraid for you, Terry," she said. I told Mom that I thought it was my turn and my duty and I had to go. I wasn't trying to be a hero. I believe in fate and "Que sera, sera", or "Whatever will be, will be". I didn't think I could do anything about it and I didn't believe that anything bad would happen to me.

I was sent to Ft. Campbell, Kentucky for my basic training and then on to Ft. Knox, Kentucky for A.I.T. A.I.T. stood for Advanced Individual Training. It was the training for the job that the Army had picked for you to do. The Army had decided, wisely I thought, to send me to Personnel School to be an Army Personnel Specialist. I was going to be an Army clerk. A desk jockey. A "chair-born ranger". "Maybe," I thought, "I'll get a job at the Pentagon." Vietnam never even entered my mind, although I had just finished eight hard weeks of training learning how to kill the Viet Cong. The Army didn't let us forget for one second what we were there training for.

The first class I was assigned to at Ft. Knox was Typing Class. "Great!" I thought to myself. "This will be a snap for me." As I started my first lessons, I listened as the other trainees slowly stumbled through their typing exercises. I zipped through mine and started wearing a path to the Sergeant's desk, turning in exercise after exercise. One day during the second week of classes, I looked up from my typing to see a First Sergeant walk into the classroom. He ambled over to our instructor's desk carrying a large package. The instructor stood, took the package, and then they quietly talked for a while, occasionally glancing my way.

"Shaw!" the instructor yelled. "Up here on the double!"

"Oh my God!" I thought to myself. "What have I done now?" I had just finished eight long weeks of basic training with people constantly screaming at me. The result was never any good. I jumped up from my typewriter and ran to the front of the room.

"Yes, Sergeant," I said, as I came to a halt at attention in front of his desk, even though it wasn't required as he wasn't an officer.

"Shaw, you'll be going with the Sergeant here," he said, motioning to the multi-striped arm of the man beside him. "He'll tell you what to do. Grab all your gear. You won't be coming back so leave your books here."

A chill went through my body as I ran back to my desk to grab my green fatigue jacket. I had no idea what was going on. Why did he say I wasn't coming back? The First Sergeant led me out of the old wood building and down the street. Finally, he turned to me, continuing to walk as quickly as he could, and said, "You're gonna be my new company clerk, Shaw."

"Oh?" I asked, struggling to keep up with him.

"We're an A.P.C. training company up the street from here." A.P.C. meant Armored Personnel Carrier. It was an amphibious tank that carries troops into battle.

"Okay, Sergeant," I muttered, immediately angry. I was going to be a lowly company clerk instead of working at the Pentagon in a nice office. "But Sarge...I'm not through with my training yet," I added quickly, thinking it might change his mind.

"You're gonna get O.J.T., Shaw." On the Job Training was what that meant. Learn as you go. Forget the proper training from school. I was getting more and more upset.

"Why'd you pick me, Sarge?" I asked, trying to cover up my anger.

"Because you were the best student and I wanted the best." He probably thought I would be happy because of that statement. I wasn't. I was mad and feeling queasy in my stomach. "I bought you for an overcoat," he added, with a snicker in his voice.

"Ah," I thought, "the package." I soon learned that that was how things got done in the Army. You traded favor for favor or item for item, if you wanted something done in your lifetime.

I quickly became the company clerk compiling and typing Morning Reports, typing up duty rosters and literally doing the First Sergeant's and Captain Leary's work for them. They just signed everything I typed and put in front of them. I was promoted to Acting Corporal. As a matter of fact, I signed that particular order for the Captain. He was rarely around and, because of that, I had learned to forge his signature at the request of the First Sergeant. Even though I was still just a Private First Class, I was given the two stripes so that I could put the trainees on K.P. or guard duty assignments. I got my own room to sleep in instead of sleeping in the bay with all of the other privates and I had keys to every building in the company, including the mess hall and the kitchen. That came in handy for late night snacks. If you've heard of Corporal Radar O'Reily on the TV show *M*A*S*H**, you know exactly what I did.

Cpl. Terry Shaw at Ft. Knox doing Army work.

Captain Leary decided, on one of the few days when he was around, that, because I was his company clerk, I should know how to drive every vehicle in the company. So I took lessons in driving the jeep and all of the monster trucks and was licensed for them all. Then the First Lieutenant, a West Point grad, started using me to drive him in the jeep out to the training sites. Looking at the troops, he told me, "You know, Shaw, all of these kids are going to Vietnam."

"Really?" I asked back. All of a sudden I saw them in a different light instead of just numbers for my Morning Reports and KP lists.

"Yep, and they're training for Recon, (reconnaissance), so most of them won't live past a month or so." I didn't know if he was telling me the truth or not. I did know that he was going to 'Nam himself in a couple of months. Every First and Second Lieutenant went, a fact I had been told in basic and a reason I turned the Army down when they came and asked me if I wanted to go to Officer's Training School.

One day the First Lieutenant had me drive him to a small lake where the trainees were taught how to drive the A.P.C.s down an incline into the water and across the lake.

"Have you driven one yet, Shaw?" the Lieutenant asked me.

"No, sir," I replied. "Don't know how."

"Well, it's about time you learned," he said. "Let's go."

I was put in the driver's seat in the belly of the beast that had a small opening in front of me to look out, and given a crash course in operating it. It was propelled and turned with two peddles on the floor. The Lieutenant sat up behind me with most of his body sticking out of a rectangular hole on the top of the A.P.C. If I had been watching the trainees closer, I would've seen that they drove the vehicle very slowly into the water. But I hadn't been paying attention.

"When you come down the hill and near the water, Shaw," the Lieutenant lied to me, "you need to gun the engines so you don't stall." I bought it and did what he said. Of course, I nose-dived into the lake pulling half of it into the small driver's area where I was sitting. The Lieutenant, of course, sitting above me, was high and dry. The trainees got a good laugh at my expense that afternoon. I was the guy who had been putting them on K.P. and guard duty and they saw it as payback. I got a soaking and I was glad to get back to my desk.

An Army A.P.C. entering the water.

The Morning Report was the worst job I had. Every day I had to send a report to headquarters listing everybody in our company, complete with the soldiers' service numbers and ranks. It was done in triplicate. It was slow and tedious and it had to be done perfectly. No mistakes were accepted or tolerated. My typing skills were really needed for that job and I was thankful I had trained myself well.

One day the Supply Sergeant came over to my desk and said, "Hey Shaw. Weren't you in that class that started Personnel School five weeks ago?" He knew I was. I had complained enough about it. I had learned that he had been in on that deal, supplying the overcoat I was bought for.

"Yeah, why?" I said, looking up from my typing, still angry at being pulled out of the class.

"Well they just graduated and guess where they're going?" he answered with a grin.

"Where?" I said, a lot more interested now than I was a moment before.

"They're all going to Vietnam. Every last one of 'em. Sarge probably saved your life when he bought you."

I don't know if Sarge had really saved my life and if I would have been in harm's way in Vietnam, but you never know. I probably would have worked in an air-conditioned office in Saigon. Who knows? But, I could have been a company clerk out in the field typing up Morning Reports with a small olive green portable typewriter; much like the one Pat and I had bought on Crazy Days. Typing lists of my dead comrades and lists of the still living. Maybe some of them would've been guys that had trained in my company at Ft. Knox. All I know is that because I had made the decision to buy that old typewriter, which caused me to make the decision to learn how to type correctly, I did not go to Vietnam. Instead, I received orders three months later to finish my service time in Pirmasens, Germany. To me it was a paid vacation in Europe.

I got married on my pre-Germany leave to my fiancée from Lake Lillian, Minnesota. She came over to Pirmasens to be with me a few months later after I had found an apartment off the base and had saved up enough money to pay for it and send for her. She was pregnant and had never been away from her parents or out of the United States before so it was a scary situation for her.

When the time for the baby arrived, late one dark moonless spring night, I loaded her in our little beat-up Volkswagen "bug" and rushed her to the local Army clinic five kilometers away to confirm it. The medics said it was time, put her in an ambulance and told me to follow them to the Army Hospital. Off we went on a wild chase up a mountain on an unfamiliar curved road. I desperately tried to keep the VW close behind the speeding ambulance, praying I wouldn't get into an accident. I could barely do fifty M.P.H. up that mountain with the gas pedal of my tiny car floored. I had some narrow misses as I blindly screamed around curves on the unfamiliar road that dark night, which had become a dark morning by now. We ended up at the U.S. Army Hospital in Landstuhl, Germany. There my tiny daughter Christine was born on April 30, 1969.

A strange thing happened that night at the hospital that would've made the hair stand up on the back of my head, had I known about it at the time. Thousands of miles from America, at a tiny Army Hospital on the side of a mountain in Germany, a woman from Lake Lillian, who had married a man who went to school in Litchfield, was giving birth on April 30th. In another room of the same hospital, a soldier from Lake Lillian, who went to the same high school I did in Litchfield, died…on April 30th. His name was Dick Vick and he had been in a car accident on a curved mountain road.

The sun had risen and it was now early in the morning. The hospital shops were just opening, so I sent telegrams to the new grandparents back in the States. "Baby girl born. Christine and mother fine." Then I went back to the Army base after shaving at our apartment. I tried to get the day off to catch some sleep but Sarge said he needed me on the job. I called the hospital and told them to tell my wife I had to work but would be there in the late afternoon. After work, I rushed back to the hospital expecting to see my first child in the arms of her mother. I walked into the room and saw my wife sitting on the edge of her bed. She obviously had been crying.

"What's wrong?" I asked. "Where's the baby?"

"I think you'd better sit down," she answered. "The doctor's going to come and talk to us. He says there's something wrong with Christine."

"What?" I was stunned. "What's wrong?"

"He says she's got Down syndrome."

A cold chill swept down my body from my forehead to my feet.

Down syndrome is a type of retardation caused by an extra chromosome from one of the parents. The children used to be called Mongoloids because of their Oriental looking eyes. They have an enlarged tongue, which causes speech problems, poor muscle tone, which means they are slow to walk and a little less than half of them have heart problems. I hadn't sat down, but I did now. The words were shocking but not unknown to either of us. My wife's aunt had Down syndrome and my mother had babysat a Down boy named David Huberty. Pat and I had played with him on the lawn to help Mom out when she was cooking.

The doctor finally came and took us to the glass windowed nursery. He went inside, picked up our baby and then held Christine up behind the glass like a puppy at "Show and Tell" in school. He pointed out the various visual symptoms, like her eyes. When he bent her little double-jointed fingers all the way back, it was like a blow to my stomach. We both cried. When the doctor came out of the room, he shocked us by telling us to consider putting Christine away in a home. The thought had never entered either of our minds.

I pushed my wife in her wheelchair back to her room. We sat and looked at each other for a while in a terribly awkward moment, not knowing what to do or say. Finally I said, "Let's write letters to our parents and tell them." So that's what we did. It was therapeutic and washed a lot of the pain right out of our bodies.

Mom wrote back to us that God had picked us to be Christine's parents because He knew that we'd do a wonderful job raising a special child. All we did was treat her like a normal child. She was our first child, so we had nothing to compare her with. Christine has brought nothing but joy to our lives. She's got the prettiest blue eyes with little "stars" or white specks in them. Down's kids are the closest you'll get to angels on God's green earth. Auntie Christine, as she prefers to be called now that my grandson has been born, has grown into a loving, gentle woman, who is "normal" in so many ways, having her trying moments along with her good moments. She goes to work every day and is not a burden to us or on society. She makes me proud to call her my daughter.

Christine at seven and thirty-three years old.

Chapter Twenty-Six
Nickels

There was the usual mid-block alley right after Reed's Printing and the Marshall-Wells store. It was followed by Cox's Market[179], yet another grocery store. Cox's was a small family run store started by Freeman Cox and passed on to his son Merlyn, whose daughter Diane or "Dee Dee" was a classmate of mine from kindergarten through high school. She married another classmate, Mick Revering, Eleanor's son, and Dee Dee still lives in Litchfield, where she had supervised my Down syndrome daughter, Christine, at one time at ProWorks.

When Dee Dee's dad retired, the store was sold to Andy Bienick, who later married my Aunt Mary Alice Shaw, Uncle Dean's ex-wife. Isn't it funny how the strands of life keep getting intertwined? Andy turned the building into a restaurant, which was the first Farmer's Daughter Restaurant. He built the present Farmer's Daughter out on east Highway 12 in late 1973 and kept the downtown one open for a year. People called it the "Downtown Café". Andy sold it and it became the Main Street Café where my step-dad Floyd would treat me to an occasional breakfast.

Dee Dee Cox played a part in my only detention stay in high school. The school had a Tuesday morning released time period scheduled in. We were released from school for an hour to walk to our churches for religion class. We Catholics went to the large meeting room at St. Philip's School. Acey Quinn, Dee Dee Cox, Marty Foss, Mick Revering, Jeannie McCarney, Mike Miller and several other Catholics walked to St. Philip's one Tuesday morning and sat in the meeting room for ten minutes, waiting for our religion teacher.

The teacher was a "no show", so Revering said, "Let's go to Dee Dee's place and play some cards." Dee Dee only lived two blocks away at the corner of Armstrong Avenue and Fifth Street. Some of the students said they were going back to school, others said they were going downtown or to other places, but I chose to go along with the majority over to Dee Dee's.

That afternoon in school I was in study hall, when Assistant Principal Harry Lindbloom called me out into the hall.

---

[179] 226 Sibley Avenue North. See page 560 of the History of Downtown Litchfield Appendix.

"Mr. Shaw," he said, "I would like the names of all of the students who skipped religion class with you today."

"We didn't skip," I said. "We went and the teacher didn't show up."

"And you didn't come back to school until the next period, is that right?" he asked me.

"No, I didn't."

"Then you skipped. Who was with you?"

"I can't tell you," I replied, not wanting to rat on my friends.

All of a sudden I was up against the lockers with clenched fists grasping the front of my shirt.

"I want the names of everyone who was with you, right now, Shaw."

I might have told him before that outburst, but his actions were uncalled for and clinched it for me. I refused to tell him, earning myself two week's detention after school. That was okay. Less time in the pool hall, more time in the books and I was a hero to my buddies.

Berquist Electric[180] was after Cox's, still walking north. I delivered the paper to Stan Berquist's new house at the outskirts of town west by Martin Huiko's place and Stan's son, Gary, was also a classmate of mine also.

The next store after Berquist's was the Gambles Store[181], which was owned in the fifties by Al Hummel. Gambles sold Hotpoint appliances and various tools. Raymond H. "Ray" Dart, a blind lawyer and son of town pioneer Charles H. "Charley" Dart, had his office upstairs. Ray had been playing with some corset stays as a youngster and the stays had sprung loose and damaged his eyes. His mother and later his wife Stella went to his college classes with him taking notes. They read Ray his reading assignments and helped him graduate and pass the bar. He won his first case, a divorce case in Minneapolis, and the judge was so impressed that he came down off the bench and shook his hand. Ray started his practice in Litchfield in 1909 and Stella went to court with him, again taking notes for him. Ray had an unbelievable memory and an unbelievable wife.

---

[180] 228-230 Sibley Avenue North. See page 562 of the History of Downtown Litchfield Appendix.

[181] 232-234 Sibley Avenue North. See page 564 of the History of Downtown Litchfield Appendix.

He chewed tobacco and he would stand up in court, make a point and then spit and hit the spittoon by his desk, as if he could see it. Ray even drove a car. The police saw him driving his big old black car around town and they never pulled him over. His wife sat next to him and steered but Ray did everything else. Ray became a Judge of Probate in October of 1931. That must have prompted a lot of "justice is blind" jokes. In May of 1955, he lost his office and home over Gambles when they caught fire. Gambles suffered some damage and couldn't reopen for a couple of months.

Christine's,[182] a woman's clothing store that was owned by J. Christine Jensen, was in the next building. She stayed at this location for only five years and then she moved across the street. I never went in there, obviously.

Harold Harding built the building north of Christine's and moved to Sibley Avenue from his Second Street location with his Harding Dry Cleaners[183] in July of 1950. Kathryn Van Nurden, Mom's close friend, worked there in the fifties.

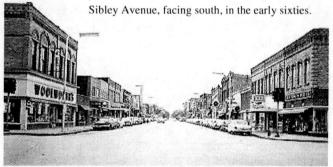
Sibley Avenue, facing south, in the early sixties.

Finally, on the southeast corner of Sibley Avenue and Third Street, was the first location for the J. C. Penney's Department Store. The building was called the Litchfield Masonic Building[184]. Old J. C. Penney himself visited Litchfield's store on September 7, 1928. When Penney's moved down the street to its new store by Johnson's Recreation in January of 1959, this building was remodeled and became the

---

[182] 236 Sibley Avenue North. See page 567 of the History of Downtown Litchfield Appendix.
[183] 240 Sibley Avenue North. It became the Litchfield Cleaners dry cleaning business. See page 569 of the History of Downtown Litchfield Appendix.
[184] 242-244 Sibley Avenue North. See page 571 of the History of Downtown Litchfield Appendix.

Woolworth and Company store in June of 1959. That pretty much put the Ben Franklin store across the street out of business.

Crossing back over Sibley Avenue, heading west again down Third Street towards my home brought me back past the "old power plant" where I started my walk around town. The old power plant was still being used, although the town had a "new power plant", built in 1948, just two blocks west of our house. During the daytime hours of the spring, summer and fall weeks, we used the immense lawns of the power plants for our baseball diamonds and football fields. But evenings and weekends, when no one was around to chase us away, things were different. The power plants provided another kind of amusement, usually involving danger and dares.

Next to the old power plant was Litchfield's water tower, erected in 1914 to replace an old wooden one. In May of 1958, large red letters stating "Class-58" appeared on the water tower under the Litchfield name. No one knew who did it and no one has ever come forward to admit to the courageous deed. But, a reliable source told me that Dave Harder was one of the culprits and class president Dick Simmons was probably involved also. At thirteen, I was really impressed that someone would do such a thing, thumbing their nose at Litchfield's authorities. It also got me thinking that if someone else could get up there, why couldn't I?

I did scale the tower but I didn't do it for the Class of '63, nor was I involved in the stunt someone else did do for my class. One morning in late May of 1963, the town woke up to large black letters spray painted on the side of the hotel, on the white concrete block pump house building near the south parking lot of the Legion Memorial Park and on one of the two storage tanks near Anderberg's DS gas station on Highway 12 East. The message painted on the hotel was "Booze is cheap. Sex is free. We're the Class of '63." Vic Forte, manager of the hotel, was livid. He had Pete Hughes get a can of spray paint and cover the graffiti up until teachers Wally Stubeda and Wayne Brix could come and do the job properly. I honestly never knew about the episode at the time. The newspaper and everyone involved must have hushed it up. In 1966, two girls did what our class didn't do. They scaled the water tower and painted "LHS '66" on it.

On a sunny Sunday afternoon, no doubt spurred on by dares and the memory of the '58 stunt, I ventured to climb that water tower. These were the days before fences, gates and locks. There was no padlocked barrier or safety enclosure to stop a crazy thirteen-year old boy from scaling the steel ladder to heights he had never been before. This was easily the tallest structure in town. This was the tallest structure in my world.

After I made the long climb up to the fenced circular platform that went around the cone-topped tank of the tower, tingling all over my body with fear and excitement, I didn't want to come down. What a thrill to look over and beyond the town that made up my world. There was our house and over there was Central Park. There was the Litchfield Hotel and Greep-Trueblood and way out there was Lake Ripley. With the thrill of the sights before my eyes, I was suddenly overcome by two fears. What if I got caught up here and how was I going to get back down?

Litchfield's "old" water tower, which several young men and women climbed, including Terry Shaw.

Coming back down makes you look down. That was something you could avoid going up. How was I going to swing my body over the side and get a firm foothold on the top rung of the steel ladder? What if I missed? My friends down below started taunting me so I slowly swung one leg over the side, gripping the fence rail tightly with both of my hands. "Is that the ladder I feel under my foot?" I wondered to myself. I was afraid to look down. "It feels like the ladder," I thought. "Here goes…" Rung by rung, I slowly climbed down. I finally made it down to solid ground, shaking with a wide grin and receiving pats on my back from my friends. The thrills I felt at the top of the world far outweighed the fears, so the tower beckoned me back several more times that summer to throw off homemade parachutes with a rock tied to them or other items, just to watch them fall, seemingly forever. The story has been told that a couple of boys threw a cat off once; just to see if it would land on it's feet. I wasn't one of them and I never saw what was left of the cat.

My stepfather, Floyd Young, would climb the tower to do maintenance like changing Christmas light bulbs. Mom was outside hanging clothes on the line one day and she kept hearing her name being called from up above.
"Hel...en....Hel...en...," the voice kept calling her.
Was it God? No, just Floyd having fun.

There was a little pump house by the power plant. It also was never locked and, because of the motor inside, it was relatively warm. Therefore, it served as a motel for unfortunates in the winter. We would see tracks in the snow up to the door in the winter and once in a while someone would come out for a smoke. Dennie saw them as he walked by in the early Sunday morning hours on his way to pick up his newspapers at the paper shack in the winter.

Close to the tower was a mountain of black coal. We would make the difficult climb up the rocky pile of coal pieces to play *King of the Hill*. I'm sure our mothers appreciated washing those clothes. Mom never said a word though, which makes one think that it was more normal than not for us to be that dirty at that age. Next to the black mountain was an elevated conveyor belt. It rose from the ground at a steep angle to the top of the two-story power plant next to it. It became a giant slide with the aid of a flattened cardboard box to sit on. Next to the coal mountain was the cooling tower.

The cooling tower was an ancient gray wooden structure that looked like a simple three story box. Earlier, when it had been erected in the late twenties, it had been at least twice as high with other increasingly smaller wooden "boxes" with slanted walls stacked on top of each other. The bottom half of one of the four walls that remained consisted of a wooden frame around a giant fan. Inside the shell of a building, (remember there were no locks back then), was nothing. Well, nothing except for a skeleton of wooden boards and beams crisscrossing over our heads. It was a favorite place for pigeons to roost. How they got in there, I do not know. I remember Dennie and Snooky Young climbing up onto the beams to shoot at them with a BB gun or poke at them with a stick.

"I'm gonna tell Mom!" I yelled, more to get them out of there than anything else. Pat and I and our friends thought this was our special place.

Instead of a floor, there was a room-size concrete water pool. The pool was only about six inches deep with scummy cold water still in it. There was a narrow two-foot walkway along the fan side of the pool. What fascinated our group was that giant fan. Apparently water had been pumped to the top of the building and then allowed to "rain" down to the pool, passing by the blowing fan. Somehow the cooled air was then collected and transferred inside the power plant to cool the giant turbine engines.

The shape the cooling tower was in told us that it was no longer being used. We would climb onto the fan, lock our small arms and legs around a blade and hold on for dear life, while our "friends" attempted to spin it. I never made it all of the way around. "Stop! Stop! I'm gonna fall! I'm slipping!", I'd yell, my arms squeezing tighter around the blade while my legs dangled backwards from my upside-down body.

In the background, the cooling tower in 1936.

My mother didn't know about any of these adventures. She worked everyday to raise us four boys and was gone most of the daylight hours. Grandpa Bill Shaw, my absent father's father, lived with us for a few years, in the mid-fifties, to watch after us so Mom could work. He had moved to town in 1949 to live in a small house three blocks north of us at 511 Swift Avenue North. When Mom needed someone to watch us so she could work at the Produce, Grandpa rented his house out and moved in with us when he was sixty-two.

Grandpa had been a janitor at the old power plant before he retired. When I was nine years old, Pat and I went up to the old brown brick power plant one early summer morning to see Grandpa, who was still working part-time there. We stood in the long cool grass by a concrete window well under the open corner window and yelled for him to come and talk to us. He did and introduced us to another man named Claude Hamilton[185]. Claude was the plant's chief engineer and his wife Celia was the cook at our parochial grade school. She made the best beef and potato hash I've ever eaten.

The window well we stood at seemed big and deep to us because of our relatively small size. I remember standing in it and my eyes came just to the top of the well. Often we would jump down into the well to retrieve frogs and salamanders that had found themselves a cool dark home there. We would take the frogs home so we could blow them up with firecrackers or put them in an old round cardboard oatmeal box to torture later at our leisure.

After the introduction to Claude, we began to go up to the power plant and yell for him too. He was fun to talk to. He had been in Litchfield forever doing a lot of different jobs. At one time, a long time ago, he did house moving for a livery stable in town. Claude was old. He'd come to the window and we'd talk. He probably enjoyed the break from his work or, more likely, the cool breeze from the open window. It was always unbearably hot inside the power plant. A couple of years later, I arranged my paper route so that the new power plant was my last delivery stop. Then, I could thaw out standing next to the giant turbines.

One day, as Claude was talking to us, he reached into his pocket and took out a shiny nickel. He held it up for us to see and then, all of a sudden, he threw it down into the window well, laughing as we jumped into the well to get it. A nickel was a huge amount of money to us. You could buy a Snickers candy bar for a nickel or a handful of penny candy.

The "nickel hunts" started that day and continued through the summer, becoming an almost daily occurrence. Frequently, when my friends weren't around, I'd go up to the power plant on my own. I sat in the cool grass next to the window well and Claude and I talked. I can't remember what we talked, maybe some of these tales I've told, but the conversations always ended with Claude saying, "Well, I'd better get back to work." Then he would reach into his pocket and dig around for that precious nickel. He always seemed to have one. I think Claude enjoyed my visits as much as I did and he was rewarding me for spending part of my summer days with him.

One hot summer night, I had a vivid dream as I slept. In the dream I had run up to the power plant as usual to see Claude. When I got there, I

---

[185] See Claude's picture on page 280.

noticed that the window was closed. The window was never closed during the day, even in the winter. I scratched my head and looked down to the window well. To my amazement, it was full of shiny nickels! Right up to the top. I couldn't believe it! I had found the treasure of my life. It was the pot of gold at the end of the rainbow.

I remember being so happy that my excitement woke me up with a start. I was overcome with a chilling question. Was it a dream or wasn't it? I didn't know. It had seemed so real. What if it was true? What if the window well really was full of nickels? What if the dream was one of those dreams that foretold the future? I had to get up to the power plant as fast as I could. I had to get up there before my younger brother Pat, lying next to me, woke up. I had to get up there before any of my friends got up there.

I couldn't dress fast enough! I ran down the stairs, through the living room, around the corner of the kitchen and out the side door of our house. I don't remember if my feet actually touched the steps down to the driveway or not. I ran towards the garage and through the opening between our garage and our neighbor's garden. I ran past McCormick's garden behind our garage and then his house. I whipped across Miller Avenue, jumped over the curb and onto the green grass of the power plant. Rounding the corner of the old brick building, I soon stood in front of the window well. The empty window well. There wasn't even a frog down there. What a disappointment! Huffing and puffing, I looked up to the open, but also empty window. I had to tell Claude about my strange dream. Wouldn't he think it was weird?

I started yelling Claude's name. I yelled it over and over, but Claude didn't come to the window like he usually did. Finally a different man I didn't know came up to the window. He looked around and then down to the nine year old boy standing below him by the window well.

"What's all this yelling about?" he asked.

"I'm looking for Claude," I gasped.

"Claude? Oh...sorry son," the man said, his voice dropping down. "Claude died in his sleep last night."

I will never forget how Claude's last goodbye touched me. I can't begin to explain it. Was it a coincidence that I had that dream on the very night that Claude had died? Or did God give me a gift of a precious memory? I think it was a gift given to me so that I would never forget Claude or my childhood growing up under the guidance of my mother in my hometown of Litchfield, Minnesota.

When my brothers and I grew older and had families of our own, we always made it back to Mom and Floyd's in Litchfield for every Christmas Eve, just as Mom had made sure that she had made back it to her parent's house in LeSueur every Christmas. After arriving in the afternoon, Dennie and I would always bring out our guitars and play and sing Christmas carols in the dining room with everyone while Mom cooked for us in the kitchen and sang along. Our step-dad, Floyd, played with the grandkids, helped Mom, and sang too.

After we had eaten, done the dishes and all the presents were opened, we'd clean up the paper and gifts in the living room and go to Midnight Mass with Mom and Floyd, early enough so that we could sit in the front pew, just as we had done with Mom as little boys, and hear the choir sing Mom's favorite Christmas carol, *O Holy Night*.

When Mom died in the fall of 1991 from Pancreatic cancer, we were uncertain if Floyd would want to carry on the traditions that Christmas. I spoke with him and he said he wanted to. We offered to help with the cooking and decorating but Floyd said, "Just come like always. I'll take care of everything." I pulled my car into the driveway a little apprehensively that Christmas. Not knowing what to expect inside the house, I loaded my three teenage kids up with gifts and we knocked on the door. Floyd greeted us, we hugged and kissed cheeks, and then he took off with the kids to help them put the presents under the tree. I said "Hi" to Dennie and his wife, who had arrived the day before. Of course, it didn't feel right in the kitchen that Christmas. Mom wasn't standing there in her apron by the stove.

I walked over to Dennie and said, "How's Floyd doing?"

"Fine," he answered me. "I think he's gonna be all right."

We were still talking when my daughter Andrea came running into the kitchen and grabbed my hand.

"Come here, Dad. You've got to see Grandpa's tree!"

"I'll see it honey," I said. "I'm talking to Uncle Dennie right now."

"No, Dad, you've got to come and see it now!"

"Oh…okay…" I told her. "I'll be right back, Dennie."

Andrea pulled me into the living room and I looked across the room to the tree. It was pretty, as usual, but I couldn't see what had made her so excited.

"Isn't it neat?" she said, pulling me across the room. Something was different about the tree but I couldn't put my finger on it. Some different decorations, maybe? Yes…that was it. Floyd was standing by the tree, with his arms around Christine and Adrian.

"Isn't it neat?" Andrea repeated. I looked again at the tree's new and different decorations.

"It's all your mother's jewelry," Floyd said, turning to me and referring to all the strands of different colored beads all over the tree. It was beautiful. They looked like they were right at home on that Christmas tree.

I don't think Floyd could have given us four Shaw boys a greater gift on our very first Christmas without our mother. Because of him, Mom was still with us. The rest of that magical night, I found my eyes drifting up to that beautiful Christmas tree over and over. Floyd, who gave my mother thirty years of well-deserved happiness, died two years later, but we Shaw boys still get together around Christmas. Pat has continued Mom's tradition of giving all her grandchildren a brown bag of candy, nuts and fruit. We toast Mom and shed a few tears every time we hear or sing *O Holy Night*. One of us makes the trek back to Litchfield every year to put a little Christmas tree on Mom's grave.

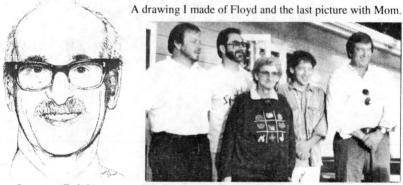

A drawing I made of Floyd and the last picture with Mom.

I must finish my song about music in our family that I've been including throughout the chapters.

THE SONG GOES ON
Now time has passed and Mick and I have gone our separate ways.
We now play in different bands, unlike the early days.
Pat and Dennie work in business, gainfully employed.
Dad's been gone for many years and so are Mom and Floyd.
Dennie and I get together and we write some songs.
Mick's three boys now have a band...the music marches on.
Though our family's spread apart, the memories sure aren't gone.
Our love for music's stayed with us and so the song goes on...
Oh yes, the song goes on.

After reading my stories, my brother Dennie reminded me of one of his stories about Mom. He wrote it up for me for inclusion in my book.

Chapter Twenty-Seven
Dennie's Chapter
The Gun

I wanted to write a story that would bring into focus the qualities and grace of the woman my mother Helen Shaw Young was and the depth of her love and commitment to her children. I will try with a story about a gun.

My mother and father were divorced when I was six and a half years old. I remember some of the arguments that went on in our house, but God's grace spared me from many of those painful memories. I remember that Mom never seemed to win, and she was always the one hurt and humiliated, crying in the bedroom, and left alone with her four boys.

Helen Shaw and her boys: Mickey, age 8, Pat, age 6, Terry, age 7 and Dennie, age 10.

Mom worked hard at protecting us from this unpleasantness. I used to justify disobedience and flippant attitudes, passing them off by saying that I was "just a normal kid, just growing up", as all kids do, questioning authority and testing boundaries. The plain truth of the matter is that I was not obedient and it pains me today to think of the things I put Mom through. I now believe God had a plan to teach me an important lesson about forgiveness through my mother.

My buddies always delighted in telling me about going hunting and fishing with their dads. As a thirteen-year old boy, I was very envious. My father did not participate in my life. I was blessed that one of Mom's brothers, my Uncle Bud, tried hard to fill in from time to time as my surrogate father. Still, Bud lived about seventy miles away and at this point in his life he was dating his wife-to-be, Frances. Rightfully, he did not have time to spend with me nor did he owe me any special attention.

One fall day, after Mom had worked all day at her job and was cooking supper, I was again being a pest. Instead of helping her do the dishes, I sat at the table and started my campaign to get something I wanted, a shotgun. I knew in my heart that I didn't have a need for it, but I asked Mom if I could buy one. I had asked for this many times before. The answer was always "No!" followed by some very sound reasons as to why not.

"Honey, you're not old enough to own a shotgun. We can't afford one right now and, besides, it's just too dangerous to have one in the house with your little brothers around." The final answer would always be, "I do not want you to ever bring a gun into this house. It is simply too dangerous...period. End of discussion." Obviously, Mom didn't like guns.

I changed my tactics and worked on my absent father. I saw him once in a while when he came to Litchfield on business. I had begged, petitioned, implored and put him on a guilt trip before. I had finally succeeded in getting him to give me a Daisy BB gun for Christmas. This too was against my mother's wishes. But, by then, it was too late and, as usual, Mom lost and my father won. I got to keep the BB gun. But this time it didn't work, so I went back to work on Mom. I reminded her that I was making my own money. I had a paper route and I made over $2.00 a week. I also saved some money from various odd summer jobs and I had about $28.00 put away in the "Bank of Mom". Thank God, Mom had invoked "penalties for early withdrawal of funds", because I know in my heart I would have blown the whole account on some worthless junk had she not imposed those rules.

I knew where a shotgun was that I wanted. It was at the Coast To Coast hardware store. It was a .16 gauge, single shot, bolt action, clip fed, Widgeon brand shotgun. If it can be said that a gun is "beautiful", then this was the one. It had a genuine walnut stock and was highly blued, except for the bolt-locking device, which had highly polished concentric swirls burnished into the steel.

Daily, I would trek to the store on my way home from school, going in the front door of the store past the paint, household items and linoleum piece goods, and march directly to the gun rack. Now and then I asked a busy Wally Hanson if I could hold the shotgun. He would let me as he stood by watching me carefully. I caressed the gun, rubbing and touching the beautifully hand stained stock, playing with the bolt action, and pretending to shoot a big Ringneck pheasant which was pictured in a Winchester Shotgun Shell poster on the wall above the ammunition stacked up on the other side of the store. The gun was on sale for $37.99. It was a good deal and I wanted it!

Coast To Coast ad from the October 16, 1955 issue of the Independent Review with a cheaper model of the Widgeon shotgun.

"Could I pay for it on time at $1.00 a week?" I finally asked Wally.

"Sure," he said, "but you will have to get your dad to come in when you pick it up". I explained to him about my dad.

"Well then, Mrs. Shaw will have to come in."

Through the fall, this scenario became a daily event for weeks on end. Wally tired of seeing me when I stopped in to look, touch, and then go home. I am sure Mom was also tired of my begging and arguing and her having to go through the whole discussion over and over. The debate always ended with the same result. Mom refused me. My heart would harbor unkind thoughts about it. I would brood and so it went.

One Friday, after school before Thanksgiving vacation, I was on one of my daily visits to see "my shotgun" before I picked up my newspapers for my paper route. I saw an older boy, John Weber, standing there looking at the guns too. He was buying bullets for his .22 rifle. I didn't know him very well, but I knew who he was. About five years older than I, John, the oldest son of Clarence Weber, lived about four blocks north of our house on Swift Avenue. I explained my "situation" to him.

"I had the same problem with my folks," he said sympathetically. "You just have to show them that you know how to handle guns and then it won't be such a hard thing to convince them to let you have one."

"Sound advice," I thought to myself. I asked him how I do that since all I owned was a dumb BB gun.

"That's no problem," he replied. "I'll rent you my gun."

I agreed and gave him $3.00 for a box of bullets and a "day's rent" out of my paper route moneybag. We made our plans for the weapon transaction.

My plan was to wait until Mom went to work on Saturday morning, as she sometimes did in the early days at the Farmer's Produce. I would go to John's house and pick up his scoped .22 semi-automatic rifle and then sneak out to the railroad tracks by way of walking along Jewett Creek. I would walk and hunt on the railroad tracks to Chicken Lake woods, about two and a half miles west on the Great Northern track. I had racked up a high score of robins, Mourning Doves and pigeons with my Daisy BB gun, so, being the great hunter that I was, I would be able to bag all kinds of critters, such as rabbits, ducks and pheasants with a "real gun". I was going to clean them, bring them home and have Mom cook them up for supper. My twisted theory was that Mom would be so impressed with my abilities to put food on the table that she would let me get the shotgun right on the spot and even help me pay for it. I would become a provider and she would have to see how responsible I was. My faulty logic gave little thought to the fact that I had never shot a rifle with a scope before, I had no hunting license, and it is illegal to shoot those game birds with a rifle.

I dreamed about my big hunting adventure all week. Saturday morning finally came. I got up and dressed for the hunt. Mom went off to work, telling me to watch over my brothers and be good, as she always did, and I always did not. After I saw her go out the door, I waited about three minutes and then I dashed out of the house. I got to the Weber's house only to find that John was not at home. I was mad and upset but I couldn't tell his mother why. She informed me that he would not be home until later that day. He had gone ice fishing. I slowly walked home thinking, "I hope the ice breaks and he drowns."

I sat around moping most of the day and waited until I thought he would finally be home. Mom had come home at noon, asked me to watch the brats again, and gone out to run some errands. About four in the afternoon, I walked to John's house again. He was there and came to the front door. When I reminded him about our agreement, he said, "Oh yah. I forgot. Come on out to the garage." I followed him.

"You know how to use this...right?" he asked me.

"Oh sure," I lied. "My uncle has one just like it. He let me shoot it a couple of times. Nice gun!"

"Okay. Be sure you bring this back to me Sunday night and clean it or I'll have to give you an ass kicking!"

"No problem," I assured him.

I started down the street towards home with the gun in its carrying case slung over my shoulder. I felt like the Great White Hunter. It was snowing, blowing and cold. A storm had come in during the afternoon and it was now a full-grown Minnesota blizzard. The sidewalk I had walked to the Weber's just a little while earlier was now in need of a shoveling. I didn't care. I was grateful that it had become dark so no one would see me with the gun and I could sneak it into the house. My little brothers were watching television in the living room and didn't see me bring the gun in through the kitchen door. I went right down to the basement and put it in my favorite hiding place under the stairs.

I busied myself thinking about all of the important things I would need for the hunt making a mental list; gloves, scarf, hat, candy bar, matches, my genuine Army canteen filled with warm water so that it wouldn't freeze. More importantly, I was wondering how I would get the gun out of the house again and go hunting on Sunday. I would have to go to Mass with the family and talk my brother Mick into selling my Sunday papers on the bank corner after church. I began to scheme up some really good reasons to be gone that Sunday afternoon. My mind was racing. I was sitting under the stair in the dim light holding the gun trying to figure out how to load it, working the action, dreaming of the big hunt and trying desperately to come up with a workable plan, when the light came on over the basement steps. Mom had just come home. She was stomping snow off her boots in the entryway to the kitchen at the top of the stair and she was upset. I could hear it in her voice.

"Where is Dennie?" she asked my brothers.

How could she know? I just knew I was in big trouble. What was really on her mind was that she had almost fallen coming into the house because I had neglected my chores and not cleaned the snow off the steps. Cowering in my hiding spot, I heard one of my brothers say, "I think he's in the basement, Mom." She started down the steps.

"I'm just getting the shovel to clean off the steps Mom!" I yelled up to her.

"Good," she said. I started up the steps with the coal shovel.

I didn't stay up and went to bed early that night. I had to get up early to deliver my Sunday papers and go to church. But of course, more importantly, I had a big day of hunting planned. I woke up early, without Mom having to yell up the stairs the usual five times to get me out of bed to deliver my papers. Old man winter had come in with a vengeance that night and at least two feet of fresh snow was drifting all over the place. It wasn't snowing now, but it was blowing and bitterly cold, not the most pleasant kind of a day to go hunting. But, it was the only day I had and I was going. I raced up to the paper shack with my sled, got my papers and rushed around my route, setting a new record for the delivery, in spite of the snow and winds. I got home earlier than normal and Mom even remarked, "What's the matter?"

"Nothing. Why?", I answered her.

She looked quizzical and came back with, "You normally don't get home for another twenty minutes."

After a while, Mom reminded me that I had to get dressed for church. While I was changing my clothes upstairs, I heard Mom walking around in the kitchen doing something and then I heard the sound of the basement door opening up and her footsteps going down. I held my breath. "Oh, oh!" I thought, "She's going down to get the shovel to clean off the steps." I had failed to do it in my haste. When I came down the stairs from my room, Mom was sitting at the kitchen table crying.

"What's the matter, Mom?"

"How could you? Why would you?" she said.

"What?"

"Where'd you get the money?"

"For what?"

"For this," she said, sobbing, standing up, grabbing my hand and pulling me into her bedroom. Then I saw it lying on her bed in its black carrying case. The gun! Before I could even close my open mouth, the interrogation began. Mom was crying and sobbing heavily asking me one question after another in rapid succession.

"Dennie, what store sold you this? How much did you spend for this? Can you get the money back? Why'd you disobey me? Was your father here yesterday? You know I hate guns. Did you do this just to hurt me? Why would you bring this thing into our house? For your little brothers to kill themselves with it? You are supposed to be the man of the house and take care of things. Set an example for them. What were you thinking?"

I would get a "but…" in every once in a while. I even got a "Mom, let me explain…." in, but she didn't hear me.

"Where are the shells? Are you crazy? Is this thing loaded? What if Pat or Terry or Mickey had found it first and shot each other? Have you shot holes in the house already? Were you in my closet?"

The small metal box for the Bank of Mom was in the closet. I honestly never knew about it until that morning. There were more questions to which I kept replying, "but…" and "Oh Mom." and "Let me explain…" and "Can I talk?"

Finally Mom said, "We have to leave and go to church. I want you to ask God for forgiveness for this. You and I will talk more about this when we get home, Dennie. Do you understand me?" The tone and the way this was phrased gave me no options and no opportunity for any dialog. There was only one acceptable answer, "Yes, Mom."

Church was hard that Sunday morning. I remember squirming a lot. When Mass ended, Mom grabbed my arm and we started the walk through the snow for home. She was silent. My brothers threw snowballs and laughed, but she didn't say a word. When we got to the corner at Sibley Avenue by the park, she reminded me that I had to do my job and sell papers at the bank corner. I didn't protest or bring up my deal with Mickey. It would give her some time to cool down.

When I got home later that morning, Mom was staring out the kitchen window. I could tell she had been crying again.

"Mom, I'm sorry, but I didn't buy the gun. I rented it."

She was flabbergasted. "You rented it? From who?"

I explained the scheme to her. Mom went to the phone to call the Webers, but then stopped dialing and hung up the phone. She turned and said, "Why didn't you just come to me about this?"

"Because you would have said 'no'."

"Maybe. Does this gun really mean that much to you?"

"Yes" I answered through my tears. "I want to go hunting."

"Can't it wait until you can go with your Uncle Bud?"

I told her that that would be fine but I wanted to go today. I had paid my money and told my friends about what I was going to do that Sunday.

"Where were you going to go?" she asked.

I told her.

"What were you going to hunt for?"

"Rabbits and pheasants."

Standing in the kitchen that cold Sunday afternoon, Mom softened, came up to me and put her arms around my neck.

"If this means that much to you Dennie, I will go hunting with you. Let's get ready." I started to cry. I don't know why, because I was getting my way after all. Looking back I think that Mom forgave me at that point.

It was cold outside, I am sure it was well below zero, and it was still blowing snow. Mom had no suitable clothes for these conditions but she didn't complain. She put on some slacks, a sweater, and her little winter boots that had a fuzzy fringe around the top. As she stood waiting by the kitchen door for me to get ready, she told my brothers that she had called her friend Katherine who would come over and stay with them. Mom put on her wool knit mittens and a scarf on her head, which she tied under her chin. We set out on the expedition and walked the railroad tracks out of town. Nothing was moving except for Mom and I. My mother was worried about me shooting myself and made me carry the gun unloaded all of the time as we walked along. She kept the bullets. Most of the time the snow was up over her boots but she didn't complain.

We reached the intersection of the railroad tracks and Vern Worden's north field behind his mink farm sheds. I was cold, getting very discouraged and about ready to turn around and start walking back towards town. The wind was fierce and biting and my cheeks were burning, even though the sun had emerged. It was still cold and now the bright white snow was blinding us. The big hunt was not producing much in the way of game and about the only thing we were going to get was a cold. We were both shivering, but not once did Mom complain. Not once did she discourage me. In fact, Mom was the one who suggested that I walk down into the heavy weeds along the ditch at the bottom of the tracks to get out of the wind and scare up a rabbit.

361

Years later, I was told by Uncle Bud that Mom used to go hunting with him when they were kids. Her role was to be the "bird dog", flushing out game. She was no stranger to what to look for in the way of cover. I followed her instructions and almost immediately I caught the movement of a cottontail jumping up and running. I pulled up the gun, but never having used a telescopic site before, I had forgotten to take the lens cap off. By the time I had fumbled my way through that maneuver and chambered my one shell, quickly handed to me by Mom, the poor scared rabbit was three hundred yards away.

I ran towards him only to encounter a barbwire fence full force, ripping my parka. To further complicate things, climbing the fence, I put a nasty scratch in my right forearm. I got over the fence, stood, aimed and fired, missing the rabbit. I called to Mom for more ammunition. She was up on the tracks with all of the bullets in her pocket. She came running down the steep bank and fell in the snow. She got up and handed one more bullet to me. With my wet cold hands, I promptly dropped the shell into the snow. She handed me another one, which I got into the rifle. I looked into the scope and couldn't find the bunny. Mom pointed off in the distance and I aimed, but between the adrenaline and the shivers from the cold wind, I missed the rabbit again. He sped off, never stopping to allow me another shot.

"We can still walk the tracks for a little while longer if you want," Mom said. The sun was starting its decent toward the horizon.

I shivered a "Yes" and we walked for another mile. When we crossed the railroad trestle over frozen Jewett Creek, I saw two more rabbits and, of course, they saw me. Mom and I were in the ditch on the side of the tracks, running after them. I stopped, shot, and missed and asked Mom for another bullet. I loaded, shot, and missed, and asked for another bullet. Loaded, shot, and missed, and ran in the direction I had last seen the rabbits. On and on it went and Mom never complained.

We never did get a rabbit. The setting sun had caught up with us, but my mother taught me something about love and how much she cared for me. I tried hard after that to be the son my mother wanted me to be, but, of course, I failed many times. As I would fail, I would remember her love and I would always ask for forgiveness. She would always forgive me. It is funny but Mom never told this story about our hunt to anyone. She could have done it to get a laugh, but she didn't. She could have told it to demonstrate the length she would go to for her kids, but she didn't.

I still have the scene etched in my heart and I have never forgotten that cold Minnesota Sunday afternoon when my mother went hunting with me. At first I thought Mom did it because she wanted me to be happy. Now I think it was for a much more important reason. She did it out of love and God used her unselfishness to teach me about forgiveness. Mom forgave my disobedience. Instead of taking a well-deserved rest from the trials of her life on the one day she didn't work, she took time to teach me a lesson. She could have punished me for the lies I had told about the gun. She didn't. She could have ignored me and sent me to my room. She didn't. She could have taken the time to rest her tired legs and feet on that cold Sunday afternoon. She didn't. Instead, my Mom froze her feet in the deep Minnesota snow, walking along side of me, so I could feel the warmth of her love. I still feel that love to this day.

Terry Tales Appendix
The History of Downtown Litchfield:
The First One Hundred Years
1869-1969

"My World – Litchfield 1959" Map

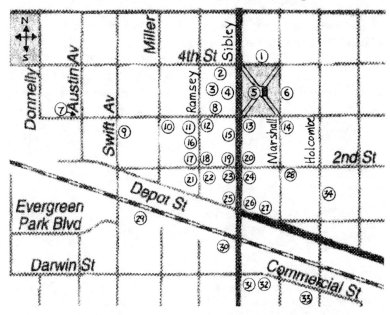

1. Floyd Warta's house	18. The Litchfield Fire Hall
2. The Meeker County Court House	19. The Northwestern Bank
3. The Meeker County Jail	20. Sward-Kemp Drug store
4. Janousek's "Eat 10¢" Café	21. The Produce – processing plant
5. The Bandstand in Central Park	22. Lund-Hydeen Pontiac
6. The GAR Hall	23. The First State Bank
7. Skeeter Anderson's house	24. Sandgren's Shoe store
8. Nelson's Buick garage	25. The Litchfield Hotel
9. The Shaw house and famous garage	26. The Greep-Trueblood store
10. The old Power Plant and water tower	27. The Western Cafe
11. The Paper Shack	28. The Community Building
12. Dahl's Goodyear Tire store/Don' TV	29. The Land O'Lakes plant
13. Becker Shoes store	30. The Railroad Depot
14. J. C. Penny/Woolworth stores	31. The Library
15. Johnson's Drug store	32. Litchfield House/Lien Apartments
16. The Litchfield Seed Company	33. The Icehouse
17. The Produce – warehouse	34. The Litchfield High School

Looking north on Sibley Avenue intersected by Second Street in about 1884.

Author's note: *To tell the history of Litchfield and its downtown stores, I will use my same "walk uptown" from my Swift Avenue home. If there's a number in front of a paragraph, it corresponds to the footnote number in a chapter of the first half of the book. If there isn't a number, then the information has been added just for this appendix. Some of the history, of course, just stays with the stories I've told. So, to really know the history of downtown Litchfield, you must read both.*

As Litchfield grew, buildings came and went. For the most part, a newer brick building replaced an older wooden one in the exact same location, but often it replaced two smaller buildings. Sometimes, new buildings overlapped a couple of old lots or old buildings straddled what we know as a present building location. Of course this caused great problems in trying to describe where a store was.

I included the present building address number to give you a general idea where the old stores were. You must know, however, that Litchfield had a couple of different numbering systems for their streets in the very early days and around World War I. Before the turn of the century, for example, stores in what we know as the 200 block of Sibley Avenue had double-digit numbers in the 40s. DeCoster's store (Smith's Appliance), for example, was 42 Sibley Avenue North and Judge Harris' confectionery (vacant today) was 46 Sibley Avenue North.

Around World War I, the 100 block of downtown was numbered in the 800s, the 200 block was in the 700s and the 300 block, across from the park was in the 600s. The numbers also ran in the opposite direction. For example, the Sibley Antiques corner was 831-833 Sibley Avenue North, instead of 100 Sibley, and Nicola's corner was 801 instead of 134 Sibley Avenue North.

365

The January 22, 1880 *Litchfield News-Ledger* newspaper stated, "Twenty-five years ago (1855), where now stands the beautiful and enterprising city of Litchfield, was an unimproved waste, inhabited only by wild beasts and wandering bands of red men." There wasn't much else here other than some thick woods. The famous "Big Woods" was just four miles away. But, the plentiful wood, nearby water and rich black earth was appealing to settlers. And the price was right...free for the homesteader. In an early historic document, our area of Minnesota was called the "Garden of the State".

In the spring of 1855, John W. Huy, Benjamin Brown and someone named Mackenzie, all employed by a St. Paul lumber company, paddled a canoe up the Crow River to the Minnesota Territory's west central area in search of pine timber. Not satisfied with their findings, they returned to St. Paul, but Huy organized another exploring party, consisting of D. M. Hanson, Thomas H. Skinner, and Rudolph "Fred" Schultz. Late that summer, the explorers took off for the same area and in the fall they stopped in what is now the township of Harvey. There they planned to start a town and call it Karishon, Sioux for "crow", which is what the Indians called the area. But, for some reason, they moved on to the present day Forest City area where they met Dr. Frederick Noah Ripley. They preferred this area so Schultz and Huy made a dugout house on the banks of the Crow River where it made a junction with a creek[186] and Huy stayed in it through the following winter to make a claim on the land. He thus became the first permanent white resident of the county. The others, except for Dr. Ripley, returned to St. Paul where Hanson went before the legislature and urged them to create a new county, which would include the area he had just visited.

The legislature complied and established Meeker County on February 23, 1856. The county was named in honor of Bradley B. Meeker (1813 -1873) of Minneapolis, who was an associate justice of the Minnesota Supreme Court from 1849 to 1853. Hanson and Huy, who were appointed county commissioners, met in the newly started Forest City on May 6, 1856 and organized the county on paper. Ripley, another appointed commissioner, was to have joined them, but he had frozen to death the previous March half a mile from the lake which now bears his name. William S. Chapman found his body later in the spring. With the nearby Crow River for transportation, more and more people gravitated to Forest City. It was named the county seat.

---

[186] It was in section 13 of Harvey Township.

My hometown of Litchfield, Minnesota was originally a portion of a Congressional township named Round Lake, but most people called it Ripley after the lake one mile from its center. Prairie schooners or covered wagons brought the first white people to settle in the area in July of 1856. They were Ole Halverson of Ness, who changed his name to Ole Ness, Henry T. Halverson, Sr., Ole Halverson of Thoen, who changed to Ole Thoen, Amos Nelson of Fossen, changed to Amos Fossen, Nels C. G. Hanson, Colberg Olson, Gunder Olson and all of their families. Having previously left their homeland of Norway in 1846, the settlers came here from Orfordville, Wisconsin (south of Madison, almost to Illinois).

A prairie schooner or covered wagon.

Later that year, William Benson, Sven or Swen and Nels Swenson, Michael Lenhardt, and Ferdinand, Christian, Frederick and William Cook came, also by prairie schooner. Sarah Jane Dougherty became the first white child to be born in Meeker County. She was born in her parents' prairie schooner in July of 1856. The first white male child, born in his parents' crude log cabin on December 11, 1856, was Ole T. Halverson. I suppose Henry and Margaret Halverson's cabin was the first "house" in town, if you can call it that. More people came in 1857[187] and still more in 1858[188], including a man named George B. Waller, Sr. The pioneers, some of whom lived in nothing more than a

---

[187] The 1857 Litchfield township census had Englishman George Blackwell, Norwegians Ole and Margaret Halverson, Gunden Alson, Keeted and Carrie Harrison, Henry and Margaret Hulverson, Barbary Hendrickson, Ole Halverson, Oliver and Jane Halverson, Guider Holson, Nelsoter and Annie Johnson, Gulfan Eberson, Asmond Nelson, Oli Climinson and Swedish Ole Benson. After the census, more people came. They were Bengt Hanson, John Larson and his sons, Nels, Andrew, Peter E. and Lewis Larson, Hogen Peterson, Thorlson J. Cornelius, Ole Amundson, Nels Danielson, Kittel Haroldson, Henry J. Johnson, Ole Kittelson, Jesse V. Branham, Sr. and his sons, Jesse V., Jr., William and Edward Branham, Oscar Erickson, Nels Clements, Ola Johnson and Louis and Maximillian Cook.
[188] Iver Jackson, Bengt Nelson and John and Thomas McGannon.

"dugout", named their settlement Ness on April 5, 1858, because most of the first settlers' home church was in Ness, Hullingdahl, Norway. Minnesota became the 32nd state in the Union on May 11, 1858, coming in as a "free state" to balance to arrival of the slave state of Kansas, a move which has been thought by historians to have eventually won the Civil War. In the fall of 1858, the Ness church here was established in the Ness home, which was southwest of present day Litchfield. Norwegian Reverend William Frederickson conducted the first service and, in 1874, the settlers there built an actual church building.

The government started offering free land to homesteaders here in 1861, just as Lincoln was being inaugurated as President of the United States and the Civil War was beginning. The Indian Outbreak of 1862, also called the Sioux Uprising, slowed immigration to the area, however. The Sioux War moved further out west as the local Indians were put under control and the Civil War ended in 1865. Veterans started coming to Minnesota looking to start a new life. Immigration to our Meeker County, however, continued to be slow until the St. Paul, Minneapolis and Manitoba Railroad, which became the St. Paul and Pacific and then the Great Northern, started coming through the Ness area in 1869, just as Ulysses S Grant was becoming the president.

The first train to arrive was a construction train on August 13, 1869. Having been in service for only seven years, the railroad's first locomotive was called the William Crooks Engine No. 1. A man named Bernard Dassel paid out money to the railroad workers along the route from the train's "pay car". In gratitude for his loyalty, the railroad named a village after him. The William Crooks brought the first female residents to our town. Marietta Porter, who was married to Charles O. Porter, came on August 26, 1869 and Mary L. Pixley, wife of insurance agent B. F. Pixley, came the next day. In September of 1924, the railroad sent the William Crooks engine on a good-will tour. It stopped in Litchfield pulling two 1862 coaches and was met by a large crowd of on-lookers.

William Crooks Engine No. 1.

Litchfield was just prairie prior to 1869. An old pioneer, interviewed by the newspaper, said there was prairie grass growing down Sibley Avenue and there was a small pond where Sibley Antiques is today. The pioneer remembered shooting ducks at that pond. Another pioneer, butcher Chris Sather, remembered a big wheat field in the mid-1870s from the corner of Sibley Avenue North and Second Street all the way out to Lake Ripley.

George B. Waller, Sr. owned the original Litchfield town site land. He had a large apple orchard on the one hundred and sixty acres where he also grew beets. Born in 1804, Waller had run a steamboat up and down the Mississippi from Alton, Illinois to Fort Snelling before settling here. He deeded one half of his land to the railroad as an inducement for the railroad to locate a town here, which of course increased the value of his land. Charles A. F. Morris surveyed the land Waller gave to the railroad and platted it on June 17, 1869. The plat was filed on July 16, 1869. I suppose we could have been called Waller, Minnesota. The railroad changed the population make-up of the county. By 1871, the village of Ness had grown to double the population of Forest City. The county, at that time, had 6,610 people.

John D. and William C. "Billy" Peterson were on one of the first trains that stopped here. They eventually had a tobacco and candy shop on the west side of Sibley Avenue. They said that when they arrived, the only building in town was a little eight by ten foot shack across the street to the east from the current Post Office. That would be at the northeast corner of Marshall Avenue and Second Street (202 Marshall Avenue North). Apparently they didn't see a barn elsewhere in town that Ole Halverson-Ness had erected in the summer of 1856. Ole lived in the barn for a summer while his house was being built. Truls Peterson built the building in 1869 that John and Billy referred to. Truls conducted a tailoring business from it. He had bought the southeast corner of Sibley Avenue and Second Street but traded it for this corner.

It's no surprise then that Litchfield's first real residential house and second building was next door north of Truls' shack. George B. Waller, Sr. built the house in 1871 and it was at 206 Marshall Avenue North. The lumber to build it was shipped here from Minneapolis by rail. Ole Halverson-Ness bought the lot and it was Farmers' Insurance Company agent B. F. Pixley's residence for many years. The third building to go up was Samuel A. Heard and C. D. Ward's general merchandise store at the southwest corner of Sibley Avenue and Third Street. It was Litchfield's first store and Heard was Litchfield's eighth Village Council

President in 1879. The clothing store and Post Office building owned by Horace B. Johnson at the northwest corner of Sibley Avenue and Second Street came next. Johnson was Litchfield's third Village Council President in 1874, when the population of Litchfield was just nine hundred people. At some time J. M. Miller's house went up somewhere. Next came a lumberyard owned by Joseph James, just across the railroad tracks to the south and also his office building, which was on the west side of Sibley Avenue.

When the railroad came in the fall of 1869, the businesses in town were Ward and Heard's store, William S. Brill's hardware, which became Meeker County's first drug store, the lumber business (but not a lumberyard) owned by Joseph James, a lumberyard owned by John Esbjornsson and Charles Ellis Peterson, Clark L. Angell's photography studio, Chase and Dunn's livery stable, Charles J. Almquist's hotel called the Litchfield House, and the Railway Land Office managed by Hans Mattson. The lone doctor in town was George W. Weisel, Litchfield's second Village Council President in 1873, but there were three lawyers, Frank Belfoy, Newton H. Chittenden and Charles Henry Strobeck. Strobeck, born in New York, was the first lawyer in town and he was Litchfield's eleventh Village Council President in 1882 and seventeenth mayor in 1895.

Sibley Avenue,
looking north,
about 1870.

Some other store "firsts" were B. O. Esping's jewelry store, D. E. Potter's furniture store, Mark Baldwin's harness shop, Vanderborck (or Vanderhorck) and King's hardware store and Harrington and Lynn's Bank of Litchfield, which closed in 1877. L. A. Nyholm laid the first cement sidewalk in Litchfield in 1895 in the 200 block of Sibley Avenue. Before that, of course, any sidewalks in town were made of wood. Because there was a gentle southerly slope of the land in town towards

Daley Slough[189], by the time the sidewalk reached where True Valu hardware is today, it was four feet off the ground and required steps.

Somewhere in town, most likely by the tracks and the depot, the St. Paul and Pacific railroad put up an "immigrant's reception house." The 1871 *Meeker County News* incorrectly referred to the twenty-five by sixty foot one story building as an "emigrant" house. The railroad put them up in villages, such as Litchfield, Willmar, Benson, Morris and Breckenridge, along the railroad's lines in the 1870s. The largest one was in Duluth and it could accommodate one hundred immigrants. The houses were "fitted up with cooking-stoves, washing conveniences, and beds." The newly arriving immigrants were given shelter in the reception houses and the chance to buy food and clothing at cost from the railroad while they looked for land in the area. It wasn't that costly to come to America in the early days. In 1885, the Stevens and Company Bank offered tickets from Germany to Litchfield for $23.00. In 1886, you could get a ticket from Sweden to Litchfield for $29.50.

Litchfield got its name from three English brothers named Electus Darwin Litchfield (1817-1888), Egbert E. Litchfield (dates unknown) and Edwin Clark Litchfield (1815-1885). The Litchfields were the contractors/investors by whom the railroad line from St. Paul to St. Cloud was built in 1862 to 1864. Later, they provided the means for building a more southern line through Meeker County to Breckenridge. They also did a lot of developing in Brooklyn, New York. The main contributor in this area was Electus Darwin. That's where the town of Darwin got its name. I suppose our town could have been called Electus, Minnesota.

E. Darwin Litchfield's mansion in Brooklyn, New York.

---

[189] This was a large wet area taking up more than the block where Longfellow Square apartments are today at 416 Sibley Avenue South. It was deep enough that some old-timers remembered swimming in it.

The people of Ness were permitted to vote on the name of their town. Electus, showing his business sense, had his wife in London donate grants of $2000 each to various religious sects in town to build churches. The Episcopal and Presbyterian churches were two of them. The Presbyterian Church, Litchfield's first church, was built in 1870. Presbyterian minister Reverend D. B. Jackson had held the first religious service in Litchfield on August 15, 1869 in a small building that had no windows. It was also used as a schoolhouse. Litchfield's first school, however, was in the home of Ole Halverson-Ness in 1860. Ole employed and paid John Blackwell to teach his children and as many others who could get to his house.

The church-going three hundred and fifty-three people in town could hardly snub Mr. Litchfield and keep the name Ness. The citizens put their votes into a ballot box made out of butternut wood in 1868 by Henry T. Halverson, Sr. It was still being used in town in the early 1900s. The majority voted for the name Litchfield and the township of Litchfield was chartered as a village on February 29, 1872. The first village council meeting was held on April 5, 1872 in the railroad's land office, which was at the northeast corner of Sibley Avenue North and Depot Street. Jesse V. Branham, Jr. was elected the President of the Council, which was the same as being elected mayor.

Sibley Avenue facing north about 1871.

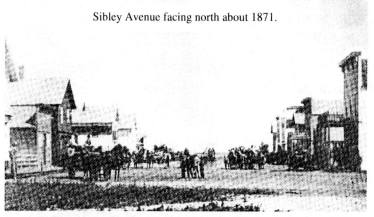

In October of 1924, E. D. Litchfield's son, also named Electus[190] Darwin Litchfield, came by train to visit the town. A telegram was sent

[190] The father went by E. Darwin Litchfield or E. D. Litchfield. The son went by the full name and never added Jr. to his name. Some history books give his father as another brother William D. Litchfield, but Electus wrote to the Independent newspaper in October of 1924 and mentioned the town being named after his father and all history books give E. Darwin as the namesake.

in advance and the city fathers mistakenly thought old man Litchfield himself was coming. They pulled out all the stops, meeting the train with dignitaries, speeches and flowers. Junior was embarrassed and he wrote the *Independent* newspaper a letter of apology for the misunderstanding.

"I am afraid the telegram..." he wrote, "may have been worded so as to give you all the impression that my father was to arrive. I hope you will again thank Mr. Branham's daughter for the beautiful flowers, which his son appreciated no less than would have his father for whom they were intended."

Remembering that Junior was an architect, the town petitioned to have him design their new Post Office. Washington, D. C. gave Junior the job in November of 1933 and so the son of Litchfield's namesake designed that brick building on the northwest corner of Second Street and Marshall Avenue.

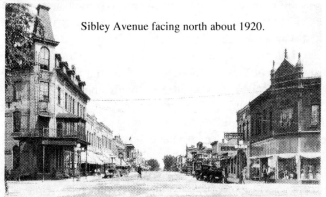

Sibley Avenue facing north about 1920.

Litchfield's entire downtown, between Depot Street[191] and Third Street, is listed on the National Register of Historic Places. Most of the store buildings were built between 1882 and 1945. Many were built with bricks manufactured between the years of 1875 to 1899 at Henry Ames and Sons' Brickyard Farm northeast of town. The first building made from Ames' bricks in Litchfield was barber Mike Weiss' residence on Sibley Avenue South in about 1877. I would say the years of 1885 and 1886 pretty much defined the look of downtown Litchfield. Many of the first brick buildings on Sibley Avenue North, especially the 200 block, went up in those years, as well as the first brick courthouse and the GAR Hall across from the park. The brickyard closed in July of 1902, moving to Paynesville.

---

[191] Once called Wall Street, today Depot Street is more often referred to as Highway 12 East.

Henry Ames
Brickyard
Farm.

An 1889 *Litchfield Ledger* article about Litchfield called it the "Queen of the Prairies" and added the statement "No Drone in Her Hive, and Every Inhabitant Full of Work and Public Spirit". Apparently the newspaper editor thought quite a bit of the city that had ballooned to a population of 2,500. Litchfield wasn't officially a city until 1943. Up until then it was a village or a town. In the early fifties, a billboard by Lake Ripley boasted that Litchfield had a population of 5000 (exactly?) and a town motto of "Large enough to serve you, small enough to know you." The north end of town had a billboard that claimed "Litchfield - The Hub Of Rural Progress". I don't think you could argue either motto. Litchfield's businesses did have every thing we needed to get by in life and everyone in town knew everyone else's business.

6. In the days before electric refrigeration in Litchfield, ice was an important commodity. It was "farmed" from Lake Ripley and other surrounding lakes and stored in icehouses. Samuel A. Heard owned an icehouse somewhere in town in 1882. His general store was at the southwest corner of Sibley Avenue and Third Street and the icehouse might have been just for his store. John H. Happ was partnered with Otto Phillip with an ice business in town in December of 1886. Their icehouse was located on the south side of Third Street between Swift and Miller Avenues, only a few feet from the site of my family's garage. John, whose woodshop was just east up Third Street, had the ice business by himself in 1902 and he sold it to Lounsbury and Curtis in January of 1909. John H. Happ was assistant fire chief from 1912 to 1914 and his Happ and Company store was near the corner of Sibley Avenue and Third Street. At some time the business closed and the icehouse was moved a few feet south to serve as a garage for someone. In July of 1917, Gust Kimpel closed down his icehouse somewhere in town. Fred

374

A. Kopplin bought it in September of 1917. This might have been the one by our house. There was another icehouse in town, south of the tracks near the Litchfield House hotel. It was Litchfield's most well known icehouse. You can read about it later in the book.

8. 114 Third Street West. Heading east from our house on Swift Avenue North up Third Street West, I passed the old power plant on the south side of the street. Across the street, on the north side, was Andy Anderson's blacksmith shop. Andy's father, Hans Christian Anderson, started blacksmithing in Litchfield in 1904 at the corner of Miller Avenue and Second Street. Hans, a black mustached huge man at six foot three inches and three hundred pounds, came from the same Danish island, Fyen, as did the famous storywriter of the same name. Hans bought A. E. Perkins' shop in April of 1911. He partnered with N. E. Nelson in September of 1924 and sold his business to a Nordquist in January of 1927. Then he built a new shop here opposite the old power plant.

Hans' son, Andrew L. "Andy" Anderson, reopened the shop at this location in May of 1939 after Hans had died. Andy was named after Hans' father Andrew. Andy sold the business to Sylvester Schmid in March of 1959 and it became Dibb's Welding & Repair later in the sixties. Today the location is the drive-thru for the Center National Bank, which is at the northeast corner of the block.

301 Ramsey Avenue North. The Okesons' house was at the northwest corner of Ramsey Avenue and Third Street where the Center National Bank is today. First Bank Center, the old First State Bank, moved there in 1978.

22. 526 Ramsey Avenue North. With all the saloons that popped up in town, (an 1885 article in the *Litchfield Independent* complained that there were seven, and soon there were eight), a supplier was needed. Litchfield had its own brewery, which will be discussed later, and a couple of bottling plants, which acted as distributors for larger out of town breweries. John Rodange and Jacob Reese started the Litchfield Bottling Works in April of 1879 at a building in the 400 block of Ramsey Avenue North, which would be north from the Center National Bank corner of Ramsey Avenue and Third Street. (The bottling plant's location was numbered 511 Ramsey Avenue North in the early 1900s). Rodange was from Luxemburg. Reese left in January of 1882 and Rodange had the business alone until he sold it in October of 1892 to Nels A. Johnson

and Alexander D. Ross. Ross, who was from Canada, had a saloon in town with J. A. C. Pallmer in the late 1800s. He owned it alone in 1888. Johnson and Ross moved the pop factory to the corner of Sixth Street and Ramsey Avenue. Ross sold his saloon to Nels Frederickson in December of 1898. John H. Happ had another bottling plant on Miller Avenue by the railroad tracks in the early 1890s.

In November of 1900, Nels A. Johnson bought out Ross. The bottling works was sold to Clifford W. Johnson around 1915. Johnson sold it to photographer Clyde G. Crosby in June of 1917. Clyde sold it to Leslie L. "Les" Berens in October of 1921, who sold it to Tom Wandok, Litchfield's famous cigar maker. Wandok sold it to Oscar and August "Auggie" Anderson in May of 1924. After a few years, Auggie sold his share to another brother named George. In March of 1946, the bottling plant was moved to its new building at 526 Ramsey Avenue North. Eventually the Nazarene Church bought the old bottling plant site to expand their church building. George Anderson died in February of 1959 and Oscar went alone in the business even though he went blind in 1950. I remember you could buy a case of glass bottled Orange Kist Soda for $1.00 there in the fifties. The "pop plant" was also the Hamm's Beer Distributing Company in our area. Oscar sold to the Lacher Bros. Distributing Company in January of 1966. Today Doug's Auto Repair is in the building where the bottling plant was last.

There were several cigar factories in Litchfield but the most known was Tom Wandok's. In 1870, a house was moved from Greenleaf to Litchfield to the 500 block of Armstrong Avenue North. It had been the U.S. Land Office in the town of Greenleaf, run by William Henry Greenleaf. Greenleaf was born in New York. The land office itself was moved downtown, but not the building. The building was moved to this location. It was moved again across the street to 508 Armstrong Avenue North where it became Litchfield's "first schoolhouse". Litchfield's actual first school was held in the Trinity Episcopal Church until the town got this schoolhouse. Later, the little building became a furniture and repair shop, and in February of 1889, it was sold to W. A. Mooney for his cigar factory. He sold the factory to Fred Reitz in May of 1894. Reitz had been on Ramsey Avenue between Second and Third Streets.

Thomas "Tom" Wandok had the cigar factory in March of 1907, complete with a cigar store Indian. He closed the doors in January of 1928. The tobacco used in these cigar factories was imported but some cheaper stuff grown by Eden Valley was also used. In the forties and fifties, the Wandok sisters lived in the house.

376

Tom Wandok's cigar factory house yesterday and today.

227 Ramsey Avenue North/111 Third Street West. A roller rink was once at the southwest corner of Ramsey Avenue and Third Street, on the lot where the paper shack ended up (near the old power plant). C. M. Tileston had the roller rink here in January of 1885. Another source gives the owners as Charles A. Brasie and J. D. Hayford and the location as west of Josiah Payne's residence. Payne had a shoe repair business just east of here, so this could have been the location. Eventually a house was moved to the lot and the Baumgartners lived in it in the thirties. The Baumgartner house was another of several houses that had been moved here from Forest City by a man named E. M. Eastman. After the Baumgartners moved out, the city bought the buildings and the lot to use for as a site for a new city office building, but sold the house and barn in June of 1946. Then for a few years this corner location was simply a vacant lot, as the new city office idea fell through. Of course, the paper shack was here for many years. Today the Litchfield Fire Department is at this location.

31. 221 Ramsey Avenue North. To the south of the lot, where the present VFW Post 2818 is located, was almost always a seed business. Oren Wilbert "Bert" Topping bought the old office of the Flynn & Bros. farm machinery business and moved it here in September of 1884 after he had bought lots 23 through 26 of this Block 60. Oren was born in Greenleaf, Minnesota, making him a rarity among early Litchfield businessmen. Most were from out of state. Topping leased the building out to Col. C. M. Lovelace for a fruits and confections business in October of 1884. Harry Harmon and Sam Wilson had a carpentry shop here in December of 1885. In January of 1894, Erhardt Lenhardt, the brewer and hotel owner, erected a building on Ramsey between Second and Third Streets for storing his beer. Might the large building that ended up here have been that building? The first seed business I found at this site was sold to a Mr. Loven in 1923. I don't know who owned it first but it became Loven's Seed Company. Loven sold it to L. C.

Wogenson in October of 1939. Then Alden Martinson bought it in December of 1957 calling it the Litchfield Seed House. Walter Wogenson owned it in the late fifties and early sixties until he went out of business. Then the Admiral Benson VFW club bought the site in May of 1965 and started building their new club here in November. The building was completed in March of 1967. The VFW had been on Depot Street in the fifties, but met in the GAR Hall until 1943, then in the Community Building.

217 Ramsey Avenue North. A gas station went up in February of 1931 to the south of the present VFW. Joe Baden owned it and he sold "Lightning" brand gasoline for 16¢ a gallon. In February of 1932, the Baden Oil Station was sold to A. T. Johnson and his son Vernon. Baden had moved to the Kopplin garage at the corner. The Johnson station was called the Bonded Gas Station. In January of 1946, Dr. Walter P. "Walt" Haugo moved his veterinary business into the rear of the same building as the gas station. He was there until 1960. In 1947, Norbert O. Kohmetscher bought the service station. The location is a part of the VFW building today.

213 Ramsey Avenue North. There was an alley to the south of the service station and after it was a small building which housed the Quinn (Tom) & Reitz (Fred) cigar factory in April of 1891. Quinn quit the business in July. Reitz moved to Armstrong Avenue North in 1894.

Leo L. Baumgartner and W. K. Dyer's Litchfield Chick Hatchery was here in the fall of 1926 until it was moved to a new building where Wells-Fargo bank is today. Baumgartner was Litchfield's mayor in 1939.

Pat Woods' Black & White Café was here next. It had originally been on Sibley Avenue across from central park where Janousek's café went and on Depot Street. It was moved here in the late thirties. Pat Woods and his wife Borghild "Borgie" split up. Pat left the business to her in the divorce settlement. Jim Gunter, who had worked for Pat, married Borgie and then ran the Black & White. Jim started a sign painting business in the rear of the café in 1955.

Duane's Auto Body shop went into the rear of the building in 1965. Mary Ramthun bought the restaurant in the late sixties and called it the Hide-A-Way Café. I don't know what happened to it, but of course the building went the way of the Produce next door to the south. It's all gone today. I'll write more about the Produce site later in the book.

378

216 Ramsey Avenue North. Across the street from the present site of the VFW, at in the middle of the 200 block of Ramsey Avenue, was A. Fred Grono's City Marble Works in the late summer of 1890. The lot had been vacant until Alex Cairncross moved his wooden store building here from Sibley Avenue to make room for his new brick building. Then the building here housed the Sigfrid W. Nelson and Sons' Nelson Implement business. I'm not sure when they moved to this location from Depot Street but they were here in the mid-thirties and on. Today this site is a city parking lot.

58. 224 Ramsey Avenue North/35 Third Street West. Back at the southeast corner of Ramsey Avenue and Third Street was Dahl's Goodyear Tire Company for many years. Before that A. W. Dodge owned the first blacksmith shop in town at this corner. He had a twenty-four by forty foot building that cost $350 to build. It was actually owned by W. L. Sales and it was sold to Samuel A. Heard in September of 1871. Charles A. Brasie moved the Clough lumberyard office here in February of 1884. Frank W. Maetzold took it over in March of 1886. He was a partner with Joseph A. Happ, who had his woodworking shop right across the street. In March of 1887, Joe Barth and Frank Maetzold erected a machinery warehouse somewhere on this block. Being "west of Barth's old blacksmith shop", it was probably here at the corner. Charles A. "Charley" Laughton owned a machine shop here in 1887 before taking on a partner named K. Webster in April of 1889. Laughton was from Wisconsin. Webster had the shop alone in June of 1890 and put up a new ten by thirty-two foot building here.

Minar Motor built a new brick building here in March of 1946 to house their Litchfield Implement Company, which sold the Allis Chalmers brand of machinery. M. Raleigh Dahl eventually bought the brick building from Minar in May of 1957. He moved into the building in July of 1957 and for years it was Dahl's Tire. His business had been uptown north of Bull Johnson's Pool Hall. Around the same time, Don's TV, owned by Don Test, moved into the Ramsey Avenue corner of this building. Connie Olmstead, my brother Dennie's friend, worked for Don as a technician.

In July of 1963, Percy Larson bought out Dahl's. He also owned the parking lot to the south on Ramsey, which he sold to the city in September of 1969. The parking lot opened to the public in November, just in time for Christmas shoppers. Today, the Binsfield Tire Inc. business is here.

The tires Dahl sold at the corner were needed for all the cars in town sold by all the dealerships. You will encounter many of them in just a few paragraphs, but one was right across the street north of Dahl's. I will get to that after finishing this side of the block up to the alley. Joseph "Joe" Barth's blacksmith shop was just to the east of the corner building starting in April of 1882 and was torn down in August of 1938. It became part of the larger building erected at the corner. Next door to the east of the blacksmith shop was Josiah Payne's shoe store in the pioneer days. It became a vacant lot and still is.

67. The dealership across the street was Nelson's Buick, which eventually took up half of the block. The corner site was the used car lot. There was an old wooden building at the corner housing the Clough Brothers lumberyard, which started in September of 1882. Charles A. Brasie, the manager, worked out of his store, which was on Sibley Avenue, but eventually had an office just across the street. Clough's was sold to William Henry Greenleaf and Son (Charles A.) in the spring of 1884. They had also bought the Flynn Brothers lumberyard in late 1878 and H. B. Brown's in 1880. The Flynns, from Illinois, went into the farm machinery business. The Greenleafs leased the Flynn elevator in September of 1889. Charles A. Greenleaf took over the lumberyard from his father in September of 1897. Charles was Litchfield's twentieth mayor in 1899 and he sold his Greenleaf Lumber Company in June of 1900 to Fred A. Kopplin. Kopplin sold coal and lumber there until 1921. Then he got into the fuel oil and gasoline business before adding LP gas.

There had been a residential house here at this corner in the thirties. Then Guy Maxson bought the lot in April of 1943. He needed it for his used cars.

61. 24-28 Third Street West. Joseph "Joe" A. Happ had an old wooden building here for his woodworking shop. He started his business in 1881 and moved to this site in May of 1883. He did any kind of woodwork, but he specialized in boats. He made rowboats and "gasoline launches". He also had a cigar box factory here starting in September of 1891. He was a partner of Frank Maetzold, who had a blacksmith shop across Third Street. They made wagons together. At some time the *Ledger* newspaper was printed here and Henry Isaac "H. I." Peterson owned the building and lot. Peterson was born in Red Wing, Minnesota. E. M Eastman eventually owned the building.

H. O. Folkestad opened a furniture mart in the building in June of 1931. Harry Madson bought the old building in March of 1934 and put up a newer building. It was called Madson's Garage. Harry Madson had been a partner with Baldis H. Koenig with a garage west of the old fire hall. The business here then became the Reisinger Motor Company when A. F. Reisinger bought it. Reisinger sold it to Guy E. Maxson in February of 1940 and it became Maxson Motors. Maxson had been in the Kopplin building. Maxson died suddenly and James Nelson bought Maxson's from Guy's widow in November of 1949. He brought in his brother L. Miles Nelson. Nelson's Buick became Nelson's Buick and Pontiac. When Nelson's finally folded, the building housed a toilet seat factory called Sperzel. It then had the Farm Bureau Insurance and today the entire half block is called Courthouse Square and contains the Meeker Title Services, Inc.

62. Dr. Henry C. Peters owned the first automobile in Litchfield in July of 1903. I'm not sure who sold it to him. There were eight car dealerships in Litchfield in the late fifties. At times, there were even more. Here are the various cars sold in Litchfield over the years and who sold them:

BUICK: Arthur W. Peterson's Implement business sold Buicks in the 1910s. Borden and Hanson's Motor Supply sold Buicks and Pontiacs also in the early years. Peterson sold the Buick dealership part of his business to Hans O. Evenson and Martin E. Spelliscy, Jr. in March of 1910. They moved west on Depot Street by the hotel. They sold Buick, Rambler, Durant, and Reo cars and farm machinery.

1915: Evenson & Spelliscy Farm Implements shop on Depot Street West.

Evenson took on different partners, one was Charles Sundahl, and they sold Chevrolet, then Buick and Dodge from their new garage in September of 1916. Then Harry Madson sold Buick with Baldis H. Koenig. The business became the Reisinger Motor Company. A. F. Reisinger sold it to Guy E. Maxson in February of 1940 and it became Maxson Motors. James Nelson bought Maxson's in November of 1949 and started Nelson's Buick, bringing in his brother L. Miles Nelson. Later they also sold Pontiacs.

CHEVROLET: As mentioned in the Buick paragraph, Evenson sold Chevrolets in the 1910s. In 1917, Peterson Implement sold Chevrolets. Starting in 1921, the Kopplins sold Chevrolets and Oldsmobiles from their garage across the tracks. The garage became Economy Gas. R. L and A. K. McDonald got that business in January of 1927 and called it Litchfield Motors, Inc. They started on Depot Street, moved to the Kopplin garage on the northwest corner of Second Street and Ramsey Avenue in January of 1928 and opened their new garage, where Fenton's and Brock's ended up at 627 Sibley Avenue North in November of 1930.

1950s ad for Fenton's.

In 1873, Civil War veteran E. M. Eastman had a pump and well business at that Sibley Avenue location. Eastman also had a building moving business and this town kept him quite busy. Across the street from that building, by the way, was a miniature golf course. The Chevy business was sold to Karl A. Danielson, Jr., son of Dr. Danielson, in January of 1932. It became the Danielson Motor Company, also known as the Danielson Chevrolet Company. Ben H. Carpenter bought it in April of 1936. Carpenter sold it to Hugh D. Fenton in February of 1939. Al Fenton took over the business in 1950.

CHRYSLER and PLYMOUTH: In the 1930s, Gust Chellin's garage sold Chrysler-Plymouth. Quinn Motors sold in the thirties and on, as will be mentioned in the Dodge paragraph. There was Stock Motors Chrysler-Plymouth in the late fifties.

DESOTO: In October of 1928, Harry Carlson and Reuben Johnson had a Desoto dealership. They called it Harry Carlson Motors, and they also sold a car called the "Roosevelt".

DODGE: Hans O. Evenson & Co. sold Dodges in 1916, as mentioned in the Buick paragraph. Alvin L. Lagergren's Dodge Brothers Motor Vehicles started in the Chellin garage and then moved to the McGowan building across from the park in June of 1926. They moved in October of 1927 to the Litchfield Laundry building, and to where the Essex had been sold in February of 1928. Harlan Quinn and Jack G. Beerling started a business called Quinn Motors across from the Community Building in April of 1934. They sold Dodge and Plymouth vehicles. Beerling bought out Quinn in 1960, but the business remained Quinn Motors.

Left: 1924 Brecht ad.
Right: Evenson and Co. Buick ad.

ESSEX: A. A. Fallon sold Hudson and Essex cars in 1926.

FORD: Around the turn of the century, there was the Evenson-Spelliscy Implement and Ford dealership, owned by Hans O. Evenson and Martin E. Spelliscy, Jr.   George G. Mill sold Fords in January of 1908. Henry Ford introduced the Model T automobile in 1908. It sold for about $850 and, as Ford said, "Can be purchased in any color the buyer wishes, as long as the buyer wants black." Colors were added in the next year. By 1926, the price dropped to $310. Nelson Implement sold Fords after that and then sold their Ford dealership to Horace J. Minar and L. E. Larson in August of 1917. Nelson Implement started selling Overland cars and Republic trucks.

65. Minar was Litchfield's oldest lasting dealership. It was first called Larson-Minar Ford. In January of 1923, Horace and his brother Cushman bought out Larson. Minar started out in the Welch garage, later known as the Chellin garage, where the Wells Fargo bank is today

at the corner of Marshall Avenue and First Street East, and then moved west of the hotel on Depot Street. In 1924, you could buy a Lincoln or Ford touring car for $295, a runabout for $265, and a Fordson tractor for $420. Minar had dealerships in Dassel and Kimball also.

In September of 1936, Minar Ford displayed Bonnie and Clyde's 1934 V-8 Ford Model 730 Deluxe Sedan in their showroom for their customers' amusement. It was riddled with over 167 bullets.

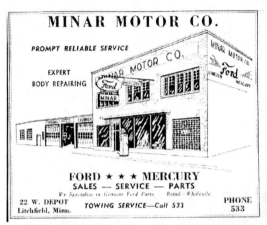

Bonnie and Clyde's car.

John H. Miller bought the business in January of 1959 and it became Miller Motor, but lots of people continued calling it Minar for years. During that same month, Alaska became the 49th state admitted to the Union. In 1969, Miller Motor became Anderson Ford. There's more about Minar and the Depot Street location later in the book.

HUDSON: Around 1916, A. A. Fallon's motors sold Hudson and Essex motorcars from the location where Hans Christian Anderson's blacksmith shop had been at the corner of Miller and Second Street, where Lindquist Sheet Metal went. Sundahl died in October of 1918 and Evenson had the business by himself. Fallon had moved there from across from the park in June of 1927. Then Krout Motors sold Hudsons in the late forties on east Highway 12, where the REA building went in 1950. Roy Swanson's Hudson started in November of 1950 at the corner of Second Street and Miller Avenue. The sign for it still hung above Chet's Machine Shop in the fifties.

KAISER and FRASIER: P. W. and Harold H. Bergmann sold Kaiser and Frazer cars in early 1946. Ed Hamm bought out P. W. in March of 1948.

MAXWELL: Dick Berens sold them around 1915.

NASH: Meeker Motor Company sold Nash in 1921. O. R. Schwartzwald's Motors sold them from the late forties and on.

384

OVERLAND: The Chellin Brothers combined with Peterson Implement in May of 1911 to sell Buick and Overland together. Nelson Implement sold them in 1917. Nelson sold the dealership to Ferdinand "Frank" H. Brecht. Brecht sold Willys-Knight, Willys-Overland and Hupmobile cars in 1924. He sold out to George Evenson in November of 1925.

PACKARD and OLDSMOBILE: Read the Studebaker paragraph.

PONTIAC: In the thirties, there was Borden and Hanson's Motor Supply, which sold Buicks and Pontiacs. In the fifties and sixties, Lund-Hydeen Pontiac sold them. Nelson's Buick and Pontiac sold them in the late sixties.

RAMBLER, DURANT and REO: See the Buick paragraph.

ROOSEVELT: The Roosevelt car was really a cheap Marmon, made from 1929 to 1931 in Indianapolis and named after Teddy, an old "Rough Rider", just like the car. See the Desoto paragraph.

STUDEBAKER: In the early 1900s, there was W. Richard "Dick" Berens' Maxwell and Studebaker dealership on main street. In 1910, Philip H. Hartman sold the cars from the Kopplin garage. Dick Berens sold just Studebakers out of a room in the Settergren building in May of 1919. Edwin H. Kopplin sold the cars himself and auto accessories out of his building in the early 1920s. Thomas A. Thompson leased part of a downtown building in February of 1926 to sell the cars.   In the late forties and early fifties, there was Dewey Johnson's Studebaker on Depot Street. It became Harold Warren's Studebaker. Kvam's Oldsmobile-Packard-Studebaker and Oliver tractors were on Sibley Avenue North in the late fifties.

WILLYS and HUPMOBILE: See the Overland paragraph.

Of course with all the dealerships selling cars in town, Litchfield needed gas stations. And we got them. Between 1959 and 1960, Litchfield had an unbelievable seventeen gas stations in town. I won't list all the gas stations down through the years, as I am dealing pretty much with just the history of downtown Litchfield, but I'll list the seventeen we had in that period. There was the Skelly station at the Lund-Hydeen Pontiac at 37 Second Street West, Art Anderson's Service Station at 33 Depot Street East, Dale's Pure Oil at 107 Depot Street East, Lind's Mobilgas at 203 Depot Street East, Minar Service Station at 225 Depot Street East, Brunken's Cities Service at 322 Depot Street East, Meeker County Oil at 326 Depot Street East, R. W. Anderberg's Direct Service at 601 Depot Street East, the East Side Shell Station out on east Highway 12, Uptown Skelly Service at 317 Sibley Avenue North,

Beckman's Standard Service at 415 Sibley Avenue North, Sid's Mobil Service at 426 Sibley Avenue North, Holen's Apco at 505 Sibley Avenue North, the Renhult & Nelson Phillips 66[192] at 618 Sibley Avenue North, Ollie's Cities Service at 702 Sibley Avenue North, Litchfield Texaco at 823 Sibley Avenue North, and Norb's Cut Rate or the Independent Oil Company at 124 Marshall Avenue North. By the way, there were thirteen churches in Litchfield in 1959.

Continuing with my walk uptown on Third Street West, I pass a vacant lot on the north side of Third Street, between Ramsey and Sibley Avenues, just before the red brick building at the corner. Charles "Charley" H. Dart moved his feed store into the lot behind the corner building in January of 1881 after starting the business with partner George Gordon in April of 1880. Dart was born in Forest City, Minnesota, a rarity among the early Litchfield businessmen, as most were from other states or countries. Dr. C. B. Spencer's office had been in a wooden building on that lot in the early 1880s. Daniel McLane also had owned a small building on the lot for a tin shop. He sold it to William Grono in March of 1886 for Grono's marble shop. There was also a warehouse building on the lot. McLane partnered with Luke D. Crowe in 1886 in an implement, farm machinery and wagon business behind McLane's store, which was at the corner. In March of 1887, the warehouse building was moved to the rear of Josiah Payne's shoe shop, across the street to the west, for a storeroom. Daniel McLane and Luke D. Crowe had a new building put up in April of 1887 for their machinery business. McLane and Crowe, both from Ireland, then sold the machinery business to A. Wall in January of 1889. In May of 1891, D. A. Roos and James F. Maher had a feed and flour business on this back lot. Roos quit the business in July of 1891. The Peterson brothers, John D. and William C. "Billy", bought the feed and flour business in October of 1891. They also owned the corner lot and the one to the north of it.

When the Robertson building was built at the corner in 1906, it covered most of this lot. I reach the northwest corner of Sibley Avenue and Third Street where a large brick building still stands across from Central Park.

68. 301 Sibley Avenue North. (50-52 Sibley in the early days.) (12-14 Third Street West in the rear.) This corner lot originally had a

---

[192] It was removed in the spring of 1963 so that a new municipal liquor store could be built on the site. The liquor store didn't materialize and the lot was sold at a loss by the city to Sands' Safety Center.

building on it eventually owned by Hiram S. Branham, son of Village Council President Jesse V. Branham, Jr. and co-owner of the Stevens and Company Bank. Jesse V. Branham, Jr. partnered with Edward A. Campbell to have a dry goods, clothing, and grocery store here in the fall of 1869. Branham had come to Meeker County with his father in 1857. In August of 1870, they sold just the grocery part of the business to Judge John M. Waldron and Capt. J. C. Braden and moved kitty-corner from here. During that same month, Colorado was the 38th state admitted to the Union. Waldron, by the way, was Litchfield's fifth Village Council President in 1876. In April of 1871, Waldron and Braden sold the business to L. S. Weymouth and William Henry Greenleaf. James H. Morris and someone named Bradford built a twenty-two by thirty-six foot two story building somewhere on this lot in March of 1871. Morris was born in New York.

William H. Greenleaf and James H. Morris in the 1880s.

Weymouth sold his interest in the grocery business to a man named LaCross in August of 1871. Greenleaf eventually bought out LaCross and changed the store over to a hardware store. Couch's restaurant was also here in the late 1870s. In March of 1875, Phineas "Pat" Cary leased the building that Greenleaf and LaCross had been in for his shoe business. Cary moved down closer to the railroad tracks in the summer of 1875. In April of 1877, Mrs. John Blackwell, wife of Litchfield's first teacher, re-opened the Blackwell music store here, again sharing the building or lot. During 1877, Edison invented the phonograph. Sharing the first floor of the building here was C. M. Tileston's dry goods store in 1878. Tileston owned the building at that time. W. P. Todd bought the goods of his brother J. G. Todd and bought the Tileston building. In 1880, Daniel McLane came here with a general store. Wait H. Dart became his partner shortly after and together they erected a new wooden building on this corner in 1881, sharing the lot, which McLane bought.

McLane and Dart's Wholesale Store sold wholesale and retail general merchandise, hardware, groceries and feed.

Otho H. Campbell, Silas W. Leavett and Wait's son Charles "Charley" H. Dart.

A fire in April of 1882 destroyed Tileston's building. Woman helped the fire brigade and they were able to remove the entire stock from Tileston's. Dart moved kitty-corner across the street to east Sibley Avenue. Dart was Litchfield's nineteenth mayor in 1898. Miss Mary Fitch's millinery was here in May of 1883. In August of 1885, the J. N. Nelson and Andrew Winger tailor shop moved into the room Mrs. Fitch had occupied. They dissolved their partnership in March of 1886 and Winger moved elsewhere. The two got back together in 1888. By 1886, McLane still owned this lot and the one to the north of it. The UTK store, owned by G. S. Butler and managed by Peder Winger, moved into a part of the building here in November of 1886. Winger went out of business in February of 1888 and McLane put a hardware in his room. D. B. and William H. Johns had their Johns Brothers hardware here in April of 1887 at "McLane's old stand" after buying out the McLane Hardware. From Kentucky, the Johns brothers moved around town a lot, both having different partners and they were together at a couple of the locations. McLane still had the grocery part of the business here. Johns Brothers moved out in August of 1887, buying out Rankin hardware at the southwest corner of Sibley Avenue and Second Street. Wait H. and Charles H. Dart bought McLane's grocery part out at this location in September of 1887. James and John McLaughlin and W. J. O'Brien bought this lot and the one to the north from McLane in May of 1888 to locate a hardware store in the corner building. The McLaughlins were born in Massachusetts. McLane and Crowe kept the machinery business on the rear lot and Dart kept the grocery here in the corner room. The McLaughlin Brothers Mercantile Company or hardware was here north of Dart in June of 1888. The McLaughlins had a fire in December of 1891, moved to the next block and went bankrupt in June of 1901. M.

Neville brought in a notions store called the New York Racket Store in May of 1893. He sold dry goods from bankrupt stores.

In June of 1901, Tipton F. McClure bought the building and lot and the one to the north also. McClure had built a home at 215 Sibley Avenue South in 1890, which is still there today. (In 1985, Rennie's Hand Painted China was in that house.) H. A. Rygh's co-operative grocery, called the Little Store, started here in October of 1901. Miss J. S. Barrett leased the room adjoining Rygh's for a millinery in March of 1902. She closed in December of 1902. At some time the name of the Rygh store was changed to the Meeker County Co-operative Store. On February 17, 1906, Rygh had a fire, which put him out of business and destroyed the building. Was the corner cursed? That was the third fire at this corner location. In March of 1906, Independent publisher Henry Isaac "H. I." Peterson bought the building. He sold the lot to Dr. James Wright Robertson in April of 1906 and Robertson built the large brick building, which is still here, in June of 1906. The building included the lot next door to the north. Robertson was Litchfield's mayor in 1905 and 1907. He rented out the downstairs and had Litchfield's first hospital upstairs.

Doctors James W. Robertson, Frank E. Bissell and dentist Edward B. Weeks.

The Emil C. Gross Jewelry moved here in February of 1909. He moved a clock to the sidewalk here also. It had been in front of his other place of business. Gross kept his business going at locations around town until October of 1930.

Emil C. Gross

In January of 1915, Henry O. Morrison moved the Selz Royal Blue Shoe Store here, but left by March to another location. In February of 1915, Joseph P. Engstrom moved his photo studio into the rear of the building. The K & H Theater, owned by P. C. "Carney" Koerner and Ernest V. Harris, was in the corner room here in September of 1915. The K & H closed down in April of 1917. The Citizens State Bank came here for a short time in June of 1917, where the theater had been. The bank was still here in 1924, although it closed for a while in November of 1922. The bank closed permanently in January of 1928. Attorney Ray H. Dart and his father Charles H. Dart, who had their offices in the bank in the mid-twenties, had to move. The National Tea Company had a grocery here in the part of the building the bank had occupied starting in October of 1928.

National Tea Company closed their store here in June of 1933. E. J. Eliason started Litchfield's first Coast To Coast store here in June of 1934. Also in November of 1936, Mrs. William P. Robertson brought her Knit Shop here into the front of the room where the Coast To Coast had been. Helen and Aurelia Shamla started their Shamla Apparel Shoppe here in February of 1937. During the previous month, Franklin D. Roosevelt was sworn in as President for his second term. Walter G. Johnson opened a barbershop in the rear of Shamla's in December of 1938. State inspectors closed him down in April of 1939. Dewey E. Johnson, son of town businessman Andrew Johnson, bought the building but not the businesses in August of 1944. Then in May of 1945, E. J. Morris' Jerdon Shop, (a branch of Gamble-Skogmo Corporation), a clothing store with dresses and furs managed by Bonnie Caylor, was here in the room the Shamlas had occupied. In October of 1948, the store's name was changed to the Jane Morris Apparel Shop, but the ladies called it "the dress shop". Jane Morris closed in early 1951 and the Litchfield Credit Association or Production Credit Association moved into the store's location in March of 1951. Their address, with an entrance around the corner, was 12 Third Street West. Eugene Tobkin's Jewelry business came in July of 1951, sharing the building with Tom's Decorating Service, also called Tom's Paint Store, which came in October of 1951 and was run by John T. "Tom" McGraw. Tobkin took on a junior partner named Marvin "Bill" Stewart. In May of 1953, Tobkin bought out Tom's part of the building and he expanded his jewelry store. Marvel Nelson's Kurlelox Beauty Salon was also in the back on the Third Street side later. Lawyer Taylor C. Waldron moved his law office into the rear of the building next to the PCA office in March of 1955. Robert Sparboe moved his Sparboe Chick Company office here in 1957. Someone sold Penn Mutual Life Insurance out of a room here also in 1957.

Mrs. George Anderson had the Budget Beauty Shop around the corner in the back at 10 Third Street West in the early sixties. The Western Saddlery shop moved here in early 1962 and then moved out to another location in September of 1962. Glenn Fitzloff and Ed Olson moved into this corner building in 1963. They had the Olson & Fitzloff Agency and the Olson Realty & General Insurance businesses. It eventually became just the Ed Olson Agency. Shamla's must have moved back in at some time because they had a fire here in 1968. It was the fourth fire for this location. Possibly the building was vacant with the Shamla name on the window? Meeker County Farm Bureau was around the corner at 12 Third Street West in the early seventies.

The building stood empty for a long time until April of 2003 when Lillith's Natural Health & Beauty and Heavenly Hands Massage moved in from Library Square for a short time. Then Mortgages on Main came. Paul's Audio Video Service is in the rear at 14 Third Street West.

There were businesses upstairs at the last location. Dr. W. E. Chapman had his office above McLane's store in 1884 before moving over the Meeker County Bank. In July of 1895, F. R. Schwie started his "Factory No. 909" cigar factory upstairs. It closed in February of 1898.

James W. Robertson's sons, Dr. Archibald W. "Archie" Robertson and Dr. William P. "Bill" Robertson, who both played football for the University of Minnesota, had a hospital upstairs starting in December of 1908. James Robertson had erected the new building here and he rented the downstairs out to businesses. The hospital rooms upstairs were made into apartments in February of 1915

303 Sibley Avenue North. The also were businesses in the basement of the previous location. William "Billy" Hanley's two-lane bowling alley was downstairs in the early 1900s. Hanley had another bowling alley just west of the hotel in a building he constructed in 1901. Hanley also had Litchfield's first roller rink in 1905, according to a source, although C. M. Tileston had a roller rink in town west of here in January of 1885. Another source gives the owners as Charles A. Brasie and J. D. Hayford and the location as west of Josiah Payne's residence. Still another says there was a roller rink run by Col. C. M. Lovelace in the middle of the 200 block of Marshall Avenue on the west side of the street. In June of 1927, the Pastime Roller Rink, run by B. G. Pierce, began business in the 600 block of Sibley Avenue North. There was a

vacant lot there where tent shows came and went. This roller rink was basically a portable one, which was a huge tent with a wooden floor. In May of 1942, the same kind of roller rink was put in a vacant lot in the middle of the block where the Litchfield Machine Shop went. E. G. Munson owned it. R. H. Bugenhagen tried the same thing south of Highway 12 on Davis Street in May of 1952, but a month later he literally pulled up stakes and went to another town. Back to this basement location, Daniel Morrisey had a restaurant here in April of 1911, but closed it in August. Mrs. Archie A. Cole and Mrs. John Ackerman had a bakery and lunch counter in this basement in November of 1911. Leo C. "Bud" Hanseman moved his Bud's Café restaurant here in December of 1915. He moved out in March of 1916. In August of 1917, the Commercial Club, a forerunner of the Chamber of Commerce, moved to the north basement room here. It had been in the Watson building. World War I ended in November of 1918 and in December, a new short-lived *Meeker County News* was in this basement. A man named Kelso decided to resurrect the paper. What he actually did was move the *Dassel Anchor* newspaper and presses here. The original *Meeker County News* was Meeker County's first newspaper. Frank Belfoy started it in Forest City in the spring of 1868 with Minnesota's first printing press. The original *Meeker County News* was moved to Litchfield, where it merged with the *Litchfield Ledger* in April of 1882, becoming the *News-Ledger* in the next building. In March of 1920, the Woman's Literary Club took over that basement room to provide a rest room for the town's ladies. The Commercial Club had moved out. In October of 1923, F. J. Koktavy's Electrik Maid Bake Shop was in the basement until he moved two doors north in January of 1927. Albert E. Kronzer's Cash Shoe Store moved into the basement in September of 1928 and he changed the business's name to the Basement Shoe Store.

Someone named Hahn leased the basement in October of 1930 for another bowling alley. Morris J. Bronson's furniture repair business was in the basement in the mid-thirties. Bronson took on a partner named Carl Wickstrom in November of 1937.

Hub Schiro moved his Schiro's Shoes to the basement here in the early seventies.

70. 305 Sibley Avenue North. (54 Sibley in the early days and then 626 Sibley Avenue in the early 1900s.) Judge John M. Waldron was the owner of this next lot and one south of here in 1871. A house owned by Justice of the Peace James Benjamin "Ben" Atkinson, Jr., the druggist, was at this location. It burned down completely in a fire in April of

1882. Another building was erected. It had the *Meeker County News* publishing firm in it. The newspaper started in the spring of 1868 in Forest City by Frank Belfoy with the first press in Minnesota. It stopped publishing in 1944. The *News-Ledger* was published here in the early 1880s in the north half of the building. Sharing the building was C. M. Tileston's store, which had moved in briefly after the fire had forced him out of his previous building next door. Tileston quickly moved out to the DeCoster building in May of 1882. There was a millinery here in September of 1882. Charles A. Brasie's general store was here in late 1882 in the south half of the building. He took orders for and managed the Clough Brothers lumberyard, a block west of here, from his store here. In June of 1883, a new building was put up here for the UTK Clothing and Dry Goods House, which was managed by Peder Winger and owned by G. S. Butler. The other building must have been moved off. The UTK store moved in here in September of 1883. Then it moved down by the hotel. Phineas "Pat" Cary moved his dry goods business here from his wife's millenary store building in July of 1884. Charles W. Johnson's "Cheap Charley" store was in the room occupied by Brasie in early 1885 before moving down the street in October of 1885. By 1886, McLane owned this lot and the one to the south. In February of 1889, Isadore Gruenberg's "Chicago Bankrupt Store" came here. It was called the "Chicago Bargain House" store in April and later the "Great Chicago Bargain Store". The store was moved in April of 1892 and the McLaughlin Brothers Mercantile Company or hardware moved their business in here in April of 1892. They were in another location in 1896. They went bankrupt in May of 1901. In April of 1893, Mrs. H. E. McKeen bought Mrs. A. M. Caswell's millinery and Caswell moved to the Snell building. Attorney H. S. McMonagle took over her room. Frank G. Simmons bought the lot in late 1891. The Peterson brothers, John D. and William C. "Billy", owned this lot in 1892. McMonagle moved his office upstairs because Greenleaf and Grono moved into the room in June of 1894. Then later in the month, they dissolved their partnership. B. Krause's bakery was here in June of 1894. Porter and Traue's bakery and lunch shop were here in January of 1897. Mary McGowin moved her millinery in here in March of 1897. During that month, William McKinley was sworn in as the 25th President of the United States. John H. Happ moved his grocery and dry goods store here in February of 1899.

Charles S. Boom ran the Litchfield Business College upstairs starting in July of 1900. C. A. Horton took it over, managing for G. A. Golden, and went out of business in November of 1905. In June of 1901,

Tipton F. McClure bought the building and lot and the one to the south. Julia Anderson had a millinery here in April of 1903. She had a fire in January of 1905. Miss O. L. Madison had a millinery here in September of 1905, which she closed in November of 1905. J. H. Happ and Company, a grocery and dry goods store owned by John H. Happ was still here in the north half of the building in January of 1909. Happ was assistant fire chief from 1919 to 1926. Around this time, dentist L. M. Benepe was upstairs. In April of 1915, John E. Hartinger had his New Bakery here. The "Jake" sign painting business was in a room in this building or next door to the south in 1916. I think the owner was George "Jake" Jacobson who had owned a hardware briefly with Jens J. Juul in the Settergren building. Hartinger ran into some anti-German sentiment in town during WWI when he registered and was announced as an alien in the newspaper. In May of 1918, he went out of business and moved out of town. A. F. Stubbenberg moved a photo studio business into the building in April of 1919. He took on a partner named J. T. Dahl in October of 1919. Brown and Phelps Printing Company was here in some part of the building in 1922. James H. Phelps left and they dissolved their partnership in September of 1924. The *Meeker County News* continued to be printed here into the forties. Elgin B. Brown continued the business as the Brown Printing Company into the late forties, leasing the building in May of 1945. James D. Atkinson had his Litchfield Battery Shop here too in 1921. He moved down by Scarp's restaurant. A. J. Nelson had a plumbing business here next and then Alvin L. Lagergren's Dodge Brothers Motor Vehicles moved in here in June of 1926 and moved out in October. A. A. Fallon then moved in to sell Hudson and Essex cars. He moved out in June of 1927 and Chris Sather opened a grocery store here.

In the thirties, R. L Steabner had an auto painting and finishing shop here. Foster R. Lasley moved the Litchfield Woolen Company retail store into the building's basement in April of 1942. Dewey E. Johnson bought the building but not the businesses in October of 1944. The printing business here became Reed's Printing in January of 1946 when James J. Reed bought Brown Printing. Boyd Anderson bought the clothing business downstairs from Mrs. Lasley in April of 1953, before he moved down next to Viren-Johnson's store. Reed expanded and relocated in 1957 to where the Legion Club is today. Above Reed's at this location, was a chiropractor's office. The 1st State Federal bank was here in the early seventies. The building became TZ Heating and is now King's Wok.

71. 307-309 Sibley Avenue North. (56 Sibley in the early days and then 624 Sibley Avenue in the early 1900s.) Again, heading north, we had a location with quite a history. Judge John A. Waldron was the owner of this lot and the one south of here in 1871. At some point, the simple wood building was called the Kelley building. It burned down completely in a fire in April of 1882. Sivert Olson had a restaurant somewhere here in the next building put up by Thomas Keefe in May of 1882. The building had E. Crosby's feed store in it in July of 1883. The business moved here from the old Cary building on Marshall Avenue, next to the Lake Ripley House, where the business had begun in February of 1883. The Nathan C. Martin & J. M. Russell Real Estate was here in the early 1880s. Martin was from Ohio. Mrs. C. M. (Fayette) Kelley had a millinery here starting in July of 1886. Mrs. A. M. Caswell's Park Millinery was here in the late 1880s sharing the building. Mary Fitch owned this lot in 1888. Mary McGowin bought the building in April of 1889 and installed a "branch" millinery in it with Jennie S. Ringdahl running it. During that same month, Benjamin Harrison was sworn in as the 23rd President of the United States. At this time the McGowan name was always given as "McGowin" in the newspaper ads and stories. I don't know why. The first time I saw it with an "a" was in a July 15, 1911 newspaper, but it went back to the "i" version. After Mary died in April of 1920 and her sisters Elizabeth "Lizzie" and Sadie took over, the spelling of the name slowly changed back until 1922, when I saw it with the "a" all the time. William Grono bought the lot in April of 1889 and August T. Koerner bought this lot in July of 1889 to put a justice office here. I don't know if he did. Koerner was from Germany. In May of 1893, Grono sold half an interest in his marble works to Henry Feig and they had the Litchfield Marble Works here for a couple of months, but Grono was to return later. Mrs. Simmons owned the lot in November of 1891. Catherine Keller owned this lot in 1898. The Swanson and Nelson millinery was here in April of 1899.

John C. Peifer leased this building in April of 1903 and his Litchfield Cash Produce Company was here along with the first of Jack C. Hanson's many barbershop locations before the turn of the century. At that time the building was still being called the Thomas Keefe building. The produce suffered a lot of damage when the millinery next door had a fire in January of 1905.

The Litchfield Produce in the early 1900s.

A new "McGowin building" was rebuilt from the old one in April of 1907. William Grono leased the building in May of 1909 for an office for his marble works. John Beckstrand bought the lot and building from real estate investor Peter E. Hanson in October of 1907. He sold the old building to D. E. Dougherty who moved it off the lot. In September of 1909, Beckstrand moved his shoe business here after he had built a new building on the lot. In the 1910s, something called Ayer Hall was here. A. J. Nelson moved a plumbing business here in March of 1919. I don't know when the newer brick building came along, but it was here in January of 1927 when F. J. Koktavy's Electrik Maid Bake Shop moved in.

Koktavy's became H. J. Roy's Litchfield Bakery in January of 1940. In May of 1946, H. J. Roy added The Igloo to his bakery's basement. He sold ice cream sundaes and cones down there and advertised that he had forty different ice cream dishes. The bakery was sold to Leon Minard in December of 1946. Roy got it back in September of 1947, but sold it to Harry Hershey in March of 1949. Then Harold H. Bergmann got it in April of 1949. Bergmann called it the Litchfield Bakery. Ray B. Cox had his chiropractic business upstairs in 1951. For a short time in 1950, Wayne Rayppy bought the bakery and had two bakeries in town. Then Hamilton A. Johnson's Furniture store was here in December of 1951. Initially just appliances and juvenile furniture was sold here. The regular furniture was sold at Johnson's store at 21 East Depot, which had been purchased from Eddy and Fenner. Later in October of 1952, Johnson moved the entire business to this location after the VFW had purchased the Depot Street building. The VFW had originally met in the GAR Hall until 1943 when they moved to the Community Building. In the early fifties, Litchfield Laboratories, a hearing aid center, was in the basement. In September of 1958, someone started a selling service in the basement here.

Johnson's Furniture in 1955.

Johnson's Furniture closed around 1960 and the building stood vacant. Then it became the home of Wayne Rayppy's New Bakery in January of 1962, after Rayppy's New Bakery located by the First State Bank burned down. Rayppy sold the bakery to Clarence Nelson in April 1964 and finally Frank Forsberg's Bakery was here. Briefly in the nineties, Susie's was here. It was a novelty and gift store. Today this building houses Remax realty and there are apartments upstairs.

Litchfield had quite a few bakeries in its history. I counted thirty-three different owners in my book alone that I have locations for. The very first bakery owner was Eli Vachon in June of 1872. Ironically, he called his bakery the New Bakery and it was located across from the Lake Ripley House hotel on Marshall Avenue North. No doubt Wayne Rayppy knew this and named his bakery in honor of that first bakery. There were only a few bakeries that I couldn't find locations for. They were the Diamond Bakery in April of 1896, the Home Bakery, owned by Mrs. A. B. Johnson in November of 1900, and the Hartinger bakery.

72. 311-311½ Sibley Avenue North. (58-60 Sibley in the early days and then 622 Sibley Avenue in the early 1900s.) This location and the next one shared a city lot, I believe. So the stores do get a little complicated. First, Judge Waldron and attorney Bowen built a new office building here in September of 1875. It was set back a ways from the wooden sidewalk which ran along Sibley Avenue at the time. Charley Taylor had a meat market here in 1880. J. M. Russell owned the lot in the late 1880s. At some point, either there were two small

buildings on this lot or more than one business shared the building. In July of 1890, W. Birch Rowley bought the lot and in September of 1890, his wife had the Park Restaurant and confectionery here in the south building or part of the single building. She closed in November of 1892. Mrs. Ed Miller moved a confectionery here in early 1893 and added a restaurant to it in May of 1893. In April of 1893, the "1873" building, as it was called, was moved here. William "Popcorn" Miller moved into the building. He moved all over town with his business and owned the lot in 1895. F. R. Schwie had his Factory No. 909 making cigars upstairs here in July of 1895. In 1897, John Beckstrand had a shoe store here. He moved here from the Watson building and then next door after he bought the lot there and put a new building on it. Mrs. Rowley came back here in April of 1896. Frank G. Simmons owned the lot in 1899.

In the early 1900s, Miss Emma Swanson's Park Bazaar Restaurant was here. Her sign said "Tea Room" under "Park Bazaar". Ole A. "Music Ole" Olson bought the building and lot here in July of 1910. In June of 1917, Swanson moved her business to the store Greenberg's had been in. She and her sister eventually had the Silver Grill there. Tom Wandok had a cigar shop here in the twenties.

This location became the Weis hamburger stand, which was sold to H. B. Tiffany in February of 1932. I believe that there were two small restaurants here side by side for a while. Harold C. Hanson came here next and started the Black & White Inn. In June of 1936, he sold the location to Harold "Pat" Wood and moved to Depot Street. Hanson took the business back in April of 1937, and sold it to Wilfred T. Farley in May. Farley called his restaurant The Paradise. He died in July of 1938. Just a month earlier, the Eden Valley sheriff dropped over dead of a heart attack as he was bringing Farley in on a disturbance charge. Wilfred's son, William Farley, moved the restaurant to 27 West Second in 1939, between Baril's Paint and Auto Parts. Oscar Olson and Walter Mortenson opened a restaurant in half of this building in December of 1936. It was called the Olson Park Café. After Oscar died, Mrs. Olson sold the restaurant to Hans C. Hanson in April of 1937. In January of 1950, Dr. G. Cueva had a veterinary office at this location. Then this location became the famous Janousek Brothers' Eat 10¢ Café, owned by Paul and his brother Henry. It was changed in the late fifties to Eat 15¢.

I don't know when it happened, but many of the restaurants here shared the building with a business on the north side. Janousek's shared with Ev's Lock & Fixit Shop, owned by Everett Roggenstein, in the fall of 1963, Leonard "Lenny" Johnson's Tri-County Water Conditioning in April of 1968, Jim and Cathy Allen's CJ Music Store in May of 1969, H

& A Television and Radio in the early seventies and A & C TV later in the seventies. One of the rooms was used for DFL headquarters in September of 1972 and it became Margaret Breitenbach's Clay Pot Floral and Gift Shop in the next year. Today the whole building is Parkview Lunch. Mark and Ann Lien owned it until they sold it to Kevin and Donna Hartmann in April of 2003.

Janousek's and CJ Music Store in 1969.

74. 313 Sibley Avenue North. (62 Sibley in the early days and then 618-620 Sibley Avenue in the early 1900s.) As far as I know, there was a vacant lot here for years. Silas Wright Leavett erected a building here in 1882. Leavett was from New Hampshire. William Grono leased the building in January of 1885 for his marble works, which he moved all around town. In March of 1885, Grono moved out and Hugh Dowling moved his harness shop into the Leavett building. Dowling was from Maine. His shop on Sibley Avenue North had just burned down. Daniel McLane brought his tin shop business here in March of 1886 after selling the building behind his store at the corner to the south. In early 1890, Mrs. H. H. Stay opened a laundry in the building.

Then Ole A. "Music Ole" or "Professor" Olson's Music House was here in 1901 with a wooden storefront stating "Pianos and Organs". It was Olson's fourth location, moving here from his location just to the north. He built a new building here. Ole was the band concert leader from 1886 to January of 1930 and his business was here for most of that time. Harry Radunz' Harry's Tire Shop moved here in September of 1928, sharing the building with the music store. Harry had his Auto Wrecking business behind the building in the alley. I don't know when Music Ole moved out, but he did before 1934, keeping ownership of the building.

Ole A. "Music Ole" Olson

After Harry left in June of 1934, the C. I. Tenney Engineering Company move in here with an office and display room for its Litchfield Gas Service, selling gas stoves and appliances. The G & K Bargain Store, managed by Morris J. Bronson, was here also, sharing the building, in late 1934. In June of 1935, Norman S. Glader and Hilding L. Wilson had their Glader-Wilson radio and TV service shop here. Yes, TV repairs in 1935. I doubt if anybody in town had a set, however. Glader got a new partner named Anderson in the summer of 1936. The Chapin Electric service shared the building for a short while, moving down the street in November. The next year, Glader and Anderson moved down by Greep's. In April of 1937, Ole A. Olson sold the building to Hans C. Hanson. Arthur Hed bought the building in May of 1938 and put a restaurant in. Then Dan Brown opened up Dan's Café here in July of 1939. In April of 1946, Dewey E. Johnson bought the building, but only as an investment. George Ley had his first Park Grocery store here in the early 1940s. He had owned the Thomas Store in the Litchfield Shoes Building. In August of 1946, George moved his grocery to 431 Fifth Street East, but kept the name, Park Grocery. He opened up there in October. The Bell-Colberg Home Supplies, owned by George Bell and John Colberg, was at this location starting in October of 1946. The business was sold to Duane and Louise Eskew in September of 1952 and it became D & L Skelgas Sales & Service. D & L moved to another location and the building had a one-year incarnation as James Otto's Milk Bar, sometimes called the Litchfield Dairy Bar, which had a grand opening on November 20, 1953. The Milk Bar sold dairy products, lunches, a few groceries like bread and canned goods, and they had a fountain service. In 1955, the building went back to Skelgas Sales and Service along with the Farm Bureau. John Colberg ran it. Then Velma Mae and Sally Mae Colberg, John's daughters, opened up the Colberg's Beauty Shop here in December of 1957. It became the Budget Beauty Shop in August of 1959 when Mrs. George Anderson bought the business.

In the early sixties, the beauty shop moved to the corner. The Litchfield Coin-Operated Dry Cleaners was here in the summer of 1963, after a fire had destroyed the previous location on Depot Street East. Ed Fitzloff and his wife owned it. In November of 1963, they were on their way home to Hutchinson from here when a train at the Sibley Avenue crossing killed them both. During that same month, John F. Kennedy was assassinated and Lyndon Johnson was sworn in as the 36th President of the United States. Frank Anderson bought the business in February of 1964. Before the building was torn down in the seventies, Anderson changed the name to Frank's Econ-o-clean.

The "300" block of Sibley Avenue.

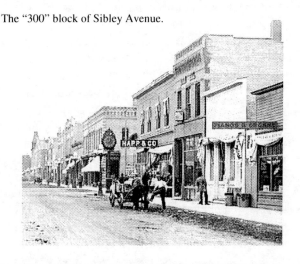

75-76. 315-317 Sibley Avenue North. (616 Sibley Avenue in the early 1900s.) An alley was next followed by this location. In the 1880s, the *News-Ledger,* owned by Frank Belfoy and W. D. Joubert, was printed in a building here. Turner and Son had a blacksmith shop in the rear of the *News-Ledger* office, probably facing the alley. After Frank Belfoy died, Joubert bought his interest in the *News-Ledger* from the heirs in April of 1882. W. D. Joubert was listed as the owner of this lot in the early 1890s. He also had a printing business. He was Litchfield's twenty-fifth mayor in 1906. Just before the turn of the century, Ole A. "Music Ole" had his music store here for a short time for another of his locations in town.

Music Ole moved next door south in 1901. H. G. Meyer leased the *Ledger* for three years from 1903 to 1906. Then Joubert took it back. When the *Ledger* ceased publication, Cal Sivright and Harry E. Wolvin leased the building in April of 1920 to sell Twin City tractors. They called their business the Meeker Motor Company and also sold Nash cars. They were here until March of 1922. John Peterson leased the building in April of 1926 for a Mohawk brand tire shop. The Masonic Lodge was in the building until their new building was built at the southeast corner of Third Street and Sibley Avenue. Harry Radunz had his first tire store and auto wrecking business here in 1926. Then there was a gas station here for as long as I can remember. The first one I find mention of was the Penn-American gas station run by Oscar A. Nelson in the May of 1927. Harry Radunz moved to a room in the rear. The station announced that it had "a very attractive rest room for the ladies." During that month, Minnesota born Charles A. Lindbergh flew his Spirit of St. Louis airplane solo from New York to Paris. G. A. Anderson succeeded Oscar Nelson. Penn-American switched over to Dutch Shell Oil in September of 1927, with C. F. Hanson as the manager. Douglas March became the manager in November of 1929. In the previous month, the New York Stock Market had crashed starting the Great Depression.

In March of 1930, Raymond Lund and Harlan Quinn took over the Shell station. A. G. Anderson had it then and Harry Anderson replaced him in July of 1930. Edwin Schelde leased the station in September of 1935. V. F. "Doc" Muelener's Shell Gas Station was here in July of 1942. In April of 1946, Dewey E. Johnson bought the station, but just for an investment. Then the gas station became the M. C. Anderson Service Station before it became the Uptown Skelly station in 1959 when Willard "Shorty" Nystrom and Roger Lien bought it.

Uptown
Skelly
in 1961.

The gas station was finally torn down in the early sixties. In October of 1971, Harper Dollerschell started a used car lot here called Harper's Auto Sales. People who bought cars from Harper didn't have

402

to go very far to register them at the courthouse. The Meeker County Court House was just north of here finishing the block.

77. The Meeker County Courthouse, which was at the northwest corner of this block and built in 1890, was torn down in 1975 and replaced with the one that's there today. The old Forest City Courthouse was moved to 15 East Fifth Street in Litchfield in 1870. That location is where Andy's Red Owl[193] had been in the sixties and seventies and the Town Square apartments' garages are today. Village Council President Jesse V. Branham, Jr. owned the building and leased it out residential, because the city decided it was too small for a courthouse. After all it was only a small wooden house painted white. A. F. Peifer lived in it for a while. The city rented the upstairs of the building next to the hotel for courtrooms until they built a new brick building at this site across Sibley Avenue from the park. Anna Swanson's father bought the "old courthouse" from Branham and moved it to 519 Ramsey Avenue North, where it stands today. Anna lived there until she died.

Going back south on Sibley Avenue, I'll cross Third Street to the southwest corner of the intersection and walk past the stores on the west side of the 200 block of Sibley.

Sibley Avenue west in the 1920s.

81. 239-241 Sibley Avenue North. (48 Sibley Avenue in the early days and then 700 Sibley Avenue in the early 1900s.) Most Litchfield citizens knew this corner building simply as "Jacks", but the very first store on this corner was Samuel A. Heard's general merchandise store. Heard was partnered with C. D. Ward and their Heard and Ward general store was actually the very first store in Litchfield in 1869. It was the

---

[193] Selmer L. Anderson opened up Andy's Red Owl at this location in October of 1965.

third building to be erected in town. Ward and Heard's store was a one-story twenty by thirty-four foot building that cost $700 to build on the lot that they owned together. They put on a rear addition in April of 1871 and Heard bought out Ward in August. Heard also had a blacksmith shop on Ramsey Avenue by the Union Hotel. Heard, who was from Canada and also owned the lot to the south of here, just had groceries in his building by 1874. In November of 1874, Frank Belfoy moved his office here. At the New Year's Festival, held at the town hall in January of 1878, Heard was voted the "Most Popular Man In Town" and he received a set of books as a prize. In the late 1870s, Lawyer Edward A. Campbell had his office somewhere in the Heard building. Heard sold his business to Delaney Ezra "Abe" Branham and George Hickcox for their City Grocery business in March of 1883. Branham was a real rarity amongst early businessmen in Litchfield. Not only was he born in Minnesota, but also he was born in Meeker County. Most of the other early businessmen in town were born in other states or other countries. By 1885, J. S. and A. P. Sherrill owned the lot and built a new building here. The Branham and Hickcox business was moved across the street that summer so that the new brick building could be erected and the wooden building was moved elsewhere to become Hugh Dowling's harness shop. Branham and Hickcox's new City Grocery opened up in October of 1885. Delaney "Abe" had the grocery store alone in March of 1888, when Hickcox sold out. Delaney's brother, Thomas F. Branham, bought an interest in February of 1891, and the store became the Branham Brothers' City Grocery. Hiram S. Angell, Clark L. Angell, Sr.'s son, and Alex Roehl bought the Branham grocery in April of 1892. Hiram also moved his confectionery here, which he then sold to Clarence A. Perry. Angell and Roehl's grocery store, still called the City Grocery, was sold to Edward L. Healy in June of 1895. Mrs. A. M. Caswell and Mrs. Flynn had a millinery here also in 1895. In November of 1895, Flynn was out and Mrs. Krueger was in. In November of 1896, D. C. Beach opened up an "auction store" here briefly. At that time the building was called the "Nelson building" for some reason. Mrs. Lewis F. Larson's millinery was also here in later 1896. When Larson moved out, Meyer Banks' Cash Bargain Store moved here in January of 1898. North Star clothing was here at some time but moved across the street in March of 1899. Mrs. Larson's re-opened in one of the rooms too in March of 1899.

Banks quit his business in January of 1900 and Nels B. Anderson put a general merchandise store here along with the baker named A. W. Sweet from next door. They called the store Anderson and Sweet.

404

Anderson traded stores with H. A. Rygh, who had a store in Dalton, Minnesota, in March of 1901. During that same month, William McKinley was sworn in as President for his second term and was soon assassinated. Rygh called his store the "New Store". In March of 1902, Louis R. Fernald brought a drug store into the building. He quit the business in November of that year, selling his stock to the Lofstrom brothers, who had opened a drugstore mid-block in the hotel block. Mrs. Larson's millinery went out of business in May of 1901. At sometime around this time, A. P. Brodeen moved his shoe repair business into part of the building. In May of 1903, B. Berman and Clarence Young started a store here called the Litchfield Fruit Store offering "fancy candies" and produce. Young was replaced by D. A. Roos and then Berman sold out to Roos in July of 1904 and moved down the street near the Johns & Lucas Hardware. James Carlton "J. C." Jacks leased the building and started his Jacks Bargain Store here in October of 1906. He later changed the name to Jacks' Ben Franklin, when he bought the second Ben Franklin franchise in the United States. J. C. raised prize-winning chickens called Buff Orpingtons.

J. C.'s son Paul took over the business when J. C. died in February of 1936. When Paul died in June of 1949, his wife Gladys took over.

Jacks closed its doors in June of 1962 after fifty-six years in the same location. In October of 1962, Marlowe Abdnor's S & Q (Service & Quality) Hardware, formerly called Marshall-Wells, moved in. Falknor's Appliance and Electronics was here in June of 1970 after Bill Falknor bought the business. Other stores in this building were The Barbers, Head Start and it is now the Ed Olson Agency, Inc.

(702 Sibley Avenue in the early 1900s.) A few businesses were upstairs over the last location over the years. In December of 1891, the Chicago Bargain Store moved in upstairs because they had had a fire at their location. Kettil Stensrud began publication of the Norwegian paper, called the *Heimdal*, upstairs in October of 1890. The paper didn't last very long. A tailor named N. P. Holmberg was upstairs in July of 1906 in a room that had been vacated by A. P. Brodeen. He closed down in November of 1906. Joseph P. Engstrom leased the rear rooms upstairs for his photo studio. In February of 1929, Hubert Dedrickson had his barbershop upstairs for a short while. Eventually the upstairs was turned into apartments and Gladys Jacks herself lived up there.

1880: Another view of City Grocery and City Drug Store on the west side of Sibley Avenue.

82. 237 Sibley Avenue North. (46 Sibley in the early days and then 704 Sibley Avenue in the early 1900s.) George Merriam owned the next lot heading south in 1871 and also the next three lots after it. He must have had a bank here because the lot was referred to later as the lot that had the old bank building. Samuel A. Heard owned the lot and the building on it in 1874. I don't know if he used it for storage or to lease, as he had his store next door. By late 1877, the building was abandoned. In January of 1878, the town band leased the building for a rehearsal hall. Then, in May of 1878, a new building was erected. One source called it Litchfield's second brick building. It had Judge Virgil Homer Harris' Confectionery and City Drug store in it. Harris[194], from Ohio, was Litchfield's twelfth Village Council President in 1883. Harris' Confectionary was sold to G. B. Upham, Jr. and Company in October of 1890. I think Harris kept ownership of the building. Then the downstairs became Atkinson Drug, owned by James Benjamin "Ben" Atkinson, Jr. in October of 1892. Judge Harris kept an office here. Atkinson took on a partner named Alex Roehl in February of 1896. They moved to the Brown building at the northeast corner of Sibley Avenue and Second Street. Sam B. Millard moved his jewelry business here in July of 1896.

---

[194] Judge of Probate Virgil Homer Harris came to Litchfield in 1871. He was a member of the GAR and his grandfather Ephraim had been a friend of Daniel Boone.

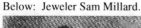
Below: Jeweler Sam Millard.

Left to right: (About 1880) A law office, Judge Harris' City Drug Store and the City Grocery (at the corner of Sibley Avenue and Third Street).

In August of 1898, Sweet and Palm returned to the bakery business and moved in here. They also sold ice cream. Sweet left Henry E. Palm in December of 1899, joining with Nels B. Anderson next door. Meanwhile, Palm moved to the rear of the building and quit retailing. He sold bakery goods wholesale as the Northwestern Baking Company. Judge Harris' son, Maro A., and Orra S. Johnston opened the Johnston and Harris New Shoe Store in the front of the building in December of 1899.

In August of 1900, Henry E. Palm took over the whole main floor after Johnston and Harris moved out. Virgil H. Harris is listed as the lot's owner in 1900. The building was occupied by O. A. Newburg's bakery around late 1902. Newburg had a big fire in February of 1907. Otho H. Campbell bought the building in February of 1903. Virgil H. Harris died in 1910. His son, Ernest V. Harris became a Judge of Probate and moved back here to have another Harris Confectionery in March of 1915. The Judge's wife had a popcorn machine in front on the street on Saturday nights when Central Park hosted the weekly band concert in the park back then. Everyone knew Harris' confectionery store more as a candy store. Judge Harris loved to play bridge in the afternoon and evening here with his cronies, such as Art Krueger, Bud Everts, Sam Gandrud, Leo Baumgartner, Bill McGee, Charles R. Clemens and Bob Farrish.

In his later years in the thirties, Harris couldn't be bothered with kids coming in for candy. He'd just yell at them to help themselves and leave the money on the counter. He quit the business in 1940 and sold to Percy E. Waller in August of 1940. Harris died in 1949. The Waller

Drug was here in the early to late 1940s. It became Johnson's Drug, when Ray Johnson took the business over in August of 1949.

Johnson's Drug in 1955.

After Ray moved to the McGowan building just down the street in March of 1964, Earl Voss had his Voss Heating and Appliances store here. It was later called Voss Electronics and then Voss Furniture, TV and Appliances. Jim and Cathy Allen's CJ Music was here for a little over a year starting in November of 1969. Lowell Ruotsinoja's service shop, called Lowell's Radio & TV, came at the same time and was in the back. When Jim left, Lowell took over the whole store. He closed, however, in December of 1971. Budget Furniture came here in February of 1972. KLFD moved here in November of 1972. It was one of four locations I knew the radio station to be at in Litchfield. The first one was the Nelson D. March house at 218 South Sibley Avenue, a few houses south of Batterberry's store. Randy "Uppercut" Leaf had a barbershop here at sometime following. The building is vacant now.

(706 Sibley Avenue in the early 1900s.) Upstairs over the last location were a few businesses. Charles Henry Strobeck and his partner S. A. Plumley moved in upstairs in November of 1878. Plumley had the office upstairs alone in the early 1880s. He was Litchfield's tenth Village Council President in 1881. Lawyer F. P. Olney had his office upstairs in 1884 and the A.O.U.W. Lodge was up there also It was very similar to the Masons, in fact the emblems and symbols used by the Ancient Order of United Workmen were steeped in Masonic attributes. Dr. W. E. Chapman had his office upstairs in October of 1886. Col. Bissell, a Justice of the Peace, moved his office upstairs in January of 1897. Bissell was from Wisconsin. Victor A. "Vic" and F. W. Sederstrom came to town and opened up a real estate office over the drug

store in January of 1897. They moved down the street in March. In the 1910s, Alva R. Hunt had his attorney office upstairs.

235 Sibley Avenue North. There were businesses upstairs over the next location also. Attorneys Edward A. Campbell and E. P. Peterson had their offices upstairs, along with the Independent printing office and the *Independent* newspaper, which moved up there in September of 1885. The law firms of John T. Byrnes and Peterson & Foster were upstairs in the early 1890s.

The Independent Printing Office and the newspaper moved out sometime after 1905 but came back later. It was upstairs from December of 1909 until 1917.

Itasca Engineering, Inc. was upstairs or in the rear in the early seventies. Today there are apartments upstairs.

94. 233 Sibley Avenue North. The basement of the next location has always housed a barbershop or beauty shop. Originally owned by pioneer barber Ray Wheeler, who moved under the Northwestern Bank, it became Jack C. Hanson's Barber Shop in 1900. Hanson had an assistant barber named Hubert Dedrickson, who moved over Jacks' Ben Franklin for a while and then under Nygaard's Jewelry. Hanson leased the barbershop to James E. Cooper in May of 1916 and moved down by Mellquist's, but came back in June of 1922.

Hanson sold his business to Sidney Munson in August of 1930 for his Munson's Beauty and Barber Shop. Munson died in July of 1942. In July of 1946, it was Mac E. Steen's, who ironically had started out under the Northwestern Bank, in Ray Wheeler's location. The barbers went 'round and 'round town. Ethel's Beauty Shop, owned by Ethel Towler Marsala, was here sharing the location in October of 1948.

Steen sold the shop to Larry Swenson in February of 1966 and it became Swenson's or Larry's Barber Shop. Larry moved out in August of 1970 to another location and Jim Allen moved his CJ Music down here in February of 1971.

88. 231 Sibley Avenue North. (44 Sibley in the early days and then 708 Sibley Avenue in the early 1900s.) George Merriam owned this lot in 1871. In 1874, Frank Belfoy had a law office here. I don't know if he occupied the whole building or shared it. In March of 1885, E. P. and Henry Isaac "H. I." Peterson, the building's owners, moved it somewhere and started construction of a new brick building. During that same month, Grover Cleveland was sworn in as the 22nd President of the

United States. The Stevens and Company bank occupied the downstairs of the new building in October of 1885. The privately owned bank was also known as the Stevens and Branham Bank, named after its owners, Hamlet Stevens, who was born in Canada and came to Meeker County in 1857, and Hiram S. Branham, born in Indiana and son of Litchfield's first "mayor", Jesse V. Branham, Jr. On the first floor with the bank was the August T. "Gus" Koerner and Company abstract and real estate office with a rear entrance. Koerner and Company dissolved their business in January of 1887 and in the late 1880s Charles "Charley" H. Dart took over the abstract business calling it Meeker County Abstracts. Then he or a son had a grocery here with a partner named A. Helgeson. Charles' blind son Ray was a lawyer in town. One of the owners of the bank, Mayor Hiram S. Branham, committed suicide in December of 1890 because of some shady dealings. The bank, which was at many locations in town, had closed in November of 1890. One of the officers was arrested for embezzlement and many people lost their money. There was another tragedy in December. Soldiers at Wounded Knee, South Dakota killed two hundred Sioux, many pushed off their land here.

August T. "Gus" Koerner

1889: Stevens and Co. bank, Harris City Drug and Branham's City Grocery.

In February of 1891, Senator George E. White bought the building and furniture and, in March, Justice of the Peace Virgil Homer Harris, the druggist from next door, opened an office here in the basement.

A turn of the century photograph of this location shows that the E. M. Eastman's Independent Printing Office and the *Litchfield Independent* newspaper was still in this building, but it was moved across the street at some time after 1905. Then it was moved back in upstairs in December of 1909 until 1917. The Meeker County Abstract & Loan Company run by Charles H. Dart was still here in the early 1920s. Dart and Helgeson dissolved their partnership in June of 1925 and leased the building to Red Owl in August of 1925. E. E. Hedlund managed the Red

Owl. Jack C. Hanson's barbershop was in the basement in the late 1920s.

The Abstract Company was still listed as this property's owner in 1933. The Red Owl was still here through the mid-fifties. Conrad W. Berquist and his son Stan J. had their Berquist Electric downstairs in this building for several months until June of 1946, when they moved over by the Auto Parts building. In June of 1949, the Red Owl started offering a Sears and Roebuck Catalog service in the store. The Red Owl was sold to S. J. "Sundy" Sjobeck in December of 1954. The Red Owl Company had owned the store. Sjobeck sold to Cy Martin, who closed the Red Owl in April of 1956. Then the building had the Thomas Furniture Mart or Litchfield Furniture Mart from May of 1956 to 1959. Frank Thomas owned it and he became the Deputy License Registrar in January of 1955. So everyone that needed new plates for their car had to go to the furniture store to get them.

Daynor Dollerschell started his Dayna's Sport Shop here in January of 1960. In December of 1960, Dayna sold his business to Jack Olson and Bob Elam and the store became Jack's Sports Center. Soon Jack had the store alone, but it was short-lived as John Kinsella moved a Sears catalog store in here in July of 1962. In January of 1971, John Wiley took over the Sears and then Glenn A. Anderson bought it in November. The building now has Cliff Schaefer's Studio and Cameras, which began in 1973.

87 & 95. 229 Sibley Avenue North. (42 Sibley in the early days and then 710-712 Sibley Avenue in the early 1900s.) William Henry Greenleaf had a general store here in early 1870. It was in a thirty-two by fifty foot two-storied building, costing $1700 to build. Greenleaf sold it to B. L. Perry and Company in the fall of 1870. George Merriam owned this lot in 1871. Judge of Probate Capt. Francesco V. DeCoster had a dry goods business here in May of 1871, buying out Perry. DeCoster was a Civil War veteran who was born in Maine. He could speak Sioux fluently. In June of 1872, DeCoster added jewelry, organs and other musical instruments and sewing machines. He bought the lot in November of 1872. There was a long wooden building here which had more than one store in it. Sharing the building were the stores next door at that time until brick buildings were built. In 1881, DeCoster added an additional shop inside his store, called it the Boston Store. It was a catalog business. In late 1881, DeCoster had a partner, George L. Swan, who left in early 1882. C. M. Tileston, who had lost his store in

the fire of April 1882, across on Third Street, moved in on May 4, 1882. DeCoster kept the jewelry business going here.

F. V.
DeCoster
in his
Civil War
uniform.

Mrs. Myron E. Baum opened a dressmaking shop over Tileston's in November of 1882. Tileston's was bought by Joseph Lawrence Wakefield in November of 1883. Joseph, from Rhode Island, sold dry goods, furnishing goods, boots, and shoes. The Woodward brothers, who were doctors, had their office over Wakefield's. Mrs. Henry L. Wadsworth's dressmaking shop moved over Wakefield's starting in November of 1884. Paul O. Olson moved his tailor shop upstairs in September of 1885. In September, he sold the tailor business to O. Wexel and G. Toreros or Thornros. L. A. Chapman moved his shoemaking and repair business into a back room here in October of 1885. Wakefield moved to another location in 1886. DeCoster got the entire business back and then in May of 1887, he took on another partner, a jeweler named Wheeler. Wheeler was in the north side of the building and DeCoster was in the south side. The partnership dissolved in January of 1889. In February of 1894, D. C. Beach moved his confectionery business into the south half of DeCoster's jewelry business. Justice Col. Bissell had his office here in May of 1894 and Clarence A. Perry bought Beach's business that same month. Then the McGowin Millinery was here in August of 1898. Mary McGowin came to Litchfield from Ireland and worked for Mrs. C. M. (Fayette) Kelley in her millinery and dressmaking shop, which started in 1873. Mary started her own dressmaking store across the street with a lady named Miss Kennedy in May of 1885. Kennedy left shortly and Mary brought in her two sisters and they started the McGowin Millinery. Mary also owned a building across from the park and bought this lot also. Mary moved out for a time in the early 1890s. I don't know why but she operated her millinery out of the McGowan house then across from the park at 28
412

Third Street East between Sibley and Marshall Avenues. At this time the McGowan name was always given as "McGowin" in the newspaper ads and stories. The first time I saw it with an "a" was in July 15, 1911, but it didn't change over permanently until 1922. In October of 1896, Helen Sorns opened a dressmaking shop in the store. The Sweet and Palm bakery, owned by Henry E. Palm, came in here in March of 1897. He had a bad fire in September of 1897.

When Mary died in April of 1920, her two sisters took over. Elizabeth or "Lizzie" had been a teacher for fifteen years and the County Superintendent of Schools and Sadie had taught in Salt Lake City, Utah. Lizzie was born in 1870. They were here from the early 1900s until late 1962. In March of 1964, Ray Johnson moved his drug store here from just down the street. The building now has Smith's Appliance and Radio Shack.

Mrs. Pixley's Millinery and DeCoster's store.

96. 227 Sibley Avenue North. (40 Sibley in the early days and then 714 Sibley Avenue in the early 1900s.) The next site had a building called the James Building because it was built by Joseph James to be used as an office for his lumberyard, which was south of the railroad tracks. The building here was the third store building to go up in Litchfield in 1869. It also had Mrs. Mary L. Pixley's millinery in 1870. Another building shared this lot. It was a fourteen by twenty foot one-story building costing $300 to build. A meat market, owned by Samuel Y. Gordon and Virgil Homer Harris, started here in May of 1871. It was a sixteen by twenty-four foot story and a half building costing $400 to build. George Merriam owned the lot in 1871. Harris bought the building in May of 1871. The Yankee Notion store owned by D. E. Potter came here in June of 1872. It was a "notions and pocket cutlery" store. Meanwhile, Gordon sold his interest in the meat market to O.H.

413

Buckwalter in July of 1872. The business became Harris and Buckwalter. Buckwalter, in turn, sold his interest to John Patten. Buckwalter had been in partnership with Al Whitmore elsewhere in town. In August of 1872, DeCoster, from next door, bought the lot for $250 and Harris sold out to Patten, who moved out to be a partner with Gottlieb "Jake" Keller in August of 1872. Harris stayed here. In June of 1873, Dr. J. S. Bell joined with Harris and opened a drug store here, called the New Drug Store. In November of 1873, Bell left and Harris continued, but moved down the street. The butcher building was moved to the rear of the lot in 1873. The small building was used as an implement business office. Dr. V. P. Kennedy had an office here for a short time in 1874. In 1873, B. L. Perry owned the lot. Mrs. Mary L. Pixley's Millinery was still here in part of the building in 1882. In 1888, a Mr. James moved his sewing machine store here. Mrs. Pixley sold her millinery to Mrs. Lewis F. Larson in April of 1892 and moved elsewhere in town. In October of 1895, Sadie Dougherty opened a grocery here. Clarence A. Perry had his confectionery here sharing the building with Oren Wilbert "Bert" Topping's barbershop, which came here in April of 1895. They both moved out after the fire next door in the bakery. A new building was put up here and Sam B. Millard moved his jewelry store into it in July of 1898.

Then in August of 1900, David Elmquist had a jewelry store here although Millard still owned the building. Elmquist decided to move to Willmar and so he sold the business to Emil C. Gross in July of 1901. L. T. Dillon & Co. leased part of the building in June of 1905. Gross added an optometry business to the jewelry store but moved down the street in 1909. Dillon was still going in early 1908, but in October he sold the jewelry business to Edward W. Gruenhagen. Gross moved to another location around that time, then bought the building in July of 1913, but he didn't move his jewelry back here until May of 1914. Dr. Walter C. Whitney bought the optometry part in December of 1919.

Gross went out of business in October of 1930. The business became the Whitney "Jeweler and Optometrist" store, when Whitney bought the entire business and the building in July of 1947. Dr. Ray B. Cox, a chiropractor, had his office upstairs in June of 1951. Whitney sold the jewelry part to Roger Setterberg in October of 1957. Setterberg moved across the street to where Irene's Fashion Shop had been in early September of 1960. The Minnesota Valley Natural Gas Company moved here in late September of 1960. The building now has Gervais Jewelry.

97. 225 Sibley Avenue North. (38 Sibley in the early days and then 716 Sibley Avenue in the early 1900s.) Continuing down Sibley, the next lot was owned by shoemaker Louis Ekbom in 1871. Ekbom was from Sweden. The building eventually on it, once owned by clothier John Birch and also Aron J. Anderson, had many unknown businesses until 1900. F. W. Thiele and Alex Cairncross had their shoe store here sharing the building with a bank in August of 1881. Mrs. Augeline Cary's millinery was also here in May of 1882. Her husband had a general merchandise store down the block towards the hotel. He moved into a room with his wife here in November of 1882 and then moved down across from the park in July of 1884 to give her more room. The Thiele and Cairncross partnership was called F. W. Thiele and Company's shoemaking business in 1883, as Cairncross, I believe, became a silent partner of Thiele. Cairncross had the business alone after Thiele left in 1884 because of poor health. He died in 1885. Clark L. Angell, who moved all over town, had his Pioneer Gallery here in early 1884. Angell was born in New York. John Palm bought an interest in Cairncross's store in January of 1885 and Angell moved down the street in August. Palm was from Sweden. Alex Cairncross and John Palm built a new building here in the November of 1886. The building cost $14,000 to build. In September of 1887, Mrs. Phelps and Miss Christine Nygren opened the New Millinery upstairs over Cairncross and Palm. Cairncross sold the building here to Louis Ekbom and A. H. Lofstrom, from next door, in March of 1889. In September of 1889, the I.O.O.F. moved in upstairs. John Beckstrand and Company bought Cairncross' boot and shoe repair business in February of 1892. In February of 1893, Cairncross and Palm was changed to John Palm and Company and it moved next door until the new building was completed. The old building was moved somewhere and Dan Post bought it from James R. Watson in August of 1900 and moved it somewhere else for a blacksmith shop. The new Palm building was completed here in June of 1894. Mary McGowin had her millinery here in 1895 for a short time.

John Birch, who was from Sweden, leased the building in October of 1909 and tried to start up his clothing store again. Ole N. Vig bought the Palm general merchandise business in February of 1912. During that same month, Arizona was the 48th state admitted to the Union. Then, Frank L. and Charles J. Anderson had a saloon here. Birch turned the clothing business to his son, J. Horace Birch who closed the business in December of 1931. Otto H. Werner moved his plumbing and heating business in the back in April of 1928. He moved to the Houd Hardware in November of 1929.

Frank Edwards moved a pool hall here later in December of 1931. A. F. Hoel's Pioneer Grocery moved here in November of 1933. It was started at another location in October of 1930. The grocery took over the whole building in March of 1935. At sometime, Hoel picked up a partner, Selon R. Salls. Hoel sold his half to Dave Vinokour in April of 1944. Ed and Ray McGraw bought the building but not the business from Kenneth Watson in May of 1944. Olaf Gerhard "O.G." Nordlie bought the business and moved into the building in August of 1944 from his other location, opening up Nordlie's Jack Sprat Grocery. His son Kenneth "Bud" came home from the war and joined O.G. as a partner in July of 1945. In 1951, O.G. changed the store's name to just Nordlie's Grocery. He sold the business to his son Bud in November of 1953. Bud moved it four doors south in December of 1954. James Otto's Milk Bar was here from early 1955 until March of 1958, when Otto closed it down. Gross Bros. Kronicks had a laundry pickup in the building in 1957. The Thomas Furniture store moved into the building in August of 1959.

Montgomery Ward's catalog and appliance store came here in November of 1964. They changed owners in January of 1969 when Kenneth E. Elstad took over. Herb and Lorna Roehn bought it in January of 1970. Then a Moose Bros. pizza place was here. Today there is still a pizzeria in the building. It is called Papa Sluigee's Pizzeria.

The "Cairncross Block" 1889. Ekbom's, Cairncross & Palm, and a millinery.

98. 223 Sibley Avenue North. (36 Sibley in the early days and then 720 Sibley Avenue in the early 1900s.) Some buildings developed a personality. That is, the types of tenants were always the same; jewelry business, drug store, or hardware, as this building had from the turn of the century and on. Louis Ekbom's shoe business was here in the next

location in 1870. Ekbom owned this lot and the one to the north in 1871. The building here was twenty by thirty feet and two-stories high, costing $1000 to build. Ekbom started his business by walking to Minneapolis to buy leather. Then he bought an ox and a cart and drove it back here, where he sold the ox and cart and started making shoes. He added groceries to his line in August of 1878. Mrs. Weems had a millinery here in the north side of Ekbom's store in March of 1879. In 1881, the Stevens and Company bank was here in the wooden building for a short time. It was also known as the Stevens and Branham Bank. At the rear of the bank was the real estate office of the Per Ekstrom and August T. "Gus" Koerner and Company in 1883. They also did loans and sold insurance. Per Ekstrom was Litchfield's first fire chief in 1877. Koerner had started in the business elsewhere in town in 1879. The bank moved up the street to the new building next to Harris Drug in October of 1985. Col. C. M. Lovelace moved his confectionery and ice cream store here in December of 1885 and then next door in March of 1886. Jim Ostrander had a barbershop here also in December of 1885. He closed in February of 1886. Alex Cairncross and John Palm built a new double brick building here and on the lot to the north in the June of 1886 and moved their general store business here. Louis Ekbom took on a partner named A. H. Lofstrom in March of 1889 and they moved down the street after buying the building from Cairncross. William H. Johns and Patrick Casey, Jr. had their Johns and Casey Hardware here in February of 1892 after Casey had bought into Johns' established business elsewhere in town. Casey was from Ireland. Johns and Casey moved out to the Welch building (Sibley Antiques) in November of 1892. J. D. Hayford leased the rear room here in December of 1892 for his feed store. In February of 1893, Cairncross and Palm was changed to John Palm and Company and it moved here while the new building was erected next door.

The Johns and Casey hardware business came back as the original Johns Brothers Hardware in the early 1900s, with owners William H. and D. B. Johns. The Johns brothers moved across the street in 1914. James R. Watson had a second-hand store here after the Johns moved out. The Palmer, Happ and Company Hardware was here next in August of 1914. Frank A. Palmer, Fred T. "Fritz" Happ and James R. Watson owned it. Palmer sold his interest to the other owners and James' brother Andrew Watson in November of 1915. It became Watson-Happ & Co. Hardware. Frank L. Lindell bought them out in January of 1917 and it became the Lindell Hardware Company. In the early 1920s, the McNulty store was here, probably sharing the building. Lindell sold the hardware business to C.A. Genet and W. E. Bates in March of 1922. The hardware store was in the north half of this building in 1924, with the Albert E. Kronzer Cash Shoe Store in the south part of the building. The shoe store came in October of 1924. Bates sold his interest to C. A. Gleason in June of 1926. Gleason, in turn, sold his interest back to Genet in December of 1927. Genet sold out to Melvin H. Robie in May of 1928. Kronzer was forced out when H.W. Houd bought the business from Robie in July of 1928 and wanted to expand. Kronzer moved to the basement of the Robertson building. E. F. Boetcher put his plumbing business into the rear of Houd Hardware in July of 1929. Otto H. Werner had the plumbing business in November of 1929.

H.W. Houd sold his business to G. W. Stevenson and J. W. Brenner in June of 1932. Their Stevenson-Brenner Hardware was here until March of 1934 when they went out of business. Litchfield Hardware, located down the street, bought their remaining goods for its store. Kenneth C. Watson moved his radio repair shop into the back in late 1933. Harry Radunz moved his Harry's Tire Shop into the building in April of 1934. Werner moved to another location in February of 1935. Radunz built a new building out on east Highway 12 and moved out there in October of 1936. Various people owned a Coast To Coast store here after that. E. J. Eliason moved his Coast To Coast here from the Robertson building in November of 1936. Martin Luedtke bought the store from Eliason in August of 1937. He called it Mart's Coast To Coast. In 1939, Ed "Eeks" Nelson's Sign & Awning Company was in the back of the building. He later moved down the alley. Ed and Ray McGraw bought the building but not the business from Kenneth C. Watson in May of 1944. Einar H. Jensen came home from the service and re-opened his radio service shop in the back in January of 1946. Luedtke sold the business to his brother and sister-in-law, Henry A. and Lucille Luedtke in June of 1948. After Henry died, Lucille sold half of the business to her manager, Bill McGraw.

In June of 1960, Bill sold his interest back to Lucille. She turned around and sold the entire business to Wallace Lloyd "Wally" Hanson in July of 1960. In the mid-fifties, Harry's Tire Shop was back behind the store in the alley. Heartland Community Action is here today.

221 Sibley Avenue North. The upstairs at the last location was known for years as Watson Hall and was used for meetings and dances. But Watson was downstairs eighteen years after the building was erected in 1886. The Odd Fellows met up there in October of 1889.

The Commercial Club was up there until 1917. It was a forerunner of the Chamber of Commerce. When the high school burned down in 1929, Watson Hall was used as a classroom. W. I. Booth moved his pool hall upstairs in late 1922 where the Knights of Columbus eventually had their meeting room.

Carl Gilbertson had a ham radio broadcasting station upstairs in December of 1931. In the mid and late thirties, the International Order of Odd Fellows had a clubroom upstairs. Watson Hall became a Youth Center for a few months in January of 1944. In May, the Youth Center was moved to the fire hall. At sometime the upstairs here became apartments. I lived up there for a few months in 1970.

100. 219-219 ½ Sibley Avenue North. I don't have much history on the next building. In June of 1876, Phineas "Pat" Cary rented the building that was here for his store but he moved out in a couple of months. During that same month, George Armstrong Custer and 250 soldiers, ignoring warnings of a massed Sioux army of 2,000 to 4,000 men, attacked the forces of Sitting Bull and Crazy Horse at the Little Big Horn. John Snell moved his furniture business into the building for a short time in 1878 while his new building was being erected. Snell, who came to Litchfield in 1877, was from Sweden. The building was sold to Charles A. Brasie in October. The wooden building here was torn down and the lot stood vacant for years. Col C. M. Lovelace built a small wooden building here in late 1885 and moved his confectionery and ice cream parlor here in March of 1886. His building was torn down or moved and the site became an alley from the late 1880s and on until the city closed it in February of 1946.

Harry Radunz had a small shop in the rear alley here, overlapping the lot to the north, and he put a new front on it in October of 1936 for his tire repair and junk business. He then moved out on east Highway 12, when he built a new building. Ray McGraw built a brick building here later in October of 1946. Berquist Electric Company occupied that new building in December of 1946 for its third location before they moved across the street. Leland Eckerman had a radio repair shop here in March of 1947. Then Tom Hasbrouck's Litchfield Furniture Mart was here in April of 1949. It was changed to the Thomas Furniture Mart after Frank H. Thomas bought Tom's business in March of 1950. Frank moved his business up the street to the Red Owl building and Tobkin's Jewelry came to this location in August of 1956.

Tobkin sold out to his junior partner Marvin "Bill" Stewart in January of 1960. Albin "Al" and Laura Tostenrud, who owned the building eventually, sold it to Bill Stewart in July of 1960. Stewart's jewelry business was sold to Lyman Dale sometime in the late sixties or early seventies. Today the Chamber of Commerce/Community Development office is here.

101. 217 Sibley Avenue North. (34 Sibley in the early days and 722 Sibley Avenue in the early 1900s.) Next I arrive at the *Independent Review* newspaper building location. Originally, Andrew P. and B. P. Nelson started a general store here) in a new building in May of 1871. It was called A. Nelson and Brother's "Skandanavian Store" (that's the spelling they used. The Nelsons were from Sweden.

Andrew
Nelson in
the 1880s.

The Nelson building, a twenty-four by sixty foot one, was built in May of 1871. B. P. Nelson built a house at 316 Sibley Avenue South in 1903. It became the Johnson-Hagglund Funeral Home. At some time the Nelson's nephew Andrew C. Johnson was brought in as a partner. He was also from Sweden. Andrew P. Nelson owned the land at this site, but, later, Andrew Johnson owned the building. He bought up several buildings as investments and years later his son, mortician Dewey E. Johnson, did the same thing. The Nelson brothers' interest was sold to the Cairncross brothers, Alex and Stewart, in August of 1874. The Cairncrosses were from Scotland. Alex Cairncross then left to venture out on his own in 1877 and Stewart Cairncross was Johnson's sole partner. In January of 1880, the Johnson and Cairncross partnership ended. The business became Cairncross and Brothers, but they moved it elsewhere in town. In April of 1886, Alex Cairncross came back and erected a new building here, moving the old one to Ramsey Avenue directly behind this location. Oddly, Andrew C. Johnson moved in and got back into the business. He took on new partners for another general store. His partners kept changing. This time the business was (Peter) Nelson, Johnson and (Lewis F.) Larson's. Lewis F. Larson had come to

420

Meeker County in 1857 from Sweden. The business moved down the street in the late 1880s. Dr. Karl E. "Henry" Cassel had his first office in Litchfield upstairs in April of 1899. In September of 1890, John Birch and Rasmus Nelson moved their clothing business here from the Masonic building. Rasmus was from Denmark. The United Workmen met upstairs starting in May of 1891. Birch bought out Nelson in April of 1892.

In May of 1909, Birch closed his store because Henry Isaac "H. I." Peterson bought the building for his printing office and moved into part of it. Birch moved his business elsewhere in November. In 1917, the newspaper took over the entire building and in the late twenties and early thirties the building's sign simply stated *Litchfield Independent*.

Litchfield's weekly newspaper, the *Independent Review* is actually a combination of two papers. One was the *Litchfield Saturday Review*, which was begun in June of 1884 by Reverend Lewis A. Pier and his brother Fred A. Pier. John T. Mullen, a local department store owner, was the editor and publisher. Fred quit the business and Lewis had it alone. Frank H. Haven bought the paper in April of 1887. It was later called the *Litchfield Review* after John T. Mullen bought it. Charles W. "Hans" Wagner bought the paper on January 1, 1898.

Frank H. Haven

The other paper was the *Litchfield Independent*, which a stock company of E. P. Peterson, Al Sanders and Nathan C. Martin began publishing on May 30, 1876. A month later, Martin was out. In 1878, Sanders sold his interest to Henry Isaac "H. I." Peterson, a brother to E. P. Peterson. E. P. traded his interest to H. I. for a cow. In March of 1920, W. D. Joubert sold his *News-Ledger* to Charles W. Wagner and H. I. John M. Harmon bought the paper from H. I. in May of 1937. The *Independent* and the *Review* merged in September of 1939, with H. I.'s grandson John M. Harmon and Charles W. Wagner as co-publishers. Wagner sold his interest to Raymond Lenhard in February of 1946. In

421

the fall of 1952, a new building was erected here. Vernon Madson bought Lenhard's interest in the paper in January of 1971. Vern was mayor in 1971 also. Stan Roeser bought an interest in January of 1973. During that same month, Richard Nixon was sworn in as President for his second term. John Harmon sold his interest to Madson and Roeser in January of 1979.

The *Litchfield Independent* had first been published in a small wooden building where the Mortenson Shoe Store and later Kate's Café was. Some of the early subscriptions to the *Litchfield Independent* were paid for with cordwood, farm produce or muskrat skins. The paper was moved to the future site of the Peterson Implement Company on Depot Street West, and then across from the Produce at the corner of Ramsey Avenue and "Wall Street". Wall Street was another name for Depot Street. I don't know why they called it that. The *Independent* began publication in 1876 during the famous Grasshopper Plague of 1873 to 1877.

Henry Isaac "H. I." Peterson

Litchfield has had nine newspapers over its early years. Four of them were the *Meeker County News*, the *Litchfield Independent*, the *Litchfield Saturday Review*, and the *Litchfield Ledger*, later called the *News-Ledger*. Frank Daggett and W. D. Joubert started the *Ledger* in 1872. It was moved to a small building (ten by twenty-two feet, costing $500) where the back part of the Masonic Building would eventually go. Then there was the *Litchfield Republican*, published by Henry G. Rising next to the Tinkham House hotel (the Lake Ripley House) on January 24, 1871 and discontinued the following autumn. There was a short-lived humorous journal called the *Rambler*, which was started in 1876 for a few months by J. D. Hayford and N. P. Olson.

LITCHFIELD NEWS LEDGER.

W. D. Joubert

Finally there were a couple of Swedish papers and a Norwegian one. One of the Swedish papers was called *Svenska Folkets Allahanda*, which means "Swedish people of all kinds". Charles Ellis Peterson, L. Gisslow and John J. Erickson published it in Litchfield after moving it from Grove City in September of 1883. They published it in the Cary building next to the Lake Ripley House hotel and went out of business in July of 1884. Charles and his brother John had a wagon making business in the 1870s. Franz Herman Widstrand published the other Swedish paper, which was called the *Rothuggaren*. That's Swedish for "root chopper" or "root lifter". It was a radical paper and Widstrand's views against women didn't set well. The paper didn't last long. Kettil Stensrud began publication of the Norwegian paper, called the *Heimdal*, in October of 1890. It also quickly folded

Today the *Independent Review* is still being published at this location along with the *Meeker County Advertiser*.

The last two buildings on the right are Silverberg-Olson/D&B and the Independent Newspaper building with "shoes" on the side from when Birch's clothing store was there.

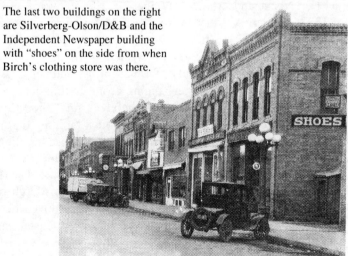

423

102. 215-215½ Sibley Avenue North. (32 Sibley in the early days.) As I said, some stores developed a "personality". The next building seemed to always have a grocery store in it. Well, from the turn of the century and on. The building I refer to had Joseph Mills' jewelry store in 1870. It was a one-story fourteen by twenty-four foot building costing $500 to build. Although Mills owned the lot, another small building was on it in a couple of years. Andrew O. Palmquist and Noreen had a tailor shop in that building for a while, starting in June of 1873. Andrew O. Palmquist was assistant fire chief from 1909 to 1912 and fire chief from 1912 to 1914. Daniel Feeney had a barbershop somewhere in the building also in 1873. Palmquist was alone in 1874. He also sold Weed and Sigwaltz sewing machines and took on a partner named Nels B. Anderson in 1874. Joseph Mills died in April of 1874, and his widow, Mrs. C. A. Mills, ran the jewelry store for a while. Then she shut it down for a short time and then re-opened the store in 1876. Clarence Jones had a jewelry store here in about 1876. Jones quit the business in February of 1880. In September of 1879, Mrs. William Richardson had a millinery here. She closed it in August of 1880. W. J. Nytes moved his jewelry store in the building in April of 1880. W. C. Waite had a music store here in 1880 selling pianos and organs. It closed in February of 1882. "Professor" Charles Griswold Topping rented the room that Nytes had occupied for his barbershop in August of 1886. Topping was from New York and had settled in Greenleaf before moving to Litchfield. John A. McColeman bought the barbershop in November of 1887. McColeman was born in Kentucky. Andrew Palmquist sold his tailor business to J. N. Nelson and Andrew Winger (Nelson & Winger) in September of 1887. Robert A. Vorys, who moved his restaurant all over town, moved it in here in May of 1890. Hiram or Clark Angell, Jr., sons of the pioneer photographer, had a confectionery here in 1890. By 1891, Otho H. Campbell owned the lot. In July of 1892, former butcher C. W. Cofield opened up a barbershop her, changing from cutting meat to cutting hair. Sam Brown then had his harness shop here for a short time in October of 1892. Then John Palm built a new brick building on the lot in 1894. It was called the John Palm General Merchandise building. Obviously, John Palm had a general merchandise store here. C. S. Sherwood had a plumbing business in the rear in the early 1890s. The (J. T.) McNulty and (A.) Helgeson hardware moved in here in March of 1898. They took on a partner, William Von Kuster, who moved here from across the street. Their store was called McNulty, Von Kuster and Helgeson.

In June of 1901, I. N. Wheeler bought out Von Kuster and joined the business. A.O. Bakken bought out Wheeler and Helgeson in May of 1903 and the hardware became McNulty and Bakken and then McNulty and Company, when the March brothers bought in. McNulty bought them out in August of 1904 and the store became J. T. McNulty & Co. Hardware. In February of 1908, McNulty sold out to Ole N. Vig and William H. Johns. The store known as Vig & Johns Hardware opened up in April of 1908. William H. Johns and D. B. Johns bought out Vig and they started their Johns Brothers' hardware here in February of 1912. After they moved out, Vig came back with a general store called Vig's Store around 1915. Vig quit the business in June of 1921 and sold the building to Clarence E. Silverberg and Nels H. Olson who had a grocery store and dry goods store here called Olson & Silverberg Inc. for a couple of years, and then Fairway. Then it became just Olson's Fairway, when Silverberg sold out in the summer of 1928. It was moved down near the hotel in March of 1929. They had shared the building with and then sold the dry goods part to Charles M. Doty and R. S. Braisted for their D & B Store Company. D & B then took over the whole store building after Fairway moved out.

Doty sold out to Braisted in September of 1931, but the store closed in April of 1932. N. J. Narum brought in an A & P, Great Atlantic and Pacific Tea Company store, here. He called it The Food Store and it was eventually run by Donald "Donnie" and Lucille Wheeler. It closed in March of 1943. Nels H. Olson bought the building in December of 1942 and the A & P moved across the street. Nels H. Olson remodeled the store and opened his Food Market, also called the Red & White store, starting in October of 1943. Then druggist Percy E. Waller's Food Market, owned by Nels, Percy, and Anton H. Schager, was here. In the forties, the *Meeker County News* was published from the basement here. Phil Palm owned the paper and he sold part of it to Lucas John "Luke" Heron. Eventually the newspaper was merged with the *Independent Review*. In February of 1946, Ed Bromberg opened his meat market in the rear of the Red & White and in March, Nels was out and Waller and Schager had the grocery. It was called Waller's Red & White. Ernest E. Heglund and his son, Wayne, took over the grocery in February of 1948, and although it was still a Red & White, they called it Heglund's Food Market. Robert W. Kruger, a buttermaker from the Kingston Creamery, bought out the Heglunds in April of 1948. In January of 1949, Theodore W. "Ted" Kohlhoff bought the business and had his second location for his Star Grocery/Super Valu. The first Super Valu had been across the street from here originally. Kohlhoff was Litchfield's mayor in 1952 and he moved in December of 1954 into his new building at 216 Marshall Avenue, where the new library is today. Kenneth "Bud" Nordlie's Groceries and Waldemar "Butch" Swenson's Meats moved here in December of 1954, sharing the building. Bud had been in the *Litchfield Saturday Review* building next door to the southeast corner of Sibley Avenue and Second Street where Nicola's is today. In November of 1955, Bud and Butch aligned with IGA. Bud then sold to the Variety Foods IGA wholesale firm in July of 1958 and Bob Olson managed his half. I knew the store simply as Nordlie's IGA. The name Nordlie cropped up many times on Litchfield businesses.

Doffing's Smart Wear, owned by Esther Doffing, opened here in March of 1960. Esther sold it to Mr. and Mrs. E. C. Chubb in the late sixties. The store closed and the building stood vacant until Maureen Jackman opened Treasured Keepsakes here.

Doffing's in 1969.

103. 213 Sibley Avenue North. (30 Sibley in the early days.) The next store location was on a lot owned by Virgil Homer Harris. Justice James Benjamin Atkinson, Jr. built and owned a building here. It was twenty by sixty-four feet, two-stories high and cost $1500 to build. In August of 1872, John Patten and Jacob "Jake" Koerner had a meat market here for a while. Patten sold his interest to Gottlieb "Jake" Keller in September of 1872. The Jake partnership of Keller and Koerner dissolved in February of 1873 and Koerner moved down the street. In the early 1870s, Louis Ekbom had a shoe shop here. In January of 1880, the Charley Taylor and Chauncey Butler butcher shop was here. Their partnership dissolved sometime in 1880 and Charley left to have a shop across from the park. Alexander Cairncross' Boots and Shoes store was here in August of 1881. He started to sell groceries and dry goods too. Charley Taylor was back here with his meat market in January of 1882. In January of 1885, John Palm became Alex Cairncross' partner and the business was called the Cairncross and Palm store. Edward J. "Ed"

426

Gould moved his harness shop in the back here in October of 1886. C. S. Sherwood moved his grocery store here in November of 1888. A furniture business owned by Fayette Kelley and George Raine was here in December of 1888, sharing the building, and the Louis Ekbom and Company shoe store moved a few doors from here. In March of 1889, Ekbom was back with the A. H. Lofstrom and their Ekbom and Lofstrom store. C. L. Anderson and Orlando Simons (in Cairncross' old stand) bought the Kelley and Raine furniture business here in June of 1889. Nels Lueken brought his shoe repair business in the rear of Ekbom and Lofstrom's here in July of 1889. The Anderson and Simons' business moved to the Howard building near the Meeker County Bank in June of 1890 while Cairncross put up a new building here. They planned to move back, but didn't. By 1891, Otho H. Campbell owned the lot here. James T. Chinnock Boots and Shoes business came here in 1890, buying Ekbom and Lofstrom's business. Chinnock was born in Ohio. The business was sold in March of 1892 after Chinnock had a fire in January of 1892. The fire ruined his stock forcing him to close in March of 1892. A. L. Shore bought his business in mid-1892. In May of 1892, Harry M. Angier moved his confectionery business in here. In July, he sold it to his brother, Quincy H. Angier. Harry Angier was Litchfield's twenty-third mayor in 1904. Quincy sold the business to Clarence A. Perry and Clark Angell, Jr. in October of 1892. Perry bought out Angell in April of 1893 and sold the confectionery to D. C. Beach. Perry came back in May of 1894. Frank McConville had a confectionery here also in mid-1893. A 1800s photograph shows a restaurant here called Bill's Lunch. There was a Bill's Lunch in the thirties and forties in town also.

Fred L. Gamer had a Phonograph Parlor here in November of 1911, selling phonographs and recordings. Gamer went bankrupt in April of 1914 and he sold his stock to Herman M. Hershey, who had a store elsewhere in town. In the early 1920s, the Albert E. Kronzer Cash Shoe Store was upstairs. Albert had to leave when Harry A. Hanson bought the lot and the old wooden building or buildings were torn down. A new brick one was constructed. In March of 1925, Hanson opened a café or Dairy Shop and he had his Litchfield Ice Cream Company in the rear of the building. During that same month, Calvin Coolidge was sworn in as President for his second term. Hanson had started his ice cream factory in 1914 elsewhere in town.

Phil J. Palm owned the revived *Meeker County News* in the basement, which was the Litchfield Printing Company in July of 1933. He took over from H. S. Johnson. The Litchfield Produce bought the ice cream factory and dairy from Hanson in February of 1934. Hanson kept the front restaurant. In 1935, Hanson changed the name of the cafe to Hanson's Tastee Shop. There was a large milk bottle sign on the front of the building with the words "Dairy Products" on it. Leslie Chapin's Electric Service moved into the basement in November of 1936. Hanson closed the café in February of 1944 and the Litchfield Ice Cream Company took over the whole building. During WWII, this building was the Meeker County Headquarters for War Loans. Olson's Hardware was here in 1949, and the Northern States Power's offices were here also. The *Meeker County News* merged with the *Independent Review* in '51 or '52. The Northwestern Bank was here for a while starting in March of 1952 while their new building at the corner to the south was being erected. Then Sederstrom's Realty or Real Estate came here in March of 1953. Victor and his brother Vern Sederstrom bought the building from Harry A. Hanson in September of 1952, when the bank moved back to its corner location. Their Sederstrom's Realty Company occupied the building, along with Chet Berg's auctioneering business. Hugo Heimdahl Insurance, Roy E. Anderson Accounting and also the State Farm Insurance office were also in here.

Larry Swenson moved his Larry's Barber Shop here in 1969. Then Larry Ackerman bought the building from Swenson and moved his barbershop, also called Larry's, in April of 1972. Alva "Al" Larson Insurance (State Farm) was in a part of the building also in the mid-sixties and on. Larry's Barber Shop, owned by Ackerman, is still here today. There are apartments upstairs.

Larry's in 1969.

105. 209 Sibley Avenue North. (28 Sibley in the early days.) The first building we come to south of Sederstrom's had more than one store occupying the building at a time, as did a lot of the buildings in town. The very first business I can find here was a book and notion store owned by W. W. Page in early 1872. Page moved down the street in

mid-1872 to partner with Alex Cairncross for a very short period. Mrs. C. M. Kelley's Millinery was here in a small wooden building in 1873. Cash C. Eddy had a confectionery here in March of 1875. He sold it to J. O. Barkham in July of 1875 and Barkham sold it to J. W. Billings in late 1875. Billings called it the Boss Confectionery and sold it to George W. Gordon in March of 1877. Gordon moved it to another location. Mrs. Kelley's husband, Justice of the Peace Fayette Kelley, owned the building and he started a photography business along with the millinery in February of 1881. James H. Morris moved his grocery business and the Post Office here in 1879. He gave up the grocery in October of 1880 to devote time solely to the Post Office. Mrs. Learned had a schoolroom in the front of the building around this time. The J. Edward Upham and Waldemar W. "Walt" Johnson Metropolitan Drug Store was here in the front of the building also starting in January of 1881, after Mrs. Learned vacated the room. Along with drugs and paints, they also sold revolvers. Upham was born in New Brunswick, Canada. Two men named Graffort and Smith had a grocery business in the back. They sold the business to Charles Griswold Topping, the barber, in April of 1881. James Garfield had just been sworn in as the 20th President of the United States in the previous month. By January of 1883, Dr. George Newland bought the Upham interest in the drug store. They soon moved to the Howard House building south of here that same year. In October of 1885, Charles W. Johnson moved into the building in a room next to the Post Office. His store was called Cheap Charley's and he sold ready-made clothes, dry goods, boots and shoes. W. S. Wooley bought the lot and put up a new brick building in April of 1886. In April of 1887, Bigelow and Topping traded places. Alexander D. Ross took over as postmaster here in July of 1887. Ross worked out of Morris' store. John D. Peterson's tobacco shop was on the south side of the building in March of 1883. Peterson brought in a soda fountain to add to his business in May of that same year. Later John partnered with his brother William C "Billy" Peterson and the business became the Peterson Brothers' Tobacco and Candy Shop in June of 1887, with an awning that stated "Tobacco and Cigars". They had bought the building and the lot in March of 1887. At some point, it became just John D. Peterson's. Miss Christine Nygren had a millinery here in September of 1888. The Cheap Charley's store was sold in March of 1889. In March of 1891, Andrew Winger, an ex-tailor, bought the confectionery from Peterson. August T. Koerner became the postmaster in May of 1891 and he moved the Post Office to the Snell building until the new office was built into the rear of the First State Bank building. Koerner was born in Germany. In August of 1891, Otho H. Campbell bought the building and lot here. Sam B. Millard's jewelry store was here sharing the building in September of 1891. In September of 1892, Millard took over the entire building for a while, but moved down the street in 1896. Isadore Gruenberg's "Chicago Bargain House" store moved in here in October of 1892. John Palm and Company bought the building in 1893.

The Peterson brothers bought their confectionery back in March of 1902. In October of 1906, the Petersons bought the fountain from the Dillner Drug store for their shop, after the drugstore moved. Henry O. Morrison moved the Selz Royal Blue Shoe Store here into part of the building in March of 1915 also. Albert E. Kronzer took over the shoe store in September of 1915 when his father-in-law, Charles H. Dart, bought the business from Morrison. According to an old photograph, the simple word "Meals" was on this building's window awning and a giant Coca-Cola sign was on the building's face.

In the thirties the Coca-Cola sign was still on the building's facing, so I assume a café was still here. J. W. "Bill" Williams' Bill's Lunch moved here in September of 1935. It was also called William's Café. Clem A. Becker's Shoe Service and harness repair came in August of 1943 and he had his second store location here up to the fall of 1952. Tostenrud Jewelry bought the building in April of 1945 as an investment, when I was born. Roosevelt had just died in January and Harry Truman was sworn in as the 33rd President of the United States. Becker moved to the corner of Marshall Avenue and Third Street in the fall of 1952, after buying the E. H. Snow Hatcheries building in September of 1952. His first store was west of the Northwestern National Bank in the Campbell building, where Fred Maass ended up. This building was torn down in March of 1954 and an addition to Whalberg's was erected. There are apartments upstairs today over Dueber's Department Store at this location and the next.

106. 207 Sibley Avenue North. (26 Sibley in the early days and then 732 Sibley Avenue North in early the 1900s.) W. W. Page and Alex Cairncross had a general store sharing this next site with another building in mid-1872. Page sold out to Cairncross in October of 1872. For some reason, one of the buildings here was called the "1873 building" and it was later moved north across from the park to make room for a new brick building here. The Greenleaf hardware store moved here in March of 1877. During that same month, Rutherford B. Hayes was sworn in as the 19th President of the United States. W. P. Todd, a brother of J. G. Todd who had a dry goods store in town, bought the twenty-five by sixty

foot two-story building from Greenleaf in September of 1877, who moved to another Sibley location. Todd traded businesses with O. B. Knapp and his brother who had a store in Darwin. The Knapps moved in here in June of 1879. In May of 1878, W. S. Wooley bought one of the buildings and his stove and hardware store was here. Fred Johnson, a black barber, moved into a part of the building in April of 1880. I believe John Paulson had a meat market here before 1882. He moved to another location. John Beckstrand had his first shoe repair store here in October of 1884. Starting in October of 1885, Theodore Ehlers and Charley Shaw, no relation to me, had a flour and feed store here to sell the grains from their mill and elevator that was over by the hotel. Edward J. "Ed" Gould moved his harness shop here in November of 1886. The Krueger brothers, Herman, August and Albert, came in with a general merchandise store in the early 1890s. It was called the Krueger Brothers Dry Goods store. Herman came to Meeker County in 1857. A. Nelson and Company's Minneapolis Cash Store was here in part of the building in the early 1890s. It went out of business in September of 1892. One of the buildings on the lot was sold to Almon Knight in December of 1892. Knight moved it to the residential area of town to convert it into a house. The other building was moved across from the park. The Krueger brothers bought the lot in February of 1893 and erected a new building here in September of 1893.

J. Skoll bought out the Krueger brothers in September of 1901 and the store became the Toggery Clothing Company. During that same month, Leon Czolgoz assassinated President McKinley at the Pan-American Exhibition in Buffalo, N. Y. and Theodore Roosevelt was sworn in as the 26th President of the United States. B. Berman had a fruit and confectionery business here in July of 1904. He called it The Arcade. He went bankrupt shortly after. The Krueger brothers came back in September of 1905, but went out of business again in November of 1906. William F. Bierman, father of Gopher legend Bernie Bierman, bought the building in July of 1908 and started his clothing business over again. William went on to be a bookkeeper for Minar Ford. Max H. Greenberg's Department Store, also called the New Store, leased the building from Bierman in May of 1912 and moved in here for a short time. He moved out in June of 1917. Emma Swanson moved her Park Bazaar restaurant here from across from the park in August of 1917. She renamed it the Silver Grill and had orchestras playing on her two opening nights and served something called Pink Tea to her guests. She sold the restaurant to George Becker in October of 1920. Emma Swanson opened the Swanson Variety Store here in October of 1922. I believe the Silver

Grill was moved into the basement at that time. Then the Swanson sisters, Emma and Esther Hanft, owned the Variety Store upstairs. Elmer O. Whalberg, Warren's dad, bought the business from Emma in December of 1925 and established his Whalberg's V Store in this building. His son Warren became a partner in 1946. In 1954, Warren bought out his dad. He expanded the store to include the building north of here. Warren kept the store going into the sixties. In January of 1928, the Judge Herman M. Hershey Music Store, also known as the Hershey Phonograph Company, was also in the building selling band instruments, phonographs and records. Hershey was a justice of the peace and he used to anger court officials because he would fine people just enough to pay for his fee or the "court costs". That was all. Whalberg wanted to expand and so Hershey left in August of 1928.

After Whalberg's closed, the store became Ohland's Ben Franklin. Today it is Dueber's Department Store.

There were some businesses upstairs over the previous location. In April of 1921, August "Auggie" Okeson's tailor shop was there over the Silver Grill and in August, Mrs. E. J. Rodange or Jennie S. Rodange moved her millinery upstairs after she had a fire down the street.

Auggie Okeson moved out and went to a room over the fire hall in July of 1936. In the 1950s, L.V. Larson, surely related to M. B. Larson the band instructor, sold band instruments upstairs. Somewhere, the National Land Bank Loans office was in the building in 1959. It was probably upstairs.

107. 205 Sibley Avenue North. (24 Sibley in the early days and then 734 Sibley Avenue in the early 1900s.) The lot in the next location, again heading south, had Robert F. Gordon and W. S. Knappen's National Billiard Hall in 1870. James B. Atkinson, Jr. owned the twenty by sixty-four foot building on the lot. It cost $1500 to build. Postmaster/clothier Horace B. Johnson owned the lot in 1871. He also owned the corner lot next door. Gordon sold his interest to Knappen in January of 1872. Knappen partnered with someone named Scott in August of 1873 and they built a new building in the next block to the south on the east side of Sibley Avenue for a "hotel" and restaurant. Conrad Juul built Litchfield's first brick building here and opened a general store in August of 1878. Other sources say the first brick building was the Bank of Litchfield's building in the next block, but that wasn't built until 1891. Andrew Tharalson bought the "Juul building" in January of 1879. He and his brother Nels opened a general merchandise

432

store here. Nels Tharalson managed it, as Andrew Tharalson was busy with his grocery store in Minneapolis. The Tharalson name was put on the building and was visible there in old photographs for many years after the business ended. Tharalson's building was twenty feet wide and sixty feet deep. A new building was erected in the rear by J. Husser and Company in September of 1882. It was a machinery warehouse. Phineas "Pat" Cary bought it. I don't know if he did anything with it other than lease it out. Peter W. Johnson had a hardware here sometime in the 1880s. Sivert Olson went into partnership with Andrew F. Nordstrom in November of 1883 selling groceries, sewing machines, pianos and organs here. In January of 1884, they sold the sewing machine and music business to DeCoster, who had a store north of here, and they closed the grocery. In February of 1890, the Tharalsons closed their business and sold their building and lot to Andrew F. Nordstrom and Company and they were back with their grocery, dry goods and shoe business. Olson and Payne had a farm implement business here, probably in the back. The building was moved next to the fire hall in late 1892 so that a new brick building could be constructed here. Nordstrom had gone out of business and a group bought his goods and sold them elsewhere in town.

Frederic William Lucas and William H. Johns started the Litchfield Hardware Company here in August of 1900. In January of 1902, the hardware expanded to include the Hanson building in the rear of the bank building to the south of here, (22 Second Street West), becoming an upside down and backwards "L" shape. The hardware building wrapped itself around the bank building next door. You could get into the hardware and the plumbing and heating business in back from Sibley Avenue or from Second Street. In March of 1908, William H. Johns retired and Lucas kept the business. It was later called Our Own Hardware. In the mid 1910s, Albin J. Nelson had his plumbing and heating business back there. Then Lucas owned the hardware himself, employing Emil W. Anderson. In July of 1913, the hardware had a fire. Coincidentally, Nelson was Litchfield's fire chief from 1924 to 1926. The hardware was moved to the middle of the 200 block of Ramsey Avenue North in the "Palm warehouse" until the building here could be fixed. In 1919, Emil Anderson bought into the business. After Lucas died, his widow sold the rest of the business to Emil and Walfred J. Lund in January of 1925.

The plumbing business in back was taken over by Earl Hutchins and Patrick J. Campbell in the mid-thirties. Earl was Litchfield's assistant fire chief from 1938 to 1940 and fire chief from 1941 to 1943. The plumbing partnership dissolved in November of 1937 and Campbell kept the shop here. In October of 1944, Dewey E. Johnson bought the building from the Peter E. Hanson estate, but didn't move a business in. He also bought the building across from the park where the *Meeker County News* had been published, after they folded. Campbell's plumbing and heating business was sold to William "Bill" Harder in March of 1949. Richard C. "Dick" Olander and his wife Lillian bought Anderson's half of the hardware in July of 1952. In February of 1956, Olander bought the other half of the store from Lund, who died shortly after that.

Olander sold the hardware to Ken Straley in April of 1967. Floyd Mottinger managed it for him. In November of 1970, Duane Larson and Dale Harmon owned the store. They turned it into a Hardware Hank store. Cynthia's Beauty Salon was here and today Patty Schultz' Styles On Sibley beauty salon is at this location.

203 Sibley Avenue North. (736 Sibley Avenue in the early 1900s.) These are the businesses that were above the last location. In 1883, Sivert Olson moved his restaurant upstairs at that location. Attorneys E. P. Peterson and William Kenney were upstairs in October of 1884. George Hickcox replaced Kenney. Dentist J. H. Bacon had his office and photography studio upstairs in 1885 in the room vacated by Peterson and Hickcox. Bacon was born in Maine and he was also a Justice of the Peace.

When a new building was completed here, the Bacon and Joseph P. Engstrom photography studio moved back in upstairs. It eventually became J. H. Bacon's dentistry and photo studio and another separate Engstrom's studio, after Bacon sold that part of the business to him. There was a dispute between those two, which resulted in Engstrom moving out and taking a lot of Bacon's things. It went to court and Bacon got his stuff back and reopened his studio in November of 1915. Clyde G. Crosby had his photo studio upstairs. He sold it to Arvid M. Rudberg in May of 1916. Rudberg moved out in 1917. Ella Leines had a beauty shop upstairs in 1926.

In November of 1951, Evelyn Pearson opened her Evelyn's Beauty Shop upstairs. Dr. J. W. Longworth moved his practice upstairs in September of 1959 into the room Dr. Bacon had been in. Today Attic Storage is up there.

From Left: First National Bank, Litchfield Hardware, Krueger Brothers' General Store and then the Peterson Brothers' confectionery.

109. 201 Sibley Avenue North. (22 Sibley Avenue North in the early days and then 738 Sibley Avenue in the early 1900s.) The last building on this block was originally Litchfield's first or second Post Office, depending on your way of thinking, and Postmaster Horace B. Johnson's clothing store in late 1869 or early 1870. The first Post Office was established on September 20, 1869 in John A. C. Waller's home. The newspaper tells us that Horace B. Johnson was the first postmaster, so Waller must not have been appointed, but he acted as a postmaster. So, Johnson's building, which was the second business building to go up in Litchfield, was the first "official" Post Office. It was a twenty-two by thirty-two foot two-story building, which cost $1850 to build. It was later expanded to twenty-two by sixty feet, with the addition going on in the rear. The Post Office was in Johnson's store, as was customary in the early days. The "Post Office" usually followed the postmaster to his place of business. Johnson's Post Office was nothing more than a wooden tool chest that the mail was deposited into when it arrived. It was dispensed to customers when they came in. Johnson was Litchfield's postmaster until April of 1874. Then he became President of the Village Council. The Post Office was moved into the Strobeck building across the street in the middle of the block in April of 1874 with Frank Daggett as postmaster. James H. Morris followed as postmaster there and he then moved the Post Office back to this side of the street a few doors north of here, where he had it for a few years. Then Alexander D. Ross took over as postmaster in Morris' building.

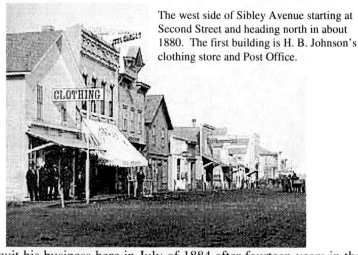

The west side of Sibley Avenue starting at Second Street and heading north in about 1880. The first building is H. B. Johnson's clothing store and Post Office.

Johnson quit his business here in July of 1884 after fourteen years in the business and he leased the location to S.W. Rankin for a hardware store in November of 1884. Rankin's Hardware had been the Rankin & Greenleaf Hardware, which started in April of 1883, at another location. Rankin had bought out Greenleaf in November of 1884. In April of 1887, a cement sidewalk was installed from the front of this corner location up to the alley north of here. It was a big deal before the turn of the century. The Johns Brothers and Charles O. F. "Charley" Youngstrom bought out Rankin and came in here in August of 1887 for one of the Johns' many locations around town. Charles O. F. Youngstrom bought out D. B. Johns' interest in March of 1889. In December of 1890, William H. Johns bought out Youngstrom, who retired, and brought his brother D. B. back into the business. So this building had the first Johns Brothers Company Hardware. Horace B. Johnson, who had built the wooden building here, moved the original front half west to the first lot after the alley (where Fred Maass had his dentistry), when, in March of 1891, the new Meeker County Bank purchased this location under Peter E. Hanson's name to build their bank on. The addition Johnson had put on was left here along with another building to its rear, which was dubbed the Hanson building. The hardware moved across the street, but construction didn't start on the bank building for a few years. Mrs. Swanson moved her restaurant into the Hanson building left here in December of 1892. Charles Henry Strobeck, pioneer lawyer, moved his office to a rear room there in February of 1893, after purchasing the building. Mrs. Swanson closed the restaurant in April of 1894. In May, Mrs. C. E. Adlerbjelke moved her restaurant in. John M. Learn moved a billiard hall into a room there

436

in July of 1896. He was assistant fire chief from 1895 to 1900 and Litchfield's twenty-second mayor in 1902. Mary McGowin moved her millinery into that room in October of 1897. Then she moved across the street. In May of 1898, the rest of the front building was moved west next to Payne and Larson's machinery warehouse in order for construction to finally begin on the new bank building. John T. Mullen and Company started a store in the rear half of the new bank building in September of 1898 and moved out in May of 1899.

In August of 1900, Col. Charles Hoyt March and Nelson D. March, brothers, moved their law offices to the rear room of the new bank building. Ned Egan had a pool hall and confectionery in the back of the building in May of 1901. He closed in December of 1901. In January of 1902, the Litchfield Hardware Company on Sibley Avenue north of the bank expanded to include the Hanson building in the rear of the bank. The Meeker County Bank became the old First National Bank in February of 1902. The name "Meeker County Bank" remained in cement over the door for a long time. Mr. Sandven bought the old Weeks' photo studio in the rear of the bank in June of 1909. The banks in town starting improving their security systems in March of 1925 after there was a rash of bank break-ins in Cold Spring, Prinsburg, Cosmos and Svea in 1924 and 1925. The newspapers referred to the robbers, who blew the safes with nitroglycerine, as "yeggs" or "yeggmen". I had read this term before in the early days of Litchfield, always referring to bad men, so I finally looked it up. The dictionary said "safecrackers or robbers", so now I know a new "old" word.

The bank's name was changed again to the Northwestern National Bank in August of 1930. The bank moved down the street to the "Ice Cream Company building" in March of 1952 for five months while this building was being remodeled. The bank moved back here in August of 1952.

The bank's ad before the front was remodeled.

437

The bank moved out in the mid-sixties. In April of 1969, the Litchfield Centennial Headquarters was here. Bill Falknor bought the building in September of 1970 and McGee Realty moved in from Depot Street. Today the Pizza Ranch occupies this building with Work Connection in the building also.

18 Second Street West. Upstairs over the buildings occupying this corner were several offices and businesses. John Nellis and J. William "Billy" Nelsan had a barbershop upstairs over the Rankin & Greenleaf hardware store in June of 1884 and Clark L. Angell had his photography business upstairs in August of 1885. By the way, Eastman invented the box camera during 1885. Nellis sold out to Nelsan in February of 1886, but the two got back together in other locations around town. D. W. Emery had his insurance, collection agency and loan office upstairs in April of 1886. In 1890, Dr. S. S. Squire, a homoeopathist, had his office over the Johns & Youngstrom Hardware. Dr. Squire was certainly a brother to S.W. Squire who owned a millinery in town. Dr. Robertson had his office here also before the turn of the century. Clark L. Angell took on a partner named William S. Weeks in his photography studio after the bank opened up. They moved in 1898 and S. H. Olson took the business over. An old photograph shows that a dentist named Alfred E. Hawkinson had his practice above the bank also.

W. Richard "Dick" Berens leased Peter E. Hanson's office upstairs in February of 1905. William Grono moved into an office upstairs for his tombstone business also. Joseph P. Engstrom's Photo Studio was upstairs in 1915. In the mid to late 1910s, Dr. W. E. Chapman, Dr. Hawkinson, the March brothers' law offices, and E. P. Peterson's law office were all upstairs.

In February of 1933, Patrick "P. J." Casey moved his law office into the office where E. P. Peterson's office had been. The Bureau of Credit Control, Inc. was upstairs in the mid-thirties and the Harold A. Olson photography studio was still upstairs in the late thirties. Olson sold his business to Kermit B. Hanson in October of 1944. Dr. John Herseth bought the dentistry business from Hawkinson in July of 1947, but sold it to Dr. H. M. Silverthorne in October. Wendell Nelson had his law office upstairs in the mid-fifties, as did attorneys Taylor C. Waldron and Leroy A. Gayner, who was also here in the mid-thirties.

When the bank was built at this corner and a basement was built, there were businesses downstairs also. In the early 1900s, the O. R. Lounsbury barbershop was in the basement with an entrance on Second

Street. The basement barbershop was sold to Clifford Wilson in May of 1907 and then bought back by Lounsbury in June. Then Lounsbury sold it to pioneer barber Ray Wheeler in February of 1908. Ray had been down the street. Wheeler sold his barbershop to G. L. Robins in January of 1910, but Robins turned right around and sold it to P. M. Danser in April of 1910. Danser sold it to Len Mellquist, who sold it back to Ray Wheeler in January of 1915. Tri-State Telephone and Telegraph Company office was in the basement, which had an entrance on the Second Street side by the door to the plumbing business and hardware next door. Rudberg sold his equipment to A. F. Stubbenberg in April of 1919 and Stubbenberg opened up in the Robertson building. Tri-State closed in February of 1919 and Northwestern Telephone bought all their equipment. In January of 1919, by the way, prohibition had just begun. Engstrom sold his business to Halver L. Olson in April of 1920.

Ray Wheeler leased his barbershop out to George Armstrong in June of 1942 and then sold it to Mac E. Steen in May of 1943. Steen moved out in 1946. I don't know what followed down here.

Occasionally, I'll leave Sibley Avenue to go to some other interesting buildings. I'll head west on Second Street around the corner from the Northwestern Bank building. Before the bank took up almost half the block, there was another small building behind Horace B. Johnson's clothing store building, just before the alley. It might have been the building I referred to as the Hanson building in the paragraph about the corner location. In 1871, the Mark Baldwin Harness Shop was in that building. It was a twelve by twenty-one foot one-story building costing $150. Baldwin quit his business in 1877. Aron J. Anderson moved a feed store building here somewhere between the small building and the next one west in May of 1879 to use as a machinery warehouse. He had a feed mill business elsewhere in town. Henry W. Adlerbjelke sold farm machinery from here in the early 1880s. In May of 1897, Charles W. Johnson (Cheap Charley) and John Thompson combined here for a machinery business under the name of Johnson and Thompson.

William "Billy" Hanley converted a building here or after the alley over to a roller skating rink in June of 1905. West of these buildings was an alley.

111. 24 Second Street West. (413 Second Street West in early 1900s.) In 1869, James Tinkham had a farm machinery business in the first building following the alley. It was Litchfield's first farm machinery business and Tinkham sold the McCormick brand. In 1872,

he took on a partner named John P. Scarp. Tinkham sold out to a man named Anderson in late 1872 and Scarp got the business himself in the mid-1870s. Scarp formed a partnership in 1879 with Albert L. McCargar and Dan Pineo. The firm was called John P. Scarp and Company. It was still here in the early 1880s. Christian Pederson came from St. Paul and started his harness shop here also in October of 1877. He moved to the Depot Street corner at Marshall Avenue and then to Sibley Avenue in July of 1878, but came back here in April of 1880 and moved Turner's old blacksmith building here. The Chris A. Bertelson & Nels "Milk" Olson Harness Shop was here in the early 1880s. Litchfield's first store building at the southwest corner of Sibley Avenue and Third Street was moved here in 1885 when a new brick building was erected on Heard's old location. After being burned out in his Sibley Avenue location, Hugh Dowling bought the building in September of 1886 and became a partner with Michael Hanses. In September of 1880, Johnny Oakes started a saloon here. In just a couple of months, he moved out to Marshall Avenue. Fayette Kelley and George Raine moved a furniture business here in November of 1888 and then out to another location in December. Litchfield's first postmaster, Horace B. Johnson, moved his clothing store to this wooden building in the early 1880s. He had started up at the corner on the lot that became the Northwestern Bank. Johnson sold his business to Nels M. Holm and Warren Johnson in January of 1884. They ran their Holm and Johnson clothing store here until they closed in March of 1885 and sold out to J. F. Fuller in April of 1885. At sometime realtor Peter E. Hanson bought the building. Henry T. Halverson, Jr.'s City Restaurant and bakery was here in 1888. S. I. Kulset rented the restaurant in 1889.

The building was leased to James Campbell[195] in May of 1914 for his harness business. Campbell eventually bought the building from Peter E. Hanson's widow in May of 1917. The Schultz Pool Hall and Bowling Alley was in part of the building in the early 1900s. Whether it was here or not, J. H. Johnson also had a bowling alley around this location which he sold in December of 1903 to G. W. Jorris. In March of 1912, Peter E. Hanson put up a new building here to lease out as a pool hall. Harry A. Hanson started his Litchfield Ice Cream Company in the rear in April of 1914. Then Elmer S. Noreen got the ice cream business, which he moved it to Sibley Avenue in 1919. He was the leader of the Noreen Orchestra that played around the area. In February of 1920, J.

---

[195] Campbell was born in Birmingham, England in 1871 and was raised in an orphanage in Canada, where he learned the harness trade. He came to Litchfield in 1893 and retired from the business in 1938.

440

William Williams had a tire repair shop in the rear where the ice cream factory had been. He moved it to the rear of the Settergren building. Delos Potter had his Central Radio Shop in the front part of the building in September of 1929 until he quit in September of 1931.

Back row: Dr. William Robertson, H. S. Johnson and James Campbell.

Front row: J. G. Morrison and Charles H. Dart.

J. Anton Johnson had a shoe store here starting in June of 1935. It must have shared the building with the harness shop. Clem A. Becker came in April of 1936 and had his first shoe repair business here along with James Campbell's harness shop. James W. Anderson had his insurance business office in the building in the mid-thirties and was still here in 1957. Campbell retired in 1938 and, in March of 1939, Becker bought out Campbell and took on both businesses. In August of 1943, Becker moved to the Peterson Brothers Building on Sibley. Mrs. Marvel Nelson brought in her Marvel Beauty Shop here in November of 1943. Harold Harding bought the building in May of 1946 for his Harding Quality Dry Cleaners to share the building with Ed "Eeks" Nelson, who had moved his sign painting shop into the rear in 1945. In April of 1946, Einar H. Jensen's radio repair shop was above Nelson. Marvel sold out to Mrs. Robert Nelson in August of 1946. Eeks took on a partner named Oliver Nordling, who had a car body repair business here in late 1947. The business was then called Nelson Sign & Body Company. John F. Decker had his Western Auto Supply or Western Auto Associate Store in the front of the building in September of 1950. Decker and Nelson were burned out May of 1951. Robert Sparboe moved his Sparboe Chick Company office here in 1954 for a short time until he moved to Second Street East in early 1956. Then Fred Maass had his dentistry at this location after his two-year stint in the army, sharing the building with the sign painting shop. Maass bought the building from Eeks in August of 1955, but Eek's sign shop remained in the rear. Right behind Maass' dentist office was Art Carlson's false teeth business. D. M. Murray, a veterinarian, had an office here also in 1957. Nelson's Sign Painting shop was still here in the rear in 1957 but it became Bill Harder's Plumbing and Heating in the early sixties.

My second cousin, Dick Birkemeyer bought Harder's business in the late sixties. He called his business Birkemeyer Plumbing and Heating. A store called Alley Boutique, owned by Claris Carlson, was in the rear in October of 1971. It sold "handcrafted artifacts". Dick Birkemeyer went into partnership with some other people in a business called J J & D Pumping Service, which headquartered here along with his plumbing business. In the late seventies, Dick took on a junior partner, Bob Grosskreitz. They had the B & G Plumbing and Heating. Bob was a brother to another classmate of mine, Richard Grosskreitz. Today the Ed Olson Rental garages are at this location.

1951: The north side of Second Street West. From the left: The vacant Maxson motors building, Ramsey Avenue, the Fire Hall, Dept. of Ag., Nelson's pool hall, Western Auto Supply, the alley and Harder plumbing and heating.

12. 26-28 Second Street West. Next, heading west, was a pool hall. At one time, around the turn of the century, Olaf M. "Feed Ole" Olson had a feed store here. I don't know what was here before that. In November of 1904, Olson bought the lot across the street and eventually built a brick building there. The earliest owner I can find of the pool hall here was Alfred Nordine in the early 1900s. Oscar Moberg opened a tailor shop here, possibly upstairs or in the rear, in July of 1908. The pool hall was sold to F. L. Peterson in October of 1910. Peterson had a lunch buffet here and C. W. Lentz moved a billiard hall in with him in April of 1912. Also in that same April, the Titanic struck an iceberg, and 1502 lives were lost because the ship did not carry enough lifeboats. Nels Bylund bought the poolroom from Lentz in December of 1912 and Clifford W. Johnson bought it in June of 1913. Peterson moved elsewhere. Litchfield went dry in April of 1914. Bylund took back the

pool hall in August of 1914 after Johnson purchased the Litchfield Pop Works from Nels Johnson. W. I. Booth had a poolroom here in February of 1922 after Bylund had moved out. Then Henry Eklund had the pool hall.

Eklund sold the pool hall to John L. Benson and Newel C. Nelson in February of 1930. In the forties, Art "Abe" Abrahamson owned the pool hall, but Newel C. Nelson got it back in May of 1951 when there was a bad fire next door. Art "Abe" Abrahamson got it back once again and it was known as Abe's Place in the mid-fifties. Milton Felt, brother to fifties and sixties high school football coach Howard Felt, owned it as Milt's Place in the sixties. Ray "Red" Oslund owned it in the late sixties and early seventies as Red's Pool Hall and Red & Joan's Pool Hall. Then it was Smokey's, owned by "Smokey" Vick, in the mid-seventies. Today there is a vacant lot here.

30 Second Street West. (403 Second Street West in the early 1900s.) Anderson Chemical and the old Fire Hall were the last two buildings on this block. Originally the David Gorman livery stable was here in one or both of the locations. Gorman was from Canada. F. P. Zimmerman and Joseph "Joe" Barth had a farm machinery business in the Anderson Chemical lot in 1886. Zimmerman committed suicide in May of 1886 by slitting his throat at the Litchfield House. Nels Olson had a harness shop at the location in the late 1880s.

Henry J. Rodange started the New Cash Produce House or the Rodange Produce Company here in March of 1908. In the twenties, the Alfred Anderson creamery was here to the west of Rodange. Anderson got out of the creamery business, leased the building to the U. S. Department of Agriculture in the forties and stayed with the chemical business, with the plant west of here, when he moved his offices here in March of 1957. Rodange closed his business in November of 1929 and sold it to Isaac N. Mayou in January of 1930. Mayou called it the Farmer's Produce.

Mayou sold his produce to Alfred Anderson next door in April of 1932. Anderson was the mayor at that time. There must have been a small building between Anderson and the fire hall at one time because Ed Lindwall had his shoe sales and repair shop there in October of 1933. He moved it into his home February of 1935. Curves, a woman's fitness center, occupied this site and the corner site to the west today.

55. The old fire hall was built in 1886. Around late 1900, whatever building was at this location, probably the fire hall, became the town hall because the new Opera House had been built in the old town hall

location. Upstairs in the building here was a large meeting room and a few smaller rooms.

The old Fire Hall in 1889.

1906: Second Street West. Lounsbury's livery (3rd bldg.) and the fire hall.

At one time, starting in July of 1936, August "Auggie" Okeson had his tailor shop up there. A youth club met up there also. There was a horseshoe pit behind the fire hall for the men to pitch shoes in. In late 1892, a building that was north of the new bank building at the Sibley Avenue corner was moved where the horseshoe pits were.

A new fire hall was built at the southwest corner of Ramsey Avenue and Third Street in 1962, the rear of it being where the old paper shack was. Anderson Chemical bought the old fire hall site at this corner in December of 1963 and was still headquartered here in the early seventies. Today the site is occupied by Curves.

100 Second Street West. E. M. Eastman had an office for his moving company and well digging business at the northwest corner across Ramsey Avenue to the west. Chris Mortenson had his Litchfield City Bakery, restaurant and boarding house at that corner, after erecting a building in June of 1886. He had returned to town in April of 1886 after operating a restaurant at another site. He sold out to Henry T. Halverson, Jr. in April of 1888. O. Wexel moved his tailor shop to a lot north of Mortenson's bakery in October of 1888. In April of 1896, A. P. Brodeen had a shoe shop here.

Dwight B. Lounsbury's livery was moved to the location at some time. At some time Harry Anderson and Alfred Anderson started their ice cream factory and dairy products store here, leasing part of the building. They sold the business to Elmer S. Noreen in the mid-1910s and then bought it back in March of 1923. In September of 1924, Alfred sold the business to Harry A. Hanson, who moved it to his new building

444

on Sibley Avenue in March of 1925. Then McDonald's Chevrolet garage was somewhere near the corner in April of 1928. Fred A. Kopplin had put up a building here at the corner where the "glass block" building and a feed house had been. That's where McDonald's moved in. Harry Madson had an auto repair here after McDonald moved out.

Madson took on Baldis H. Koenig as a partner in October of 1931, before moving to the west corner of this block. Maxson Motors was here after that in the late thirties and early forties. In January of 1941, a mattress factory was moved into the north room of Maxson's. The Surplus Commodities Credit Corporation owned it and they used surplus cotton from the south. During that month, Franklin D. Roosevelt was sworn in as President for his third term. Maxson's had to move when Fred A. Kopplin sold the building to the produce in February of 1943 for an egg procession plant. Maxson moved to Third Street West. The building here burned down in November of 1953 and a new one was erected in March of 1954. It ended up being the freezer lockers for the turkey plant when a new building was erected here in July of 1958. Today it is a vacant lot.

104 Second Street West. West of the corner building was a café named the Lunch Time Inn, which was owned by Kate Pierce. Kate sold the cafe to her son-in-law and daughter, Kenneth and Laura Mae Welsand, in January of 1949. Initially, their cafe was called Kenny's Café, but after Kenny died, it became Laura's Café. Then it was called the Lunch Time Inn again. Laura married Marlin "Bud" Carlson and started calling the business the West End Cafe. In October of 1971, Mary Ramthun bought it. Mary also had the Hide-A-Way Café around the corner on Ramsey Avenue.

Somewhere west of the café, on a vacant lot, which was probably the alley, E. G. Munson erected a portable roller rink in May of 1942. It was a huge tent with a wooden floor.

114-116 Second Street West. LeRoy "Roy" and Eldon Swanson moved into the building here following the alley in February of 1932. In October of 1957, Chester "Chet" Olson leased the former Litchfield Produce garage from Geinitz, which was just west of the alley after the café. He moved his Automotive Machine Shop there at in 1958. It burned down in February of 1963 and Olson moved it out on east Highway 12. Olson came back to this location though. Today L S Customs is here.

122 Second Street West. (305 Second Street West in the early 1900s.) In about 1915, Dr. H. C. Peters had a veterinary business at this location. In the summer of 1919, the Johnson and Hanson auto repair business went into the building here. Phil H. Brutger bought the Motor Mart owned by M. E. Johnson, G. A. Jorgenson and J. F. Johnson in August of 1920. During that same month, women are given the right to vote. In September of 1920, Brutger bought out Joe B. Weber in the Litchfield Machine Shop. He sold the Motor Mart to R. C. Finley and A. D. Piper in March of 1921. During that same month, Warren Harding was sworn in as the 29th President of the United States. Brutger sold the machine shop to Wilbur H. Geinitz in early 1922. Geinitz built a new shop here in September of 1927, called his business the Litchfield Machine Shop. Then Geinitz moved out on east Highway 12 in September of 1945. During that same month, Japan unconditionally surrendered to the United States, ending World War II. Today the Aggie's Kountry Keepsakes store is at this and the next location.

124-126 Second Street West. Hans Christian Anderson's blacksmith shop had been here at the northeast corner of Miller Avenue and Second Street. In 1953, LeRoy Lindquist opened the Litchfield Sheet Metal Works at the corner. Eventually Arvid Reinke's Sheet Metal was here. Today Aggie's Kountry Keepsakes is at this location.

Anderson Chemical was across Second Street was at the southeast corner lot and later adding on to the lot to the east of here. In February of 1951, the Farm Home Administration moved their office to the Anderson Chemical building.

37. 123 Second Street West. Noreen's Pavilion was to the east of that building. Originally, H. J. Kellman and Jeffe Schelde had a lumberyard at this location. The Noreen brothers, Elmer S. and Rudolph, bought the lot in July of 1909. They built a fifty by eighty foot dance hall in the summer of 1909. Noreen's was sold to Harry A. Hanson and Alfred Anderson in late 1922. Alfred Anderson bought out Hanson and closed the pavilion down in April of 1925. He leased it out for basketball in December of 1925. Later he converted the building over to his manufacturing business and Anderson Chemical Company.

121-119 Second Street West. (318 Second Street West in the early 1900s) The next lot, heading east, originally had the Litchfield Iron

Works. H. J. Kellman owned it in the 1890s. Then Kellman took on a partner named Parsons and they called their business P & K Iron Works. Parsons left and Kellman changed the business over to a garage and auto livery (rental) business and a machine shop, starting in March of 1908. Kellman had two automobiles he rented out. One was a Rambler touring car and the other was a Moline runabout. Kellman also sold and repaired automobiles. He sold that part of his business to O. V. Armstrong in June of 1909. Kellman kept the machine shop part of the business and they operated together in the same building. Armstrong turned around and sold the garage to J. G. Morrison and W. W. Shelp in August of 1909. John T. Toland started the Litchfield Canvas Glove Factory upstairs over the machine shop in February of 1909, but by April he was operating the business out of his house at 604 Sibley Avenue North. Kellman's Litchfield Machine Shop was sold to Phil H. Brutger and Joe B. Weber in October of 1918. This location and the ones east of here became part of the produce complex. Today all the buildings are gone.

117 Second Street West. (316-312 Second Street West in the early 1900s.) Herbert and James Atkinson built the Litchfield Automobile Company next to the previous wooden building in April of 1912. They sold out to the Vincent brothers, who sold out to W. Richard Berens in December of 1914. W. R. Coyne had the business in 1917. Fred H. Hankey moved his machinery business into the building in April of 1918. The Krueger Brothers' (Art and John) Garage was in the Hankey building in the summer of 1923 and it was still there in the mid-fifties. Then the lot became part of the turkey processing plant and today is vacant.

At one time before the turkey processing plant building at the corner was expanded towards the west, there had been a small pond between the Krueger garage and the Produce building. Ducks and geese that got loose from the plant would swim around in the pond until someone would have to wade in and retrieve them.

(325 Second Street in the old numbering system.) The southwest corner lot had H. J. Quigley's feed yard before the turn of the century. Lorenz C. Johnson had his confectionery near here, around the turn of the century. He sold it in October of 1915 to Edel Krook, who sold it to Axel E. Anderson in December. Axel was still here in 1917. Chris A. Bertelson had a restaurant called the Café Du Nord around here in July of 1921. Close by was the Funderburk Sales Stable. Martin A.

Anderson bought the Quigley feed yard in March of 1919. This location also became part of the turkey processing plant complex or the Litchfield Produce Company. This particular building was where the turkeys were killed and eviscerated and where my mother worked on the line for many years. The entire block is vacant today.

11. The Produce, with its office at the northwest corner of Ramsey Avenue and Depot Street, (325 Depot Street West was the address in the early 1900s), took up half of the 200 and all of the 300 numbered blocks of the west side of Ramsey Avenue North. The Peifer brothers, John C. and Frank A., and John's son Arthur E. moved the Produce here to that "office corner" in June of 1906 from Sibley Avenue across from the park. The Peifers, originally from Luxemburg, bought the brick Union House nine-room hotel at this corner location and converted it over. Andrew Ogren and Arthur Aylesworth had built the hotel, which actually faced Depot Street, in September of 1887 on the former site of the Charles "Charley" A. Laughton livery and farm machinery business, which was here in 1881. Laughton sold Case implements. Prior to the hotel, Andrew Ogren had a restaurant here. Andrew Ogren and Arthur Aylesworth sold the hotel to J. E. Elliott in July of 1900. Elliott immediately sold it to C. A. May, who, in turn, immediately sold it to John E. Hanley in July of 1901. Hanley eventually sold it to George A. Lee. Martin Larson and Frank Gerard also owned it at times. In November of 1902, Gerard bought out Larson. John C. Peifer sold controlling interest in the Produce to the Hutchinson Produce Company in April of 1909 and sold out completely in January of 1910. He bought the business back in March of 1912. The Produce bought and sold eggs, poultry, cream, hides, fur and wool. John C. Peifer left and moved to Benson to start another produce there. In 1918, D. B. Payne joined the partnership.

The Produce, (formerly the Union House), in 1906.

448

In the early thirties, the Produce started marketing the ELPECO brand of turkeys. It stood for E Litchfield Produce E Company. Art Peifer's son Bob was assistant manager at the plant in the fifties and his daughter Patricia or "Patty" was in my class in grade school and high school. The Produce closed in January of 1957. During that same month, Dwight D. Eisenhower was sworn in as President for his second term. The Peifers sold the plant to Earl B. Olson of Willmar, Minnesota. In September of 1957, Earl B. reopened it as the Farmer's Produce Company, headquartered in Willmar, Minnesota. He later renamed his company Jenny-O after his daughter Jenny Olson. Jennie-O suspended operations in Litchfield in the summer of 1985. The buildings were torn down in the summer of 1991 and the entire block is empty.

Halvor Berglin bought a bakery building and had it moved near Laughton's livery for his Litchfield Brass Foundry business in November of 1886. Then the bakery became a blacksmith shop owned by Chris A. Bertelson and someone named Olson. Olson sold his share to Bertelson in March of 1891. Eventually Hans C. Anderson got it and sold it to the Produce in January of 1933.

There was a grocery store run by Isaac Hines directly across the street from the hotel at the northeast corner of Ramsey Avenue and Depot Street in February of 1897. Today the Quality Craft factory is at this corner location facing south.

North of it, mid-block towards the corner to the north, was a building that was the Israel Miller feed mill, which began operations in 1885. Miller came to Litchfield in 1884 to build and operate "Lulu" the steamboat on Lake Ripley. Lulu took people across the lake to the Brightwood Beach resort on the lake's south shore. George Hinds bought the mill in May of 1890. It eventually became an ice cream plant. The Peifers bought the ice cream plant in 1934. Today Rainbow Body & Paint Shop is at this location.

54 & 112. 37 Second Street West/130 Ramsey Avenue North. The brick building that became Lund-Hydeen's angled the southwest corner of Ramsey Avenue and Second Street. Chris A. Bertelson may have had a blacksmith shop here or close by in May of 1883. Also in 1883, Josiah Payne had a shoemaking business here. In 1885, Bertelson quit the blacksmith shop for three years but came back in 1888 and started it up again. Nels Olson had a harness shop here in the early 1890s.

Fred T. "Fritz" Happ opened a plumbing business here opposite the Quigley Feed yard in March of 1917. Once the brick building was erected, there was probably always a service station in the front. Ole L. Langren owned the corner and he leased it to John Baker, Jr. and Dwight B. Lounsbury in June of 1925. They installed the gas pumps at the corner and opened a gas station called the Community Oil Station. Lounsbury bought out Baker in November of 1925 and took on another partner named Newell C. Nelson. They sold the station to Robert Wilson Crawford in July of 1926. A person named Worden sold sod from this corner in the twenties.

In February of 1932, the Baden Oil Station moved here from their former location by Loven's seed house. The Crawford station was still here in the front of the building. Mayou sold the building to Alfred Anderson in 1933. In 1933, Borden and Hanson's Motor Supply Company, owned by Anthony "Tony" Borden and Harold C. Hanson, moved into the main part of the building. They also sold Buicks and Pontiacs. Hanson bought Borden out in 1935 and Borden bought the hotel. Crawford sold the gas station to Edward E. Lund in May of 1937. Lund called it the Community Service Station. Pure Oil bought the building in August of 1940. Frank Ekbom's Auto Parts was here in the early forties, actually starting in the next building. Ed Lund built a new building at the corner here in September of 1947. In October of 1949, Ose Berg and Chester "Chet" Olson started their Automotive Machine Service Company in a room. James Nelson sold his interest in the Auto Parts business in November of 1949 to F. Edwin Nelson, Stuart "Stuey" Nelson and Burton Holt. Ekbom built his new building sharing the corner and moved in September of 1950. Lund-Hydeen Pontiac came in. At that time there was a Skelly gas station in the front. Enoch Peterson had an office for his insurance and real estate business in a room here in 1950. He moved out in late 1957, after he formed a partnership with A. E. "Bert" Eske in July of 1957.

In the late sixties, the King Koin Launderette was moved here. The Bungalow Gift Shop was added to the Launderette also. Gordon and Laura Bloomquist bought the Launderette in April of 1972. The building is now the home of Karen McCarthy's Tax Service.

113. 27-29 Second Street West. Heading east on Second Street, back towards Sibley Avenue, the first location after the corner had a feed store owned by David Gorman before the turn of the century. In June of 1900, Percy Vorys moved his tin shop to the building here and John Ziel had a rug factory here in May of 1906. At some time Clem Stiff's beer and pool hall was here. Outside on the street was the city's longest watering trough for the horses. It remained there until the summer of

1920 when the downtown streets were finally paved. A large building was erected here in March of 1912 and, because of its size, there were many occupants, making it confusing.

Bill's Lunch Wagon, owned by J. W. "Bill" Williams, was here in the early thirties. It had been on the street near Olson's grocery. Williams moved out in September of 1935. Clayton Quale moved his Clay's Eat Shop here in April of 1936. Hans Paulson took over that summer, but couldn't make a go of it. He just left, without selling the business or telling anybody. The newspaper said that he "took leave for parts unknown." So Joe Goeddertz came in and took over in August of 1936. Mrs. W. L. Caley came in October and started her Caley's Cozy Inn here. Mrs. Melvin "Kate" Pierce, who later became my neighbor, bought the café in March of 1937 for the first of her three locations in town. William Farley brought his Paradise Café here in the east part of the building in 1939. Frank Ekbom and his son Glenn had a Red & White grocery here in the west half of the building in October of 1940. It closed in January of 1941 and F. Edwin Nelson's Auto Parts moved here in April of 1941. At some time Farley sold the Paradise to Reuben Carlson who sold it to George Mihlbauer in May of 1944. Clem Stiff bought the Paradise from Mihlbauer in December of 1944 and his son Wallace ran it for him. Arthur Hed bought the café in 1945. In April of 1946, Auto Parts bought out the Paradise Café in order to expand. Auto Parts waited a while to expand though because in June of 1946, Conrad W. and Stan J. Berquist had their electric business here, having moved out from under the Red Owl store on Sibley Avenue. Tobeck Electrical and Furniture Company moved into the room where Berquist had been in February of 1947. Enoch Peterson was here in 1949 with his real estate and insurance business. Auto Parts, which had been in several locations all over town, moved next door in the summer of 1950 so that they could move the old building here to a location near William Christenson's icehouse. Then they were able to expand onto this lot. They moved into their new building in September of 1950. This is part of the previous vacant building today and also vacant.

114. 23-25 Second Street West. Charles "Charley" Shaw, no relation to me, and Theodore Ehlers had a feed store here, the next location heading east, to go along with their mill a block away to the south on Depot Street. They moved out to another location in July of 1884. John Knutson came in with a meat market that same month. He immediately took on a partner named Peter N. Dahl, but their partnership

dissolved and the business closed in August of 1884. Jacob "Jake" Koerner bought the lot and opened his meat market here in September.

Otto Gibson had a flour and feed store at this location starting in April of 1901. At some time, in the early 1900s, a Mrs. Halverson gave music lessons somewhere around here. Olaf M. "Feed Ole" Olson bought the lot in November of 1904. He moved across the street while he built a new brick building here in September of 1923. Then his general merchandise and feed store was in it with groceries in the front and feed in the back. In the previous month, President Harding died of an embolism after suffering ptomaine poisoning followed by pneumonia. Calvin Coolidge was sworn in as the 30th President of the United States.

Olson leased the front of the building to A. F. Hoel in October of 1930. Hoel called his business the Pioneer Grocery. After Hoel moved to Sibley Avenue in November of 1933, Harry W. Olson, Olaf M.'s son, opened a new grocery in the front. Harry Olson was Litchfield's fire chief from 1933 to 1935. Olaf M. Olson sold the building to Oscar W. Nelson in September of 1937, but Olaf's son Harry stayed here with his grocery store. The brick building became the original site of Nordlie's Grocery, when Harry sold out in February of 1939 to Olaf Gerhard "O. G." Nordlie, who then started his Nordlie's Cash Grocery. He started calling it Jack Sprat in late 1939. In March of 1940, Nordlie moved the business to the *Litchfield Review* building on Sibley Avenue North, where Plate's Toggery would end up. Roy E. Anderson had an accounting office here in November of 1947. In November of 1950, Flo and Don Singlestad sold their Log House café on Highway 12 and opened up the Stork and Tot Shop at this location. Wilfred F. Baril's Paint and Wallpaper Store was at this location starting in January of 1952. Berger N. Sjoquist, an attorney, had an office upstairs in the late fifties. He died of a heart attack in that office in December of 1960. This is another vacant building today.

119. 137 Sibley Avenue North. There were always hair care shops under the bank at the southwest corner of Sibley Avenue and Second Street and the next building to the south. In September of 1891, when the new bank building was completed, J. William "Billy" Nelsan had the first barbershop in the bank basement. He and barber Ray Wheeler, who was kiddy corner across Second Street from him, got some of those new "electrified" hair clippers in 1919. Also John A. McColeman had his barbershop down there too in the early 1890s. Billy Nelsan died in November of 1924 and his sons, Raymond and Harry Nelsan, sold his

shop to Martin B. Peterzen in December of 1924. Raymond was not the other Raymond Nelson in town who also was a barber under Sward-Kemp and had a brother named Harry. How's that for confusing? Peterzen's Beauty and Barber Shop was here in the late twenties. Peterzen was the leader of Litchfield's famous prize winning drum and bugle corps.

Peterzen leased the business to Ivan Jaeger in May of 1931, but took it back later. Minneapolis Laundry had a pick up office down in the basement here in the mid-thirties. In February of 1949, Peterzen sold the barbershop to Bea Determan and Vince Decker and it became Decker's Barber and Beauty Shop. In May of 1951, the shop became Fred E. Winter's Barber and Beauty Salon. A Dr. Murphy had an office down here in the early fifties. When Murphy left, Enoch Peterson moved his insurance business into the room in December of 1956. Roscoe G. Keller bought out Winter in July of 1952. Roscoe had become friends with Litchfield barber Hubert Dedrickson who took him under his wing and helped him go to school and even buy his tools of the trade. Enoch Peterson and A. E. "Bert" Eske had an office for their insurance and real estate business in a room here in late 1957, after they formed a partnership in July of 1957.

When Roscoe's shop was flooded because of the fire at the New Bakery on December 30, 1961, he bought the old Burleigh's Studio building by the Unique, tore it down in 1962, and put up a new building there for his shop.

117. 135 Sibley Avenue North. (20 Sibley in the early days.) A. A. Brown owned the Sibley Avenue and Second Street southwest corner lot in 1871. Robert F. Gordon owned a building south of the tracks and he moved it here in May of 1871. I don't know what it was used for at that time, but the building had the Gottlieb Koerner and Joseph Roetzer meat market in it in 1874. In May of 1878, Capt. James Benjamin Atkinson, Sr., a Civil War veteran, bought the building that was here, moved it to Marshall Avenue and divided it into two residential houses. Another building was either here or was then erected because the Staples brothers, Charles A., J. H. and N. P., leased the site for their general store in August of 1881. They left in 1883. There also was a bakery here at some time. Ira Brickley had a general merchandise store at this location in 1884 or 1885. The store closed in April of 1886. Then Mrs. Gottlieb C. "Caroline" Koerner had her City Meat Market here in May of 1886, after Gottlieb had died in July of 1884 leaving her with seven kids to support. Caroline, born in Wittenberg, Germany, at first leased the

market back to one of the Staples, then she moved back to her building on Marshall Avenue and Jacob "Jake" Koerner bought the lot here and moved an old building onto it that had been next to his meat market to south of here. He moved it off in March of 1887, but a building must have remained because William Diepenbrock and August Bracher had their meat market here for a while and then Mrs. Koerner and her sons Fritz and William came back and started the Sibley Meat Market here in October of 1890. After Mrs. Koerner moved out again, Otho H. Campbell bought the lot in March of 1891 and sold it in April to the Bank of Litchfield, which built a brick building here. It was completed in September of 1891. A source calls it "Litchfield's first brick building", but the brick Juul building, which became the Tharalson building, was built in 1878. I always knew this corner to have a bank. First it was called the Bank of Litchfield, which began at another location. Then, in November of 1890, the owners combined with the failing Stevens and Company bank and decided to change it to a state bank calling it the State Bank of Litchfield in December of 1890. The state bank was chartered on January 15, 1891 and they moved into the new brick building here on this site known as "Mrs. Koerner's Corner" in September or October of 1891.

Right to left: About 1900, the "new" old First State Bank building, the City Bakery, a vacant lot where Hagglund's Furniture store went, the "drug store building" and the alley.

Nelson D. and Col. Charles Hoyt March moved their law office here somewhere in the bank building in November of 1891. Charles was Litchfield's mayor in 1909 and 1912 and Nelson was mayor in 1925.

454

Col. Charles Hoyt March and Nelson D. March

An early version of Litchfield's Post Office, under Postmaster August T. "Gus" Koerner, came to the rear of the bank building in 1892. It remained here until the bank expanded. In December of 1892, John W. Wright, Litchfield's second fire chief, became the postmaster. He was born in Virginia and served as fire chief from 1895 to 1896. The bank building used to extend all the way to the alley west of this corner. In September of 1891, J. D. Hayford had a flour and feed store in the back of the new bank. In February of 1897, James F. Maher became the next postmaster.

W. D. Joubert became the postmaster in April of 1901. E. E. Peterson had a flour and feed business in the rear of the building in January of 1903 and Christian B. Nelson had a shoe repair in the rear of the Post Office in May of 1904. In February of 1905, Charles Henry Strobeck was the postmaster. The Post Office moved out from May of 1908 until October of 1908, while an addition was put on to the building to give the Post Office more room. Postmaster Strobeck died in May of 1911 and John W. Wright became acting postmaster until W. D. Joubert was appointed again in August of 1911. John N. Gayner became the postmaster in August of 1915. In the early twenties, the Litchfield Laundry was located either in the bank's basement or in the rear of the building. The laundry was sent to the cities for cleaning. Andrew Ernst Lofstrom became the postmaster in August of 1924. In March of 1925, Z. P. Hatcher and J. P. Revier bought the laundry and it closed in January of 1927. James H. Phelps became the postmaster in March of 1926 after Lofstrom had suddenly died.

The Post Office was still here in the west part of the building in June of 1931. Victor A. "Vic" Sederstrom's realty business was back there too. The Minneapolis Laundry had a pick-up/drop-off place in the rear of the bank building in the late thirties. Marvel's Beauty Shop was in the rear in the mid-thirties until it was moved across the street in 1943. (23 Second Street West) There were a lot of offices at that address in the mid-thirties. Dr. W. E. Macklin had an office here, D. F. Nordstrom and Wendell S. Nelson shared a law office here, and dentist Dr. Albert C. Nelson had his office here. He was Litchfield's mayor in 1919 and 1936. The bank's name was changed to the First State Bank on October 1, 1946. N. Thomas Woodward had his law office here and when he died in 1947, Berger N. Sjoquist and Edward F. Jacobsen formed a partnership and moved into the offices in December. Also some veterinarians, V. F. Olson in '53 and Carl Johnson in '56, had offices either in the rear of the building or in another small building behind the bank.

A new bank building was built and it opened in June of 1963. It included the building next door to the south. The public library moved in here in 1979 when the bank moved, and now the building is occupied by Sparboe Farms.

118. 133 Sibley Avenue North. In the fifties there was a doorway between the original bank and the next building, heading south on Sibley Avenue again. In that doorway and up the stairs were a bunch of offices. From 1891 to 1916, two dentists, Drs. Edward B. Weeks and Albert C. Nelson, who actually came in 1904, performed their torture in partnership up there. Weeks was born in Wisconsin. Miss Nellie Lannan had a dressmaking business over the Post Office at the rear of the bank building in October of 1892. August T. "Gus" Koerner moved his real estate office upstairs in September of 1893. Charles Henry Strobeck followed in December to an office that attorneys E. B. Hall and H. C. Salisbury had occupied. Victor A. "Vic" and F. W. Sederstrom moved their realty business over the bank in March of 1897.

Top row: Lawyer Charles Henry Strobeck and wagon maker Joseph A. Happ,

Bottom row: Barber J. William Nelsan and Shoe man John Beckstrand.

Senator Charles H. Dart had his office over the bank in December of 1902. Gus Koerner's son, P. C. "Carney" Koerner went into the real estate and insurance business and moved into his father's office over the bank in July of 1907. Dr. G. E. Hoeper had his office upstairs in June of 1908. Edward B. Weeks retired in 1916, Harold H. Peterson took his place and Nelson went on until 1939 when he became superintendent of the Litchfield Sewage Disposal Plant, of all things. Upstairs in the mid 1910s were Dr. Carroll C. Carpenter's, Luke K. Sexton's and N. Y. Taylor's law offices, J. H. Ayer's optometry business and the Kennedy Realty Company Land Office, which was also called the Litchfield Land Company. Sexton stuttered, yet became the city attorney and spoke to students at the high school every year. His daughter, Florence "Flo", married lawyer P. J. Casey. In the twenties, the Holm Tea Rooms, run by Mrs. Frank Oscar "Kitty" Holm was up here. It closed for a while because of a fire and re-opened in January of 1928. She finally closed it in October of 1928. Mrs. Elmer Langren then had the Langren Beauty Parlor upstairs. She sold it to Pearl Barquist in March of 1929. N. Thomas Woodward bought the practice of Luke Sexton in October of 1929.

Pearl Barquist closed her beauty salon in March of 1933 and Mrs. J. M. Pericle opened her Peacock Beauty Salon in the same room. During that same month, Franklin D. Roosevelt was sworn in as the 32nd President of the United States. Dr. Robert M. "Bob" Farrish had his office up here starting in May of 1939, as did dentist A. J. McCormack. Farrish had taken over Dr. Albert C. Nelson's business. In June of 1948, Arden W. Burleigh started his photographic business in Litchfield, opening his first photo studio up here. Cel's Beauty Shop, owned by Cel Munson, was up here too. In August of 1948, Marvel Nelson bought the business and, even though Marvel also owned the Kurlelox Beauty Shop elsewhere in town, she started another Marvel's Beauty Shop. She had bought that other beauty shop from the Perricles in 1937, which she called Marvel's. She sold this one to Mrs. Robert Nelson in August of 1946. Merlyn Olson had a dental laboratory upstairs in September of 1947. John W. Mostue had a dental practice up here. In 1949, Daynor N. Tharalson had his financial consulting business up here, as did Frederick E. Schultz with his accounting office in the mid-fifties. W. O. Jensen's Optical was up here too, buying William Cox's business in June of 1950. During that month, the United Nations declared war on North Korea. Mostue Optometry was also upstairs and Jensen bought his business in February of 1961. During the previous month, John F. Kennedy was sworn in as the 35th President of the United States. Then Jensen's business became Gross Optometry in May of 1961 when Gary P. Gross bought the business. Edward F. Jacobsen had an office up here in the mid-fifties. Also at some time Art Carlson had a false teeth operation up here. In the late fifties, the Litchfield Produce Company had an office upstairs.

120. 131 Sibley Avenue North. (18 Sibley in the early days and then 806 Sibley Avenue in the early 1900s.) Butcher Jacob "Jake" Koerner, Sr. originally owned this next lot heading south on Sibley Avenue. Jake erected a small building here in 1870 and had a butcher shop here for a while. At some time in the early years, the building had the Litchfield Brewery bar, a saloon selling the local brew. Erhardt Lenhardt, who eventually owned the hotel at the corner of this block to the south, owned both the brewery and the saloon. The brewery itself, started in 1873 by Lenhardt and Joseph Roetzer, was located by Lake Ripley where the Brent Nelson house stands near the lake outlet. There were caves there where the beer was stored. Speaking of Lake Ripley, the golf course, located near it, was the site of a racetrack and fairgrounds in the late 1800s. From July 1889 to July 1893, the popular Brightwood Resort was across the lake on the south shore. Hiram Branham and Charles A. Greenleaf owned and ran the resort. Guests took a steamship across the lake from the site of today's Anderson Gardens to get to it. Hiram S. Angell, Clark's son, had a confectionary at this Sibley Avenue location in the late 1880s. Peterson, Stark and Company, a quickly thrown together business selling the stock out from the Nordstrom store that went under, was here in 1893. Robert A. Vorys had yet another location here for his ever moving restaurant in March of 1894. The Peterson, Stark and Company moved out in May of 1894 to a building west of the old fire hall. Peter Peterson had a saloon here in May of 1895. Cook opened a pool hall under Peterson's saloon in March of 1898. In December of 1899, Orra S. Johnston and Maro A. Harris opened a shoe store in the building here, calling it the Johnson & Harris Shoe Store.

Henry E. Palm moved his bakery into this building in August of 1900. Palm sold the bakery to A. G. Swanson in October of 1900. In February of 1903, building owner Virgil Homer Harris sold the building along with his other downtown building to Otho H. Campbell, owner of the beautiful home known as the "Raven's Nest", the "nun's castle" or the "Conservatory" at 307 Holcombe Avenue North. Vorys quit the restaurant business in January of 1903. Then in May of 1903, Emil C. Gross moved his jewelry store here. The Peterson brothers bought the building in January of 1909, and Gross had to move elsewhere. The Peter Peterson saloon here closed in May of 1908 and the Anderson brothers bought it. Erhardt Lenhardt sold the building to his son and son-in-law, Edmund Lenhardt and William Shoultz, in November of 1907 and they conducted another saloon here, I believe. William Shoultz and Edmund Lenhardt bought the brewery from Erhardt Lenhardt in 1910 and William bought out Edmund from the brewery in February of 1911. In return, Edmund got ownership of this building. In October of 1910, Fred L. Gamer leased the building and sold phonographs here. Litchfield went dry in April of 1914 and the Bank of Litchfield bought the building from the Lenhardt at that time. Shoultz sold a half interest in the brewery to Rudolph Hoefs in March of 1916. Joseph A. "Joe" Happ leased the building in April of 1914 and in June he moved his Happ and Company Grocery and Dry Goods here. Happ had been across from the park, just as Gross' store would be. The business had started in about 1899 elsewhere. The Happ and Company Department Store was here for five of Happ's many years in the business. In the mid-1910s, Happ gave up the grocery part of the business. A fire above him in the Holm Tea Room in January of 1928 caused a lot of damage to Happ's store goods.

Lofstrom's, Wright Furniture, a saloon and the State Bank of Litchfield.

John H. Happ

Happ closed his business in November of 1939. In December, Shirley James bought the store and changed it to the Litchfield Dry Goods Company. She moved to another location in October of 1941. Wayne Rayppy's New Bakery came in November of 1941. Rayppy had a fire here on April 12, 1954. The fire only shut Rayppy down for about ten days. He had another fire on December 30, 1961 and it forced him to move down by Janousek's Café across from the park. That was the fourth fire at this location, tying the "fire record" with the Robertson building on the northwest corner of Sibley Avenue and Third Street. CJ's "store for ladies" was here for a while after that. Eventually this building was demolished when the First State Bank next door expanded and built their new building in 1962.

The New Bakery in the fifties.

121. 129 Sibley Avenue North. (16 Sibley in the early days and then 808 Sibley Avenue in the early 1900s.) Pioneer shoemaker Nels B. Anderson had a shoe shop here in the next location heading south on Sibley Avenue after he bought the lot in 1873. He was still here in 1885. Charles H. Bigelow, born in New York, and a man named Austin had a confectionery here in March of 1880. Bigelow moved to another location in June of 1881. In June of 1886, Col. Jacob M. Howard bought the lot and put up a new building. The UTK Clothing and Dry Goods House, managed by Peder Winger and owned by G. S. Butler, was here in September of 1886, then moved again to the McLane building across from the park. In March of 1888, the Golden Eagle Clothing House, managed by M. Leon and owned by the Kahn Brothers Company, was here. Leon was born in Germany. Nelson and Company's store was here at sometime in part of the building. Then C. R. Smith and Company had a furniture and undertaking business here in November of 1891, while the Golden Eagle moved to the rear of the building. Smith & Company had been in the Masonic building in 1890. In November of 1893, the Golden Eagle moved next door south. Smith and Company's business was sold to John W. Wright in June of 1897. William Grono moved his real estate and insurance office upstairs at the same time. The building was shared with Mrs. Mary L. Pixley's Millinery, which had started north of here, and Mrs. Lewis F. Larson's millinery also. Clarence A. Perry moved his confectionery business into a room here in October of 1896. Black lamplighter and Civil War veteran Van Spence opened a laundry out of his house in February of 1897 and used Perry's confectionery as a drop off place. Pixley's was damaged when the bakery next door had a fire in September of 1897.

460

Grono, who shared his office with Herman M. Hershey, sold the insurance part of his business to Alfred H. Nelson in August of 1900. Tipton F. McClure built a new building here in 1900. The large building shared the lot next door south. Wright had the business through 1912, but in July of 1911, Ole L. Langren moved his Langren Furniture and Undertaking here. Langren, mayor in 1917, bought Litchfield's first automobile hearse in February of 1917, but it wasn't delivered until August. Langren sold his business to Dewey E. Johnson in January of 1927. Johnson, who moved around town with several businesses and who bought several buildings as investments, added a "Morgue Room" in the rear. It was Litchfield's first funeral viewing room outside of the living rooms in people's houses. Johnson was still here in March of 1929 to sell the business to C. Ad Swenson and Reuben B. Hagglund. They called their business Swanson and Hagglund Furniture and Undertaking. During that same month, Herbert Hoover was sworn in as the 31st President of the United States.

Hagglund bought out Swanson in November of 1935. Finally Hagglund just had his furniture business here. His undertaking part of the business was moved to the grand house it's in today at 316 Sibley Avenue South. Hagglund bought the house from Horace J. Minar in July of 1935. B. P. Nelson had built it in 1903. Hagglund sold the funeral home and furniture business to Don Cole in June of 1957. Later Hagglund got the business back and then sold the furniture part again to Don Brock in August of 1959. This store became Brock's Home Furnishings.

Hagglund formed a partnership with Donald L. Johnson with his undertaking business and sold out to him in October of 1960. The funeral home was called the Johnson-Hagglund Funeral Home starting in January of 1964, even though Hagglund no longer had an interest in the business. Brock moved to the Fenton building in the summer of 1961 and J. Christine Jensen moved her women's clothing store called Christine's here from across the street in November of 1961. Christine's was sold to Mrs. Dorothy Radunz in August of 1966 and then to Harold and Eunice Harding in March of 1970. John Olmscheid bought the business in 1976. Finally, Margie Polingo's Sunrise On Main, which started in 1988 and closed in 2002, was here. Today Essence Of Flowers is at the location.

The two right buildings are Butterwick's and Christine's.

122. 127 Sibley Avenue North. (14 Sibley in the early days and then 810 Sibley Avenue in the early 1900s.) Just before an alley, we had another one of the "personality" buildings in town. This time it was drugstores, but not until the turn of the century. J. W. Glazier had the Litchfield Restaurant here in the early days of Litchfield. He built the sixteen by thirty-six foot two-story building with an icehouse and shed in the back for $3000. In September of 1872, Glazier's building was sold to a Mr. Franklin who had a millinery and boot and shoe business here. The lot was kept and transferred to Martha Glazier, so J. W. must have died. Martha sold it in June of 1873 to William H. Myers. Myers had a New Bakery and confectionary at "Glazier's old stand". Myers is listed as the property owner in 1874. In March of 1880, Charley Myers, William H.'s son, opened a confectionery and tobacco shop in the front room of the building. In December of 1880, Col. Howard bought the lot from lawyer A. C. Smith. Smith, who came to Meeker County in 1858, was Litchfield's seventh Village Council President in 1878. The building was moved back off Sibley Avenue so that Col. Howard could erect a new brick building here. William or "Uncle Billy" Myers had a cigar stand here in 1881. Joseph Lawrence Wakefield moved here in 1886 with his general store. In November of 1888, the Benson Brothers store was here buying out Wakefield's dry goods, furnishing goods, boots, and shoes business. The brothers dissolved their partnership in August of 1889 when Ed Benson retired and T. M. Ramsay bought his interest. The store was known as Benson and Ramsay. It closed in November of 1889. By the way, North Dakota, South Dakota, Montana and Washington had just been admitted to the Union as states. Anderson and Simons moved their furniture store in here briefly in June of 1890.

462

They closed in July. When Litchfield's first First State Bank was originally set up in December of 1890, this building was rented and became the bank before the large block building on the corner was built in the fall of 1891. The bank opened for business here on January 16, 1891 and moved to the corner in September or October of that year. The building was called the Howard Building at that time. Sometime in late 1893, the Golden Eagle Clothing House moved into the room the bank had occupied. A. Helgeson and Otho H. Campbell bought the building and the Golden Eagle stock in April of 1894. They kept the Golden Eagle name and moved down the street in October of 1899.

Left: The building in 1889. Right: An old road sign.

The building went to the Lofstrom brothers in November of 1902 for their Lofstrom Brothers Prescription Druggists store. One of the Lofstroms was Victor E. or "Vic" and the other was Andrew Ernst, who died in 1926. The Lofstrom Drug had a soda fountain.

Foster Butterwick bought the Lofstrom's business in April of 1946. Foster took out the soda fountain and called his business Butterwick's Pharmacy. He kept it going for forty years. Foster's son, Forrest, was in my high school class. The Meeker County Emergency Food Shelf is here now.

125 Sibley Avenue North. There were several offices and businesses over the previous location over the years. August T. Koerner moved his real estate office to an upper room here in September of 1887. He built a house in 1894 at the corner of Fifth Street East and Armstrong Avenue North, which is still there today. F. L. Scherer had a cigar factory upstairs and in July of 1904 he started making "Litchfield Opera"

brand cigars, named after Litchfield's new Opera House. A glove factory was up here also.

In May of 1905, Peter E. Hanson's real estate office upstairs was converted into another of Litchfield's telephone exchange offices. Hanson built a house at 405 Armstrong Avenue North in 1904. People have called the house the "Red Castle" for years. Hanson built another house next door at 413 Armstrong Avenue North in 1905 for his daughter Nellie when she married lawyer Nelson D. March. Both houses are still there. W. A. Mooney bought Scherer's cigar factory in March of 1906. In December of 1915, E. L. Alleman had an insurance office upstairs. J. I. Harrington and Walter H. McCann had a real estate office called Harrington and McCann upstairs also in January of 1916. In February of 1916, they moved across the street.

Nels Ringdahl had a tailor shop above the drugstore in 1939. Charles R. Clemens had an insurance office up here also and still did into the late sixties. There are apartments upstairs today. There was an alley next heading south from the building.

123 Sibley Avenue North. Following the alley was a building, which was called the Aron J. Anderson building in later years. The basement of that next location had occupants with an entrance in the alley. In October of 1891, D. C. Beach moved his confectionery business into the basement from next door to the south. Hubert Dedrickson moved his barbershop to the basement in April of 1929 opening Hubert's Barber Shop.

In August of 1964, John Munson bought out the Dedrickson barbershop. John was the nephew of Sidney Munson who had owned a barbershop in town in the thirties. During that same month, the United States began military presence in Vietnam. John closed down and moved out in May of 1965.

121 Sibley Avenue North. Several occupants were upstairs over the businesses before and after Tostenrud's at the next location. Miss Carrie Anderson, a dressmaker, had her shop over the Meeker County Bank there in 1883, as did lawyer F. P. Olney and the law firm of Charles Henry Strobeck and Simons. Carrie moved down the street above the Nelson, Johnson and Larson store. Dr. W. E. Chapman had an office upstairs in late 1884.

Around the turn of the century, W. A. Mooney moved his cigar factory upstairs. Axel Johnson bought it from him at sometime. Axel closed his cigar factory upstairs in February of 1908. In October of

1913, P. C. Neilson had a knitting factory upstairs and F. L. Scherer had a cigar factory upstairs in November of 1915. Scherer moved to a Depot Street location in June of 1917. For many years Harold A. Peterson had his dentistry office upstairs. He started in April of 1926 and was still here well into the sixties. Chiropractor Bernard S. Determan moved his office here also in May of 1926.

In September of 1937, chiropractor A. Mauritz Asplin bought Determan's chiropractic business and was here along with Peterson's dentistry. In June of 1942, Lowell Wilson had his second chiropractic practice here. His first was in a hotel room over Viren-Johnson's store. In September of 1959, Dr. Wilson put up an office building at 30 Third Street East for his chiropractic business and moved to it in January of 1960. His son Dean was in my high school class and became part of the staff at my alma mater, the Minneapolis College of Art and Design. Newell J. Vold opening his first optometry upstairs in October of 1950. Then he moved across the street. In March of 1950, William LaMotte had a tailor shop upstairs. There are apartments upstairs today.

Fairway,
Nygaard
Jewelry and
Lofstrom's.

124. 119 Sibley Avenue North. (12 Sibley in the early days and then 816 in the early 1900s.) In April of 1871, Clark L. Angell had his photographic gallery here at the next location heading south. He moved around town a lot and didn't stay here very long. In October of 1873, Dr. Frank E. Bissell moved his office here. Bissell was Litchfield's fourteenth Village Council President in 1886 and eighteenth mayor in 1896. Then in the summer of 1875, Phineas "Pat" Cary had his Cary's Store here selling boots and shoes. Cary, who moved around town a lot also, didn't stay here very long either. He moved to Marshall Avenue in 1877 and this became the first location of the Meeker County Bank,

which was started in January of 1878 by president Alex Cairncross. By 1880, the president was Andrew P. Nelson. B. P. Nelson was the vice-president. John Birch and Company, a clothing store, started here in February of 1881 before moving across the street. Pioneer lawyer Charles Strobeck bought the lot and building in February of 1893.

Miss N. E. Stuart moved a millinery here in April of 1900. She closed down in July of 1900. Sam J. Bundy moved his restaurant in here in October of 1904. In November of 1904, Jacob Wilson and Walter Hitzman bought the restaurant and had their North Star restaurant here. In September of 1906, F. L. Scherer bought the restaurant, changing the name to the Star Restaurant. He quit in July of 1907 and sold the business to Wesley B. Hunter. The Family Theater, starting in September of 1908, was the next business I could find here. V. Bailey and G. L. Batten leased the building to show some of those new fangled moving pictures and Jessie Conson played the piano for them. Movies were a nickel for children and a dime for adults. The theater was sold to Aron J. Anderson and his son Ben in January of 1909. Hunter sold the restaurant, which was still here, to Mrs. Mary Bloemkers in January of 1909 also. Gust Chellin, the garage man, brought a jewelry store to this location in June of 1909. The Family Theater moved out and Mrs. Mary Campbell moved here in April of 1911, leasing the room for a millinery. William Lind bought out Mrs. Bloemkers restaurant and moved it down the street. Chris O. Nygaard bought the jewelry business from Chellin in November of 1911. Wesley B. Hunter moved a poolroom into the room formerly occupied by the Campbell millinery in September of 1912. Campbell's millinery was out before the summer of 1916 because P. C. "Carney" Koerner and James H. Phelps moved their insurance and real estate business into the room she had occupied, at that time. Dr. J. E. Davis had an optometry business in Nygaard's in the twenties. Aron Anderson bought the building in March of 1925.

Nygaard's became Tostenrud's in November of 1932, when Albin "Al" Tostenrud bought the store.

At some time in the early sixties, a woman's clothing shop chain named Mode O'Day Frock Shop moved in here. Mrs. Everett L. Roggenstein owned it. In February of 1969, "Hub" Schiro bought the stock from the closed Becker Shoe Store and moved it here as Schiro's Shoe Store. Then it was the Christian Village Shop and then the Mt. Zion Bible & Book Store. It is Heritage Lace today.

The first
Meeker
County
Bank
location.

117 Sibley Avenue North. There were businesses upstairs over the next location also. It was known as Asher's Hall and later, Lyon's Hall. It was used for public entertainment and as a temporary church for the Christian Church, with Rev. L. Y. Bailey as pastor, until 1873. Later a Baptist Church with Rev. J. Thompson as pastor was up there. Miss Carrie Anderson had a dressmaking business upstairs in the early 1880s. In October of 1888, the J. N. Nelson and Andrew Winger (Nelson & Winger) tailor shop was upstairs. Dr. W. B. Robb was upstairs in May of 1889. Dr. William Dickson, a veterinary surgeon, had his office here in 1890. At sometime in the mid-1890s Oscar A. Mehner had a tailor shop upstairs. Dr. James Wright Robertson had his office up there too in the early 1890s before building his "hospital" at the northwest corner of Sibley and Third Street.

In November of 1902, Mrs. Frederick Rudberg put her dressmaking parlor upstairs for a while. Jeannie Holmes started her Holmes Beauty Parlor upstairs here in the early 1920s. She started another shop next to the Hollywood Theater in 1936, but kept this one going too. I don't know what's upstairs here today. I assume it is apartments.

125. 115 Sibley Avenue North. (8-10 Sibley in the early days and then 818 Sibley Avenue in the early 1900s.) The next building was another "personality" building, this time groceries, except for the first few owners. This location and the next one heading south were once called the "old courthouse building". Reading Asher built the first building on this lot and he had his North Star Billiard Hall here in 1870. His building was twenty-four by sixty-four feet and two stories high, costing $3500 to build. Andrew C. Johnson and Andrew P. and B. P. Nelson also had a clothing store here sharing the building in 1870. Asher

had an unknown partner but had the billiard room alone in September of 1871 and sold his business to F. Mead in December of 1871. Mead dropped the "North" part of the billiard hall name and then sold it to Joseph "Joe" Cameron in September of 1872. Cameron was the night watchman, or policeman, for Litchfield in 1873. Andrew C. Johnson bought the building and stilled owned it in 1880. He turned his business into a general merchandise business, selling dry goods and groceries. Phineas "Pat" Cary's Store, a general merchandise store selling boots and shoes, was here in October of 1882. The next month Cary moved across the street to the Ralston building. Nelson, Johnson and (Lewis F.) Larson's general merchandise store was here in 1882. They moved to the next block into the *Litchfield Independent*'s building in the mid-1880s. Charley Shaw, no relation to me, came in February of 1883 and he had the Star Restaurant and boarding house, also known as a saloon, here. He sold it in May of 1883 and opened a restaurant across from the Lake Ripley House. Pioneer shoemaker Nels B. Anderson's business was here in 1883. Some of these businesses shared the building or were in the back with an alley entrance. Anderson died in 1898. Waldemar W. "Walt" Johnson and Company (Dr. George Newland) moved a drug store into part of the building in August of 1886. Walt was initially a partner with J. Edward Upham down the street in their Metropolitan Drug Store. Along with drugs and paints, they also sold revolvers. In January of 1889, Johnson bought out Newlands and owned the drugstore himself. Nelson, Johnson and Larson came back in 1889 when they built a new building here. Anthony Anderson bought Peter Nelson's interest in January of 1890 and the business became Johnson, Larson and Anderson's general store from 1890 to 1896, Johnson, Larson and Hanson from 1897 to 1905 and Johnson, Larson and Wanvig in 1905. D. C. Beach, who moved around town with confectioneries, bought the grocery part in October of 1891 and Andrew C. moved into the alley behind the hotel. Waldemar "Walt" W. Johnson's Drug store was here until May of 1894, when it became Lewis J. Lundemo's Drug store.

Lundemo sold out to E. Theodore Dillner in January of 1902. Dillner moved to the northeast corner of Sibley Avenue and Second Street in September of 1906. In March of 1912, the Johnson, Larson and Wanvig business ended and J. W. Peterson bought the building. L. R. Kelly moved in to sell out the old stock in April of 1912. The Cramer/Lassell stock was added later that month and Kelly kept going until June of 1912. The Andrew C. Johnson and Son General Store started up here in July of 1912. The son was Reuben Johnson. After A. C. died, Garfield Cutts bought the dry goods half of the general store in

January of 1920 and had it here until he retired in March of 1929. He might have been the son of a doctor in town named George Armstrong Custer Cutts who died in 1927. In March of 1929, Olson's Fairway grocery, owned by Nels Olson, moved here. Clarence Silverberg came and joined Olson.

Nels Olson retired in September of 1937 and sold out to Silverberg, so it became just Silverberg's. Then it became Silverberg and Felling Fairway when Bernard "Bernie" Felling bought in. Leroy R. "Roy" Cook moved his meat market into the back in November of 1944. He went out of business in October of 1945. Clarence sold his interest to his son Hardy Silverberg in March of 1954, but the name stayed Silverberg and Felling until Hardy decided he wanted his own identity. So the business became the Bernie and Hardy Fairway in March of 1955. Hardy, by the way, had been a radio operator on the B-29 raids over Tokyo in WWII. He came home to Litchfield with battle stars, air medals and the Distinguished Flying Cross. Bernie Felling bought the business entirely from Hardy in July of 1957.

Bernie ran his Fairway here for quite a while until his new location around the corner on First Street (Depot Street) was remodeled from the old Minar Ford building in January of 1970. By the way, Bernie had a "politically incorrect" store motto in his ads in the fifties and sixties: "Where Ma Spends Pa's Dough". In 1971, the Litchfield Garment Company, a division of Butwin Sportswear Company of St. Paul, was here. It was moved to 412 Gilman Avenue South in the early spring of 1971. Then the Fabrific Fabric Center was here in the early seventies and the Champion Auto Store followed it in 1973. Later this store had something called New Life and today De Ann's Country Village Shoppe, owned by De Ann Rothstein, occupies the building.

Sibley Avenue facing north about 1904. The picture was taken out of a hotel window on July 4th.

126.   113 Sibley Avenue North.   (6 Sibley in the early days.)
Nearing the corner, I come to a building with quite a history.   In
November of 1880, W. S. Wooley bought "the old courthouse" building
here for $7500, but I don't believe he moved his folded hardware
business here.   The *Litchfield Saturday Review* was published here in
September of 1884 for a short time.   John T. Mullen was the editor and
publisher.   Mullen built a house at 406 Armstrong Avenue North in 1888
and it is still there today.   Ole A. "Music Ole" Olson had a music store
here in the north part of the building, which included the site to the south,
in 1886.   David Elmquist moved over here in September of 1886 from
the south side of the building, which was actually next door to the south,
and switched places with Music Ole Olson.   At that time this was the
only wooden building left on the west side of Sibley Avenue between
Depot and Second Streets.   Every other building was made of brick.
August Erickson became Music Ole's partner in December of 1886.
They called the store Olson & Erickson.   W. S. Wooley owned this
building in 1890 and he rented it to Robert A. Vorys for a restaurant.

The Anderson and Strobeck clothing store was here in the early
1900s.   In October of 1906, the Farmers and Merchants' State Bank
opened here sharing the building.

The Farmers and Merchants' closed in October of 1930 because of a
run on the bank.   Emil Mortenson moved his shoe store here in March of
1932.   In November, he went bankrupt and moved back to his former
location across the street.   Arthur Halverson came in and sold out the
shoes.   The Ole Omsrud Ladies' Apparel "ready-to-wear" dress store
was here beginning in May of 1933.   Herman A. Plate bought the
building in August of 1936 and opened his Plate's Federated Store here,
selling shoes and clothes.   Omsrud had to move.   I don't know where he
went.   Plate was mayor in 1943.   Then David C. Ramsay bought the
business in September of 1940 and it became Ramsay's Federated Store,
which opened in December of 1940.   The Federated Store was sold to R.
Orville Barber in November of 1945.   It was followed in January of 1946
by Mirth J. and H. K. "Mac" McIver's Mirmac's Store, which sold "dry
goods and ready to wear".   H. K. McIver also owned the Hollywood
Shop shoe store by the Hollywood Theater.   Mirmac's closed in
September of 1952.   George Farnquist rented the building in January of
1953 and his Marshall-Wells hardware store was here before it was
moved to the Legion building in 1954.   During that same month, Dwight
D. Eisenhower was sworn in as the 34th President of the United States.
George sold his business to M. T. Rye in October of 1953.   Mr. Rye

found that the business didn't suit him so he let it go back to George a month later. The building must have been shared because, in the early fifties, another occupant was the Northland Woolen Company. The building was leased in 1951 and the business was changed to the Singlestad's Stork and Tot Shop and then the Northland Tot Shop in 1957. Later it became Boyd's. Today this building houses Boyd's Uptown Kids, which is owned by the daughter of Boyd Anderson, the owner of Boyd's.

111 Sibley Avenue North. There was doorway between the last location and the next location. It opened to a wide stairway that went upstairs to a number of offices that were above the previous and the next locations. In 1884, Charles Henry Strobeck, the pioneer lawyer, had his office upstairs. Justice James Benjamin Atkinson, Jr. had an office there in July of 1886. In August of 1886, there were offices for county officers upstairs. O. Wexsel had his tailor shop upstairs in 1887. William Danielson had a real estate and insurance office upstairs in 1893. The telegraph business moved up there also in September of 1893.

Imogene Tuman had a dressmaking school upstairs in March of 1909. During that same month, William Howard Taft was sworn in as the 27th President of the United States.

Dentist Clarence E. Aga moved his office upstairs in April of 1933 to a room where dentist R. S. Whinnery had been. Arvid M. Rudberg opened his photography studio in the rear suite over Frank & Nate's in September of 1933. Optometrist W. O. Jensen moved in upstairs in March of 1934. Dr. V. J. Telford had his practice upstairs in the thirties. Nels Ringdahl moved his tailor shop in upstairs in October of 1936, after his brother had retired. He soon moved back across the street. Lowell Wilson came to town in July of 1941 and started his first chiropractic business upstairs in a hotel room. Clemens Insurance was upstairs in the forties. Dr. Frederick C. Brown, our family dentist, took over the business of Clarence E. Aga upstairs in November of 1946. Dr. John E. Verby was upstairs over the store in 1950 and he was the first partner of Dr. Allison in 1951. Before them, Doctors V. .J. Telford and I. J. Kelley had practices up there. Allison took over Kelley's business. Dr. Gregory Olson, our family doctor, partnered with Dr. David Allison in 1954.

127. 109 Sibley Avenue North. (4 Sibley in the early days and then 824 Sibley Avenue in the early 1900s.) The next to last store location in this block had a "clothing store personality", but it started out differently. David Elmquist had his jewelry store here in 1883 in the south half of the

building. In September of 1886, Elmquist moved to the north part of the building, next door, and Ole A. Olson moved his music store here. J. William "Billy" Nelsan and John Nellis moved their barbershop business into some part of the building in September of 1886. Then, before the turn of the century, A. Helgeson and Otho H. Campbell moved their clothing business here. Another Campbell bought out Helgeson and the business became the Campbell and Campbell Clothing Company.

Ole A. "Music Ole" Olson across from the park in 1900 or early 1901. W. H. Anderson bought out the Campbells in August of 1902 and had his Anderson Clothing Company here. His partners were lawyer Charles Henry Strobeck and E. G. Porter. Strobeck bought out Porter in August of 1903. The store went out of business two years later in August of 1904. At some time Nels Lundeen had a shoe repair in some part of the building. Lundeen moved his shoe repair across the street in August of 1905. Famous Gopher football coach Bernie Bierman's dad, William F. Bierman, leased the building in November of 1904 and had his clothing store here. He originally partnered with Charles A. Johnson in February of 1906 and their store was called Bierman and Johnson. Johnson retired in June of 1908 and Bierman had the store alone. John T. Mullen and E. O. Hammer bought the building in March of 1908. Frank E. Viren and Nathan I. "Nate" Johnson leased the building in June of 1908 and started Viren-Johnson's Clothing Store in August. The store was known in the early days as "Frank & Nate's". Both of the owners had worked for John Birch in his clothing store at different times. Frank, born in Sweden, and Nate not only sold clothes but they also sold furs. Bierman found himself looking for a new location. Frank was married to Rosa "Rose" Lenhardt, sister of Edmund, who ran the hotel. At one time, this entire half block, from the hotel to the alley, had a wooden overhang with arches and pillars at the front edge of the sidewalk. It looked very smart and elegant. Also, around this time, there were still hitching posts behind Viren-Johnson's in the alley for farmers who brought teams to town. That location was close to the parking lot for Bernie's Fairway. Max H. Greenberg's Department Store was here sharing the building with Viren-Johnson from May of 1912 to 1917, when it was moved across the street to the Greep's building. Carlsen's Drug had originally been at the Viren-Johnson location also before moving to the building where J D Framing and Gallery is now. Miss Emma Swanson's Park Bazaar Restaurant moved here for a short time in June of 1917 from her original place across from the park.

After Nate died, Frank Viren had the store by himself. In August of 1945, Frank, despondent over slipping sales because of the inability to get clothing items because of the war, left the store, went home, walked into his bathroom with his shotgun and blew a hole in his chest. During that same month, the United States dropped the first atomic bomb on Hiroshima, Japan. Frank Viren's widow Rose Lenhardt Viren sold the store to Frank's friend and fellow worker Arthur L. "Art" Tostenrud in September of 1945. Art was the first owner to change the name from Frank & Nate's back to Viren-Johnson. Donald C. "Don" Larson[196] became a partner to Art Tostenrud in the clothing store on the main floor in 1957. Larson was Litchfield's mayor in 1958 and bought Tostenrud out in 1962.

Jerry Tierney, a classmate of my older brother Dennis, owned the clothing store next. All the owners kept the Viren-Johnson name even though those gentlemen and their heirs no longer had any connection to the store. Later Nickelodeon Antiques was at this location and then Litchfield Office Supply, which moved and closed the building down. It stood vacant for a long time until Very Vintage, an antique store owned by Susan Johnson, moved into the building in May of 2003.

128. 103 Sibley Avenue North. (2 Sibley in the early days.) The corner location of this block had a building that is in almost every picture and postcard of downtown Litchfield, the Litchfield Hotel. Before the hotel was here, however, a wooden building, which very little is known about, was here. I do know that Joseph Leaser had his furniture factory in it for a while in early 1871. He moved to Marshall Avenue North in April of 1871. Civil War veteran Colonel Jacob M. Howard built the hotel at a cost of $19,000 called it the Howard House. Col. Howard was Litchfield's thirteenth Village Council President in 1885.

F. V. DeCoster, A. T. Koerner and Col. Jacob Howard in 1899.

---

[196] Don Larson's mother originally was a cook for the Dunwoodys of the Dunwoody Institute. She became a cook for the Esbjornssons when she came to Litchfield. She served many dinner parties for them, as they were members of the "400 Club", a group of well-to-do townspeople who entertained the elite.

Construction on the hotel was started in February of 1881 and finished in the fall of that year. The original size was seventy-five by ninety feet and three stories high. On November 3, 1881, the grand opening ball was held on the main floor of the hotel. Howard also owned the park, called Howard Park, across the street near the railroad tracks, where Burger King is today at 21 Depot Street West. Howard always leased the hotel out. Harry S. Lilligar was the hotel's first proprietor until 1884. In 1883, Col. Howard fixed the park up for the hotel guests to enjoy. Richard Knights leased the hotel in 1884 and then David Gorman and Richard Knights ran it until May of 1885. Gorman left first and he and a partner named Ormsbee bought the livery of Knights and McCargar. Frank A. Proctor had a real estate office in a corner room of the hotel in 1883. Frank W. Minton became the proprietor of the hotel, leasing it when Knights left in late 1885. He partnered with Ditlof Peterson in running the hotel's saloon, which was now on the main floor instead of in the basement. The Johnson drugstore, which was also in a room here, moved two doors north in August of 1886. L. H. Rawson, born in Massachusetts, leased the hotel and became the proprietor in May of 1889. Also in May, Charles A. Greenleaf and William Grono moved their real estate business into a corner room here. They only stayed a little while. Then it went to Horace B. Johnson, Litchfield's first postmaster and first clothier, in June of 1894.

The Howard House in 1889.

In June of 1894, Sam Brown opened a confectionary in a corner of the hotel. He didn't stay long. P. J. Murtha took over the saloon in the hotel in May of 1895. George H. Woodhouse ran the hotel in 1897 and

William Shoultz, a son-in-law of Erhardt Lenhardt, whose wife was the pastry cook at the hotel, ran the hotel in 1898.

In 1900, a three-story brick addition was added on to the hotel. On March 23, 1901, Erhardt M. Lenhardt, the brewer, purchased the hotel. It was renamed the Lenhardt House or just The Lenhardt. His son-in-law Frank E. Viren owned the saloon inside the hotel and ran the hotel for a while in April of 1902, before leaving to start his clothing business next door. John M. Learn bought or leased the hotel from Lenhardt in February of 1908. Walter W. Earley took over the hotel saloon in February of 1908. Learn leased the rooms over the Viren-Johnson store and the Farmers and Merchants bank in May of 1909 for an addition to the hotel. On July 4, 1911, the hotel had its first fire. I don't know the extent of the damage. Edmund "Ed" Lenhardt started managing for his father in January of 1914. Jack Ryan ran the saloon in the twenties and thirties. Then Jack Flynn ran it. Guests loved to hear the old player piano in there. After Erhardt died in 1929, Ed leased the hotel from his brother and sisters. He added a deck to the hotel after his kids were born to give them a place to play and cool off. The family lived in two apartments in the rear of the hotel, right off the deck. The hotel added the Coffee Shop in May of 1928 and bus service in August of 1929 when the Northland Transportation Company, forerunner to Greyhound, moved over here from Scarp's Café. The name Greyhound started being used in the summer of 1930.

Lenhardt nephew John M. Palmquist ran the hotel in the 1930s and car garage owner Anthony "Tony" Borden leased the hotel about 1934. Borden was fire chief in town from 1914 to 1916. Edmund M. Lenhardt bought the hotel outright in July of 1934. Allan Bronson ran a taxi service from the lobby in February of 1936. Bee Hultgren's Beauty Shoppe was in the back of the hotel in March of 1943. Homer C. Carrier owned the hotel next in the mid-forties, keeping the Lenhardt name. Dean Schultz, the newspaper business guy and postmaster, had a taxi business out front in August of 1946 and Gerald C. Holly tried the taxi thing in February of 1947, calling his business Jerry's Taxi. His brother, Dave, took over in March changing the name to City Taxi. Carrier sold the hotel to Theodore T. Wold and Joe H. Herbranson in April of 1951. The dining room went under a new manager, Ole O. Larson, in August of 1950. Ole and his wife also owned the Travelers' Inn. In November of 1950, the coffee shop's name was changed to the Colonial Coffee Shop after a contest was held to name it. In January of 1951, C. Kuefler bought City Taxi and operated it from a "stand" in front of the hotel. Gerald Buckley bought the taxi stand in February of 1956. Cecil Mies had the Litchfield Taxi Service in town in the late '60s, but I'm not sure where his headquarters was. Vic Forte managed the hotel for Wold and Herbranson from 1962 to 1968. On Christmas Eve of 1966, there was a fire in the kitchen area, the hotel's second and last fire. Jim Hannan bought the Colonial Café in February of 1969. Still called the Lenhardt, most people in town called the hotel the Litchfield Hotel, so when the hotel was sold again in 1969, that name became official. After the hotel closed down, it was torn down in December of 1978. Once of the reasons was the fact that there weren't any fire escapes. Greenbriar Floral occupied the site in a new building, which is vacant today.

As with most of the buildings downtown, the hotel had some businesses in its basement. The hotel billiard hall, in the basement, opened up in October of 1881. Austin Knight had a saloon in the basement in the early 1880s. There were also "sample rooms" down there where traveling salesmen, staying at the hotel, could put out their wares for customers to view. Barbers Graffort and Smith were the first to have a barbershop in the basement. They soon left to open a grocery store elsewhere in town. Then, pioneer barber "Professor" Charles Griswold Topping's had the barbershop in the early 1880s. Topping moved around Litchfield a lot. He started in a room attached to the Tinkham Hotel in 1870. Topping turned around and sold the barber chairs to a Mr. Brown in December of 1879 moving out to start a grocery elsewhere. Brown had a shop over at the Exchange Hotel. In April of 1885, the Independent Printing business moved to one corner of the downstairs from across the street. The *Litchfield Saturday Review* was published there for some time. In April of 1885, the Knight's basement saloon closed and soon opened up on the main floor. Two barbers, John Nellis and J. William "Billy" Nelsan, were down in the basement in April of 1887. The telegraph office moved into the basement in March of 1893 and out in September of 1893. During March, by the way, Grover Cleveland was sworn in as the 24th President of the United States. Michael Robert "Mike" Weiss, another barber, followed downstairs in October of 1893. Weiss brought in his son, Arthur, as a partner. Arthur took over and brought his own partner in. His name was Martin Oie and they called the business Art & Mart's barbershop.

In May of 1932, Arthur bought out Martin. Martin "Mike" Radtke bought the barbershop from Arthur in January of 1934 after Mike Weiss had died from a heart attack. Mike Radtke was here well into the sixties.

I will turn the corner from the hotel and head west down Depot Street. Before Minar built their large building stretching from the Depot Street alley behind the hotel to Ramsey Avenue North, several small businesses were on this street, which was often called Wall Street in the early days. Baldis H. Koenig had an auto repair in the building right behind the hotel in July of 1913. William "Billy" Hanley had a bowling alley west of the hotel on Depot Street in 1904, and probably before that also.

66. 22-28 Depot Street West. (417 Depot Street West in the early 1900s.) J. H. Spelliscy had a machinery business in a building after the alley in May of 1898. Around the turn of the century, the Evenson-Spelliscy Implement and Ford dealership, owned by Hans O. Evenson and Martin E. Spelliscy, Jr., was here. Evenson left to sell Chevrolet elsewhere with Charles Sundahl. Sigfred W. Nelson became Spelliscy's partner in October of 1911. Nelson bought out Spelliscy in May of 1914, and the business became Nelson Implement. Sigfred's brother Oscar A. Nelson was brought into the business. Nelson Implement sold their Ford dealership to Larson-Minar Motor Company in August of 1917 and started selling Overland cars and Republic trucks. Larson-Minar bought the Nelson Implement building in April of 1919. Nelson Implement moved two buildings to the west to sell out their vehicles and machinery and in June of 1919 bought the building that Ed Lindwall was in at the corner. In February of 1920, Sigfred bought out his brother Oscar in the implement business. Sigfred sold the Overland and Republic dealerships to Ferdinand "Frank" H. Brecht, who sold out to George Evenson in November of 1925. Horace J. Minar's brother Cushman bought out Larson's interest in the firm in January of 1923.

Minar Motor bought the rest of the block in February of 1946 from their building to Ramsey Avenue. Eventually Minar had a building, which covered the half block, before they moved out on East Highway 12.

After Minar moved, the city bought the building and tore most of it down in March of 1967 to use as a parking lot. The Charmoll Manufacturing Company leased the remaining part in October of 1969 to make men's and boy's winter jackets and vests. It didn't last long and Bernard "Bernie" Felling bought the building, remodeled it and moved his Bernie's Fairway here in January of 1970. Today the Quality Craft, Inc. business is at this location.

The Minar Ford building, which became Miller Ford.

(411 Depot Street West in the early 1900s.) Peter E. Hanson had a real estate office somewhere in this block in late 1881. I believe it was in the building just west of the implement dealership. Pioneer shoemaker Nels B. Anderson moved his shop somewhere on the block in the May of 1886. Again, I believe it was here or at the corner. Carpenter Nels J. Hawkinson was in this building in the 1880s and 1890s. Nels and his brothers Andrew J. and Henry started a woodworking factory in town in March of 1898. I'm not sure of the exaction location but I believe it was here just west of the implement.

Henry Hawkinson, the factory and Andrew J. Hawkinson

William "Billy" Hanley opened a fruit business and confectionery in Hanson's building in April of 1899. Jack C. Hanson had a barbershop somewhere on this street before he moved downstairs under the Northwestern Bank. Once again, I believe it was here.

In April of 1902, Mrs. Ber had a laundry business in the building that Hanson had been in. William Grono leased the old Hanson land office building for his marble works in November of 1904. Grono was born in Michigan. Chester Clements opened a tire repair shop here in March of 1913. During that same month, Woodrow Wilson was sworn in as the 28th President of the United States. In March of 1916, Albin J.

478

Nelson, a plumber who moved all over town, moved into the building. F. L. Scherer moved his cigar factory in July of 1917 to the building. Edward Lindwall had his shoe repair business here in September of 1918. Nelson Implement bought the building in June of 1919 and Lindwall moved away. He came back later though and leased the building again. In 1933, he moved his shop over by the City Hall.

Realtor Peter E. Hanson and the 1890 businesses on Depot Street leading up to Sibley Avenue and the Howard House.

Another one of the businesses on Depot Street West, the *Litchfield Independent* newspaper, which moved around town a lot, was right at the corner of Ramsey Avenue and Depot Street in October of 1881 for their third location. The building was moved here from Depot Street East across Sibley Avenue. Lawyers E. P. Peterson and William Kenney formed a partnership in August of 1882 and shared the building until they moved out in October of 1884. Peterson was a rarity in town amongst the early Litchfield businessmen. He was actually born in Minnesota. The Independent Printing Office expanded into the lawyers' room until it was moved to the 200 block of Sibley. Chester Arthur had just been sworn in as the 21st President of the United States, by the way. In 1881, Christian B. Nelson had a boot and shoe repair shop here. He was the son of John E. Nelson, and he was still in that same building in 1884. A. H. Lofstrom had a painting shop in this block also in the early 1880s through the 1889. O. Wexel and Paul O. Olson had a tailor shop next door in May of 1886. I'm not sure if that meant they shared the building or were in the Hanson building east of here. Nels and A. Lueken had a boots and shoes business on the corner in 1888. James F. Maher and August Palm started a farm machinery and wagon business somewhere near the corner in March of 1888. In March of 1889, Archie A. Cole and H. H. Stay rented the painting business from Lofstrom.

Lofstrom eventually died from lead poisoning, an occupational hazard. The Cole & Stay partnership ended in June of 1889 and Stay kept the business. W. B. Cutler had a barbershop at that corner in the early 1890s.

C. M. Bakken and A. L. Baklund, two young gentlemen from Willmar, started up a motorcycle shop here in April of 1917. They sold Excelsior and Indian motorcycles. During that same month, President Wilson asked Congress to declare war on Germany and the United States entered World War I on the side of the Allies.

25 Depot Street West. Across Depot Street, by the railroad sidetrack, was the Roller Mill, which was built in 1872 by J. C. Braden, A. Adams, William S. Brill and John M. Waldron. In 1873, Adams and Brill sold out their interests to their partners. Robert S. Hershey & Co. bought the mill in 1874 from the partnership and called it the Litchfield Flouring Mill. Charles "Charley" Shaw, no relation to me, and Theodore Ehlers purchased the mill in November of 1877 and built the Shaw & Ehlers elevator in September of 1885. Ehlers was from Germany. Then A. Berkner and Son owned it. The official name was the Litchfield Roller Custom Mill and it was the "B" mill of the Berkners' three mills, the others being in Waverly ("A") and Long Lake ("C"). The mill, remodeled in 1882, turned out one hundred barrels of Pride of Litchfield, Fancy Patent, and baker's flour and twenty-five barrels of rye and graham each day, mostly sold in the British Isles.

The Roller Mill in 1898.

In the mid-thirties, the elevator was called the Farmer's Elevator and the Litchfield Elevator in the sixties. Today the First District Ag Service/Cheese Store is at that site.

49. I'll leave the 100 block of Sibley and head south across the tracks to visit a few places. Of course we had the train depot right after the tracks. The depot was built in August of 1901 and dedicated on January 9, 1902. The original wooden depot was east of it across Sibley Avenue. It burned down in 1899. Sadly, this depot was torn down in October of 1985. Commercial Street was south of the depot. A lumberyard has always been across that street.

The depot in the 1920s.

129. 126 Sibley Avenue South/25 Commercial Street West. (918 Sibley Avenue in the early 1900s.) In the spring of 1870, Chauncey Butler had a lumberyard here in a small fourteen by twenty-four foot one-story office building that cost $200 to erect. The lumberyard was sold to James H. Morris in September of 1873. After selling the lumberyard, Butler and his partner, W. M. Campbell, had an Agriculture Implement business here also, possibly in a building in front of the lumberyard. I do know that at sometime a building was erected in front of the lumberyard. Butler was Litchfield's sixth Village Council President in 1877. Morris sold the lumberyard to Michael J. Flynn in late 1873 and Michael Flynn's brother Daniel from Illinois joined with him in March of 1874. Flynn also bought the lumberyard.

Michael J. Flynn in the 1880s.

In late 1874, Butler and Campbell added W. M. White to their machinery business, calling it Butler, Campbell & White. They sold out to the Flynns in late 1878. The Flynns, in turn, sold the lumberyard to William Henry Greenleaf. The Michael J. Flynn and Brother Company sold carriages and buggies, farm machinery, and Studebaker wagons from that building starting in early 1879 and into 1886, at least. Their "specialty" was Marsh Harvesters and Deering Twine Binders. The Flynns also bought the Butler elevator in 1880. Michael J. Flynn was Litchfield's fifteenth mayor in 1887 and a Civil War veteran of the 2nd Calvary. Technically he was the first mayor as the mayors were called Village Council Presidents before 1887. The Kopplins built a new building at this location. Fred Kopplin also built a home at 210 Sibley Avenue South in 1894. The house is still there today. Another Kopplin house is the beautiful home at 724 Sibley Avenue South. Called the "Rosemary Home", it was built in the 1890s and was gifted as a home for nursing students, nurses and businesswomen by Dorothea Kopplin, in remembrance of her daughter Rosemary.

In April of 1900, the Settergren brothers expanded their hardware, which was downtown, with an additional storeroom here. Jens J. Juul and George "Jake" Jacobson bought the Settergren hardware here in December of 1915. They called it the Juul Hardware. Jacobson left in the spring of 1916 to do sign painting elsewhere and, in June of 1916, Juul sold out to Thomas S. Hull. He called his business the Hull Hardware Company. It was sold to P. W. Barthel in July of 1917. John Esbjornsson and Fred A. Kopplin bought the Simpson Lumber Company, which was on the southeast side of Sibley Avenue across the tracks, in March of 1901. It was moved to the Kopplin location here, eventually becoming just Kopplin's. John Esbjornsson was Litchfield's sixteenth mayor in 1888. Philip H. Hartman had an automobile repair shop and garage in the Hanson warehouse either here or just north of here in April of 1910. He also sold Studebakers. Hans O. Evenson bought the Hartman garage in November of 1911. Hans O. Evenson and his new partner Emil M. Nelson had their Buick dealership here in February of 1919 and left in March of 1922 to go to the Welch garage at the east corner of Depot Street and Marshall Avenue. Edwin H. Kopplin moved his auto accessories and Studebaker dealership here in March of 1922. Fred A. Kopplin sold the lumberyard to the Neuman Lumber Company in March of 1922 and they sold it to J. F. Anderson in June of 1924.

The Kopplin building was leased to Charles Quist in July of 1932. When Chauncey Butler left in October of 1935 to go into the alley of the

300 block of Sibley Avenue North, L. E. Christofferson succeeded him. Anderson Lumber put up a new office building here in October of 1936. F. Edwin Nelson's Auto Parts was in the Kopplin building at some time before 1941, when they moved to Second Street West. The Litchfield Body Shop, owned by Gene Louisiana and Arthur Draxton, was opened in front rooms of this building in March of 1942. Berg Supply was here in the early forties. Culligan Water Softener Company, owned by L. C. Kalberg and M. H. Johnson, came here in the room formerly occupied by Berg in April of 1946. Stanley Wiebers had a laundry business here in part of the building in May of 1947. At some time the Kopplins took back the building and Ed Kopplin started the Economy Gas Company here in July of 1952. The Anderson Lumber Company was sold to Al Nelson in September of 1959. Hamm Implement was here later. Eventually Ideal Lumber Company took over the front building and the lumberyard.

Economy Gas moved out to a new building on South Davis in March of 1965 and the Fleet Wholesale Supply Company, the Fleet Distributing Supply Company or the Fleet Farm Supply, depending on the ad, moved into this building in August of 1965. The Ideal Lumber yard or Ideal True Valu Home Center has taken over the entire complex and is still at this location today.

The basement of this building also had other businesses, as did most of the downtown buildings. Victor Mickelson leased the basement in December of 1921 for an auto repair. E. M. Leines bought the car repair business from Mickelson in October of 1925.

LeRoy "Roy" Swanson had his auto repair in the basement around 1932. He moved to another location in February of 1932. Starting in September of 1947, the American Legion was in the basement.

The Litchfield Thermo Plastics Company, started by Robert Everts and Arvid Reinke, moved into the basement in October of 1964.

130. 200-202 Sibley Avenue South. South of the lumberyard, across the street, was a house with a grocery store inside and gas station out in the front. In the early twenties, Mrs. R. Reynolds had the grocery there. She added the filling station out front in October of 1925. Leon Albright bought it in October of 1930 and sold it to Hugh I. Batterberry in December of 1931. Hugh called it the Eagle Grocery and Service Station. It was also called the Southside Grocery, but everyone just called it Batterberry's, even after Batterberry sold it to Roy Nelson in

September of 1953. Roy sold it to Ralph Wick in May of 1962. Ralph had worked at Bernie's Fairway. Today this is a private residence.

The late 1800s: The left house became the site of the library and the right one became Batterberry's. In the background is Lake Ripley.

201 Sibley Avenue South. Directly across Sibley Avenue South and kitty-corner from the lumberyard was the Carnegie Library. The library was built in 1904 with $10,000 donated by Andrew Carnegie on a site where Louis Larson had his house. There was an auction of the house, nobody bid and Louis got it back for under $800. He moved it south down Sibley Avenue. Lawyer Alva R. Hunt applied for the Carnegie grant in 1902. The library was dedicated on April 27, 1904 and the doors were opened to the public on Tuesday, May 17, 1904. The contractor was Phil Schelde's dad, Jeffe. Phil Schelde, who also studied engineering, was married to Genevieve "Gen" Osdoba and was the Greep-Trueblood store's general manager after Pete Osdoba bought the store. The first librarian was Alice Lamb. In October of 1915, the Christian Science church leased the basement for a while for their services.

After Alice Lamb retired in November of 1937, Bess Harmon, mother of the *Independent Review's* John Harmon, became the next librarian. Then came Marie Erickson and then Gertrude Johnson. Gertrude ran the library for about twenty years.

In the 1980s, a couple of different restaurants were here. Bill and Laura Harper's Library Square Restaurant, originally called Library Restaurare, opened here in June of 1983. Also in the building were the New York Life Insurance agency and something called Hidden Manna. Today it is still called the Library Square Building and the Barberettes Salon & Rejuvenating Center and Bohn Consulting Associates are a couple of the businesses located here. Lillith's Natural Health & Beauty and Heavenly Hands Massage was here until it moved in April of 2003.

132. (508 Darwin Street East in the early 1900s.) East of the library was a long tall white building called the Litchfield House. It was a hotel and was built by Charles J. Almquist and his brother Solomon M. "Sol" Almquist. The hotel opened for business in August of 1869. It was the first "big" building to be built in Litchfield. It was leased to L. W. Perkins immediately and then to M. T. Hayford in 1870. Charles Almquist died in December of 1870. In 1871, the Litchfield House newspaper ad stated, "Dinner from 12 o'clock till 2 o'clock 25 cents". Almquist's widow sold the building to Hayford, in August of 1873. In December of 1877, Hayford bought a building that J. B. Hatch had used as a furniture store on Marshall Avenue and moved it to the rear of the hotel to be used as a kitchen. Hayford leased the hotel for a year to C. C. Sturdevant or A. H. Sturtevant in September of 1880 and then got it back in November. Hayford died in the early fall of 1885. His wife Eunice A. Hayford leased the Litchfield House to Myron E. Baum in September of 1885 and then sold it outright to him in October of 1888. Myron was born in Indiana. E. A. Baum, a physician and probably a brother of Myron, had his office in the hotel in the early 1890s. There was a blacksmith shop, owned by a Peterson, one block to the south of here. Ide F. Brown bought it in December of 1891.

Myron E. Baum was Litchfield's twenty-first mayor in 1900 and assistant fire chief from 1900 to 1905. Ironically the Litchfield House had a fire on December 20, 1911, which put Baum out of business for a while. Baum closed the dining room in August of 1913. Mrs. J. W. Gilbert owned the hotel in April of 1926, after Myron Baum died in 1921. An interesting sideline about Myron Baum is that he committed suicide by purposely drinking a cup of muriatic acid, (hydrochloric acid), and burning out his throat.

Mrs. Gilbert sold the building in May of 1931 to John M. Palmquist, the owner of the Lenhardt Hotel. A. J. Hanson bought the Litchfield House in May of 1936 and turned it into a boarding house. Harold Lien bought it in 1948 and it became the Lien Apartments and Rooms until 1979 when the business closed. Today one of Ideal Lumber's buildings is on the site.

16. 100-124 Commercial Street East. At the corner, heading east from the Litchfield House, was Litchfield's very first lumberyard. John Esbjornsson and Charles Ellis Peterson started the lumberyard here in August of 1869. It went out of business that winter. Silas Wright

Leavett then had a lumberyard here in 1871 and he sold it to Esbjornsson in September of 1876. John called it the Pioneer Lumber Yard.

The lumberyard burned down in June of 1919 and was rebuilt. John passed it on to his son Hugo who passed it down to his son John Esbjornsson II. Stanley "Stan" Holmquist bought it in March of 1954, changing the name To Holmquist Lumber. He added a partner named Glenn Doering in January of 1955 and changed the name to the Litchfield Lumber Company.

15. 200 Commercial Street East. Across Holcombe, again heading east was an icehouse business. G. A. Neuman started an ice business in 1905. That small icehouse's location is unknown, but the ice business was moved into the larger icehouse at this location. The icehouse here was built in 1910 by a group of stockholders consisting of John M. Learn, William Shoultz and A. W. Kron. They hired Henry J. "Hank" Martens as their manager. Henry eventually took the business over. He was assistant fire chief from 1926 to 1929 and Litchfield's fire chief from 1929 to 1930. Kron was Litchfield's thirtieth mayor in 1914.

Martens sold the business to William Christenson in January of 1949. During that same month, Harry Truman was sworn in as President for his second term. A man named Lawrence Miller, dressed in leather chaps, did home delivery of the ice. Another home deliveryman was Ernie Gunter. They had a leather "saddle" looking thing over their shoulders to rest the ice block on. It had a pouch in the back to collect drippings so that they didn't get any water on the customer's floor. The icehouse building was torn down in May of 1962, after Consumer's Co-op Oil Company purchased the lot.

One block away, at the corner of Marshall Avenue and Commercial Street, was William Henry Greenleaf and Son's lumberyard in the early 1880s.

125 Sibley Avenue South. Heading back to the 100 block of Sibley Avenue from the library, I passed another lumberyard, which I remember as Weyerhauser. It originally was the J. F. Anderson Lumber Company, which became the Liberty Lumber Company and then Thompson Yards Inc. in February of 1916. But before all these lumberyards, there was an elevator here called the Minnesota & Dakota. It was either owned by or managed by George Raine. I'm not sure when it was built, but it burned down completely in June of 1890. Thompson Yards became

Weyerhauser Lumber in September of 1959 and today it's a warehouse for Ideal Lumber.

North of the railroad tracks, still on Sibley Avenue, was the Meeker County Elevator in the late 1870s and early 1880s. There were a lot of elevators around Litchfield in the 1880s. Commodore Davidson built the first elevator in town for the railroad in 1869 and it was very small. I'm not sure of the location but I'll bet it was on the south side of Depot Street between Sibley and Marshall Avenues. It was sold to the Millers' Association of Minneapolis who enlarged and improved it in 1879. In the late 1880s, Alexander D. Ross took it over. Col. John M. Howard built an elevator in 1872 on Marshall Avenue South, south of the tracks. The Cargill Brothers bought it in 1884 and A. J. Berry managed it for them. It's now at 106 Depot Street East. There was an elevator across Sibley Avenue, south of the tracks, which Chauncey Butler built in 1876. It failed in 1877 and James B. Atkinson, Sr. bought it. Michael J. Flynn and Brother bought it in 1880. It was bought by William Henry Greenleaf and Son and managed by H. H. Hine in September of 1897. The Farmers and Merchants Cooperative Association's elevator was built in the fall of 1886 and was managed by John Lindgren. I don't know the location of it. Shaw and Ehlers had an elevator with their Litchfield Roller Mill across Sibley Avenue, north of the tracks, which they built in 1885. The Northwestern Elevator Company was where the old "Railroad Elevator" had been on Marshall Avenue. The Northwestern, managed by Swan Peterson, was moved to Sibley Avenue North where the old depot had been, in the early 1890s. The Minnesota & Dakota elevator, constructed and owned by the Litchfield Elevator Company in 1883, was near the Litchfield House. The Litchfield Elevator Company was comprised of Alexander Cairncross, Andrew P. Nelson, W. W. Rollins, Nels Larson, B. P. Nelson and others. They sold the elevator in 1887 to an unknown buyer and it burned down in June of 1890. Also in the early 1890s, the total went up to five, adding the Farmer's elevator on Ramsey Avenue, run by Daniel McLane, and Daniel McLane's own elevator on Marshall Avenue North. In July of 1891, McLane leased the Flynn brothers' old warehouse on the south side of town but he didn't move into the building until March of 1892.

Still walking north on Sibley Avenue, I come to the east corner building, which is almost as famous as the hotel building.

133. 100 Sibley Avenue North. (1 Sibley in the early days and then 831-833 Sibley Avenue in the early 1900s.) One of the first non-residential buildings to go up in Litchfield was at this corner of Sibley Avenue and Depot Street. The St. Paul and Pacific Railroad put the building up for a land office in 1869. Hans Mattson was the land agent. In 1870, another small building was added to the lot and used as county offices. On April 5, 1872, Litchfield's Village Council met here for the first time and elected Jesse V. Branham, Jr. as the President. Lawyer Henry Hill had his office here. Then it became Meeker County's courthouse containing offices of the registrar of deeds, the county auditor, and one or more other officials. The county board held its meeting here also. County auditor Hamlet Stevens, a co-founder of the Stevens and Company bank, had his office in the building. In 1875, the St. Paul and Pacific Railroad still owned this lot. In late 1876, Stevens dug a pit behind the building to bury locust in during the Grasshopper Plague. The city paid a bounty on the pests. In the mid-1880s, the same small wooden building housed a livery and implement dealership. The building had a sign on the roof that stated "Studebaker Wagon".

Looking north at the east side of Sibley Avenue from the eastern corner of Sibley and Depot Street.

Frank Belfoy owned the building and had a printing office here briefly in late 1870 before moving elsewhere in town. Frank Belfoy was a pioneer lawyer and publisher of the *Meeker County News*. In 1873, J. W. Knight started his small "pump" business here in a little building. In July of 1882, J. W. Knight and Company built a "pump office" and feed grinding mill here. Then Knight had a plumbing and hardware store here. Christian B. Nelson leased part of the building in March of 1887 for a confectionery and restaurant. In April of 1887, Knight sold the hardware portion of the store to William H. Johns. That was the start of the Johns name being associated with hardware stores at locations all

488

over town. The small building used as the courthouse was moved a few doors east of here on Depot Street to be used as a harness shop. Knight moved a few doors up the street. Richard Welch bought the lot from Frank Belfoy's widow in April of 1889. Daniel McLane moved here in June of 1890, selling general merchandise. During that same month, Idaho and Wyoming were admitted to the Union. McLane moved out and sold his business to W. E. Tait and O. N. Ruden in March of 1891. They called their business O. N. Ruden and Company. In 1892, Welch built the famous big red brick building that's still here. Helgeson Brothers and Company, a general merchandise store, moved into the front part of the new building in May of 1892. The "Company" part of their name was S. W. Krueger, who had bought into the business in Mary of 1891. They called their store "The Grand". Late in 1892, the store took over the entire ground floor and added a partner named J. T. McNulty. They moved out in March of 1898. William H. Johns and Patrick Casey, Jr. rented the north room of the building in October of 1892. Their Johns and Casey Hardware came here for a short time. In October of 1893, the Chicago Bargain House moved upstairs, after their fire elsewhere in town in 1891. The business had moved all over town and finally closed in January of 1894. The brick building was the site of the Helgeson, Wells and Company store in 1894, as A. Helgeson invested in the store. The name was changed to Wells Brothers and Company General Store or the Wells Bros. Company Department Store in March of 1895. The Wells brothers, Alpheus and Alfred, sold groceries here also. Originally the store included the building next door where the Unique Theater went. It was called the "Big Store".

Left: The Wells store corner. Center and right: Alpheus and Alfred Wells

A fire gutted the store on November 11, 1908, but it bounced back in a few months and reopened in March of 1909.

The hotel and the Depot Street side of Wells the morning after the fire.

The Wells Bros. store closed in February of 1917 after twenty-two years. Richard Welch ran a general store here for a couple of months and then leased the building to Max H. Greenberg for his Greenberg's Department Store in June of 1917. Greenberg opened for business in October of 1917. Greenberg's had been in the Bierman building (Viren-Johnson's) across the street for five years. Greenberg went bankrupt in October of 1925. Welsh sold the building to Dewey E. Johnson in December of 1925. In January of 1926, L. J. Larson and Sons leased the building. Larson and Sons added groceries to the merchandise. Greep-Trueblood Company bought the business from Larson and Sons in June of 1926, installed Peter Osdoba as the manager, and took out the grocery part of the business out.

Pete Osdoba bought the business in the 1930s, but decided to leave the name as it was. After Pete died, his sisters, Genevieve "Gen" Osdoba-Schelde and Margaret "Peg" Osdoba-Palmquist assumed ownership. The Osdoba family ran Greep's for forty-eight years. In the late sixties, the store's sign simply stated "Greep's". Mike Mihlbauer's Sibley Antiques is here today.

134. Once again I will leave Sibley Avenue to walk east down Depot Street. The next building, after the Welch building on the corner was erected, was Litchfield's second telephone office. Before that, someone sold McCormick machinery from a building on this lot. Edward J. "Ed" Gould had his first harness shop here in February of 1886. He moved five more times to other locations in town, besides having a couple of different locations for saloons.

The first telephone office was in back of the corner drugstore downtown. The building here still has "R. Welch 1906" on the top of its front. Richard Welch built and owned this building, plus the Greep's building and the Unique Theater building. The Litchfield Telephone Exchange moved into the building in early 1906. The VFW bought the building in 1959, but continued to rent it to the telephone company. Today a body piercing and tattoo shop is here.

135. 21-23 Depot Street East. (Today Depot Street is more often referred to as Highway 12 East.) The *Litchfield Independent* was printed at this site before 1881, heading east from Sibley Avenue. A building was moved here from around the corner on Sibley. This was the *Independent's* second location. The building and the *Independent* moved again to the corner west of the hotel. In 1889, Daniel McLane and Luke D. Crowe had their machinery business here or in a wooden building closer to the west corner. The business had been behind McLane's store at Sibley Avenue and Third Street for many years. McLane took sole ownership of the business in December of 1890 and moved it in June of 1894 to the old Simpson-Jenkins Lumber Company building southwest of the depot. The James Campbell Harness shop was here in February of 1894. Campbell had moved to Litchfield in late 1893. Then Sam Brown had his harness shop here. After he moved down the block, A. Fred Grono moved his marble shop here in March of 1897. Edward J. "Ed" Gould bought the building for his harness shop in July of 1899.

In May of 1900, Mike J. Owens bought Gould's harness business for his Owens Harness Shop. Owens moved his shop a couple of doors east to the building Scherer's restaurant was in and Scherer moved here in the summer of 1911. Scherer sold the restaurant to Leo C. "Bud" Hanseman in August of 1915. A fire at the livery stable building next door to the east damaged this building in November of 1915. Hanseman moved to the Robertson building. Hanseman was back here in March of 1916 with his Bud's Café when the building was repaired. Then it was torn down. After F. L. Scherer put up a new building in June of 1917 for his cigar factory, a series of restaurants were here. The first was Bud's Café again, which closed in January of 1918. Scherer reopened his restaurant here in February of 1918. He called it the Boston Oyster and Chop House. At that time you could get a complete T-bone steak dinner for 50¢ at the restaurant. Next came Ole Hillstrom's restaurant in November of 1920. Ole quit in November of 1922 and Scherer took over with his Dairy Lunch Room, early in 1923. Scherer sold that restaurant to Oscar Warner in September of 1923. In March of 1929, A. G. Lewison had a sporting goods store here called the Gopher Store, breaking the chain of harness shops and restaurants. Besides sporting goods, the Gopher Store sold batteries and tires.

O. B. Gilbertson bought the Gopher Store in May of 1932 and changed the name to the Litchfield Auto Supply. For some reason he used both names in his newspaper ads, but went out of business in August of 1934. The G. L. Herman Furniture Store was in this building in March of 1935. I don't know if my high school classmate, Wayne Herman, was related to him. The business became the Eddy and Fenner Furniture store in April of 1946. Litchfield's future Chief of Police George A. Fenner was the partner of C. I. Eddy in that venture. Hamilton A. Johnson Furniture took over the business in August of 1951. Somewhere in the building, Bell-Colberg had their home supplies business until October of 1946, when it was moved across from the park. Johnson conducted his furniture business both here and across from the park in the early fifties until the VFW purchased this building in October of 1952 to have their clubroom upstairs. They rented the downstairs out to Johnson Furniture until Johnson left and moved his entire business across from the park next to Janousek's that month. Then the Meeker County Implement Company, sellers of John Deere and bought from Otto Sundahl, was here in the mid-fifties through 1959.

The business was sold to Boyd Weseman and Dennis Buck in November of 1960. In 1962, they moved the implement business to Highway 24 northeast of town. Hi-Way Supply, owned by Ralph Barrick and Floyd Hoel, moved into the building next, around 1965. Earl's Body Shop was also in the building at that time, probably in the rear. Barrick acquired the business himself and then sold it in June of 1970 to Gerald Gartner and Jeff Benson. Today this building stands vacant.

136. 25 Depot Street East. (Today Depot Street is more often referred to as Highway 12 East.) There were two buildings on this next lot to the east, so the information here may get confusing. The Chase and Dunn (R. W.) Pioneer Livery Stable was Litchfield's first livery and it was started here in the fall of 1869. Charles O. Porter owned all the lots from this point to the corner at Marshall Avenue in 1874. Sometime after that, Chase sold out to Dunn and Dunn took on a partner named Damuth. Dunn then sold his interest to Albert L. McCargar and Damuth and McCargar ran the livery. In November of 1881, they sold out to David Gorman and someone named Ormsbee. The Gorman and Ormsbee partnership dissolved in March of 1882 and Gorman bought Ormsbee out. Gorman still owned the livery in 1890. It was sold to the Wheeler brothers, Frank E. and I. N., in November of 1892.

Frank E. Wheeler

I. N. Wheeler

John M. Learn and Henry J. "Hank" Martens, future owner of the icehouse, leased the business from the Wheelers in June of 1900. They advertised that they sold "buggies and bicycles". Wesley B. Hunter bought out one of the Wheelers. Then Mike Ryan bought Hunter out. The other Wheeler sold his interest to Jack A. Hunter and the livery firm became Ryan and Hunter. Ed Olson bought out Ryan in May of 1907 and then Olson sold out to Jack Hunter in December of that year. In July of 1909, Hunter sold the livery to carpenter Nels J. Hawkinson. During that same month, Congress passed the 16th Amendment and income tax started. Hawkinson sold the livery to Ed Curtis and Dwight B. Lounsbury in December of 1909. Richard Welch became the owner of the building in the 1910s. The livery became the Hunter and Lounsbury livery in April of 1914, when Dwight B. Lounsbury consolidated with Hunter because of decreased business because of automobiles. The building got into disrepair and, in October of 1915, Welch was told by the city to tear it down, as it was a fire hazard. Guess what? It mysteriously caught fire and burned down in November. The livery was rebuilt and owned by Lounsbury and Son in 1916, just missing getting burned down again when the Wells store on the west corner had their big fire in the late fall of 1916. Oscar W. Nelson bought the horses and the equipment owned by Lounsbury in September of 1919 and moved the business to a barn by Hans C. Anderson's blacksmith shop. From September of 1926 until April of 1928, R. L and A. K. McDonald had their Litchfield Chevrolet business here. In April of 1928, Hans O. Evenson sold cars here. Evenson had given up his Buick dealership and was now selling Graham-Paige cars. The John Becklund-Roy F. Crosby auto repair garage was here in the rear in December of 1928.

Evenson moved out in 1931. Becklund and Crosby leased the whole building in October of 1931 and moved to the front. Harry Carlson had an "exchange market" here in March of 1933. It was a buying-selling service. In March of 1934, Betty O'Malley moved her dressmaking shop in here, calling it Betty's Shop. The Elgin B. Brown printing office was moved into some part of the building in November of 1937 after he had a fire at his other location over the Unique Theater. Robert Kaping came in May of 1936, calling his business the Litchfield Electric Shop. He moved out in April of 1938. George Bruce McClellan's Mac's Coffee Bar was here in May of 1938 McClellan, with some partners, had a chain of Coffee Bars in Willmar, South St. Paul, and Benson. Adolph E. Nelson took the restaurant over and had it for several years before leasing it to Clair Snyder and Evelyn Vargason in June of 1944. Elgin B. Brown moved out in May of 1945. Then the restaurant became Cecil Langhoff and Frank Madera's C & F Coffee Bar in September of 1945. Also, possibly in the rear, there was a building called the "White Front" garage or building here. Dewey E. Johnson Motor Sales was in it in March of 1947, selling Studebakers. In September of 1952, Harold Warren bought the dealership from Dewey. In October of 1968, the Red Door Thrift Store, owned by Don Anderson, moved in here and in July of 1969 it moved back out. During that same month, Neil Armstrong became the first human to walk on the moon. This building is gone today.

137. 27 Depot Street East. (Today Depot Street is more often referred to as Highway 12 East.) Sam Brown had a harness shop in the next location heading east in the early 1900s. The building itself had been at the corner of Sibley Avenue and Depot Street and had been used as the courthouse and city government building for a while. F. L. Scherer had a cigar factory here and sold the cigars in a shop here in April of 1910. He added a restaurant to the front of the building in September of 1910. Peterson Implement, at the corner east of here, also owned this building and it was sold to Mike J. Owens for a harness shop in the summer of 1911. Scherer moved to Owens' previous location with his restaurant. A fire gutted the building in November of 1915. Fires seemed to plaque buildings on Depot Street East. Owens moved elsewhere until a new brick building could be built here. Then he moved back here in June of 1916. Edward Lindwall had a shoe repair here for a while in September of 1918. He moved around town a lot. A plumbing business owned by Albin J. Nelson was here, and then Thomas A. Thompson leased part of the building in February of 1926 to sell Studebakers, sharing the building. In July of 1926, Scherer took the building back and re-established his restaurant, but not for long. W. Richard "Dick" Berens had a Chrysler business here in February of 1927. He moved out in January of 1928. Scherer did the restaurant here again and then closed again in November of 1928. He was persistent if not

successful. Charles H. Fitschen leased part of Mike J. Owens harness shop for a sporting goods store in March of 1929. Nelson's Eat Shop, owned by Harlow and Curtis Nelson was here after that until they closed in November of 1930. They were the sons of Alfred E. Nelson, who also owned a café in town.

In 1931, E. O. Redmond leased the building and put in his Model Eat Shop. J. W. Stiff took over in August of that year. A man named Stiff had owned a saloon about where Baril's Paint store went on Second Street West. I don't know if it was the same man. This business was sold to W. C. Donaldson in February of 1932. Donaldson called it the Rainbow Eat Shop. For some reason, Donaldson was under the scrutiny of the local officials. One night he just closed up the shop and left, leaving dirty dishes on the counter and in the sink. Walter Keller reopened the restaurant immediately and had his Model Eat Shop or Walt's Eat Shop here. He sold it to V. F. "Doc" Muelener in January of 1934. Muelener called it "Doc's Place" and turned right around and sold it to Otto and Dorothy Anderson in April of 1934. They called it the "Dorotto Café". They sold it to Ludvig Olson in October of 1936. It was the Stockholm Café until it was sold in October of 1937 to A. D. Bohnen and Bertha Wyttenhove to become the B & W Café. When it was sold to Harold "Pat" Woods, Woods kept the B & W letters but changed the name to the Black & White Inn. Pat moved the restaurant over by the produce and seed house at 213 Ramsey Avenue North where the Litchfield Hatchery had been in the mid-thirties. Walter McHugh had a restaurant here, which he sold to Frank Trappani in May of 1939. Trappani's beer license was taken away in July of 1939 and the FBI and the Secret Service investigated him. He had a suspicious-looking fire in August and he sold the building to the Askeroth brothers in October of 1939 before skipping town. He was later charged with counterfeiting. Clarence M. "Skip" and Vernon Askeroth built a new building here and installed a bowling alley in April of 1940. They leased the front of the building out to Frank L. Fransein in April of 1940 and he had the Bowling Café here. The Askeroths dissolved their partnership in April of 1945 and Clarence kept the bowling alley while Vernon took over the paint shop. The bowling alley was sold to Walt Schranz at some time and Ray and Jacob "Ollie" Olson bought it from him in May of 1949. It was sold to Art Krout and Warren Plath in November of 1954. This bowling alley had four lanes and my brothers, Dennie and Mick, worked there as pinsetters for a while. Art heard that a group from the cities was going to build a new bowling alley in town so he and Warren Plath quickly put up the Ripley Lanes[197] south of town by Lake Ripley in September of 1956. Of course, this bowling alley closed down. Vic Baldwin and Marv Nesterud took over the café part of the old bowling alley here in December of 1956, renaming it the Western Café. In September of 1957, there was new management of the Western, but I don't know who the owner was. Dances were held in the back bowling alley part.

Ralph Opatz, a teacher in another town, started Litchfield's first pizza parlor here in August of 1960. Although the Western Café offered pizza on its menu in May of 1958, I had my first restaurant pizza, (the "food of the gods"), here in September of 1960. Then the building housed the Litchfield Coin-Operated Dry Cleaners in October of 1961. After another Depot Street fire in May of 1963, the dry cleaning business was moved across from the park. Jerry Beckman's Appliance store followed here in the late sixties and seventies. In September of 1968, Pat Joyce started his Litchfield Radio and TV in the building sharing it with Beckman. Today it is America's Racquet & Fitness Center.

1916: The hotel, Wells store, the telephone office, an unoccupied building, Lounsbury livery, Scherer's restaurant and Peterson Implement.

138. 33 Depot Street East facing south, and 101 Marshall Avenue North facing east. (Today Depot Street is more often referred to as Highway 12 East.) Originally the Mitchell and Waller (John A. C.) Lumberyard was here at the corner of Marshall Avenue and Depot Street in 1870. The building was torn down in July of 1871 and the lot became vacant. It was used as an ice skating rink. In March of 1885, the GAR's old wooden armory building was moved here. The building, erected in

---

[197] Art and Warren sold the Ripley Lanes to Martin Pedley in September of 1961 and he sold it to Joe Nelson who had it for many years. An earlier bowling alley in town was where the King's Wok is now.

1874, had originally been in the middle of the east side of Marshall Avenue North between Second and Third Streets, where it had used as the armory and also as a roller rink. I don't know who moved it here but most likely it was for a machinery business. This corner of Depot Street and Marshall Avenue North, owned by Charles O. Porter, had a lot of different businesses here facing either Depot or Marshall, but most of the ones facing Depot had to do with farm equipment. I'll take the businesses facing Depot Street at this point, as I cover the ones facing Marshall in another part of the book. In 1894, George G. Mill's Implement was here. Then the Peterson Implement Company moved into the building.

Arthur W. Peterson leased the building, (it was called the Elliot building), in December of 1904 for his machinery business which had been a couple of doors west of here. He had bought the business from J. H. Spelliscy in 1904 when it had been on Depot Street west of the hotel. Peterson sold the Buick dealership part to Hans O. Evenson and Martin Spelliscy in March of 1910. They moved west on Depot Street by the hotel. Arthur W. Peterson and his brothers, Flanders H. and O. S., bought the George G. Mills' John Deere business. Arthur's brothers sold out to him in October of 1922. Arthur called it the Litchfield Implement.

After forty-eight years in the implement business, Arthur sold out to Otto Sundahl and J. Forrest Yetter in May of 1952. They changed the name to the Meeker County Implement Company. The building was torn down in May of 1953. A new building was erected and it became John O'Fallon's Sinclair Oil and Lennart Holen's Sinclair gas station in September of 1953. Meeker County's first outdoor phone booth was put in front of that gas station in late September of 1953. O'Fallon sold to Bart Hoard at some time. Holen sold to Eldon Johnson in the summer of 1958. In 1959, it was the Anderson Service Station.

In November of 1970, William S. "Mac" or "Bill" McGee, mayor of Litchfield in 1963, had a realty office in a building at this corner facing Marshall and, in May of 1973, the Benage Jewelry store was in a building facing Marshall. I don't know if it was the same building or not but it stayed only months before moving to Sibley Avenue North. Later my classmate John Ferguson had used cars here before moving his dealership out on east Highway 12. Eventually the Dave Pierce Insurance Agency occupied this space and next to it today are the Litchfield Therapeutic Massage and Exotic Specialty Travel/Lucky Mindy Adventures businesses.

24. There were many restaurants in Litchfield over the years. Most of them were downtown, but a couple had unique locations where Depot Street split into Highway 12 East on one side and First Street on the other. In the next block heading west was Ole Larsen's Travelers' Inn in the forties and fifties at the point of a triangular block. The block, at the junction of Depot and First Streets, had Capt. Miller's feed mill in August of 1885. Then Daniel Flynn's farm implement business was here in the early 1890s.

The "triangle" with the Travelers' Inn at the point.

C. O. Davis' Travelers' Café was built here in September of 1929. It was open all night. Gordon Langhoff owned it in the early forties, but he lost his beer license in December of 1944, hurting his business. Julia O. and Ole M. Larsen bought it in the mid-forties and changed it to the Travelers' Inn. In 1950, Ole ran an ad in the *Independent Review* calling notice to his "specials" at the Travelers'. The Friday special was fried turtle and the Saturday and Sunday specials were lutefisk. The Larsens ran it up to 1951, when they sold it to Russ and Doris Peterson.

The Petersons sold it to Donovan and Irene Blaha in January of 1966 and then bought it back in January of 1967. They sold it to Ervin and Margaret Jensrud in the late sixties. It is now Langmo Farms.

107 Depot Street East. (Today Depot Street is more often referred to as Highway 12 East.) East of the restaurant in 1879 was an old blacksmith and wood working shop building. Morris and Henry Neuman built it. Morris was the blacksmith. He had started on Marshall Avenue around 1873. In October of 1890, Nels Edward Anderson bought it and had his blacksmith shop there. Nels was uncle to Andy Anderson whose blacksmith shop was across from the old power plant at 114 Third Street West. M. B. Hudson and Company rented the Neuman building in December of 1892 for a flour and feed mill.

Nels Edward Anderson

Nels E. Anderson sold the shop to M. H. Yost in March of 1922. Fred A. Kopplin built his Super Service gas station here in September of 1929 after he tore down Anderson's old wood building. Across the street were the old stockyards used by the railroad. Someone named Halverson ran it. Both the gas station and the Travelers' Inn, first called the Travelers' Café, were open all night. It was the only all night gas station between here and the Dakotas. Dale's 76 Service was here in the late sixties and early seventies. Today Prints Charming is just east of the site of the Travelers' Inn.

215-225 Depot Street East. The Kopplins had a miniature golf course for a while east of the station where the Green Lantern was and the Super America station is today. The Green Lantern café was where the Super America gas station is today between Holcombe and Armstrong Avenues at 215 Depot Street East. It was owned by Henry Hanson, and was sold to Fred R. Butte or Butke or Buddes in May of 1939. Because it was so near to the old high school, maybe a hundred yards at the most, it was said that Coach Millard Horton used to slip in there during practice for high school sports for a quick beer. It was sold to Mrs. George Bauer in January of 1942. She called it the Eat Shop then. The Super America station came in the early sixties and is still here today.

19. Just like the railroad, Highway 12 runs right through the middle of Litchfield. Highway 12 was once called Highway 10. Highway 10 came into town out by Ripley Cemetery. There were a few businesses on Highway 12 on each end of the town. One of the businesses out on Highway 12 East was Sylvester "Spotty" Loehr's A & W Drive-In, for example. In 1947, Spotty started his A & W Drive-In at the corner of Sibley Avenue North and Tenth Street where the gas station parking lot is for the closed Tom Thumb convenience store today and McCarthy's

499

Drive-In had been in the sixties. In May of 1952, Spotty moved his drive-in out on east Highway 12, about where Taco John is today. Another drive-in, The Shack, also started in 1947. It was out on east Highway 12, between the DS station and Harry's Tire Shop.

Near the A & W was the Red & White grocery store, where Super Valu is today. Two businesses out by Spotty's that didn't stay, but kids liked, were the trampoline pits and go-cart racing. The trampolines didn't stay because of accidents and insurance problems. Fred Berke opened the "Jumpo-Jym" up May of 1960. Fred was mayor in 1961 and 1970. In June of 1960, Roger Nelson and Eldon Tritabaugh put up a go-cart track by the A & W drive-in. The track lasted about six weeks. The city council put them out of business because of too many complaints about the noise and the dust.

Harry Radunz built his new Harry's Tire Shop out there in 1936. He couldn't keep his business going at that location and he sold the building to Art Krout, who started Krout Motors there. The REA bought the building from Krout in December of 1949 and had their office at that location. By the way, the first farm to get electrified was the Charles Ness farm in June of 1937. In July of 1949, Phil Berg opened the Dairy Freeze, which became the Dari-Way, next to Anderberg's D-S gas station. Anderberg had bought out Henry Plocher in September of 1940. Berg sold the Dairy Freeze to Nathan Fullerton in 1960.

The oddest-looking business on east Highway 12 was a small, yellowish log cabin. Called the Log House Café, it was owned by Don and Flo Singlestad. They started the business in October of 1948. Located where the Super Valu parking lot is, it was a café and a drive-in complete with carhops. The Singlestads sold the log cabin to Mr. and Mrs. R. Johnston in 1950 and, in May of 1952, the Johnstons sold it to Bob Basten. Then, in February of 1954, it became the Litchfield Municipal Liquor Store, which was managed by Rudy Hoffman.

Bill and Ida Johnson started a restaurant at the East Side Shell gas station in May of 1959 at the very east edge of town. They called it Ida Johnson's Café. The gas station was built in January of 1955.

140. 104-106 Sibley Avenue North. (3 Sibley in the early days and then 827 Sibley Avenue in the early 1900s.) Back on Sibley Avenue North, heading north from the Greep's corner, was Solomon "Sol" M. Almquist's saloon in 1870. Sol was a brother to Charles J. Almquist who owned the Litchfield House. The saloon was twenty by thirty feet and two-stories high. Mr. Hulbertson, a blacksmith in town, built the building for $1500 and then leased it out. In 1875, the St. Paul and

500

Pacific Railroad still owned this lot. Solomon moved a few lots up the street in late 1876 to a larger building he had erected. Phineas "Pat" Cary's Store, a general merchandise store also selling boots and shoes, was here from November of 1882 to 1901. In 1887, August T. Koerner's wife Catherine "Katie" was listed as the lot's owner. Mrs. Augeline Cary's Star Millinery was here in the late 1880s. When the basement was dug for the new Welch building next door to the south in 1892, some quick work was needed to keep Mrs. Augeline Cary's building from toppling into the hole. In 1897, the first movie theater was opened in the United States, foretelling a future for this location.

J. Codden leased the building here in March of 1910 and started something he called the New Store. He sold clothing and changed the name to the St. Paul Bargain Store. Then Welch and Company (W. H. Welch and Emil Gross) had a store here called the Litchfield Racket Store. 1901 was a big year for the building with a lot of changes. Mrs. Cary went out of business in April of 1901 and Mrs. John Johnson and Julia Anderson took it over. Mrs. Cary kept ownership of the building. Johnson and Anderson called their business the Litchfield Millinery Company and they moved out in June, at the same time that the Litchfield Racket Store was being sold to L. T. Amunds and Company. Amunds changed the name of the store from the Racket Store to the Royal Cash store in July. Mrs. M. Bears leased a room in the building for a millinery in September and closed it in December. The American Amusement Company leased the building in December of 1910 and by February of 1911 they had started the famous Unique Theater. Some town people got up in arms about the movies and formed a censorship board, demanding to preview the movies. The theater was leased to Boyd Helgeson and Ray Maher in May of 1911. By the way, in 1913 Edison invented "talkies" or movies with sound. The Noreen brothers, Elmer S. and Rudolph, bought the theater in April of 1914. Being musicians, they doubled as the accompaniment for the silent movies along with their pianist Hardy A. "Snooky" Bronson. Snooky, who worked at the Silverberg-Olson store, played the Kimball grand piano and the Noreen brothers often played horns for many years up front to the side of the silent movie screen. When the people saw Snooky come down the aisle they knew the show was about to begin. Snooky was still playing right up to the day C. F. Schnee brought in sound equipment in 1929. In the summer of 1915, two young men from Litchfield were hired to take a camera and shoot short films about towns in the area. They were H. C. Griffith and Arthur Scherer. On August 30, 1915, Unique Theater patrons were treated to a very short silent film that began with county officials parading in front of the camera on the courthouse lawn. Then there were some views of Sibley Avenue facing south. The next sequence followed the city band marching to the train depot to meet a delegation from Atwater, which included Atwater's baseball team. The entire group was then shown marching to the ballpark on the southeast corner of town where the teams were filmed standing in lines for the camera. Mayor Peter Rodange was shown throwing out the first ball for the game and that was the end of the film. No one knows what happened to the film but I do know that Atwater defeated Litchfield that night by a score of 11 to 1. The United Theatres Company, headed by Bart Foster, leased the Unique in October of 1917, but Rudolph Noreen still owned and managed it. Elmer Parsons bought Noreen's share of the theater in December of 1917, then the lease with United Theatres was cancelled and the theater was sold to David T. Hobson in January of 1918. Hobson, who also owned a confectionery and cigar shop next to the Hollywood theater's future site, changed the name to the Hobson Theatre in May of 1918. He sold the theater to G. W. Brown in December of 1919. Brown changed the name back to the Unique and then sold it to A. F. McLane in October of 1920. In June of 1922, E. V. Freid bought the theater. At this time the "Unique Orchestra", led by E. V.'s brother Leonard Freid, provided the background music. They also played some dance jobs around the area. I don't know who was in the orchestra and if Snooky Bronson was still playing piano at this time. He was still a member of Elmer Noreen's orchestra. C. F. Schnee bought the Unique from Freid in July of 1924 and opened up in September. Donald "Donnie" Wheeler, son of Litchfield pioneer barber Ray Wheeler, went to work for Schnee in 1927 helping his cousin Floyd Wheeler, who was the projectionist. At one time or another, the entire Wheeler family, Donnie, Lucille, Jerry and Yvonne worked for the Schnees. In October of 1927, *The Jazz Singer,* starring Al Jolson, debuted as the "first" talking picture, and its success spelled the beginning of the end for silent movies. The Unique was finally allowed to show movies on Sundays on April 14, 1929. Litchfield citizens were treated to their first successful "talkie" at the Unique on December 1, 1929. It was *The Rainbow Man* starring Eddie Dowling and Frankie Darro. The admission price jumped up to 20¢ and 50¢.

The Schnees remodeled the theater in 1948, putting a new front on the building. Both of their theaters were sold to Dean Lutz in April of 1978. The Unique was torn down in May of 1996. It is just a vacant lot and a lot of great memories today.

108 Sibley Avenue North. (829 Sibley Avenue in the early 1900s.) There were a few businesses upstairs over the previous location. In August of 1902, Mrs. Frederick Rudberg had her dressmaking parlor upstairs for a couple of months. J. I. Harrington and Walter H. McCann had a real estate office called Harrington and McCann upstairs in February of 1916. It was changed to the McCann Land Company selling "Farm Lands", according to Walter McCann's sign.

The Longworth Beauty Parlor opened up over the Unique in 1931. Elgin B. Brown had his Brown Printing office upstairs in the mid-thirties but moved out in November of 1937 after he had a fire.

142. 110 Sibley Avenue North. (5 Sibley in the early days and then 825 Sibley Avenue in the early 1900s.) Next door to the north of the Unique was a poor little wooden building busy with its many tenants. M. Arthur Brown started out in this building in the early days of Litchfield. He sold hardware in his little shop and was a "turner" or lathe operator. In 1875, the St. Paul and Pacific Railroad still owned this lot and Mrs. A. Waggoner, a dressmaker, was here in the back of whatever store was here in 1883. In September of 1884, Birch and Nelson Clothing moved in here from across the street. John Birch was partnered with Rasmus Nelson and the business advertised that they had "gent's furnishing goods". Robert A. Vorys opened a confectionery and bakery here in March of 1886. Vorys moved his restaurant all over town over the years. In June of 1888, pioneer Nels C. G. Hanson had a small hardware here in some part of this building. By 1889, he had a partner named John Johnson. In mid-1893, Christian B. Nelson had a confectionery here. J. W. Knight and Company had a plumbing business in the rear in the early 1890s.

The Ringdahl brothers, Ole and Nels, came here around the turn of the century with their tailoring business. Miss Christine Nelson, who ended up marrying Ole Ringdahl, leased half of the building in March of 1902 for a millinery and then bought the building in July of 1907. Elsie V. Ralston bought the millinery in August of 1913. She had been on Marshall Avenue. In 1913, a sign here stated "Ringdahl Bros. Merchant Tailors". Ole retired in 1936, and Nels kept the business going by himself here and in different locations around town, usually above stores. He also sold grave markers and monuments. He took the ones he made mistakes on and made a walkway in the rear. Eventually the markers got covered with dirt and when they were uncovered a few years later, people thought they had found an old graveyard. At first the tailor business was here in the north side of the building. The Ralstons' millinery was in the south side. The Ralston Sisters' Millinery, which began here in the early 1900s and was still going through the 1920s, shared the building with the S. H. Skartvedt's Electric Service Company in April of 1920. The electric service was in the north half of the building. In the mid-1910s, the millinery was called Miss Elsie V. Ralston's Millinery, as one sister left, but then came back. Mrs. Parson and Mrs. William P. Robertson had a dressmaking and knitting shop here in the late twenties.

In August of 1936, William Linne, the baker, opened an office here to sell McConnan & Company products. I assume they were like Watkins products. Glader and Anderson moved their electric shop here in the north half in October of 1936. The business was now called Glader, Inc. The Brown Printing Company sharing the building in early 1937 but moved above the Unique next door. Charles West bought out Glader in November of 1937 and called his business West Electric Company. In April of 1938, Robert Kaping brought his Litchfield Electric Shop here, sharing the Ben H. Anderson owned building with the Ralstons. One of the Ralston sisters left again in 1939 and the business once more became Miss Elsie V. Ralston's Millinery. Chet Berg bought West's half of the building and his Berg Electric Sales and Service, also called the Litchfield Electrical and Motor Works, was here in 1938. One can only assume or hope that some of these businesses were upstairs or in the back. In December of 1941, Shirley James brought her Litchfield Dry Goods store into part of the building. She sometimes advertised the business by just her name. During that same month, the United States declared war on Japan. Shirley James closed in February of 1942. In late 1942, Axel A. Gordhammer moved his dry cleaning business into the room where the Electric Shop had been. In 1946 Chet Berg, bought the whole building and Ralston had to move. She moved the business to her house at 340 East First Street. Leland Eckerman had a radio repair business in a corner of the building in the mid-forties. He moved out in May of 1947. In March of 1948, George D. Tuttle bought the building and had his Tuttle's Sport and Gift Shop here. Tuttle was the city's mayor in 1949. Barber Martin B. Peterzen started selling Prudential Life Insurance in an office in the building in February of 1949. Tuttle's store closed in December of 1950. Arden W. Burleigh bought the building from Tuttle in January of 1951 and he had his photography studio here until June of 1962 when he moved down by the greenhouse to 718 Sibley Avenue North where my uncle, Allen Johnson, had had his small grocery for a while.

Roscoe G. Keller bought the building, tore it down and put his new barbershop, the Keller Barber Service, and office building up in the summer of 1962. The Western Saddlery shop moved here to one of the rooms in September of 1962, as did Dr. J. H. Navratil, a chiropractor. When Navratil left, Dr. M. L. Speckman moved his chiropractic business to that room in November of 1967. In the late sixties, Gloria Werre and Carol Keller had their Coiffure Beauty Salon in the rear of the building. My wife worked for them when we came back from Germany. Cynthia Tongen bought the salon in August of 1970 and it became Cynthia's Wig & Beauty Salon. My classmate Sue Wisdorf Eisenbacher worked along side of my wife for them. Today, the building at this location houses the Bruce Kellogg's Kellogg Barber Shop and H & R Block.

143. 112 Sibley Avenue North. (7 Sibley in the early days and then 823 Sibley Avenue in the early 1900s.) A little store called Axel's Candy and Tobacco store or Axel's Place, owned by Axel Johnson, was the next store heading north in my day. It was in half of the building where John E. Jorgenson Realty is now. In 1875, however, the St. Paul and Pacific Railroad owned this lot and in the mid-1870s, a building housing the Rail Road Bonds and Real Estate Agency was here. In the summer of 1879, Per Ekstrom, August T. "Gus" Koerner and Company (Frank E. Viren) had a real estate office here. Viren left the partnership in October of 1881. The Stevens and Company bank bought out his interest. A small saloon owned by S. A. Thorp was here in 1883. In 1891, John Creighton owned the lot that included this building and the one to the north of it. Nels Fredrickson had a "temperance bar" here in the early 1890s.

Christian B. "Christ" Nelson had a confectionary here in 1921, which he sold to Walter Nelson, John M. Palmquist and Clyde G. Crosby. It was called the Palmquist Confectionery. Nelson left, retaining ownership of the lot, and John M. Palmquist sold his interest to Clyde G. Crosby in March of 1923. Nelson's daughters, Sophie, Daisy and another whose name I don't know, inherited the building and the one to the north. Axel Johnson bought the building here from the Nelsons and the business from Crosby in September of 1923. Because of his ties to "Music" Olson, (his wife was Olson's daughter), the Litchfield Music Center was here also. After Axel retired, Vold's Optometry came in here in September of 1956. Today John E. Jorgenson's Realty is at the location of both Kate's and Axel's.

146. 114 Sibley Avenue North. (7 Sibley in the early days and then 821 Sibley Avenue in the early 1900s.) Another tiny building followed Axel's. In 1875, the St. Paul and Pacific Railroad owned this lot. In May of 1876, the site had the Independent Printing Office, which published the *Litchfield Independent* newspaper. The Nelson sisters owned this tiny twelve and one-half foot wide building. In 1891, John Creighton owned the lot that included this building and the one to the south of it.

At one time in the early 1900s, the *Litchfield Saturday Review* was also published here at the Litchfield Printing office. William Miller had a plumbing business here around the turn of the century. After he left, Nels Lundeen moved his shoe repair into the room from across the street in August of 1905. Emil Mortenson bought Lundeen's business in September of 1911 and started his shoe repair business.

Mortenson moved across the alley to the Settergren building north of here in August of 1930 and the L. W. Adams Electric Service Shop moved in here, trading locations. Sandy's Shine Shop and newsstand owned by L. F. "Sandy" Sandberg was here in September of 1931, but he closed his business in April of 1932. Mortenson moved across Sibley Avenue in February of 1932, but came back here with his repair shop in November after his shoe store across the street went bankrupt. After Mortenson moved out again, J. Fish moved his Cut Rate Store here in February of 1935. He sold "cut rate" fruit. The business must not have lasted long because Walter G. "Walt" Johnson moved his barbershop here in August of 1935. In October, Johnson moved across the alley to the rear of the Settergren building. Mrs. William P. Robertson had a yarn store here called the Knit Shop in November of 1935. Walt Johnson came back in August of 1936, buying the building. Leo Shaffer bought the shop in December of 1937 and his Shaffer's Barber Shop was in the building sharing it or just occupying it. In April of 1940, Leo added a beauty shop to his business, calling the business Shaffer's Beauty and Barber Shop. Lucille Hanson managed the beauty salon. John Becklund had a Fix It Shop in the back room in the mid-1940s. Leo Shaffer wanted to go into the Navy during the war, so he leased the shop out to Gust Korinta in April of 1944 and left. That deal fell through or something because W. H. Eid and S. C. Berg had their Refrigeration Service here until Leo came back in October of 1944. The Navy had rejected him. Eid's Refrigeration Company was in the back in the mid-forties, so Eid must have gotten full control of the business by then. Dave Holly moved in and had the Taxi Inn here in the later forties. In April of 1948, Holly sold the little building and his taxi service to Lyle and Martin Thomas. Kate and Melvin Pierce bought the site in February of 1950. They built a new brick building here in 1951 and moved in, starting Kate's Café or the Quick Lunch. It was later called Kate's Lunchroom.

Kate retired and sold the building to Laura Tostenrud in July of 1960 and the business became the Food Box. Today John E. Jorgenson's Realty is at the location of both Kate's and Axel's. An alley followed Kate's. As far as I can tell, there was always an alley or vacant lot at there.

147. 116 Sibley Avenue North. (9 Sibley in the early days and then 817 Sibley Avenue in the early 1900s.) The lot north of the alley had a couple of buildings on it; maybe one was straddling the eventual alley location. Andrew P. Nelson and Andrew Winger had a tailor shop here in 1876. In September of 1876, the Elmquist brothers came from Minneapolis and started the Elmquist Brothers' jewelry store in one of the buildings here. On the 7th of that month, the locals were shocked to hear that Jesse James and his gang robbed a bank in Northfield, Minnesota. Dr. V. P. Kennedy had an office in one of the buildings. In November of 1876, Solomon "Sol" M. Almquist started building a twenty-five by sixty foot saloon building here where Dr. Kennedy's office had been. His Solomon Saloon was finished in February of 1877. One of the Elmquist brothers, P. J., left and David, the other one, moved across the street in the early 1880s. At some time the buildings were combined or the smaller of the two was removed. Almquist turned the saloon over to his nephew Frank Dahl and bartender Ditlof Peterson in January of 1886, but retained ownership. D. A. Roos, who also owned a bottling plant, bought the saloon from Almquist in April of 1888. He quickly sold the saloon and bottling plant to Nels Frederickson in December of 1888. The Johnson and Wanvig hardware was here at some time in part of the building. August A. "Gus" and Frank Settergren bought out Johnson and Wanvig in January of 1893. The business became the Settergren Brothers Hardware. Their father, Carl J. Settergren, was a tanner in town. Pioneer lawyer Charles Henry Strobeck bought the lot and buildings in February of 1893. In 1894, the saloon became the J. A. C. Pallmer saloon. F. R. Fredrickson moved into part of the building in May of 1894 for another saloon, possibly a "temperance" one. The Tuscarora Salvage Fire Company, which sold damaged clothes, moved into the building in August of 1897. John M. Learn moved a billiard hall and temperance saloon into a room here in October of 1897. He also partnered with Charles H. Dart in the

Litchfield Collection Agency in 1897. It probably was headquartered here.

The old "Exchange barn" was in the alley behind Settergren's. It was left here when the Exchange Hotel moved to Marshall Avenue. R. K. C. Brown bought the barn and changed it into a feed, transfer and sale stable in December of 1909. Brown sold it to a Shoutz who sold it to T. W. Stewart in May of 1915. Tom Quinn had a dry cleaning business here in May of 1916, which he sold to C. J. Stephansen in October of 1918. He called the business the Litchfield Cleaning Works. Richard Welch leased the building and moved here in January of 1918 to sell Paige, Mitchell and Saxon automobiles. Edward G. "Ed" Gates opened a tire vulcanizing shop in a rear room here also in January of 1918. W. Richard Berens sold Studebakers out of a room in the building in May of 1919 after Welch left in March. The Settergren brothers bought the building around 1920, but people called it the Settergren building way into the fifties. Richard Welch moved back here in March of 1922. He moved out again that summer. In 1921, Jake's Army Store, selling army surplus goods, was here for a short time. The building was split with Rudolph C. Peters and George R. Johnson's store called The Clothes Shop, which came here in Welch's part on the right side of the store in September of 1922 and Wright Electric, which came in June of 1920, on the left. H. M. Wright owned the electric business. At that time, Wright was sharing W. Richard Beren's showroom. Victor Mickelson had a car repair business in the rear of the building at the same time. Johnson sold his interest in The Clothes Shop to Louis G. Marquard in January of 1925. Marquard eventually bought out Peters in May of 1925 and the L. G. Marquard Clothing was here until it closed in September of 1928. More than one business was in this building at one time, as you can tell. Also there were businesses to the rear of the building, probably across the alley. Ed Bohls had a feed barn there, which he sold to William Huberty in October of 1922. In late 1922, J. William Williams had his tire repair shop in the rear of the building. In December of 1926, Algot Lindholm had a shoe repair business in the part of the building where Welch had sold cars. Olaf O. Askeroth and his son Clarence M. "Skip" Askeroth moved in with their paint and wallpapering business until they moved into their more known location on Second Street. In August of 1929, Kronzer's Cash Shoe Store was here in the part of the building where Marquard Clothing had been.

The shoe store went out of business in 1930. At some time in the early thirties, Clinton Caylor had a woman's wear shop named the Lydia Darrah Shop in a room here. In July of 1930, Ray Allison moved his

Allison Electric shop in here. His store became Adams' Electric Shop, which moved to where Mortenson's shoe store had been in August of 1930. Emil Mortenson moved in here exchanging locations with him. Adolph M. Olander brought a fruit and vegetable business to the building in April of 1931. Frank's Café, owned by Frank Williams, was here in 1931. Clara Olson's Flavo Korn Shop was here in the early thirties. It closed in January of 1932 and Clint and Agatha's Kandy Kitchen moved here to the room Olson vacated. Clinton and Agatha Caylor owned it. In December of 1931, Olaf Nelson had his Home Cafe here in the back room where Allison Electric had been. Olof leased his restaurant to Arnold Larson in May of 1932. Frank Williams came back with his cafe in November of 1932 and moved into the room formerly occupied by Clinton Caylor's shop. Also in November of 1932, the Tiger Store owned by L. C. Kortie and his sons, one was Jim, was in the front of the building. Al E. Hummel managed it. The Tiger Store, a variety store with hardware, became Gamble's later.

1933: Sandgren's Shoe Repair, Beach's gun repair, Arvig's Bee Hive Café and the Tiger Store.

In July of 1934, the Tiger store and a pool hall, which had once been owned by my great-uncle Ed Birkemeyer at the other end of town, switched locations. So now the pool hall was here and the building was back to what it began as, a saloon. Walter G. Johnson had his barbershop here in the rear in October of 1935. The locals called him the "25¢ barber". L. E. Christofferson bought the barbershop from Walter right away. The pool hall became Feig and Edwards Recreation Parlor, which changed to Mons and Edwards in the early forties and then just Edwards Recreation Parlor, when Frank Edwards bought the lot and pool hall from O. A. Settergren in May of 1941. John O'Neil moved his plumbing business to a small building in the alley behind the pool hall in early 1946. In November, he was working late at night when something

509

exploded and he was engulfed in flames. Night patrolman Tiny Fredrickson was checking the alley and saw the fire. He rushed in and covered John with his jacket and smothered the flames, saving John's life. In the late forties, Edwards took on a partner named Willard "Bill" Putzier. Melvin "Bull" Johnson bought out Edwards in July of 1953 and Johnson and Putzier's Recreation was born. Johnson bought out Putzier in January of 1958, and the "saloon" became Johnson's Recreation.

Melvin Johnson sold the recreation hall to Patrick "Barney" Barnes in March of 1962 and it became Barney's Rec. Then it was Dale's Rec in 1966, when Dale Lee bought it. It's a vacant lot today. The two stores that followed this one were where Penney's built their new store.

150. 118 Sibley Avenue North. (11 Sibley in the early days and then 815 Sibley Avenue in the early 1900s.) The first occupant of the next lot heading north was the Litchfield Exchange Hotel, built in 1870 by George Teigen, and sold to W. S. Knappen in early 1873. In December of 1873, Knappen added a restaurant to the hotel. In January of 1875, it was sold to Thomas Ryckman. H. W. Simons bought it in 1878 and moved it to the middle of Marshall Avenue on the east side of the street in June of 1879. While here on Sibley Avenue, a barber named Brown had his business in the hotel in the mid to late 1870s. The John Birch and Andrew P. Nelson clothing store, which moved all over town, moved here in the early 1880s for a short time, sharing the building as did Andrew O. Palmquist's tailoring business. Birch and Nelson moved out in the spring of 1885 and Palmquist moved to another location in town. Birch and Nelson were advertising that they would trade clothing for wheat at that time. Money must've been in short supply. Palmquist came back with a partner, Olof P. "Ole" Ringdahl in March of 1889. Ole Ringdahl's brother Nels worked for Andrew and Ole at another location in 1887. An 1897 photograph shows Palmquist as a tailor somewhere else in town. Possibly it was after then that he moved in here as partner to Ringdahl.

Ringdahl, Palmquist and two of their tailors in 1899.

Nels left and went to Minneapolis to work, then came back and bought out Palmquist in April of 1901. The business became the Ringdahl Brothers Tailor Shop. Nels was assistant fire chief from 1906 to 1909. Around the turn of the century, the Ringdahls moved back down the street to their original location. Edward G. "Ed" Gates had a tire repair business here in later 1918, moving here from next door. It became the first location of Clarence F. "Dugan" Deilke's Cleaning Works, when Deilke bought out Stephansen in April of 1923. The Caylor Candy Shop was here in some part of the building at some time. Deilke moved out in early 1930 after building a new shop elsewhere. In March of 1922, James D. Atkinson moved his Litchfield Battery Shop here from the old *Ledger* building. Atkinson sold the battery shop to Harry N. Carlson in May of 1923. Paul M. Olson and Reuben Wenberg had a tire repair shop here in March of 1925. C. W. Rudolph opened an electrical supplies store in the Gates Tire Shop in July of 1926.

S. M. Arvig brought a café here in April of 1933 and called it the Bee Hive Cafe. Arvig sold the Bee Hive to Hugo H. Boetcher in March of 1937. He called his restaurant Hugo's Café. The Sederstrom Realty was here upstairs in the mid and late thirties. F. A. Myers' shoe repair shop was next to Boetcher in the other half of the building. O. A. Settergren sold the building to Boetcher in May of 1941. Axel A. Gordhammer's Dry Cleaning moved into a room in March of 1942. He moved down the street in late 1942. In April of 1944, Conrad W. Berquist moved his electric shop into the half that wasn't occupied by Hugo's Café. It was the first of many locations around town for Berquist. W. H. Eid and S. C. Berg had their Eid and Berg Refrigeration Service in the rear of the building in November of 1944. The building had the Rau and Dahl Tire Company in the north half starting in April of 1945. M. Raleigh Dahl was actually in the service but came home in April of 1946. In June, Dahl bought out Rau and the store was changed to the Dahl Tire Company. Don's TV service, owned by Don Test was here in 1953. Dahl moved to the corner of Third Street and Ramsey Avenue in 1957 and Don Test followed Raleigh to that location. The J. C. Penny Company then built on this lot and the one to the north in 1958. The store opened up in January of 1959. Today, True Valu hardware is here.

In 1916 and 1923 photos of this street, there was a tiny twelve and a half foot wide building between the last building and the next. George Homer Beach had a gun repair shop in this little building in the late

1880s and added a shooting gallery in October of 1886. During that same month, the Statue of Liberty was dedicated in New York Harbor.

Beach's business and the building were still here in the early thirties. This was the original drop off point for the Twin City newspapers. Beach died in the fall of 1936, after celebrating fifty years of business in the same place.

1923: Gordhammer meats, Scarp Café, White Cross laundry, Beach gun shop, Deilke's cleaning/Gates tire shop and Wright Electric/Clothes Shop.

151. 120-124 Sibley Avenue North. (13 Sibley in the early days and then 813 Sibley Avenue in the early 1900s.) In October of 1876, Samuel Hollingsworth's Uncle Tom's Cabin Saloon was in the building north of the last location. The Litchfield Music Company was here at one time also. In 1877, creditors closed the saloon but it re-opened in October of 1878 next door. At some time before 1885, Mrs. A. Waggoner had a dressmaking shop in a room here. John Hanson and J. A. Olson sold McCormick machinery from an office in that room in April of 1885. In the early 1890s, Edward J. "Ed" Gould had a "temperance" pool hall here. That meant he sold no liquor. In 1895, Andrew O. Palmquist was listed as the owner of this lot. By then he had his tailoring shop here. Palmquist was another person in the clothing business who moved all over town. By 1897, Ole Ringdahl was his partner here.

In September of 1921, Harry Wisner's White Cross Laundry was here. I believe it became Hatcher's Litchfield Laundry, which closed in January of 1927. Scherer's cigar factory was upstairs over the laundry in the early 1920s. Andrew W. Sandgren's shoe repair shop was here for a while in the late twenties and early thirties. Ole Hillstrom started selling new shoes in the south side of the room along side Sandgren in May of 1928. Richard Welch had an office there also until he died in the late 1920s.

512

In August of 1933, Andrew Sandgren committed suicide. His son George came home and took over the business. Vic and Vern Sederstrom's Realty was upstairs but they moved down to the ground level in April of 1943 after Sandgren's had moved to the north corner of this block. Leonard A. Hobert moved his insurance office into the building at the same time. Vold's Optometry's second location was above the business. Vold moved south down the street in September of 1956. This building stood vacant after Sederstrom's moved by the *Independent Review*'s building. The Litchfield or Production Credit Association was here for a short time in the late forties or 1950 but moved out in March of 1951. The building was torn down in October of 1956. The J. C. Penny Company then built on this lot and the one to the south in 1958 and opened up for business in January of 1959.

After Penny's closed, the building became Bob Hanson's Coast To Coast. It's the True Valu hardware store today.

Penney's in 1969.

152. 126 Sibley Avenue North. (15 Sibley in the early days and then 811 Sibley Avenue in the early 1900s.) The building north of the Penny's site sat on a lot originally owned by M. Arthur Brown and Clark L. Angell. H. B. Brown had a lumberyard in town under the name of Brown and Brown and he erected a building here in September of 1878 after Angell had left the location. Samuel Hollingsworth moved his saloon and billiard hall here from next door in October of 1878. James Hooser leased the building in October of 1879 and turned it into just a temperance billiard hall, taking out the bar. That lasted just two years. In December of 1881, Swan August "Gus" Scarp bought the building for his saloon. Scarp, from Sweden, built a new wooden building here and leased the saloon to John Burns in January of 1887. Later that month, John Paulson and Charles C. Sather bought the saloon business from Scarp. In October of 1887, John Paulson sold his interest in the saloon back to Scarp. Jacob "Jake" Koerner, Sr. had an old wooden building

also on the lot here to the rear. It connected with a smoke house in the rear alley. In 1887, he moved the building to his lot at the southwest corner of the Sibley Avenue and Second Street intersection, tore down the smoke house and had it rebuilt on the lot with the meat market. In May of 1894, Edward J. "Ed" Gould and Nic Meisenberg bought the saloon. Gould and Meisenberg sold the saloon in May of 1898. I believe it was to Soren Hanson.

Next, I have conflicting facts. Hanson sold the saloon to Tom A. Courtney in July of 1906 according to one source. Another source says that Andrew G. Carlson bought it in December of 1906. After Carlson died, Dave Swanson took over. At some point around this time, Fred H. Hankey had his saloon here. Litchfield went dry in April of 1914. The wooden building was torn down and F. Edward "Ed" Scarp, son of town pioneer Swan August Scarp, erected a new brick building in August of 1916. The first business in the new building was Scarp's Café in February of 1917. The Northland Transportation Company used Scarp's as a bus stop in the mid-twenties until they moved to the hotel in August of 1929.

Frank Fransein, who had managed the restaurant for Scarp, leased it in November of 1930. Fred A. LaLonde, Jr. bought the café and building in November of 1935 and Fransein moved down the street. LaLonde called his restaurant LaLonde's Café for a while and then he changed the name to the Black Cat Cafe. In the mid-thirties, Auto Parts Inc. was started in the rear where the harness shops had been. It had an alley entrance. Ed Hamm's Litchfield Supply Company followed it, before Hamm moved to the north end of town. Culligan Softwater Service Company was back in the late forties, sharing the rear with Schmidt and City Club Beer Distributing.

When the Black Cat closed down, (for some crazy reason, I went to their auction), the building stood vacant for a while. Then, in November of 1965, it housed Thorp Loan and Thrift. Finally Litchfield Chiropractic Center (Steven Bachman) moved into the building.

128 Sibley Avenue North. (809 Sibley Avenue North in early 1900s.) The businesses upstairs over the previous location were few. F. R. Schwie moved his Factory No. 909 cigar factory upstairs in April of 1896.

In the early 1910s, the Blossom Land Company and Dr. A. J. McCormack's Dentistry were up there. Dr. Bernard S. Determan, a chiropractor, had his office upstairs in the 1920s.

In the thirties, LaLonde advertised his Black Cat as a café and a hotel. He had turned the rooms upstairs into hotel rooms and rented them out. Although they were quite nice rooms, there was a quirk in that the guests were not given keys. You were on the honor system. In the late forties, the American Legion Club room was upstairs.

1933: Linne's bakery, an unoccupied building, Larson's Cash Meat Market and the first version of Fransein's Café.

154. 130 Sibley Avenue North. (17 Sibley in the early days and then 807 Sibley Avenue in the early 1900s.) Time for another "personality" store. This one had to do with meats eventually, and it gets confusing. There were a couple of small buildings on this lot north of the previous location. A Mr. Parker built one. It was sixteen by twenty-eight feet with a twelve by sixteen foot ell. At one and a half stories, the building cost $1500. D. E. Potter did his furniture construction in it for a short time before moving to one of his several other locations in town. Two gentlemen named C. B. Howell, a real estate agent, and Campbell eventually owned the little building and they sold it to George B. Lyon in March of 1871. John Lofvquest's meat market was here in 1871 also in the other building. It was an eighteen by twenty-five foot, one and a half story building, costing $600 to build. In August of 1871, Jacob "Jake" Koerner, Sr. moved his New Meat Market here in Lofvquest's building. His sons Jacob Jr. and John helped him. In late 1871, M. Arthur Brown shared the location, selling farm implements here. M. Caswell got the meat business here and Mrs. Gottlieb Koerner, Caroline, bought it from him in September of 1889. She closed it in April of 1891. The 1893 *Litchfield Independent* stated that the Reuter brothers then had the

business here and sold their meat market back to Mrs. Koerner and her sons Fritz and William in July. But the *News-Ledger* had Mrs. Gottlieb Koerner here in September of 1893. What is confusing here, I believe, is there were three Mrs. Koerners in Litchfield, Caroline, Mrs. August T. Koerner or Catherine "Kate" and Jacob "Jake" Koerner's wife, C. C.

Caroline's son, Fritz C. Koerner, by the way, served as the fire chief for the fire department from 1900 to 1905. In March of 1900, Mrs. Koerner moved her meat market back here. Mrs. Koerner and her sons were here on Sibley Avenue in the mid-1910s. The Koerners called their business the Pioneer Meat Market. The J. R. Blossom Land Company was upstairs in the mid-1910s. Dr. J. A. Ledell had his chiropractic office upstairs in around 1915. The meat market was sold to the Gordhammer brothers in October of 1920, but they couldn't move in right away. They started their Gordhammer Meat Market in February of 1921. The story told was that an agreement in the sale stated that the Koerners couldn't open another meat market on Sibley Avenue, so that's why they ended up in the alley of this block.

The Gordhammers closed in February of 1933 and sold to Guy I. Larson in April. The store became Larson's Cash Meat Market. Then Sam Peterson bought it in November of 1941 and for quite some time the business here was Sam's Meat Market. Larson committed suicide by gassing himself in the spring of 1951.

In the early seventies, the Hub Fabric & Fashion store was here. The Brodin Studio, a bronze casting business, is here today.

155. 132 Sibley Avenue North. (805 Sibley Avenue in the early 1900s.) Starting out as a vacant lot with a fence facing Sibley, this next location, still heading north, was owned by William S. Brill, who had a drugstore next door to the north. In April of 1871, D. E. Potter put up a twenty by sixty foot story and a half building here for his furniture business. In June of 1871, Potter took on a partner, an undertaker named W. J. McNair. They dissolved their partnership in June of 1872 and Potter sold his stock to Joseph Leaser. Potter then started the Yankee Notion shop here but he quit in August of 1872 selling out to O. C. McGray, who had a dry goods cash store. But McGray moved to Forest City in February of 1873. Nathan C. Martin and Henry L. Wadsworth bought the building in 1873. They had a real estate and insurance business here for a short time. Their partnership dissolved in August of 1874 and Wadsworth kept the business and the location. The partnership of John Knutson and Peter N. Dahl was here in the early-1880s. At some time a man named Chandler came and had a small building here. I don't

know what Chandler did with it, but he did lease it out to James Campbell, who used it as another of his many harness shop locations in the late 1890s. Campbell moved out in January of 1898, when Chandler built a new building here. The Cornelius brothers moved their confectionery here from next door in July of 1899. Charles W. "Hans" Wagner's *Litchfield Saturday Review* newspaper moved here the same month occupying the second floor and the basement. Wagner built a home at 403 Armstrong Avenue South in 1889 and it is still there today. David Elmquist moved his jewelry store into a room here in July of 1899.

The Cornelius brothers quit their business in February of 1900. Wagner bought the lot in September of 1912 and put up a new brick building. The *Review* stayed here into the 1920s. Then the building housed a restaurant in the thirties. It had a simple sign "Lunches" on the front of the building.

Olaf Gerhard "O. G." Nordlie moved his Jack Sprat grocery here in March of 1940. In August of 1944, Nordlie moved to the John Palm building, selling this building to his brother Amos B. Nordlie who had Nordlie's Toggery here in August of 1944. After Amos died, the business became Gale Plate's Toggery in March of 1958. Gale was the son of Federated Store owner Herman A. Plate.

After Plate's left in November of 1971, Something Special, a gift store owned by Askeroth's Interiors came here in November of 1972. Then a jeans store was here and finally a fire gutted the building. It stood vacant until Nicola's made it into the patio it is today.

156. 134 Sibley Avenue North. (19 Sibley in the early days and then 801 Sibley Avenue in the early 1900s.) Drug stores, bakeries and shoe stores were the odd combinations and personalities of the corner store of this block. First it was a drugstore. The Saint Paul and Pacific railroad, which owned this lot, sold it to M. S. Holm for $50 in February of 1870. Holm turned a quick profit by selling it to William S. Brill for $150 in April of 1870. Brill had the first drugstore in Meeker County down the street in 1869. He erected a new building here in September of 1870 and moved in. Brill was here until he sold the store to Nathaniel Frank "Happy" Revell in September of 1882 for $2850. Revell called his store the Meeker County Drug Store, but the locals called it the Pioneer Drug. Then it became the Revell Bros. Drug store in 1883 when Happy's brother, A. J. Revell, became a partner. They were both born in Wisconsin. Jeweler David Elmquist, who moved all over town, was in a corner of the building in 1882. Happy Revell left in February of 1889

and the drugstore became the A. J. Revell Drug store. A. J. put a pole up on the roof that was used to signal the town folk about the weather conditions and for "signal service flags". I imagine it was a forerunner to Civil Defense. Frank McConville had a fire at his old location and moved his confectionary to a back room here in January of 1896. During that month, Utah was the 45th state admitted to the Union. McConville sold his business to the Cornelius brothers in early 1899. They moved a couple of doors away and William Brown and O. W. Alger moved their confectionery into the room in April of 1899. Alger was also the manager of the Western Union telegraph office, which he moved here too. Brown sold out in July of 1899.

The Revell Drug and A. J. Revell

In January of 1900, Litchfield's Women's Christian Temperance Union installed a ladies' "Rest Room" in the building where women could come and "rest" and have conversation, and probably use the facilities, while shopping in downtown Litchfield. Ironically, Kellgren's saloon was right around the corner in the building to the rear. Erhardt Lenhardt bought the "Revell corner" in April of 1904, but didn't do anything with it. Erhardt Lenhardt sold the buildings to his son, Edmund "Ed" Lenhardt, and son-in-law, William Shoultz, in November of 1907. O. A. Newburg moved his bakery in here in March of 1907 after he had a fire down the street. B. Wold and Chris Mortenson bought the bakery in June of 1909 and called it the Palace Bakery. Then they sold the business to William Linne in March of 1910. Linne added a confectionery and luncheon to the bakery. It became, of course, Linne's Bakery, but it was still called the Litchfield Bakery in the phone book. William Shoultz sold his interest in the building to his brother-in-law Edmund Lenhardt in January of 1911 in exchange for getting full ownership of the brewery they had bought together from Erhardt. William was married to Mina "Minnie" Lenhardt. William Linne bought

518

the corner location in March of 1914. Linne leased the bakery to R. H. Oscarson and O. B. Trigstad in July of 1921. He kept the confectionery part of the business however.

Linne sold his entire bakery business to Wayne and Arne "Arnie" Rayppy in November of 1933, but kept ownership of the front building. The Rayppys had their first New Bakery here. Wayne's brother, Arnie, was killed in an accident with a bread truck he was driving for a Minneapolis bakery in July of 1934. Linne sold the building to George Sandgren in November of 1942, but George didn't move his store up the street to this location until March of 1943. Wayne moved his bakery across the street next to the bank. The National Farm Loan Association was in the rear of the store starting in December of 1942, next to where Louis Vossen had his shoe repair service. Sandgren's announced the purchase of a new "X-ray" machine to check the fit of shoes in July of 1947. It was called a fluoroscope and a picture of it can be seen in Chapter Twenty-Two. Sandgren's closed down the repair shop in the rear in February of 1958. Roy Lindeen leased the store in 1959, but the store was still called Sandgren's Shoes. Five years later, George Sandgren died.

Sandgren's in 1969.

Lindeen owned the building and lot in April of 1970. Later this location became John's Shoe Corner. Chester Saxby owned the building and lot in January of 1983, Music Plus was here, Paul Boushard owned the corner in November of 1891, Ron Nicholson bought the lot in August of 1895 and then Nicola's came to the location.

Upstairs over the corner location and the building stretching around the corner were a few business offices. Smith D. King had a dentistry office upstairs in early 1879 and Dr. Frank E. Bissell had his doctor office up there. King had owned a hardware in town, partnered with a man named Vanderborck or Vanderhorck and later one named Whyborn. Dentist Edward B. Weeks was upstairs in the late 1880s. Dr. Bissell still had an office upstairs in 1893, as did veterinarian and dentist A. M.

Skinner. In March, Dan Hanson moved a barbershop in upstairs over the pool hall. He specialized in 10¢ haircuts. It's time for another detour from Sibley Avenue. Turning the corner and heading east on Second Street, the next building was known as Askeroth's.

157. 18-24 Second Street East. (512 Second Street East in the early 1900s.) A couple of small wooden buildings had been to the east behind the corner building. The first of the two lots had pioneer Clark L. Angell as its occupant. Clark L. Angell had his first photography business here in the next location just before the alley. At first Angell's gallery was a portable one. I assume that meant nothing more than a tent. Clark came and went and in March of 1873, Barott's Photograph Rooms was here. I assume that by that time a wooden structure had been put up. Barott left in May of 1873. Then in the late 1800s, the Clark L. Angell Photo Gallery was in the small wooden building here where the west part of the Askeroth Paint and Wallpaper store building was. Angell was forever coming and going, but when he put down roots he lived in a house at 318 Holcombe Avenue South. "Doc" J. H. Bacon had bought Angell's business when he left once in March of 1879. Bacon was also the librarian for Litchfield's Circulating library, which boasted it had over one thousand books in 1880. Clark came back and got the business again. He took on a partner, Fayette Kelley, in November of 1881 and then Doc Bacon again in February of 1882. At this time there was just a long wooden fence where posters were displayed in the next lot to the east, extending into the alley that wasn't there then. Bacon quit the business here and sold his share of it to William S. Weeks, who was a partner of Angell by 1889. Weeks was born in Wisconsin. They called their business the Old Pioneer Studio. Nels Frederickson bought the Jim Lemen saloon here in October of 1886, so Lemen must have been here somewhere sharing the building. He had a shooting gallery in the rear in May of 1886. In October of 1889, J. H. Nayes added an oyster and lunch house in the rear of the saloon. Frank McConville brought in his confectionery in October of 1893 and moved to the A. J. Revell Drug Store building at the corner in January of 1896.

The S. A. Kellgren saloon was here in April of 1900. It was sold to Erick Peterson in February of 1901. Ole B. Olson leased the building in September of 1901 and moved his pool hall here. George A. Lee became his partner later in the same month and they opened a bowling alley in their part of the building. Mr. Cole was the next to have the poolroom and his son, Charles R. Cole, joined him in April of 1903. In April of 1904, Erhardt Lenhardt bought the "Revell corner", which included this

520

building, but he didn't do anything with it. Fred H. Hankey had a saloon here in 1905. Hankey was assistant fire chief from 1914 to 1918. Clark L. Angell came back to Litchfield and leased the site in November of 1905. He put up a new building. After a new building was erected here, Angell started his business up again, moving his gallery upstairs. In May of 1906, John and William Duffy bought the poolroom. They left the business in July of 1906 due to credit problems. Herman M. Hershey took over, but the Duffys came back and re-opened in August. K. E. Johnson bought the upstairs gallery in September of 1906. Harold Bondeson had the photographic gallery following Johnson. The Duffys went bankrupt in November and Hershey had the downstairs again. Ole B. Olson bought the pool hall business back in March of 1907. Erhardt Lenhardt sold the buildings to his son, Edmund "Ed" Lenhardt, and son-in-law, William Shoultz, in November of 1907. Wesley B. Hunter took over the pool hall in February of 1909. In May of 1908, Clyde G. Crosby leased the photography business. He moved to the rear of the First National Bank in December of 1910 and sold the business at this location to L. P. Weller in January of 1911. William Shoultz sold his interest in the building to his brother-in-law Edmund Lenhardt in January of 1911 in exchange for getting full ownership of the brewery they had bought together from Erhardt. In October of 1911, Lorenz C. Johnson leased a room in the downstairs for a confectionery for his son Clifford W. Johnson. In May of 1913, a new building here was completed. It took up the two lots behind the corner building and went all the way to the alley to the east. It was called the "Shoultz Building" although Edmund "Ed" Lenhardt, son of Erhardt, built and owned it. William "Bill" had a pool hall here. He was a son-in-law of Erhardt Lenhardt. Eventually another son-in-law, Frank E. Viren, owned it. Oscar O. Lindblom bought the confectionery business in May of 1914 and Johnson moved over by the H. J. Quigley Feed yard. Also in 1914, August Erickson had the saloon, but Litchfield went dry in April of 1914. Judge Herman M. Hershey's Music Store or the Hershey Talking Machine Company was here in 1915. Carl F. W. Schultz came here next and had a confectionery selling malts and soft drinks and also a poolroom, which he sold to O. C. Frederick in July of 1916. Frederick moved it to another location. William Shoultz was back here in November of 1919 with a shop selling malt products and soft drinks and owning the building. He added a pool hall in April of 1920. The Fashion Shop occupied the west end of the building. Marie Palmquist, niece of the Lenhardts and John's wife, and Amy Eastman owned that business and it opened in August of 1922. Frank E. Viren bought the

Shoultz building in the rear in May of 1923. In March of 1925, Eastman sold out to Palmquist. Smith's Appliances was here before the Askeroths bought the building.

The Askeroths, Olaf O. and his sons Clarence M. "Skip" and Vernon, bought it from Frank E. Viren of Viren-Johnson in March of 1931. It became Askeroth's Paint and Wallpaper Store or Askeroth's Paint Shop. The Askeroth family had been involved with painting and decorating since 1885 when Andrew O. Askeroth started a business in town at an unknown location. In 1893, his son Olaf O. came into the family business. Andrew retired in 1912. Olaf brought in his sons Clarence in 1917 and Vern in 1921. Olaf retired in 1941. The Askeroths dissolved their partnership in April of 1945. Vernon kept the paint shop here and Clarence "Skip" took the bowling alley. Later Askeroth's became Smith's Appliances. The Litchfield Video store is at this location today. At some time this location was combined with the next one to the east.

Askeroths' in 1961.

After the new brick building was built at the Askeroth location, a few businesses were upstairs. In July of 1938, Fred Maass came to town and opened his office up there. In the mid-forties, the Hanson Studio photography business, owned by Kermit B. Hanson, was upstairs.

Lowell Wilson moved upstairs in 1950. James Anderson had an insurance office here also. Walter C. Whitney opened up another optometry shop upstairs in April of 1962 and Frederick C. Brown had his dental office upstairs in the mid-sixties and early seventies.

158. 26-30 Second Street East. (514 Second Street East in the early 1900s.) For many years, the large building after the alley was called the

Snell Block because it initially had John Snell's furniture and undertaking business and was large enough to accommodate several other businesses. Snell started his business in 1877 at another location and built a new building here in May of 1879. He also had a photography business here. The building took up two lots and had three large rooms for stores. Eventually, there was a building in the rear facing the alley, so I'll include the businesses there with this building. So there were a lot of businesses in and out of the buildings here at the same time. Charley Taylor moved his butcher shop here to the small building in the back in November of 1881. Because the Snell building was so long, the small rear building actually ended up being behind Scarp's Café or where the Black Cat ended up. Taylor moved all over town and didn't last long here. He closed the shop soon and moved elsewhere. Jim McMahon leased a room in the Snell building and moved his saloon here from Marshall Avenue in late 1882. In October of 1883, Mrs. H. E. McKeen moved her millinery to a corner room of the Snell building. Later she moved to Sibley Avenue where Mrs. A. M. Caswell's millinery was and Mrs. Caswell moved here. Paul O. Olson opened a tailor shop in the rear of Snell's building in April of 1885. Then he moved to Sibley Avenue by the Stevens and Company bank. The Koerner meat market was in the rear building in the summer of 1885. C. S. Sherwood rented the west side of the Snell building in April of 1888 for his grocery business. Snell sold the building to Daniel McLane in August of 1888 and sold his furniture stock to Fayette Kelley and George Raine in December. They moved it elsewhere. In June of 1889, Boudette and T. J. Cauley had the New Meat Market in the building in back. Cauley was a rarity amongst early Litchfield businessmen. He was actually born in Minnesota. Most of the other businessmen in town weren't. Boudette left in August of 1889 and the market went out of business in December of 1889. In August of 1890, the William Diepenbrock and August Bracher meat market moved to the building in the rear from Mrs. Koerner's Marshall Avenue building. They closed in February of 1891. A. O. Lawson brought a meat market into the northeast corner of the Snell building in May of 1891. D. C. Beach brought his confectionery into a room here in July of 1891. He moved to another location in October. In July of 1891, August T. Koerner became the postmaster and he moved the Post Office here that August until the new Post Office was built into the rear of the First State Bank building. The Harrison Variety Store Company opened up in a room of the Snell building in December of 1891. In 1892, John Hagen became the owner of the lot here. In April of 1892, Ross and Worrell bought the Lawson business but moved out in a couple of months. The C. W. Cofield and James Stuart City Meat Market went into the west room of the Snell building in January of 1892. Cofield retired and the business was called Stuart and Company in July of 1892. The "Company" part was Fritz C. Koerner, son of Gottlieb and Caroline. Mrs. Nels Swanson's restaurant was in the east room here in October of 1892. In April of 1893, Mrs. A. M. Caswell moved her millinery into a room here. She had a partner named Krueger in 1896. Also in April, the A. Nelson and Company dry goods business moved in here. Mrs. McKeen moved her millinery to a corner room in September of 1893. The Henry H. Rappe and Frank Sykora meat market was in the rear building in July of 1893. Henry was Litchfield's third fire chief, serving from 1896 to 1900. In January of 1894, some men in town rented a room here and set up a gymnasium, which was really some boxing equipment. In April of 1894, Swanson's restaurant closed and Mrs. C. E. Adlerbjelke took it over, getting back in the restaurant business. Reigel and Minderhout bought the meat business in the rear in September of 1894. Sykora and Rappe bought it back in October of 1894, calling the business Sykora and Company as Rappe only had an interest. The Campbell harness shop moved into Brown confectionery room in September of 1894. The east room had the William Von Kuster tin shop in May of 1894. He moved to Sibley Avenue. W. H. McCarthy's "Marble Works" was in some part of the building in 1895. He took on a partner named M. L. Thompson in 1898.

M. L. Thompson and W. H. McCarthy

By 1895, Gottlieb Koerner was still listed as the owner of the lot and the building in the rear of the Snell building, although he had died in July of 1884. Rappe sold his interest in the meat market to Sykora in January of 1898. He moved out in September and opened another market elsewhere in town in October of 1899. In May of 1898, F. E. Wolfenden had a photography business here. He quit in June. Henry Hedberg moved a laundry into a back room at sometime before the turn of the century.
524

Carl J. Settergren came here in November of 1898 with a fur and hide buying business. He was a tanner also. Tom Wandok had his cigar factory in a room here in the late 1890s, as was Ole B. Olson's pool hall. In May of 1890, Edward J. "Ed" Gould had a saloon in the building and in June the Snell building, now owned by Tipton F. McClure, burned and was gutted inside. The fire started in Hedberg's laundry in the back and the laundry was lost along with the marble works and the cigar factory. It was fixed up enough so that Hedberg moved back in with a partner named Nelson in July of 1900. Tom Wandok moved his cigar factory back into the building in September of 1900. Olson moved his pool hall out in September of 1901. Sam J. Bundy and a partner named Moede opened a restaurant here in the west room in January of 1902, calling it the Horseshoe Café because of the horseshoe shape of their lunch counter. Bundy bought out Moede in April of 1902. The Thompson and McCarthy partnership ended in April of 1903 and Thompson took on a new partner named Schultz for the marble works. The Thompson and Schultz partnership dissolved in July of 1904. Bundy sold the restaurant to Mrs. Eva Doyle in May of 1904. Eva died in October of 1905, and her daughter Grace sold it back to Bundy. Hanson and Eggleson were the next owners in September of 1910 and they sold it to Jack A. Hunter in February of 1911. Hunter sold to Miss Cora Steffen in July of 1911. All the buildings from the alley to Marshall Avenue, mostly known as the Snell Block, were sold to Tipton F. McClure by Silas Wright Leavett and August T. Koerner in December of 1911. The Steffen restaurant closed in April of 1913 and Sam J. Bundy bought it again, but he sold it to Edgar "Ed" Curtis in January of 1914. Meanwhile behind the building in the alley in 1919, Fritz C. Koerner, his mother Mrs. Gottlieb Koerner or Caroline and her son-in-law Charles A. "Charley" Neuman built a new cement block butcher shop where the old meat market building was and they started another meat market. They called it the Koerner and Neuman Market. Fritz C. Koerner took over his mother's interest in June of 1924. Neuman was Litchfield's fire chief from 1922 to 1924. Elsewhere in the Snell building, the Ramus Furniture Company was here for a short time in the late 1920s. It went out of business in September of 1928. The Horseshoe Restaurant was sold to Ray McGraw in March of 1929.

Ray McGraw still owned the restaurant in the late thirties through the late forties. He sold it to his son John Thomas "Tom" McGraw in October of 1945. Tom sold it to George Bauer in August of 1949. Charley Neuman died in 1940 and his son Louis F. Neuman got Charley's interest in the meat market business in the block building in the rear. Neuman bought out Fritz C. Koerner in January of 1942 and later took on a partner named Paul Olson in October of 1946. Neuman bought out Paul Olson in October of 1951 and the business became just Neuman's Meat Shop.

George Bauer sold the restaurant to George Schoultz in November of 1960. It later became a law and doctor's office in the late sixties. In June of 1961, Roy Nelson, owner of Nelson's Grocery, (the old Batterberry store), bought the Meat Shop in the rear from Neuman while still keeping his grocery store across the tracks. He then moved the butcher shop to the 1st District Association Building south of the railroad tracks by the Swift Avenue crossing. The law office of Olson (Leland), Nelson (Wendell) & Nagel was here and Dr. Lennox Danielson had his office here. Today the Second Street Business Center is at this location. Dr. R. E. Patten has his chiropractic office here along with Franklin Insurance and Jill Miller Insurance Agency.

159. 32-34 Second Street East. (518 Second Street East in the early 1900s.) This location was actually the west part of a large building that ran to the east corner. F. Edward Scarp and Company's Litchfield Laundry was here initially in the late 1800s or early 1900s. W. F. Schrader bought it in 1907. The Gundlock-Johnson Millinery moved here when W. F. Schrader leased their location next door in February of 1911 to expand his operation. The Johnson sisters sold out to Minnie Gundlock in December of 1912. She called it Gundlock Millinery. Minnie Gundlock married Clyde G. Crosby in the summer of 1915 and changed the name of her millinery to Mrs. C. G. Crosby's Millinery. Mrs. Crosby shared the building with her husband's photography business and Schrader's Litchfield Steam Laundry in about 1915. The laundry had a fire in January of 1918. When it moved in 1919, Judge Herman M. Hershey's Music Store or the Hershey Phonograph Company moved into the part that was vacated in November of 1919. Mrs. Crosby bought all the fixtures from the Rodange Hat Shop or millinery when it went out of business in July of 1923 and moved them into her shop here, expanding it. Hershey moved to another location in late 1927 and soon folded. When he did, Mrs. Crosby sold his record inventory in her millinery. After Hershey had moved out, Frank L. Christenson's Easy Washing Machine Company came in January of 1928. Frank took on a partner, James Caylor, in February of 1928.

In April of 1930, John O. Larson moved his furniture repair and flooring business and the office to his funeral home here in the room the washing machine company had been in. Larson moved out in October of

1931 to sell out of his house. Clinton and Agatha Caylor moved their Kandy Kitchen in the room Larson had vacated in December of 1931. It was moved out in January of 1932. In February of 1935, C. W. LaTourelle had an electrical repair shop here. He moved out in April of the same year to the Litchfield Machine Shop building. Litchfield Production Credit Association was here in the mid-thirties. The Bell Telephone Company had an office here in the west part of the building in the late forties until they built the new building on Ramsey in 1956. Mrs. Crosby finally retired in March of 1953 after forty-five years in the business. D & L Skelgas moved here from across from the park in 1953. In May of 1956, the Walter Olson Real Estate office moved into the room that the telephone office had been in. Robert Sparboe moved his Sparboe Chick Company office here in 1956 also for a short time.

In June of 1961, Harlan Quinn put up a new brick building here and leased it out to the Meeker County Soil Conservation Service on the left and the law partnership of Wendell Nelson and Leland Olson on the right. Dr. Robert M. Farrish, the dentist, and Dr. Gary P. Gross, the optometrist, moved their offices into the building in March of 1962. The Meeker County Abstract Company, American Family Insurance, Rebecca M. Rue's law office and Olson (deceased Leland), Nelson (deceased Wendell), Wood (Mark P.) and Berry (David G.) law offices share this location today.

160.   40 Second Street East. (520-522 Second Street East in the early 1900s.)   Eventually a large brick building that became Quinn Motors was at the southeast corner of the block, at Second Street and Marshall Avenue, but before that there was a small building on the lot that Chris Mortenson leased and moved his Litchfield City Bakery into in October of 1884. Mortenson left the building and town for a while but returned to a different location in 1886. William Grono started a marble works in January of 1885 in the Silas Wright Leavett building across from the park, but moved in here in November. From here Grono moved to the rear of McLane's store in McLane's old tin shop in March of 1886. William "Popcorn" Miller started a popcorn factory here in May of 1889. He moved around town. Possibly William Grono or his brother Fred, who was also a marble worker, became a partner to W. H. McCarthy in October of 1894 and he bought out McCarthy in 1895. McCarthy moved up the street to the Snell building. M. L. Thompson owned the business called the Litchfield Marble and Granite Works in 1897. He became partners with McCarthy in the Snell building and ended up a partner of Grono after the turn of the century. Carl F. W. Schultz got ownership of

the marble works at sometime. In the mid-1890s, A. F. Edson and Company had a feed store here. In October of 1891, "Popcorn" Miller was back here after his other location's building was torn down. Miller had been here before and then in the southeast corner of the Howard Park between the hotel and the railroad tracks.

A. J. Mellgren had the Litchfield Carriage Works here in November of 1900. In December of 1902, this building and Edson's feed business was sold to Leslie Barrick. A few weeks later it was sold to E. E. Peterson, who moved the business behind the Bank of Litchfield in January of 1903. From December of 1902 to 1910, August "Gus" A. Settergren and W. S. Tooker had the Litchfield Glove Factory at this location. Mrs. Jack A. Hunter leased the room vacated by the glove factory for a bakery in April of 1907. Charles Henry Strobeck, the town's postmaster, moved the Post Office to the west part of the building here for a few months in May of 1908, while an addition was added to their location behind the First State Bank. The Post Office was moved back to its location in October of 1908. Jennie S. Ringdahl opened a millinery here in March of 1909. This building was quite big, so her millinery was towards the center of this half block. She took a partner on named Minnie Gundlock a year later in March of 1910. Ringdahl sold out to Mabel and Selma Johnson and it became the Gundlock-Johnson Millinery. They moved to the room where Jack A. Hunter had his bakery and W. F. Schrader, who had the Litchfield Laundry next door, leased the room to expand his operation in February of 1911. Carl F. W. Schultz' Litchfield Marble and Granite Works went out of business in January of 1912. During that same month, New Mexico was the 47th state admitted to the Union. The marble and granite works was sold to the Melrose Granite Company, managed by Harold C. Hanson, in September of 1914. At some time Gust Chellin had a garage here in the east part. The Chellin Brothers sold Overland cars and combined with Peterson Implement in May of 1911 to sell Buick and Overland together. Gus Chellin took on a partner named J. William Williams who sold his interest to Fred Sundler in January of 1913. Chellin sold the corner to Anthony "Tony" Borden, Harold C. Hanson and Victor Mickelson in December of 1915. Mickelson left in February of 1917. Chellin moved to the Welch garage when it was finished in March of 1917. The new company here was the Motor Supply Company. During that same month, Woodrow Wilson was sworn in as President for his second term. Victor J. Davis opened a tire repair business in part of the building. In August of 1917, L. E. Larson and Horace J. Minar moved their new Ford dealership in here for a short time. Schrader sold the laundry to C. E.

Williams in August of 1920, and Williams sold it to A. E. Nagel in October. Hans O. Evenson moved his Buick dealership to the corner building in the fall of 1926. He moved out and Motor Supply took over the Buick dealership in September of 1928.

In March of 1934, Motor Supply moved to the Kopplin building at the northwest corner building at Ramsey Avenue and Second Street (210 Ramsey Avenue North), because Harlan M. Quinn bought this building in February of 1934. He and Jack G. Beerling started the business I always knew at this corner called Quinn Motors in April of 1934. They sold Dodge and Plymouth vehicles. Curtis W. LaTourelle opened an electrical repair and appliance shop in a room west of the office of Quinn's in February of 1935. Harlan Quinn bought all of the buildings from this corner to the Horseshoe Café in February of 1946. In June of 1959, Loren Caskey moved his Caskey's Shoe Repair into part of this building.

Jack Beerling bought out Harlan Quinn in 1960, but the business was still called Quinn Motors. When Quinn Motors closed in the late sixties, the L & P Selling Service, owned by Laura and Paul Clouse, moved in. Today Dee's Family Hair Styling is here.

Turning the corner onto Marshall Avenue and heading north, there was a small building facing Marshall just to the south of the corner building, sharing this corner lot. It originally had J. W. Bartlett's Billiard Hall in it in 1875. He advertised that he sold no liquor. "Doc" J. H. Bacon had a dentist office and photography studio at this location in 1882. He partnered with Clark L. Angell in a photography business at this location about the same time. It was called Bacon and Angell. The owner of the building in 1888 was Albertina Thiele. Angell left and Bacon took on a new partner, John E. Nordstrom, in January of 1892. This location eventually became the part of the Quinn Motors building that faced Second Street.

125 Marshall Avenue North. Heading south from the previous location, there was a building almost directly across from the city hall building, but not at the corner lot. It had Gottlieb C. Koerner's meat market in it. The market started in February of 1873. Koerner built the twelve by twenty-five foot building for $200 and leased it to Jacob "Jake" Koerner in January of 1874. Gottlieb took it back in July of 1875. Jake had a shop called the City Meat Market on Sibley Avenue by the railroad tracks. He sold it to M. Aune and H. P. Olson in September of 1879. Gottlieb died in July of 1884. The business closed here and then

his widow Mrs. Gottlieb C. Koerner or Caroline opened the meat market up again in May of 1885. She moved to the southwest corner of Sibley Avenue and Second Street in May of 1886 and sold this Marshall Avenue location to August Bracher and Diepenbrock in July of 1887. They closed in September of 1887. In September of 1887, Charles C. Sather and Swan August "Gus" Scarp re-opened the butcher shop in this building. In December of 1887, they moved the business to their saloon building. Mrs. Gottlieb C. Koerner still owned the building and she sold it to C. W. Cofield and James Stuart in December of 1891. They called their meat business Cofield and Stuart and moved it to the Snell building. The Reuter brothers opened a meat market at this location in January of 1892. Today Litchfield Office Supply is at this location. Some historians say that at one time, Marshall Avenue was the main business street in Litchfield. I refute that statement and will take you by all the businesses on Marshall Avenue and let you be the judge.

About in the middle of Marshall Street, between Second and Depot Streets, was B. G. Murch's saloon in 1883. In April of 1892, Duane H. Duckering moved yet another building either here or between here and the corner building for a feed store. It had been the old GAR armory building and had stood across the street from where the new library is today. M. B. Hudson leased it for his feed business immediately. Then Duckering got it back and took on a partner name Pennoyer for a feed store business. A. F. and Elmo Edson bought the business in February of 1894, calling it A. F. Edson and Company.

Herb Markle and Jacob A. Lenhardt had a livery here around the turn of the century. Markle sold out to Lenhardt in August of 1906. Lenhardt sold out to J. E. Elliott, who sold out to I. N. Wheeler, who sold it back to J. E. Elliott. All that happened in the span of a month.

Somewhere in the middle of the block was the Litchfield Welding and Machine Company. It was here for quite a long time, beginning before the turn of the century as a blacksmith shop and still going today as Litchfield Welding.

115 Marshall Avenue North. Somewhere near the last location, across from the hotel on Marshall Avenue, were lots owned by H. W. Simons. W. M. White had a farm machinery business on one of the lots here or near here in April of 1871. Also in April of 1871, A. H. Lofstrom built a small building here for his paint shop, before he moved to Sibley Avenue in 1874. Morris Neuman and his brother Henry had a

blacksmith shop around this location in 1872, but they moved to Depot or First Street. In February of 1873, Charles Forester had a blacksmith and wagon making shop here. Someone named Vanderwalker took it over in July. In October of 1875, J. B. Hatch built a shop on one of the lots for his furniture business. It was "the first door north of Topping's". Neuman built a brick building on his lot in 1876. John Snell bought the furniture business in 1877. He moved out in 1878 and Charles Forester moved into the "old Snell building" with a saloon.

101 Marshall Avenue North. A couple of buildings were just north of the western corner of Marshall Avenue and Depot Street. One was known as the Topping building because "Professor" Charles Griswold "Charley" Topping was one its most well known occupants. He began business here in June of 1871. Eli Vachon had the first "New Bakery" in Litchfield here along with a restaurant, which sold ice cream and lemon beer starting in June of 1872. Topping moved his barber business here in June of 1872 from at the Ripley House hotel, which was across Marshall Avenue. Vachon sold the lot next to his bakery to a Mr. Hoyer in July of 1872. Vachon quit his bakery in the spring of 1873. F. W. Thiele had his first shoe store here in November of 1872, and a man named Hays had a grocery store here. The building was eighteen by twenty feet and cost $200 to build. Prior to 1874, Dr. V. P. Kennedy had an office in one of the buildings around here, as did real estate broker Nathan C. Martin. Mr. Hoyer had his building next to Thiele's in 1874. Chauncey Butler bought the Hoyer building in July of 1875 for a bank. It closed in December of 1877. In 1875, Topping added a bath that families could rent for 50¢ an hour and a confectionery and grocery business. In May of 1879, he added a soda fountain to his confectionery. In November of 1879, Topping leased his barber chairs to Fred Johnson[198], a black man from Minneapolis, and his son, Oren Wilbert "Bert" Topping, but he kept the confectionery, which he sold to William Stocking. Two sisters-in-law, Mrs. W. White and Mrs. E. E. White opened a music store here in December of 1878. In a couple of months they moved to Sibley Avenue. Johnny Oakes moved his saloon here in November of 1880. He opened a restaurant in the saloon in a few months. Then Frank Williams had a saloon here, which he sold to Martin Smelsle in March of 1882. Charley Shaw, no relation to me, had a saloon on Sibley Avenue, which he quit in May of 1883 and fixed up this building for another restaurant and bakery. The City Saloon was here, sharing the building, in June of 1882. I don't know who ran it. The bakery and restaurant were sold to

---

[198] The Litchfield News-Ledger gave his name as Charles Jones.

Hanscom and Johnson in November of 1884. They called it the New Brunswick Bakery. John Nellis had his barbershop over the bakery for a short time starting in January of 1885 before moving to Sibley Avenue in February of 1885. Sometime in early 1885, John Beckstrand started his first shoe repair business here. There was a fire in the bakery in early 1886 and Hanscom was brought to trial in May of 1886 for starting it. Halvor Berglin bought the bakery building and had it moved near Charles "Charley" A. Laughton's livery for his Litchfield Brass Foundry business in November of 1886. Oren Wilbert "Bert" Topping, the barber, was listed as the owner of the lot in 1888. C. S. Sherwood moved his grocery into the "Topping building" in February of 1894 and put a plumbing warehouse into a small building on the lot. After a fire in September of 1897, Topping moved under the Atkinson Drug, after selling the shop here to John A. McColeman. The businesses here today face Depot Street.

Marshall Avenue in the 1870s.
Lower right: Lake Ripley House. Lower left, across Marshall Avenue, left to right: a livery, a saloon, the alley, Koerner's meat market and a marble works.

100 Marshall Avenue North/100 Depot Street West. At the eastern corner of Marshall Avenue and First Street, where the Wells Fargo Bank is today, was the Lake Ripley House hotel. William Gould & Co. built the hotel in 1870 on Gould's lot and it was leased to James Tinkham. He called it Tinkham House. Tinkham advertised it as "the largest hotel in town". It was an odd claim in that Charles J. Almquist built his Litchfield House hotel across the tracks in the late summer of 1869 and it easily dwarfed this hotel, which was built at a cost of $7000. It was in the shape of an "L" with front balconies at the second and third floors. Several of Litchfield's eligible bachelors, such as lumberyard owner
532

John Esbjornsson and lawyer Charles Strobeck, lived at the Tinkham House. In early 1871, "Professor" Charles Griswold "Charley" Topping had a barbershop and washroom in the hotel. Topping eventually had shops all over town at different times. He moved across Marshall Avenue in June of 1871. W. S. Knappen had a saloon in a room attached to the hotel. P. E. Christian leased the hotel next. Then, in May of 1871, William Gould & Company changed the name to the Lake Ripley House. The Nelson brothers leased the hotel in December of 1871. The "hot potato" hotel was passed to John Scarp and Gordon in May of 1872. That fall, Otho H. Campbell and Myron W. Damuth bought it. The building got into disrepair around this time. Doctor Frank E. Bissell had an office in the hotel but left in June of 1873. Campbell bought it from Damuth in September of 1873, repaired it and sold it to R. W. Dunn[199] in October of 1873. O. D. Webb had it in October of 1874 and then George H. Fountain had it in 1875. In March of 1876, L. D. Marshall leased it and then Z. B. Fifield leased it in November of 1876. Fifield had a meat market in town in 1877. W. A. Baldwin leased the hotel in December of 1877.

The Lake Ripley House in 1878 and 1885.

Peter Meisenberg owned the hotel next in 1880. He died in January of 1884 and his widow and son Nicholas took it over. Johnson and Chevre or Chevere rented the eastern part of the hotel building in June of 1889 for the Deering Farm Machinery business. In the early 1890s, Mrs. Meisenberg was still listed as the owner.

---

[199] R. W. Dunn and Myron W. Damuth had a livery stable at the Holcombe Avenue corner behind the hotel. Dunn sold his interest to Damuth, who sold the building in May of 1875 and then put up a new one. He took on a partner named Albert McCargar in 1877. Frank Belfoy bought the building and moved it to Sibley Avenue in September of 1875. A new building was erected and the McCargar and Knight livery was still at the corner location. In 1881 they moved to a location on Depot Street between Sibley and Marshall Avenues.

A. H. Bishop had the hotel from March of 1905 up to 1907 when he shut it down. In October of 1908, Dell McMillan reopened the hotel. At some time Fred Cook ran the hotel. The hotel shut down shortly after and stood vacant until James Ward opened an auto repair shop in it in September of 1911. H. A. Walker started his Litchfield Tire Vulcanizing and Repair Company in the rear of the hotel building for a temporary headquarters in August of 1912. Floyd Depew reopened the hotel in 1913, but after it was inspected by the State in May of 1914, there were rumors that it was going to be condemned. Of course, it mysteriously burned down on August 8, 1914 and was removed from the lot. Richard Welch put up a garage here and rented it out. It didn't go up easily, however. First, during construction, a fire broke out in the building. Then in March of 1917, it collapsed. Gust Chellin's garage was the first at this site in late March of 1917 and Minar Motor was here in August of 1917. Richard Welch moved here in March of 1919 to sell Paige, Mitchell and Saxon cars. Chellin bought the site in November of 1921, tore down the Welch building and put up his own building. He moved into it in March of 1922. Then Hans O. Evenson had his Buick dealership here in 1926. He had been in the Kopplin building across the tracks with partner Emil M. Nelson. Nelson quit the business in February of 1924. The Becklund-Crosby repair shop was here in the rear but moved to the Welch garage on Depot Street in December of 1928.

Charles Emery had an auto repair shop in the rear of Chellin's garage here in 1941. He turned his garage into a machine parts factory for the New Brighton munitions plant in June of 1942. The Litchfield Hatchery, owned by Leo Baumgartner, bought the Chellin Garage in October of 1942.

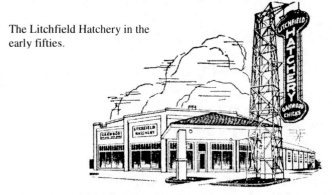

The Litchfield Hatchery in the early fifties.

Emery's war shop continued to be in the rear. The Litchfield Produce Company became the occupant here in 1957 with a turkey hatchery.

Then the Litchfield Ice Cream Company was here. In June of 1958, the building was sold at an auction.

Dick Stewart moved his King Koin Laundry here in February of 1960. In 1967, the building was torn down and the Northwestern Bank put up a new building in November of 1968. It became the Wells-Fargo Bank that it is today.

Next to that corner lot, heading north, was the building where Henry G. Rising published the *Litchfield Republican* newspaper starting in the January 24, 1871. He discontinued the paper in the following autumn. At some time the building was torn down and the lot became vacant.

In June of 1902, John M. Learn and Henry J. "Hank" Martens moved the old depot to the lot for their farm machinery warehouse. Frank E. and Melvin Wheeler bought them out in January of 1903. They called their business Wheeler and Company.

One door north of that lot was the Joseph Leaser furniture factory. It was a twenty-five foot square story and a half building that cost $500 to build in 1870. Mr. Leaser used it to make and sell furniture and coffins, which he started selling in the spring of 1871 on Sibley Avenue. He added a twenty by forty foot building for a sales room in February of 1873. I think Gottlieb "Jake" Keller and Jacob "Jake" Koerner had a meat market here for a short time before moving to Sibley Avenue. Chauncey Dart might have had a feed store in the area also, before he moved to Sibley Avenue. Phineas "Pat" Cary, who bounced around town, bounced into this building with his shoe business in late 1878. Otto Marr had a general merchandise store here in September of 1885. Crosby and Harry M. Angier had a carpentry shop here in January of 1887. Dr. S. S. Squire, a homoeopathist, bought this building in September of 1890 and turned it, making it into his home and office.

114 Marshall Avenue North. A house was moved to the next lot, heading north, in 1869 from Forest City. Adam Klass owned the house. It was twenty-five by thirty-six feet and two-stories high. It had been Klaas' saloon in Forest City and became the same here, plus a boarding house. It eventually served as a unit of the Exchange Hotel, which was next door to the north. The original house is still at this location today.

The Exchange, another one of Litchfield's hotels, was moved from Sibley Avenue to the next site in June of 1879 by its owner H. W. Simons. A Mr. Brown had a barbershop business in the hotel in October of 1879. "Doc" Upham used to extract teeth "with little or no pain" in a room at the hotel in the fall of 1880. Charley Shaw (no relation) leased the hotel in January of 1882. Shaw left in February of 1883. J. B. Hatch bought the hotel in May of 1883 but couldn't make the payments and it went back to Hatch. Hatch sold it to Swan August "Gus" Scarp in July of 1884. The hotel closed in August of 1884 and George A. Lee leased and reopened it in September. Scarp took the hotel over again in January of 1887. Henry E. Freeman leased the hotel in October of 1887. Leander L. Wakefield, who came to Meeker County in the fall of 1856, leased it in June of 1889 and Thurston A. Richardson leased the hotel in September of 1890. It became the American House hotel in April of 1895, when Ludvig Schultz bought it. C. Edward "Ed" Markle and Jacob A. Lenhardt leased it in April of 1906. During that same month, there was the famous San Francisco earthquake. George Hatch bought the hotel in August of 1911 and turned it into two residential houses. A. Barth bought one in 1919.

20. Next door to the north is a parking lot today, but when the old town hall was at the corner location, W. W. Rollins' saloon was here in 1870. It was eighteen feet wide by twenty-five feet long and two-stories high. It cost $1000 to build. In 1874, the building was moved somewhere to the north side of town. Then a roller skating rink was here. I don't know what kind of building was used to house the rink but eventually, in October of 1898, a strange looking building went onto this lot. It was wooden and it was round. The Olson brothers had a steam-powered Merry-Go-Round business here in July of 1898 and they built the building to house it. They moved the Merry-Go-Round into it in December of 1898. It opened for winter business in January of 1899. A young black man worked inside grinding out music for the carousel from of a large music box. A ride cost 5¢.

In September of 1921, the Olsons sold the Merry-Go-Round to some people in Kimball, Minnesota, but the wooden building stayed here. The Litchfield Horseshoe Courts moved into the building in November of 1921. The son of one of the Olsons, Louis, owned the building later and leased it to Nicolas C. "Nick" Weber in March of 1926. Weber had his Weber Implement Company in this odd looking building selling International machinery. Clarence Weber took over from his dad and moved to a new building on east Highway 12 in July of 1947. Norbert O. "Norb" or "Norm" Kohmetscher moved his Norb's Cut Rate Service gas station here from the 300 block of Ramsey Avenue in 1949. In May of 1953, he sold the business to Gailand Wright who had his Independent Oil Company here. Then it became Jesse's Cut-Rate Station. Kohmetscher got it back in August of 1957. The building was torn down in May of 1961 and is a parking lot today.

161. 126 Marshall Avenue North. In the early days of Litchfield, a wooden City Hall building stood where the Community Building stands today at the corner of Marshall Avenue and Second Street. The "town hall" was built in the fall of 1874 by the city and the Masons to be used conjointly as a city meeting place and the Mason's Golden Fleece Lodge. It was twenty-six feet wide, seventy-two feet long and two stories high. The Masons used the upstairs. In 1875, Robert S. Hershey & Co. owned the lot. On February 1, 1878, women's rights leader Susan B. Anthony spoke at the hall for the benefit of the library association. They made a whopping $10 that night from audience donations. Susan was touring the country campaigning for the National Woman Suffrage Association's promotion of a federal woman's suffrage amendment. After much urging from the local newspapers in the late 1890s, the city finally decided to get rid of the old building and put up a new brick Opera House.

The old city hall was sold at an auction in May of 1900 to George G. Mills and moved off the lot to make room for the new building. Mills moved it to the lot opposite the Litchfield House hotel (a warehouse for Ideal Lumber is there today) where it was used as a warehouse for his Deere, Webber and Company business. He eventually sold the building to the Peterson Implement Company and it was torn down in the 1920s for the lumber. The new Litchfield Opera House was designed by architect William T. Towner and built in late 1900. Opening night was Thursday, November 8, 1900. The William Owens' traveling troupe performed *The Marble Heart* that night. Two years later, they staged *Othello* there.

The
Opera
House
in
1908.

From 1900 to 1924, operas, plays, dances and band concerts were held in the building, but in October of 1917, the United Theatres Company, headed by Bart Foster, leased the building to show movies and stage vaudeville shows. E. J. Gates and Floyd Rothlisberger leased the building in May of 1920 to show movies also. Finally David T. Hopson, who owned the Unique Theater downtown, had enough and appealed to the city to stop being his competition. When they didn't listen, he sold the Unique. Mrs. Ernest Campbell donated the huge red velvet curtain that had hung on the stage at the Opera House. She is also credited with saving the Bank of Litchfield by depositing a huge sum of money when it was on the brink of failure. In November of 1920, Gates and Rothlisberger gave up their lease on the building and it went back to being used for local plays, band concerts, dances, roller skating, non-school basketball games and city meetings. The Opera House was remodeled in 1935 to be used exclusively as the city's Community Building and that's the name most people have always known it by.

In 1962, part of the back of the building was turned into an extended art classroom for the high school. I was in the first art class, taught by Jerry Trushenski, to use that classroom. The police department and Mayor's office were moved to the front of the building in April of 1963. The offices had been over the old fire hall. The city offices were in the building for a long time but the building is vacant today because of mold problems. In the spring of 2003, the Preservation Alliance of Minnesota named it to its list of the Minnesota's ten most endangered historic properties.

162. 202 Marshall Avenue North. Straight north of the Opera House at the corner is a residential home that was converted for a period of time into a funeral home. This location was the site of the first residential building in Litchfield in 1869. It was an eight by ten foot shack owned by Truls Peterson, who conducted a tailoring business out of it, besides living there. Saloon owner Nels Clements and butcher T. J. Cauley owned the house that was built to replace it at different times before the turn of the century. Clements was born in Meeker County, a rarity among early Litchfield businessmen.

I don't know when the present house was built. I would assume the twenties. Dewey Johnson's Funeral Home was in the house in the thirties. Johnson took on a partner named E. Lee Buckley in March of 1943. The business was called the Johnson-Buckley Funeral Home. Buckley left and Johnson took on another associate named Sherwood S.

Doody in September of 1943. Lennart Erickson bought the business from Dewey Johnson in January of 1946.

The funeral home was finally closed in October of 1967. Today the house is back to being a regular home.

210 Marshall Avenue North. There was another residential house north of the funeral home, the fourth lot from the southeast corner of Marshall Avenue and Third Street. But in 1959, the National Farm Loan Association and Production Credit Association bought the lot. They put up a new brick building for offices. They moved into the building from their other locations in July of 1959. The Farm Loam Association changed to the Federal Land Bank Association of Litchfield in January of 1960. Today it is called the Farm Credit Services of Minnesota Valley.

93. 216 Marshall Avenue. This lot to the north of the last one had once had a building on it that had been erected in 1874 by Nels Pearson, but I don't know what kind of business he had. Litchfield's first Village Council President Jesse V. Branham, Jr had owned it. Later the building on it was used as an armory for the National Guard and also as a roller rink before it was moved to the corner of Marshall Avenue North and Depot Street where it became an implement dealership. In November of 1906, Carl F. W. Schultz bought the vacant lot here and put up a building for his marble works.

Theodore W. "Ted" Kohlhoff built a new Super Valu store here in December of 1954. In September of 1966, Ted sold his interest to his son Gene V. and retired. Ted had brought his Gene into the business as a partner several years before. Gene sold half of the business to his manager Bruce Cottington in November of 1968. Super Valu moved out on Highway 12 East and became Cottington's Country Foods. This building stood vacant for a long time until Litchfield's new library was put into the remodeled building in 2003.

226 Marshall Avenue North. In 1870, Charles Forester, a carpenter/wheelwright, had a one-story sixteen by thirty-four foot building costing $500 to build, here at this southeast corner of Marshall Avenue and Third Street. The St. Cloud House hotel was here in the early 1880s and was still here into the early 1900s. Mrs. Michael L. O'Laughlin owned the hotel. She leased it to C. Ed Markle and Jacob A. Lenhardt and they had it for years. T. O. Risdon leased the St. Cloud House in October of 1906. Sometime before 1908, the hotel was closed.

In October of 1908, Dell McMillan reopened the hotel. Then William M. Olson bought the hotel and leased it in January of 1916 to John Granahan. Granahan couldn't make a go of it. Olson turned the front half into a grocery store in March of 1918.

Olson ran the grocery until October of 1930. At some time the E. H. Snow Hatchery came to the building. Clem A. Becker bought it in September of 1952 for his shoe repair business. Gene Kohlhoff and partner Bruce Cottington bought the Becker store site for an addition to their parking lot and they turned the store into a Gold Bond Gift Stamp Redemption Center or Golden Gift Center in January of 1969. During that same month, Richard Nixon was sworn in as the 37th President of the United States. Today this is the parking lot for the new library.

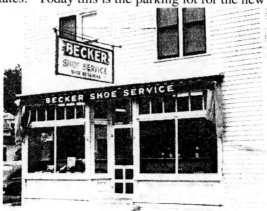

Becker Shoes on Marshall Avenue and Third Street.

30 Third Street East. Across the street, at the southwest corner of Marshall Avenue and Third Street, was F. G. Alvord's blacksmith shop in the early 1870s. It became Dave Condon's blacksmith shop, which became Dan Post's in September of 1882. Dan Post's shop became Nick Post's blacksmith shop in the twenties. Nick sold the shop to Ben Sandberg and Charles Osbeck in July of 1932. I don't know what other businesses followed, but eventually, in September of 1959, Dr. Lowell Wilson put up an office building here for his chiropractic business. He moved into it in January of 1960.

26-28 Third Street East. West of Wilson's building on Third Street, where the McGowan house had been, another building was erected in the early sixties. It was called the Hugh Wegner building, so I assume that he put the building up for his insurance business. Lawyers Edward F. Jacobsen and George H. Neperud and Dr. Donald Dille had their offices here also starting in January of 1964. In October of 1966, dentist Roger

540

A. Dahlseid moved into a room in the building. Lucille's Beauty Shop moved into the building in September of 1968. National Securities Underwriter was here in the early seventies along with State Farm Insurance. Dee's Beauty Salon was here in the mid-1980s. The Backyard, a tanning center, is in the building today.

Wayne Rick put up a building to the west of the Wegner building for his Rick's Plumbing and Heating business in the late 1960s. He is still at this location today.

Back on Marshall Avenue was a lot just to the north of the corner. The building on the lot was called the McGee building. McGee and Fracker's livery was in it at the turn of the century. In 1919, Oscar A. Nelson had his livery stable in the building. Oscar sold it to his brother Harry in April of 1920. Harry sold a half interest to W. I. Kitts in April of 1923. W. H. Mortenson's automobile repair shop was in the building in September of 1925.

163. 35 Second Street East. (515 Second Street East in the early 1900s.) At the northwest corner of Marshall Avenue and Second Street is the Post Office. There was a livery at this corner for a long time. In July of 1886, John Knights, from Canada, bought the corner lot here from the owner Nathaniel Frank Revell and started a livery in August. He had a partner name Bryant initially but then Knights took on a partner named Alexander D. Ross that same year. Knights retired and sold out to Ross in February of 1891. Ross took on another partner from up the street named Henderson M. Angier. They were still here in the late 1890s. Still later, Henderson M. Angier and Jack A. Hunter's Livery and Feed Stable was here so Ross must have sold out to Hunter. Angier's interest was then sold to Dan B. Lasher.

Alexander D. Ross and Henderson M. Angier

In March of 1904, Lasher sold his half of the livery to Wesley B. Hunter, brother of Jack A. Hunter. James J. Nelson, Jr. bought out Wesley Hunter's interest. In November of that year, Seth C. Caswell bought out James J. Nelson, Jr., who retired. Caswell sold out to William Watkins in January of 1907. During that same month, Oklahoma was the 46th state admitted to the Union. B. P. Nelson owned the lot and he sold it to the March brothers in March of 1919. They leased it out to Standard Oil, which built an oil station here in the late summer of 1919. Henry McGannon's Standard Oil business opened up in December of 1919 selling kerosene. The livery was moved to the northeast corner of Ramsey Avenue and Second Street. James Ryan took over the Standard business and started offering gasoline for the cars in town, all four of them. It was Litchfield's first service station. Standard Oil moved the service station to Sibley Avenue North, away from downtown, in November of 1929. This lot stood vacant.

The new Post Office was built on the vacant lot and it was opened to the public in September of 1935. An interesting sideline to the Post Office is that the architect from New York was none other than Electus Darwin Litchfield, Jr., the son of the man that Litchfield was named after. He was given the job of designing the Post Office in March of 1933. Roy Peterson became the new postmaster in August of 1936 and A. G. Johnson took over in August of 1941. Johnson retired in late 1959, but the new postmaster, Dean Schultz, wasn't appointed until September of 1961. This is still the site of Litchfield's Post Office today.

164. 27-29 Second Street East. Heading back west on Second Street towards Sibley Avenue from the Post Office corner, the next location before the alley had an odd mixture of occupants. First there was a feed mill owned by John Knights. In July of 1885, he traded it to Capt. Miller for a house. In August, Miller moved it next to Neuman's wagon shop on Depot Street. West of the feed mill was a smaller building. In May of 1885, Miss L. R. Moore's Ladies Bazaar was in it. Tommy and Lulu Branham bought Moore's stock and opened a stationery, notions and artist's goods store here in March of 1886. Then there was a meat market owned by D. W. Barker and J. Q. Andrews in the building in December of 1887. They closed in July of 1888 and A. M. Caswell and Sons moved their meat business here in the same month. Caswell was from Canada.

In the early 1900s, the Ed Curtis and Dwight B. Lounsbury Feed and Sale Barn was here and then in 1917, the Sugden Dray Line was here. Then I lost track of what was here in the 1920s.

Part of the building was torn down and there was a business here called the Trading Post in the mid-forties. John Colberg's Skelgas was here in the early fifties. Colberg went across from the park and then the small building here was occupied by Sando's TV in September of 1955. Leonard "Len" Sando sold TVs and Baldwin and Thomas organs and was an auctioneer also. He went out of business in October of 1957. Today a lawn for the Post Office site is here.

165. 23 Second Street East. (513 Second Street East in the early 1900s.) Samuel Y. Gordon's old butcher shop was moved here in April of 1873 on the next lot heading west. Then Nels C. G. Hanson and Nels Elofson used it as an office for their farm implement business. In 1877, P. Borstrom made and sold boots and shoes from the small white building, which was right behind the "drugstore building". In 1883, Ole A. "Music Ole" Olson opened his first music store here. He moved to Sibley Avenue down by the hotel in 1886. Eldo H. McGannon rented the building in September of 1889 for a flour and feed store. He sold the business to J. D. "Dick" Hayford in January of 1890. Sam Brown opened a harness shop here in October of 1892 and then turned right around and moved. The Litchfield Bakery, owned by A. McPherson, was here in mid-1894. James Campbell moved his harness shop here in January of 1898 from the Chandler building on Sibley Avenue.

Olaf M. Olson had a feed store here in August of 1902. Then it was E. E. Peterson's feed store. The real estate office of J. H. Spelliscy was the next business here. He left sometime before December of 1915, because Mike J. Owens moved his harness shop to the building at that time after he had a fire at his location on Depot Street. In 1917, the Carl F. W. Schultz general store was there. He closed in May of 1919, but reopened in August of 1919. Frank Williams and Fred Sperling bought the building in May of 1922 for their grocery business. I believe Floyd D. Lyons had his White Grocery here in September of 1923. In April of 1926, Walter E. Buren moved his grocery here for a short time. John O. Larson moved his furniture repair and linoleum business here along with an office for his Litchfield Funeral Home in February of 1929. He quickly moved across the street.

Hans O. Evenson moved his car business to the location in August of 1931 from his former location in the White Front garage. After Evenson left, Frank Williams came with his Frank's Cafe in September of 1932, but moved to the Settergren building in November. Otto H. Werner moved his plumbing and heating business into the rear of the little building in February of 1935. In the late forties, Dick Baldwin bought the building for his radio and TV repair shop. He also sold and repaired guns, but didn't advertise that part of his business.

When Baldwin died in January of 1964, Gary Johnson bought the business and building in March. He closed the business in October of 1967. Gib Smith then brought in his Gib's Shoe Repair here in April of 1968. Likens Studio, a photography business, was here in 1971 and Jeannie's Place, an antique store, was here in May of 1973. Today there is a small parking lot here.

167. 200 Sibley Avenue North. Before arriving back on Sibley Avenue, I passed a stairway on the south side of the building at the northeast corner. The stairway led down to an entrance under the corner store where there has always been a barbershop. Oren Wilbert "Bert" Topping, son of pioneer barber "Professor" Charles Griswold "Charley" Topping, had the first shop down there in February of 1885, after the Brown building was erected in November of 1884. He quickly moved out. J. William "Billy" Nelsan had the in September of 1885. He had been upstairs over the Rankin and Greenleaf Hardware store in June of 1884. John A. McColeman was here in October of 1891. Oren Wilbert "Bert" Topping moved back in here in December of 1897 after a fire damaged his shop elsewhere.

Walter W. Earley bought out Topping in August of 1902. Walter's son Albert became the Meeker County sheriff. Walt sold the business to Anthony "Tony" Bordan in April of 1908. Bordan moved out in September of 1912. W. C. Daniels came here in January of 1915 after he had been burned out at another location, but he immediately sold to J. Filbach and J. Carlson that same month. Walter W. Earley bought the barbershop back in June of 1915. Another son of Walt, George Earley, had the shop in the twenties and early thirties.

Raymond A. "Ray" Nelson went to work for George and then bought the shop from him in March of 1935. Ray kept it for twenty years. He had a shower stall down here that could be rented. Ray sold out to Jim Murphy in July of 1955 and went up north to run a resort. Ray came back and bought the shop back in August of 1959. Larry Ackerman bought the business from Ray in October of 1965 calling it Larry's Barber Shop. Then Larry moved the shop up to street level across the street to where it is today.

166. 202 Sibley Avenue North. (23 Sibley Avenue North in the early days, and then 741 Sibley Avenue North.) Back on Sibley Avenue, the corner building was another of my "personality" buildings. This was

another drug store building, but it took a while to become that. M. Arthur Brown built a large twenty by eleven foot two-story wooden building with a twenty by sixteen foot addition here, at a cost of $1800. It was for his hardware and implements store. William "Billy" Patterson had a feed store in the front at this location, which he sold to Chauncey F. Dart in March of 1874. The hardware was in the rear. In the spring of 1880, a man named Lindquist held weekly jewelry auctions here. Peter W. Johnson and M. Arthur Brown had a hardware here in July of 1880. David Elmquist, who moved all over town, briefly had his jewelry store here in 1880. Johnson bought Brown's share of the hardware business in 1881, and he was still here in the early 1890s. Brown kept the implement business. About this time, the remaining old wooden building was torn down and a new brick one was erected with bricks made in Litchfield. The building has "Brown's Block 1884 J. M. and P. Peterson Builders" on the top facing. It was completed in November of 1884. M. Arthur Brown built it and continued his tinware and farm implement business here. In June of 1885, Birch and Nelson Clothing rented the storeroom in the back for their business. They had been in several locations around town. By September of 1889, Birch and Nelson had moved out to the Masonic Building down the block. Just Brown was here and his awnings advertised clothing and furnishings.

Von Kuster Hardware and Birch and Nelson Clothing in 1889.

In December of 1889, Brown opened a grocery and dry goods business in the room in back where Birch and Nelson had been. Lawyer H. S. McMonagle had his office in the rear of the building in the early 1890s, but moved upstairs in April of 1893 when W. H. McCarthy rented the room for his Meeker County Marble Works. In November of 1893, Brown went out of business. Mrs. Ida Davis had her Home Bakery here somewhere in the building in November of 1893 and closed it in June of

1894. An office for the Minnesota Telephone Company, Litchfield's first telephone company according to the *Litchfield Independent*, was in the back starting in December of 1897. A confusing bit of information is that an October of 1882 issue of the *Independent* stated that the Revell brothers got Litchfield's first telephone and it ran from their residence to their store across Second Street. But, the October of 1885 newspaper states that David Gorman got the first telephone running from his house to his livery. At some point, Otho H. Campbell bought this building. After Peter Johnson's hardware closed, tinsmith William Von Kuster moved into the room in April of 1896. James B. Atkinson, Jr. and Alex Roehl moved their drug store here in March of 1897, combining their stock with the Revell drugstore stock they bought. Their drugstore was the first one at this corner. Mary McGowin moved her millinery into the back room in late 1897 or early 1898. Charles A. Anderson bought Roehl's interest in the drugstore in January of 1899. The store became Atkinson-Anderson Drug and then just Anderson Drug when Anderson bought out Atkinson. In May of 1898, A. M. Standish had a restaurant in the back room. The McLane Commercial Company moved into the back storeroom in March of 1899.

Tipton F. McClure bought the building from Otho H. Campbell in August of 1906. The Ziemann poolroom was in the back in the early 1910s. Carl F. W. Schultz bought the poolroom in April of 1913.

Anderson sold the drugstore to Henry W. Carlsen in June of 1944. Home Gas was in the rear in the early fifties. Del Peltier, in partnership with men named Sward and Kemp, then bought the drugstore in August of 1955 and it became Sward-Kemp Drug. It was Ringhold Drug for a while. Recently it was the Raeann Rose Photography business and the J D Framing Store. When the framing store closed in early 2003, Mary Moore opened up her Mutt's Bath and Bakery in March of 2003.

169. 204-206 Sibley Avenue North. (739 Sibley Avenue in the early 1900s.) Several businesses have been upstairs over the previous corner building over the years. In 1872, Clark L. Angell had the first photography business in town upstairs. In June of 1872, T. R. Briggs bought out Clark briefly but he moved to Willmar and Angell was back in August. Dr. Frank E. Bissell was also upstairs in 1872. Sivert Olson and Andrew F. Nordstrom had a sewing machine and musical instruments store in late 1882 in rooms over Johnson's hardware. They moved to DeCoster's store in early 1883. Judge S. A. Plumley moved his office in upstairs right after the building opened up. August "Gus" T. Koerner had his justice of the peace office upstairs in 1885. Lawyer E.

B. Hall and notary public H. C. Salisbury had offices upstairs in 1890. Mrs. C. E. Adlerbjelke rented the second floor in February of 1891 for a boarding house, which she called the Eagle Hotel. In February of 1892, Hattie Anderson had a dressmaking business upstairs. In May, Mrs. Adlerbjelke added more rooms over Peter W. Johnson's hardware store, which was in the back of the building. Lawyer H. S. McMonagle had his office upstairs in April of 1893 after having been in a room downstairs in the rear of the building. Upstairs at that time also was E. W. Campbell's law office, and Doctors Karl A. Danielson and John J. Donovan's offices. Campbell was mayor in 1921 and 1927. Danielson built a home in 1910 at 805 Sibley Avenue South and it is still there today.

At some time in the early 1930s, Dr. Harold Wilmot had his office upstairs and his brother Cecil A. joined him in September of 1937. They moved out when they built a clinic by the park in March of 1950. After the Wilmots moved out, Dr. K. J. Kelly was upstairs here.

171. 208 Sibley Avenue North. (25 Sibley Avenue North in the early days and then 737 Sibley Avenue in the early 1900s.) I head north again on Sibley Avenue, where the next building had mostly restaurants after it's resurrection from being a vacant lot. Originally James M. Morris, a grocer, built a small building here in 1871. It was a twenty by thirty foot two-story one with a twenty by thirty foot addition. It cost $800 to build. The U. S. Land Office, managed by John M. Waldron and J. C. Braden moved upstairs over the grocery in the Morris building in July of 1871. W. P. Todd leased the old Morris building for a general store in April of 1875. In September of 1876, the land office left Litchfield. George W. Gordon had the Boss Confectionery here in March of 1877. He had bought the confectionery from J. W. Billings and moved the business here. That June, Gordon sold out to A. Wirt, who had had a gun shop in the Babcock hardware store. Wirt sold the confectionery to Samuel Y. Gordon in October of 1877. In March of 1887, Andrew J. Anderson and Nels C. G. Hanson had a hardware store here. The partnership dissolved in June of 1888 and Hanson sold his interest to Charles Windle. William Von Kuster had a hardware store here in the mid-1890s. When Von Kuster moved out in early 1898, Mary McGowin moved her millinery here for a short time in April of 1898, as the Spanish-American War was just beginning. Mary went out of business at this location in July of 1898 and moved to her final location. Sykora's meats moved in here in September of 1898.

Ole B. Olson owned the north half of the lot in 1912. Richard "Dick" Berens bought the building from Aron J. Anderson around 1915 and he sold his Maxwells and Studebakers here. His window sign read "W. R. Berens Autos". Henry Klauser owned the building in October of 1916. A restaurant run by Carl Christensen and Elmer Lorass was here in early 1917, sharing the building. I think it was first called the Litchfield Restaurant and then the Carl Christenson Cafe. Nettie Pearson had it in 1917. Berens moved out in 1919. Elmer S. Noreen leased the building for his Litchfield Ice Cream and Dairy Company in November of 1919. At this time the building was called the "Klauser building". Aron J. Anderson sold the back lot to W. Richard "Dick" Berens in September of 1920 for selling cars. He moved to the Scherer building on Depot Street in June of 1921. Harry Hansen took over the ice cream factory and moved across the street in December of 1924, when he built a new building there. Ole Hillstrom's Home Café was here starting in April of 1925. He had been in the Scherer building on Depot Street. He sold the restaurant to Olaf Nelson in February of 1927.

Olaf Nelson left to go to one room of the Settergren building in November of 1931. E. Stavig had a shoe repair shop here for less than a month in December of 1931. Then in February of 1932, A. G. Johnson's Litchfield Flower Shop was here until he rented the building at 713 Ramsey Avenue South for a greenhouse in July. The flower shop was followed by Judge Herman M. Hershey's music store and gift shop in October of 1932. He moved out in January of 1936. Frank Fransein bought the lot and moved in here in November of 1935. Frank also had a restaurant in Atwater, which he sold to Herman Brulla and Loretta Wischmann in August of 1961. His son Wallace "Wally" took over the restaurant here in the early fifties while Frank ran the other restaurant, but Frank took this one back in April of 1957.

Fransein's in the fifties.

The Shamrock Café, owned by Jan and Jerry O' Keefe was here in the early sixties. They moved elsewhere in town after Don Burke bought the building in November of 1971. Burke moved his jewelry store here in February of 1972. After having been a Sears Catalog Store, the building stood vacant and today a business called S & R Everything Store is in it.

548

173. 210 Sibley Avenue North. (27 Sibley Avenue North in the early days and then 731 Sibley Avenue in the early 1900s.) It seems that the Hollywood Theater has been at the next site forever, but that's not true. In 1871, George B. Lyon owned the lot and in 1874, Joseph Roetzer, a brewer with Erhardt Lenhardt, owned it. I don't know if either did anything with it. Roetzer also owned the lot next door. Albert Vitzthum Von Eckstaedt (Albert Vitzthum) partnered with John Rodange in 1880 in a saloon here and bought Rodange's half of the saloon in January of 1883. Albert was from Germany. John Konsbrick's wine, liquors and cigar business, (a saloon), moved in here in December of 1885, after Konsbrick's previous saloon down the street had burned down. Konsbrick was also from Germany. The saloon moved to the basement and the building was leased to the Jacob Kahn, of the Kahn Brothers Company, (Louis was his brother), for their Golden Eagle Clothing Store in March of 1886. The store was managed by M. Leon. They soon moved down the street to the hotel block. The D. D. Cole and Co. general store was here in 1888. It closed in January of 1889. Mrs. Adlerbjelke moved her restaurant into the building that same month. Henry T. Halverson, Jr. sold farm machinery from a room here in the spring of 1891. It was still here in 1894, but by that time it was called Halverson and Anderson. The McLaughlin Brothers Mercantile Company or hardware moved their business here in December of 1891, because of a fire at their other location. Fred Reitz had a cigar factory here in November of 1896 and suffered some damage in 1898 when Chapman's, next door, burned down. It seems that fires had a connection with this location.

John Turck had the White Front saloon here in early 1907. Vitzthum had a fire in April of 1907, which put him out of business. Turck's also closed in 1907 and F. M. Brown reopened it in February of 1908. Jerry Sherwood owned the saloon in August of 1908 and he sold it to John Gaasterland in September of 1908. The Minneapolis Brewing Company actually owned the saloon license, which Gaasterland lost for them in December of 1910 by selling to minors. A. J. Davidson and Sam M. Hanson moved a shoe store here in September of 1911. It was called Davidson's Selz Royal Blue Shoe Store. Selz was a shoe brand. Henry O. Morrison bought the shoe business in July of 1914 and called it Morrison's Selz Royal Blue Shoe Store. During that same month, World War I began as the Ottoman Empire declared war on Bosnia. Henry's father, Jim, helped him out in the store. One night when Jim was walking home, he got killed at the Holcombe Avenue railroad crossing when he didn't see the speeding mail train going through town. Henry Morrison then moved the business to the Robertson building. James Copouls' Litchfield Candy Company Store and Vitzthum's saloon were here in the early 1910s. David T. Hobson's Cigar Shop and confectionery came here in May of 1918. Hobson's confectionery was still here in March of 1920 and George H. Rethlake bought it, changing the name to George's Confectionery. C. B. Damuth sold phonographs in the confectionery. At some point in 1920 or 1921, the building was removed and this location became a vacant lot. Another building was put up and in September of 1922, Frank O. Holm bought it. His wife Kitty had a "tea room" over the First State Bank. Holm sold the building to S. P. Kelly in May of 1923. Kelly sold the building in the same week to William Lallis, who had The Elite Candy Shop or confectionary here. Lallis sold his confectionery to A. D. O'Neil in July of 1926. O'Neil sold it to T. W. Langin in January of 1927. T. W. Langin's Goodie Shop, which was like a deli with a fountain, sandwiches and homemade mayonnaise, was here until Langin sold his business to L. A. Webster in July of 1929.

Mid-1910s: Johns Hardware, an empty lot, Hobson's with the Litchfield Candy Co. and Berens' auto.

In February of 1930, Harry Radunz, the tire and junk man, bought the building from John Rodange, who had owned it. Harry didn't move here however. Tom Wandok had a saloon here in 1930. Webster sold his restaurant business to R. S. Kroona in 1931. Louis G. Marquard had a restaurant and confectionery here called the Oasis Café in the early thirties. He sold it to Oscar Olson in November of 1933. C. F. Schnee bought the site from under the occupant's noses and they were evicted. Schnee then built the Hollywood Theater here. He opened it on Tuesday, November 24, 1936. On the Grand Opening night, the movie shown was *Libeled Lady* starring Jean Harlow, William Powell, Myrna Loy and

Spencer Tracy.   In the late thirties, the Holmes-Hollywood Salon, a beauty shop owned by Jennie Holmes, which became Bee's (Hultgren) Hollywood Salon in January of 1947, was above the Hollywood.   C. F. Schnee died in July of 1955 and his sons continued on with the business. In the fall of 1955, they bought some land on the Lloyd Turck farm, at the junction of highways 12 and 22, and started construction of the Starlite drive-in theater, which opened up on June 28, 1956. The first car to drive in was the Chester Madson family car. The Hollywood had a fire in the lobby in May of 56, so the "good" movies were shown at the Unique Theater until the Hollywood could be fixed up.   The theater reopened in October of 1956.   The Federal Land Bank had an office upstairs over the theater in 1957.   National Farm Loan Association, probably the same business, was there also. It moved out in July of 1959 to its new building on Marshall Avenue North.

Maurine's Fabrics had this address in the early seventies so it must have been upstairs at that time. The Hollywood theater was sold to Dean Lutz in April of 1978 and it's still going today.

174. 212-212½ Sibley Avenue North. (29 Sibley Avenue North in the early days and then 729-727 Sibley Avenue in the early 1900s.) The building north of the Hollywood had the same façade as the Hollywood. It was done on purpose when the Hollywood was built. At that time the building also took on the same street number as the Hollywood for some reason. So we have a little confusion here but not with the location of the businesses. Originally several different stores in a couple of small wooden buildings had been in this location. In 1874, Joseph Roetzer owned the lot but I don't know if he did anything with it. He also owned the lot next door. Around 1876, all that was here was a vacant lot with a wooden fence facing the street. I believe the following is correct. Chris Mortenson started his Litchfield City Bakery here in April of 1884. His newspaper ad stated, "I claim to be making the best bread, biscuits, cakes, pies, etc. to be found in Litchfield, try my work, and see if my claim is not true." Mortenson moved to another location in the fall of 1886. George H. Chapman's harness shop was here at sometime in the late 1880s. Chapman was from England. There was a space between this building and the one to the south. George Kline put his shooting gallery in that space in October of 1891. Emma Anderson owned the lot in 1893. Chapman's harness shop burned to the ground in March of 1898. A new building was built, which Edward J. "Ed" Gould leased in July of 1898 and started another harness business in. The Charles Edblom Saloon and confectionery business followed. There were rooms

upstairs rented out to men only, mostly salesmen who came to town. The Swanson and Nelson millinery moved into the downstairs room vacated by Gould in July of 1899.

William Henry Greenleaf moved his real estate office into a room here in March of 1902. The saloon was sold to E. B. Paulson in April of 1902. N. P. Holmberg had his tailor shop here in November of 1902. William Gordon and George W. Alexander bought the stock from the Krueger Brothers store, which closed elsewhere, and sold the stock here as the Litchfield Mercantile Company in September of 1908. H. A. Plath bought the remainder from them in October of 1908 and continued selling the stock here. Anthony "Tony" Borden and Chris A. Bertelson moved into the building September of 1912. Borden had a barbershop in his half and Bertelson had a confectionery in his half. Bertelson sold the confectionery to Clifford W. Johnson in February of 1913. Johnson sold it to Oscar O. Lindblom and bought a pool hall across town. Borden sold his barbershop to W. C. Daniels in June of 1914. Daniels had a fire in January of 1915, which ruined the confectionery also. This building was smaller than it ended up being and a very small wooden building that had Mrs. Ida Agnew's hamburger eat shop was to the north of it. Ida's shop started as a waffle shop in November of 1929.

1933: Deilke's, Hanson's hamburgers, Oasis Café (Goodie Shop), and Hershey's music shop.

The hamburger shop was sold to Raymond A. Hanson in April of 1932. Clayton Quale had his Clay's Eat Shop here in the early thirties. When Fransein's was moved into a building down the street, Clayton was seen running in the alley one night in February of 1936 just before a fire started between Fransein's and the Oasis Café next door. The fire was put out and Quale was charged with arson. He got off for lack of evidence. The Schnees bought the lot and tore the buildings down in February of 1936. A new building was put up with the same façade as the Hollywood Theater next door. The store in the new building became

Silas L. Radant, William G. Goldberg and H. K. McIver's Hollywood Shoes store in September of 1937. In June of 1950, McIver bought out his partners and changed the name to the Hollywood Shop. He shut the business down in July of 1956 after the Hollywood Theater had their fire, which badly damaged his shoe inventory. Then the building became Irene's Fashions and Bridal Shop in November of 1957. Mrs. Jack (Irene) Strand owned it.

Irene's closed in the summer of 1960 and Roger Setterberg moved his Setterberg's Jewelry here from across the street in September of 1960. Lowell Paffrath brought in his Paffrath Jewelry store in November of 1964. Don Burke ran it. It became Burke Jewelers in January of 1967 when Don bought the business. Burke moved next door in February of 1972. In March of 1972, Gerald F. Foote appropriately brought a shoe store here called Gerald's. He should have named it Foote Shoes, don't you think? Frederick E. Schultz had an accounting office somewhere here in the early seventies. Then, it was the Dragon Shop and finally Jenni's Consignment. Today it is a vacant building.

About 1880: The Forester Saloon, Chapman's Harness, small buildings, another saloon, a confectionary, a feed store, and, across the street, the Brill drug store.

175. 214 Sibley Avenue North. (31 Sibley Avenue North in the early days and then 725 Sibley Avenue in the early 1900s.) Originally I believe there were a couple of small buildings at this next location heading north. In 1869, the M. Arthur Brown Hardware was here (one of the first three businesses in town) and D. E. Potter had his furniture business (Litchfield's first) here also. Potter moved out to another location in early 1870, and, in May of 1870, George H. Chapman bought
553

the building Potter had been in. Chapman had his Pioneer Harness Store of Meeker County here sharing the lot. In 1871, Chapman is listed as the lot's owner. In 1879, he built a new building here. It was a sixteen by twenty foot one-story building that only cost $200 to build. In 1879 Judge John M. Waldron owned the lot here and neighboring lots. In 1876, the John Rodange saloon was here in the Brown building. Charley Taylor opened a meat market somewhere in the building in May of 1881. In August of 1881, Taylor bought McGuire's butcher shop next door and consolidated the two. At some time Chapman moved his harness shop next door. C. G. Wennerlund had a jewelry store here in May of 1887, managed by Christian B. Nelson, followed in that same year by the New Fruit Store owned my Matthew Blumer and someone named Seeley. In August of 1887, the fruit store was changed to a confectionery. They sold the confectionery to Christian B. Nelson in January of 1888. Edward J. "Ed" Gould moved his harness shop here in June of 1888. In November of 1888, Gould became partner with Michael Hanses. He closed in February of 1893. In May of 1893, the Reuter brothers moved their meat market here. Mrs. C. E. Adlerbjelke, whose husband, Henry W., had a farm machinery business in town, moved her Eagle Restaurant and Confectionery here late in 1889. She quit the business in December of 1891. Leslie Dart came in and sold out her remaining confectionery stock until Harry M. Angier bought the Eagle Restaurant and Confectionery in January of 1892. He moved across the street in May. In July of 1892, Robert A. Vorys moved his City Bakery and Restaurant into the room where Mrs. C. E. Adlerbjelke had been. He also bought A. M. Caswell's greenhouse property, in May of 1901, and changed it into a chicken ranch, no doubt to stock his restaurant. Church and Weber had a flour and feed store, managed by Olaf M. "Feed Ole" Olson, in March of 1895. William Henry Greenleaf and his son Charles A. moved an office for their lumberyard here in the front in March of 1895. In the late 1890s, Christian B. Nelson back here again with his confectionery, owned the building and the one north of here. He suffered a lot of damage when the Chapman building to the south burned down in March of 1898. Ed W. Swanson moved his confectionery here in the fall of 1898. He sold his stock to William Brown and O. W. Alger in January of 1899. They moved down the street.

H. I. Carlson opened up his City Restaurant here in January of 1904. Sam J. Bundy, former owner of the Horseshoe Café, bought the restaurant along with Herman M. Hershey in August of 1904, but they moved out to the old Meeker County Bank building in October. J. W. Miller bought the building in March of 1905. During that same month,

Theodore Roosevelt was sworn in as President for his second term. Miller sold the building to Albert Mortenson and Charles Forberg in May of 1906. Their business closed in July of 1906. In August of 1906, Leona and Louise Schultz and Mrs. J. M. Palmquist opened up another millinery here, which they called Misses Schultz Millinery Parlors. William Lind opened another restaurant here in June of 1911. He had bought out the Bloemkers restaurant, which was down the street and he moved it here. I don't know what he called it, but a good name would have been the Hot Potato, the way it changed hands. Lind sold it to Mrs. Boegen in January of 1913 and Albert H. Berndt bought it in February of 1913. The Harris brothers leased the building for their New York Cafe after Berndt moved out in May of 1913 to the Dart building. In October, they sold it to Fred Cook, who sold it to Thomas "Tom" Reed in June of 1914. Reed was indicted for illegally selling liquor and the building mysteriously burned down in September of 1914. Then after World War I, there was just a vacant lot here. The present building was erected in 1929 to house Clarence F. "Dugan" Deilke's Dry Cleaning and Dyers business, which had been down Sibley Avenue next to the Settergren building in 1923.

Clarence Deilke moved into the new building in February of 1930. In October of 1946, Deilke's son-in-law, Howard "Howie" Koehn, bought a half interest in the business. In March of 1947, they sold the business to Ernest Berg. So we had the Berg Dry Cleaners. Deilke, his daughter Ruth and her husband Howie bought the business back in January of 1949. Ruth and Howard Koehn bought Clarence out completely in 1949.

Deilke Dry Cleaners in 1955.

It became the Benage Jewelry store in 1973 and then Margaret Breitenbach's Clay Pot Floral and Gift Shop after the dry cleaners closed. Then it was the Pizza Factory, Campus Life and now it's the Crow River Area Youth For Christ.

Reed's Printing combined the next two stores into one store and today the Legion keeps them together. But for a long time there were two separate stores next, just before the mid-block alley. There are apartments upstairs today at 214 ½ Sibley Avenue North.

176. 218 Sibley Avenue North. (33 Sibley Avenue North in the early days and then 723 Sibley Avenue in the early 1900s.) Litchfield's first hardware store was here in the fall of 1869. Smith D. King and Vanderborck or Vanderhorck owned it. The Smith D. King and Whyborn Hardware was here in the early 1870s in a twenty-two by thirty-six foot two-story building that cost $1500 to build. They had a coupon in a January of 1871 *Litchfield Republican* newspaper for "Good For Five Cents On A Dollar King and Whyborn". That was very rare for those days and the only coupon I saw in the early newspapers until after the turn of the century. King left in March of 1873 and Whyborn sold the business to Z. B. Fifield, who didn't last in the business very long. William H. Greenleaf bought his stock. By the way, in March of 1873, Ulysses S Grant was sworn in as President for his second term. Dr. V. P. Kennedy owned the lot here in January of 1874 and he had his office here in a new small wooden building which shared the lot. Kennedy left before the end of the year. George M. Babcock and Co. built a new hardware store here in 1975. It was a twenty-four by forty-one foot two story one. A. Wirt had a gun shop in the hardware, which he sold to Harrington and Clark in summer of 1877. S. W. Frasier had a restaurant upstairs in August of 1877. The small building was moved in November of 1878. In 1879, Judge John M. Waldron owned the lot here and neighboring lots. Nels Swanson had a farm machinery depot here in 1879. He sold Osborn and Buckeye farm machinery. A man named McGuire had a butcher shop here for a short time in the early 1880s. In March of 1882, the Flynn brothers opened a "branch office" to their wagon and carriage making business here. They owned a lumberyard in town and had branched out to the other business. At some point, probably just prior to 1890, two wooden structures, this building and the one to the north were torn down and a vacant lot was here until a new brick building was erected that covered both lots. According to old photographs, John Paulson and someone named Peterson owned the City Meat Market here on the south lot in October of 1882. Paulson retired in July of 1885, but came back in 1887. Henry T. Halverson, Jr. bought Peterson's interest in November of 1887. Charles C. "Charley" Sather bought Halverson's interest and the business became Paulson and Sather.

556

Paulson eventually owned the meat market by himself in October of 1889 and he sold it to William Diepenbrock and August Bracher. They moved in September of 1890. Then C. Ad Swenson had the business here. Christian B. Nelson had his confectionery here in May of 1892 and Ross and Worrell moved a meat market here in June of 1892. They closed in July. Christian Nelson still owned this building in the late 1890s. The Sather Brothers meat business was back here in October of 1899 when his brother Chris joined Charles C. Sather.

C. Ad Swenson was back with another partner named J. W. Miller and they bought out the Sather brothers in February of 1905. Swenson bought out Miller in March of 1905 and then sold his meat business to M. J. Molitor and Z. F. Moser in April of 1907. They called their business the City Meat Market and sold it to Joseph and Nick Leither in June of 1908. It was sold to Forsberg and Rosenquist in February of 1909. In April of 1911, Daniel Shaughnessy and Sons bought the meat market and turned right around and sold it to Henry J. Boedecker in July of 1911. Boedecker still called it the City Meat Market. He sold it back to Forsberg and Rosenquist in October of 1911. They sold it to Freeman Cox in January of 1914. The Johns brothers, William H. and D. B., bought this lot and the one to the north in April of 1914 for a new building for their hardware business. This forced Cox to move north of here. So the Johns Brothers and Company Hardware was here after the new building was erected. D. B. Johns and G. E. Logan (the company part of the partnership) sold their interest in the hardware to G. L. Horton, J. W. Eberts and Oscar W. Ringdahl in January of 1920. Now the business was just called Johns Hardware. Ringdahl bought William H. Johns' interest in the hardware in February of 1925 and sold it to George B. Bohrer in February of 1929. Otto H. Werner had a plumbing and heating business in the back of the hardware. Otto sold the plumbing business to Tony Beerling and Ole Nelson in March of 1928 and moved to another location in back of Houd Hardware.

Beerling and Nelson dissolved their partnership in November of 1935 and Beerling kept the shop in the back. In the June of 1935, F. F. Faut bought the hardware store. Also in the mid-thirties, something called the R & N Motor Express operated out of some part of this location. In October of 1938, Earl Olson bought the hardware but Faut kept it going for a while until Olson had his opening in March of 1939. John O'Neil's plumbing and heating business went into the rear of the building in July of 1945, but the next year he was down the street. Jerry Nelson had the plumbing shop in April of 1949. In November of 1950, Wayne Rick's tin shop and repairs was added to the rear. In February of

1951, the hardware became the Olson-Upham Hardware when George Upham became a partner to Earl Olson. Then Olson had it alone again in July of 1952, when he bought out Upham. For years Olson Hardware was famous for its "Santa Land" in the basement at Christmas time. In August of 1952, the American Legion Nelsan-Horton Post 104 bought the building. The Legion moved in upstairs and continued to rent the downstairs to businesses. Olson Hardware closed in June of 1957. Then Wilson's Hardware was here. Finally James J. Reed came in 1957 and he eventually bought the building. The Legion Club upstairs was used on some Fridays in the spring of 1958 for a Teenage Canteen. Students in the high school were allowed to come from 8pm to 11pm on certain Fridays and play the jukebox and have sodas. Later in that year, the Canteen was moved to the Armory. The Junior Chamber of Commerce sponsored it. The Legion Club remained upstairs and when Reed went out of business, they finally moved downstairs where they are today.

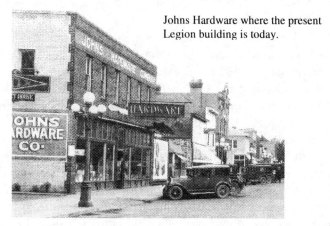

Johns Hardware where the present Legion building is today.

177. 220-222 Sibley Avenue North. (33 Sibley Avenue North in the early days and then 721 Sibley Avenue in the early 1900s.) I believe more than one building occupied this lot in the early days. In September of 1873, W. S. Knappen and a Mr. Scott built a small twenty-two by forty foot two-story building costing $1750 on this lot to be used as a hotel, billiard hall, saloon and restaurant. The hotel was actually a boarding house. In November of that year, Knappen sold the saloon part to Scott and kept the restaurant. In December, Knappen moved down the street to a different building. In August of 1878, Dr. S. L. Barr had his office upstairs. Charles Forester moved into the building in December of 1878 for his saloon, which he opened in January of 1879. In 1879 Judge John M. Waldron owned the lot here and neighboring lots. Charles H.

Bigelow moved his confectionery and stationery business here in a part of the building in June of 1881. Charles Forester's saloon was still here in the mid-1880s. In March of 1882, there was a "Chinese" laundry in the rear of the saloon, but a Chinese man didn't run it. The history gets confusing here. Possibly some of the stores in the other building that became Reed's were here. As I said, more than one small building occupied a lot. Also in 1889, Hiram S. Angell bought the stationery and confectionery business of Bigelow. John Paplow had a saloon here in the early 1890s, which he sold to Peter "Pete" Peifer.

John H. May's cigar factory was started over Peifer's saloon in May of 1904. Harry M. Angier moved his grocery to this location in March of 1911 after putting up a new building here. He sold it to Walter E. Buren in March of 1914. The Johns brothers bought this lot and the one to the south later in April of 1914 for a new building for their hardware business. This forced Buren to move north of here. So the Johns Brothers Hardware was here after the new building was erected. The National Tea Company, another grocery, started here in 1929.

Litchfield's Post Office came here on the north part of the building in May of 1931, while the current Post Office was being built. In November of 1935, Henry Weidenheft and Company moved a general store, Wiedenheft's Cash and Carry Store, in here along with Leroy R. "Roy" Cook's Meat Market, who had been at another location in the 1920s. In the phone book the business was called Wiedenheft & Cook. In December of 1939, Cook moved down the street. In 1940, it became just Wiedenheft's Grocery. Wiedenheft tried something new in January of 1940. He went to a "self-service" grocery. The customers had to actually go down the aisles and pick up the food they wanted themselves! Wiedenheft sold his grocery to Ed Hefty in February of 1941. His A & P was here in the north half of the store in July of 1943, it closed in May of 1954 and then it became Farnquist's Marshall-Wells in January of 1953. Marshall-Wells, which sold paint and hardware, moved here from their former location next to Viren-Johnson's. In March of 1956, Marlow Abdnor bought Marshall-Wells from Farnquist. Abdnor dropped the Marshall-Wells name and called his store the S & Q (Service & Quality) Hardware in February of 1959. Then he moved to the Jacks building.

Eventually the whole confusing mess became just Reed's Printing, when it was expanded to include the entire building. KLFD radio moved upstairs in the early sixties. The Legion Club is here today.

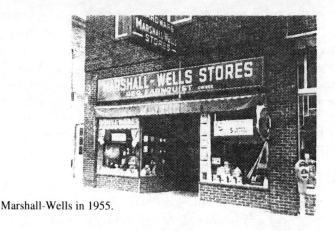

Marshall-Wells in 1955.

179. 226 Sibley Avenue North. (35 Sibley Avenue North in the early days and then 719 Sibley Avenue North in early 1900s.) There was an alley next and then a lot that at first held two small wooden buildings in late 1869. Pioneer lawyer Charles Henry Strobeck owned both buildings. The very first occupant of part of the lot was William S. Brill, who came to Litchfield from Red Wing, Minnesota. He had the first drugstore in Meeker County here in 1869 in a twenty-two by thirty-three foot two-story wooden building. It cost $3000 to build, quite a sum in those days, and was one of the first four businesses in town. Brill actually started out with a hardware store here but turned it into a drugstore, calling it the Meeker County Drug Store. Brill moved down the street when he erected a new building at the southeast corner of Second Street and Sibley Avenue. Brill was in the south side of the lot here and Strobeck occupied the north side with his law office. Lawyer Charles Henry Strobeck erected the north building, a sixteen by twenty-four foot two-story one that cost $750 to build, in the October of 1869. A watchmaker named B. O. Esping had a window in Strobeck's for his business. T. K. Gray and Ludwig F. Damm brought in a drug store in Brill's old location in February of 1871. The Gray brothers from Minneapolis owned it, but Damm managed the drug store. Damm's newspaper ad called the store "Svenskt Apothek" (Swedish Drugstore) and stated it was a "Skandinaviska Familje Medikamenter" meaning a "drugstore for Scandinavian families." Frank Daggett became the postmaster in April of 1874 and he moved the Post Office into Strobeck's building from Johnson's building. Lawyer Edward A. Campbell had his law office over one of these buildings in September of 1874. J. G. Todd had a dry goods store in the Strobeck building. I find no more mention of the other building for many years, so it's possible

that some of the businesses to follow might have been in it. James H. Morris became the postmaster and moved his grocery business here to be with the Post Office in May of 1875. He moved into the room vacated by J. G. Todd. Todd's brother W. P., who started another dry goods and hardware business elsewhere in town, bought Todd's goods. I think Todd and Morris just traded locations. John Blackwell had a music store here also in March of 1975, sharing the building. Blackwell was also a teacher, one source states he was Litchfield's first, and he either quit the business or died, because his wife re-opened in a couple of years at another location. Morris bought a large shelf with slots from the town of St. Anthony, Minnesota to improve the way the mail was handled. "Professor" Charles Griswold "Charley" Topping moved a branch of his confectionery and grocery here to a room in Strobeck's building for a short time also in November of 1875. Dr. L. P. Foster had his office over the Post Office for a while. The Knapp Brothers dry goods store was here in October of 1878. Morris moved across the street in late 1879. James B. Dougherty moved in here in December of 1879 and started another grocery at this location. He had been a resident of Meeker County since 1856. W. P. Todd bought the Knapp business and went back into business in March of 1880. T. Channell and Thompson dry goods bought out the Todd business in February of 1881 and it changed to Thompson and Rexford in April of 1881. In 1876 Strobeck took on a partner, S. A. Plumley. S. W. Frasier moved his restaurant here in November of 1878 and Strobeck and Plumley moved down the street. The restaurant must not have lasted long because two sisters, Mrs. W. White and Mrs. E. E. White moved their music store here in early 1879. They quit the business in February of 1880. Hugh Dowling's harness shop was here in September of 1879 in one of the buildings, as was the Independent Printing Office. Alex Cairncross had a dry goods and grocery store here in the early 1880s. He was in several locations around town with different partners, including his brother Steven. In January of 1883, John Nockels purchased the old wooden building and lot here. He moved the old building towards the back of the lot and he and John Konsbrick had a saloon here in the south building in 1883. He owned the other building too. Dowling's harness shop burned down on March 4, 1885, destroying the Konsbrick saloon next door also. Dowling opened up in a building south of Central Park. The Independent Printing office moved across the street to their present building in April of 1885, so that the destroyed old buildings here could be torn down. Mrs. John Nockels put up a new two-story brick building, twenty-five by seventy feet, in September of 1885. The Konsbrick saloon was back here then.

It was here for a picture in 1889. Tom Wandok started his cigar factory upstairs here in February of 1889. He moved out in June of 1890.

Konsbrick sold his saloon to O. M. Nelson in June of 1908. In 1912, Edmund M. Lenhardt had the saloon here. Sam J. Bundy bought the building in January of 1913 and Lenhardt moved out because Litchfield went dry in April of 1914. Freeman Cox's City Meat Market shared the building with Walter E. Buren's Square Deal Grocery store in May of 1914. Dr. A. W. Hanson had his office upstairs in August of 1818. Freeman bought the building from Bundy in September of 1922. In 1923, Cox got refrigeration for his meats. Before that, of course, they had to use ice. Freeman had one huge icebox that held six tons of ice. It had to be filled once a week. Buren sold his grocery part to Freeman in March of 1926 and moved to another location. Freeman began calling his business Cox's Market House. Eventually Freeman's son Merlyn had the business until he retired.

Andy Bienick started the first Farmer's Daughter restaurant here in February of 1970. He built the present Farmer's Daughter out on east Highway 12 in late 1973 and kept this one open for a year. People called it the "Downtown Café". It was Harold's Restaurant in the 1990s, when Harold Gendron bought it from Andy. Today it is the Main Street Cafe.

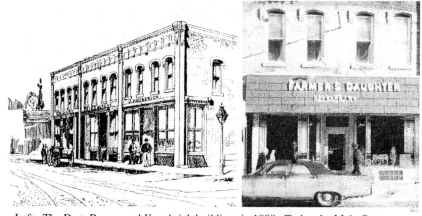

Left: The Dart, Berens and Konsbrick buildings in 1889. Today the Main Street Café is in the right building. Right: The original Farmer's Daughter restaurant.

180. 228-230 Sibley Avenue North. (37 Sibley Avenue North in the early days and 717 Sibley Avenue North in early 1900s.) Continuing north on Sibley Avenue brings me to a lot with originally more than one building again. Justice of the Peace Fayette Kelley owned the lot in 1874 and had an office in one of the buildings. Chauncey F. Dart's feed store was here in the early 1870s in the other. B. O. Esping

moved his jewelry and watch repair business upstairs over Dart's in the early 1870s. In March of 1874, Daniel Feeney moved his barbershop somewhere in the building from his previous location. He moved out in 1875. Also in 1874, when more than one small wooden building occupied the lot, I believe the Harrington and George B. Lyon bank, Litchfield's first bank was here. It was most likely in the Kelley building and it was called the Bank of Litchfield. Harrington sold his interest to George F. Snow and then Chauncey Butler bought out both in October of 1875. The bank closed down in December of 1877. In November of 1876, Dr. L. P. Foster moved into the building Kelley had occupied. In 1880, Chauncey F. Dart's Furniture and Undertaking was here. Peter Berens bought the business in November of 1884, giving up his blacksmithing business on the west side of Marshall Avenue near Third Street. Peter Berens, who then lived upstairs, built a new brick building here in April of 1886, moving the other building off the lot, and in August he moved in. John Johnson and Nels C. G Hanson had a hardware here also in 1888, but an 1889 picture shows that Berens was still here, so the hardware was probably in the rear.

His sons, W. Richard "Dick" and Leslie L. "Les", joined Berens in August of 1902. Peter took on Dick as a partner in June of 1906, calling the business Berens and Son. Dick Berens added automobiles to the inventory in 1911. Dick moved his automobile business out in 1915. In October of 1917, Les bought the building and business from Peter. Dewey E. Johnson bought the furniture and undertaking business in June of 1921, buying the building from Les.

On September 20, 1930, the I.G.A. Star Grocery store opened here, owned by Theodore "Ted" W. Kohlhoff and Frank Miller. I.G.A. meant Independent Grocers Alliance. Ted bought out Frank in 1942 and he changed the store from I.G.A. to Litchfield's first Super Valu in 1946, although it was stilled called Star Grocery. In December of 1948, Ted moved the business across the street to where Doffing's Smart Wear eventually went. Berquist's Electric came into this building in February of 1949. Stan took over the business from his father in January of 1955.

Stan was Litchfield's mayor in 1968. Berquist's moved out to 412 Gilman South and a store called Gibson's Discount Center was here in September of 1969 before Pamida moved in. Natural Food Co-Op or Natural Foods Market is here today.

East side of Sibley, about 1875: From the left: The Bank of Litchfield (Natural Food Co-op), Dowling's harness shop and Strobeck's law office (Main Street Cafe), alley, Forester's saloon (Legion Club), and Flynn Brothers (Legion Club)

181. 232-234 Sibley Avenue North. (39-41 Sibley Avenue in the early days and then 711 Sibley Avenue in the early 1900s.) Elizabeth Rust owned the next lot to the north in 1871. She had the Mrs. E. Rust Millinery here in May of 1971. She was the wife of Frank M. Rust who had a masonry business in town in partnership with E. D. Townsend. In 1874, John Malmquist owned the lot and had a dry goods store here. I believe there was more than one building on this lot, because Mrs. Rust sold the property to A. W. Swenson in October of 1875 and moved to Marshall Avenue. Swenson had a dry goods store here until 1879. Phineas "Pat" Cary moved into the same building as the Rust millinery in November of 1877 selling shoes. Cary leased it out to someone for a grocery in June of 1878. Christian Pederson moved his harness shop here in the other building from Depot Street in July of 1878. He went under later in the year and rose up again at another location in town. Charles H. Dart had his feed store and grocery here in the autumn of 1882. "Charley" partnered with Clark L. Angell, Jr. in February of 1883 and with Robert S. Hershey afterwards selling cigars in a shop in his store. Miss Kennedy and Mary McGowan opened a dressmaking shop upstairs in May of 1885. Kennedy left shortly and Mary brought in her two sisters and they started the McGowin Millinery, moving it across the street. Charley H. Dart bought the lot in December of 1885 and put up a "double-block" or combined building here with Peter Berens next door in April of 1886. Andrew Winger moved his tailor shop upstairs in the spring of 1886. Christian Pederson closed his harness shop in August of 1886. Dart bought out Hershey in January of 1887 and gave up the grocery part of his business in the fall of 1887. At some time Robert A. Vorys had one of his restaurants here. I believe it was in the late 1880s.
564

The Litchfield Greenhouse took over one window of the restaurant to display its goods in September of 1887. J. William "Billy" Nelsan rented a room under Vorys' restaurant for a barbershop in April of 1888. Hugh Dowling opened a new harness shop in the room where Dart had had his grocery in July of 1888. Vorys restaurant closed in August of 1889 and he moved to the Wadsworth house on Marshall Avenue North in September. Jacob "Jake" Koerner had a confectionery and grocery in the main building in September of 1889, which he sold to Wait H. Dart in December. In an 1889 picture, the sign still shows just the Charles H. Dart grocery here. There was a space on the lot next to Dart's. "Popcorn" Miller had his stand in that space in the late August of 1890. George Kline had a shooting gallery in the rear of "Popcorn" Miller's stand in June of 1891. When "Popcorn" Miller moved out of the space between the buildings in October of 1891, Justice James Benjamin Atkinson, Jr. put a small building there for an office (41 Sibley Avenue North) and Kline moved out. Wait H. Dart and Company's grocery was still here in early 1893. J. D. Hayford bought Charley H. Dart's flour and feed business in January of 1896. Around this time, A. A. Atkinson bought the lot. A Chinese man named A. J. Joy came back to Litchfield to try his laundry business in town again and opened up here in May of 1897. In August of 1897, Isadore Segal had his Litchfield Bazaar business here. When Segal moved out, the North Star clothing business leased the building in March of 1899. In June of 1899, Oscar A. Mehner had a tailor shop in the small Atkinson building.

Mehner quit his tailoring business in September of 1900. Phillip A. Addy had a shooting gallery in the Atkinson building in November of 1901. Ironically Mr. Addy and his younger brother were both picked up on suspicion of murder but it couldn't be proven. Phillip was released, but the younger brother went through a long trial and was found not guilty. Ole L. Langren moved his undertaking and carpet and wallpaper business here in the main building in February of 1900. Langren took on a partner named D. E. Dougherty, in August of 1900. Dougherty had been in a different building with McLaughlin Mercantile. Langren and Dougherty called their business the Palace Furniture Company. Dougherty was Litchfield's twenty-eighth mayor in 1910. Christian B. Nelson had a shoe repair business in the small Atkinson building, which he sold to Sam M. Hanson in January of 1910. In September of 1911, Chris A. Bertelson leased the small building for a candy and cigar store. Ole L. Langren left Dougherty in July of 1911 and he moved down to the hotel block. Dougherty and his Palace Furniture went out of business in September of 1912. In February of 1913, Lorenz C. Johnson bought

Bertelson's confectionery. In May of 1913, Albert H. Berndt bought the building from Charles H. Dart and moved his Kaiser Hoff restaurant here. It closed later in the year and Edward W. Gruenhagen moved his jewelry business here in January of 1914. Gruenhagen moved out and O. C. Frederick moved a poolroom and confectionery here in the autumn of 1916. Frederick sold his business to William Couette in May of 1917. Harry L. Coons bought the pool hall in October of 1920. George Pike and John Hannan took it over in July of 1921 and Pike bought out Hannan in January of 1922. Federal agents arrested Pike in October of 1922 for selling bootleg. He spent forty-five days in jail for that. W. I. Booth leased the building for his pool hall in March of 1923 after Pike had moved out. August Holtz and A. G. Armen bought Booth's pool hall in May of 1923. At sometime, the Eklund brothers had a pool hall here too. My great-uncle Edward "Ed" Birkemeyer and his brother Alfred G. Birkemeyer owned the Birkemeyer Brother's Pool Hall on this location from 1926 to 1932. Alfred also sold and serviced radios in the basement of the pool hall, starting in February of 1929. His business was called the Litchfield Radio Shop.

The Birkemeyers dissolved their partnership in July of 1930. In June of 1931, Alfred left the pool hall business and moved next door with his radio repair business. Ed, who also ran a well drilling business in town, sold the pool hall to James Madden and his son in June of 1932 to devote full time to the drilling business. Madden sold the pool hall to Gust Xenedes in September of 1932. Gust closed it in January of 1933. Frank Edwards had his pool hall here then with a partner named Mons and in July of 1934, they swapped locations with Jim Kortie, who had been next door to the future Penny's store location in the next block. Thus, the Tiger Store came here. The original Tiger Store had been owned by L. C. Kortie and his sons and was managed by Al E. Hummel. It became the Gamble's store around 1939. Al bought it from the Korties in June of 1950. There was a bad fire here in early 1955 and the store was closed for repairs until July of 1955.

Shopper's Guide and Gambles in 1969.

Gamble's added Alden's Catalog Sales in the early seventies. Bill Olson bought Gamble's in March of 1977. Today the building houses the KLFD radio studios and Bright Star Cleaning Company.

Above: Penney's, a vacant lot, the closed Dan's Eat Shop, Gamble's, IGA Grocery and Cox's Market in 1939.

182. 236 Sibley Avenue North. (2 Sibley Avenue North in the very beginnings of the town, 43 Sibley Avenue North in the early days and then 709 Sibley Avenue in the early 1900s.) Village Council President Jesse V. Branham, Jr. owned this next lot in 1871. Mrs. C. M. (Fayette) Kelley's Millinery was here in a small wooden building in 1873 before she moved across to the west side of Sibley Avenue. Miss Lizzie Caswell was a dressmaker in the building with Mrs. Kelley. Now, the history of the lot becomes vague. The building here was called the Litchfield Shoes building after that because that store was one of the first occupants in the 1870s. I don't know who owned the shoe store, however. Then the building was called the N. Thomas Woodward building because lawyer Woodward had his office here at some time. The building once housed a restaurant owned by a man named Thompson. This was the site of Sam B. Millard's jewelry store in the late 1870s. Charles Forester owned the building in the late 1880s and moved his saloon here. He sold it to Ditlof Peterson in July of 1889. Mrs. H. E. McKeen's millinery was here in part of the main building in June of 1893. She moved to various locations around town. Mrs. S. W. Squire had a millinery where McKeen's had been in late 1893. Another source says that McKeen sold out to Mrs. A. M. Caswell, who got back into the business in December of 1894. Charles A. Greenleaf and William Grono moved their real estate business here either in late 1894 or early 1895 and Grono moved out in 1897. I believe Mrs. Lewis F. Larson's millinery was also here in the late 1890s. She moved around

town also. A. A. Atkinson owned the building and the lot before the turn of the century.

Henry Isaac "H. I." Peterson, the publisher, bought the building and the lot in October of 1907 from Mrs. A. A. Atkinson. Harry M. Angier had a grocery here in October of 1910. J. B. Cramer opened a general store, called the New Bargain Store, here in March of 1911 after Angier had moved out. Cramer sold the business to John W. Lassell in March of 1912. Lassell immediately went out of business in April and sold his stock to L. R. Kelly, who sold the goods elsewhere in town. Peter Makris sold his homemade candies here in November of 1912 until Mrs. M. Hunter leased the building for a bakery in April of 1914. Mrs. Mildred Thompson had a restaurant here in the twenties.

Dan Brown bought the building in September of 1931 and it became Dan Brown's Tavern and Restaurant. He started the Harvey Tavern just outside of town in Harvey Township in August of 1937. Then he changed the name to the By-Way because it was located at the intersection of highways 12 and 22. The story told was that Dan Brown's brother ran a still at his place just out of town. I don't know if he ever supplied Dan with stuff during the prohibition or not. Alfred G. Birkemeyer moved his Litchfield Radio Shop in the back of the building with an alley entrance in June of 1931. Alfred closed his business in April of 1932. Kenneth C. Watson bought Arthur out and had the radio repair shop back there in June of 1932. Dan bought Watson out in October of 1933 so that he could expand. Watson moved across Sibley Avenue. Dan moved the building here to the alley so that he could put up a new brick building at this site in 1938. He had a grand opening in September for his new Dan's Eat Shop. Apparently Dan got himself overextended, because in May of 1939, he closed and left the building. He then opened Dan's Café next door south of the Shell Station by the courthouse in July. Leroy R. "Roy" Cook's Meat Market came here in December of 1939. The Thomas Store, owned by George Ley, came here in July of 1940. He soon moved across from the park also. The Shamla sisters bought the building in October of 1944 and Cook moved his meat shop out in November. The Shamlas moved their Shamla Apparel Shoppe here in December of 1944. Florence Kammerer bought the business in July of 1947, but kept the Shamla name for a while. Then she changed it to Florence Fashions in 1950. Florence sold the business to J. Christine Jensen in February of 1956 and it became Christine's.

Christine's was moved across the street in 1961. F. E. Rooney's Real Estate office came here in February of 1962. The Shopper's Guide, owned by Fred and Norma Berke, was here in the late sixties and early seventies, sharing the building with the Rooney Real Estate office and Tri-County Conditioning. The Heritage Bake and Coffee Shop or Heritage Café and Bake Shop, run by baker Clarence Nelson's daughter and son-in-law, and Beauty Haven were here in later years. Today it's the attorneys' offices of Robert Schaps and Brad A. Kluver.

238 Sibley Avenue North. (707 Sibley Avenue in the early 1900s.) There were a couple of businesses over the next location. Tom Wandok moved his cigar factory upstairs there in June of 1890.

Dr. Karl E. "Henry" Cassel moved his office upstairs over the main building in December of 1902 and attorney Ray H. Dart and his father Charles H. Dart had their offices upstairs starting in March of 1928.

183. 240 Sibley Avenue North. (45 Sibley Avenue North in the early days and then 705 Sibley Avenue in the early 1900s.) In 1869 Wait H. Dart had a dry goods store here on the next lot heading north. He sold it to W. D. Stanton in 1870. It was in a two-story twenty by thirty foot building with a one-story sixteen by twenty foot addition. All of it cost $1200 to build. Stanton owned this lot and the next corner lot. He died in 1874 and his wife, Rosa Mary Stanton, was listed as the owner of this property in 1875. I don't know if she continued the business or not. Mrs. H. H. Stay had a laundry here in May of 1890, foretelling how the location would end up. James Stuart and Company moved their City Meat Market here in December of 1892. In April of 1893, the meat business closed and the Grono and Feig Marble Works moved into this location in November of 1895. It was called the Litchfield Marble and Granite Works. William Grono is listed as the property owner in 1895. A couple of shoemakers moved in here too. M. L. Thompson bought the marble works from Grono in late 1897. Grono sold his tombstones out of his house for a while. The house was located on Sibley Avenue a half a block north of the park. By 1899, Mary McGowin owned this lot.

The marble works moved out in February of 1900 and a saloon moved in. Mrs. John Johnson and Julia Anderson moved their Litchfield Millinery Company here in June of 1901. A. P. Brodeen had his shoe repair business in here in November of 1901. Then N. P. Holmberg had his tailor shop here but was out in time for Emma Mikkelson to open her millinery here in April of 1906. Jennie S. Ringdahl took over in September of 1906. She called her business Miss Ringdahl and Company, because she had a partner, Mary McGowin from across the street, who still owned the lot. In October of 1906, a dog got locked inside the store overnight and tore the goods apart. The millinery was put out of business. In November of 1906, the local Republican Party used it for their headquarters until elections were over. Then A. W. Sweet leased the building for his candy kitchen in late November of 1906. C. J. Ruud's shoe shop was here also and when it closed, the inventory was sold in March of 1907 to the Nels Lundeen general store, which was near Settergren's. Sweet went out of business in August of 1907. Allen K. Wheeler of the Litchfield Nursery Company leased the building in June of 1908 for a flower shop. Mrs. M. Arthur Brown opened another millinery here in February of 1909 and then Mrs. Archie A. Cole and Mrs. Marshall took it over in June of 1910. Peter Makris had a Second Hand Store here from 1915 to 1916, when he had a fire. P. C. Koerner and James H. Phelps had an insurance business here, sharing the building, in April of 1916. Then Albert H. Johnson had a meat market here in April of 1918 but he went out of business in August of 1918. Jennie S. Ringdahl came back as Mrs. E. J. Rodange after having married and opened another millinery here in February of 1919, calling it the Rodange Hat Shop. It shared the building because, in March of 1919, Andrew Anderson opened his tin and plumbing shop here in the back. The plumbing shop might have been in the alley in another smaller building. My source said it was near Mellquist's, which was next door to the north. There probably was another small building on the lot because Rodange had a fire in July of 1921 and the main building was destroyed. She moved out to over the Silver Grill restaurant. But Jack C. Hanson still had a barbershop in a small building here in 1922. He moved to the basement of the building where the Meeker County Abstract & Loan Company was in June of 1922. Ed Lindwall moved his shoe repair business in here in October of 1922. Eventually the old wooden building was torn down and this site was a vacant lot for many years. The small building to the south remained. Jack Thompson had a hamburger wagon that he sold out of on Third Street East next to the last building on this street until he was asked to move off the street. He moved it onto the vacant lot here in December of 1929. J. W. "Bill" Williams was allowed to keep his hamburger wagon on Second Street West near Olson's grocery store, for some reason.

Betty O'Malley moved her dressmaking shop, Betty's Shop, into the small building left on the lot in early 1936. Harry Carlson and Christ Kallevig started a used car lot here in the vacant lot in June of 1936. Harold Harding bought the lot in January of 1950 and built a new brick building here. He moved in from his Second Street location with his Harding Dry Cleaners in July of 1950.

H. Robert "Bob" Wannow bought the cleaning business in March of 1968. Then it became the Litchfield Cleaners dry cleaning business and is called Litchfield Dry Cleaners today.

I finally arrive at the corner building on this block, my walk around Litchfield nearly completed. The building at the corner has been called the Masonic Building for years.

184. 242-244 Sibley Avenue North (1 Sibley Avenue North in the very beginning of the village, then 47 Sibley Avenue North in the early days of the town, and then 701-703 Sibley Avenue in the early 1900s.) The first general store in Litchfield was here on this corner lot. But it wasn't the first store. That was across the street. Wait H. Dart owned the general store in 1869. He came to Meeker County in August of 1857. In August of 1870, Jesse V. Branham, Jr. and Edward A. Campbell moved their grocery store here to somewhere on the lot from kitty-corner across the street. Branham bought out Campbell in January of 1871. The Masonic Hall was over Branham's store. The local chapter was called the "Golden Fleece Lodge No. 89". In June of 1872, Dart started a flour and feed store here. He sold his interest to M. Arthur Brown in October of 1873. Brown moved it to another location. W. D. Stanton owned this corner lot and the one to the south of it, but not the store. In April of 1873, Branham started calling his store the New York Store. I don't know when Branham moved out. Rosa Mary Stanton was listed as the owner of the property in 1875, as her husband W. D. had died in late 1874. A. W. Swenson rented the building in August of 1874 for a general store, but moved to another location in October of 1875. Also in August of 1874, Rosa Mary Stanton put a different building on the front of the lot and William H. Greenleaf rented it for the Greenleaf Real Estate Office. Hiram S. Branham, of the Stevens and Company bank, bought the building in the late summer of 1881. The bank was here for a short time. In 1880, John Birch started his Birch and Nelson's Square Dealers Store on this lot. He was partnered with Andrew P. Nelson but Andrew sold out to his brother Rasmus in the spring of 1884. The name was changed to just Birch and Nelson Clothing and they moved away in June of 1885. At that time the Branham and Hickcox's City Grocery building from across the street was moved here so that a new brick building could be built there. Mrs. C. M. (Fayette) Kelley had a millinery here in July of 1886, sharing the building. Each December for the next couple of years, someone brought in "The 5 & 10 Cent Bargain Store" here. Ola Salmonson opened a feed store in the rear of the

building in June of 1887. A new brick building, designed by an architect named Phelps, was built on the lot in the summer of 1889. It was fifty feet by one hundred feet and the Birch and Nelson Clothing store moved back here in September of 1889. They occupied the north corner of the building, while the Krueger Brothers dry goods, groceries and boot and shoe store occupied the south side.

The corner building in 1889.

The C. R. Smith and Company furniture store moved here in October of 1890. Then the building was vacant for a while before it was leased to Star Clothing in November of 1891. Star Clothing sold "seconds" and cheaply made clothes and they were forced out in January of 1892 because they didn't make their lease payments. The McLaughlin Brothers Mercantile Company or hardware moved their business here in February of 1892 after moving around town because of a fire in their first location. They were gone in April. The Chicago Bargain House moved to a corner room here in September of 1892. Birch was back and had his clothing business here again in 1897. Clarence A. Perry moved his confectionery here in December of 1897 after a fire at his location, which was across the street. Daniel McLane got back in the general store business when he formed a partnership with Charles H. Dart, David Gorman and Richard Welch in early 1898 and moved the McLane Commercial Company into a room here in May of 1898. In August of 1898, Ed W. Swanson bought the confectionery here from Clarence A. Perry and quickly moved it out to the Nelson building. The John T. Mullen Dry Goods and Groceries store came here in May of 1899.

Mullen closed in February of 1905 and his business was sold to Anthony Anderson, Olof Brusven and Harry M. Angier in April of that year. The store became the Brusven-Anderson Company. J. D. Wilson bought into the store in March of 1911. Then in February of 1912, Victor N. Mellquist bought the building from the owners Peter Berens, Mrs. August T. Koerner and John W. Wright. He brought in his Mellquist's Department Store or the Mellquist Company mercantile.

572

Mellquist's was a forerunner of the "super" department stores of today. They had a grocery store in the back with an entrance on the north side facing Third Street and they used the second floor of the building also. Jennie M. Holmes also opened up a beauty shop in the rear of the building in April of 1925. Mellquist closed the second floor in November of 1926 because of money problems and shut the entire store down in March of 1927. The Masonic Building Association bought the building in April of 1927 and leased the downstairs to the J. C. Penney Company. Penney's, with Henry Stoetzel as the first manager, opened in October of 1927.

Below: Victor N. Mellquist
To the right: Penney's in the
"Masonic Block" in about 1940.

When Penney's moved down the street in January of 1959, Woolworth and Company leased the building in March of 1959 and opened up in June.

In April of 1983, Lyle and Judy Hames brought Hardware Hank back to Litchfield, opening up their store here. Today Partners Hardware Hank is at the site, owned by the partnership of Jim and Cindy Theis and Larry and Deb Valiant.

18 Third Street East. There were a few occupants to tell you about upstairs over the corner building. The Masonic Hall was upstairs over Branham's store in the early 1870s. The Masonic Hall again moved upstairs over the building after the new one was erected in 1889. Sorenson and Cokley moved their Model Bakery upstairs to a room over the building in March of 1898. Mellquist's department store expanded to include this upstairs in the 1920s. The Masonic Lodge bought the building in 1927 and is still up there today.

There were a couple of small buildings behind the corner building in the early days. In May of 1873, a small building was built on the rear of the lot, with an entrance facing either Third Street or the alley. The *Litchfield Ledger*, started in April of 1872 by Frank Daggett and W. D. Joubert in Forest City, was published there. Daggett was from Vermont and Joubert was from Wisconsin. The little building was eighteen by twenty feet and cost $500 to build. Daggett's interest was sold to Frank Belfoy at some time. In May of 1875, Frank Belfoy bought the building occupied by the Dunn and Damuth livery across town and moved it here in September for an office. By the early 1880s, however, the *Ledger* office had moved to west of the park on Sibley Avenue. William Grono started his marble works in this building in January of 1885, but then moved elsewhere. His brother A. Fred had another marble business elsewhere in town and he moved in here in July of 1890 with his City Marble Works. He quickly moved out to Ramsey Avenue across from the seed house, but in February of 1891, he moved back here and his City Marble Works and his brother's Litchfield Marble Works were combined to become the Litchfield Steam Marble and Granite Works. I don't know how long it stayed at this location, but they took on a man named M. L. Thompson as a partner in 1893.

Orphans

There were a number of other stores or businesses in Litchfield that I uncovered in my research. Unfortunately, I couldn't find a home for them. In other words, I couldn't find their exact locations. So I call them my "orphans". The year that precedes the paragraph of the orphans is the first year that I found mention of them.

1870: The Andrew M. Swanson tailor shop in a fifteen by eighteen foot one-story building costing $400. The N. Hintze tailor shop in a fourteen by sixteen foot one-story building costing $100. The Peter Knudson boots and shoe business in a twelve by eighteen foot one-story building costing $160. C. B. Howell had a real estate office on Marshall Avenue. It was a small eleven by sixteen foot building, which cost $125 to build. The William Heath tin and hardware shop in a twenty by thirty foot one story building south side of tracks, costing $400. The N. A. Viren wagon shop in a twenty by twenty-four foot one-story building. The M. S. Anderson & Vanderwalker blacksmith shop in a twenty by twenty-two foot one-story building costing $100. Their partnership dissolved in February of 1870. Anderson continued with the business. The Edward Sweet carpenter/wheelwright shop in a twelve by twenty-four foot one story building. Mr. T. J. Wheeler's millinery starting in December of 1870. Mr. Hulbertson's blacksmith shop, costing $100 to build.

1871: The Joseph James lumberyard. It was near the old depot. Dr. J. H. Bacon's office in a fourteen by twenty-one foot one-story building costing $200.

1872: The Nelson Boarding house on First Street. G. W. Fuller started the Litchfield and Meeker County Nursery in the spring of 1872. It was on the site of the original Litchfield Nursery started by George B. Waller and his son.

1873: The Nathaniel Antahel shoe shop in an eighteen by twenty-five foot building costing $500. Dr. George W. Weisel moved from his office to A. N. Grenier's building.

1874: The A. H. Lofstrom painting shop on Sibley Avenue. Next door, Judge Smith and his partner S. A. Plumley built an office building that was fifteen by forty feet in November of 1874. Per Ekstrom build an office near their building. John Blackwell bought the lots they had been on. John Smith bought a billiard saloon in November.

1875: Charles Bishop Billiard Saloon on Sibley Avenue.

1876: George W. Gordon and Co. leased their meat market to Samuel Hollingsworth He opened it up on Sibley Avenue across from the park for a few months and then sold it to Edward Hull who moved it across from a bank. In October, Z. B. Fifield bought the meat market. Mrs. Harris' millinery was in the Dayton meat market.

1877: The Peterson brothers' blacksmith shop was on the south side of tracks.

1878: E. J. Hatch gun shop. Mr. Cable opened a restaurant in the Rust building on Marshall Avenue in October.

1879: Thomas Hamilton opened a cigar factory in November. J. L. Chadwick and Co. started the Minnesota Bed Spring and Lounge manufacturing business. Elevator owner H. H. Harris skipped town with debts and money. Christian Pederson built new harness shop on Third Street in April. Turner and son built a blacksmith shop north of Pederson's in late 1879. (They closed and sold the building in April of 1880 to Pederson who moved it to Second Street.) Pederson's went under again in November of 1879 and the stock was turned over to Hugh Dowling.

1880: Charley Shaw had an ice cream restaurant in June. Christine Nelson millinery. Jacob "Jake" Koerner sold dry goods, boots and shoes in April in a new brick building. He started selling groceries in November of 1881. The J. W. and W. B. Gordon grocery. The Henry L. Wadsworth and Frank A. Proctor partnership dissolved in November. Then Proctor owned the business. Charles H. Dart and George W. Gordon started a flour and feed store in April.

1882: Samuel A. Heard icehouse. Haight Bros. vacated Otho H. Campbell's store building and C. J. O'Brien moved in. Chauncey F. Dart furniture store on Sibley Avenue was between Depot and Second Streets. Clark Angell, Jr. and Charley Dart's confectionery business was sold to Charles H. Bigelow in March.

1883: Matthews and Baum started a broom making business in February. Payne and Waller "Artic Feed Mill" was in the northwest part of town. The Wilcox and Eastman feed mill was near the circus grounds.

1884: Andrew J. Anderson bought the property of Oren Wilbert "Bert" Topping. Chris Backer closed his saloon on Marshall Avenue in December. He died in January. Jim Ostrander and Woodward built a forty-two by one hundred foot indoor skating rink in November.

1885: The W. J. Whittington greenhouse was at corner of Holcombe Avenue and Third Street in October. In October of 1885, E. L. Parker leased a building for a general store. In 1886, E. L. Parker took on a partner named Samuel Cossairt. The Edward Mantor and Hitz farm machinery business. John Konsbrick reopened his saloon in Chris Backer's old stand in March of 1885.

1886: Mrs. Augeline Cary bought the old Halvor Berglin shop for her millinery in November.

1887: O. Wexel's tailor shop was next to Peter E. Hanson in July. He moved north of Josiah Payne's shoe shop in December and in January, he sold the business.

1888: O. B. Knapp leased a hotel and called it the "Grand Hotel" in October. The Nash Bros. cigar factory opened in February. J. W. Johnson farm machinery, implements and wagons business started.

1889: The real estate partnership of Peter Johnson & Co. (Per Ekstrom) dissolved in January. I don't know their location or when the partnership started. In April, Virgil "Virge" Baum reopened the old Peter Berens' blacksmith shop on Marshall Avenue North. The Waller Bros. feed mill, which was in K. Webster's old mill on the south side of the tracks, was west of Chris Bertelson's blacksmith shop in early 1889. The Cofield Mattress Factory started up in June somewhere.

1890: Frank H. Haven printing. D. A. Roos bought Pearson's feed store in March. Robert Shaw flour and feed store.

1891: Daniel McLane rented the Flynn warehouse to sell machinery in July. The Wheeler Bros. rented the warehouse in May.

1893: John Nordstrom moved his saloon to Dassel.

1896: The Diamond Bakery had new quarters in April.

1900: The Vitzthum saloon moved to the Carlson building. The Carlson saloon moved to the Kellgren saloon location before he went to Revell's building. Nels Lueken moved his shoe shop to the building vacated by Mrs. Gottlieb Koerner. In November, there was a Home Bakery owned by Mrs. A. B. Johnson. Ham Tom ran a Chinese laundry.

1901: The George Worthington paint shop was on the corner opposite the Scandia Hotel (Depot and Marshall?) next to Virgil "Virge" Baum's blacksmith shop. A. E. Knight and Miller partnership dissolved when Knight retired. In November, Thurston A. Richardson sold his feed mill and bought Oscar Spatz' in January of 1902.

· 1903: Louie Hanson sold a half interest in his barbershop to Pat McGowin in January. Alexander D. Ross and Henderson M. Angier leased a warehouse on the south side of the track for a machinery firm.

1907: J. H. Spelliscy bought the Thurston A. Richardson feed mill in October.

1908: Oscar and Al Skoog bought the old Anderson brothers location for a saloon in May.

1913: The Hendrickson and Son General Merchandise store.

1918: Nels Bylund bought the poolroom occupied by John Conson.

1919: In March, Andrew Anderson opened a plumbing shop in the former Kinlund restaurant building.

1928: Harry Carlson Motors sold the "Roosevelt" car and Case tractor.

1929: Alfred E. Nelson's Eat Shop.

1932: Danielson-Nelson Mercantile Company.

1940: Green Gable rooms. Mrs. Joseph Nelson's rooms.

Acknowledgements

In the beginning, I relied on my own and my brothers' recollections for accuracy in my stories and the downtown stores' locations. I wish to acknowledge my three brothers' contributions and confirmations concerning those things. They are Dennis William, Michael Eugene and Patrick Francis Shaw. Dennie contributed in an additional way. Inspired by my stories, he sent me one of his own, which I've included. Thanks Dennie for the great story that supports my tales of how wonderful a woman our mother was. Our childhood friend Eugene "Skeeter" Anderson gave me the same support and help through many emails. Another friend, Peter Hughes, gave me many contributions. Some of his written memories sent to me by email were added to the book almost verbatim. Pete was an inspiration to me and gave me numerous leads.

To back up our faulty memories and get additional information, I went to the GAR Hall (the Meeker County Historical Society) in Litchfield and met Dona Sheridan Brown and Cheryl Caswell Almgren. They were genuinely interested in my endeavor and offered me a tremendous amount of help, especially Dona. Every day that I walked into that building, I picked her brain. I'm sure I became a nuisance. Thank you ladies for putting up with me and giving me "Carte Blanc" in the building. Thank you also for letting me use the many pictures of early Litchfield entrusted to you. Other pictures I've used came from postcards and pictures sold on ebay.com and from my private collection.

My three main sources for store locations and Litchfield history at the GAR were the old newspapers, the old phone books and a short but very helpful paper written by Don Larson and Vern Madson. Several times I ran into strangers or old acquaintances either at the Hall or in downtown Litchfield and our little conversations helped me too. The Litchfield Area Oral History Project tapes, made by Joe Paddock several years ago, were helpful with my stories also. I thank one and all.

Finally, this book wouldn't have gotten off the ground if not for the urgings of my daughter, Andrea Bree Peterson. She also helped me with ideas for the way the book has been put together and how each chapter should unfold. She paid me a compliment one day after reading and editing a section of the book for me. It went right to my heart. "You have a wonderful way with words, Dad," she said. "You are such a great storyteller." You have no idea, Drea, what those words said to me.

The real motivator, however, was Ethan Ryan Peterson, my first grandson, who might never have known anything about my wonderful home town or what Grandpa did as a kid there, if not for his mother's urgings and my desire to get it down in print for him to read.

About the Author

Terry R. Shaw was born in Mankato, Minnesota in April of 1945 but he grew up in Litchfield from the age of two years old and on. He has a Bachelor of Arts from the Minneapolis College of Art and Design and a Bachelor of Science from St. Cloud State. He taught art in Glencoe, Minnesota for twenty-five years and was a full-time substitute teacher in the Willmar, Minnesota schools for six years before retiring. He has played drums in various rock bands steadily since 1963, except for his two-year stint in the Army. Two of those bands were with his brother Mick. The most known of those two was called Shaw-Allen-Shaw. Terry has written over eighty songs and two other books, one about the Beatles and one about Buddy Holly, which are on the Internet. They can be found at:

Beatles: http://homepage.ntlworld.com/p.moorcroft/
Buddy Holly: http://www.pmoorcroft.freeserve.co.uk/tshaw1.htm

Terry Shaw researching this book at the Meeker County Historical Museum and sitting on the steps of the old house at 222 Swift Ave. No.

Index

F

T

W

Wacker
Marie   317

Wadsworth
Henry L.   417, 577
Mrs. Henry L.   412

Waggoner
Mrs. A.   503, 512

Wagner
Charles W.
  "Hans"   240, 421, 517
Harriet   240

Waite
W. C.   424

Wakefield
Joseph Lawrence 412, 462
Leander L.   536

Waldron
John M. or A.   387, 393, 395, 397,
       480, 547, 554, 556,
       558
Taylor C. "T. C." 152, 391, 438

Walker
H. A.   534

Waller
George B., Sr.   304, 367, 369, 575
John A. C.   304, 435, 496
Percy E.   407, 425

Walstad
Loren "Wally"   *31, 222*

Walters
Hazle   114, 215, 216

Wandok
Thomas "Tom"   281, 376, 398, 525,
       550, 562, 569

Wannow
H. Robert "Bob" 571

Ward
C. W.   369, 403, 404
James   534

Warden
Herbert E.   *64*

Warren
Harold   385, 494

Warta
Floyd   *109,* 110, 111, *112,*
       113, 172, 242, 364

Waterman
?   153

Watkins
Alvin Cecil
  "Alvie"   32, 95, *96,* 97, *141,*
       292
Arnold "Ray"   97
Donald   97,
Dorothy   97
Emery   97
Harold   97
Marvin "Muck"   97
Maynard   97
William   543

Watson
Andrew   417
James R.   415, 417
Kenneth C.   416, 418, 568

Webb
O. D.   533

Weber
Clarence   356, 536
Joe B.   446, 447
John   356
Judy   232
Mick   138
Nicolas C. "Nick"536
Teddy   138
? (Feed store)   554

Webster
K.   379, 577
L. A.   550

Weeks
Edward B.   *389,* 456, 457, 519
William S.   438, 520

Weems
Mrs.   417

Wegner
Hugh   540

Weidenheft
Henry   559

Weisel
George W.   370, 575

Weiss
Arthur   476
Michael Robert
  "Mike"   373, 476

Welch
Richard   266, 489, 490, 493,
       508, 512, 534, 572
W. H.   501

Weller
L. P.   521